Bremer · Jarnut · Richter · Wasserstein (Hg.)
Language of Religion – Language of the People

MittelalterStudien

des Instituts zur Interdisziplinären Erforschung des Mittelalters
und seines Nachwirkens, Paderborn

Herausgegeben von
Ernst Bremer, Jörg Jarnut, Stephan Müller
und Matthias Wemhoff

Schriftleitung:
Nicola Karthaus, Susanne Röhl

Band 11

München 2006

Ernst Bremer · Jörg Jarnut
Michael Richter · David J. Wasserstein (Hg.)

Language of Religion – Language of the People

Medieval Judaism, Christianity and Islam

unter Mitarbeit von Susanne Röhl

Wilhelm Fink Verlag

Gedruckt mit Unterstützung der Gerda Henkel Stiftung, Düsseldorf

Bibliografische Information der Deutschen Nationalbibliothek

Die Deutsche Nationalbibliothek verzeichnet diese Publikation in der Deutschen
Nationalbibliografie; detaillierte bibliografische Daten sind im Internet über
http://dnb.d-nb.de abrufbar.

Gedruckt auf umweltfreundlichem, chlorfrei gebleichtem und alterungsbeständigem
Papier ⊗ ISO 9706

© 2006 Wilhelm Fink Verlag, München
(Wilhelm Fink GmbH & Co. Verlags-KG, Jühenplatz 1, D-33098 Paderborn)

www.fink.de

Satz: Thomas Eifler, Berlin
Umschlagabbildung: Yvonne Junge-Illies, Mannheim
Einbandgestaltung: Evelyn Ziegler, München
Herstellung: Ferdinand Schöningh GmbH & Co. KG, Paderborn

ISBN 978-3-7705-4281-9

Contents

Foreword

This book derives from the conference of the same name that took place in Paderborn between 5 and 9 July 2003. At that meeting, numerous scholars from home and abroad discussed the most important cultural communities of medieval Europe, Jewry, Christendom and Islam, and offered inter-cultural and inter-religious comparisons between them.

Many people contributed to the success of the symposium, and we are indebted to them. Our thanks go to all those who presented papers, who took part in the discussions, who sat in the audiences, to the organisers, the assistants and other helpers, to the Institute for Interdisciplinary Research on the Middle Ages and its Aftermath (*Institut zur Interdisziplinären Erforschung des Mittelalters und seines Nachwirkens*/IEMAN) and the University of Paderborn, to the *Liborianum* and the *Museum in der Kaiserpfalz* in Paderborn, which hosted our meeting, and to the City of Paderborn; and also to the authors of the papers in this publication, as well as to Thomas Eifler in Berlin and Yvonne Junge-Illies in Mannheim, to Ansgar Köb, Manuel Koch, Susanne Röhl and Uta Westphal in Paderborn and to the Wilhelm Fink Verlag who helped to make the results available to a wider public.

Our special thanks go to the Gerda Henkel Stiftung, whose generous financial support made possible the organisation of the event and the publication of this volume.

The Editors

Introduction

MICHAEL RICHTER AND DAVID J. WASSERSTEIN

The term 'Latin Church' expresses a fundamental aspect of the Christian religion of the Middle Ages and the modern period: it denotes the official and exclusive language of the liturgy, of the standardized celebration of divine worship. In the Roman world of Antiquity, Latin was also the language of the people. It became the *lingua sacra* outside 'Romania', first in Ireland from the fifth century, finally and completely also in 'Romania', after the Romance languages separated themselves from Latin in the course of the early Middle Ages. The Latin Church is one of the monuments of the European Middle Ages and became the inheritance also of the modern period, perhaps even strengthened by the reaction to the Reformation. Latin remained in this period the predominantly used *lingua sacra*, while Hebrew and Greek, which were ideologically at least ranked equal with it, in fact found less use.

The use of a uniform sacred language in a geographical area of great linguistic variety had both benefits and costs. Of benefit was certainly that it was easier to maintain unified forms of divine worship and preaching, an important precondition for the claims of the Church to universalism. The unavoidable consequence was, however, that central aspects of the Christian message were not directly accessible to the overwhelming majority of those concerned. That made the clergy separate from the people in a religious sense, a separation that can be understood most easily in terms of language. A further consequence was the partial distancing of the faithful. The desire for a deeper understanding of this set of circumstances provided the occasion for the holding of a conference in Paderborn in July 2003.

The conference was organized by the editors of this volume with the help and support of IEMAN, the Medieval Institute of the University of Paderborn, and of the Gerda Henkel Stiftung in Düsseldorf. It brought together scholars from a dozen countries, and almost as many linguistic backgrounds. More importantly, it assembled representatives of a broad selection of disciplines – medieval European history and linguistics in all their variety, Hebrew and Jewish studies, Islam and Arabic, Coptic, Gothic and Irish and Welsh, and even Syriac as witnessed in the writings of Christians in India. Nearly a week of intensive work and discussion permitted the participants to explore the comparisons and parallels (and also the differences) between and among all of these linguistic and religious cultures.

The question that we wished to explore in this meeting was whether a comparison with the other great religions of the West, Judaism and Islam, looking at the links between language of religion and secular language, might clarify the enduring character of the Latin church. It became obvious that both in the Jewish religion and in the Islamic, the language of divine worship was much more accessible to broader layers of those concerned, because in each case it was expressed in a high register of a single language which could be understood by the faithful passively at least to some extent. While the Jewish religion remained exclusively 'national', Islam was a faith with extensive claims. Alongside the growth of Islam the Arabic language and its associated culture spread very broadly too. In comparative perspective the Islamic religion appears consequently of more all-engaging effect than the Christian. In the Latin church a translation of the Christian message into the vernacular was an unavoidable consequence, which, while the translation of the Bible itself was not necessarily at the start of this process, took very varied forms. These results had extremely positive effects on the vernaculars as well, which were almost all reduced to writing using the Latin alphabet. In the Islamic world, by contrast, the language of the population oriented itself to the language of religion, so that the language of the holy book was seen as possessing a quality which towered unattainably above the daily language of Muslims. And this in its turn provided reasons for the study of the Arabic language on a broader basis.

Lingua sacra had as a result in the Jewish and Islamic worlds a completely different function from the one it had in Christian societies, and it can be considered one of the results of this conference that the endurance of the religious message in the Latin West of the Middle Ages is seen to have been more limited than in the other religious communities, where the official language of the faiths played an, if not indeed the, decisive role.

All 26 sessions of the conference *Language of Religion – Language of the People* were concerned with the interplay of religion and language, both spoken and written, in the various societies under study. In some of these societies the language of religion was the same as that of speech, in others not. In some the language of religion was not necessarily the same as that of culture in more general terms. In most the registers of language in use in religious contexts differed from those in other contexts. The value of the meeting for many of the participants clearly lay in the discovery or the awakening of a passive understanding of the fact that the problems experienced in the study of one culture, one geographical area, one people, one religion, could be seen to be paralleled elsewhere, within and outside the confines thus somewhat arbitrarily set to such study. On occasion this was in contexts completely detached and distant, both in time and in geography – for example in late medieval India from the perspective of early medieval Ireland – at others in contexts close by in both senses – for example, for medieval European Christians, among their Jewish neighbours. The conference thus had a fertilizing effect on the thinking and, it is to be hoped, also on the research work of participants from many fields.

For the organizers, perhaps more than for the other participants, the fruits of the meeting included not only the general realization of the value of inter-disciplinary co-operation, via such meetings and via collaborative research projects. Another benefit lay in the deeper understanding of the value of another kind of cross- but not inter-disciplinary work: the project, so to say, of this meeting was the study of language in society in the past. A huge variety of different societies and different languages, with different functions and structures for all, does not necessarily mean that the study of languages in societies of the past must be a set of separate studies meeting only marginally at conferences like this: quite the contrary, the study of language(s) in history should be a single unified discipline, with all the difficulties that that implies, precisely because, as this meeting showed, the fundamental problems and questions in such studies are the same everywhere. Radical differences that appear on the surface – of time and place, of specific language or society or religion – should not obscure the underlying unity of the problems encountered or of the methods and approaches to be used in trying to understand and resolve these. While the examples studied at this meeting were of use in arousing both awareness and interest, it became clear that not enough work had been done on the questions raised in any of the areas considered here. The study of historical sociolinguistics has much to do before we can claim to understand the full range of the problems which it presents.

A further gain from this meeting was a deepened understanding of the meaning of the term 'sacred language', "Sakralsprache", for different societies. A sacred language necessarily possesses both an element of 'otherness' and one of belongingness ("Zugehörigkeit") for the participant-observer within the relevant community. This may be because of register, or it may be because of literary style, or it may be because of the character of the language itself. But it draws also on the character of the sacred texts which it carries, to make of them, and of itself, something separate, though still belonging to the community. In this the "Sakralsprache" differs from (what may be) the same language used as the language of culture, or occasionally of speech, where the element of 'otherness' does not pose such a problem. Here it is clear that much more work is necessary in order to place such understanding in a more detailed context both of historical example and of explanatory analysis. The problems in this area differ from those in the more general area of historical sociolinguistics, though they overlap with them too, but any explanatory theory will have to take account also of the special character of the religions studied at this meeting, both as being monotheistic and as belonging to individual traditions. It is not self-evident that similar results would emerge from study of different types of sacred language in different types of sacred systems.

A third area where the meeting produced elements for future questioning lay in the borderlands of language. Different languages considered at our meeting seemed somehow identified, to varying degrees and in varying ways, with particular religious traditions. It became abundantly clear that languages were not simply empty vessels, passive vehicles for the expression of religious and social messages; they function also as boundary markers between different religions and cultures – and at the same time as bridges by which new messages can be expressed and transmitted across dividing lines. On one hand they can be used for the expression of ideas and material for one group which it is desired that another group should not have access to – for example in accounts of the dominant religion in a society in texts written by and for members of a minority group in the same society. On the other, multilingualism, or at least access to more than a single language, among members of different groups within a single society can serve as the means of access (in either direction) to the texts and messages of the 'other'. Here too the character of the levels of multilingualism that are to be found everywhere calls for much further exploration, and seems to call both for new methods for the extraction of the information that we need and for new ways of laying that information out usably for scholarship. Language atlases of the medieval world are all too rare, and the methodologies for their construction are not yet available.

All in all, therefore, the Paderborn meeting offered its participants a fruitful experience, feeding and challenging at the same time, one that opened new vistas at the same time as it cleared paths in the historical undergrowth. Yet in seeking to explore new problems in this way, all the participants were giving witness to old truths. Muslims read in their holy book "Surely We have revealed it – an Arabic Qur'an – that you may understand" (Qur'an 12:2); Jews read in their Scripture that "I will make known my words unto you" (Proverbs 1:23); and Christians in theirs, "Go ye into all the world, and preach the gospel to every creature" (Mark 16:15).

Michael Richter

Concept and evolution of the *tres linguae sacrae*

The justification for the presentation of this topic, and, to be more precise, for bringing together this conference, is the need for greater evaluation of the use of the Latin language as the virtually exclusive language of the liturgy in the Western half of Christianity throughout the Middle Ages and indeed before as well as after that time.[1] This is one of the great divides between Catholic and orthodox Christianity. It must be historicized as well as contextualized. A wide comparative framework is called for. Its ideological background will be outlined in what follows. It points to the concept of the *tres linguae sacrae*.

I shall range over eight centuries and many parts of Western and central Europe. It can be stated at the outset that the sources for my topic are quite meagre. This is all the more surprising in view of the fact that a large proportion of the printed sources to be consulted is available electronically.[2] Thus I work on the assumption that the sources I present are more representative than in other earlier discussions known to me; these, however, are also few.[3] The small basis of source references is surprising if one takes into account the fact that the Church was the leading institution to make use of writing, and predominantly so in Latin. I suggest that even in our field the surviving sources can hardly be regarded as representative of the daily realities.

Our point of departure has to be the report, found only in St John's Gospel (19: 19–20), about one aspect of Christ's crucifixion:

---

1 This is one of the fundamental differences between Catholic Christianity and Islam. The Koran was recited and received in a particularly arcane register (for this concept see further below in note 23) of Arabic; (see the contribution of Hanna KASSIS in the present volume) for mainly Arabic-speaking believers. The Christian religion was celebrated in Latin, a foreign language for the majority of the believers, for which, however, avoidance of the features of classical rhetoric was advocated and the use instead of the *sermo humilis* in analogy to the educational standards of Christ's disciples was encouraged. AUERBACH, Erich: Literatursprache und Publikum in der lateinischen Spätantike und im Mittelalter, Bern 1958, (Literary language and its public in late Latin antiquity and in the early Middle Ages, London 1965), esp. ch. I; cf. also RICHÉ, Pierre: Éducation et culture dans l'occident barbare, VIIᵉ au VIIIᵉ siècle, Paris 1962, pp. 135–39, 194–98, and see further below, notes 25, 26.

2 The following electronic data bases have been consulted: CETEDOC I–III, CTLO Archives, Library of Latin texts, moderante TOMBEUR, Paul, CLCLT 5 (2002); Royal Irish Academy, Archive of Celtic Latin literature, Brepols 1994 (this is still incomplete).

3 SCHWERING, Julius: Die Idee der drei heiligen Sprachen im Mittelalter, in: Festschrift August Sauer, Stuttgart 1926, pp. 5–11; LENTNER, Leopold: Volkssprache und Sakralsprache. Geschichte einer Lebensfrage bis zum Ende des Konzils von Trient (Wiener Beiträge zur Theologie V) Wien 1964, esp. pp. 35–39; RESNICK, Irven M.: Lingua Dei, lingua hominis: sacred language and medieval texts, in: Viator 21 (1990), pp. 51–74.

> Scripsit autem et titulum Pilatus: et posuit super crucem. Erat autem scriptum: JESUS NAZA-
> RENUS, REX JUDAEORUM. ... et erat scriptum Hebraice, Graece, et Latine.

The end point of our discussion for the present purposes is Hugh of St Victor in the mid-twelfth century with the statement:

> Notandum quod tribus linguis, Hebraica, Graeca et Latina, missa celebratur, quia his titulus passionis Domini nostri Jesu Christi ... scriptus fuisse legitur.[4]

I have not found such a specific statement anywhere else. Hugh's assertion should be qualified in the following manner: Mass was celebrated in Latin, and the liturgy included a few terms which had been taken into the Latin rite from Hebrew and Greek. I suppose that this fact was so widely known as not to be worth mentioning in most cases.

In between these poles we place the articulation of these three languages as sacred languages, which first appears in[5] (though perhaps it was not originally formulated by) Isidore of Seville in the seventh century:

> Tres sunt autem linguae sacrae: Hebraea, Graeca, Latina, quae toto orbe excellunt. His enim tribus linguis super crucem Domini a Pilato fuit causa eius scripta. Unde et propter obscuritatem sanctarum Scripturarum harum trium linguarum cognitio necessaria est, ut ad alteram recurratur dum siquam dubitationem nominis vel interpretationis sermo unius linguae adtulerit.[6]

When we find the very same statement in Bede[7] in the eighth century, Clemens Scottus[8] and Rabanus Maurus[9] in the ninth, as well as in Rupert of Deutz[10] in the twelfth, we can postulate direct or indirect borrowing, aware as we are of the wide reception of this work of Isidore.[11]

However, the authorities who were to be referred to time and again on this issue, and on whom Isidore also leaned, were Jerome and Augustine who expressed

---

4 De officiis ecclesiasticis II, xii, ed. by J. P. Migne, in: Patrologia Latina 177, p. 418, and see also Speculum Ecclesiae, PL 177, p. 358D; similarly from around the same time Honorius Augustodunensis, Gemma animae, I, xcii: ... *Hoc igitur Graece canitur quia missa tribus linguis, Hebraica, Graeca et Latina cantari praecipitur, sicut et titulus in passione Domini scriptus fuisse legitur*, PL 172, p. 574.

5 BORST, Arno: Der Turmbau von Babel. Geschichte der Meinungen über Ursprung und Vielfalt der Sprachen und Völker, 4 vols., Stuttgart 1957–63, III, p. 454. See also below in note 27.

6 LINDSAY, W. (ed.): Isidori Hispalensis Episcopi Etymologiarum sive originum Libri XX, IX, 3, Oxford 1911.

7 Bedae Presbyteri de linguis gentium, PL 90, p. 1179.

8 TOLKIEHN, J. (ed.): Clementis ars Grammatica XXXVII, Leipzig 1928, p. 22.

9 De universo libri XXII. Liber Sextus Decimus, caput primum, PL 111, p. 435.

10 Commentariorum in Apocalypsim IV, vii, PL 169, p. 965. For another interpretation by Rupert see in: Iohannis Evangelium XIII, ed. by Rhabanus HAACKE, in: C(orpus) C(hristianorum) C(ontinuatio) M(edievalis) 9, Turnhout 1969, p. 740.

11 FONTAINE, Jacques: Isidore de Séville et la culture classique dans l'Espagne wisigothique, I–III, Paris 1983; id.: Isidore de Séville: génèse et originalité de la culture hispanique au temps des Wisigoths, Turnhout 2000; BISCHOFF, Bernhard: Die europäische Verbreitung der Werke Isidors von Sevilla, first in: Isidoriana. Estudios sobre San Isidoro de Sevilla en el XIV centenario de su nacimiento, León 1961, pp. 317–44, repr. in id.: Mittelalterliche Studien I, Stuttgart 1966, pp. 171–94.

the special position of the three languages in somewhat different ways. What we can see in their reception is that in the insular world, which was to be of seminal importance in this matter, Jerome would appear to have been the principal authority on this issue in Ireland, Augustine in Anglo-Saxon England. Irish Christians contributed a great deal to the christianisation of the Anglo-Saxons, and Irish and English to the spread of Christianity on the continent.

As far as Jerome is concerned, it would appear that no detailed exegesis by him of the Gospel of St John has survived. He raises the issue of the three languages only in a commentary on Isaiah; we may quote his statement there:

> Et ideo in tribus principalibus linguis quibus titulus dominicae scriptus est passionis, tribus generibus appellatur.[12]

Thus the scholar who worked most intensively with the three languages in reality theorized least about them.

In Ireland, we find the first echo of this in Cummian's paschal letter, which can be dated to ca. 630, in which he refers explicitly to Jerome when he states that < *Aebreos, Gregos, Latinos* –> *quas linguas, ut Ieronimus ait, in crucis suae titulo Christus consecravit.*[13] Another Irish work, Ps.-Augustine (Augustinus Hibernicus), *De mirabilibus sacrae scripturae,* one generation after Cummian, states that these three languages have eminent status: *tribus linguis principatus committitur.*[14] This concept emerges likewise in the earliest treatise on languages in Irish (written most likely in the later ninth century), *Auraicept na n-Éces,* that is to say, outside the strictly religious sphere.[15]

In his detailed commentary on the Gospel of St John, St Augustine gives an explanation why these three languages were used in the titulus:

> Et erat scriptum hebraice, graece et Latine: Rex Judaeorum. Hae quippe tres linguae ibi prae ceteris eminebant; hebraea, propter Iudaeos in Dei Lege gloriantes; graeca, propter Gentium sapientes; latina, propter Romanos multis ac pene omnibus iam tunc gentibus imperantes.[16]

---

12 Sancti Hieronimi presbiteri commentariorum in Esaiam libri I–XI, CC S(eries) L(atina) 73, (1963), p. 459.

13 WALSH, Maura/Ó CRÓINÍN, Dáibhí (ed.): Cummian's letter *De controversia paschali* and the *De ratione conputandi* (Pontifical Institute of Medieval Studies, Studies and Texts 86) Toronto 1988, pp. 56–58 (= PL 87, p. 969).

14 De mirabilibus sacrae Scripturae, PL 35, p. 2161: *Harum vero omnium linguarum novi Testamenti tempore, tribus linguis, hebraicae utique, graecae et latinae, principatus committitur, quia in eis crucis Christi titulus litteris hebraicis, graecis et latinis scriptus, Evangelica auctoritate perhibetur.* See further LAPIDGE, Michael/SHARPE, Richard: A bibliography of Celtic-Latin literature, 400–1200, Dublin 1985, here no. 291, p. 79.

15 *Auraicept na n-Éces.* The scholars' primer, ed. by G. CALDER, Edinburgh 1917, pp. 12/13: *Coigiur sechtmoga[i]t a lin na filed .i. fear gach berla 7 na tri saidhi .i. sai gach primhberla dona tri primberlaibh .i. Eabra 7 Greic 7 Laidean.* "The poets numbered seventy-five, that is one for each language, and the three sages, to wit, a sage for each of the three principal languages, Hebrew, Greek and Latin."

16 In Iohannis evangelium CXVII, 4, Corpus Christianorum Series Latina 36, p. 653 (= PL 35, p. 1946). For another explanation see Augustine, Sermo CCXVIII, PL 38, p. 1085: *Non quia graeca et latina solae sunt gentium linguae, sed quia ipsae maxime excellunt; graeca, propter studium litterarum, Latina, propter peritiam Romanorum.*

This explanation of St Augustine was taken up in several places by Bede.[17] He obviously placed the authority of St Augustine above that of Isidore. The same formulation is found in Alcuin,[18] and because of his education in the north of England it is just as likely that he drew on Bede as directly on Augustine. It also occurs in the exegetical work of Christian of Stablo a century after Alcuin.[19] A variation of it is used in Pseudo-Bede, Collectanea.[20]

A somewhat different explanation for the use of the three languages by Pontius Pilate is found in Hilary of Poitiers who stressed that the Christian religion was widespread predominantly in the Roman empire:

> Romana quoque lingua media inter Hebraeos Graecosque conlecta, quia his maxime tribus linguis sacramentum voluntatis Dei et beati regni expectatio praedicatur; ex quo illud Pilati fuit ut his tribus linguis regem Iudaeorum Dominum Iesum Christum esse praescriberet. Nam quamvis multae barbarae gentes Dei cognitionem secundum apostolorum praedicationem et manentium hodie illic ecclesiarum fidem adeptae sint, tamen specialiter evangelica doctrina in Romano imperio, sub quo Hebraei et Graeci continentur, consistit.[21]

Hilary wrote before either Jerome or Augustine, but his writings did not find the same echo as those of the other two. In any case, he wrote while the Roman empire was still in existence.

Sociolinguistic context

Here our point of departure is the fourth century when Latin was the main language of the liturgy in the Western part of the empire;[22] this was shortly before Christianity acquired the status of the exclusive religion of the empire. In the empire Latin had been and continued to be the language of secular government. In this field the sociolinguistic concept of registers of language[23] synchronically is useful. The various registers need not be mutually incomprehensible – on the con-

---

17 Bede, In S. Iohannis Evangelium expositio, PL 92, p. 910; In Lucae Evangelium expositio, Bedae Venerabilis Opera, Pars II, Opera exegetica, ed. by D. Hurst in: CCSL 120, Turnhout 1960, p. 404 (= PL 92, p. 618); In Matthaei Evangelium Expositio Lib. IV, PL 92, p. 124.
18 Alcuin, Commentaria in S. Joannis Evangelium, PL 100, p. 982.
19 Christiani Druthmari Corbeiensis monachi expositio in Matthaeum, PL 106, p. 1490.
20 PL 94, p. 547: *Tria vasa sunt linguarum: Hebraeum, Graecum, Latinum. Tres enim hae linguae in titulo crucis Christi consecratae sunt. Prima Hebraea, propter legem, secunda Greca propter sapientiam Graecorum, tertia Latina propter regnum Romanorum. Et ideo hae tres linguae primatum in omnibus linguis obtinent: nam erat scriptum Hebraice, Graece, Latine: Jesus Nazaraenus rex Judaeorum.*
21 Instructio Psalmorum, ed. by J. Doignon, Turnhout 1997, CCSL 61, p. 13 (= PL 9, pp. 241f.).
22 The transition from Greek to Latin in the liturgy in Rome is normally dated to ca. 350-380, see Klauser, Theodor: Der Übergang der römischen Kirche von der griechischen zur lateinischen Liturgiesprache, in: Miscellanea Giovanni Mercati (Studi e Testi 121), I, Roma 1946, pp. 467–82; for a later summary see Fischer, Bonifatius: Beiträge zur Geschichte der lateinischen Bibeltexte, Freiburg 1986, pp. 165 ff., and passim.
23 See Hymes, Dell: Foundations in sociolinguistics. An ethnographic approach, Philadelphia 1974, p. 59; Spolsky, Bernard: Sociolinguistics, Oxford 1998, p. 33.

trary: a distinction between active and passive command of a language is helpful here.[24]

Half a century ago a lively discussion raged on the topic of the Latin of the Christian religion in late antiquity, in the terms of the Dutch Latinist Christine Mohrmann, as "eine altchristliche Sondersprache";[25] she in turn built on the earlier work of her compatriot Joseph Schrijnen.[26] This position has not found general acceptance. It is true that the language of the Christian liturgy, in using the Latin of pre-Christian times, produced some semantic changes, but these modifications did not then transform Latin into a 'Sakralsprache' of the kind it was when Hugh of St Victor wrote. On the contrary, the Latin of the liturgy in the fourth century would have been widely accessible to citizens of the Roman empire without their having had a formal education. This aspect has not, hitherto, received the attention it deserves. In the light of the sociolinguistic dimension of Latin it is not surprising that Hilary, Jerome and Augustine did not use the expression *linguae sacrae* for the languages used in the *titulus* on the cross. What needs to be elucidated, on the other hand, is the use of these words by Isidore. They cannot be taken to carry the same connotation as the *lingua sacra* 'Sakralsprache' in later times, even in the Romania.[27] The issue of Latin turning into a *Sakralsprache* in the *Romania* has been a topic of the wider issue of the transition from Latin to the Romance languages, discussed most recently in depth by Michel Banniard[28] and Roger Wright.[29]

The sociolinguistic context was completely different outside the borders of the Empire. I will here confine myself to the West. The first society so affected was that of the *Scotti*, to use the contemporary Roman term, the Irish, if we use our current terminology. Irish society received Christianity from ca. 400 onwards, most likely from Britain and Gaul.[30] In both these countries Latin was the legacy of the Roman past, and that a very recent one. Those missionaries among the Irish whom we know by name, Palladius from Gaul, Patrick from Britain, would have been

---

24 RICHTER, Michael: À quelle époque a-t-on cessé de parler latin en Gaule? A propos d'une question mal posée, in: Annales, E.S.C. 38 (1983), pp. 439–48, repr. in: Studies in medieval language and culture, Dublin 1995, pp. 109–19.

25 Altchristliches Latein. Entstehung und Entwicklung der altchristlichen Sondersprache, first published in 1939, reprinted in: MOHRMANN, Christine: Études sur le latin des chrétiens (Storia e letteratura 65, 87, 103, 143), Roma 1958–77, I, pp. 3–19. For a posthumous assessment by sympathetic scholars see Sacris Erudiri 32,1 (1991). This stance has been taken up uncritically by RESNICK: Lingua Dei, lingua hominis (as above note 2).

26 SCHRIJNEN, Jos.: Charakteristik des altchristlichen Latein, Nijmegen 1932.

27 It would appear significant that no other text from Spain is found on this issue, and none whatever, apparently, from early medieval Italy.

28 BANNIARD, Michel: Viva voce. Communication écrite et communication orale du IVe au IXe siècle en Occident Latin (Collection des Etudes Augustiniennes, Série Moyen-Age et temps modernes 25) Paris 1992 summarises the research of two decades.

29 WRIGHT, Roger: Late Latin and early Romance in Spain and Carolingian France, Liverpool 1982; id.: A sociophilological study of late Latin, Turnhout 2002.

30 For the most recent synthesis see CHARLES-EDWARDS, T. M.: Early Christian Ireland, Cambridge 2000, with a rich bibliography. For all the qualities of that study, I disagree with the author on the

familiar with Latin as the language of the liturgy. In Palladius's Gaul Latin was also the language of everyday life. In Patrick's Britain Latin had been the language of the Roman government while the bulk of the population would have spoken British Celtic as their native language, though with a fair sprinkling of Latin.[31] Palladius and Patrick appear to have imposed that language as the language of the liturgy also in Ireland. In this case, Latin there became a *Sakralsprache* for the first time in the manner almost universal in later medieval Europe. How this related to the non-Latin native languages, in Britain as well as in Ireland, is discussed in further contributions at this gathering. In more than one respect, Ireland functions as a laboratory to understand better the Western Middle Ages. It is necessary to add that early Christian Ireland benefited much from early Wales.

Further discussions on these and related issues, namely of the crucial role of Ireland as the hinge linking late antiquity and the medieval West, were the *leitmotiv* of the conferences on Ireland and Europe in the early Middle Ages which I had the privilege to run for two decades jointly with Próinséas Ní Chatháin.[32]

The reality of trilingualism in the Church

The question of the practical application of the doctrine of the *tres linguae sacrae* is very difficult to answer. Here the narrow limits of our sources are particularly evident.

One obvious point of reference is a ruling of the synod of Frankfurt of 794, convened by Charlemagne and thus applicable to the territories under his rule. There we find:

> 72. Ut nullus credat quod nonnisi in tribus linguis Deus orandus sit; quia in omni lingua Deus adoratur, et homo exauditur, si iusta petierit.[33]

---

important issue of the thorough Christianisation of early Irish society, as I make clear in my review in Deutsches Archiv 57 (2001), pp. 832f.

31 A notable witness is St Patrick, Confessio 9: *Quapropter olim cogitavi scribere, sed et usque nunc haesitavi; timui enim ne incederem in linguam hominum, quia non didici sicut et ceteri, qui optime itaque iura et sacras litteras utraque pari modo combiberunt et sermonem illorum ex infantia numquam mutarunt, sed magis ad perfectum semper addiderunt. Nam sermo et loquela nostra translata est in linguam alienam, sicut facile potest probari ex saliva scripturae meae qualiter sum ego in sermonibus instructus atque eruditus, quia, inquit, sapiens per linguam dinoscetur et sensus et scientia et doctrina veritatis.* BIELER, Ludwig (ed.): Libri epistolarum Sancti Patricii episcopi, in: Classica et Mediaevalia 11 (1950), pp. 61–62.

32 Ní CHATHÁIN, Próinséas/RICHTER, Michael (ed.): Irland und Europa/Ireland and Europe, Die Kirche im Frühmittelalter/The early Church, Stuttgart 1984; iidem: Irland und die Christenheit/ Ireland and Christendom. Bibelstudien und Mission/The Bible and the Missions, Stuttgart 1987; iidem: Irland und Europa im früheren Mittelalter/Ireland and Europe in the early Middle Ages. Bildung und Literatur/Learning and Literature, Stuttgart 1996; iidem: Ireland and Europe in the early Middle Ages/Irland und Europa im früheren Mittelalter. Texts and transmission/Texte und Überlieferung, Dublin 2002.

33 Monumenta Germaniae Historica LL 3, Concilia 2,1, p. 171 (ed. by A. Werminghoff, Hannover/ Leipzig 1906); for inferior version see PL 97, p. 198.

The use of all languages for prayer was authorised in the New Testament on a wide basis, especially with regard to Pentecost.[34] However, we must note that the Carolingian ruling applied only to prayer, not to the liturgy generally.[35]

Reaching beyond the *tres linguae sacrae* for the entire liturgy, however, was the work of Constantine and Methodius in Moravia in the 860s, and it found a short-lived acceptance even in Rome.[36] The Life of Constantine, probably written by his brother Methodius, devotes an entire chapter to a dispute in Venice in 867 on this issue, and there the concept of the *tres linguae sacrae* is called a heresy.[37] However, the subsequent destiny of the Moravian Church shows that by then the Latin Church was firmly established in the West, including the territory of the Western Slavs.

We saw at the outset that the doctrine of the *tres linguae sacrae* was not really put into practice in the post-Roman West, and that what emerged instead was the Latin Church based on a sacral language which was understood only by the initiated, which gave the Middle Ages in the Western part of Europe its very peculiar flavour; this has too long been taken for granted. This phenomenon was first formulated in Ireland before 807 with the statement concerning the Christian Church in Ireland: *Aeclessia Scotorum immo Romanorum, ut Christiani ita ut Romani sitis.*[38] *Romanus* here can be read as a synonym of *Latinus*.

It can be proposed therefore that the use of Latin as *Sakralsprache* in Western Europe throughout the Middle Ages reduced the chances of the Christian religion permeating the societies in which this was practiced[39] to the extent that this happened in Islamic societies with their religion.

---

34 For *omnis lingua* see especially St Paul, Philippians 2:11.

35 The remarkable interest expressed by Walahfrid Strabo in his De exordiis et incrementis rerum ecclesiasticarum in the links between Hebrew, Greek and Latin, esp. ch. 7, MGH Capitularia II, 481, may be due to Irish influence, see RICHTER (forthcoming).

36 A wide-ranging collection of the relevant sources is available in Magnae Moraviae Fontes Historici, 5 vols., Praha 1966–77. See especially the letter of Pope John VIII to Prince Svatopluk "Industriae tuae" of 880 (JAFFÉ, Reg. Pont. Rom. 3319), vol. 3: *Litteras denique Sclavinicas a Constantino quondam philosopho repertas, quibus Deo laudes debite resonent, iure laudamus et in eadem lingua Christi domini nostri preconia et opera enarrentur, iubemus. Neque enim tribus tantum, sed omnibus linguis Dominum laudare auctoritate sacra monemur, que precipit dicens: "Laudate Dominum omnes gentes et collaudate eum omnes populi.",* p. 207. From the very rich literature I cite here only: DOSTÁL, Antonín: Sprachenprobleme in der Zeit Cyrills und Methods, in: GRAUS, Frantisek/ FILIP, Jan/DOSTÁL, Antonín (ed.): Das grossmährische Reich. Tagung der wissenschaftlichen Konferenz des Archäologischen Instituts der Tschechoslowakischen Akademie der Wissenschaften 1963, Praha 1966, pp. 329–55; VLASTO, A. P.: The entry of the Slavs into Christendom, Cambridge 1970, pp. 20–85.

37 Vita Constantini c. 16, see the French translation by DVORNIK, Francis: Les légendes de Constantin et de Méthode vues de Byzance (Byzantinoslavica Supplementa 1), Praha 1933, pp. 375–78; see also the contribution of Anna KUZNETSOVA in the present volume.

38 BIELER, Ludwig (ed.): The Patrician texts in the Book of Armagh (Scriptores Latini Hiberniae X), Dublin 1979, vol. IV,4, p. 124. My interpretation of this phrase differs somewhat from Bieler's.

39 This subject has not yet been sufficiently investigated due to the unbalanced nature of the source material at our disposal, see RICHTER, Michael: The formation of the medieval West. Studies in the oral culture of the barbarians, Dublin/New York 1994, esp. ch. 2. I definitely include here

It would appear furthermore that an exceptional interest in the Hebrew and Greek languages by Christians was fairly widespread in early Ireland. This may be accounted for in part by the early arrival of Christianity in this country, but also by the vibrant oral culture that persisted after the introduction of Christianity alongside Christian Latin learning[40] and that maintained great reverence for cultivated language as such.[41]

A number of exegetical works, not all available in print yet, have passages where it is explained what various terms are "in the three languages".[42] These works begin to surface in the seventh century. It must be said that the command of the two more exotic languages was not sound. However, it may be pointed out that Adomnán in his Life of Columba, completed shortly before 700, gives the name of Columba in Hebrew, Greek and Latin, without any ideological flavour:

> Nam licet diverso trium diversarum sono linguarum unam tamen eandemque rem significat hoc quod ebreice dicitur jona, grecitas vero peristera vocitat, et Latina lingua columba nuncupatur.[43]

Already about a century earlier, in other words, before Isidore's Etymologies were compiled, familiarity with the three languages as something special, *tres linguae principales*, as they were referred to in Ireland, is attested in two of the letters of the Irishman Columbanus, one to Pope Gregory I ca. 601 written from Luxeuil, the other to Pope Boniface IV written ca. 613 perhaps in Bobbio, in both of which

---

Ireland, see RICHTER, Michael: Ireland and her neighbours in the seventh century, Dublin/New York 1999, esp. ch. 1, pp. 28ff.

40 See RICHTER, Michael: The personnel of learning in early medieval Ireland, in: Ní CHATHÁIN/RICHTER (ed.): Irland und Europa im früheren Mittelalter/Ireland and Europe in the early Middle Ages. Bildung und Literatur/Learning and literature, pp. 275–308.

41 See RICHTER, Michael: Formation, esp. ch. 9. See also the – presumably ninth-century – treatise in Irish of the grammar of the Irish language *Auraicept na n-Éces,* mentioned earlier; on this treatise, cf. AHLQVIST, Anders: The early Irish linguist, in: Commentationes Humanarum Litterarum 73 (1982), Societas Scientiarum Fennica.

42 BISCHOFF, Bernhard: Wendepunkte in der Geschichte der lateinischen Exegese im Frühmittelalter, first in: Sacris Erudiri 6 (1954), pp. 189–279, esp. at pp. 207–08, 216, 227, 238, 243, 254, 259, 270 revised in id.: Mittelalterliche Studien I, Stuttgart 1966, pp. 205–73; id.: Das griechische Element in der abendländischen Bildung des Mittelalters, first in: Byzantinische Zeitschrift 44 (1951), pp. 27–55, reprinted in id.: Mittelalterliche Studien II, Stuttgart 1967, pp. 246–75; McNALLY, Robert: The "tres linguae sacrae" in early Irish Bible exegesis, in: Theological Studies 19 (1958), pp. 395–403; the Irish computus in Brussels (unprinted) poses in a stereotyped manner the question of several terms *in linguis principalibus,* a clear reminiscence of Jerome: *Sciendum nobis quomodo sol, numerus, dies, ebdoma, in principalibus linguis vocatur*; LAPIDGE,/SHARPE: A bibliography of Celtic-Latin literature, B 324, pp. 1, 3, 22, 27, 63. On this subject see further GORMAN, Michael: The myth of Hiberno-Latin exegesis, in: Revue Bénédictine 110 (2000), pp. 42–85, as well as Ó CRÓINÍN, Dáibhí: Bischoff's Wendepunkte: fifty years on, in: Revue Bénédictine 110 (2000), pp. 204–37.

43 ANDERSON, A. O./ANDERSON, M. O. (ed.): Adomnan's Life of Columba, Edinburgh 1961, Secunda praefatio, p. 180.

he gives his name in Hebrew, Greek and Latin![44] In this (as in other features) Columbanus clearly displayed his Irish education and the influence of Jerome. One may suggest therefore that Jerome's works had been absorbed in Ireland and by Columbanus before he left his native country in 590. Adomnán is not likely to have known Columbanus's letter, and this speaks all the more strongly in favour of a shared Irish educational foundation which existed in the late sixth, the late seventh century, and indeed beyond.

It emerges that the attraction of the concept of the *tres linguae sacrae* was strongest in those countries in which Latin as the language of the liturgy was a *Sakralsprache* from the very beginning, and in this field Irish Christianity held the lead.

---

44 WALKER, G. S. M. (ed.): Sancti Columbani Opera (Scriptores Latini Hiberniae II), Dublin 1957, repr. 1970, Ep. 1, p. 2 and Ep. 5, p. 54. On Columbanus see most recently LAPIDGE, Michael (ed.): Columbanus. Studies on the Latin writings, Woodbridge 1997; RICHTER, Ireland and her neighbours, ch. 5.

Johannes Niehoff-Panagiotidis

Towards a history of communication in Byzantium: the Greek church and the vernacular(s)

Since the seminal works of Clanchy and Richter,[1] communications history has developed into an integral part of medieval studies. The interest in questions dealing with oral and written communications, literacy vs./and orality, non-verbal communication in gestures, symbols and rituals, has seen such far-reaching and successful projects as the former "Sonderforschungsbereich 321: Übergänge und Spannungsfelder zwischen Mündlichkeit und Schriftlichkeit" in Freiburg, directed by W. Raible, the research group "Pionier project Verschriftelijking" in Utrecht directed by M. Mostert and the works by G. Jaritz and his crew situated at the academy for research in medieval everyday life culture (*Medium Aevum Quotidianum*) in Krems (Austria).

Given this situation in (Western) Medieval studies, the general question underlying this paper is the following: how did literary communication and its counterpart, oral communication, function in medieval South Eastern Europe, the area once dominated by Byzantium and then by the Ottoman Turks? If one looks at the leading bibliographies on this topic, e.g. the one published by M. Mostert in 1999,[2] one easily realises that research in this field has not been very active, and that there are actually very few items listed. Since that publication, the situation has not changed greatly, even if we take into consideration the latest article by M. McCormick[3] on this subject: it deals almost exclusively with non-verbal communication: travels, the mobility of local elites, shipping and the transfer of populations so far as can be detected by DNA-analysis.

In reading the current handbooks/introductions to Byzantine studies,[4] as a rule one finds there, if anything, a condensation of research done on this topic in the first third of the 20th century, expressed in truisms, viz. that in Byzantium

---

1 M. T. CLANCHY: From Memory to Written Record. England, 1066–1307, Cambridge 1979; M. RICHTER: Sprache und Gesellschaft im Mittelalter. Untersuchungen zur mündlichen Kommunikation in England von der Mitte des elften bis zum Beginn des vierzehnten Jahrhunderts, Stuttgart 1979.

2 M. MOSTERT: New Approaches to Medieval Communication, with an Introduction by Michael Clanchy, Turnhout 1999.

3 M. McCORMICK: Byzantium on the move: imagining a communication history, in: Travels in the Byzantine World. Papers from the Thirty-fourth Spring Symposium on Byzantine Studies, Birmingham April 2000, ed. by R. MACRIDES, Aldershot 2002, pp. 3–29. I will consider his article in a more detailed manner at the end of this paper.

4 Cf. A. DUCELLIER: Byzance et le monde orthodoxe, Paris 1986 (German translation: Byzanz. Das Reich und die Stadt, Frankfurt 1990); J. HALDON: Byzantium. A history, Sutton 2000; P. SCHREINER: Byzanz, München 1994, and W. TREADGOLD: A history of the Byzantine state and society, Stanford 1997.

ancient Greek (in the sense of "Medieval Latin", viz. Latin and not the vernacular) was still in use as the official language of church, court and imperial representation, that Modern Greek or its medieval forerunner was not written regularly before the fourth crusade, and that this state of things (called *diglossia* in Greek) continued until the late 20th century when *katharevusa* was abandoned in favour of *dimotiki*. If the reader turns to older works, like Beck and Mango,[5] it becomes evident that these display more sensitivity in this field than more recent publications, even if they lack – understandably enough - the framework furnished by modern theories for the study of communication that has been applied recently, and highly successfully, to medieval studies. Why is this so?

There are several possible answers to this and related questions, and I will give but a brief sketch of an explanation of this state of our field here. First, Byzantine and to a lesser degree Modern Greek studies are notoriously hostile to 'modern' theories stemming from literary criticism, communication theory and linguistics: the linguistic turn is still almost unknown here, and it is only recently that there have been some tentative steps in this direction.[6] One reason for this is the fact that so much grassroots work remains to be done in Byzantine studies – many important texts are still not edited and the number of scholars working in this field is still very limited.

Secondly, as is usually the case, the history of the field of Byzantine and Modern Greek studies shapes the interest of the scholars doing research in this area to a great extent. When Byzantine and Modern Greek studies began as an academic subject in its own right in the late 19th century, diglossia was a live phenomenon in Greece, and the subject of a bitterly fought struggle in Greek society, a struggle that had political as well as social and literary aspects and was not finally resolved until well into the 1980s. In consequence views of social levels of language and social encoding of spoken/written language in Byzantium remained dominated by current political discussions in Greece, and this interest dominated the study of literary communication, chiefly in the field of vernacular vs. literary literature in Byzantium.[7] That this 'demoticist' perspective on Byzantium can model even contemporary research is shown clearly by the work of H. Eideneier, one of the few Byzantinists in Germany to do research in this field during recent decades: his roaming *Dichtersänger* of Byzantium seem to be modeled closely on modern Greek *rembetiko*-singers, and I am not sure if this presents a historically satisfying explanation of the many problems of Medieval Greek literature in the vernacular.[8]

---

5   H.-G. BECK: Das byzantinische Jahrtausend, München 1978; C. MANGO: Byzantium, the empire of New Rome, New York 1980.

6   One should mention here at least the names of M. Mullett, P. Agapitos and the late J. Ljubarskij.

7   K. KRUMBACHER: Das Problem der neugriechischen Schriftsprache, München 1902.

8   As an introduction to Eideneier's somewhat odd views one might consult H. EIDENEIER: Leser- oder Hörerkreis? Zur byzantinischen Dichtung in der Volkssprache, in: Ellinika 34 (1982/83), vol. 1, pp. 119–150, and EIDENEIER 2000. A much more balanced approach is given by JEFFREYS, E./JEFFREYS, M.: The Oral Background of Byzantine Popular Poetry, in: Oral Tradition, 1,3 (1986), pp. 504–547.

When I dealt, at some points for the first time, with the social dimension of Byzantine 'diglossia',[9] communications history in the field of medieval studies was at a relatively early stage in its development. For Byzantine studies, even ten years later, it seems that this situation has not changed very much. It is impossible in this short paper to give even a brief sketch of what could be called a modern communcations history of Byzantium, a field that would interpret language as social behaviour, whose interpretation as symbolic action furnished the model for different, non-verbal acts of comunication, e.g. those investigated by McCormick. Thus, my aim here cannot be to establish Byzantine communcations history as a branch of historical research that would use the methods furnished by modern linguistics (chiefly sociolinguistics, orality/literacy questions, problems of performance, narrativity etc.).

All that I can do here is select one problem from the vast field of Byzantine communications history: the attitude of the church towards the vernacular. Did the Greek church really oppose so radically its use in writing among its flock as it did in the 19th and 20th centuries? In other words: to what extent is the Great Church (*megali ekklisia*) the heir of the Byzantine empire in the Balkans in its sociolinguistic approach? Is modern Greek diglossia in fact the continuation of Late Antique diglossia, which in turn could be seen as the 'prehistory' of the modern situation as Eideneier suggests?

In looking at this question, I shall try to use caution in applying 'modern' theories to Byzantine/post-Byzantine studies. It seems important to me, in doing so, to strengthen the dialogue with adjacent medieval studies: as far as the 'Western' middle ages are concerned in this context, we should remember that these studies represent generally speaking a more developed stage of research; for the Jewish and Islamic middle ages, on the other hand, it seems evident that something comparable could be done, but it is still in the beginning – it suffices here to mention the beautiful volume *Communication in the Jewish Diaspora*[10] (ed. Menache).

The Greek church possesses the oldest sacred language of Christianity. This language, when adopted by her, was already the heir of an age-old tradition, the Greek *paideia*, whose roots reached back very much into the 'pagan' past. It has to be stressed, however, that the church in undergoing the process of accommodation to the social values of the surrrounding society was preceded by the hellenized Jews when they decided e.g. to translate the Torah into the language of the then leading civilization of the ancient world. After the third century B.C.E., there is a whole range of Jewish-Hellenistic writings which were preserved almost exclusively by the church and comprised many levels of literary style and thus of adoption of social values of Greek civilization. The New Testament, clearly, stands in this tradition, and its writers clearly chose the lower strata of Judaeo-Greek writings.

As is well known, the Roman Empire in its eastern part did not disappear but was transformed into Byzantium. A lot has been written on the process of assimi-

9 J. NIEHOFF-PANAGIOTIDIS: Koine und Diglossie, Wiesbaden 1994.
10 S. MENACHE (ed.): Communication in the Jewish Diaspora: the pre-modern world, Leiden 1996.

lation to the 'pagan' society surrounding the church, and the adoption of its literary models is but one aspect of this process. As a result, Byzantium as a historical phenomenon has been happily described by one of our greatest scholars, G. Ostrogorsky,[11] as the synthesis of Greek *paideia*, Roman state and Christian faith. For this paper, it is of crucial importance that this synthesis, achieved in Late Antiquity, survived the fall of Byzantium for a further five hundred years in the framework of the Ottoman empire, up to the (re)naissance of the modern Balkan national states and national languages (generally speaking, in SE Europe the concepts of language and nation are even more closely intertwined than in other countries). Thus, up almost to the present day, the Byzantine past has its impact on the region, even if it seems still difficult for most of the Balkan nations to accept this as a common (but not *per definitionem* Greek) heritage, going beyond nationalist bias. Therefore, I shall treat the Byzantine-post-Byzantine period as a unity in this paper.

As is often the case with success stories, the Byzantine synthesis tended to immobility: Early Christianity's critique of *paideia* and its plea for simple language, which in the East had been weaker already in the beginning, moved into the background in the course of time. There are, of course, voices that confront *alievtikos* (fisherman-like) with *attikos/aristotelikos* (in the manner of Aristotle or Attic grammar), but these are only a few voices in the polyphonic concert that is early Byzantium: the imperial court is the mightiest, but not the only, stronghold of *paideia*, even to a certain extent secular *paideia*. Augustine's loud protest against the identification of Roman empire and *civitas Dei* is not heard in the east, at least well into the late Middle Ages. It is no wonder, thus, that we find the Byzantine court involved in projects of re-writing the Bible. Emperess Evdokia herself, wife of Theodosios II and born as a pagan, reformulated the holy texts into the 'holy' language of Hellenism, the language of Homeric verse, and later Nonnos of Panopolis did the same with the gospel of St. John. A precursor in this peculiar re-writing that to most scholars appears to be nothing more than a philological oddity was Apollinarios of Laodikeia who did the same thing, if the writings attributed to him are genuine, for the Psalms already in the fourth century. There he declared the Holy Spirit, whose message he put into Homeric verses, creator of the 'Ionian' dialect, viz. the epic language.[12]

In the long run, this attitude, of combining the holiness of the text with the sanctity of its original language, did not win out, even in Byzantium. This kind of identification has prevailed only among the Arabs: even today it is almost forbidden to recite the Quran in any other language than the original, and there are no translations of it, only 'paraphrases'. The reason for this is, that for Islam the Arabic Quran IS the uncreated word of God, and once again one sees how closely

---

11 G. OSTROGROSKY: Geschichte des byzantinischen Staates, München ³1963.
12 Joseph GOLEGA: Der homerische Psalter. Studien über die dem Apollinarios von Laodikeia zugeschriebene Psalmenparaphrase, Ettal 1960, esp. 43 in combination with 36.

Islamic theology fulfils the thought of late antique theology, taking a different direction.

Nevertheless, in the east, the question of liturgical vs. vernacular language was shaped in stark contrast to the west, because the long-term historical-political conditions were so different. Throughout Late Antiquity, and this before the Arab invasions and the loss of almost all the Near East to the empire, the economic decay and the subsequent disruption of communication routes, Greek was by far not the only language written for liturgical purposes on Byzantine soil. During all this period from the third century onwards we can observe a process which is still difficult to analyze in its social, historical and linguistic aspects: the gradual identification of dogmatic, social and protonational movements which stood in opposition to the dominant Graeco-Roman civilization and which in the long run led to the formation of the 'national' oriental churches: the Nestorians who choose Syriac, the Monophysites who adopted the western variant of the same language, the Copts and the Armenians. As historians looking back and finding ourselves confronted with a university scene where Christian Oriental, Byzantine, Classical and Slavonic studies belong to different departments, it is very difficult to assess these processes. In the beginning, and this seems clear, the results of this "culturalization of dogmatic differences"[13] were far from clear cut: the Monophysite John Philoponos in the early sixth century wrote in Greek, and Greek remained the language of Coptic liturgy well into the Islamic period. On the other hand, it is evident that in the course of time the non-use of Greek in a liturgical context became increasingly identified with heresy, that is: what the imperial governement considered dangerous. The official church thus fostered Greek and tolerated the liturgical use of 'barbarian' languages only when their speakers dwelled outside the empire or at least on its margins, as in the case of the Georgians. The only exception to this rule that I know is that of 'orthodox' Syriac, the language that is normally called Christian Palestinian Aramaic. In this case, it was the competition with Edessene Syriac (the language of Monophysitism *per definitionem*) and the odour of heresy that made the Greek church in Palestine more lenient. From inscriptions in this Christian Palestinian Aramaic we learn that Greek was displayed as the dominant language even in this case.

All this has to be kept in mind when we want to explore the historical setting and preconditions of the *mise par écrit* of Old Church Slavonic. As has recently been pointed out by G. Schramm, without this late antique background the move of the ecclesiastical hierarchy of Byzantium towards a new liturgical language seems hardly comprehensible.[14] But even taking into account the personal achievements of Cyril and Methodius, it is clear that this new means of liturgical communication was designed for areas outside the empire: Moravia was beyond any direct

---

13 This is the expression Peter Brown used in a private conversation; I am not sure whether this characterization, if it implies the priority of dogmatic differences, is right.

14 G. SCHRAMM: Slawenmission als Fortgang der Heilsgeschichte, in: Στέφανος. Studia byzantina ac slavica Vladimiro Vavřinek ad annum sexagesimum quintum dedicata, Prag 1995, pp. 535–546.

imperial grip, and even in the Bulgarian empire Old Church Slavonic only very gradually replaced Greek. The Slavs living on Byzantine soil were in contrast heavily hellenized, and after the reconquest of Bulgaria at the turn of the 10th century the coexistence of Greek and Slavonic as languages of the liturgy was a problem in the newly created quasi-patriarchate of Ohrid. Thus the specific Byzantine conditions are crucial for understanding the genesis of the church Slavonic language as well as the conditions for literary communication in the Near East and the Balkans in general.

Turning back to Byzantium proper, even if positions like that of the empress Evdokia did not prevail and at least up to the Macedonian renaissance we find voices of the western type (*melius nos reprehendant grammatici quam non nos intendant populi*) – one example would be Theodoros Studites whose correspondence (from the first half of the ninth century) is a step further in the direction of *dimotiki*. With the revival of classical studies and the reformulation of imperial doctrine in the framework of classical hellenism, the *sermo piscatorius* comes to an end in Byzantium for many centuries.[15] After the ninth century, the ecclesiastical and liturgical use of the vernacular seems to have had gloomy perspectives – at least at first sight. So, paradoxically, while in the ninth century church Slavonic emerged as a fully fledged liturgical language, it was the setting in the Macedonian renaissance that barred this way to Greek for the next three centuries– and it is in my view a consideration worth noting that church Slavonic is the last liturgical language that emerged still under the conditions of late antiquity, not of the imperial centuries of Byzantium. For Greek itself, it is not before the fourth crusade that the social-political conditions of the empire changed so drastically that vernacular Greek slowly became a language of Christian ritual, in the beginning mainly for territories dominated by the Latin conquerors or exposed to massive western acculturation. Thus, the material itself recommends that we arrange it according to three different stages of chronological evolution: before 1204 (with some chronological exceptions), before 1453, and before 1700, that is before enlightenment sets in definitively.

1. Before 1204 it is only Jews and Muslims who write religious texts in vernacular Greek. While the Jews were living among Greek-speaking populations since early hellenistic times, it was the battle of Manzikert in 1071 that led to the loss of inner Asia Minor for the Byzantine state. These non-Christian Greek texts are of crucial importance for the rise of liturgical languages in Greek, and it is quite astonishing that they have not been studied as they deserve to be done. This is the more remarkable because all Christian texts in vernacular Greek before 1204 are highly problematic as far as authorship, literary devices, language and date are concerned: works like Digenis Akritas or the Ptochoprodromika are still far away

---

15 That it is Constantine VII Porphyrogennetos, the most prominent representative of the Macedonian renaissance, who for the books he wrote or committed to writing sometimes used a language close to the vernacular is well known among Byzantinists, but still not sufficiently explained.

from any scholarly consensus, and it is quite common among scholars of Byzantine vernacular literature to contest even such basic questions as date and authorship. It was thus the publication of the Jewish documents containing Greek material by N. de Lange in 1996 that provided ample material for the study of this tradition.[16] All 16 documents published by de Lange contain material in vernacular Greek, almost exclusively written in Hebrew script. Among these documents is a very old translation of the book of Ecclesiastes into the vernacular, probably for liturgical purposes: the oldest text in 'modern' Greek. Of comparable importance is the use of the Greek vernacular in the Passover *haggadot* published by de Lange (docs. 5–8), where the text to be *recited* during the ritual is in Hebrew, of course, but the 'stage directions' are in Greek – since the manuscripts can be dated partially to the eleventh century, these texts most probably represent the oldest prose in 'modern' Greek that is not a translation (as in the case of Ecclesiastes). It is strange, and one hopes only a coincidence, that the Judaeo-Greek evidence has been so poorly studied by most of the specialists in Byzantine vernacular Greek. There can be no doubt: the oldest texts known so far that can be declared as written in modern Greek are of Jewish origin, they come from a religious, sometimes liturgical, context, and they present many of the features of medieval spoken Greek that had been posited since the beginning of such studies.

While this 'Judaeo-Greek' can be labelled as an auxiliary language taken into use by the rabbis for better understanding of Hebrew sacred texts, the case of Islamic Greek for liturgical purposes is quite different, except for the fact that those who were writing in Greek were religious outsiders, even non-Christians.[17] Whereas most of the Greek-Jewish texts are anonymous, we know the author of the early Muslim Greek literature: it was the Persian poet and founder of the order of the Mevlevis, Ğelāl ed-Dīn Rūmī and his son (and properly speaking the founder) Sultan Walad who wrote poems in the Greek language and Arabic script to give more verve to his mystical Islamic preaching in late Seljuk Cappadocia. I shall not cite an example here, but it is clear that the liturgical-didactical aspect is dominant in this poetry, even if the form is metric. The language is, in stark contrast to the Jewish texts, the local idiom, while the literary topics are Muslim. This effort was a pioneering work: we have products of Islamic, mostly poetical, inspiration written in the Greek vernacular but in Arabic script from all over the Greek world up to the 19th century. We have a *mevludname* (a popular poem in praise of the birth of the Prophet), and even a translation of the Quran into the dialect of Janina is attested, even if it seems to be lost. Once again, it is strange that our literary histories do not take these texts into account, and again this is, it is to be hoped, only a coincidence.

---

16 Cf. N. DE LANGE: Greek Jewish Texts from the Cairo Genizah, Tübingen 1996, and my article dealing with this material from a sociological perspective: J. NIEHOFF-PANAGIOTIDIS: Byzantinische Lebenswelt und rabbinische Hermeneutik. Die byzantinischen Juden in der Kairoer Genizah, in: Byzantion 74 (2004), pp. 1–59.
17 Cf. J. NIEHOFF-PANAGIOTIDIS: Übersetzung und Rezeption, Wiesbaden 2003, ch. IV.

2. As I have said already, the fourth crusade and its aftermath mark a strong break in Byzantine history generally speaking and in the history of liturgical languages, too. *Latinokratia*, as the Greeks still call this period, and the definitive splitting up of the Empire, which was never to recover again, posed a strong challenge to the Byzantine 'mentality', mainly in those regions which were in the long run dominated by Venetians, Genoese or French dynasties like the Lusignans. A new élite of hellenized Franks, that is to say Catholics and catholicized Byzantine groups, was formed, sometimes called *Gasmouloi*. It is mainly on the islands that we find these classes and their literature: Crete, Rhodes, Cyprus and the Ionian islands, Chios, etc. Everywhere it was the Latin church, directed via remote control by the popes, that took power and was protected and favoured by the Venetian etc. authorities.

The Catholic church possessed already at this time a religious literature in the rising vernaculars of Europe – thus it can be said that the time of the conquests, or of European expansion, was a time of expansion for the vernaculars, too. However, the bulk of the rising Franko-Greek literature is more secular in character, if that is possible in the Middle Ages. But a manuscript from Cyprus, Cod. Vat. Pal. 367, contains the scenario for a passion play in Greek language with some Cypriot flavour.[18] This piece, which is highly controversial because it is unclear how many parts can be distinguished, surely follows a western model, since there was no religious theater in Byzantium. Another text, the *logoi paregoritikoi* (words of consolation) on the passion of Christ, stems from Venetian Crete and is dramatic, too.[19] It is highly probable that this and comparable texts stand at the beginning of the 'Cretan theatre' of Renaissance and baroque types that flourished in the 16th and 17th centuries and that can be characterized roughly as an attempt to emulate contemporary, mainly Italian, literature in the West.

On the borderline between the Byzantine and postbyzantine periods stands the figure of the theologian Johannes Plusiadenos (1429–1500) who from his native Crete became bishop of Methone (Modon) which was a Venetian stronghold, too.[20] He fought – first against then equally fiercely in favour of – the union of the churches and wrote a poem in demotic Greek, a *threnos* of the *theotokos* on the passion in 189 *dekapentesyllaboi* (verses of 15 syllables, typical for vernacular poetry) which has been preserved in autograph.

Another strong enemy of the Latins was Joseph Bryennios who was active at the turn of the 14th century as a missionary in Crete, then under Latin domination.[21] In his *kephalaia heptakis hepta* (seven times seven chapters) he relates a number of horrible stories concerning the Latins; this work claims to be but an abbreviated

---

18 Cf. H.-G. BECK: Geschichte der byzantinischen Volksliteratur, München 1971, pp. 112f.

19 Ibid., p. 191.

20 Ibid., p. 191 and G. PODSKALSKY: Griechische Theologie in der Zeit der Türkenherrschaft (1453–1821), München 1988, pp. 83f.

21 N.B. ΤΩΜΑΔΆΚΗΣ: Ὁ Ἰωσὴφ Βρυέννιος καὶ ἡ Κρήτη κατὰ τὸ 1400, Athen 1947; H.-G. BECK: Kirche und theologische Literatur in Byzanz, München 1959.

version of the homilies he delivered there. But it is striking that it is exactly the Catholic rival that leads a fierce orthodox like Bryennios to the revival of a genre that had long since fallen into disuse among the orthodox: the homily. His language is simple and touches *dimotiki* very often.

3. In dealing with these few, sketchy examples we have already touched on the post-byzantine era: the 16th and 17th centuries are for the Greek church the main period of confrontation with the western churches, and it is mainly the Catholic competition that stimulated trade; and the question to what extent demotic Greek has to be given room in liturgy is one of the lines of conflict.[22]

The case of Joannikios Kartanos may serve as an example here. He stemmed from Corfu/Kerkyra, that was Venetian and remained so up to 1797. His entire life is an adventure, and it is only since the happy findings of E. Kakoulidou Panou that we know enough about his life, one that was lived between Venice, Corfu, Avlona/Vlorë and Constantinople. To understand his work it is important to know that Kartanos lived for a long time in Italy, mainly in Venice. One of his several stays in prison – he had insulted a Greek priest who had converted to Catholicism in S. Giorgio dei Greci – gave him the opportunity to write his main work. This was a retelling, thus not a translation, of the Old and New Testaments in demotic Greek, entitled: *Palaia te kai Nea Diathiki*. Even if Kartanos wisely does not mention his prototype, E. Kakoulidou has succeeded in identifying it:[23] it is the "fioretto di tutta la Bibbia historiato", which in turn is but a translation into Italian of the *Historia Veteris et novi testamenti*, a *biblia pauperum*; even Kartanos's illustrations stem from this book. The Modern Greek translation by Kartanos was printed in 1536 in Venice and provoked a scandal, partly because its author had used apocryphal material, partly because of its language. Kartanos suffered trial as a heretic and his most radical enemy, the priest Pachomios Roussanos (he, too, was a Venetian subject, from Zakynthos) wrote three treatises against him, one under the title *Hai tou kataratou Kartanou Haireseis* (the heresies of the cursed Kartanos), where there is clearly a pun on his adversary's name. As in late antiquity, heresy is identified with the use of 'aberrant' linguistic form.

Nevertheless, Kartanos's work became so popular that the famous and 'orthodox' preacher Damaskinos Studitis (who died in 1577 as metropolitan of Arta-Naupaktos) took seven of his 36 preachings from the condemned work of Kartanos into the famous collection of his homilies *thisauros* (first printed in 1570), that uses equally the spoken language – tactfully without mentioning Kartanos.[24] Later, the Slavonic translation of this *thisauros* became so widespread that popular homilies and edifying literature in Bulgaria and among the South Slavs were

---

22 PODSKALSKY 1988, the best work in this field, has ample material on these questions, but does not treat it as a topic in its own right.
23 E. KAKOULIDOU-PANOU (ed.): Ἰωαννίκος Καρτάνος: Παλαιά τε καὶ Νέα Διαθήκη, Βενετία 1536, Ἐπιμέλεια κειμένου – Εἰσαγωγή – Σχόλια – Γλωσσάριο, Athen 1988.
24 PODSKALSKY 1988, pp. 101f.

labelled simply 'Damaskini': the pioneering role of the Greek church for the emergence of religious literature among the Balkan Christians is thus evident again. Lack of space prevents me from showing this for Albanian, too.

This and many other similar examples show clearly the conflicts that the orthodox church encountered in the competition from the Catholics and Protestants. In trying to draw the oriental Christian to their side, the 'westerners' made room for the almost neglected vernacular. The model for this was the role of the vernacular in the West. Thus, the catechism of cardinal Bellarmin was translated into Modern Greek and first printed in Rome in 1616 (then in Paris 1633, etc.) under the title *didaskalia christianiki* (Christian instruction). The orthodox could in turn only regain lost territory by adapting themselves to western models – but this could lead to the insult of 'heresy'. By this token, the scheme I. Kartanos – Pachomios Roussanos – Damaskinos Studitis (thus: heretical revolutionary – traditionalist critic – conservative compromise under the roof of orthodoxy) was repeated several times later. The most famous case is that of a martyr-rebel, Cyrillos Lukaris, patriarch of Constantinople from 1620 to 1638 who converted formally to Calvinism and had a complete translation of the New Testament into Modern Greek printed in Geneva – where I studied a copy in 1996. Less well known than this cause célèbre is the fact that already his uncle and predecessor in the see of Alexandria, Meletios Pigas, had printed homilies in the popular language, under the name of orthodoxy.[25] This state of things was valid mainly for the territories dominated by the Venetians; elsewhere, on Ottoman soil, the reactionaries had access to much more drastic means: they used the Ottoman authorities to keep the embarrassing westerners far off. Thus, the murder of Cyrillos Lukaris by Ottomans was done at the instigation of his fellow-churchmen, much to the grief of the Dutch ambassador at the Porte who could not help him.

One factor might have been decisive for the fact that ecclesiastical literature in vernacular Greek almost disappeared at the end of the 17th century: the decline of Venetian rule in south eastern Europe after the war of Crete brought the situation of competition to an end, and the Catholic communities on the islands shrank or disappeared altogether.

Before finishing this paper, I should add some comments on the possibilites of a linguistic turn in the emerging field of Byzantine communications history. It would be a misunderstanding, even a complete mistake, to take these remarks as a negative critique of the more archaeological or 'positivist' approach pleaded for by M. McCormick in the article cited. My remarks should be considered more as a contribution from the side where the original meaning of 'communication' was situated: that of language. This does not mean that I am arguing as a fervent supporter of modern linguistics. The linguistic turn has to be taken into account for

---

25 On Kyrillos Lukaris cf. G. Hering: Ökumenischer Patriarchat und europäische Politik, 1620–1638, Wiesbaden 1968, and Podskalsky 1988, pp. 128ff. and passim. On Pigas cf. ibid., pp. 162ff.

Byzantine studies and the considerations of some of my colleagues point in that direction. But history has to be the principal interest of a historian.

To avoid the disintegration of Byzantine studies, I should instead argue for a reintegration of language data into questions that are normally answered by purely archaeological findings or, more recently, by DNA-analysis: McCormick himself points in this direction on p. 19 of his article, where he shows the importance of genetic analysis in combination with Old Norse toponyms for elucidating the population history of north-eastern Derbyshire. Exactly the same thing is possible on Greek soil. More concretely, we can envisage a collaboration of specialists in Slavic toponymy with archaeologists (and perhaps specialists in DNA-analysis) for the history of Slavic settlements in Greece.[26] The study of these placenames once stood at the centre of the sources at the disposal of the historian, e.g. Vasmer and Bon[27] (the latter for the Peloponnesus only). But since that time, archaeological data have increasingly been taken into consideration, in the long run to the disadvantage of the study of linguistic material.[28] But as language is the principal means of communication, words can be transported, too, rather like other objects of cultural exchange. It would be a fascinating topic to study the loanwords in the Greek language concerning oriental trading goods alongside archaeological findings. For questions concerning movements of population and the dialectics of isolation/opening to communication roads we have at our disposal a source that for many decades has been studied apart, but it could easily be taken into account: the modern Greek dialects. I tried this at a very early stage in an earlier paper,[29] but the field is still open to research, since it is of course easy to view the Greek dialects of Southern Italy as spoken counterparts to the idea of "imperial edge" (McCormick), or the aberrant role of Pontic on the shores of the Black Sea as corresponding to the special role of this geographical region since antiquity. With a bit of simplification it could be suggested that the modern Greek dialects are to a large extent the results of exactly the communications history that McCormick envisages. Of course, research is not easy in this field, but it can serve as a complementary source for a Byzantine *histoire du quotidien* with equal or even superior importance to archaeological evidence (as in the case of the Slavs, where I find it still very difficult to identify any archaeological object with a given ethnic stratum).

---

26 McCORMICK 2002, p. 20 underlines that the same research as for medieval England could be possible for Bithynia or Thrace, but he does not mention the toponymic evidence of these areas.

27 A. Bon: Le Péloponnèse byzantin jusqu'en 1204, Paris 1951; M. VASMER: Die Slaven in Griechenland, Berlin 1941.

28 The latest important article that gives full account of toponymic evidence for Slavic settlement in Greece, is that by J. KODER: Zur Frage der slavischen Siedlungsgebiete im mittelalterlichen Griechenland, in: Byzantinische Zeitschrift 71 (1978).

29 J. NIEHOFF-PANAGIOTIDIS: Archäologie und Sprachwissenschaft. Byzantinische, Neogräzistische und sprachwissenschaftliche Bemerkungen zu H. Lohmanns "Atene" (Zur Möglichkeit historischer Anthropologie des griechischen Raumes anhand von Ortsnamen, archäologischen Daten und neugriechischer Dialektverteilung), in: Klio 77 (1995), pp. 339–353.

Let me sum up the findings in this paper as follows: a future history of Byzantine communication has to take into account the methodological achievements of the linguistic turn but must adapt them to the specifically Byzantine conditions. Concerning the tension between the written language and the vernacular, this holds especially for the role of the enduring empire and the history of the orthodox church that did not share many developments of the Western churches such as church reform, etc.

Again differently from western medieval studies, a great amount of grassroots work on language material remains to be done. Apart from the cases mentioned above, we still have no history of Byzantine semantics, i.e. language in its social contexts from an historical perspective, dreamed of already by Dölger.

Modern Greek diglossia is only a very distant echo from the Byzantine past; to understand the former, one has to take into account the special communications history of the Ottoman Empire and the special role of the church as displayed in its framework. The role of spoken Greek in Byzantium is different from the role of the vernaculars in the West, but is not to be seen in the light of the Psyharis-controversy of the 19th century. In any case, it is a true mirror of the historical circumstances of the Byzantine empire and can be treated as a source for historical studies just like other sources.

Johannes Pahlitzsch

Griechisch – Syrisch – Arabisch.
Zum Verhältnis von Liturgie- und Umgangssprache bei den Melkiten Palästinas im 12. und 13. Jahrhundert

Die griechisch-orthodoxe Kirche von Jerusalem im Mittelalter zeichnete sich durch ihre besondere Multilingualität aus. Nach der islamischen Eroberung setzte spätestens ab dem Ende des 8. Jahrhunderts eine sprachliche Arabisierung der Melkiten, wie die orientalischen Christen orthodoxen Glaubens genannt wurden, ein. Diese Arabisierung wurde allerdings in Palästina keineswegs von einem breiteren Islamisierungsprozess begleitet.[1] Bis zu den Kreuzzügen dürfte zumindest in einigen Regionen die Mehrheit der Bevölkerung noch christlich gewesen sein.[2] Spätestens ab dem 11. Jahrhundert stammte dagegen der höhere Klerus sowie ein großer Teil der in den zahlreichen Klöstern Palästinas ansässigen Mönche aus Byzanz und war somit griechischsprachig.[3] Zudem gab es in Palästina noch zahlreiche Niederlassungen von Gemeinschaften aus anderen orthodoxen Ländern wie Georgien, das schon ab dem 4. Jahrhundert enge Beziehungen zum Heiligen Land unterhielt, oder ab dem 13. Jahrhundert aus Serbien und Russland.[4]

Wie mit dieser Vielfalt an Sprachen und Völkern im Bereich des Geschäftslebens umgegangen wurde, zeigt ein Kaufvertrag von 1169, in dem neben den als

---

1 Mango, Cyril: Greek Culture in Palestine after the Arab Conquest, in: Cavallo, Guglielmo/ de Gregorio, Giuseppe/Maniaci, Marilene (Hg.): Scritture, libri e testi nelle aree provinciali di Bisanzio. Atti del seminario di Erice (18–25 settembre 1988), Bd. 1, Spoleto 1991, S. 149–160; Schick, Robert: Christianity in the Patriarchate of Jerusalem in the Early Abbasid Period, 132–198/750–813, in: Adnan al-Bakhit, Muhammad/Schick, Robert (Hg.): Bilād al-Shām. During the Abbasid Period. Proceedings of the Fifth International Conference on the History of Bilād al-Shām (7–11 Shaʻban 1410 A.H./4–8 March 1990), Amman 1991, S. 63–80, S. 66; Griffith, Sidney: From Aramaic to Arabic: The Languages of the Monasteries of Palestine in the Byzantine and Early Islamic Periods, in: Dumbarton Oaks Papers 51 (1997), S. 11–31; allgemein siehe Schick, Robert: The Christian Communities of Palestine from Byzantine to Islamic Rule. A Historical and Archaeological Study (Studies in Late Antiquity and Early Islam 2), Princeton 1995.
2 Ellenblum, Ronnie: Frankish Rural Settlement in the Latin Kingdom of Jerusalem, Cambridge 1998, S. 253–276.
3 Pahlitzsch, Johannes: Graeci und Suriani im Palästina der Kreuzfahrerzeit. Beiträge und Quellen zur Geschichte des griechisch-orthodoxen Patriarchats von Jerusalem (Berliner Historische Studien 33, Ordensstudien 15), Berlin 2001, S. 43.
4 Siehe Pahlitzsch, Johannes: Die Bedeutung Jerusalems für Königtum und Kirche in Georgien zur Zeit der Kreuzzüge im Vergleich zu Armenien, in: L'idea di Gerusalemme nella spiritualità cristiana del medioevo. Atti del Convegno internazionale in collaborazione con l'Istituto della Görres-Gesellschaft di Gerusalemme (Gerusalemme, Notre Dame of Jerusalem Center, 31 agosto– 6 settembre 1999) (Pontificio Comitato di Scienze Storiche. Atti e documenti 12), Vatikanstadt 2003, S. 104–131.

Käufern agierenden georgischen Mönchen des Hl. Kreuz-Klosters bei Jerusalem einheimische arabische Christen als Verkäufer auftreten. Von besonderem Interesse ist die griechische Unterschrift eines Presbyters der Anastasis namens Gabriel. Die ganze Breite der im Heiligen Land lebenden, der orthodoxen Kirche angehörenden Nationen zeigt sich in diesem Dokument: Der einheimischen arabischsprachigen Bevölkerung stehen Mönche georgischer Herkunft und die die Spitze der Hierarchie verkörpernden Griechen gegenüber. Obwohl die Urkunde zur Zeit der Herrschaft der Kreuzfahrer in Palästina abgefasst wurde, weist das verwandte Formular dennoch eine weitgehende Übereinstimmung zu dem islamischer Kaufverträge auf, wie es sich in den Handbüchern der Rechtsgelehrten zur Abfassung von Urkunden, den sogenannten *šurūṭ*-Werken, und in den erhaltenen islamischen Dokumenten findet. Die arabischsprachigen orthodoxen Christen folgten also auch siebzig Jahre nach der Eroberung Jerusalems durch den Ersten Kreuzzug unbeeinflusst von westlichen, lateinischen Rechtsformen ihren eigenen, noch aus der Zeit der islamischen Herrschaft stammenden Traditionen.[5]

Das Beispiel der Urkunden der jüdischen Gemeinde Kairos aus der Geniza zeigt, dass der starke Formalismus islamischer Kaufverträge auch die Verträge der andersgläubigen Minderheiten unter islamischer Herrschaft bestimmte.[6] Wenngleich die nicht-islamischen Minderheiten in ihren internen Angelegenheiten autonom waren, so war die Verwendung islamischer Formen bei Rechtsgeschäften mit Muslimen selbstverständlich. Dass man aber auch, wie in den Geniza-Dokumenten belegt, bei Rechtsgeschäften zwischen zwei Juden auf das islamische Formular zurückgriff, dürfte seinen Grund unter anderem darin gehabt haben, dass es zur Absicherung im Falle eventueller Rechtsstreitigkeiten nur von Nutzen sein konnte, das Rechtsgeschäft auch nach islamisch-rechtlichen Vorstellungen gültig abzuschließen, da als letzte Instanz doch immer der *qāḍī* fungierte.[7] Auf vergleichbare Weise werden sich auch die arabischsprachigen Christen Palästinas vor der Errichtung der Kreuzfahrerherrschaft islamische Rechtsformen angeeignet haben. Da aber die Muslime ihre Rechtstraditionen unter christlicher Herrschaft weiter pflegen konnten und die Strukturen zur Selbstverwaltung zumindest auf lokaler Ebene bestehen blieben,[8] erklärt sich auch für die Melkiten die Beibehal-

---

5   PAHLITZSCH: Graeci und Suriani im Palästina der Kreuzfahrerzeit (Anm. 3), S. 181–188 und S. 314–324 (Edition mit Übersetzung und Kommentar).

6   Zum Formalismus der islamischen Kaufverträge siehe WAKIN, Jeanette A.: The Functions of Documents in Islamic Law. The Chapters on Sales from Ṭaḥāwī's Kitāb al-shurūṭ, Albany/New York 1972, S. 38; LITTLE, Donald P.: Six Fourteenth Century Deeds for Slaves from al-Ḥaram aš-Šarīf, in: Zeitschrift der Deutschen Morgenländischen Gesellschaft 131 (1981), S. 297–337, S. 335f., weist ebenso hin auf die „remarkable similarity in the basic form and even certain key phrases of all published purchase deeds, which […] means that there was a degree of continuity in Arabic notarial practice which extends over a period of six centuries".

7   KHAN, Geoffrey: Arabic Legal and Administrative Documents in the Cambridge Genizah Collections (Cambridge University Library, Genizah Series 10), Cambridge 1993, S. 1.

8   FAVREAU-LILIE, Marie-Luise: „Multikulturelle Gesellschaft" oder „Persecuting Society"? „Franken" und „Einheimische" im Königreich Jerusalem, in: BAUER, Dieter/HERBERS, Klaus/JASPERT, Nikolas (Hg.): Jerusalem im Hoch- und Spätmittelalter: Konflikte und Konfliktbewältigung –

tung solcher Formulare in internen Rechtsgeschäften im lateinischen Königreich von Jerusalem.

Als eigentliche Muttersprache der einheimischen griechisch-orthodoxen Christen, der Melkiten, muss im 12. und 13. Jahrhundert das Arabische gelten. In diesem Sinn heißt es dann auch bei Jakob von Vitry, dem lateinischen Bischof von Akkon vom Anfang des 13. Jahrhunderts, sie würden „in der alltäglichen Rede die sarazenische Sprache gebrauchen. Sarazenische Buchstaben und Schrift verwenden sie in Verträgen, geschäftlichen Dingen sowie allem anderen außer in den heiligen Schriften und anderen geistlichen Angelegenheiten, wofür sie griechische Buchstaben benutzen. Daher verstehen die Laien unter ihnen, die nur die sarazenische Sprache kennen, im Gottesdienst diese Texte nicht."[9] Damit beschreibt Jakob von Vitry nicht ohne polemischen Unterton offensichtlich die Situation in den großen Küstenstädten, also vor allem in seiner Bischofsstadt Akkon, aber auch in Jerusalem. Als Liturgiesprache diente dort entsprechend der griechischen Herkunft des höheren Klerus Griechisch, das als offizielle Sprache des orthodoxen Patriarchats von Jerusalem gelten kann.[10]

II

Generell trifft die Aussage Jakobs von Vitry über den rein profanen Gebrauch des Arabischen durch die Melkiten jedoch nicht zu, wie die rege Übersetzung kirchlicher Literatur durch arabischsprachige Christen ab dem Ende des 8. Jahrhunderts belegt. Und auch auf dem Gebiet der Liturgie kann Jakobs Beobachtung nur zum Teil bestätigt werden. Zwar blieb das Griechische als Liturgiesprache bis in das 13. Jahrhundert und darüber hinaus in Gebrauch, zumal ab dem 11. Jahrhundert die Präsenz griechischer Mönche und Kleriker in Palästina wieder stark zunahm,[11]

Vorstellungen und Vergegenwärtigungen (Campus Historische Studien 29), Frankfurt a. M./ New York 2001, S. 55–93; PAHLITZSCH, Johannes/WELTECKE, Dorothea: Konflikte zwischen den nicht-lateinischen Kirchen im Königreich Jerusalem, in: ibid., S. 119–145; KEDAR, Benjamin Z.: The Subjected Muslims of the Frankish Levant, in: POWELL, James M. (Hg.): Muslims under Latin Rule, 1100–1300, Princeton 1990, S. 135–174; RILEY-SMITH, Jonathan: The Survival in Latin Palestine of Muslim Administration, in: HOLT, Peter M. (Hg.): Eastern Mediterranean Lands in the Period of the Crusades, Warminster 1977, S. 9–22. Zu muslimischen Amtsträgern siehe RILEY-SMITH, Jonathan: Some Lesser Officials in Latin Syria, in: English Historical Review 87 (1972), S. 1–26.

9 Jakob von Vitry: Libri duo quorum prior orientalis sive Hierosolymitanae alter occidentalis historiae nomine inscribitur, ed. v. Franziskus MOSCHUS, Douai 1597 (Neudruck Farnborough 1971), S. 139.

10 NASRALLAH, Joseph: La liturgie des Patriarcats melchites de 969 à 1300, in: Oriens Christianus 71 (1987), S. 156–181, S. 160. Vgl. auch Milka Rubin zitiert bei GRIFFITH: From Aramaic to Arabic (Anm. 1), S. 23.

11 Siehe etwa das in Jerusalem geschriebene Typikon von 1122, PAHLITZSCH: Graeci und Suriani (Anm. 3), S. 191ff. GRIFFITH: From Aramaic to Arabic (Anm. 1), S. 23f. und 28f., betont, dass vom 9. bis zum 11. Jahrhundert Griechisch zwar als *lingua sacra* sein Prestige und seine „iconic functions" behalten habe, es ansonsten aber kaum Belege für die Abfassung irgendwelcher größerer

aber schon für das 9. Jahrhundert ist die Verwendung arabischer Übersetzungen für die Lesung der biblischen Texte im Gottesdienst belegt.[12] Doch handelt es sich hierbei eben nur um die Texte der Schriftlesung, nicht um die eigentliche Liturgie. Als Liturgiesprache diente den einheimischen arabischsprachigen Orthodoxen vor allem in den ländlichen Gebieten Palästinas dagegen Syrisch, bzw. genauer der als christlich-palästinisches Aramäisch bezeichnete lokale Dialekt des Syrischen, der sich zumindest als Liturgiesprache bis in das 13. Jahrhundert hinein gegenüber den herrschenden Arabisierungstendenzen behaupten konnte. Vollständige arabische Übersetzungen liturgischer Bücher sind daher erst ab dem 13. Jahrhundert belegt. So enthält der Sinaiticus arabicus 237 unter anderem einen liturgischen Kalender, ein Horologion sowie die Chrysostomos-, Basilios-, Petrus- und Jakobsliturgie.[13] Dies ist insofern bemerkenswert, als dass ab dem Ende des 8. Jahrhunderts die Zahl nicht-liturgischer palästinisch-aramäischer Texte abnimmt, während für die Zeit vom Ende des 8. bis zum 11. Jahrhundert mehr als 60 solcher christlich-arabischer Handschriften aus Palästina bekannt sind. Inhaltlich besteht dabei eine signifikante Übereinstimmung zwischen den syrischen und arabischen Texten: In beiden Fällen handelt es sich vor allem um Übersetzungen kirchlicher Literatur, wie etwa der Bibel, von Hagiographie oder von Predigten, die für eine breite Leser- bzw. Hörerschaft gedacht waren.[14] Das Arabische löste somit das Aramäische nicht nur als Umgangssprache, sondern auch als kirchliche Literatursprache mit Ausnahme der Liturgie ab. Der Grund für diese Sonderstellung der Liturgie dürfte darin bestanden haben, dass auch die Melkiten die Sprache, die für Gebete und Liturgie gebraucht wurde und als Mittel der Kommunikation mit Gott diente, in gewisser Weise als heilig ansahen.

Dennoch drang das Arabische allmählich in die syrischen liturgischen Texte ein. Als Entgegenkommen für den Benutzer wurden ab dem 10. und verstärkt ab dem 11. Jahrhundert Rubriken und Marginalien mit liturgischen Anweisungen

---

Texte auf Griechisch in Palästina gebe. Erst ab dem 11. Jahrhundert setzte dann wieder eine Belebung der griechischen Literatur im Heiligen Land ein.

12 Graf, Georg: Geschichte der christlichen arabischen Literatur (Studi e testi 118), Bd. 1, Città del Vaticano 1944, S. 142–146; Leeming, Kate: The Adoption of Arabic as a Liturgical Language by the Palestinian Melkites, in: Aram 15 (2003), S. 239–246, 242 und 244.

13 Nasrallah, Joseph: Histoire du mouvement littéraire dans l'église melchite du Vᵉ au XXᵉ siècle. Contribution à l'étude de la littérature arabe chrétienne, Bd. 3, T. 1 (969–1250), Louvain/Paris 1983, S. 379–381. Kate Leeming: The Adoption of Arabic as a Liturgical Language (Anm. 12), S. 243ff., verweist zwar auf die Existenz einer im Sabas-Kloster angefertigten arabischen Übersetzung von zwölf kurzen Troparia aus dem 9. Jahrhundert für den Morgengottesdienst am Karfreitag. Ihre Schlussfolgerung, dass dann auch andere Gottesdienste in Gänze auf Arabisch abgehalten worden seien und die arabischsprachigen Christen über eine eigene Kirche verfügt haben müssten, wird jedoch durch die Quellen nicht gestützt.

14 Blau, Joshua: A Grammar of Chrisian Arabic Based Mainly on South Palestinian Texts from the 1st Millenium (Corpus Scriptorum Christianorum Orientalium 267, subsidia 27), Bd. 1, Louvain 1966, S. 19–33; Griffith: From Aramaic to Arabic (Anm. 1), S. 18f.; Rubin, Milka: Arabization versus Islamization in the Palestinian Melkite Community during the Early Muslim Period, in: Kofsky, Arieh/Stroumsa, Guy (Hg.): Sharing the Sacred. Religious Contacts and Conflicts in the Holy Land, First-Fifteenth Centuries CE, Jerusalem 1998, S. 149–162, S. 153f.

auf Arabisch eingeführt und zunehmend auch arabische Paralleltexte hinzugefügt. Als ein Beispiel kann ein syrisches Evangeliar von 1030 (Vat. Syr. 19) dienen,
das in 'Abūd, einem Dorf in der Nähe Jerusalems verfasst worden ist und Marginalien in *karšūnī*, also auf Arabisch in syrischer Schrift enthält. Dies stellte typi-
scher Weise die erste Phase der Einführung der eigenen Sprache noch im Gewand
der sakrosankten Liturgiesprache dar.[15] Eine Sammlung von Weiheriten aus dem
11. Jahrhundert bietet ein anschauliches Bild vom Gemisch der Sprachen und
Quellen in dieser Übergangszeit. Die Handschrift umfasst sowohl Formulare für
Kirch- und Altarweihen im palästinisch-aramäischen Dialekt als auch Übers5-
zungen aus dem Griechischen sowie Texte für die Priesterweihe im edessenisch-
syrischen Dialekt und andere griechische Formulare. Überschriften und Anweisungen finden sich auf Arabisch wie auch in anderen Sprachen.[16]

Die arabisierte Gemeinschaft der ursprünglich aramäischsprachigen Melkiten
in den ländlichen Gebieten Palästinas war sich dieses Sprachwechsels sehr bewusst
und dieses Bewusstsein trug sicher zu der langen Beibehaltung des Syrischen in
der Liturgie bei. Der palästinisch-aramäische Dialekt scheint tatsächlich einen
zentralen Punkt ihrer Identität ausgemacht zu haben, leitete sich davon doch ihre
Selbstbezeichnung als *as-suryānī*, als Syrer, ab. Unter dieser Bezeichnung werden
sie dann auch in den Listen der verschiedenen christlichen *nationes* im Heiligen
Land in lateinischen Pilgerberichten und bei Jakob von Vitry als eigene Gruppe, gesondert von den Griechen aufgeführt. Allerdings betonen die lateinischen
Quellen sehr deutlich, dass die *suriani* ansonsten derselben Kirche wie die Griechen angehören.[17] Der Stolz, über eine eigene heilige Sprache zu verfügen, führte den Autor einer arabischen Handschrift von 1164 zu der Behauptung, *suryānī
filasṭīnī*, das heißt Palästinisch-Syrisch, sei die Sprache gewesen, in der Gott mit
Adam gesprochen habe, also die erste Sprache überhaupt. In der zweiten Hälfte
des 12. Jahrhunderts, zur Zeit der Herrschaft der Kreuzfahrer und der damit verbundenen Unterstellung der griechisch-orthodoxen Kirche unter die Suprematie
der lateinischen Kirche, muss diese Äußerung als Mahnung, die Identität und den
Zusammenhalt der eigenen Gemeinschaft zu bewahren, verstanden werden.[18]

---

15 NASRALLAH: La liturgie des Patriarcats melchites (Anm. 10), S. 160; RUBIN: Arabization versus
   Islamization (Anm. 14), S. 157f.
16 Rituale melchitarum: a Christian Palestinian Euchologion, ed. und übers. v. Matthew BLACK
   (Bonner orientalistische Studien 22), Stuttgart 1938; GRAF: Geschichte der christlichen arabischen Literatur (Anm. 12), S. 626f.
17 VON DEN BRINCKEN, Anna-Dorothee: Die „Nationes christianorum orientalium" im Verständnis
   der lateinischen Historiographie von der Mitte des 12. bis in die zweite Hälfte des 14. Jahrhunderts
   (Kölner historische Abhandlungen 22), Köln/Wien 1973, S. 76–103.
18 RUBIN, Milka: The Language of Creation or the Primordial Language: A Case of Cultural Polemics in Antiquity, in: Journal of Jewish Studies 49 (1998), S. 306–333, S. 330, die hier einen Beleg
   für einen Gegensatz von arabischsprachigen Melkiten zur griechischen Hierarchie sieht. Es handelt sich um cod. sin. arab. 391, dessen Abfassungszeit von Milka Rubin fälschlich mit 1264 angegeben wird, siehe aber RUBIN: Arabization versus Islamization (Anm. 14), S. 158, wo sich in Anm.
   48 der arabische Text findet. Zur Lage der orthodoxen Kirche unter lateinischer Herrschaft siehe
   allgemein PAHLITZSCH: Graeci und Suriani im Palästina der Kreuzfahrerzeit (Anm. 3).

III

Aber auch im städtischen Milieu, wo im 12. Jahrhundert das Griechische durch die aus Byzanz stammenden Mönche und Kleriker als Liturgiesprache vorherrschend gewesen sein dürfte, drang das Arabische anders als von Jakob von Vitry geschildert im Bereich der Liturgie allmählich vor. In einem griechischen Typikon der Liturgie der Karwoche, das 1122 in Jerusalem geschrieben wurde, heißt es in einer Rubrik zu einer Predigt des Joannes Chrysostomos, dass diese Predigt im Anschluss an die Verlesung des griechischen Originals noch einmal vom 2. Diakon in arabischer Übersetzung vorgetragen werden soll. Auf den folgenden extra freigehaltenen Pergamentseiten wurde dann auch die arabische Übersetzung dieser Predigt hinzugefügt.[19] Somit fand das Arabische zumindest im Rahmen der Predigt, bei der es in besonderem Maße auf die Verständlichkeit ankam, Verwendung in der Liturgie.

Dies zeigt sich auch am Beispiel des nur auf Arabisch überlieferten Homiliars des Jerusalemer Patriarchen Athanasios II. aus dem 13. Jahrhundert. Insgesamt gehört das dem Athanasios zugeschriebene Homiliar formal und inhaltlich ganz der byzantinischen Tradition an. Der Autor benutzte sicher griechische Vorlagen, beherrschte also die griechische Sprache. Zwar gibt die sprachliche Form der in einem flüssig geschriebenen Mittelarabisch verfassten Predigtsammlung keinen eindeutigen Hinweis auf eine Übersetzung aus dem Griechischen. Die Verwendung griechischer Namen und Begriffe in arabischer Umschrift ist allerdings auffällig. Weiterhin könnte so die sprachliche Form der Bibelzitate erklärt werden, die zum einen durch eine prinzipielle Übereinstimmung mit der ägyptischen Vulgata charakterisiert sind, andererseits aber signifikante Abweichungen aufweisen, die auf eine direkte Übersetzung aus dem Griechischen hindeuten. Vielleicht ließ sich der sicher aus dem kirchlich-monastischen Milieu stammende Übersetzer bei der Übertragung der Bibelverse von seiner Kenntnis der arabischen Standardbibel leiten, wurde aber gleichzeitig von seiner griechischen Vorlage beeinflusst.[20]

Aus dem Charakter des Homiliars lassen sich Rückschlüsse auf das potentielle Publikum ziehen, liegt es doch im Interesse eines jeden Predigers, verstanden zu werden, um seine Zuhörer überzeugen und belehren zu können.[21] Es ist anzunehmen, dass die Homilien von Athanasios für seine eigene Predigttätigkeit in

19 PAPADOPOULOS-KERAMEUS, Anastasios: Hierosolymitike Bibliotheke, Bd. 3, St. Petersburg 1897 (Neudruck Brüssel 1963), S. 98–101; PAHLITZSCH: Graeci und Suriani (Anm. 3), S. 208.

20 Zur Predigtsammlung des Athanasios siehe ausführlich PAHLITZSCH: Graeci und Suriani (Anm. 3), S. 270–289 und S. 359–382 (Edition mit Übersetzung und Kommentar).

21 LONGÈRE, Jean: La Prédication médiévale, Paris 1983, S. 12. Allgemein zur noch in den Anfängen befindlichen Erforschung der Zuhörerschaft byzantinischer Predigten siehe CUNNINGHAM, Mary B./ALLEN, Pauline (Hg.): Preacher and Audience. Studies in Early Christian and Byzantine Homiletics (A New History of the Sermon 1), Leiden/Boston/Köln 1998, besonders die Einleitung der beiden Herausgeberinnen, S. 1–20.

der Sonntagsmesse vor der versammelten Gemeinde verwandt wurden.[22] Es liegt daher nahe, von einer ungefähr zeitgleichen Entstehung der arabischen Übersetzung auszugehen, da nur so etwas für die eigentliche Gemeindepredigt gewonnen war. Dies entspräche der eben geschilderten Praxis einer Verlesung der Predigt in Griechisch und Arabisch im Typikon von 1122. Ein konkreter Hinweis auf die fortschreitende Zweisprachigkeit im Gottesdienst in der Jerusalemer Kirche findet sich im Homiliar selbst in der Predigt zum 4. Sonntag der Vorfastenzeit, in dem Athanasios das Fasten am Karsamstag behandelt und seine Gemeinde auffordert, diesen Tag in der Kirche zu verbringen, wobei „derjenige von euch, der lesen kann, ein Buch bei sich haben soll, sei es nun Griechisch (*rūmī*) oder Arabisch, um darin zu lesen."[23]

Andererseits besteht die Möglichkeit, dass es sich bei dem griechischen Original zunächst um eine Sammlung von Musterpredigten handelte, die der Patriarch zur Verbesserung der Predigt als Leitfaden für seine Priester und Mönche verfasste. Dazu würde auch das fast vollständige Fehlen konkreter Bezüge zur eigenen Gegenwart passen. Die Predigten sollten allgemeine Gültigkeit haben und zur Verwendung für möglichst viele Gelegenheiten offen sein.[24] Auch für diesen Zweck wäre die baldige Anfertigung einer arabischen Übersetzung vonnöten gewesen. In der Folge erfreute sich das Homiliar des Athanasios großer Beliebtheit, wie sich aus der recht beachtlichen Zahl arabsicher Handschriften ergibt. Zudem wurde die Sammlung im 18. Jahrhundert in überarbeiteter Form gedruckt.[25]

Insgesamt zeigen die hier geschilderten Beispiele, dass die orthodoxe Kirche von Jerusalem entgegen der polemisch gefärbten Aussage Jakobs von Vitry, wonach die arabischsprachigen *suriani* gar nichts vom Gottesdienst verstünden, durchaus mit der Mehrsprachigkeit innerhalb der melkitischen Gemeinde umzugehen wusste.

IV

Die sprachliche Arabisierung der Liturgie ging aber keineswegs mit einer personellen Arabisierung des höheren Klerus des Patriarchats von Jerusalem einher. Es gab zwar durchaus arabische Bischöfe wie den für die zweite Hälfte des 11.

---

22 Allgemein dazu CUNNINGHAM, Mary: Preaching and the Community, in: MORRIS, Rosemary (Hg.): Church and People in Byzantium, Twentieth Spring Symposium of Byzantine Studies Manchester 1986, Birmingham 1990, S. 29–47, S. 45ff.

23 PAHLITZSCH: Graeci und Suriani (Anm. 3), S. 288. Zur Verwendung des Adjektivs *rūmī* siehe auch SERIKOFF, Nikolai: Rūmī and Yūnānī. Towards the Understanding of the Greek Language in the Medieval Muslim World, in: CIGAAR, Krijnie N./DAVIDS, Adelbert/TEULE, Herman (Hg.): East and West in the Crusader States. Context – Contacts – Confrontations (Acta of the congress held at Hernen Castle in May 1993), Leuven 1996, S. 169–194.

24 Vgl. LONGÈRE: La Prédication médiévale (Anm. 21), S. 13.

25 Joseph NASRALLAH: Histoire du mouvement littéraire dans l'église melchite du Vᵉ au XXᵉ siècle. Contribution à l'étude de la littérature arabe chrétienne, Bd. 3, T. 2 (1250–1516), Louvain/Paris 1981, S. 53f.

Jahrhunderts belegten Sulaimān al-Ġazzī.[26] Anfang des 12. Jahrhunderts sind aber griechisch-stämmige Metropoliten von Tyros und Sidon und Caesarea zu Patriarchen von Jerusalem gewählt geworden.[27] Einen interessanten Fall für die Bedeutung des Griechischen für den hohen Klerus stellt eine lateinische Urkunde von 1173 dar, in der der Meister des Johanniterordens das Georgskloster in Bait Ǧibrīn dem *surianus* Meletos, dem Erzbischof der *suriani* und Griechen in Gaza, Zeit seines Lebens überließ. Die vom Kloster erwirtschafteten Überschüsse waren dafür als Almosen zur Versorgung der Armen im Jerusalemer Johanniter-Hospital zu verwenden. Als besonderer Nutznießer des geistlichen Lohns für die Verrichtung dieser guten Werke wurde der byzantinische Kaiser genannt, auf dass er mit Gottes Hilfe im jetzigen Leben zum Wohle der Kirche sein Amt ausübe, in Zukunft aber in das *regnum eternum* eingehe. Darüber hinaus wurde Meletos in die Gebetsbruderschaft (*confratriam*) des Hospitals aufgenommen.[28] Einerseits fällt in dieser Urkunde die ungewöhnliche Nähe des orthodoxen Erzbischofs zu den Johannitern auf, andererseits zeigt die starke Ausrichtung auf den byzantinischen Herrscher, dass hier keineswegs ein einheimischer Bischof ohne Rücksicht auf die Interessen der orthodoxen Kirche agierte. Interessant ist aber die Bezeichnung des Meletos als *surianus*, das heißt als Christ orientalischer Herkunft. Meletos hat diese lateinische Urkunde eigenhändig unterschrieben, nicht aber auf Arabisch, sondern auf Griechisch. Seine auf dem Original der Urkunde erhaltene Unterschrift weist dabei keinerlei Anzeichen auf, nicht von einem griechischen Muttersprachler abgefasst worden zu sein.[29] Ein griechischer Name und die Kenntnis des Griechischen scheinen also die Vorraussetzung für die Übernahme eines Bischofsamtes in Palästina gewesen zu sein.

Vielleicht in konkretem Zusammenhang mit dieser Betonung der Griechischsprachigkeit des Meletos steht die etwa zur selben Zeit einsetzende Byzantinisierung der palästinensischen Kirche. Mit dem Begriff der Byzantinisierung wird hier die engere Anbindung des Patriarchats von Jerusalem an Konstantinopel auf rituellem und kirchenrechtlichem Gebiet bezeichnet. Bis in das 12. Jahrhundert hinein konnten die drei orthodoxen Patriarchate des Orients, Antiochia und Jerusalem mit der Jakobs- sowie Alexandria mit der Markus-Liturgie, jeweils ihre

---

26 DICK, Ignace: Samonas de Gaza ou Sulaiman al-Gazzi, Évêque melkite de Gaza, XIᵉ siècle, in: Proche-Orient Chrétien 30 (1980), S. 175–178.

27 PAHLITZSCH: Graeci und Suriani (Anm. 3), S. 102–109 und S. 134–138.

28 Regesta regni Hierosolymitani, 1097–1291, ed. v. Reinhold RÖHRICHT, Innsbruck 1893, Nr. 502; der Text wurde ediert von Joseph DELAVILLE LE ROULX: Trois chartes du XIIᵉ siècle concernant l'Ordre de S. Jean de Jérusalem, in: Archives de l'Orient Latin (1881), S. 413ff. Zur Institution des Charistikions in den Kreuzfahrerstaaten siehe MAYER, Hans Eberhard: Varia Antiochena. Studien zum Kreuzfahrerfürstentum Antiochia im 12. und frühen 13. Jahrhundert (MGH Studien und Texte 6), Hannover 1993, S. 138–161, zur hier behandelten Urkunde S. 160f.; sowie MAYER, Hans Eberhard: Bistümer, Klöster und Stifte im Königreich Jerusalem (Schriften der Monumenta Germaniae Historica 26), Stuttgart 1977, S. 406–409; MAYER, Hans Eberhard: Latins, Muslims and Greeks in the Latin Kingdom of Jerusalem, in: History 63 (1978), S. 175–192, S. 191f.

29 PAHLITZSCH: Graeci und Suriani (Anm. 3), S. 196–199. Eine Abbildung der Urkunde findet sich in der Edition von Delaville Le Roulx zwischen den Seiten 414 und 415.

eigene Form des Ritus bewahren. In der Folge strebte das Patriarchat von Konstantinopel verstärkt die Vereinheitlichung der Liturgie durch die Übernahme der in der Hauptstadt üblichen Joannes Chrysostomos-Liturgie an. Die Durchsetzung der Chrysostomos-Liturgie als allein gültige Form zog sich zwar bis in das 13. Jahrhundert und darüber hinaus hin,[30] dürfte aber dennoch wesentlich dadurch begünstigt worden sein, dass sich vom Beginn des 12. bis zum Anfang des 13. Jahrhunderts die Patriarchen von Jerusalem und Antiochia ständig in Konstantinopel im Exil aufhielten.[31] Mit Theodoros Balsamon übernahm ca. 1185 ein Vertreter dieser Byzantinisierungspolitik das Amt des Patriarchen von Antiochia im konstantinopolitanischen Exil. Als sich der Patriarch von Alexandria im Rahmen eines ganzen Katalogs von Fragen bei ihm erkundigte, ob die in Jerusalem und Alexandria üblichen Jakobs- und Markus-Liturgien von der „heiligen und katholischen Kirche" akzeptiert würden, antwortete Balsamon daher eindeutig ablehnend. Als Grund führte er an, alle Kirchen Gottes müssten im Brauch dem Neuen Rom, also Konstantinopel, folgen und gemäß der Lehre des Johannes Chrysostomos und des Basileios die Liturgie feiern.[32]

Byzantinisierung und Arabisierung stellten dabei keineswegs einen Gegensatz dar. Vielmehr ist von einem lebendigen Nebeneinander griechischer und arabischer Einflüsse auszugehen. Mit Bezug auf die Feier des Gottesdienstes äußerte sich Joannes von Chalkedon, ein Zeitgenosse Balsamons, in einer ersten Fassung der Antworten auf die erwähnten Fragen des Patriarchen von Alexandria dahingehend, dass die orientalischen Christen, die kein Griechisch verstanden, die Liturgie in ihrer eigenen Sprache feiern sollten. Entsprechend der geforderten engen Anbindung an Byzanz verlangte Balsamon dann in seiner Überarbeitung, dabei genaue Übersetzungen aus dem Griechischen zu verwenden.[33] Dass in einer aus

---

30 KARALEVSKY, Cyrille: Histoire du Patriarcat Melkites (Alexandrie, Antioche, Jérusalem) depuis le schisme monophysite du VIᵉ siècle jusqu'à nos jours, Bd. 3: Les institutions, liturgie, hierarchie, statistique, sources du droit canonique et organisation, Rom 1911, S. 156–181; NASRALLAH: La liturgie des Patriarcats melchites (Anm. 10), S. 156–181; DALMAIS, Irénée-Henri: Liturgies d'Orient, Paris 1980, S. 33; EVERY, George: Syrian Christians in Jerusalem, 1183–1283, in: Eastern Churches Quaterly 7 (1947/48), S. 46–54, S. 53, weist darauf hin, dass in der im Parisinus Suppl. gr. 476 aus dem 15. Jahrhundert enthaltenen Jakobsliturgie in den Diptychen des Patriarchen Leontios II. (1176–1185) gedacht wird, so dass der Pariser Kodex die Kopie einer im 12. Jahrhundert in Palästina entstanden Handschrift sein dürfte; siehe BRIGHTMAN, Frank Edward: Liturgies Eastern and Western, Bd. 1: Eastern Liturgies, Oxford 1896 (Neudruck Oxford 1967), S. L.

31 So wurde nach Theodoros Balsamons Kommentar zum 32. Kanon des Trullanums der Patriarch von Alexandria während seines Aufenthalts in der Hauptstadt offenbar in Anwesenheit von Balsamon dazu aufgefordert, die Chrystomos-Liturgie zu verwenden, Syntagma ton theion kai hieron kanonon, ed. v. Georgios A. RHALLES/Michael POTLES, Bd. 2, Athen 1852 (Neudruck 1966), S. 377.

32 Syntagma ton theion kai hieron kanonon, ed. v. Georgios A. RHALLES/Michael POTLES, Bd. 4, Athen 1854 (Neudruck 1966), S. 448f.; NASRALLAH: La liturgie des Patriarcats melchites (Anm. 10), S. 163 Anm. 38. Siehe allgemein GRUMEL, Venance: Les réponses canoniques à Marc d'Alexandrie, leur caractère officiel, leur double rédaction, in: Echos d'Orient 38 (1939), S. 321–333.

33 PITSAKES, Konstantinos G.: He ektase tes exousias henos hyperoriou patriarche ho patriarches Antiocheias sten Konstantinoupole ton 12o aiona, in: OIKONOMIDES, Nikolaos (Hg.): To Byzantio kata ton 12o aiona, Athen 1991, S. 91–139, S. 100f. Die Annahme von GRIFFITH: From

dem 12. oder 13. Jahrhundert stammenden griechischen Handschrift nun gerade der Markus-Liturgie die arabische Übersetzung am Rand beigefügt worden ist, mag allerdings nicht ganz den Vorstellungen Balsamons entsprochen haben.[34]

Darüber hinaus wurden die von den byzantinischen Kaisern erlassenen Gesetzesbücher von den orthodoxen Christen im Orient ab Anfang des 13. Jahrhunderts in das Arabische übersetzt und tradiert, auch wenn sie mit ihren weitreichenden Bestimmungen zu allen Fragen des öffentlichen Lebens nur zu einem geringen Teil für die Regelung der internen Rechtsprechung der Melkiten relevant waren. Lediglich das Ehe- und Erbrecht konnte unter muslimischer Herrschaft im Rahmen der rechtlichen Autonomie in internen Angelegenheiten Anwendung finden.[35] Entsprechend der Byzantinisierungspolitik auf dem Gebiet der Liturgie heißt es in einer Antwort des Theodoros Balsamon auf die Frage des alexandrinischen Patriarchen, ob es verwerflich sei, dass die *Basilika*, das Rechtsbuch Leons VI., seiner Gemeinde nicht bekannt sei: „Diejenigen also, die sich einer orthodoxen Lebensweise rühmen, seien sie aus dem Orient, aus Alexandria oder von anderswoher, werden Rhomäer genannt und müssen gemäß den Gesetzen regiert werden."[36] Auch die orientalischen arabischsprachigen Christen galten somit als Byzantiner und sollten in allen Lebensbereichen Byzanz folgen.

Diese arabischen Übersetzungen der byzantinischen Rechtsbücher stellen einen weiteren Beleg einer im Palästina der Kreuzfahrerzeit lebendigen griechisch-arabischen Tradition dar. So wurden mehrfach ältere Übersetzungen mit Rückgriff auf das griechische Original neu überarbeitet. Als Vorlage dienten dabei zweispaltige, auf Griechisch und Arabisch verfasste Handschriften. Als eigentlicher Ort dieses Austausches können die orthodoxen Klöster gelten, in denen im 12. und

---

Aramaic to Arabic (Anm. 1), S. 29f., der sich dabei auf Dagron, Gilbert: Formes et fonctions du pluralisme linguistique à Byzance (IXe–XIIe siècle), in: Travaux et Mémoires 12 (1994), S. 219–240, S. 228ff., stützt, dass im 11. und 12. Jahrhundert „an earlier linguistic pluralism gave way to an insistence on Greek in matters of faith and cult", scheint mir Balsamons Aussage überzuinterpretieren. Auch wenn das griechische Original als Garant für die Orthodoxie der jeweiligen Texte angesehen wird, so gestattet Balsamon ja dennoch die Feier der Liturgie in anderen Sprachen, Syntagma ton theion kai hieron kanonon (Anm. 32), Bd. 4, S. 452f.

34 Brightman: Liturgies Eastern and Western (Anm. 30), Bd. 1, S. LXIV. Erst Brakmann, Heinzgerd: Zur Bedeutung des Sinaiticus graecus 2148 für die Geschichte der melchitischen Markos-Liturgie, in: Jahrbuch der österreichischen Byzantinistik 30 (1981), S. 239–248, S. 243, hat diese Handschrift als Sin. gr. 2148 identifiziert. In Kamil, Murad: Catalogue of all Manuscripts in the Monastery of St. Catherine on Mount Sinai, Wiesbaden 1970, S. 117, serial no. Greek 1500, wird die Handschrift auf das 13. Jahrhundert datiert und fälschlich als Sin. gr. 2147 bezeichnet, siehe Brakmann, S. 243, Anm. 25. Interessanterweise enthält der Sin. gr. 2148 bei der anaphorischen Fürbitte für den Patriarchen von Alexandria am Rand die auf Griechisch nachgetragenen Namen zweier Patriarchen von der Mitte des 13. Jahrhunderts, womit belegt wird, dass im Patriarchat Alexandria trotz aller Byzantinisierungstendenzen auch noch im 13. Jahrhundert die lokale Markusliturgie beibehalten worden ist, Brakmann, S. 246ff.

35 Zur rechtlichen Stellung der Christen unter muslimischer Herrschaft siehe allgemein Fattal, Antoine: Le statut légal des non-musulmans en pays d'Islam, Beirut 1958.

36 Syntagma ton theion kai hieron kanonon (Anm. 32), Bd. 4, S. 451.

13. Jahrhundert Handschriften in beiden Sprachen verfasst wurden.[37] Auch griechisch-arabische liturgische Handschriften sind aus dieser Zeit überliefert.[38] Die Übersetzungen byzantinischer Rechtsbücher bilden keinen Widerspruch zu der eingangs geschilderten Übernahme islamischer Rechtsformen. Bei Kaufverträgen war eben eine Intervention der muslimischen Obrigkeit immer denkbar, während die in den byzantinischen Rechtsbüchern behandelten Ehe- und Erbrechtsfragen der eigenen kirchlichen Jurisdiktion unterlagen. Zudem ging der Wert dieser Übersetzungen weit über ihren praktischen Nutzen hinaus. Hiermit demonstrierten die *suriani*, dass sie unbestreitbar Teil der orthodoxen Welt waren.

Die Identität der Melkiten im 12. und 13. Jahrhundert wurde nicht durch ihre Arabischsprachigkeit bestimmt.[39] Als *suriani* hielten sie bis in das 13. Jahrhundert trotz der fortschreitenden Arabisierung der Liturgie an ihrer eigenen palästinisch-aramäischen Liturgiesprache als Kennzeichen ihrer auf diese Weise regional definierten Gemeinschaft fest. Als *rhomaioi/rūmī* fühlten sie sich dagegen dem byzantinischen Reich zugehörig und scheinen der von Byzanz geforderten Vereinheitlichung von Liturgie und Recht ohne größeren Widerstand gefolgt zu sein. Beide Aspekte stellen somit zwei sich einander ergänzende Facetten ihres Selbstverständnisses dar.

---

37 Siehe dazu LEDER, Stefan (Hg.): Die arabische Ecloga. Das vierte Buch der Kanones der Könige aus der Sammlung des Makarios (Forschungen zur byzantinischen Rechtsgeschichte 12), Frankfurt a. M. 1985; und demnächst PAHLITZSCH, Johannes (Hg.): Der arabische Procheiros Nomos (Forschungen zur Byzantinischen Rechtsgeschichte), Frankfurt a. M.

38 GRAF: Geschichte der christlichen arabischen Literatur (Anm. 12), S. 625f.; NASRALLAH: Histoire du mouvement littéraire (Anm. 13), Bd. 3, T. 1, S. 366.

39 Dementsprechend muss auch die nur schwach belegte Auffassung von VILA, Daniel: The Struggle over Arabisation in Medieval Arabic Christian Hagiography, in: al-Masāq 15 (2003), S. 35–46, die orientalischen Christen hätten auch gerade gegen die Muslime ihre eigene arabische Identität betont, abgelehnt werden. Dass sich arabischsprachige Christen ausdrücklich als Araber bezeichnet hätten, ist mir nicht bekannt.

David J. Wasserstein

Language and prayer among Muslims, Christians and Jews in the early Islamic world

How did people pray in the world of early Islam? What language or languages did they use to do so? What was the relationship between the languages of regular, everyday speech and the languages of prayer? Were they the same or varied? What did it mean to a worshipper to pray in a language other than that of everyday life? And what did it mean to offer prayer to God in words which the worshipper perhaps did not understand, or did not understand very fully? Did the register of the language used in the liturgy – often very high – have significance for understanding (clearly yes), for effect (less clearly, but still yes), and for meaning (fairly clearly also yes, but rather in a negative sense)?

These questions are not all as easy to answer as they might appear to be. For the period after the rise of Islam, in the first few centuries, in the area that became the Arab-Islamic empire, we tend to associate the worship of Islam with the use of the Arabic language, that of the God of the Jews with Hebrew, and that of the Christian God with Greek (or Latin or Syriac/Aramaic). It is an easy set of assumptions, and one which consorts well with the languages of the holy writings of these groups. But if God is in the details then easy assumptions are also risky ones. The period following the rise of Islam, largely because of the rise of Islam, was also a period of massive change of language and massive change of religion among the peoples of the territories conquered by the Arabs in the seventh Christian century. Iran became almost wholly Muslim in faith and its linguistic character became heavily influenced by Arabic. The territories conquered from Byzantium and further west became almost wholly Muslim and wholly Arabic linguistically.

These two processes, religious and linguistic change, together with a third one, ethnic transformation, are closely intertwined with each other. But they are not identical, and it remained possible down to modern times to undergo one or two of them without the third. Thus one could be Arabic in language and Arab in ethnicity, but not Muslim in religion (the last foreign minister of Iraq under Saddam Hussein, Tariq Aziz – a Christian – is a good example of this); one could be Arabic in language but neither Muslim in faith nor perceived by anyone as Arab in terms of ethnicity – Jewish. One could be Muslim in religion, but neither Arabic in language nor Arab by ethnic affiliation – a Persian Muslim, for example. And there are other possibilities. The relationships between and among these processes at the start of Islam is obscure; in particular, it is difficult to penetrate the fog surrounding the chronological relationship between processes of linguistic change and religious change: did conversion to the God of the Arabs entail as a preliminary and as a prerequisite knowledge of the language in which He had sent His message to them? Did you have to understand what He had said to Muhammad, preserved in the Qur'an, before you could accept its truth? Put the other way around: could you accept the message of God without understanding it? The question is more complicated than one might imagine, particularly in the conditions of a society sometimes aggressively missionising towards its own minorities, such as we find, for example, in the Near East of a thousand years ago.

Take the case of conversion: did a Jew or a Christian who converted to Islam, and then by definition changed his language of prayer, know what he was doing? Or we can turn this question inside out, and ask whether and how far non-Muslims who used Arabic as their language of prayer remained non-Muslims: to what extent is prayer to the God of Christians, in the Islamic world as elsewhere, a function of the retention of the (or a) language of the Christian Bible, Latin or Greek or Syriac/Aramaic? And for which purposes? The problem presumably arose in a number of places. And the same, *mutatis mutandis*, could apply also to Jews.

A well-known Muslim *fatwa*, or religious-legal opinion, tells us that prayer is permitted in any language, including Berber, 'because God understands all languages'. It is a relief to know this, especially, one assumes, if one happens to be a Berber. But Muslim *fatwas* do not have automatic applicability or truth value among non-Muslims, and Christians, at least non-Berber ones, in classical Islam may have wondered about the matter. In al-Andalus, Christian Spain, we have the famous example of Alvarus of Cordoba in the ninth century, complaining about the widespread attraction to Arabic experienced by young Christians there: despite the feeling with which Alvarus expresses his plaint, we do not know much in detail about what this really meant for people then, and we do know that forms of spoken Latin, what we call Romance, were in use in the Islamic parts of the peninsula long after.[1] But there certainly did come a time when Christians in al-Andalus lost literary command of Latin, and probably also Romance as a speech-form, too. What did this mean for their prayers? What did this mean for public prayer, in the mouths of priests, and what did it mean for private, personal prayer by individuals? Translations of the Scriptures into Arabic, and the translation/composition of works of canon law in that language, demonstrate less and less ability to use Latin/Romance; this decline is confirmed by the complete cessation of writing among these Christians in Latin; they may not prove total loss of Latin/Romance as a vehicle of speech in prayer, but they certainly show which way the wind, a veritable tempest, was blowing. That direction was, quite literally, southwards, for we hear, at the start of the twelfth century, of the expulsion of some thousands of

---

1 For Alvarus' plaint, see WASSERSTEIN, D.: A Latin Lament on the Prevalence of Arabic in Ninth-Century Islamic Cordoba, in: Arabicus Felix, Luminosus Britannicus, Essays in Honour of A. F. L. Beeston on his Eightieth Birthday, ed. by A. JONES, Reading 1991, pp. 1–7; for the broader linguistic picture in Islamic Spain, WASSERSTEIN, D: The Language Situation in al-Andalus, in: Studies on the Muwassah and the Kharja, ed. by A. JONES and R. HITCHCOCK, Reading 1991, pp. 1–15 (repr. in M. FIERRO and J. SAMSÓ [eds.]: The Formation of al-Andalus, Part 2: Language, Religion, Culture and the Sciences [= The Formation of the Classical Islamic World, general ed. L. I. CONRAD, vol. 47], Aldershot 1998, pp. 3–17).

Andalusi Christians to north Africa, where, we have to assume, they spoke Arabic and soon forgot any Romance that they may have retained up till then.

This comes out if we look at the legal aspect of conversion, too: the evidence comes from the tenth century, but we have no good reason to doubt that something broadly similar, if not in the technical details then in the overall pattern which it reveals, was happening earlier, too. From tenth-century Cordoba we have a legal formulary which contains a standard "document for the conversion of a Christian" (it contains others too, for members of other faiths, and for women as well as men).[2] This is a purely legal document, which the convert probably needed mainly for tax reasons (God could presumably tell what he believed, without a piece of paper to prove it). But in order to get this certificate of conversion to Islam, he had to appear before a *qadi*, or judge, and go through a legal procedure in which, among other things, he had to confirm that he was in good mental health and understood what he was doing, and explicitly renounce his former faith and take on the new one, along with all its obligations, in particular those of prayer. This is more than simply a matter of saying "la ilaha illa Allah", something that we all know is sufficient to make one a Muslim for certain purposes; it is more than simply throwing a few drops of water on someone's head. It is a legal step, performed in Arabic and written down in Arabic in a formal legal document; it is a step weighted with much social and legal, as well as merely religious, consequence, and it was seen as such, and this in a society in which legal acts of much consequence were accorded the respect that they deserve. We may with some justice assume large-scale arabicisation of these Christians, while still Christians, at greater or lesser speed depending on their physical and social location.

Something similar seems to have happened among the Jews too. The Islamic conquests brought virtually all the Jews of the world west of India under a single rule. We know scarcely anything of the real effects of the initial period of Islamic rule for the Jews, though we can deduce much from what was going on before and what happened later. One of the effects was the rapid acquisition of Arabic by Jews in the territories that became the Arab world (including Islamic Spain). Perhaps the best single indication of this is the translation of almost the whole of the Bible from the original tongues into Arabic by Sa'adya Gaon in Egypt and Iraq in the first half of the tenth century. As we are often reminded, the translation of the Bible is a massive and hugely costly task; no one undertakes it unless there is a pressing need for it. There was such a need among the Jews of these centres at that

---

2 See Ibn al-'Attar: Formulario notarial hispano-árabe, ed. by P. CHALMETA and F. CORRIENTE, Madrid 1983, p. 406. For a translation see Pedro CHALMETA and Marina MARUGÁN: Ibn al-'Attar, Formulario notarial y judicial andalusí del alfaquí y notario cordobés (m. 399/1009), Madrid 2000 (see also the review of this work by C. DE LA PUENTE, in: Journal of the Economic and Social History of the Orient 45 (2002), pp. 524–26). See further CHALMETA, P.: Le passage à l'Islam dans al-Andalus au Xe siècle, in: Actas del XII Congreso de la U.E.A.I. (Malaga 1984), Madrid 1986, pp. 161–83; ABUMALHAM, Monserrat: La conversión según formularios notariales andalusíes: valoración de la legalidad de la conversión de Maimónides, in: Miscelánea de Estudios Arabes y Hebraicos XXXIV (1985), pp. 70–84.

time, and it was filled by the work of Saʿadya. But what does it mean to say that there was such a need among them? It means, *inter alia*, that they could not, or no longer, understand the Scriptures in the original, and needed to have them in a language which they could understand. It meant that they had by then already largely abandoned (a) other languages that they had been using until that time – the languages of their social environments, Greek, Aramaic (in its various forms), Latin; and (b) the language of the Scriptures itself (Hebrew, with some Aramaic). The latter explains the need for the new version of the Bible; the former makes us ask what language they were now using to pray. And did they understand their prayers? It also raises questions about the comprehensibility to these Jews of the Bible readings in the synagogue, as well as about the use and function at this stage of the *targumim*, the Aramaic translations of Scripture which had been made to begin with because of the inability of Jews to understand the Hebrew original. How were these now regarded and used?

The simple answer to these questions is that the Jews largely went over to Arabic. But the language of public prayer among them remained ever Hebrew (with a small admixture of Aramaic), and Hebrew, as part of Jewish religious and cultural life in general, was vastly re-born under the umbrella of Islam. But although Hebrew thus enjoyed a renaissance, and was known to the culturally active elite among the very small numbers of Jews in the various centres, this does not mean that all, or most, Jews understood their prayers. It would be difficult to justify such a claim. In fact we do not know how much most of them can have known. Hebrew seems to have functioned among certain elements of the Jewish population as an important second language. However, how large these segments were is impossible to say; how deep the knowledge went is not much easier to judge; and what we mean by 'second' in such contexts is open to question. And lastly, we can be pretty sure that for most Jews, almost all women, most children, the majority of the men, Hebrew was in many ways a closed book.[3]

These changes among Christians and Jews of the early, classical Islamic world are the product of wider changes in their societies. Those changes in their turn are the product, not just of conquest by Arabs, with their new faith, but also of massive conversion by Christians (and perhaps just a very little by Jews, as I have argued elsewhere) to the religion of their conquerors.[4] In other words, if the Chris-

---

3   See, e.g., OLSZOWY-SCHLANGER, Judith: Learning to read and write in medieval Egypt: children's exercise books from the Cairo Geniza, in: Journal of Semitic Studies 48 (2003), pp. 47–69; ead.: Karaite linguistics; the "renaissance" of the Hebrew language among early Karaite Jews, and contemporary linguistic theories, Beitraege zur Geschichte der Sprachwissenschaft 7 (1997), pp. 81–100.

4   For an exciting and attractive, if not necessarily correct, picture of how the conversion process affected the entire populations of the new Islamic empire, see BULLIET, R. W.: Conversion to Islam in the Classical Period. An Essay in Quantitative History, Cambridge, Mass., 1979 (see also the long review by Y. Friedmann of another book on the topic, in Asian and African Studies 14 (1980), pp. 81–90, discussing Bulliet's thesis); for my reservations about the application of any such models to such small minorities as the Jews, see WASSERSTEIN, D: Islamisation and the conversion of the Jews, in: Conversions islamiques, Identités religieuses en Islam méditerranéen, ed. by Mercedes GARCÍA-ARENAL, Paris 2001, pp. 49–60.

tians went over to Arabic, it was because other Christians had gone over both to Arabic and to Islam, helping to make Arabic the language of those sections of the population that were dominant not only politically but now also numerically. As I have suggested, we cannot know in any individual case, and it is also impossible to be definite in respect of whole areas, whether religious change brought linguistic change in its wake or linguistic change led to religious change. The two are very intimately related but we cannot be clear about a chronological link between them. What is clear, though, is that the one implied the other in some form, and what that means is that islamisation implies arabicisation; and that tended to mean the abandonment of other languages.

Because of this it is worth wondering just a little about the character, in particular the linguistic character, of the Islam of the early generations of the Islamic world outside Arabia. We should not make the easy mistake of imagining that the linguistic character of the Near East on the eve of Islam was either uniform or static. Quite the opposite. In a recent article, I argued that at least in one place, Nessana, on the edge of the desert frontier of the Byzantine empire, now just on the Israeli side of the border with Egypt, there was in process a long-term transformation of the character of the population.[5] On the basis of the written material found there sixty five years ago by the Colt expedition, inscriptional and documentary, it seems to me that the people of Nessana were moving over from paganism to Christianity, from Arabic to Greek, and in consequence also from Arab ethnicity to something that we can call Greek too. This flies in the face of some current orthodoxies, especially one which sees, first, much Arabic in the region, and secondly ongoing large-scale osmosis of Arabic outwards from the Arabian peninsula into the settled areas of the two great empires. I am unpersuaded both of the truth of all this and of its significance. In the first place, the evidence of Nessana, onomastic and linguistic, demonstrates the abandonment of Arabic and the adoption of Greek, as well as the abandonment of paganism and the adoption of Christianity. In the second place, it is not to be supposed that, without the massive transformation of Arab society wrought by the coming of Islam, Arabic would ever have amounted to anything significant outside the fringes of the peninsula or been able to mount any meaningful challenge to Greek or to Aramaic-Syriac or to Persian. Why should anyone, before and without the coming of Islam, to put this very simply, have taken on Arabic, and at the price of Greek? To counter this one would need very special forms of special pleading.

Now Nessana is just one small place, and it is not the whole of the Near East. Nevertheless, it both exhibits a certain linguistic richness and illustrates the fact that languages and language use are ever in flux. That richness and that flux at Nessana were, *mutatis mutandis*, the character of the Near East as a whole, and after 632, as before, richness and flux remained. However, there were new elements now, principally Arabic, and if what happened was essentially the expulsion

---

5 WASSERSTEIN, D.: Why Did Arabic Succeed Where Greek Failed? Language Change in the Near East After Muhammad, Scripta Classica Israelica XXII (2003), pp. 257–72.

of the rest by the cuckoo of Arabic, nonetheless the Near East thereafter still displays much linguistic variety and movement. One of the great lacks in our field is a linguistic atlas of the area in the period after the rise of Islam. It would be technically very difficult to produce, but there can be no doubt that it would be a worthwhile and instructive project to undertake.

Not only in the realm of religion, this significance of Arabic can be seen in the overall attractive power of imperial rule by those of Arab speech among the ruled, in the formal imposition of Arabic as the official language of administration towards the end of the seventh century, in the foundation of a new imperial capital dominated by Arabs and Arabic in Baghdad in the middle of the eighth century, in the invention of a glorious Arab past, the pre-Islamic *jahiliyya*, in the development of Arabic as a new world-class language of culture, via the creation of a massive new written literature, partly through translation, of belles-lettres, in the sciences, in the religious fields too, in that language, in the canonisation of the Arabic language and its study itself, in the migration of large numbers of Arabs out from the peninsula and their settlement all over the empire, a veritable *Voelkerwanderung*, in the creation of a new world market system in which Arabic came rapidly to serve as a world language, allied to a religion in which travel, for pilgrimage and in search of learning, *fi talab al-'ilm*, was a rapidly accepted norm.[6] In this context, Arabic also filled, better than any other, the need for a single common language. And all of this as background to a society or a set of societies in which the full acceptance of Arabic and of Islam served also as an admission ticket into a new identity for the convert, as an Arab.

Both in these early generations and later too, new arrivals, whether from within the society or from outside (such as slaves or mercenary or slave soldiers) abandoned their languages and took on Arabic, partly for these reasons and partly for others such as the need for integration and sheer communication. This does not apply to the Ottoman Turks, who came very much later and very differently;[7] nor does it apply with the same force to Iran, for other reasons. It did not work either for one large group of earlier converts, the Berbers, for reasons which remain slightly obscure. But it does represent the broad lines of what happened. People

---

6 See for example, from a huge literature, MORONY, Michael G.: Iraq After the Muslim Conquest, Princeton 1984; LASSNER, J.: The Topography of Baghdad in the Early Middle Ages, Detroit, 1970; LAPIDUS, I. M.: The evolution of Muslim urban society, in: Comparative Studies in Society and History XV (1973), pp. 21–50; DRORY, Rina: The Abbasid construction of the Jahiliyya: cultural authority in the making, in: Studia Islamica 83 (1996), pp. 33–49; the various volumes of the Cambridge History of Arabic Literature; GUTAS, Dimitri: Greek Thought, Arabic Culture. The Graeco-Arabic Translation Movement in Baghdad and Early 'Abbasid Society (2nd–4th/8th–10th centuries), London/New York 1998.

7 See for example, for the Mamluks and the Turks, HAARMANN, Ulrich: Arabic in speech, Turkish in lineage: Mamluks and their sons in the intellectual life of fourteenth-century Egypt and Syria, in: Journal of Semitic Studies 33 (1988), pp. 81–114; id.: Ideology and history, identity and alterity: the Arab image of the Turk from the 'Abbasids to modern Egypt, in: International Journal of Middle East Studies 20 (1988), pp. 175–96.

had plenty of good reasons to take on Arabic; they had correspondingly few good reasons to retain their old languages. I shall return to this below.

I return at this point to the questions that I began with: the relationship between the languages of prayer and religion and those of daily life. Among the Greek texts dug up at Nessana, which I mentioned a few moments ago, the excavators found one text, written on the back of a used piece of papyrus. It was a prayer, and was one of the pieces of evidence which come together to persuade me of the Greek language of the inhabitants of the little desert town in the seventh century, many of them originally of Arab stock. The prayer was fairly well-known, taken from the *euchologion mega*, in the Byzantine prayer book. It says the following:[8]

> God of spirits and of all flesh, Who hast banished death, trampled Hades under foot, and bestowed life upon the world, give repose to the soul of Thy servant in the region of light, in the region of respite, whence pain and grief and lamentation have fled. Forgive all done by him in word or deed or thought, for Thou art good and lovest mankind. Thou knowest there will never live any man who will not sin, [for Thou alone art God, free of all sin and Thy justice is the justice of eternity. Thy word, O Lord, is truth. Thou art the sleep and the resurrection of Thy servant and we hymn Thy glory to the Father, the Son and the Holy Ghost, now and forever and to the eternity of eternities. Amen.]

It is difficult to know what to make of this: was it some sort of aide-mémoire, or an amulet (but on the back of a torn bit of papyrus?), or what? Because of its contents, the prayer is common in the context of death, but in this case it seems not to have any specific application; contrary to what one might expect, no name is inserted after the words "to the soul of Thy servant". It remains a little puzzling.

By a curious and happy chance, a variation, or a set of variations, on the same prayer is used on a number of tombstones found in what was once Christian Nubia. The inscriptions on the tombstones can (with some difficulties) be dated to the period 993–1243, perhaps even 858–1243 CE.[9] Here the mortuary context is very clear: in each case, the prayer is used, on a tombstone, as a prayer for the deceased. What is Greek doing all that way down in Africa? More to the point here, can I apply the same reasoning as in the Nessanan case to argue that Nubians spoke Greek?

---

8   Taken from Casper J. KRAEMER, JR.: Excavations at Nessana, 3, Non-literary papyri, Princeton 1958, pp. 309–10, no. 96, with references to the relevant bibliography.

9   For what follows see FREND, W. H. C./MUIRHEAD, I. A.: The Greek manuscripts from the cathedral at Q'asr Ibrim, in: Le Muséon 89 (1976), pp. 43–49; FREND, W. H.C: A fragment of the "Acta Sancti Georgii" from Q'asr Ibrim (Egyptian Nubia), in: Analecta Bollandiana 100 (1982), pp. 79–86; id.: Some Greek liturgical fragments from Q'asr Ibrim in Nubia, in: Studia Patristica 15 (= Texte und Untersuchungen 128) (1984), pp. 545–53; id.: Fragments of an Acta Martyrum from Q'asr Ibrim, in: Jahrbuch fuer Antike und Christentum 29 (1986), pp. 66–70; id. and George DRAGAS: A Eucharistic Sequence from Q'asr Ibrim, in: Jahrbuch fuer Antike und Christentum 30 (1987), pp. 90–98; more generally, ADAMS, William Y.: Nubia, Corridor to Africa, Princeton 1977, pp. 485–88, 745–46. For the inscriptions themselves see Preisigkes Sammelbuch Griechischer Urkunden aus Ägypten, III, 1926, no. 6035; IV, 1931, nos. 7428–7432, 8235–8241; and the entries on Nubian topics in ATIYA, A. S. (ed.): The Coptic Encyclopedia, New York 1991 vol. 6, pp. 1800–22, with plentiful further bibliography.

This is much more difficult. Nubia was converted in the sixth century, in the time of Justinian, and was always Monophysite. Like Ethiopia, the church there was always dependent on the Coptic church of Egypt; unlike Ethiopia, it was not a separate church. Its bishops and priests were largely named from Egypt, trained there, and sometimes actually came from there too. Egyptian influence was always strong – in dogma, in personnel, in church architecture – and in language. The Nubian church was also quite unusually polyglot. We find (remains of) texts there in Old Nubian (even after that language had been succeeded in popular use by others), in Coptic, even in Latin (we have from the first half of the eighth century a battered version of the famous palindrome *sator, arepo, tenet, opera, rotas*), Greek and, later on, Arabic too. It is the Greek that is puzzling here, not just because of the Monophysite dogma and connection of the local church, but also because we seem to have a good deal of it.

Greek is present in Christian Nubia from the start down to at least the thirteenth century, and may even have enjoyed a slight revival, under Byzantine influence (though we must wonder about the mechanisms of that), in the eleventh century. We find Greek in use in the liturgy, we find the clergy knowing Greek and writing it and using it for rubrics and instructions in their liturgical manuscripts, possibly also in speech, and we find it in use on local tombstones, including the formula from the *euchologion mega* that I have just mentioned. The Greek would often not have satisfied Porson, but that is the character of a living language. And this seems, with all its barbarities, because of all its barbarities, to have been living.[10] What is going on here?

It seems to me that the medieval Christian Nubians, about whom we still know far too little, represent an example, perhaps an extreme example, of a cultural-linguistic phenomenon which we may call indifferent multilingualism. This is very different from what we are used to in the Arab world in general in later periods. There we encounter the phenomenon known as diglossia. By diglossia we usually mean the use of two registers of a given language for different, specific purposes in a given society. In the case of Arabic it refers to the use of spoken and of written Arabic for speech and writing respectively. These are very different from each other, but they are also varieties of the same language. And on the written side, too, different registers of Arabic are assigned different functions. What is now called Middle Arabic, a sub-classical and not very highly regarded register of the written language, was reserved for types of writing that were of little artistic or literary significance; the higher registers of Arabic were reserved for poetry, for such elegant and difficult writing as the *maqamat*, and, of course, the highest of all is reflected in the Qur'an.[11] Among Jews in the classical Islamic world, we find the

---

10 We should distinguish between levels of excellence of knowledge of a language to which we have testimony in our sources, and levels of textual excellence, or a particular form of a text. Thus, Frend and Dragas (loc. cit. pp. 97–98) point out that "the Nubian Eucharistic sequence, though following the same pattern as the Liturgy of St. Mark is often simpler and more direct than the latter." As they remark, this points merely to acquaintance with an earlier version of the text.

11 See Encyclopaedia of Islam, 2nd edition, I, pp. 561–603.

same, but with the complex addition of Hebrew and Aramaic, in different forms, at different levels and with particular functions.[12] Thus Biblical Hebrew (as a parallel to Qur'anic Arabic) was used, very occasionally alongside literary Arabic, for the production of poetry, as a supreme form of literary creativity. On the analogy of diglossia, we can call the resulting Jewish linguistic situation polyglossia. And in general we can say that if we know what sort of literary work by Jews or Arabs we are dealing with, then we can be pretty sure that we know also what language or linguistic register it is written in.[13]

In Nubia, unlike in the classical Islamic world, the use of a variety of languages seems to represent little more than the accidental collocation of individuals of different languages in a single society. We may assume that for many activities of ordinary life Nubians used local languages. However, in the church in Nubia, and in related areas of life, there were liturgical and other influences coming from Egypt, and Coptic, as the language of the geographically close mother church, was as a consequence always important. But Greek was always important there, too; we know of personnel coming from Constantinople, and of literary contacts with Byzantium, and the authority and prestige of the great city played a role too, possibly in some tension with that of Coptic.

What we cannot know in many cases is how these languages functioned. Specifically, it would be interesting to know how broadly each of them was understood: in many cases it seems clear that they cannot have functioned as much more than vehicles for what Richard Ettinghausen called, in the field of Arabic epigraphy, "symbolic affirmation".[14] Whatever this means in terms of social behaviour, it does not mean much in linguistic terms. In the cases of the Nubian tombstones with Greek inscriptions, the presence of a couple of lines of Old Nubian above or below the Greek may indicate something similar for the Greek there. But we cannot be sure. It seems rather that in Nubia the different languages or registers of language were not reserved to specific functions, and that different linguistic forms were used, far rather, on the basis of who the speaker or writer or user happened to be

---

12 See especially RABIN, Chaim: Hebrew and Arabic in medieval Jewish philosophy, in: Studies in Jewish Religious and Intellectual History Presented to Alexander Altmann on the occasion of his seventieth birthday, ed. by S. STEIN and R. LOEWE, Alabama 1979, pp. 235–45.

13 DRORY, Rina: Al-Harizi's *Maqamat*: a tricultural literary product?, in: ELLIS, R./EVANS, R. (eds.): The Medieval Translator 4 (Binghamton Medieval and Renaissance Texts and Studies 123), Exeter 1994, pp. 66–85; ead.: Literary contacts and where to find them: on Arabic literary models in medieval Jewish literature, in: Poetics Today 14 (1993), pp. 277–302; ead.: 'Words beautifully put': Hebrew versus Arabic in tenth-century Jewish literature, in: Genizah Research after ninety years: the case of Judaeo-Arabic. Papers read at the third congress of the Society for Judaeo-Arabic Studies 1987 (University of Cambridge Oriental Publications 47), ed. by J. BLAU and S. C. REIF, Cambridge 1992, pp. 53–66; ead.: Models and contacts: Arabic literature and its impact on medieval Jewish culture (Brill's Series in Jewish Studies 25), Leiden 2000; ead.: The earliest contacts of Hebrew literature with Arabic literature in the tenth century, Tel Aviv 1986 (repr. 1988, 1996) (in Hebrew).

14 ETTINGHAUSEN, Richard: Arabic epigraphy, communication or symbolic affirmation, in: Near Eastern numismatics, iconography, epigraphy and history: studies in honor of G. C. Miles, ed. by D. K. KOUYMJIAN, Beirut 1974, pp. 293–317.

and what his or her linguistic competences were. Thus I call this kind of multilingualism indifferent, rather than functional. This is very different from the situation which we have in classical Islam. There the situation was similar rather to that of Charles V: Je parle espagnol à Dieu, italien aux femmes, français aux hommes, et allemand à mon cheval. This was di- or polyglossia. Everything is defined by the context.

In the first generations of the Islamic empire and as conversion proceeded, both among the learned, the literate, the elite, and among the ignorant, the uneducated, the otherwise monoglot peasants, we cannot imagine such a clear set of definitions and divisions. We cannot imagine that things were so clear, or so well arranged in that period. Nubia offers the pattern. Everything was in flux. During the long process of conversion to Islam, as people needed to perform such central religious obligations as prayer, there must have been a great deal of experimenting with the linguistic forms and competences which people possessed. They must have tried to use some Arabic, but they must equally have been cabined, cribbed and confined by the limits on their knowledge of Arabic, as they must also have been driven by their other linguistic competences. This is confirmed for us by what little evidence we have. Not only the testimonies from al-Andalus demonstrate this; the apparently very rapid changeover to Arabic among the Melkites of Palestine seems to demonstrate this too.[15] In a sense, the Christian changeover to Arabic shows how little the linguistic dress of prayer, as distinct from its theological content, appeared to matter. But the best illustration of it must be the survival and later resurgence of Persian in Iran.[16] From the beginning Arabic prospered mightily in Iran, as a language of religion and of culture more generally, and we find evidence of it as a spoken language there, too. But numerous forms of Persian survived, and it re-emerged in the tenth century as a separate literary language, New Persian, gravid with influence from Arabic. By that time, Arabic had come to occupy a large, though never total, and clearly defined place in the linguistic framework of the country.

This was in the tenth century, more than three hundred years after the arrival of Islam. At the start things cannot have been so clear. The struggle for the re-emergence of Persian, like that for the (re-)emergence of Middle English, needed time for the new definitions of linguistic space. In the meantime, as in medieval Nubia, where there was no language possessing authority in clearly defined spheres, we find the phenomenon that I have called indifferent multilingualism. Conversion

---

15 See GRIFFITH, Sidney H: Arabic Christianity in the Monasteries of ninth-century Palestine, Aldershot 1992; id.: From Aramaic to Arabic: the Languages of the Monasteries of Palestine in the Byzantine and Early Islamic Periods, in: Dumbarton Oaks Papers 51 (1997), pp. 11–31; id.: The Gospel in Arabic: An Enquiry into its appearance in the first Abbasid century, in: Oriens Christianus 69 (1985), pp. 126–67; id.: The monks of Palestine and the growth of Christian literature in Arabic, Muslim World 78 (1988), pp. 1–28.

16 LAZARD, G.: The rise of the New Persian language, in: The Cambridge History of Iran 4 (The Period from the Arab invasion to the Saljuqs), ed. by R. N. Frye, Cambridge 1975, pp. 595–632, with further bibliographical references.

to Islam, the growth of the significance of Arabic in all spheres of social existence, the relative decline of the importance of those spheres in which other languages operated with any exclusivity – all of these in the end settled things via the application of a socio-linguistic inversion of Gresham's law: the useless language was driven out by the useful.[17]

17 This paper was prepared while I was a Fellow of the Institute for Advanced Studies at the Hebrew University of Jerusalem, as one of the leaders of the Research Group there in 2002–03, on "Greeks, Romans, Jews and Others in the Near East from Alexander to Muhammad: A Civilization of Epigraphy". I am grateful to the Institute, to its staff and to the other fellows there during my stay for the creation of an ideal working environment and for the friendships which developed there. I am also grateful to the participants in the colloquium in Paderborn for their comments on my paper, which have contributed much to its final form. I remain responsible, of course, for the conclusions offered here.

Hanna E. Kassis

"We have sent it down as an Arabic Qur'an"
An Arabic Qur'an: An examination of sources and implications

For the believer, the recitation of the Qur'an, the sacred book of Islam, in the language of its revelation is what Marmaduke Pickthall described it to be: an "inimitable symphony, the very sounds of which move men to tears and ecstasy".[1] Pickthall is speaking of the interaction of people and language within the perimeters of faith, an interaction that, rising from the foundation of faith, requires acknowledgement, though not necessarily knowledge, of the language as a vehicle for the expression of that faith. Muslims are gratified, indeed elated, at hearing the sacred text recited, notwithstanding the fact that, lacking the requisite command of the language, a majority among them would not be able to comprehend what they hear. Their satisfaction arises from the assurance that what they hear is the embodiment of the Word of God. This does not mitigate the significance of mastery of the language of revelation for maintaining the faith by means of understanding and communicating the content of the sacred text. The overriding assumption in this regard has always been that, while recitation avails the believers at large of the divine word, the analysis and articulation of the tenets of the faith may be entrusted only to those who, as a starting point, possess a firm command of the language in which the Qur'an was revealed. For Muslims, as one non-Muslim scholar puts it, the Qur'an "is what Mohammed felt it to be, and orthodoxy has always maintained it is, one whole and indivisible divine book, equal in all its parts, its parts being equal to its whole, an eternal Arabic expression of God's final message to mankind".[2] There is valid emphasis on "Arabic expression" in this assessment. For indeed, if the Qur'an is the lifeline of Muslim faith, thought and institutions, the language in which it was revealed is the fibre of that lifeline. Religion and language are empowered each by the other.

My purpose in this brief presentation is to address the question of whence came the language that became the means of revelation, and to examine the hypothesis asserting that 'Classical Arabic', the language of the Qur'an, and its script are of Christian Arab origin. Needless to say, this question of language does not imply an influence in the shaping of the doctrine conveyed by the language. In other words, to suggest that the language may have sprung from a Christian Arab foundation should not imply that the doctrines of the revealed text were consequently drawn from or influenced by this external source. In fact, it would be very safe to say that Christianity had no influence on the birth and development of the Qur'an. But if the hypothesis is correct, it inevitably raises the question of whether

---

1 PICKTHALL, Muhammed Marmaduke: Meaning of the Glorious Koran, New York 1930, p. vii.
2 ARBERRY, Arthur John: The Holy Koran: An Introduction with Selections, London 1953, pp. 5–33.

or not a language can be appropriated. Does it become exclusively the language of one religion? The question gains further consequence when, in defining their identity, Christians living under Muslim rule turn their backs on Greek (in the East) and Latin (in the West) in favour of 'reclaiming' Arabic, when it is convenient to them, as the language of their Christian scriptures and the articulation of their faith.

Two attributes characterise Islamic thinking as far as prophecy and revelation of scriptures are concerned; both emerge from the Qur'an. The first is that all messengers sent by God were to deliver the message in the language of the people for whom it was intended, in order that they might understand it clearly: "We [God speaking] have sent no Messenger save with the tongue of his people, that he might make all clear to them" (Qur'an 14:4). This applies to bearers of an oral message as well as to those entrusted with the sacred written text.[3] Accordingly, the message (written or oral) sent through Moses (al-tawrāt, the "Torah") would be in the language of the Children of Israel, and that sent through Jesus (al-injīl, "the Gospel") would be in the language of those to whom Jesus was sent.[4] In regard to the latter, Muslim writers oscillated between Hebrew and Aramaic as the language of the revelation of al-injīl, the "Gospel" that was revealed to Jesus, but never defined the language of that revelation as Greek.[5]

The second attribute, which is a consequence of the first, is that the revelation sent through Muhammad, the Qur'an, was in Arabic. Thus Arabic became *lingua sacra*, alongside Hebrew and Aramaic, the only other languages of textual revelation acknowledged by Muslim scholars. Here, the Qur'an is unique among world scriptures in that the language in which it was revealed is identified in the sacred text itself. There is nothing in the Hebrew Bible that identifies Hebrew (or in some cases Aramaic) as the language of revelation. Hebrew is referred to as the "sacred tongue" only in the later Rabbinic literature to distinguish it from the "vulgar tongue".[6] Certainly, there is nothing in the New Testament that speaks of Greek as the language of revelation or inspiration, notwithstanding the fact that

---

3   The Qur'an lists eight Messengers preceding Muhammad: Noah, Lot, Ishmael, Moses and Jesus, as well as Hūd (sent to 'Ād), Ṣāliḥ (sent to Thamūd), and Shu'ayb (sent to Madyān). There is no certainty regarding the identity of the last three, who may be quasi-Biblical figures. Of all these messengers, only Moses and Jesus were entrusted with a revealed book, as was later Muhammad. There is reference in the Qur'an to David receiving a revealed book, the *zabūr* ("Psalms"?), but like Abraham who, according to the Qur'an, possessed *ṣuḥuf* "scrolls", David was a Prophet, not a Messenger.

4   There is no indication in the Qur'an about whom Jesus was sent to other than that his followers were known as *naṣārá*, the Qur'anic term for "Christians".

5   Here we have to acknowledge the Muslim premise that Jesus was only a Messenger, as were Moses and Muhammad, and not a divine figure as affirmed by Christian orthodoxy. As prophet and messenger, he is seen by Islam as the recipient and transmitter of a revealed text, the *Injīl* ("Evangel" or "Gospel"). The text in the hands of the Christians is generally regarded as inauthentic.

6   Jeffery, Arthur: Hebrew Language, in: The Interpreter's Dictionary of the Bible, vol. 2, E–J (1962), p. 553.

the Christian text in its entirety first appears in Greek. In the Qur'an, on the other hand, the language of that specific revelation, the Qur'an, is unambiguous; it was revealed "in a clear, Arabic tongue" (Qur'an 26:195).

At the same time, the bearer of the message, Muhammad, was not extraneous to the community for whom the message was sent. According to Muslim tradition, Muhammad was the first, and final, messenger (entrusted with a revealed book) to emerge outside the Biblical tradition, acknowledged and foretold by his prophetic antecedents. In the eyes of some Muslim interpreters, Moses was speaking of Muhammad when he said, "The Lord your God will raise up for you a Prophet like myself, from among yourselves, from your brothers; to him you must listen" (Deut. 18:15). Similarly, Muslim tradition maintains that Muhammad was the embodiment of the Paraclete of whom Jesus spoke (John 14:26, 15:26, 16:7). Muhammad, who was neither a Jew nor a Christian, had to convey the message entrusted to him in the language of the polytheist Arabs to whom he was sent. That message is perceived to be a restatement of what had been revealed previously through antecedent Messengers. Indeed, the Qur'an speaks of itself as being a confirmation in Arabic of what had already been revealed to Moses (Qur'an 46:12).[7]

When Muhammad's detractors hinted that someone else, most likely a Christian,[8] was instructing him, a Qur'anic text came to his defence, "And We [again God speaking] know very well that they say, 'Only a mortal is teaching him'. The speech of him at whom they hint is barbarous ['ajamī, non-Arabic]; and this is Arabic speech, intelligible" (Qur'an 16:103). The Arabic term 'ajamī, translated here as "barbarous", implies, among other meanings, someone whose tongue is other than Arabic. A further affirmation of the language of revelation states, "If We had made it a barbarous Koran, they would have said, 'Why are its signs [or verses] not distinguished [or explained clearly]? What, barbarous and Arabic?'" (Qur'an 41:44).

Thus, a messenger from the people and a language understood by them come together to convey the divine message. According to the Qur'an, it was primarily for the sake of clarity that the sacred text was revealed in the language of the people for whom it was intended. People would not have accepted Muhammad or believed the message he delivered had the revelation been in a foreign tongue, "If We had sent it down on a barbarian and he had recited it to them, they would not have believed in it" (Qur'an 26:198–199). But now that it was revealed in Arabic, it was intelligible to them, "We have sent it down as an Arabic Qur'an; haply you will understand" (Qur'an 12:2). As a result, people may heed the message (Qur'an 19:97 and 20:113), and retain it (Qur'an 44:58).

---

7   The text reads, "Yet before it was the Book of Moses for a model and a mercy; and this is a Book confirming, in Arabic tongue, to warn the evildoers, and good tidings to the good-doers". Any discrepancy between the Qur'an and the Biblical text (Old or New Testament) is generally seen in Islam as being the result of adulteration of the Hebrew or Christian scriptures by their respective adherents.

8   ṬABARĪ: Tafsīr al-Qur'ān ("Commentary on the Qur'an"), Cairo 1904, vol. 12, p. 84; SUYŪṬĪ, Jalāl al-Dīn: Tafsīr al-Jalālayn, Cairo n. d., p. 366.

As the dominion of Muslim polity expanded in the course of the 7th and early 8th centuries, so did the religion, Islam, and the language of that religion, Arabic. But the rise of the language to prominence and its proliferation in the vast new realm was fraught with problems. First, Arabic had to contend against well-established languages with long-standing traditions, such as Syriac, Persian and Greek in the East, and Latin in the West. Second, unlike the Greek of the New Testament and the Latin of Jerome's Vulgate, each of which possessed a rich literary precursor, Arabic was precarious in that it did not possess a substantive body of pre-Islamic literature. In fact, the extant corpus of this sparse literature was largely limited to an oral poetic tradition whose authenticity has been subject to scrutiny by Muslim and non-Muslim scholars alike. In addition, when the Qur'an was written down, Arabic script was defective: several consonants were represented by the same written symbol and were indistinguishable; the *hamza* (glottal stop), arguably a consonant if treated as an equivalent to the Phoenician *alif*, as well as the vowels, were not written.

Under such circumstances, the chances of the success of Arabic as an imperial language were rather limited. Its triumph, in spite of these drawbacks, has been described as a "true wonder of Arab expansion".[9] What should be emphasised is the fact that the success of the language was an effect of the spread of the religion that, as much as some people may suggest otherwise, was due more to conviction than coercion.

One major problem arises from this otherwise uncluttered depiction of the triumphant history of the language of the revelation: the difficulty of identifying the Arabic language in which the revelation came. Was there, at the beginning of the seventh century, a language in common usage known as the "Arabic language"? If such existed, was it a spoken as well as a written language? Was there a divergence or an agreement between the spoken and 'literary' forms of the language? Was it uniformly intelligible by all?

For the believer the question would be extraneous in that if the Qur'an is said to be revealed in intelligible Arabic, it follows that "Arabic" was a language already in existence. This is well expressed by the lexicographer Ibn Manẓūr (1233–1311) who argued that "there were five prophets among the Arabs: Muḥammad, Ishmael, Shuʿayb, Ṣāliḥ and Hūd, which demonstrates that the Arabic tongue is ancient".[10] But Ibn Manẓūr does not explain what he means by the "Arabic tongue". We should interject here that insofar as evidence is concerned, the Qur'an is the earliest body of written literature in Arabic. Arab culture was heavily dependent on oral preservation and transmission. We have no evidence whatsoever that anything of pre-Islamic literature – odes (*muʿallaqāt*, *mufaḍḍalīyāt*, or the like), legends, or *gesta* narratives (*ayyām al-ʿarab*, "days of the Arabs") – was put into writing until well into the Islamic period.

---

9 LEWIS, Bernard: The Arabs in History, London 1958, p. 132.
10 IBN MANẒŪR: Lisān al-ʿarab ("The Language of the Arabs"), Beirut 1955–56, vol. 1, p. 587.

The claim of Ibn Manẓūr to the antiquity of the "Arabic tongue" notwithstanding, the question of the identity of the language of the revelation, to which should be added the question of the origins of the script, occupied the attention and energy of Arab grammarians and historians in the various centres of learning of the Islamic world. Similarly, Western scholars engaged in developing their respective hypotheses regarding the development of the language within the context of the history of the text of the Qur'an. The details of the debate should not detain us here. Suffice it to say that, at the risk of oversimplification, we may summarise the suggestions or hypotheses put forward under three broad groupings.

The first, the traditional view of several Muslim writers, proposes that the language of the Qur'an was the spoken dialect of Quraysh, the tribe of the Prophet. Some among this group suggested that this language was akin to or influenced by that of the poets of the nomads of Najd, a region quite removed from Mecca, the birthplace of the Prophet and the locus of the earlier revelations, or Medina, the centre of Muslim power and the locus of later revelations. This view acknowledges the existence of other Arabic dialects while emphasising the primacy of that of Quraysh. Needless to say, this view prevailed, and still prevails, primarily in the domain of piety.

In the second group – largely comprised of Western scholarship – there is agreement that a universal Arabic language did not exist, and that the language of the Qur'an bears resemblance to that of the poets of Najd. There is further agreement, more or less, that "Classical Arabic was to some extent a foreign idiom which had to be acquired".[11] Beyond that, opinions are vastly varied regarding the extent of the interaction between various spoken dialects and oral literary expression.[12]

Drawing support from epigraphic sources and literary attestations, the third hypothesis advances the view that 'Classical Arabic' and its script found their origins outside the Arabian Peninsula, among Christian Arabs living in the bordering regions of Syria, Iraq, and Sinai. This should not necessarily question the possible existence of some form of writing, or at least an awareness of its existence, in the main centres of trade and pilgrimage in Arabia (such as at Mecca). The verse in the Qur'an enjoining believers to write down a debt would be meaningless if some form of writing were not practised in Medina during the prophetic age.[13] At the same time, however, it is evident from the Qur'an itself that the craft was largely limited to a few scribes (Qur'an 2:283). The primary 'writer' in the Qur'an is God Himself.[14] The question then is not that of the presence of writing among

---

11 RABIN, Chaim: Ancient West Arabian, London 1951, p. 17.

12 For a cogent resumé, see RABIN, Chaim: The beginnings of Classical Arabic, in: Studia Islamica 4 (1955), pp. 19–37.

13 The crucial verse reads: "O believers, when you contract a debt one upon another for a stated term, write it down, and let a writer write it down between you justly, and let not any writer refuse to write it down, as God has taught him; so let him write, and let the debtor dictate, and let him fear God his Lord and not diminish aught of it" (Qur'an 2:282).

14 With the exception of Qur'an 2:79, which condemns those who "write the Book with their own hands, then say 'This is from God' that they may sell it for a little price", the remaining verses point to God (3:181, 4:81, 5:83, 19:79, 21:94 and 36:12) or his heavenly servants (82:11) as the "writer".

the Arabs; the many inscriptions in various forms of Arabic found in the Arabian Peninsula are testimony to that. In addition, Johannes Pedersen has assembled the evidence of the presence of imageries of writing in the work of some pre-Islamic poets.[15] Rather, the question pertains to the idiom in which the revelation was cast, and the specific script to which it was initially committed.

It is evident that the earliest extant pages of the Qur'an were written in kufic, "the liturgic script par excellence".[16] To specimens cited so far in competent writings on Qur'anic calligraphy,[17] we should add the copy of the Qur'an from Samarqand (now in Bukhara), with its claim to antiquity,[18] as well as the finds from San'ā' (Yemen) currently under study.[19] The debate on whether or not kufic was preceded by other scripts for writing down the sacred text is best summarized by Grohmann.[20]

There is regrettably no complete history of Arabic palaeography.[21] However, the few pre-Islamic epigraphic discoveries may shed some light on the history of the development of 'Classical Arabic' script prior to the rise of Islam. In addition to graffiti found in the Sinai and dating from around AD 300,[22] mention should be made of a number of inscriptions recently discovered at Faw (Saudi Arabia), carved by members of the Christian Arab Kindite dynasty that was vanquished by the Lakhmids.[23] But the earliest meaningful specimen of Arabic writing so far known to us is the funerary inscription at Namāra (south-eastern Syria) of the Lakhmid king Imru'al-Qays (d. 328),[24] the self-styled "king of the Arabs",

15 PEDERSEN, Johannes: The Arabic Book, Princeton 1984, pp. 7ff.

16 SCHIMMEL, Annemarie: Calligraphy and Islamic Culture, New York 1984, p. 4.

17 See, for example, LINGS, Martin: The Quranic Art of Calligraphy and Illumination, London 1976, and LINGS, Martin and HAMID SAFADI, Yasin: The Qur'ān – A British Library Exhibition, London 1976.

18 KRACHKOVSKII, Ignatii IUlianovich: Among Arabic Manuscripts – Memories of Libraries and Men, Leiden 1953, p. 150.

19 PUIN, Gerd-Rüdiger: Observations on early Qur'ān manuscripts in San'ā', in: WILD, Stefan: The Qur'ān as Text, Leiden 1996, pp. 107–11; and Id.: Methods of research on Qur'anic manuscripts – a few ideas, in: Masahif San'a', Kuwait National Museum 1985, pp. 9–17.

20 GROHMANN, Adolf: The problem of dating the early Qur'āns, in: Der Islam 33 (1958), pp. 213–31.

21 Mention should be made of the incomplete but indispensable work of GROHMANN, Adolf: Arabische Paläographie, 2 vols., Vienna 1967, 1971. See also MORITZ, Bernhard: Arabic Palaeography – Texts from the First Century of the Hidjra till the Year 1000, Cairo and Leipzig 1906; and particularly SOURDEL-THOMINE, Janine: khaṭṭ, in: Encyclopaedia of Islam, 2nd ed., vol. 4 (1978), pp. 1113–22.

22 GRIMME, Hubert: A propos de quelques graffites du Temple du Ramm, in: Revue Biblique 45 (1936), pp. 90–95.

23 ANSARY, A: Qaryat al-Faw: a Portrait of a Pre-Islamic Civilization in Saudi Arabia, Riyadh 1982. See also SHAHID, Irfan: Byzantium and the Arabs in the Sixth Century, vol. 1, part 1, p. 156.

24 DUSSAUD, René: Inscription Nabatéo-arabe de 'En-Namāra, in: Revue archéologique 2 (1902), pp. 409–21. SHAHID, Irfan: Philological observations on the Namāra inscription, in: Journal of Semitic Studies 24 (1979), pp. 33–42 (reprinted in: Byzantium and the Semitic Orient before the Rise of Islam, Variorum 1988).

described by the historian al-Ṭabarī as being a Christian.[25] While its primary significance for our purpose lies in the fact that it demonstrates the antiquity of the association of Christian Arabs with the development of written Arabic, it should be noted that the script in this inscription bears no resemblance either to the kufic script employed in the transcription of the revelation or to later forms of Arabic writing.

An inscription from Zabad (northern Syria), dated 512, carved in memory of the founders of a *martyrion* dedicated to St. Sergius, is more akin to cursive script.[26] But the inscription of a single word, *bi-salāmih* ("in His peace"), on the mosaic floor of the southern sacristy of the Church of St. George at Khirbat al-Mukhayyaṭ (the town of Nebo in southern Jordan), dated 535/6, is written in a style much closer to the kufic script.[27] The same is true of the dedicatory inscription from Ḥarrān (Syria), from the *martyrion* of St. John the Baptist, dated 568.[28]

The Lakhmid successors of Imru' al-Qays, whose capital was at Ḥīra and whose power extended well into Syria, oscillated in matters of religion between polytheism, which they favoured, and Nestorian Christianity, toward which they were by and large at best neutral. The Lakhmid public, on the other hand, gradually favoured Christianity. However, by the second half of the sixth century Christianity prevailed at the court. Queen Hind, the Christian mother of the Lakhmid king 'Amr (554–569), described herself in a dedicatory Arabic inscription over a convent she built in the capital Ḥīra during her son's reign, as "the maid of Christ and the mother of His slave ['Amr b. al-Mundhir] and the daughter of His slaves [the Christian royal Ghassanid household from which she descended]".[29]

As patrons of poetry, the Lakhmid kings recognised the power of poetic language, and their court was visited by some of the distinguished poets of pre-Islamic Arabia (Labīd, Ṭarafah, and al-Nābighah, among others). It boasted its own distinguished Christian Arab poet, 'Adī ibn Zayd (d. 600) who, we are told, mastered Persian and Arabic and was appointed to the chancellery of Chosroes, the Persian emperor (late 6th century), with the responsibility of writing letters in Arabic.[30] The role played by the court at Ḥīra in standardising the language of the poets cannot be overestimated.

25 Ṭabarī: Annales, Leiden 1879–1901, p. 834. Bosworth, Clifford Edmund (tr.): The History of al-Ṭabarī, vol. 5, The Sasānids, the Byzantines, the Lakhmids, and Yemen, State University of New York 1999, p. 44.

26 Kugener, M. A.: Note sur l'inscription trilingue de Zébed, in: Journal Asiatique 9 (1907), pp. 509–24 and: Nouvelle note sur l'inscription trilingue de Zébed, in: Revista degli Studi Orientali 1 (1907), pp. 577–86.

27 Saller ofm, Sylvester J. and Bagatti ofm, Bellarmino: The Town of Nebo (Khirbet el-Mekhayyat), Jerusalem 1949, reprint 1982, Pl. 30:1 and pp. 76, 105 and 171f.

28 Waddington, William Henry: Inscriptions grecques et latines de la Syrie, Paris 1870, pp. 563ff.; Shahid, Irfan: Byzantium and the Arabs in the Sixth Century, vol. 1, part 1, Political and Military History, Dumbarton Oaks 1995, pp. 325–28; see also Rabin, Chaim: 'Arabiyyah. Arabic language and literature, in: Encyclopaedia of Islam, 2nd ed., vol. 1 (1960), p. 564.

29 The text is preserved by Yāqūt: Mu'jam al-buldān ("Geographic Dictionary"), Beirut 1977, vol. 2, p. 542.

30 Al-Iṣbahānī: Kitāb al-Aghānī, Beirut 1955, vol. 2, pp. 34ff.

There is no denial that Lakhmid Ḥīra had an inestimable cultural and religious impact on Quraysh. According to Ibn Rustah, it is from Ḥīra that Quraysh acquired the art of writing and the system of false or heterodox belief (*zandaqa*).[31] It is likely that starting from Ḥīra, Christian missionaries utilised the language of the pre-Islamic poets to develop an idiom for the preaching of the Gospel among the Arabs of the Arabian Peninsula. If indeed an Arabic translation of the Gospels existed in pre-Islamic times, it most likely would have been produced at Ḥīra. Admittedly, this remains conjectural as we do not possess the definitive literary evidence needed to support the hypothesis. Arguable as the case may be, the suggestion is made that the eloquent homiletic oratory of such Christian preachers as Quss ibn Sāʿidah of Iyād[32] (d. 600?) – a matrilineal relation of the Lakhmids – left an impression even on the Prophet Muhammad himself. According to tradition, the Prophet heard him preach, praised him, and memorized some of what he had said.[33]

Later Arabic sources are not reluctant to assert that the Christians were in the forefront of developing the language which was to become the vehicle of the revelation as well as the script in which it came to be written. As we have already noted, al-Iṣbahānī points out that Zayd ibn Ḥamād and his son the poet ʿAdī were among the first to write in Arabic. Father and son were Christians from Ḥīra. The historian al-Ṭabarī reports that Khālid ibn al-Walīd, the Muslim conqueror of Syria, was surprised to find that the Christians of al-Anbār "wrote in Arabic and were learned in it", having acquired it from Iyād, their co-religionists.[34] The assertion is made by al-Iṣbahānī that the script in which the Qurʾan was written was derived from the Christians of Ḥīra and al-Anbār.[35]

A remark by Sībawayhi, author of the founding text of Arabic grammar (d. 796), merits examination here, albeit briefly. But for purposes of clarification it should first be noted that Sībawayhi employs the synonymous terms *kalām* ("speech") and *lugha* ("idiom") which must be distinguished from *lisān* ("tongue" or "language"). As used by Sībawayhi, *lugha* is the "manner of realising an element of language by an ethnic group, a tribe or a locality".[36] This may be manifested by various characteristics, including methods of constructing the plural of

---

31 IBN RUSTAH: Al-aʿlāq al-nafīsah, ed. de Goeje, Leiden 1892, pp. 192 and 217. See also HITTI, Philip K: History of the Arabs, Macmillan 1974, p. 84, where he identifies *zandaqa* with Zoroastrianism.

32 A confederation of Christian Arab tribes centred at al-Anbār, north of Ḥīra and the Lakhmids. They are described as "highly competent in writing in what came to be called the Kufic script". See TRIMMINGHAM, John Spencer: Christianity among the Arabs in Pre-Islamic Times, London 1979, pp. 177f.

33 AL-IṢBAHĀNĪ: Kitāb al-Aghānī, vol. 14, pp. 86–91; MASʿŪDĪ: Murūj al-dhahab, Beirut 1978, vol. 1, pp. 82ff.; CHEIKHO, Louis: Shuʿarāʾ al-naṣrānīyah fil-jāhilīyah (Les poètes arabes chrétiens "avant l'Islam"), new edition, Cairo 1982, pp. 211–218; PELLAT, Charles: Ḳuss B. Sāʿida, in: Encyclopaedia of Islam, 2nd ed., vol. 5 (1986), pp. 528f.

34 ṬABARĪ: Annales, p. 2061. BLANKINSHIP, Khalid Yahya (tr.): The History of al-Ṭabarī, vol. 11: The Challenge to the Empires, State University of New York 1993, pp. 51f.

35 AL-IṢBAHĀNĪ: Kitāb al-Aghānī, vol. 5, p. 191.

36 HADJ-SALAH, A.: Lugha, in Encyclopaedia of Islam, 2nd ed., vol. 5 (1986), pp. 803f.

nouns or the use of a grammatical particle in forming a sentence. In section 68 of his "Book",[37] Sībawayhi contrasts idiomatic usage (*lugha*) in the Qur'an with that of the Bedouin Arabs.[38] In the course of discussing an unusual usage, he explains that the Qur'an was revealed in the speech (*kalām*) or idiom (*lugha*) of al-'*ibād*,[39] an assertion which he restates later.[40] It is not immediately clear what Sībawayhi means by al-'*ibād*. The term (plural of '*abd*), translated as "the faithful" by Michael Carter,[41] primarily means "servants, slaves (of God)" and by extension "worshippers", or "people at large". It is not likely that Sībawayhi has any of these groups in mind as each possessed a range of speech (*kalām*) or idiom (*lugha*). It is more probable that Sībawayhi is making reference to al-'*Ibād* of Ḥīra, one of the three homogenous groups of the population of that city and the most sedentary among them,[42] who were Christian.[43]

Thus, early Muslim writers did not hesitate to acknowledge the contribution of Christian Arabs to the development of the language and script in which the revelation was cast. Similarly, Western scholars such as Julius Wellhausen[44] and, more recently, Chaim Rabin[45] and J. Spencer Trimmingham,[46] among others, concluded that Classical Arabic was developed by Christians of Ḥīra and its adjacent centres. Nabia Abbott says that she "has for some time accepted the possibility that Arabic scripts were used in literary works in pre-Islamic times, especially among the Christian Arabs of Iraq and Syria and among Arabic-speaking Christian and Jewish colonists in Arabia itself".[47] She cites references in later sources to the Prophetic age in which people, both men and women, are described as being able to read and write. These undoubtedly include rivals of the Prophet, such as Umayyah ibn Abī al-Ṣalt (d. 624),[48] as well as proponents such as Waraqah ibn Nawfal, the cous-

37 DERENBOURG, Hartwig (ed.): Kitāb Sībawayhi/Le Livre de Sîbawaihi – Traité de Grammaire Arabe, Paris 1881, vol. 1, pp. 138f.

38 Sībawayhi cites a text from the Qur'an in which he merges two distinct verses into one by adding the conjunction *wa* ("and"): Qur'an 52:11 and 83:1 *wayl^un lil-mukaḏḏibīn^a wa-wayl^un yawma'iḏ^in lil-muṭaffifīn^a* ("woe unto those that cry lies [and] woe that day to the stinters").

39 *wa-lākinna-l-ibād^a kullimū bi-kalāmihim wa-jā'a l-qur'ān^u 'alá lughatihim* ("the '*ibād* were addressed in their own speech, and the Qur'an came in their idiom"), SĪBAWAIHI, vol. 1, p. 139, line 7.

40 *fa-'innamā ujriya hāḏā 'alá kalām^i l-'ibād^i wa-bihi unzila al-qur'ān* ("this was brought about in the speech of the '*ibād* in which the Qur'an was revealed"), SĪBAWAIHI, vol. 1, p. 139, lines 12–13.

41 CARTER, Michael G.: Sībawayhi, in: Encyclopaedia of Islam, 2nd ed., vol. 9 (1997), p. 526.

42 ṬABARĪ: Annales, p. 822. BOSWORTH: The History of al-Ṭabarī, vol. 5, pp. 21–2 and n. 78.

43 DODGE, Bayard: The Fihrist of al-Nadīm, Columbia University Press 1970, vol. 2, p. 693.

44 WELLHAUSEN, Julius: Reste arabischen Heidentums, gesammelt und erläutert, reprinted in Berlin 1961, p. 232.

45 RABIN, Chaim: The beginnings of Classical Arabic, in: Studia Islamica 4 (1955), pp. 19–37 and 'Arabiyyah, p. 565.

46 TRIMMINGHAM: Christianity among the Arabs, p. 227.

47 ABBOTT, Nabia: Studies in Arabic Literary Papyri, vol. 2: Qur'anic Commentary and Tradition, Chicago 1964, p. 5.

48 AL-IṢBAHĀNĪ: Kitāb al-Aghānī, vol. 2, pp. 357–67; CHEIKHO: Les poètes arabes chrétiens "avant l'Islam", pp. 219–37; also reported by Ibn Qutaybah, cited by MONTGOMERY, J.: Umayya B. Abi 'l-Ṣalt, in: Encyclopaedia of Islam, 2nd ed., vol. 10 (2000), p. 839, as having "read the ancient books of the scriptures of Allāh".

in of Muhammad's wife Khadijah, who were credited with the "study of books".[49]
They also include Ḥafṣah and ʿĀishah, two of the later wives of the Prophet. But
aside from the wives of Muhammad, and excluding Umayyah ibn Abī al-Ṣalt, who
was described simultaneously as a pretender to prophecy and a *ḥanīf*,[50] the examples cited in Nabia Abbott's argument are in the main Christians.

And as the new religion developed, so did the language of the polity that was
guided by the revelation. The revelation nourished and enriched the language,
which in turn became the vehicle for the communication of the revelation. The
two, revelation and language, became inseparable. The language that was brought
forth by the faith became at the same time the lifeline of that faith, as well as the
medium for scholarship in the various fields of study emerging from the faith.
There is validity in the remark (made in 1942) by the Punjabi scholar Shaykh ʿIna-
yatullah when he summed up the significance of Arabic in the life of Islam and
Muslim communities. He said, "Without Arabic Islam would be only imperfectly
intelligible. For any understanding of the thoughts that sway the life of the Muslims, the beliefs they hold most sacred, and the principles of theology and ethics in
which they are brought up, we must have recourse to Arabic, which is the original
and the main repository of all the religious sciences of Islam."[51]

But as Arabic and Islam became two inseparable aspects of one religious and cultural reality, two new problems arose. The first pertained to the translatability
of the Qur'an for the benefit of those whose religion was Islam but who did not
possess a command of Arabic, and the second pertained to the Christians and
their use of the language.

It is true that Arabic became the language of religion and of the vast body of
literature generated during the classical age of Islamic civilization. But, as pointed
out earlier, it is a fact that the sacred language of the revelation of Islam remains
beyond the grasp of the vast majority of Muslims. At the same time, hearing the
Qur'an recited without necessarily understanding what is said evokes an ecstasy at
the satisfaction of hearing the sound of the divine word, seeking its meaning and
interpretation subsequently.[52] In other words, not unlike Hebrew for Judaism and
Latin for pre-Reformation Western Christianity, it may appear that comprehending the sacred text becomes secondary to the sanctity of the language in which the
text was revealed. Unintended as this may have been, it did not obviate the need

---

49 Waraqah ibn Nawfal is described by al-Ṭabarī as follows, "He had become a Christian, read the
   Scriptures, and learned from the people of the Torah and the Gospel". ṬABARĪ: Annales, p. 1151.
   WATT, Montgomery/McDONALD, Michael V. (tr.): The History of al-Ṭabarī, vol. 6: Muḥammad
   at Mecca, State University of New York 1988, p. 72.
50 One who, in his search for religious truth, scorns false belief; see the discussion by TRIMMING-
   HAM: Christianity among the Arabs, pp. 261–64.
51 INAYATULLAH, Shaikh: Why we learn the Arabic language, in: Muslim World 39 (1949), p. 242,
   cited by CHEJNE, Anwar: The Arabic Language: Its Role in History, University of Minnesota Press
   1969, p. 13 n. 9.
52 KASSIS, Hanna: The Qur'an, in: COWARD, Harold (ed.): Experiencing Scripture in World Religions, Orbis 2000, pp. 63–84.

for a translation of the sacred text, an issue that gradually came to be a subject of debate among Muslim scholars.

When the Muslims conquered North Africa and parts of the Iberian Peninsula, they did not hesitate to inscribe their coins with a verse from the Qur'an translated into Latin. But this was not to be the standard to emulate. "If the text of the Qur'an is revealed in Arabic, how can it be rendered in any other human language?", argues a contemporary Muslim scholar.[53] While favouring an interpretation of the content of the Qur'an, Muslim scholarship, by and large, envisaged a translation of the sacred as being impossible. Without exception, Muslim schools of jurisprudence argued for the liturgical recitation of the Qur'an in Arabic. As a minimum, every Muslim is required to be able to recite the opening chapter in Arabic, whether or not that person knows the language. But there is certainly no consensus among Muslim scholars as far as translating the text for purposes of study or religious instruction is concerned. For example, a few argued in favour of rendering the sacred text in Persian and subsequently in other languages for that purpose; others supported the translation of only those verses that offered a single, unambiguous meaning. But the majority has always tended to be opposed to translating the sacred text. Underlying all this was the justifiable fear that translation gives a single definite interpretation to the text, limiting the meaning of the revelation to the learned opinion of the translator. Nonetheless, translating the text, without diminishing the sanctity of the language of revelation, had its champions.

I wish to cite as an illustration the position taken by the late Muḥammad Aḥmad al-Ghamrāwī, one of the leading scholars of al-Azhar, in this regard. The majority of the *shuyūkh* ("religious masters") of al-Azhar were opposed to the translation of the Qur'an, but accepted the view that an interpretive paraphrase of the text, supervised by an authorised committee, could be rendered in languages other than Arabic. Ghamrāwī was a member of a minority group that endorsed the right to translate the sacred text itself rather than producing only an authorised paraphrase.[54] To bear out his position, he cited a narrative from the life of the Prophet which relates that the Prophet sent a letter to the Byzantine emperor Heraclius inviting him to accept Islam. Let me quote the text as reported by Bukhārī, in translation:

> In the name of God the Merciful, the Compassionate. From Muhammad, God's servant and His Messenger, to Heraclius the ruler of the Byzantines. [And] Peace be upon him who follows the guidance. I invite you to Islam that you may be safe, and God will double your reward. But if you decline, you will bear the guilt of the "Ariusites".[55] [Say] 'People of the Book! Come now to a word common between us and you, that we serve none but God, and that we associate not

---

53 AL-BUNDĀQ, Muḥammad Ṣāliḥ: The Orientalists and the Translation of the Coran [in Arabic], Beirut 1980, p. 49.
54 GHAMRĀWĪ, Muḥammad Aḥmad: The problem of translating the Holy Qur'an [in Arabic], in: Majallat al-Azhar 39 (1967), pp. 185-89.
55 The identity of the "Ariusites" and their possible association with the Arians are not established.

aught with Him, and do not some of us take others as Lords, apart from God.' And if they turn
their backs, say: 'Bear witness that we are Muslims.'[56]

Ghamrāwī points out that in this letter the Prophet cited the text of three verses
of the Qur'an: one verbatim (the *basmallah*), and two only in part, omitting the
conjunction "and" (*wa-*) in one (Qur'an 20:47), and the verb "Say" (*qul*) in the
other (Qur'an 3:64). Ghamrāwi then draws two conclusions from this episode.
First, it is obvious that Heraclius did not know Arabic and therefore had to rely
on a translation of the Qur'anic passages. Second, the three verses chosen by the
Prophet represent three degrees of difficulty in interpreting the text of the Qur'an.
"By including them in the letter that was to be translated for Heraclius, one finds
a legal authorisation to translate all levels of difficulty that may be found in the
Qur'an". "The Prophet", he concludes, "chose to use the exact text of the Qur'an
in addressing Heraclius, the mighty ruler of the Byzantines, rather than an interpretation of the text.... All this clearly indicates which of the two methods is more
beneficial in calling people to Islam: following the example of the Prophet as he
cited the exact text of the Qur'an, albeit knowing that it would inevitably have to
be translated, or inviting non-Arabic speaking people to Islam solely by means of
interpreting the text". In adopting this position, Ghamrāwi did not abandon the
primacy of the integral text in the language in which it was revealed. Rather, he
defended the need to open up the message contained in the text through trustwor-
thy translation and interpretation. For him the language of revelation becomes a
gateway rather than a defensive wall.

If the Arabic of the Qur'an came to be perceived as the sacred language of Islam,
the question of the continued and growing use of the language by non-Muslims
(particularly Christians and Jews) became at times vexing. While Christians like
al-Akhṭal, a distinguished poet of the seventh century, maintained their position
of artistic and philological respectability among Muslim grammarians and literati,
there was a growing isolation of the Christians that most likely first peaked when
the Caliph 'Umar II (717–720) set in motion a programme of attracting Christians and Jews to convert to Islam as well as removing them from office in a policy
of 'islamising' the state. It was at this time that John of Damascus was compelled
to abandon his position as official representative of the Christian community and
retire to monastic life, writing his views of Islam in Greek, rather than Arabic, for
the benefit of the wider church. When this programme of inducement to convert
was later vigorously reactivated during the Abbasid caliphate (750–1258), particularly during the reign of al-Mutawakkil (847–861), several Christian writers
began composing apologetic treaties in defence of Christianity and, as Sidney Griffith has pointed out, the primary purpose of "their effort was to translate Christi-

---

56 BUKHĀRĪ: Ṣaḥīḥ, Part 1: The Beginning of the Revelation, cited by GHAMRĀWĪ: The problem of
translating the Holy Qur'an, p. 188.

anity into Arabic".[57] If the hypothesis so far presented is correct, namely that the Arabic style that was developed at Ḥīra and that contributed to shaping the idiom of the transcription of the Qur'anic revelation was employed to preach Christianity in pre-Islamic Arabia, the earliest Christian polemicists were simply reverting to the use of the language not only to 'translate' their doctrine to Arabic but as a vehicle for preaching it to the Muslims. These polemicists knew the language and content of the text of the Qur'an far better than their Muslim counterparts knew the Bible (Jewish or Christian), and employed that knowledge to their advantage in their polemical writings.[58]

The official Muslim reaction was swift. The core of the problem was seen to lie not so much in matters of doctrine as in language. Arabic was the language of the revelation of the Qur'an, not a tool to be employed by the learned Christians for their religious or polemical purposes. As a result, the Caliph al-Mutawakkil, whose attitude towards the Christians was shaped by his inclination towards the traditionalist Ibn Ḥanbal and his school of jurisprudence, attempted to prohibit them from teaching Arabic or the Qur'an to their children.[59] And as the stipulations of the traditional peace treaty with the Christians, while protecting the rights of the Christians in matters of religion and person, were mute in regard to language, the new policy eventually found expression in a recension under the misnomer "the Pact of 'Umar" which circulated in some Muslim writings. It proposed prohibiting the Christians from teaching the Qur'an to their children or from using Arabic on their seals.[60]

This did not deter Christians from continuing to use the language, especially in their writings, religious or scientific. But while some maintained or adopted an affiliation with Arabic, others appear to have distanced themselves from it. As an illustration, one may contrast here the attitude of two Arabic-speaking Christian religious writers from two different regions of the Islamic world.

When, by the 10th century, Arabic had become the common language employed by the Christian church in al-Andalus (Muslim Spain), the anonymous translator of the Book of Psalms into Arabic adopted a stance contrary to that prevalent in the Western Church. While the Western Church favoured the use of Latin, the translator – who may have been 'arabicised' rather than of Arab descent – favoured the use of the vernacular (Arabic) in prayers and lectionaries.

---

57 GRIFFITH, Sidney: The Gospel in Arabic: an inquiry into its appearance in the first Abbasid Century, in: Oriens Christianus 69 (1985), p. 127.

58 See GRIFFITH, Sidney: The Prophet Muaammad, his scripture and his message according to Christian apologies in Arabic and Syriac from the first Abbasid century, in: La vie du Prophète Mahomet – Colloque de Strasbourg, Strasbourg 1983, pp. 99–146, reprinted in: GRIFFITH, Sydney: Arabic Christianity in the Monasteries of Ninth-Century Palestine, Variorum 1992, section I.

59 ṬABARĪ: Annales, p. 1390; KRAEMER, Joel (tr.): The History of al-Ṭabarī, vol. 34: Incipient Decline, State University of New York 1989, p. 90.

60 AL-ṬURṬŪSHĪ (1059–1126): Sirāj al-mulūk ("The Lamp of Kings"), Cairo 1872, pp. 135–138; BAYĀTI, Jaafar (ed.), Sirāj al-mulūk, London 1990, p. 401. See TRITTON, Arthur Stanley: The Caliphs and their Non-Muslim Subjects – A Critical Study of the Covenant of 'Umar, London 1930 (1970), pp. 5-17.

In the introduction to his translation he justifies his position by paraphrasing passages from St. Paul's first Epistle to the people of Corinth (I Corinthians 14) in a manner that makes Paul's teachings support his view. The case as he puts it warrants citation, in translation, at length:

> The Apostle [St. Paul] said, "If a believer utters his prayers in his own tongue, he benefits himself with the spiritual gifts. Whosoever instructs the community and proclaims and interprets to them in his own tongue, realizes the spiritual benefits both for himself and the community".
> The Apostle further said, "I wish you all to speak in your own tongue. But more than that I want you to understand the interpretation of the prophecies".
> The Apostle further said, "Unless the inanimate cymbals and horns are sounded, how can listeners comprehend what they intone? For trumpets are sounded only when one is readied for battle. It is likewise with you my brethren if you do not understand your own speech and prayers; how would you comprehend what you utter and your supplications to God? If you do not understand what you say, you will only feel it within yourselves. There are many families of languages in the world and each has its own sound and intonation".
> The Apostle said, "If I, then, do not comprehend the meaning of a sound and its interpretation in that [specific] language, I shall be a barbarian to the one with whom I converse; similarly, the one who addresses me in a language I do not understand would appear to me to be barbarian. So it is with you if you do not understand your own prayer."
> After that the Apostle said, "What then do you do, brethren? When you gather together each of you has a hymn, a law, and a revelation, each has a language, eloquence and interpretation. Let everything you possess be for the edification, good and benefit of others."
> The Apostle informs us that the first to believe – the Greeks, the Jews, the foreigners [al-'ajam] and the Romans – declared their faith and prayed to their Lord in the language they each knew: the Greeks in Greek, the Syrians in Syriac, the foreigners [a'jamī] in Latin, in order that each tongue may be strengthened in the faith in God. Similarly, the prayers of the Christians in the East and the West, whether they be bishops, kings, patriarchs, monks, or the masses of their laymen, be they Franks, Arabs or Syrians, those who believe in Christ, they all pray using the Psalms that are translated from Hebrew into many languages. These include Greek, Latin, Syriac, Indian (?), and Arabic. Understand this, may God prolong your life.[61]

This contrasts with writers such as Paul of Antioch (1140–1180) who relied on the question of language to evade the continuing inducement to convert to Islam, although at the time he was living in territory held by the Crusaders. In his "Letter to a Muslim" he wrote (in Arabic):

> We know that he [the Prophet] was not sent to us, but to the polytheistic Arabs of whom he said there had come to them no warner before him. We know that he did not obligate us to follow him because there had come to us before him prophets who had preached and warned us in our own languages, and who handed on to us the Torah and the Gospel in our own languages.[62]

Certainly, Paul of Antioch was not speaking on behalf of the Jews when he referred to the Torah, and although writing in Arabic, he was most likely alluding to either Syriac or Greek when speaking of "our own languages".

---

61 Kassis, Hanna: The Arabicization and Islamization of the Christians of al-Andalus-Evidence of their Scriptures, in: Brann, Ross (ed.): Languages of Power in Islamic Spain, Bethesda, Maryland 1997, pp. 136–155.
62 Khoury, Paul: Paul d'Antioche, Beirut 1964, p. 61; Michel SJ, Thomas (ed.): A Muslim Theologian's Response to Christianity: Ibn Taymiyya's al-Jawab al-Sahih, New York 1984, p. 88.

It would be misleading to give the impression that Arabic Christians – native or 'arabicised' – may be grouped solely under either one or another of these two examples. There were Christian writers who not only engaged in the translation of Syriac and Greek scientific and philosophical works into Arabic, but made their own contribution to one or another of the sciences. One example is Yaḥyá ibn ʿAdī (893–974), who twice transcribed Ṭabarī's Commentary on the Qur'an,[63] and whose *Kitāb Tahdīb al-Akhlāq* ("The Reformation of Morals") is fit reading for Muslim and non-Muslim alike.[64] Similarly, the anonymous collator and translator of Sacred Canon Law of the Arabic-speaking Christian Church in al-Andalus (mid-11th century) did not draw back from using Qur'anic expressions in conveying Christian ideas.[65] For him, as for others, Qur'anic Arabic was a living language well-suited to the expression of sublime Christian ideas. At the same time, a marginal gloss warns against reading "the Arabic [Book]". I doubt that he ever heard of Ḥira or the Lakhmids and their fellow Christian Arabs, or contemplated in his translation a repatriation of a lost heritage.

Not unlike their Muslim counterparts, Christians too chose to hear their own sacred scriptures read to them in the respective language (Syriac, Greek, Latin, or perhaps Arabic) deemed fit to convey the sacred word. For them as well, hearing the text recited or chanted in its liturgical setting was – and in many instances remains – more important than comprehending it. Ideally, it was left to the homily to elucidate what was heard. There is an inevitable sanctity that accrues to the language of sacred scriptures; the vessel is sanctified by its content. And Islam, in this regard, is not any different from Judaism or, to a lesser extent, Christianity. What is unique about Islam is that the language seems to have been sanctified by the Source of the revelation which in turn sustained that sanctification. For the believer, the One who revealed the message chose the language and the idiom deemed most suitable for conveying the message: *innā anzalnāhu qur'ānan ʿarabīyan* "We have sent it down as an Arabic Qur'an". For the non-believing scholar, Muhammad made that choice, and chose well.

---

63 Dodge, Bayard: The Fihrist of al-Nadīm, vol. 2, p. 631.
64 Griffith, Sidney (ed./tr.): The Reformation of Morals, Brigham Young University 2002.
65 Kassis, Hanna: Arabic-speaking Christians in al-Andalus in an Age of Turmoil (Fifth/Eleventh century until A. H. 478/A.D. 1085), in: Al-Qanṭara 15 (1994), pp. 401–22.

CLEOPHEA FERRARI

Die Sprache der Wissenschaft.
Christlich-arabische Lehrtradition im Mittelalter

Die Stadt Bagdad ist heute nicht nur als Zentrum und Opfer tragischer Ereignisse besonders präsent, sondern auch in ihrer Rolle als Ort kultureller Bedeutsamkeit, der durch die Jahrhunderte und Jahrtausende hindurch eine Ausstrahlung globaler Reichweite hatte. Als Ort des Kulturtransfers von der griechischen Antike und ihrer hellenistischen Umformung zur Adaption in der arabischsprachigen Lebenswelt war Bagdad Hort von Aktivitäten und Entwicklungen, deren Nachwirkungen man bis heute aufspüren kann. Das Zusammenspiel von Rezeption und Innovation in verschiedenen Bereichen der Wissenschaften und der Technik machten dies möglich.

Ein Ausschnitt aus dieser langen und fruchtbaren Wirkungszeit soll im Folgenden beleuchtet werden. Es handelt sich um die Zeit rund um das Jahr 1000. In dieser Zeit fand die Rezeption des hellenistischen Erbes zu einer neuen Blüte. Dabei waren es vor allem aus der Erziehung in syrischen Klosterschulen hervorgegangene christliche Gelehrte und ihre Schüler, die sich mit dem griechischen Erbe auseinander setzten.[1]

Ein Bereich, in dem sich die Aktivitäten der christlichen Gelehrten besonders ausgeprägt äußerten, war die Medizin. Gerade in Bagdad, wo es schon seit dem 8. Jahrhundert, als unter Hārūn ar-Rašīd ein Krankenhaus gegründet wurde, eine Reihe von angesehenen Krankenhäusern gab (so beispielsweise das berühmteste, das im Jahre 368/978 von ʿAḍud ad-Daula eröffnet worden war), deren Wirken als Heil- und Lehrstätten gefördert und gepflegt wurde, waren viele christliche Ärzte tätig. Für Muslime erwies es sich sogar als schwierig, als Arzt eine Position zu erreichen. Dies zeigt ein Beispiel, das im Kitāb al-Buḫalāʾ (Buch der Geizhälse) von Ǧāḥiẓ (gest. 255/869) berichtet wird. Ǧāḥiẓ erzählt darin von dem Bagdader Arzt Asad ibn Ǧānī, der, als seine Praxis schlecht ging, einmal Folgendes gefragt wurde: „Dies ist ein Pestjahr, und Krankheiten sind weit verbreitet; Du bist ein gelehrter Mann, hast Geduld, Diensteifer, Beredsamkeit und Sachkenntnis. Wie kommt es, dass deine Praxis so schlecht geht? Da antwortete er: Erstens bin ich

---

1 Die Entwicklung der Überlieferungsgeschichte vom Griechischen ins Syrische behandeln BROCK, Sebastian: From Antagonism to Assimilation: Syriac Attitudes to Greek Learning, in: BROCK, Sebastian: Syriac Perspectives on Late Antiquity, London 1984; HUGONNARD-ROCHE, Henri: Les traductions du grec au syriaque et du syriaque à l'arabe, in: FATTORI, Marta/HAMESSE, Jacqueline (Hg.): Rencontres de cultures dans la philosophie médiévale: traductions et traducteurs de l'antiquité tardive au XIVᵉ siècle, Louvain-La-Neuve 1990, S. 131–147; ENDRESS, Gerhard: Die wissenschaftliche Literatur, in: Grundriß der Arabischen Philologie, Bd. 2: GÄTJE, Helmut (Hg.): Literaturwissenschaft, Wiesbaden 1986, S. 407–412.

für die Patienten ein Muslim; und bei ihnen war, schon bevor ich Arzt wurde,
ja, bevor ich erschaffen wurde, der Glaube eingewurzelt, dass die Muslims in der
Heilkunde nichts taugen. Und zweitens ist mein Name Asad, und er sollte Ṣalībā,
Maraʾil, Yuḥannā oder Bīrā lauten; ferner ist mein Beiname (kunya) Abūʾl-Ḥāriṯ,
und er sollte Abū ʿĪsā, Abū Zakariyyā oder Abū Ibrāhīm sein. Ich kleide mich in
ein Obergewand aus weißer Baumwolle, und es sollte aus schwarzer Seide sein.
Und schließlich ist meine Aussprache die arabische, und meine Sprache sollte die
der Leute von Gundisapur sein!"[2]

Asad ibn Ǧānī stellt also mit bitterer Ironie fest, dass seine Praxis nur dann
Erfolg haben würde, wenn er ein Christ syrischer Erziehung wäre oder eine Aus-
bildung an der persischen Schule in Gundisapur genossen hätte. Als muslimischer
Arzt hingegen habe man keine Chance.

Standen die christlichen Ärzte in hohem Ansehen, waren sie gleichzeitig auch
Träger einer Lehrtradition, die sich an das Vorbild der alexandrinischen Tradition hielt. Deswegen war die Vermittlung ärztlichen Wissens nicht nur auf die
Weitergabe von praktischen Erfahrungen beschränkt, sondern sie speiste sich
vornehmlich aus Büchern, in diesem Falle vor allem aus übersetzten Werken des
Hippokrates und Galen. Da seit Ḥunain ibn Isḥāq, einem der wichtigsten Übersetzer medizinischer Texte, also schon seit dem 9. Jahrhundert Hippokrates und
Galen zugänglich waren, konnte das medizinische Wissen auf dieser Grundlage
aufgebaut werden.[3] Die Auseinandersetzung mit dem griechischen Erbe war fundamental, da es zum Ideal des Arztes gehörte, sein ärztliches Wissen in der antiken Lehrüberlieferung eingebettet zu haben. Die Ausbildung der Ärzte war denn
auch auf dem alten Curriculum aufgebaut, das als Propädeutikum die Logik des
Aristoteles zur Voraussetzung hatte, was wiederum die Beschäftigung mit dessen
Werk lebendig erhielt.[4]

So scheint es denn auch natürlich, dass es in Bagdad im 10. Jahrhundert über
mehrere Generationen hinweg eine aristotelische Schule gab, deren erster bekann-
ter Lehrer Mattā ibn Yūnus (gest. 940) war. Mattā ibn Yūnus war nestorianischer Christ. Er wurde in der syrischen Klosterschule erzogen und entwickelte
sich zu einem bedeutenden Übersetzer und Kommentator, der zum Schulhaupt
der Bagdader Philosophen wurde. In seinen Übersetzungen übertrug er aus dem
Syrischen ins Arabische und gab damit der Rezeption der aristotelischen Texte
neuen Schwung. Dies hatte eine große Wirkung einerseits im Falle der *Analytica*

---

2 Vgl. Ǧāḥiẓ, K. al-Buḫalāʾ, hg. v. Gerlof van Vloten, Leiden 1900, S. 109, hg. v. A. ʿAbd al-Sātir,
   Beirut 1987, S. 138.
3 Ḥunain ibn Isḥāq wurde besonders wegen seiner philologischen Methoden und der großen Zahl
   der von ihm hergestellten Übersetzungen zu einem wichtigen Träger der Überlieferung. Er
   selbst verfasste eine Schrift über seine Arbeitsweise bei der Übersetzung der Galen-Schriften, siehe Ḥunain ibn Isḥāq: Über die syrischen und arabischen Galen-Übersetzungen, hg. und übers. v.
   Gotthelf Bergsträsser (Abhandlungen für die Kunde des Morgenlandes 17,2), Leipzig 1925.
4 Die Entwicklung der Ärzteschule und die Biographien einzelner Gelehrter werden in einen größeren Zusammenhang gestellt und ausführlich geschildert von Endress: Die wissenschaftliche Literatur (Anm. 1), S. 400–472, besonders S. 440–448.

posteriora, die bisher aus dogmatischen Gründen in den syrischen Klosterschulen nur zu einem Teil gelesen wurde, durch Mattā ibn Yūnus (und später durch Al-Fārābī) jedoch wiederentdeckt und ans Licht gezogen wurden.

Zum anderen wandte sich Mattā ibn Yūnus auch den zugänglichen griechischen Kommentaren zu und übersetzte sie mit dem aristotelischen Text zusammen. Dies änderte den Zugang zum Text und brachte der Auseinandersetzung mit ihm eine neue Perspektive. Die bibliographischen Quellen, allen voran das Bücherverzeichnis Ibn an-Nadīms mit dem Titel *Al-Fihrist*, sprechen von einer Übersetzung der letzten Bücher des Kommentars von Themistios zu den *Analytica priora* und *Analytica posteriora*.[5] Von Mattā ibn Yūnus stammt auch die erste Übersetzung der *Poetik*, die seit den Alexandrinern zum *Organon* gezählt wurde, und er übertrug weitere Texte samt deren Kommentare von Alexander von Aphrodisias, Olympiodor und Themistios. Die meisten seiner Übersetzungen von griechischen Kommentaren zu Aristoteles-Werken sind allerdings verloren, sie waren indes folgenreich für die Lehrtradition der Folgezeit.

Der bedeutendste Schüler von Mattā ibn Yūnus, Yaḥyā ibn ʿAdī, (gest. 363/974) war jakobitischer Christ.[6] Er wirkte als Lehrer in Bagdad und übersetzte Kommentare und Originaltexte, wie zum Beispiel die *Kategorien*, die *Topik*, die *Sophistici Elenchi* und die *Poetik*, zu Teilen auch die *Physik* mit dem Kommentar von Alexander, *De anima* und Teile der *Metaphysik*. Auch Werke von Platon wurden von ihm übersetzt, nämlich die *Leges* und der *Timaios*, er verfasste aber auch eigene Kommentare zu Aristoteles. Yaḥyā ibn ʿAdī ist auch der Autor zahlreicher Schriften zur Propädeutik, zu Ziel und Zweck der Logik, zu Problemen der Physik und der Mathematik und zu einzelnen Fragen der Metaphysik und Psychologie. Auch zur Ethik hat er sich in einigen Traktaten geäußert. Fruchtbar war auch seine Tätigkeit als christlicher Dogmatiker und Kommentator. In diesen Werken versuchte er auch, die Logik zur Verteidigung seiner dogmatischen Auffassungen ins Feld zu führen, im Besonderen in einer Vielzahl von Traktaten zur Apologie der Trinität.

Schüler von Yaḥyā ibn ʿAdī und sein Nachfolger als Oberhaupt der Schule war Abū Sulaimān as-Siǧistānī (gest. nach 391/1001), ein Muslim, der weniger durch die Hinterlassenschaft philosophischer Werke als vielmehr als das Zentrum eines Kreises von Gelehrten bekannt ist.[7]

Der eminent wichtige muslimische Gelehrte Al-Fārābī, der nach Aristoteles der „zweite Lehrer" genannt wurde, war ein überaus produktiver Kommentator und Autor eigener Werke, die sich mit dem antiken Erbe auseinandersetzten.

---

5 Siehe Ibn an-Nadīm, Al-Fihrist, hg. v. R. Taǧaddud, S. 322.

6 Die Werke von Yaḥyā ibn ʿAdī werden gesammelt und vorgestellt in Endress, Gerhard: The Works of Yaḥyā ibn ʿAdī. An Analytical Inventory, Wiesbaden 1977, S. 25–28.

7 Die Gedankenwelt des Gelehrten Abū Sulaimān as-Siǧistānī und seiner Umgebung ist untersucht worden von Kraemer, Joel L.: Philosophy in the Renaissance of Islam. Abū Sulaimān as-Siǧistānī and His Circle (Studies in Islamic Culture and History Series 8), Leiden 1968.

Fārābī hatte wohl Kontakte zu diesen Kreisen, gehörte aber nicht wirklich dazu.[8] Er war es indes auch, der die griechische Philosophie in die islamische Lebenswelt zu integrieren suchte. Ob sein Abstand von der Gruppe auf seine Religionszugehörigkeit zurückgeht, ist nicht mit letzter Klarheit zu sagen, es deutet jedoch einiges darauf hin. In dem Bemühen, sich von der christlichen Schule zu distanzieren, kritisiert er öfter seine Lehrer, im Besonderen Mattā ibn Yūnus. Aber die Haltung der Trennung Fārābīs war unzeitgemäß. Für zwei Generationen nach ihm galt noch eine enge Kooperation zwischen Christen und Muslimen. Erst später trennten sich die Schulen, mit dem Resultat, dass Christen und Muslime in ihren Kommentaren nur noch auf Autoren ihrer eigenen Religion zurückgriffen.

Zu Yaḥyā ibn ʿAdī's engsten Schülern gehörte auch Abū ʿAlī ʿĪsā ibn Isḥāq ibn Zurʿa (gest. 398/1008), ein jakobitischer Christ. Er setzte dessen Tätigkeiten fort mit Übersetzungen der *Zoologie* und *Sophistik*, von Kommentaren zu Aristoteles und eines Buches von Nikolaos von Damaskus über aristotelische Philosophie. Außerdem ist er auch der Verfasser eines Kompendiums der gesamten Logik.

Von den Tätigkeiten des Kreises um Yaḥyā ibn ʿAdī zeugen auch die Werke, die von Ibn Suwār (geb. 942) überliefert sind. Er gehörte zu den jüngeren, christlichen, Schülern Yaḥyā ibn ʿAdīs. Nach den Berichten übersetzte er die *Meteorologie*, die *Ethik* und andere Schriften des Aristoteles aus dem Syrischen ins Arabische. Er kommentierte aber auch und verfasste eigene Schriften (beispielsweise sind von ihm Prolegomena zur Kategorienschrift erhalten). Er war es auch, der die Fassung des *Organons* seines Lehrers Yaḥyā ibn ʿAdī redigierte. Ibn Suwār trat in fortgeschrittenem Alter zum Islam über und starb als erfolgreicher und berühmter Arzt.

In ihren Kommentaren zu den aristotelischen Schriften übernahmen die arabischen Gelehrten zumeist das Vorgehen ihrer griechischen Vorgänger. Die Bedeutungen einzelner Wörter werden erklärt oder Argumente zur Erläuterung umschrieben. Oft zitieren sie die Ansichten früherer Kommentatoren. Dabei werden die Meinungen der griechischen und der arabischen Autoren auf der gleichen Ebene gegeneinander angeführt. Einerseits geschieht dies, um der eigenen Ansicht durch die Autorität des Vorgängers Unterstützung angedeihen zu lassen. Oft jedoch geht es darum, der anderen Meinung zu widersprechen. Meistens ist es in diesem Fall das Anliegen des Kommentators, Aristoteles gegen den anderen Kommentator zu verteidigen. Nicht immer aber bleibt Aristoteles von Kritik verschont. So wird zum Beispiel oft darauf hingewiesen, dass Aristoteles sich selber widerspricht, sei es in einem anderen Buch, sei es in der Argumentation selbst. Wie schon die griechischen Kommentatoren sind auch die arabischen zum Widerspruch bereit, allgemein kommt dies allerdings nicht häufig vor. Eher ist die Tendenz festzustellen, unklare Stellen durch Aristoteles selber zu erklären. Die höchste Autorität ist Aristoteles, gewissermaßen auch sich selber gegenüber.

---

8 Auf das Verhältnis Fārābīs zu den Gelehrten seiner Zeit geht ZIMMERMANN, Friedrich W.: Al-Farabi's Commentary and Short Treatise on Aristotle's De Interpretatione, S. CX ein.

Mögen Rückgriffe auf frühere Autoren auch häufig sein, sind sie doch nicht immer zuverlässig. Es kommt vor, dass ein Argument jemandem zugeschrieben wird, um sich dessen Autorität zugunsten des eigenen Gedankens zu versichern, und andererseits kann auch die Herkunft einer Fragestellung oder eines Argumentes einmal unterschlagen werden. Der Grund für Letzteres ist nicht unbedingt Ehrsucht. Durch die Situation der mehrfachen Kommentierung der einzelnen Texte kann es auch manchmal schwierig sein, die Urheber einzelner Argumentationen zu unterscheiden.[9]

Der letzte der bekannten Bagdader Lehrer war Abū l-Faraǧ ibn aṭ-Ṭayyib, der selber Schüler der oben genannten Ibn as-Samḥ und Ibn Suwār gewesen war.[10] Ibn aṭ-Ṭayyib ist nicht nur der letzte der Reihe von bekannten Aristotelikern in Bagdad, er ist, das ist durch die Kommentare zu *Isagoge* und den *Kategorien* bezeugt, auch der letzte, der sich in Form und Inhalt seiner Kommentare an das Vorbild der griechischen neuplatonischen Vorgänger hält. An seiner Person lässt sich daher auch besonders deutlich das Bildungsideal und seine Beziehung zum Christentum in jener Zeit sichtbar machen. Nestorianischer Christ, war er Sekretär des Katholikos von Bagdad und als Arzt an dem von ʿAḍud ad-Daula gegründeten Krankenhaus tätig. Im Jahre 1043 starb er. Neben seinen praktischen Tätigkeiten verfasste er zahlreiche Kommentare, Übersetzungen und Traktate. In seinen schriftlichen Werken scheint die ganze Bandbreite seiner Tätigkeiten auf. Überliefert ist, dass er der Autor großer Kommentare zur Bibel und dogmatischer Traktate ist, dass er aber auch Kommentare zu Werken von Hippokrates, Galen und zu Aristoteles verfasst hatte. Viele dieser Schriften sind nicht mehr erhalten. Seine beiden Kommentare zur *Isagoge* und zu den *Kategorien* und die zur *Physik* sind jedoch vollständig überliefert.[11]

Seine Werke schrieb er mit dem Anspruch, alles bisher Gesagte zusammenzufassen und auf den Punkt zu bringen, um damit alle anderen Kommentare überflüssig zu machen. Als Grund dafür nennt Ibn aṭ-Ṭayyib, dass er in seiner Umgebung mit Schrecken sehe, dass nichts mehr gelesen würde, und dass es deswegen notwendig sei, die Dinge so aufzubereiten, dass die wichtigsten Dinge mit dem Wenigen, was überhaupt noch gelesen würde, abgedeckt werden. Eine uns wohlbekannte Klage also, der Ibn aṭ-Ṭayyib aber mit einigem Pragmatismus begegnet.

Für wichtig hält er Folgendes: An erster Stelle stehen natürlich das *Organon* des Aristoteles zusammen mit der *Isagoge*, die *Metaphysik* und einige seiner phy-

---

9 Zur Zitierweise der arabischsprachigen Kommentatoren siehe ZIMMERMANN: Al-Farabi's Commentary, S. LXXVIII–XCII.

10 Zu Ibn aṭ-Ṭayyib siehe FERRARI, Cleophea: Der Kategorienkommentar von Abū l-Faraǧ ibn aṭ-Ṭayyib. Text und Untersuchungen, Leiden 2006; ebenso ENDRESS: Die wissenschaftliche Literatur, S. 431 und S. 461f.

11 Editionen – Kommentar zur Isagoge: GYEKYE, Kwame: Arabic Logic. Ibn al-Ṭayyib's Commentary on Porphyry's Eisagoge, Albany 1979 (Übersetzung); Ibn al-Tayyib's Commentary on Porphyry's Eisagoge. Arabic text edited with introduction and a glossary of greek-arabic logical terms, hg. v. Kwame GYEKYE, Albany 1979; Kategorienkommentar: FERRARI: Der Kategorienkommentar von Abū l-Faraǧ ibn aṭ-Ṭayyib; Physik: Al-Ṭabīʿa. Ḥaqqaqahū wa-qaddama lahū ʿAbdarraḥmān Badawī, al-Qāhira 1384–5/1965–6.

sikalischen Schriften. Des Weiteren die hippokratischen Schriften und die Kommentare Galens. Wie man an den erhaltenen Kommentaren zu *Isagoge* und den *Kategorien* sehen kann, hält er sich dabei in Form und Inhalt eng an die neuplatonische Schule. Aufgebaut sind die beiden Kommentare nach dem Vorbild der alexandrinischen Vorlesungsnachschrift (ἀπὸ φωνῆς), wie es besonders von Olympiodor und seiner Schule geprägt worden ist. Der aristotelische Text wird in Lemmata aufgeteilt, die eins nach dem anderen erläutert werden. Dem Kommentar vorangestellt sind nach griechischem Vorbild die Prolegomena. Die gesamte Schrift ist in Lehreinheiten aufgeteilt (taʿālīm), die den πρᾶξεις der griechischen Vorbilder, vor allem Olympiodor, entsprechen. Weiter wird im arabischen Kommentar, ebenso wie bei Olympiodor, getrennt zwischen Teilen, die einer allgemeineren Einführung dienen, und solchen, die den Text Wort für Wort kommentieren, es wird also zwischen θεωρία und λέξις unterschieden.[12]

Beispiele für den Lemma-Kommentar nach alexandrinischem Vorbild sind nur in den erhaltenen Kommentaren von Abū l-Faraǧ ibn aṭ-Ṭayyib überliefert. Die beiden Texte sind ein sprechendes Beispiel für die Übernahme der Form griechischer Aristoteleskommentare in der arabischen Schule und gleichzeitig der Beleg dafür, dass in der Bagdader Schule die Vertrautheit mit den griechischen Kommentaren des 5. und 6. Jahrhunderts groß gewesen sein muss.

Ob die Logik Teil oder Instrument der Philosophie ist, war eine vieldiskutierte Frage. Bei den Peripatetikern, und damit auch bei den Bagdader Philosophen, hat die Logik den Platz eines Werkzeuges der Philosophie. Deshalb steht sie im *cursus studiorum* auch am Anfang. Begonnen wurden die Studien also mit der Logik, das heißt mit den *Kategorien*. Danach folgen die übrigen Werke, die zum *Organon* gezählt wurden, worunter seit den alexandrinischen Lehrern auch die *Poetik* und die *Rhetorik* gezählt wurden.

Ein Stück der arabischen Kommentierung des *Organons* ist uns erhalten in dem in Paris aufbewahrten Manuskript, das das ganze Textcorpus des *Organons* enthält (Paris, Bibliothèque nationale de France, ar. 2346). Die Handschrift enthält die Übersetzungen aller Teile des *Organons*, inklusive der *Rhetorik* und der *Poetik*, versehen mit Marginalnotizen verschiedener Generationen von Bagdader Philosophen vom 10. bis zur Mitte des 11. Jahrhunderts. Alle darin versammelten Texte (außer der *Rhetorik* und der *Poetik*) wurden direkt von einem Autograph des Ibn Suwārs kopiert, der wiederum Teile davon direkt von einem Autograph seines Lehrers Yaḥyā ibn ʿAdī abgeschrieben hatte. Dieser seinerseits hatte seine

---

12 Zum Kommentar in der griechischen neuplatonischen Tradition nenne ich nur HADOT, Ilsetraut: Le commentaire philosophique continu dans l'Antiquité, in: Antiquité tardive 5 (1997), S. 169–176; HADOT, Ilsetraut: Les introductions aux commentaires exégétiques chez les auteurs néoplatoniciens et les auteurs chrétiens, in: HADOT, Ilsetraut (Hg.): Simplicius. Commentaire sur les Catégories, Bd. 1, Leiden 1990, S. 21–182. Zur griechisch-arabischen Tradition HEIN, Christel: Definition und Einteilung der Philosophie: von der spätantiken Einleitungsliteratur zur arabischen Enzyklopädie (Europäische Hochschulschriften: Reihe 20, Philosophie 177), Frankfurt a. M. 1985.

Autographen von den *Kategorien* und von *De Interpretatione* mit dem originalen Manuskript des Übersetzers, Isḥāq ibn Ḥunain, kollationiert.[13]

Die Bagdader Philosophen beschränkten sich jedoch nicht ausschließlich auf das *Organon*. Wir haben Zeugnisse dafür, dass sie auch die physikalischen Schriften des Aristoteles studierten. Die Kommentare von Philoponos, Themistios und Alexander von Aphrodisias sind ins Arabische übersetzt und studiert worden, sie sind allerdings im Allgemeinen nicht erhalten. Themistios' Paraphrase ist verloren, der Kommentar von Philoponos hat nur in Fragmenten überlebt, die arabische Übersetzung seines kompletten Kommentars ist nicht erhalten und der Physikkommentar von Simplikios war in der arabischen Welt nicht bekannt. Die einzige überlieferte Übersetzung der *Physik* stammt von Isḥāq ibn Ḥunain (gest. 910), man weiß aber auch von einer Übersetzung durch Qusṭā bin Lūqā.[14]

Nicht nur zum *Organon*, auch zur *Physik* ist ein Zeugnis der Lehre erhalten: die heute in Leiden aufbewahrte Handschrift der *Physik*, eine Vorlesungsnachschrift, die ins Jahr 395/1004 datiert ist.[15] Die Handschrift geht auf ein Exemplar zurück, das Abū l-Ḥusain al-Baṣrī (gest. 1044, Schüler von Ibn as-Samḥ), ein Theologe, hergestellt hatte. Es umfasst den Aristotelestext nach der Abschrift von Yaḥyā ibn ʿAdī, daneben Kommentare von Johannes Philoponos, Mattā ibn Yūnus, Ibn as-Samḥ und Ibn aṭ-Ṭayyib (diese beiden Letzteren waren die direkten Lehrer von Ḥusain al-Baṣrī). Ibn as-Samḥ hat den Kommentar von Philoponos benutzt, aber auch eigene Ideen und Beispiele beigefügt. Ebenso verfuhren auch Mattā ibn Yūnus und Ibn aṭ-Ṭayyib. Trotzdem gilt die aristotelische Grundlage als Fundament für das gesamte Wissen. Kommentare und Glossen dienen am Ende dazu, die Argumentation des Aristoteles zu stärken. Widerspruch gegen den „Ersten Lehrer" kommt zwar vor, im Ganzen geht es aber mehr darum, das System von innen her zu erklären und mit den eigenen Argumenten gegen Angriffe von außen zu stärken.

Durch die Treue zur Tradition kam es aber auch dazu, dass nicht ein ‚reiner', unangetasteter Aristoteles überliefert und weitergegeben wurde, sondern, durch die neuplatonischen Kommentatoren, ein Aristoteles in neuplatonischer Färbung. Dazu gehört auch, dass Aristoteles als Systematiker und Dogmatiker dasteht, nicht zuletzt durch die spätantike Kommentierweise. Denn ein markanter Charakterzug dieser Kommentare ist die betonte Systematisierung des Stoffes, die der Form eines Lehrbuches nahe kommt. Die Themen und Argumente in den aristotelischen Schriften erfuhren durch die Kommentatoren Einteilungen und Unterordnungen, die sich über mehrere Ebenen hinweg erstrecken und ein System bilden. Wie dieser Zugang zu Aristoteles übernommen wurde, lässt sich am Kategorienkommentar von Ibn aṭ-Ṭayyib zeigen.

---

13 Zu dieser Handschrift siehe HUGONNARD-ROCHE, Henri: Une ancienne „édition" arabe de l'Organon d'Aristote: Problèmes de traduction et de transmission, in: HAMESSE, Jaqueline (Hg.): Les problèmes posés par l'édition critique des textes anciens et médiévaux, Louvain-La-Neuve 1992, S. 139–157.

14 Sie wird erwähnt bei Ibn an-Nadīm, Al-Fihrist, S. 310.

15 Leiden, Bibliotheek der Rijksuniversiteit, Ms. Or. 583, Edition siehe oben Anm. 11.

Die Gliederung des überaus langen Kommentars ist streng. Die Einteilungen der oberen Ebenen in Lehreinheiten, einführende und erläuternde Teile habe ich schon erwähnt. Es ist aber auch so, dass die Aporien, die, wie beispielsweise bei Olympiodor und dessen Schule, im Laufe der Kommentierung auftauchen, im arabischen Kommentar immer den gleichen Ort einnehmen, nämlich unmittelbar vor dem Lemmakommentar. Darin ist Ibn aṭ-Ṭayyib weit strenger als seine griechischen Vorbilder, bei denen die Aporien auch mal im laufenden Kommentar abgehandelt werden. Dabei ist festzustellen, dass die Aporien als eine Art Unterrichtsfragen behandelt werden, indem sie mit System aufgereiht sind. Sie werden nämlich oftmals innerhalb einer Gruppe immer schwieriger und beziehen sich zunehmend auf Details.[16]

Da das aristotelische System dasjenige ist, auf dem das ganze Wissen aufgebaut ist, kann es auch nicht erlaubt sein, grundsätzliche Kritik zu üben. Es ist deswegen nur folgerichtig, dass Ibn aṭ-Ṭayyib höchstens einmal an der Formulierung eines Satzes etwas auszusetzen hat. Aber auch diese Kritik macht er gewissermaßen nur zugunsten von Aristoteles, damit es zu keinen Missverständnissen komme und der wahre und richtige Sinn der aristotelischen Gedanken unverfälscht zum Leser gelange. Ebendiese Kritiklosigkeit forderte seinen Zeitgenossen Ibn Sīnā (Avicenna) dann auch zum Widerspruch heraus. Dieser äußerte sich allgemein negativ über die Bagdader aristotelische Schule, deren Vertreter er für beschränkt und ignorant hielt, und Ibn aṭ-Ṭayyib war ihm ein besonderer Dorn im Auge. Von einem Schüler Ibn Sīnās ist denn auch überliefert, dass er „noch nie etwas noch Konfuseres und Abwegigeres gesehen habe als die Kommentare des Ibn aṭ-Ṭayyib".[17] Es ist ganz klar, dass Ibn Sīnā einen ganz anderen Zugang zu den überlieferten philosophischen Texten hatte und auch, im Gegensatz zu Ibn aṭ-Ṭayyib, nicht nur an der überkommenen Tradition hängen, sondern etwas Neues schaffen wollte. Ganz ohne Ressentiments werden aber auch seine Aussagen über den Kollegen nicht zustande gekommen sein. Immerhin ist zu bedenken, dass Ibn aṭ-Ṭayyib durch seine Stellung als ‚Chefarzt' und Lehrer am ʿAḍudī-Krankenhaus in Bagdad eine prominente Stellung innehatte, die anderen wohl auch zugesagt hätte.

Ibn aṭ-Ṭayyib ist nicht nur als Kommentator ein besonders eingängiges Beispiel für eine Lehrtradition, die diejenige der Spätantike in Bagdad fortsetzt indem Aristoteles in derselben Weise verstanden und kommentiert wird wie bei den griechischen Vorgängern. Ibn aṭ-Ṭayyib ist darüber hinaus auch ein gutes Beispiel für den Lehrbetrieb innerhalb dieser Bagdader Schule. Er war Christ und die meisten

---

16 Die Behandlung der Aporien bei Ibn aṭ-Ṭayyib wird anhand eines Beispiels im Detail untersucht in FERRARI, Cleophea: Der Duft des Apfels, in: Aristotele e i suoi esegeti neoplatonici. Logica e ontologia nelle interpretazioni greche e arabe. Atti del convegno internazionale (Roma, 19–20 ottobre 2001) (Elenchos 40), a cura di Vincenza CELLUPRICA/Cristina D'ANCONA con la collaborazione di Riccardo CHIARADONNA, Napoli 2004, S. 85–106.

17 Mubāḥaṯāt, in: Ibn Sīnā, Mubāḥaṯāt, hg. v. M. Bidārfār (1992), S. 82. Ins Englische übersetzt ist der Brief in GUTAS, Dimitri: Avicenna and the Aristotelian Tradition, Leiden 1988, S. 64–72.

seiner Lehrer waren Christen, aber wie schon seine Lehrer hatte auch er muslimische Schüler. Dass die Religion die Lehre nicht behinderte, wurde erst dadurch möglich, dass die Philosophie, vorzüglich natürlich die Logik, in ihrer Funktion als Grundlage der Erkenntnis überhaupt, als ein Wert universaler Geltung also, betrachtet wurde. Christliche Lehrer (z. B. Yaḥyā ibn ʿAdī) hatten muslimische Schüler (z. B. Siǧistānī), und muslimische Lehrer gaben ihr Wissen an christliche Schüler weiter. Auch innerhalb des Christentums konnten auf diese Weise verschiedene Glaubensrichtungen (Orthodoxe, Nestorianer, Jakobiten) miteinander verkehren. Es ist den Berichten von Abū Ḥayyān at-Tauḥīdī (gest. 1010) zu entnehmen, dass die „Schule von Bagdad" Männer von nah und fern anlockte, Muslime wie Christen aller Couleur.[18]

Die Philosophie, wie sie in diesen Kreisen betrieben, das heißt unterrichtet und diskutiert wurde, blieb jedoch außerhalb der islamischen Lehrinstitutionen. Es ist deshalb nicht erstaunlich, dass die Vertreter der islamischen Orthodoxie zuweilen auch kritisch auf das philosophische Treiben schauten. Als ein Zeugnis dafür kann die Debatte über Logik und Grammatik zwischen Abū Bišr Mattā und al-Sīrāfī im Jahr 932 gelten, wo Bedenken gegenüber den unislamischen Grundlagen des Denkens der Logiker laut werden. Denn dadurch, dass die alexandrinische Schule das Programm des Unterrichts weiter bestimmte, blieb die Logik die methodische Grundlage des ganzen Lehrgebäudes.

Das blieb nicht ohne Widerspruch: Überliefert sind einige Belege für den Widerstreit zwischen den Verteidigern der Logik als Instrument und propädeutische Disziplin aller Wissenszweige und den Verteidigern der Grammatik als Fundament der (islamischen) Grundlagen des Wissens. Dabei ist ein ebenso wichtiges Argument für die Logik, dass sie das Instrument (ὄργανον) ist, um Gut und Schlecht zu unterscheiden. Damit wird es erst möglich, ein richtiges und gutes Leben zu führen. Folglich ist die Logik also das Instrument, um richtig (in bezug auf Gott) und glücklich (εὐδαιμονία) zu leben. Der Weg dahin, nämlich das Richtige vom Falschen zu unterscheiden, ist, die Natur der Dinge zu erkennen. Letztlich hat also das Ziel der logischen Studien etwas Metaphysisches.

Einer der berühmtesten Berichte über den Streit zwischen Logik und Grammatik wird bei Abū l-Ḥayyān at-Tauḥīdī überliefert. Im Jahre 932 soll ein Disput in Bagdad stattgefunden haben, auf Aufforderung und im Beisein des Wezir, und zwar zwischen dem uns inzwischen gut bekannten Abū Bišr Mattā ibn Yūnus und dem Grammatiker Abū Saʿīd as-Sīrāfī.[19]

---

18 Diese Berichte stehen in den beiden Werken Al-Muqābasāt, hg. v. Ḥ. as-Sandūbī, Kairo 1929 und dem Kitāb al-Imtāʿ wa-l-muʾānasa, hg. v. A. Amīn/A. az-Zain, Kairo 1939–1944, 1951.

19 Eingeleitet, übersetzt und kommentiert ist dieser Text in ENDRESS, Gerhard: Grammatik und Logik. Arabische Philologie und griechische Philosophie im Widerstreit, in: MOJSISCH, Burkhard (Hg.): Sprachphilosophie in Antike und Mittelalter (Bochumer Studien zur Philosophie 3), Amsterdam 1986, S. 163–299. Ins Französische übersetzt von ELAMRANI-JAMAL, Abdelali: Logique aristotélicienne et grammaire arabe. Étude et Documents (Études musulmanes 26), Paris 1983.

In der Begegnung kommt der Vertreter der Logik, Mattā ibn Yūnus, nicht gut weg. Seine Argumentation ist schwach, er kann seinem Gegner, dem Grammatiker as-Sīrāfī, keinen Widerpart bieten. Die Argumentation von Mattā ibn Yūnus beruht darauf, dass er behauptet, für die Logik sei Sprachkenntnis nicht notwendig, was as-Sīrāfī widerlegt. Mattā ibn Yūnus wird auch dafür angegriffen, dass er selbst, obschon er die griechische Logik vertritt, lehrt und verbreitet, selbst das Griechische nicht beherrsche. Tatsächlich übersetzte Mattā ibn Yūnus, der eine syrische Erziehung genossen hatte, aus dem Syrischen. Seine Position wird noch um ein Mehrfaches geschwächt, weil er nicht gut Arabisch kann. Dieser Vorwurf war allgemein bekannt. Auch Fārābī hat seinen Lehrer wegen der mangelhaften Sprachbeherrschung, vor allem, was die Aussprache betrifft, kritisiert.

As-Sīrāfī betont denn auch, dass diese griechischen logischen Texte ja nichts Gutes sein könnten, sehe man sich die unbeholfene und arabisch unkorrekte Ausdrucksweise an. Mattā ibn Yūnus wird ganz grundsätzlich schon wegen seiner mangelnden Sprachkenntnisse angegriffen. Durch das ‚minderwertige' Arabisch der Übersetzungen, das oft den Regeln der klassischen arabischen Grammatik nicht genügt, bekamen die Texte in den Augen der islamischen Gelehrten den Geruch des Mediokren. Die ‚Sprache der Wissenschaft', das heißt die Sprache, in der die christlichen Übersetzer das antike Erbe weitergaben, war also auch eine Sprache, durch die sie sich von den islamischen Gelehrten abgrenzten. Keinesfalls ist dies zu hoch zu bewerten, ist es doch eine Tatsache, dass die sprachlichen Schwierigkeiten auch durch die schwer in Übereinstimmung zu bringenden Ausdrucksformen im Griechischen, Syrischen und Arabischen entstanden. Für die Gegner der griechischen Philosophie war jedoch diese sprachliche Schwäche Wasser auf ihre Mühlen.

Neben der Frage der Sprachbeherrschung ist es auf der Seite der Logik-Gegner auch klar, dass Logik unnötig ist für jemanden, der gesunden Menschenverstand besitzt. Die Grammatik sei nämlich selbstgenügend, die Logik dagegen sei abhängig von der Grammatik. Damit ist auch klar, dass die Grammatik gegenüber der Logik Vorrang hat.

Im Gegensatz dazu stellen die Logiker in den Vordergrund, dass die Sprachen jeweils verschieden, das Denken hingegen für alle gleich sei. Deshalb stehe die Logik, indem sie universal ist, über der Grammatik. Die Logik ist gewissermaßen die Grammatik des Denkens.

Das Thema wurde mehrfach auch von Schülern und Enkelschülern des Mattā ibn Yūnus behandelt. Letztlich ging es darum, das rationalistische Denken auch in einem islamischen Kontext als Grundlage zu verteidigen, was teilweise gelang, bediente sich die islamische Theologie doch auch der Logik, um ihre Dogmatik zu verteidigen. Der Disput aus dem Jahre 932 zeigt, dass sich hinter griechischer Logik und arabischer Grammatik durchaus auch die zwei Religionen gegenüberstanden, auch wenn das in dem Bericht über den Disput nicht erwähnt wird.

Trotz dieser Differenzen ist das einigende Medium die arabische Sprache geblieben, obschon sie für viele eine Fremdsprache geblieben ist und als Zielsprache der Übersetzungen aus dem Griechischen und Syrischen manche Verbiegung hinnehmen musste. Die uns überlieferten Zeugnisse in dieser Sprache stammen aus einer versunkenen Welt. Nicht nur fand die Schultradition in Bagdad nach dem ersten Drittel des 11. Jahrhunderts ihr Ende: Die Zeitläufte taten das ihre, um auch letzte Spuren davon zu vernichten.

SVETLANA I. LUCHITSKAYA

Muslim-Christian polemics concerning images.
Visual tradition as the language of religion

In the medieval Christian tradition central messages of religion were conveyed to the uneducated not only with the help of writings and sermons (written and oral tradition), but also – and even first and foremost – with the help of images. So the role of the visual tradition can hardly be overestimated. Figurative thought and medieval religious symbolism, the foundation of which was the idea of joining the visible and the invisible world, favoured the perception of Scripture through images.

Throughout its history, Christianity sought to overcome the Old Testament ban on the creation of images of God and on their veneration. Christians usually invoked the doctrine of Incarnation (as well as of the Trinity) in support of their conception of images. The Incarnation of Christ was interpreted as the main principle and the model of mediation between the visible and invisible worlds. The idea of the Incarnation, of the Incarnated Logos (Christ), implied a quite different attitude to the visual as compared with the Old Testament. The Christian point of view enhances the notion that the medieval image repeats the mystery of the Incarnation by attributing a material corporeal aspect to all that is transcendent and inaccessible. The cult of the images was justified in the Christian tradition and the theory of images was thoroughly elaborated. Holy icons and the Cross embodied the presence of God and the saints among the faithful, so sacred images – the representations of God and the saints – were indispensable items in the churches. These images were venerated by the Christians who believed in their power to intercede for people. In both Eastern and Western Christian culture the representation of the divine, the visualization of the invisible God, is a form of mediation between God and believers. Both Eastern and Western Christian civilization became civilizations of images.

This was not true of Islam. The strategy of the visual in Islam differs in many respects from the Christian one. On the one hand, there is no explicit ban on representation in the Quran (as there was in the Old Testament). The opinion that Islam with its absolute monotheism in principle puts images under a ban seems to be rather a stereotype than the truth. On the other hand, we should note the scarcity of Muslim reflection on images. We do not find any theory of images (as there was in Christian culture) elaborated in the Quran and *hadīth*; no special texts codify precisely the sphere of the visual in the Muslim tradition. As a matter of fact, the starting point for the aniconic exegesis of Muslim thinkers is a small set of texts which discuss images of false deities, that is to say, idols. The Quranic sūras "Abraham" (14) and "Prophets" (21) speak of the struggle of Abraham against the adoration of idols (*al-sanam, as-asnam*). According to the Quran only false images deserve to be destroyed, not every image. The faithful should avoid veneration of images without being strict about image-making. Nevertheless some authorities were opposed to (but did not ban!) the depiction of all living beings that possessed the "breath of life" (*al-rūh*) (except for trees and plants, which were regarded as inanimate objects) on the grounds that such depiction was a blasphemous imitation of the creative act of God.[1]

The point is that in Muslim tradition the act of making an image (*al-taswīr*) is expressly associated with the divine activity of creating (*al-khalq*). Muslims believe that to breathe in the spirit of life, to create living beings, is the unique prerogative of God. He is the "Creator, the Fashioner" (sūra 59:24), *al-musawwir*, and as the sole Creator he cannot admit of competitors. So *al-taswīr* is an activity which is proper to God, and it must have been this idea which became the basic theological rationale for the Islamic antipathy to image-making. By the time of the first Umayyads, Muslims were already threatening Christians with punishment on the Last Day for their use of images of living beings.[2] The doctrine of Islam turned away from the translation of faith through images, so representation is thoroughly excluded from the religious sphere (it is noteworthy that the Quran was never used as a source for illustrations as was the case with the Christian Bible). Images not of human making – *acheiropoētai* – were also not known in the Muslim tradition. The visual or verbal representation of God as well as the representation of Deity in any concrete form is not possible. "No vision can grasp Him", says the Quran, "but His grasp is over all vision: He is above all comprehension, yet is acquainted with all things" (sūra 6:103). The visualization of God is excluded, "for there is no God

---

1   Contrary to Aristotle, the Muslims thought that plants had no souls so the Muslim tradition excluded from the general Islamic disapproval of images representations of plants and trees and – as a consequence – of inanimate objects in general. Hence the development of the art of arabesque suits Muslim tradition. There were other means to avoid creating images of living things. In order to keep to the injunction painters changed the size of the living things represented, did not depict the real individuals, tried to stylize and not to copy or imitate. These means were typical of miniature and calligraphy. See CLÉMENT, Jean-François: L'image dans le monde arabe: interdits et possibilités, in: L'image dans le monde arabe, ed. by Gilbert BEAUGÉ et Jean-François CLÉMENT, Paris 1995, pp. 1–23.

2   The Islamic attitude to images has been extensively discussed by modern scholars. According to Creswell the prohibition of depictions of people and animals appeared approximately at the end of the 8th c. His reason is that the Arabic tract of Abu Qurra written in the 80s of the 8th c. refers to this injunction (so that it is a terminus ante quem) while John of Damascus, who died in the middle of the 8th c., does not mention it in his polemics with Muslims (thus giving a terminus post quem). See CRESWELL, Keppel Archibald Cameron: Early Muslim Architecture: Umayyads A.D. 622–750 (vol. 1, pt. 2), Oxford 1969. Grabar shares in general the opinion of Creswell, who based himself on the argumentum ex silentio (GRABAR, Oleg: The Formation of Islamic Art, New Haven 1973, pp. 48–67). Paret in his analysis of the Muslim authorities (including hadith) showed that the issue came up earlier than Abu Qurra's day – perhaps, in the reign of the caliph Abd al-Malik (685–705), who tried to islamicize public life in the caliphate, and that by the early years of the 8th c. the precept had generally been agreed upon; PARET, Rudi: Die Entstehung des Islamischen Bildverbots, in: Kunst des Orients 11 (1976–1977), pp. 158–81. Van Reenen has now challenged the validity of these conclusions. See VAN REENEN, Daan: The Bildverbot, a New Survey, in: Der Islam, 67 (1990), pp. 27–77.

except one Allah" (sūra 5:72). In the eyes of the pious Muslim any visual representation of God can be perceived as His copy or double, an attempt to ascribe partners to God (sūra 13:36). Unlike Christians, for whom the Incarnation is a model of mediation between the visible and invisible worlds, Muslims could not recognize the idea of the Incarnation of God, since for Muslims this is like transgressing the dogma of the absolute exclusiveness of God ("He is God alone! God the Eternal! He begets not and is not begotten! Nor is there like unto Him any one!" sūra 112:3–4). Given what has been said, Christians are in Muslim eyes the ones who ascribe partners to God. Accordingly the idea of the Trinity is also rejected: "Say not 'Trinity': desist: it will be better for you: or Allah is one Allah. Glory be to Him: (for exalted is He) above having a son" (sūra 4:171). Consequently the Passion and the death of Christ on the Cross are not recognized (sūra 4:157: "That they say (on boast): We killed Christus Jesus, the son of Mary, the Messenger of Allah, but they killed him not, nor crucified him"). On the whole, the Deity cannot be visualized, images are not accepted and not venerated (including the Cross, because the Crucifixion is rejected). To sum up, Muslims consciously refused to represent God in any concrete image which could be venerated, strictly observing the Old Testament injunction (Deuteronomy 15): "Take ye therefore good heed unto yourselves; for ye saw no manner of similitude on the day that the Lord spake unto you in Horeb out of the midst of the fire."

From the very beginning the Christian and Muslim traditions differed greatly in their approach to images. Permanent mutual misunderstanding between the two cultures and two religious mentalities were due partly to these differences between the Christian and Islamic conceptions of imagery. A misunderstanding in regard to the significance of images gave rise to polemics and discussions on the cult of the 'Other'. Sacred images played an important role in the Muslim-Christian polemics, viewed sometimes as a symbol of Christianity against the Infidel, sometimes as a proof of the Christians' 'idolatry'.

Christians were aware of the vulnerability of their position, for the Christian definition of the sacred image was rather loose. Indeed, how was the Christian to venerate God in His images without venerating these very images? There were no firm criteria for distinguishing between licit and illicit images. This problem puzzled medieval intellectuals. In fact for medieval believers literacy signified sometimes being able to distinguish between true and false images (idols). Rather frequently Christians had to justify their conception of images in the face of Jews and Muslims who kept to the Old Testament ban on creating images and venerating them and who accused Christians of idolatry.[3] If in literature great consideration has been given to the Judeo-Christian polemics regarding sacred images (Gilbert of Crispin, Guibert of Nogent, Hermann Judas),[4] the role of the Muslim

---

3 See CAMILLE, Michael: The Gothic Idol. Ideology and image-making in medieval art, Cambridge/ New York 1989, pp. 1ff.

4 See e.g. SCHMITT, Jean-Claude: La conversion d'Hermann le Juif. Autobiographie, histoire et fiction, Paris 2003.

critics of images in the formation of the Christian conception of the cult of images has not yet been studied. Yet the conception of the sacred image is at the core of a religion.

My purpose here is to examine the encounter between Christianity and Islam in the sphere of imagery and to look in detail at the possible impact of Muslim polemics on Christian attitudes towards images and the Christian view of the relationship between Image and Word, written or spoken.

The first intellectual and spiritual encounter of Christians and Muslims occurred in the Byzantine empire. The initial clash over images and the doctrine which they proclaim dates from the middle of the 8th century. The theoretical discussions on this subject are to be found in the treatises of the Byzantine writer Yuhannâ b. Mansûr, better known as John of Damascus. In 743 he completed in the Palestinian monastery of Mar Sabbas his "Fount of knowledge", a vast three-part theological compendium. The second part of it is titled "On the heresies" (περὶ αἱρεσεῶν).[5] In this work the Byzantine writer describes one hundred heresies in as many chapters. What has been considered as an original contribution in this work are only the last three chapters dealing with Islam, Iconoclasm and the sect of the Aposchites. One of these chapters – chapter 101 in the printed edition – touched on the "religion of the Ishmaelites, precursor (πρόδρομος τοῦ Ἀντιχριστοῦ) of the Antichrist which is still prevalent today, leading the people astray".[6] This chapter from his "Fount of knowledge" as well as his very short "Disputation between a Saracen and a Christian" laid the foundations of the Christian perception of Islam.[7] Both works testify to the fact that John of Damascus had a thorough knowledge of the theology and the christology of the Quran. He was the first to begin the discussion of these problems with the Muslims.[8] The main aim of John of Damascus was to provide the Christians with simple and practical arguments to parry the thrusts of the adherents of the other faith with its disapproval of religious images. The Muslim objections were rooted in problems of Christology, namely the dogma of Incarnation which was accepted in Christianity. From this perspective Muslims also criticized the Christian veneration of the Cross and other

---

5   Ioanni Damasceni, Liber de haeresibus, in: Die Schriften des Johannes von Damascos, ed. by P. B. Kotter O.S.B., Berlin/New York 1981, vol. 4, p. 20–67.

6   Ibid. p. 60.

7   See Tolan, John: Saracens. Islam in the Medieval European Imagination, New York 2001, pp. 50–55; Id.: Réactions chrétiennes aux conquêtes musulmanes. Étude comparée des auteurs chrétiens de Syrie et d'Espagne, in: Cahiers de Civilisation Médiévale 44 (2001), pp. 349–67.

8   His works had a great influence on the Muslims. See Ducellier, Alain: Chrétiens d'Orient et Islam au Moyen âge, Paris 1996, pp. 103–20; Abel, Armand: La polémique damascienne et son influence sur les origines de la théologie musulmane, L'élaboration de l'Islam. Colloque de Strasbourg, Paris 1961, pp. 61–85; Sachas, Daniel: John of Damascus on Islam, the "Heresy of the Ishmaelites", Leiden, 1972; Id.: The Arab Character of the Christian Disputation with Islam: The Case of John of Damascus (ca.655–ca.749), in: Religionsgespräche im Mittelalter, Wiesbaden 1992, pp. 185–205; Meyendorff, John: Byzantine Views of Islam, in: Dumbarton Oaks Papers 18 (1964), pp. 117–118.

images. John of Damascus explains convincingly the reasons for disapproval of images on the part of Muslims regarding Christology. First and foremost Muslims accuse the Christians of being "associators": from their point of view Christians introduce an associate to God by saying that Christ is the Son of God and God: "they call us associators (ἑταιριαδτάc)" – complains John of Damascus – "because they say, we introduce beside God an associate to Him by saying that Christ is the Son of God and God (λέγοντεc εἶναι τὸν Χριστὸν υἱὸν Θεόν)."[9] In order to answer this charge, John of Damascus adduces the following argument. The prophets announced Christ's coming and the Gospels confirmed it; if Christians are wrong, the prophets are wrong: "this is what the prophets and the Scripture have handed down to us" – he says – "and you, as you claim, accept the prophet."[10] Then, to resist the attacks of Muslims, he accuses them of being "mutilators" – he calls them "κόπτας τοῦ θεοῦ" (cutters of God) – because they cut away from God the Logos and the Spirit. "Since you say that Christ is Word and Spirit of God, how do you scold us as Associators? (πῶς λοιδορεῖτε ἡμᾶς ὡc ἑταιριαστάc)," he asks.[11] He argues that the Word and the Spirit are each inseparable from the one in whom it has its origin. So if the Word is in God it is obvious that he is God as well; if, on the other hand, this is outside of God, then God, according to Muslims, is without word and without spirit (ἄπνουc). So he comes to the conclusion that Muslims, in trying to avoid making associates to God, have mutilated Him. Thus, he summarizes, Muslims, trying to avoid making associates to God, have mutilated Him as if He were a wood, a stone (λίθον ἤ ξύλον).[12] By deploying these arguments, John of Damascus does his best to defend his coreligionists. So this is a reply to the Muslim accusation directed against Christians that they are "those who admit partners to God". His aim is to silence his opponent and to justify the practice of his religion. He knows that the Muslims accuse Christians of idolatry because they venerate the Cross. Though the Cross is not mentioned clearly, the Christian symbol is, however, indirectly rejected by the Quran and despised by the Muslims, because the Quran is known to reject the divinity of Christ and the Crucifixion (sūra 4:57). Thus, that which the Christians venerate as the symbol "through which the power of the demons (δαιμόνων ἰσχὺc) and the deceit for the devil had been demolished"[13] is, actually, considered by the Muslims as a gross insult against God and disbelief in God's messengers. John of Damascus realizes that not only the veneration of the Cross but also that of any representation or image is despised by the Muslims. It is noteworthy that the discussion takes place at the time of the iconoclasm controversy. At this time religious and political factions fought with each other over images. John of Damascus is known for defending the arguments of the pro-image faction. His friendly view of

---

9 Ioanni Damasceni Liber de Haeresibus ...p. 63: "Καλοῦσι δὲ ἡμας ἑταιριαστάc".

10 Ibid. p. 63.

11 Ibid. p. 63.

12 Ibid. p. 63.

13 Ibid. p. 64.

images had a great influence on his attitude towards Islam. John of Damascus uses arguments in defence of crucifixes and icons from the iconoclastic dispute against Islam. He says that Muslims "defame us as being idolaters because we venerate the cross (τὸν σταυρὸν) which they despise".[14] But the Cross reminds Christians of the Crucifixion and of the sufferings of Christ who is the Incarnated Word. Further he returns the accusation of idolatry onto the Muslims, pointing at their veneration of the Ka'ba. In this context John of Damascus wants to tell his readers about the religious practice of the Muslims connected with the Ka'ba. According to him even the Muslim ritual of pilgrimage is permeated with idolatry. The destination of their pilgrimage is the Ka'ba in Mecca. According to John of Damascus the Ka'ba is a stone which the Muslims embrace and kiss in their Χαβαθὰν. "How is it, he asks his opponent, that you rub yourself up against a stone and kiss it?"[15] John of Damascus tells that this stone is in fact a head of Aphrodite whom they used to venerate and whom they used to call Χαβὰρ which stands for great (ὅπερ σημαίνει μεγάλη).[16] Earlier he mentions that until the time of Heraclius, when their false prophet Muhammad appeared, Muslims worshipped the morning star and Aphrodite. That some cult of the morning star existed among the pre-Islamic Arabs seems certain, but John of Damascus attempts to find traces of paganism in Islam itself. John of Damascus identifies Χαβὰρ with both Aphrodite herself and the Ka'ba. Upon this stone, even to this day, traces of an engraved image are visible for those who know about it, he asserts. So can the Muslim compare this to veneration of "the Cross of Christ" (τον σταυρὸν τοῦ Χριστοῦ) before which the Christians bow down.[17] Thus in rejecting the Muslim accusation of veneration of the icons and the Cross, which they consider a kind of idolatry, John of Damascus describes the Muslim rite of the veneration of the Ka'ba as idolatrous and makes an attempt to prove that the Muslims were themselves originally idol-worshippers.

According to the other Byzantine writer Nicetas of Byzantium (8th c.), Muhammad was also in fact a devotee of the goddess Khabar, and her idol is still to be seen in Mecca where it is worshipped by the Muslims.[18]

John of Damascus, Nicetas of Byzantium and other Byzantine writers create a traditional image of pagan idolatry ascribed to pre-Islamic Saracens by Christian authors starting from Isidore and other Christian writers. John of Damascus suggests that if one scratches the monotheism of the Muslims who impute idolatry to Christians, one will find a pagan stone-worshipper. But as a matter of fact, his accusations of idolatry conceal his fears that the Muslims could ascribe idolatry to Christians. He is deploying mainly defensive counter-arguments in the hope of

---

14 Ioanni Damasceni Liber de Haeresibus ...p. 64.
15 Ibid.
16 Ibid. p. 60.
17 Ibid. p. 64.
18 Nicetae Byzantini, Confutatio falsi libri quem scripsit Mohamedes Arabs, ed. by J.-P. MIGNE in: Patrologiae cursus completus. Series graeca 94 (1860), cols. 669–842.

justifying the Christian practice of venerating images. At the time of the iconoclastic controversy, John of Damascus, one of the most ardent defenders of the
sacred images, describes the sacred objects of the Muslims as idols and justifies the
cult of the crucifixes and veneration of the Cross.

On the other hand, Christian-Muslim polemics may have supplied John of
Damascus with some evidence for Byzantine definitions of sacred images and the
relative merit of Scripture and images. The Byzantine response to the Muslim criticisms of the Christian images contributed to the formation of the conception of
image in the Byzantine tradition. It is not our intention to discuss the possible
interrelation of Byzantine and Muslim iconoclasm, which is rather complicated.[19]
Iconoclasm in the Byzantine tradition on the one hand and aniconism in Islam,
on the other, are certainly quite different phenomena; nevertheless, in the opinion
of the Byzantine Fathers the Islamic disapproval of images and of their veneration
represented perhaps a certain parallel to Byzantine iconoclasm. It is not by chance
that the council of 787 attacked the opponents of icons in order to indicate their
imitation of Muslim beliefs and practices.[20] John's position as defender of images
was perhaps reinforced thanks to the Christian-Muslim polemics regarding the
veneration of the sacred images. "Images and sermon serve the same purpose",[21]
this famous statement is a tacit recognition of the equality of images and texts,
word and image.

That Muslim polemics influenced to some extent Christian reflections on images proves another fact. At that time apart from the real adversaries, polemical or
apologetical correspondence between Muslims and Christians was common.[22]
Early in the 8th century – so it is assumed – an exchange of letters on the question of the respective merits of Christianity and Islam took place between the
Umayyad Caliph 'Umar II (717–720) and the Byzantine Emperor Leo III the Isau-
rian (717–741). Leo III is known to belong to the anti-image faction in the iconoclastic controversy. This discussion was opened earlier by the Muslims. According
to the Muslim tradition Muhammad had sent a letter to Heraclius inviting him
to convert to Islam and laying out the doctrine of Islam. 'Umar II is said to have
sent such a letter to the Byzantine Emperor Leo III. Modern researchers assume
that the letter attributed to 'Umar II was in fact written by a Muslim author of

---

19 It is not possible to share the view of Patricia Crone who thinks that "Byzantine iconoclasm was
    a response to the rise of Islam". See Crone, Patricia: Christianity and Byzantine Iconoclasm, in:
    Jerusalem Studies in Arabic and Islam 2 (1980), p. 68.
20 See Lossky, Nikolaï/Boespflug, François: Nicée II 787–1987. Douze siècles d'images religieuses,
    Paris 1987.
21 Mansi, Jean-Dominique (ed.): Sacrorum conciliorum nova et amplissima collectio, vol. XIII, col.
    361.
22 Jeffrey, Arthur: Ghevond's Text of the Correspondence between 'Umar II and Leo III, in: The
    Harvard Theological Review 38 (1944), pp. 269–333; Gaudel, Jean Marie: The Correspondence
    between Leo and 'Umar: 'Umar's Letter Re-discovered?, in: Islamochristiana 10 (1984), pp. 109–
    52.

the 9th century.[23] Muslim sources do not mention of it. The only Christian source to mention it is the Armenian historian Ghevond who wrote in the 10th century. In his "history of the caliphs" he cites a number of quotations from the letter of Leo III.[24] It is not possible either to assert definitely that this exchange of letters did take place or to reject it outright.[25] But what makes its subject matter particularly attractive here is that the correspondence in question is an excellent example of Muslim polemical views of Christianity and Christian images. In his letter 'Umar II gives a brief description of Christian doctrine and reproaches Christians for having falsified Scriptures and regarding Jesus rather as a God than as a messenger sent by God. What is more important for us is that he attacks the cult of relics and the cult of the Cross and images. Thus he challenges the emperor in the discussion. First of all 'Umar II asks Leo III about the validity of the Christian veneration of the Cross and of icons: "Why do the Christians adore the bones of apostles and also pictures and the Cross?"[26], the caliph writes to the emperor. Leo's reply is an exposition of the conception of images in the early period of iconoclasm. A large part of Leo's letter is devoted to the problems of cult and worship, in reply to 'Umar's attack on the Christian doctrine of images. There is also a serious passage concerning the veneration of the Cross and the icons, in which it is noteworthy that the use of images is constantly justified in his letter by Old Testament texts: "We honour the Cross," says Leo III, "because of the sufferings of that Word of God incarnate...borne thereon as we have learned from a commandment given by God to Moses and from the prophets..."[27] Further he refers to the corresponding passages in the Bible (Exodus 18 and Isaiah 60,13). He writes that the metal plate which Moses, bidden by God, placed on the forehead of the pontiff or high priest bore the image of a cross having the form of a living being, and it is in imitation of this symbol that Christians according to Leo III sign their foreheads with the cross. "As for pictures," says Leo III, "we do not give them a like respect, not having received in Holy Scripture any commandment whatsoever in this regard. Nevertheless, finding in the Old Testament that divine command which authorized Moses to have executed in the Tabernacle the figures of the Cherubim, and, animated by a sincere attachment for the disciples of the Lord who burned with love for the Saviour Himself, we have always felt a desire to conserve their images, which have come down to us from their times as their living representations".[28] And he goes on: "Their presence charms us, and we glorify God who

---

23 Ibid. Jeffery ascribed this letter to the Byzantine emperor Leo VI (866–912) for he had found the Latin summary of this letter among the works of Leo VI. See: JEFFERY, Arthur: Ghevond's Text, pp. 273–74. See on this subject: TOLAN, John: Saracens in the medieval imagination, New York 2001, pp. 37, 60.

24 GHEVOND, Vardapet: History of the caliphs, Saint Petersburgh 1862 (in Russian).

25 It is noteworthy that Leo III spent his childhood in the Arab Mar'ash and could speak both Greek and Arabic fluently. See: JEFFERY, Arthur: Ghevond's Text, p. 277.

26 GHEVOND, Vardapet: History of the caliphs, p. 30.

27 Ibid. p. 63.

28 Ibid.

has saved us by the intermediary of His Only-Begotten Son who appeared in the world in a similar figure, and we glorify the saints. But as for the wood and the colours, we do not give them any reverence...etc., etc."[29] In the letter of Leo III we can find the main elements of the Christian conception of images and justification of icons. He invokes the Old Testament and the doctrine of Incarnation, he reminds us of specific functions of the images, to incarnate the presence of God and the saints. Leo's text is an amazing example of Christian apologetics, based upon minimizing the role of images (in contrast to the attitude to images of his Christian opponents).[30] But even if Leo III is known to belong to the anti-image faction he attaches an educational and sentimental significance to the images; in the face of the Muslim polemics he insists on the veneration of the Cross (as we know this was preserved by the iconoclasts themselves). He tries to *evade* the criticism of the veneration of the Cross by ascribing paganism to the cult of Islam. In this respect Leo III's criticism of the Ka'ba cult deserves special attention. His reply to the charge of veneration of the Cross by a counter-charge of Muslim veneration of the Ka'ba is commonly used: "But you, do you feel no shame to have venerated that House that is called Ka'ba, the dwelling of Abraham, which as a matter of fact Abraham never saw nor so much as dreamed of, in its diabolical arid desert? The House was existing long before Muhammad, and was the object of a cult among your fellow citizens, while Muhammad, far from abolishing it, called it the dwelling of Abraham".[31] In fact, the Ka'ba in pre-Islamic days had been a pagan shrine, and the circumambulation and the kissing of the Black Stone which were taken over into the Islamic ceremonial of the pilgrimage derive from the pagan practice, so Leo III had some knowledge of Islam. "Muslims," says Leo III further, "reproach Christians for not turning when they pray to the region indicated by the Qur'an" (sūra 11, 136–140).[32] Sūra 2 of the Quran is known to order the Muslims to change the *qibla*, the direction of prayer, from Jerusalem to the Ka'ba in Mecca (sūra 2, 136: "Now shall We turn thee to a Qibla that shall please thee. Turn then thy face in the direction of the sacred Mosque: wherever ye are, turn your faces in that direction"). The Quran also explains that the Ka'ba was built by Abraham and his son Ishmael. But Leo III considers the objections of Muslims to be completely vain and full of folly. He tries to show that the Muslim cult is a veneer covering the true idolatry: "The region to which the prophet turned when they made their prayers is not known", he says in his letter, "It is you alone who are carried away to venerate the pagan altar of sacrifice that you call the House of Abraham. Holy Scripture tells us nothing about Abraham having gone to place".[33] So his response to the Muslim criticism of the Cross contained intense criticism of the veneration of the Ka'ba and he tried to ascribe idolatry to his opponents.

---

29 GHEVOND, Vardapet: History of the caliphs, p. 63.
30 MEYENDORFF, John: Byzantine Views of Islam, in: Dumbarton Oaks Papers 18 (1964), pp. 115–32.
31 GHEVOND, Vardapet: History of the caliphs, pp. 63–64.
32 Ibid. p. 53.
33 Ibid.

It is clear from both Islamic and Christian sources that in the VIIIth and early IXth centuries, the issue of the veneration of crosses and images was a matter of contention between Muslims and Christians in the caliphate.

While John of Damascus as well as other writers parried the accusations of Muslims from a Greek Christian perspective as a Christological heresy, his pupil Theodore Abū Qurrah (d. c. 820) defended the Christian practice of venerating images against the charge of idolatry also in terms of Muslim theology.[34] He lived in Muslim-occupied territory, in Syria, and played a role at the court of the Abbasids. So he acted in a quite different context.[35] A Melkite Christian, a monk at the monastery of Mar Sabbas in Palestine, then the orthodox bishop of Harran, he was a Christian theologian who wrote some of his treatises in Arabic and he was among the first Christians to exploit the apologetic potential of the new Arabic medium of public discourse.[36] His works maintain strictly negative attitudes towards the faith of Islam, but the arguments he uses are conceived in such a way as to be understood by his opponents.[37]

---

34 See: Arendzen, Johannes: Theodori Abū Kurra De cultu imaginum libellus a codice Arabico nunc primum editus Latine versus illustratus, Bonn 1897. It has been translated into different languages: Griffith, Sidney H./Robin D. Young (ed.): Abu Qūrra Theodore, A Treatise on the veneration of the Holy Icons, Louvain 1997; Dick, Ignace: Theodore Abuqurra, Traité du culte des icones, Rome 1986; Pizzo, Pietro (ed. & trans.): Theodoro Abu Qurrah. Difesa delle icone. Trattato sulla venerazione delle immagini, Milano 1995; Bacha, Constantin: Les œuvres arabes de Theodore Aboucarra évêque de Harran, Beyrouth 1904; Graf, Georg: Die arabischen Schriften des Theodor Abu Qurra, Bischofs von Harran (ca. 740–820), in: Forschungen zur christlichen Literatur- und Dogmengeschichte 10 (1910), S. 278–333; Griffith, Sidney: The First Christian Summa Theologiae in Arabic: Christian Kalam in 9th c. Palestine, in: Gervers, Michael/Bikhazi, Robert (ed.): Conversion and Continuity. Indigenous Christian Communities in Islamic Lands, Eighth to Eighteenth Centuries, Toronto 1990, pp. 15-31.

35 The most significant feature of monasticism in this period was the beginning of the shift from writing in Greek to writing in Arabic. While John of Damascus had written in Greek, a few decades later his pupil Theodore, also a monk in the monastery of Mar Sabbas, wrote in Arabic or Syriac. See: Schick, Robert: Christian Communities of Palestine from Byzantine to Islamic rule. A historical and archaeological study, Princeton 1995, p. 99.

36 His Arabic works were not known until the end of the XIXth century and it was Graf who undertook a thorough study of eleven of his tracts. Graf made up a list of the manuscripts of the works of Abū-Qurrah, though he had no access to the monastery on Mt. Sinai. See: Graf, Georg, Die arabischen Schriften des Theodor Abū Qurrah, pp. 278–333; Griffith published a notice on the two short theological treatises of Abū Qurrah discovered in the monastery of Mount Sinai (Sinai Arabic MS 72), Griffith, Sidney: Some unpublished Arabic sayings attributed to Theodore Abū Qurra, in: Le Muséon. Revue d'études orientales, Louvain 1979, pp. 29–35.

37 Bishop of Harran since 795, he had collisions with the patriarch of Antioch Theodoret and, having been deposed by the patriarch, he probably regained the see with the accession of Job to the patriarchal throne in 799 (Job was an iconophile). See Griffith, Sidney: A Treatise on the Veneration of the Holy Icons, Louvain 1997, p. 16. See also: Krachkovski, Ignace: Abū Qurra, in: Christiansky Vostok 3 (1916), pp. 301–09. Sablukov wrote an article in the review "Missionar" published in Kazan: Sablukov, Georgii: Abū Qurra, in: Missionar 6 (1879), pp. 148–51, 157–59, 172–75, 181–84, 190–93. Both I. Krachkovski and G. Sablukov mentioned that the Moscow Patriarchal Library possessed some works of Abū Qurrah unknown in the West. See also Vladimir, Archimandrit: The systematic description of the manuscripts of the Moscow Patriarchal Library, Moscow 1894, p. 852 (in Russian).

John of Damascus and other Byzantine writers (such as Theodore Studites) as well as the authors of the acts of the VIIIth ecumenical council are known to have defended the veneration of holy icons in the Christian Church. But the Byzantine debate over images was rather irrelevant to Theodore Abū Qurrah. He expressed the troubles of the Melkite Christians living within the *dār al-islām* (territories under Islamic rule) and speaking Arabic. These were deciding factors influencing Christian attitudes towards images. They had been subjected to the constant criticism of Jews and Muslims for their practice of bowing down before crosses and images. According to the scholarly Islamic tradition the Christian practice of venerating images and crosses was tantamount to idolatry. Abū Qurrah had to resist the charges of Muslims who ascribed idolatry to Christians. His treatise on the veneration of the Holy Icons was a response to their criticisms.[38] It was probably written in 799.[39] The treatise gained a very high reputation and was popular among the fathers of the church.[40]

It stands to reason that the public veneration of the symbols of Christianity in an Islamic environment created great problems for the Christians.[41] The opposition of Jews and Muslims (*al-barrāniyyūn* – "outsiders" as Abū Qurra calls them) stemmed from their opposition to the direct dogmatic statement about Christ's Incarnation and His death and the resurrection that they imply.[42] In the first instance Muslims imputed to Christians the worship of idols and the transgres-

---

38 Even the Melkite patriarch of Alexandria Eutychius knew his tract and refers to it in his vast Chronicle finished in 935. See SAMIR, Khalil Samir: Le traité sur les icônes d'Abu Qurra mentionné par Eutychius, Orientalia Christiana Periodica 58 (1992), pp. 461–74. Abū Qurrah's treatise includes 24 short chapters dealing with the Christian practice of veneration of icons. In the Arabic original we see a long description of the content of the tract rather than a title or, perhaps, the title is replaced by the exposition of the main argument of the treatise. See SAMIR, Khalil Samir: Le traité sur les icônes d'Abu Qurra, pp. 461–74.

39 For a long time historians held that Abū Qurrah must have composed his treatise before the year 787, since nowhere in it does he refer to the 2nd Council of Nicea. In an article published in 1963 Dick pointed to the fact that Abū Qurrah mentioned the martyr Anthony Ruwa who was beheaded on Christmas day 799 and deduced from this note that the treatise had been written at the very beginning of the 9th c. According to I. Dick Abū Qurrah served as Melkite bishop of Harran between the years 795 and 812 and it is between these years that he must have composed his treatise. See: DICK, Ignace: Un continuateur arabe de St. Jean Damascène: Theodore Abū Qurrah évêque melkite de Harran. La personne et son milieu, in: Proche Orient chrétien 12 (1962), pp. 209–23 and 13 (1963) pp. 114–129.

40 Abba Yannah, probably an official at the church of the Icon of Christ in Edessa, asked Abū-Qurrah to compose a treatise on the holy icons. At least it was Abba Yannah who informed the theologian that many Christians were abandoning the prostration before the icon of Christ the Saviour in Edessa – the most famous *acheiropoiētos*. See: GRIFFITH, Sidney: A Treatise on the Veneration of the Holy Icons, Louvain 1997, p. 8.

41 The Islamic campaign for the public display of the symbols of Islam in the conquered territories began already in the reign of the caliph Abd al-Malik (685–705). See: GRIFFITH, Sidney: Theodore Abu Qurra's Arabic Tract on the Christian Practice of Veneration of Images, in: Journal of the American Oriental Society 165,1 (1985), pp. 53–73.

42 There is archaeological evidence that in Palestine and Syria in the early 8th c. the destruction of images and crosses was carried out. See: SCHICK, Robert: The Christian Communities of Palestine from Byzantine to Islamic Rule, pp. 164ff.

sion of what God commanded in the Pentateuch and the Prophets. The concern of Abū Qurrah was to shore up the confidence of Christians who were abandoning the practice of venerating the holy icons because of the reproaches of Jews and Muslims.[43]

In order to persuade Christians of the correctness of their practice of venerating images, Theodore Abū Qurrah puts forward several arguments. These arguments give an insight into Christian thoughts on images and the Christian conception of images. First, Abū Qurrah is convinced that a person who refrains from making the prostration to icons should logically disavow other mysteries of Christianity. As in the case of the rest of the mysteries, so must holy icons, just like other items, receive honour comparable to the honour accorded to them.[44] To reject them because there is no mention of them in the New Testament would require one logically to reject other things not mentioned there, concerning the apostolic foundations of which one has no doubt – e. g. the eucharistic formulae and various other liturgical practices.[45] Further, Abū Qurra tries to find the inconsistencies in the Muslim criticism of Christianity. In the first place he tries to refute the Muslim views of Christian images. It is not a valid contention against images, he says in his treatise, to allege that they imply the attribution of corporeality to God. He refutes the Quranic prohibition on representing God in a concrete visual image. According to him, all scriptural languages, whether in the Old Testament, the Gospels, or even the Ouran, speak of God in terms that of themselves imply corporeality.[46] To prove this, he lists several arguments from the Old and New Testaments: that God walked in Paradise (Gen 3:8), that he visited Abraham and ate and drank (Gen 18), that God stood atop a ladder and from there spoke with Jacob (Gen 28:13), etc.[47] Therefore, the corporeality which images imply is no more attributable to God than is the corporeality which the language of the Scriptures spells out. Further Abū Qurrah argues that the very practice of the veneration of images must be apostolic in origin even if we cannot find a scripture to speak of it, but images are found in all of the churches of every country. Their ubiquity proves that they have come down from the beginning. We may not find a firm basis for images, but their use has come down to us as an inheritance, as has also, for instance, the liturgy of Baptism or the consecration of sanctuaries, the veneration of the Cross and similar things. The icons, says Abū Qurra, are in the church at the direction of the apostles.[48] He also cites different passages from the works of

---

43 Two copies of this tract have survived. The first is the British Library Oriental MS 4950 copied in 877 by Stephen of Ramlah, a monk of the monastery of Mar Chariton in Palestine. The other is the 10th c. Arabic manuscript now in the monastery on Mount Sinai (Sinai Arabic Ms 330, ff. 315–336). Dick has published an article on this copy of the tract. See: DICK Ignace: Deux écrits inédits de Theodore Abū Qurra, in: Le Muséon LXXII (1959), pp. 53–67.

44 ARENDZEN, Johannes: Theodori Abū Kurra De cultu imaginum libellus a codice Arabico nunc primum editus Latine versus illustratus, Bonn 1897, p. 34 (Latin).

45 Ibid. p. 2.

46 Ibid. pp. 8–9.

47 Ibid. pp. 7–9.

48 Ibid. pp. 11–12.

the Fathers, the "teachers" of the Church (St Athanasius, Eusebius, bishop of Caesarea, and St Gregory the Theologian) as he calls them. Their works, he says, attest
to the early presence of images in the church and to the legitimacy of venerating
them.[49] Basing his judgements upon the statements of the "teachers", Abū Qurra
defends in his treatise the veneration of holy icons and in the first place the Cross.[50]
Then comes his next argument. The Christian habit of venerating images does not
come under the ban against idols which is recorded in Exodus 20:2–5 and in Deuteronomy 6:13. First and foremost, says Abū Qurra, the scriptural prohibition of
idolatry is addressed to the ancient Israelites but not in order to prohibit the veneration of images of God and saints. God said "You shall not make prostration to
them" (Exod. 20:5) – to steer prostration in the right direction. But God inspired
the apostles to give permission to venerate images to Christians, about whom no
one fears what used to be feared for the Israelites.[51] Secondly, the adoration or the
honour which one's act of proskynesis expresses is addressed either to God, who
deserves adoration, or to his saints who deserve honour. With their prostration
to icon or cross Christians simply show love and affection for the person whose
image it is. This is not like worshipping idols. In making prostration to the icons
of the saints, not by way of adoration, but by way of honour, all believers are giving
the saints what they deserve. The saints are intermediaries between God and man.
Prostration is the act that puts man into contact with the saints.[52]

Like many Christian writers before him Abū Qurrah tries to justify his statements with the help of the Old Testament.[53] Image-making, he says, is in accord
with the actions of Moses, Solomon and other spiritual characters. Even though
God commanded the Israelites not to make any likeness, he commanded Moses to
make two cherubims and the serpent of bronze (Exod 25:18, Num 21:8–9). In the
Temple Solomon made images of palm trees and lilies and likenesses of a lion and
of oxen (I Kings 7:19, 23, 25, 36).[54] So God did not mean to forbid making images
of anything at all. Abū Qurrah also knows that according to Islamic teaching,
anyone who has made an image of a living thing will be obliged on resurrection

---

49 ARENDZEN, Johannes: Theodori Abū Kurra, pp. 12–15.
50 It should be noted that the veneration of the Cross still remains one of the main points of discord
  between Muslims and Christians. "The word of the cross is foolishness to those passing away" (I
  Cor.1:18) – Abū Qurra cites the words of St Paul, ibid. p. 12. He recalls the sufferings of Christ
  who was Word and Spirit of God: ibid. p. 14.
51 Ibid. pp. 37–38.
52 Ibid. p. 20.
53 In this respect his argumentation does not differ materially from the theological justification
  deduced from the Old and New Testaments by Leontius, bishop of Neapolis in Cyprus (7th c.) who
  was trying to parry the charges of idolatry made by Jews against Christians in his "Sermo contra
  Judaeos". To defend the Christian conception of images he mentioned Moses and Ezekiel, pointed
  to the Second Tables of the Law and to the Cherubims (Exodus), the Temple with forms of palms
  and lions (Ezekiel). As for the Cross and icons, they remind Christians – according to Leontius
  of Neapolis – of God and in His honour they are set in the churches and adored. He also pointed
  to the evidence of the miracles performed through the icons, see BAYNES, Norman H.: The Icons
  before Iconoclasm, in: The Harvard Theological Review XLIV (1951), pp. 93–207.
54 ARENDZEN, Johannes: Theodori Abū Kurra, p. 18.

day to blow the spirit into this image. In his opinion Muslims are at variance with Holy Scripture because Solomon and Moses will not be required to blow the spirit into the likenesses they made.[55] Besides Muslims themselves make picture of plants and so they contradict their own statements for these people should also be punished for their making pictures of plants, since they would be required to inspire their pictures and to make them grow, to produce fruit.[56] So Abū Qurrah tries to find inconsistencies in the Muslim statements about images and he shows that their judgement would be valid against themselves. Therefore, he concludes, Muslims have no right to impute idolatry to the Christians for their veneration of images.

Abū Qurrah resorts to a refined argumentation in order to prove the significance of images in the practice of faith and to justify the use of images in Christian practice. According to him, icons and writings are equivalent (Ezek. 41–43; Jer. 51:59–64), or even icons are better than writing, because they are more eloquent than writing for their purpose of instruction.[57] This is the main conclusion he comes to at the end of his long debate.

Though in another context Abū Qurra finds himself under pressure from Muslim critics, he comes to the clear recognition if not of the primacy of Image over Word in the transmission of faith, at least of the relative merit of icons and the Cross. Imagery was an unavoidable subject in the Muslim-Christian polemic. These debates may be termed "polemics" only in a conventional sense; the treatises represented not polemics so much as apologetics. Even if the Christian Eastern writers acted in different contexts – in the circumstances of the iconoclastic crisis or amidst the growing iconophobia of the Christians living within the *dār-al-islām* – regardless of the fact whether they wrote from different perspectives – from the Greek Christian perspective and from the perspective of the Muslim theology – their goal was the same – not to convert their Muslim opponents, but to silence them and to be left alone, to practise the Christian faith and to defend the Christian veneration of images. For ages Byzantine Christianity was kept on the defensive. However the polemics with the Muslim opponents intensified the Christian reflection regarding images and supplied them with the exquisite arguments Christians used in later discussions. The Byzantine attitude to images was shaped in the course of opposing the accusations of Muslims who accused Christians of idolatry. In order to strengthen their position, Christians living side by side with Muslims made the significance of the image fundamental and recognized the equality of Word and Image as worthy of worship. Images are not devoid of spiritual value – this was the statement they were trying to prove, each in his own manner. In a semiotic sense the visual tradition was a very important language which also served to transmit sacral knowledge to medieval believers.

---

55 Arendzen, Johannes: Theodori Abū Kurra, pp. 19–20.
56 Ibid. pp. 25–27.
57 Ibid. p. 41.

Mayte Penelas

Linguistic Islamization of the 'Mozarabs' as attested in a late ninth-century chronicle

The distance between the language in which the religious texts of a certain community were written and the language spoken and understood by the uneducated people entailed translations from the sacral language into the vernacular to make those texts available to everyone. In the particular case of al-Andalus, the arabization of the Christians resulted in the translation of a number of texts important for this community into a language so far from Latin as Arabic.[1]

Several testimonies indicate an important degree of arabization and cultural islamization undergone by the Christians of al-Andalus in the late 9th century, and especially from the early 10th century onwards. Albarus of Cordova (d. 861) gives us a good testimony to this process in the well-known passage of the *Indiculus luminosus* in which he talks about the practice of circumcision among Christians[2] *ob improperantium ignominiam deuitandam* (in order to avoid the ignominy of being insulted), and he complains about the attraction the young Christians felt towards the Arabic language. He even states that among the Christians of al-Andalus it was easier to find someone who knew the Arabic metrical rules than someone who could write a letter in Latin correctly.[3]

Be this statement true or, as it seems, a "declamatory exaggeration", as Ramón Menéndez Pidal puts it,[4] the fact remains that in al-Andalus Arabic ended up by prevailing, and, if Christians such as Albarus of Cordova resisted the spread of Arabic among them, others made open defence of its use, as it was the language understood by common people. Thus, in the introduction preceding the three extant Arabic translations of the Psalms made in al-Andalus,[5] translation is defended on Saint Paul's authority. In the first Epistle to the Corinthians (ch. 14) the apostle asserts that only the person who is understood can be of benefit to

---

1 As David Wasserstein has pointed out, translations from Latin into Arabic in al-Andalus "answer some sort of need in their intended audiences", i. e. the Christians, see WASSERSTEIN, David: The Language Situation in al-Andalus, in: JONES, Alan/HITCHCOCK, Richard (eds.): Studies on the Muwaššaḥ and the Kharja (Proceedings of the Exeter International Colloquium), Reading 1991, pp. 1–15, p. 6 (repr. in: FIERRO, Maribel/SAMSÓ, Julio [eds.]: The Formation of al-Andalus. Part 2: Language, Religion, Culture and the Sciences, Aldershot 1998, pp. 3–17).

2 This practice is also attested in the *Vita Johannis Gorzensis*, in: SIMONET, Francisco Javier: Historia de los mozárabes de España, Madrid 1897–1903, p. 609.

3 Indiculus luminosus, 35, in: GIL, Juan (ed.): Corpus Scriptorum Muzarabicorum, Madrid 1973, pp. 313ff.

4 MENÉNDEZ PIDAL, Ramón: El idioma español en sus primeros tiempos, Buenos Aires 1942, p. 36.

5 As we shall immediately see, three different Arabic translations of the Psalms survive: those of the Vatican Library, the British Library and the Ambrosian Library. All three of them are preceded by the same introduction in prose, with slight differences.

the Church; on the contrary, the person whose words are incomprehensible is like
a barbarian to the others. In short, relying on St. Paul's words, the champion of
the Arabic translation of the Psalter claims that people can obtain spiritual good
(*al-fawā'id al-rūḥāniyya*) from prayers and be of benefit to the community only
if their words are comprehensible and they themselves understand what they are
reciting, and the only way to achieve that is by using their own tongue.[6]

Therefore, in the Iberian Peninsula the acculturation of the Christians under
Muslim rule meant their progressive adoption of Arabic, and the consequent
translation into this language of a number of texts regarded as important for
them, mainly but not exclusively religious ones. Moreover, these translations
show us that this arabization was accompanied by an islamization of their language, through the assimilation of Islamic words and formulae. This fact has
already been demonstrated by Hanna Kassis and Marie-Thérèse Urvoy – among
others – in some articles[7] dealing with the production of the Andalusi Christians: specifically, the Arabic canons of the Church in al-Andalus preserved at
the Library of El Escorial (ms. 1623); the three Arabic translations of the Psalms
extant at the Biblioteca Apostolica Vaticana (Arab. 5), the Biblioteca Ambrosiana
of Milan (codex & 120 sup.) and the British Library (Add. 9060); and the Arabic translations of the Gospels preserved at the Bayerische Staatsbibliothek of
Munich (Arab. 238) and the Biblioteca Nacional of Madrid (ms. 4971). To a certain extent all of them show the degree of Islamic influence on the language of the
Mozarabs.[8] Along with their arabization, Urvoy, who has edited and studied in
depth the Milan translation of the Psalms, refers to "une certaine islamisation de
leur religiosité."[9] Kassis for his part has analysed the translations of the Bible[10] and
the Arabic collection of canon law,[11] and he says with regard to the latter: "The

---

6 Le Psautier Mozarabe de Hafs le Goth, ed. and transl. by Marie-Thérèse URVOY, Toulouse 1994,
   pp. 2f. See the English translation of the passage by KASSIS, Hanna: The Arabicization and Islamization of the Christians of al-Andalus. Evidence of Their Scriptures, in: BRANN, Ross/OWEN,
   David I. (eds.): Languages of Power in Islamic Spain, Bethesda 1997, pp. 136–155, pp. 147f.
7 Two of the articles appeared in the monographic section, Cristianos de al-Andalus y mozárabes, in:
   Al-Qanṭara 15 (1994).
8 On this term and the problems it raises, see HITCHCOCK, Richard: El supuesto mozarabismo andaluz, in: Actas del I Congreso de Historia de Andalucía, diciembre de 1976. Andalucía medieval.
   Vol. 1: Andalucía islámica, pp. 149ff.; CHALMETA, Pedro: Mozarab, in: Encyclopaedia of Islam.
   New edition (EI²) 7 (1993), pp. 246–249; URVOY, Dominique: Les aspects symboliques du vocable
   "mozarabe". Essai de réinterprétation, in: Studia Islamica 78 (1993) pp. 117–153; LAPIEDRA, Eva:
   Cómo los musulmanes llamaban a los cristianos hispánicos, Alicante 1997, pp. 308–312.
9 URVOY, Marie Thérèse: Influence islamique sur le vocabulaire d'un Psautier arabe d'al-Andalus, in:
   Al-Qanṭara 15 (1994), pp. 509–517, p. 517.
10 KASSIS: Arabicization and Islamization (n. 6).
11 KASSIS, Hanna: Arabic-speaking Christians in al-Andalus in an Age of Turmoil (Fifth/Eleventh
   Century until A.H. 478/A.D. 1085), Al-Qanṭara 15 (1994), pp. 401–422. Hanna Kassis, who is
   preparing an edition of the canons in Arabic, thinks that this collection, compiled in 1049 under
   the title *Kitāb al-Qānūn al-muqaddas* (Book of the Holy Canon), is not a translation of the Latin
   Hispana Systematica but an independent Arabic work, parallel to it, ibid., pp. 415f. On this text,
   see also DERENBOURG, Hartwig: Notes critiques sur les manuscrits arabes de la Bibliothèque

first striking feature of the codex is the degree of arabicization and islamicization undergone by the Christian community, not only among the laity [...] but more particularly among the educated clergy".[12]

This paper is intended to add a further example: the text known as *Kitāb Hurūshiyūsh*, which is the only extant non-biblical translation from al-Andalus.[13] As a first approach to the linguistic islamization of the *K. Hurūshiyūsh*, I will show here that many of the features underlined by Kassis and Urvoy are also found in this text.

A copy of the *K. Hurūshiyūsh* dating from the 13th or 14th century is preserved at Columbia University of New York (X, 893.712 H), but the original was completed in al-Andalus at the end of the 9th century or the beginning of the 10th. The Columbia manuscript contains a world history from the Creation up to the Arab conquest of the Iberian Peninsula,[14] based mainly but not exclusively on the *Historiae aduersus paganos* by the 5th-century presbyter Orosius. At the request of his master Saint Augustine, Orosius wrote a world history with the explicit aim of demonstrating that pre-Christian times were much worse than those following Christ's birth, and that divine providence was behind every historical event. From the contents of the Arabic text it is evident that one of the translators, at least, was a Christian,[15] as Christians were the intended audience: on the one hand, he rendered more or less accurately Orosius' comments in defence of Christianity;[16] on

---

Nationale de Madrid, in: Homenaje a D. Francisco Codera en su jubilación del profesorado, Zaragoza 1904, pp. 571–618, pp. 607–610; ABU-HAIDAR, Jareer: A Document of Cultural Symbiosis. Arabic Ms. 1623 of The Escorial Library, in: Journal of the Royal Asiatic Society (1987), pp. 223–235.

12 KASSIS: Arabic-speaking Christians (n. 11), p. 415. Kassis demonstrates his statement by analysing the language and the structure of this document, where each entry is ordered according to the *ḥadīth* literature. As for the language, Kassis points out that a "number of Latin words that were incorporated into the Arabic vocabulary of the Mozarabs [...] are entirely ecclesiastical and liturgical in nature", without an equivalent in Arabic, ibid., pp. 416f; on the transliterated words, see also ABU-HAIDAR: A Document of Cultural Symbiosis (n. 11), p. 229. But, besides these transliterated terms from Latin, he shows that the Christian jurist used other Islamic Arabic words, as we shall see.

13 For information on this text beyond that given in this paper, see the introduction to the edition: Kitāb Hurūšiyūš ([= Hur.] Traducción árabe de las *Historiae adversus paganos* de Orosio), ed. by Mayte PENELAS, Madrid 2001 (Fuentes Arábico-Hispanas 26).

14 The Columbia manuscript finishes with the reign of the emperor Valens (r. 364–378) but internal and external testimonies show that the Arabic text went on to narrate the imperial history until Heraclius (r. 610–642), and added the history of the Gothic rulers in Hispania up to the last Visigothic king, Roderic, that is until the arrival of the Arabs in 711.

15 In another article I have pointed out that there is evidence suggesting that Ḥafṣ b. Albar al-Qūṭī, known for being the author of the Arabic Psalms preserved at the Ambrosian Library, is also the translator of Orosius' book, possibly in collaboration with Qāsim b. Aṣbagh, cf. PENELAS, Mayte: A Possible Author of the Arabic Translation of Orosius' *Historiae*, in: Al-Masāq. Islam and the Mediterranean 13 (2001), pp. 113–135.

16 On this, see PENELAS, Mayte: Del latín al árabe. Una traducción 'mozárabe' del siglo IX/X, in: Actas III Congreso Hispánico de Latín Medieval (León, 26-29 de septiembre de 2001), vol. 1, coord. by Maurilio PÉREZ GONZÁLEZ, León 2002, pp. 423–432.

the other, he completed and continued Orosius' book by turning to the Bible and other sources, such as the *Chronica* or the *Etymologiae* of Isidore of Seville.[17]

Notwithstanding, the text shows an important degree of acculturation, which is reflected, for example, in the way proper names are constructed according to the Arabic onomastic system,[18] or in the interpolation of data or reports belonging to the Islamic tradition. For instance, following the *Chronica* of Isidore of Seville, the *K. Hurūshiyūsh* reports that Noah's Ark (*al-safīna*)[19] rested on a mount of Armenia called *Arārāth*.[20] The Arabic compiler explains that "it is the mount *al-Jūdī*" (*jabal al-Jūdī*), as it appears in the Quran (11,44), thus identifying – not for the first or the last time – the Biblical Mount Ararat with the Quranic Mount al-Jūdī.[21] Furthermore, the *K. Hurūshiyūsh* gives the Quranic form of those Biblical names also mentioned in the Quran. Thus, *Ṭālūt* stands for Saul, *Jālūt* for Goliath and *ʿUzayr* for Ezra. Likewise, Abraham is called *Ibrāhīm Khalīl Allāh*, or *al-Khalīl*[22] (cf. Quran 4,125), the *amicus Dei* of the Bible.

There are quite a few other instances in the *Kitāb Hurūshiyūsh* that demonstrate the influence of Islamic culture on the Christians of al-Andalus. In his fundamental article on the Arabic translation of Orosius' *Histories* Giorgio Levi Della Vida explained this fact by the possible participation of a Muslim, namely Qāsim b. Aṣbagh,[23] in the translation.[24] However, in a subsequent article he stated that it was difficult to determine how much was due to the Muslim collaborator and how much to the permeation of Islamic culture into the Christian environment.[25] But

---

17 This fact may indicate that he intended to provide the arabized Christian community of al-Andalus with an Arabic world history from the Creation until the Arab conquest, written from a Christian point of view. This is in my opinion the main goal of this compilation-cum-translation.

18 Thus the name is made up by the *ism*, or individual name, and the *nasab*, or list of ancestors' names, each introduced by *ibn* (son of), besides other elements that do not concern us here. E.g. Joseph is called *Yūsuf b. Yaʿqūb b. Isḥāq b. Ibrāhīm* (Hur., p. 58), that is, Joseph son of Jacob son of Isaac son of Abraham. In this instance the *nasab* would be real but in many others it appears to be a mere invention by the author. On this, see PENELAS, Mayte: Introduction, in: Kitāb Hurūšiyūš (n. 13), pp. 45f.

19 Here the translator uses the word *al-safīna* for Noah's Ark, but the term *al-tābūt* is also employed with this sense (Hur. I, par. 143–147). The usual term in the Quran is *al-fulk* (e.g. 7,64; 10,73), although *al-safīna* is used once (29,15). However, in the Arabic literature *al-safīna* appears more frequently than *al-fulk*. As regards the term *tābūt*, its meaning is 'chest', 'box', 'Ark of the Covenant', and with this latter sense it is also found in the *K. Hurūshiyūsh* (e.g. Hur. I, par. 323f; VII, 42). The Arabic translation of the Bible used by the 11th-century Cordovan polygraph Ibn Ḥazm also employed *tābūt* for Noah's Ark, and Ibn Ḥazm is compelled to explain that it is the *safīna*, Al-Fiṣal fī al-milal wal-ahwāʾ wal-niḥal, vol. 1, ed. by A. SHAMS AL-DĪN, Beyrouth 1996, p. 147.

20 Isidori Hispalensis Chronica (= Isid. Chron.), ed. by José Carlos MARTÍN, Turnhout 2003 (Corpus Christianorum. Series Latina 112), p. 17; Hur. I, par. 145.

21 See STRECK, M.: Djūdī, in: EI² (n. 8), vol. 2 (1965), pp. 573–574.

22 See, e.g., Hur., p. 52.

23 See n. 15.

24 LEVI DELLA VIDA, Giorgio: La traduzione araba delle Storie di Orosio, in: Al-Andalus 19 (1954), pp. 257–293, pp. 285ff. (repr. in: NALLINO, Maria [ed.]: Note di storia letteraria arabo-ispanica, Rome 1971, pp. 79–107, pp. 101f.).

25 LEVI DELLA VIDA, Giorgio: I Mozarabi tra Occidente e Islam, in: L'Occidente e l'Islam nell'Alto Medioevo (Settimane di studio del Centro italiano di studi sull'Alto Medioevo 12), Spoleto 1965, pp. 667–695, p. 690, (repr. in: NALLINO: Note di storia letteraria [n. 24], pp. 55–77, p. 72).

it is particularly with the linguistic islamization of the *K. Hurūshiyūsh* that this paper is concerned, with the Islamic terms and formulae used by the late-9th-century Andalusi Christian author. And the fact is that the same Islamic words and expressions are found in the rest of the Arabic production of the Mozarabs, from which we can infer that they adopted them and used them in their own way.

Let us examine first the texts studied by Kassis. If with respect to the Arabic canons of the Church in al-Andalus he stressed "the degree of arabicization and islamicization undergone by the Christian community", with regard to the translations of the Psalms of the Vatican and the British Library Kassis says: "Each demonstrates in its own way the degree of Islamic influence on the translators".[26] As for the main remaining copies of the Gospels, a distinction must be made between the translations deriving from that completed in 946 by Isḥaq b. Bilashku of Cordova, a copy of which survives at the Bayerische Staatsbibliothek of Munich, and others whose main representative would be the translation of the Biblioteca Nacional of Madrid. The degree of linguistic islamization is much higher in the translations that derive from Isḥāq's, which fact leads Kassis to conclude: "The translation by Ibn Bilashku portrays a society very much at home in its Muslim environment, fully arabicized and not uncomfortable with being islamicized. On the other hand, the Madrid manuscript portrays an Arabic-speaking Christian community that appears to have defined its arabicization to exclude or minimize its islamicization".[27]

Most of the words and formulae underlined by Kassis in the two aforementioned articles are also found in the *K. Hurūshiyūsh*. The *basmala* – the introductory Islamic formula *bi-sm Allāh al-Raḥmān al-Raḥīm* ('in the name of God the Compassionate, the Merciful') – is used both in the Munich translation of the Gospels[28] and in the Arabic canons of El Escorial.[29] In the *K. Hurūshiyūsh*, after the index of contents, the *basmala* serves to open the translation itself, followed by a formula of seeking assistance from God, *'awna-ka yā rabb* ('your help, O God'),[30] as is also found in the manuscript of the Vatican Library.[31]

The formula *'azza wa-jalla* ('Mighty and Exalted'), which follows the mention of God, is used twice in the *K. Hurūshiyūsh*: in this order, or the other way round,

26 Kassis: Arabicization and Islamization (n. 6), p. 152.

27 Ibid., p. 155.

28 Ibid., p. 154. The translation of Madrid uses the Christian formula *bi-sm al-Āb wal-Ibn wal-Rūḥ al-Quddūs* [In the name of the Father, the Son and the Holy Spirit], the same as the prose introduction to the Arabic Psalms of London and Milan; Le Psautier mozarabe (n. 6), p. 1; Kassis: Arabicization and Islamization (n. 6), p. 152.

29 Simonet: Historia de los mozárabes (n. 2), p. 728; Abu-Haidar: A Document of Cultural Symbiosis (n. 11), p. 227; Kassis: Arabic-speaking Christians (n. 11), p. 418; Koningsveld, P. Sj. van: Christian Arabic Literature from Medieval Spain. An Attempt at Periodization, in: Christian Arabic Apologetics during the Abbasid Period (750–1258), ed. by Samir Khalil Samir/Jorgen S. Nielsen, Leiden/New York/Cologne 1994, pp. 203–224, p. 222.

30 Hur., p. 17.

31 Kassis: Arabicization and Islamization (n. 6), p. 153.

far less usual, *jalla wa-ʿazza*.[32] This formula is also found in the collection of canon law of the Church in al-Andalus.[33]

In the Arabic canons the term *muṣḥaf*, pl. *maṣāḥif* ('volume', 'book'), designates each of the ten books into which the text is divided, as well as the Gospels and books in general.[34] In the translation of Isḥāq each Gospel is referred to as *muṣḥaf*.[35] This term usually refers to the Quran, the Book *par excellence*.

For 'book' the most frequent word in the *K. Hurūshiyūsh* is *kitāb* and its plural *kutub*, which may refer to both normal and special books.[36] In addition to this neutral term the translator employs *muṣḥaf*, pl. *maṣāḥif*, as well as *sifr*, pl. *asfār*, a word that normally designates a holy book, especially for the Jews. And when he employs these terms it seems that he does so in reference to books that are in some way special. Thus, the translator uses them to denote books that, in Orosius' words, were composed "with the solicitude and the zeal of ancestors" (*maiorum cura studioque*).[37] *Muṣḥaf* applies to books with religious or legal significance such as the Book of the Maccabees, or the Book of Wisdom (*Muṣḥaf al-ʿilm*) by Jesus son of Sirach.[38] *Sifr*, or its plural *asfār*, refers not only to the Pentateuch or to books of the Old Testament,[39] e. g. the Book of the Maccabees again, but also to books in a way special, such as the Sibylline Books (*asfār Shabīla*),[40] the Christian apology by the 2nd-century philosopher Justin Martyr,[41] or even Orosius' book and the translation itself.[42]

Another Islamic feature of the Mozarabic writings is the use of Yaḥyā for John instead of the Christian form Yūḥannā, as is attested in the Arabic canons, the Munich manuscript,[43] and the *K. Hurūshiyūsh*. Thus, John the Evangelist is called *Yaḥyā b. Sabadhāy al-ḥawārī*,[44] that is 'John son of Zebedee, the disciple'. The term *ḥawārī* is also employed in Isḥāq's translation of the Gospels for disciple.[45] The use of this word, instead of *rasūl*, pl. *rusul*,[46] is noteworthy as it is the term

---

32 Hur. II, par. 1 (*jalla wa-ʿazza*) and 4 (*ʿazza wa-jalla*).

33 KASSIS: Arabic-speaking Christians (n. 11), p. 418.

34 DERENBOURG: Notes critiques (n. 11), p. 609; ABU-HAIDAR: A Document of Cultural Symbiosis (n. 11), p. 228; KASSIS: Arabic-speaking Christians (n. 11), p. 415; KONINGSVELD: Christian Arabic Literature (n. 29), p. 222.

35 The Madrid translation employs *kitāb*, a neutral term for book, KONINGSVELD, P. Sj. van: The Latin-Arabic glossary of the Leiden University Library, Leiden 1977, p. 55b.

36 It is used, e. g., to refer to the Pentateuch (*Kitāb al-Tawrāʿ*) and books of the Old Testament; see, e. g., Hur. I, par. 117.256; IV, 2.

37 Hur. VI, 74 (cf. Orosius, Historiae aduersus paganos [= Oros. Hist.], ed. and trans. by Marie-Pierre ARNAUD-LINDET, 3 vols., Paris 1990, VI,15,31); Hur. VII, 123 (cf. Oros. Hist. VII,16,3).

38 Hur. II, 54; IV, 69.

39 E.g. Hur. I, 282; II, 76.115; III, 114.

40 Hur. III, 118; IV, 24.

41 Hur. VII, 114.

42 Hur. IV, 185; V, 69; VII, 21.

43 KASSIS: Arabic-speaking Christians (n. 11), p. 418; KASSIS: Arabicization and Islamization (n. 6), p. 154.

44 Hur. VII, 96.103.

45 KASSIS: Arabicization and Islamization (n. 6), p. 154.

46 See GRAF, Georg: Verzeichnis arabischer kirchlicher Termini, Louvain 1954, p. 52.

employed in the Quran in the plural, *ḥawāriyyūn*, to refer to Jesus' disciples (3,52; 5,111f; 61,14).

Another word largely employed in the writings of the Mozarabs to designate the Book of Psalms is *zabūr*, a term used in the Quran in reference to a scripture given by God to David (4,163; 17,55). Kassis points out that in the collection of canon law "the Qur'anic term *zabūr* is often used instead of *mazmūr*".[47] *Zabūr* is also the word employed in the *K. Hurūshiyūsh* to refer to the Psalter, whereas each Psalm is rendered as *mazmūr*.[48]

Imām, pl. *a'imma*, denotes a person who is at the head of a group, whose example is followed, and, particularly in the mosque, the person who leads the prayer. In the Arabic canons this term is employed with the meaning of 'priest'.[49] Similarly, in the *K. Hurūshiyūsh imām/a'imma* stands for someone with religious authority, whereas the only time the word *imāma* – that is, the rank of *imām* – is used, it renders the Latin *sacerdotium*.[50]

The *K. Hurūshiyūsh* also has some features in common with the Arabic translation of the Psalms in verse, a 17th-century copy of which is currently preserved in the Biblioteca Ambrosiana of Milan. This manuscript contains an introduction and a translation of the Psalms both in verse, completed by Ḥafṣ b. Albar al-Qūṭī in Cordova in 889. Both introduction and translation in verse are preceded by an introduction in prose by an unknown author, which is also included in the other two extant Arabic translations of the Psalms, those of the Biblioteca Apostolica Vaticana and the British Library. As said before, the Islamic influence on the vocabulary of the Milan manuscript has been analysed by its editor M.-Th. Urvoy in an independent article.[51] Urvoy provides several examples classifying the vocabulary under three sections: juridical vocabulary, cultural concepts and expressions, and divine names.

With regard to the first section, Urvoy points out that in the prose introduction to the Arabic translations of the Psalter, ethical vocabulary is classified in accordance with the criteria of *fiqh* or Islamic jurisprudence, and adduces a paragraph in which virtues and vices are qualified according to *al-aḥkām al-khamsa*,[52] i. e. the five qualifications into which religious law classifies every human act: obligatory, recommended, licit/indifferent, reprehensible and forbidden.[53]

---

47 KASSIS: Arabic-speaking Christians (n. 11), p. 418. On *mazmūr* see GRAF: Verzeichnis (n. 46), p. 55.
48 Hur. I, 349.365. In the Arabic Psalms of London and Milan, Psalter is referred to as *zabūr* and each Psalm as *mizmār*, cf. Le Psautier mozarabe (n. 6), p. 1: "the *zabūr* contains one hundred and fifty *mizmār* (Vatikan: *sūra*)". See also KASSIS: Arabicization and Islamization (n. 6), p. 153.
49 KASSIS: Arabic-speaking Christians (n. 11), p. 418.
50 Hur. I, 436 (cf. 4 Regum 12,2); VI, 31 (cf. Oros. Hist. VI, 6,2–4); VII, 218.
51 The influence of the Quranic style on the translation of the Psalms by Ḥafṣ al-Qūṭī had already been dealt with by SAMIR, Khalil: Al-Turāth al-'arabī al-masīḥī al-qadīm wa-tafa'ulu-hu ma'a al-fikr al-'arabī al-islāmī, in: Islamochristiana 8 (1982), pp. 1–35, pp. 20f.
52 URVOY: Influence islamique (n. 9), pp. 510f.; Le Psautier mozarabe (n. 6), p. 11.
53 On this, see FARUKI, Kemal: Al-Aḥkām al-Khamsah. The Five Values, in: Islamic Studies 5 (1966), pp. 43–98.

Urvoy notes this "juridisation de l'éthique" in the verse translation of Ḥafṣ al-Qūṭī, particularly in the frequent use he makes of the word *farḍ* to render the Latin *praeceptum, mandatum* or *lex*.[54] In the *K. Hurūshiyūsh* this term is also found with the usual albeit not exclusive meaning of 'religious duty', always denoting an order or decree issued by someone with authority.[55] For instance, following Isidore of Seville's *Chronica*, the compiler reports that the founder of Athens, Cecrops, whose name is rendered as *Jīrush* – the same form as that for Cyrus –, was the first to sacrifice a bull as an offering to Jupiter, as well as to order his subjects to worship this god. He uses the verb *faraḍa* ('he ordered') to render the Latin *praecepit*.[56]

Jupiter is referred to as *Yūbish* in the Arabic translation. Two brief comments on this rendering must be made: first, the form *Yūbish* is clearly a transliteration of Jupiter's Latin name in the genitive case, *Iovis*; secondly, the translator explains that "*Yūbish* is a god (*wathan*) by the name of the shining (*al-durrī*) *Mushtarī*", *al-Mushtarī* being the Arabic name for the planet Jupiter. He does the same thing every time he mentions both this god and Saturn – the planet named after this god is called *Zuḥal* in Arabic –,[57] possibly out of consideration for an audience that would not recognize the supreme god of the Romans or his father by their Latin names. Both are given the epithet *al-durrī* ('shining'), a frequent epithet for self-luminous stars, but at times also used for planets.[58]

The next section according to Urvoy's division concerns Islamic cultural formulae and concepts.

Ḥafṣ al-Qūṭī employs the usual formula for thanking God *wal-ḥamd li-Llāh*, literally 'praise be to God', to close the poem in *rajaz* metre (i. e. *urjūza*) preceding his Arabic translation of the Psalms.[59] In the *K. Hurūshiyūsh* this formula closes the first, second and third Books (*juz'*, pl. *ajzā'*, lit. 'part').[60]

One of the most frequent words used by Ḥafṣ to translate *lex* is *kitāb*, besides others such as *sharī'a* and *nāmūs*,[61] the Arabic transliteration of the Greek *nomos*.[62] These three terms are also found in the *K. Hurūshiyūsh* with the meaning of 'law'. It is noteworthy that the word *nawāmis*, plural of *nāmūs*, refers here to a legal sys-

---

54 URVOY: Influence islamique (n. 9), p. 511.

55 Hur. I, 185; II, 46; IV, 55; VII, 19.

56 Isid. Chron. (n. 20), 50; Hur. I, 212. Similarly, this word denotes an imposition of worship in Hur. I, 171; and VII, 40.

57 Hur. I, 175.249.261; III, 80; IV, 9.

58 Thus, in the exegetical work by al-Qurṭubī (d. 1272–73), we are told that the *kawkab durrī* (shining star) of Quran 24,35 is *al-Zuhra* (Venus) and, further on, *al-Mushtarī* (al-Jāmi' li-aḥkām al-Qur'ān, Cairo 1987, XII, p. 258 and p. 263).

59 Le Psautier mozarabe (n. 6), p. 20. As for the introduction in prose, it is closed by the same formula in a larger form *al-ḥamd li-Llāh rabb al-'ālamīn* (praise be to God, Lord of the Worlds). See Le Psautier mozarabe (n. 6), p. 13; URVOY: Influence islamique (n. 9), p. 512.

60 Hur., p. 125, p. 160, p. 201.

61 URVOY: Influence islamique (n. 9), p. 513.

62 Apart from the Greek loanword, there is another genuine Arabic word *nāmūs* with various meanings: 'hiding place', 'mosquito', 'confidant', as an epithet for the archangel Gabriel, etc.; see PLESSNER, M./VIRÉ, F.: Nāmūs, in: EI², vol. 7 (1993), 953–956.

tem of Ancient Greece or of a related people, and on just one occasion of another people, specifically the Romans.[63]

Sharī'a, or its plural *sharā'i'*, is employed to render 'religious law' or simply 'religion'. For instance, in conjunction with *al-kitāb* it is once used to refer to 'Moses' law',[64] and the Latin *uera religio* is rendered as *al-sharī'a al-ṣādiqa* ('the true religion'),[65] namely Christianity for both Orosius and the translator. However, this word is not exclusively applied to Christianity or a monotheistic religion, but also to paganism.[66] Thus, when the translator renders *pontifices* as *a'immat*[67] *sharā'i'i-him*, he is obviously referring to the religious laws of the Romans.[68]

Sunna, pl. *sunan*, denotes a rule or custom derived from tradition, and *par excellence* from the Prophet Muhammad's or his followers' way of behaving. In the *K. Hurūshiyūsh* this term is also used with the meaning of 'law' or 'customary practice'. It is obviously with this sense that it is employed along with *kitāb* in the next instance. The *K. Hurūshiyūsh* reports that *"Markush* with his brother *Awrāliyush"* – that is, Marcus Aurelius Antoninus Verus and Lucius Aurelius – were the first to levy tributes in accordance with the law (*al-sunna wal-kitāb*).[69] It seems that the rightness of rulers in collecting taxes was a matter of special concern to the translator, as the Latin original does not mention taxes at all: *hi primi rempublicam aequo iure tutati sunt* ('they were the first to watch over the Republic with equal authority'), says Orosius.[70]

Just as in the translation of the Psalms by Ḥafṣ al-Qūṭī,[71] *al-hudā* is used with the meaning of 'right path' in the *K. Hurūshiyūsh*. For instance, Orosius reports that Titus destroyed the Temple of Jerusalem because, being exhausted and empty (*effetum ac uacuum*), it could not be of usefulness in a time when the Church of God was germinating everywhere.[72] But, according to the Arabic rendering, in Titus' times the religion of Christ was not in its incipient phase but had already spread throughout the world so that God was worshiped *'alā al-hudā*, with the exception of the Temple of Jerusalem, where it was done *'alā al-ḍalāl*:[73] the 'right way' as opposed to the 'wrong way'.

Therefore, Titus – the Arabic text goes on – set fire to the temple: *fa-aḥraqa Ṭīṭush al-miḥrāb wal-bayt*, says the *K. Hurūshiyūsh*, thus rendering the original *templum in Hierosolymis incendit*. What is meant by the words *al-miḥrāb wal-*

---

63 Hur. I, 198; II, 79; V, 76; VI, 23.

64 Hur. I, 218 (cf. Isid. Chron. [n. 20], 55).

65 Oros. Hist. I, prol.,14; Hur. I, 6.

66 For different uses of the term *sharī'a*, see Hur. I, 236.393; II, 9.14.55; V, 9; VII, 29.223.

67 On this word, see *supra*.

68 Oros. Hist. V, 18,27; Hur. V, 106.

69 Hur. VII, 116.

70 Oros. Hist. VII, 15,1. This is not the only instance in which the translator says that a certain ruler 'levied tribute fairly' (*'addala al-maghārim*) where Orosius only mentions the ruler's moderation (see, e.g., Oros. Hist. VII, 18,8; Hur. VII, 148).

71 See URVOY: Influence islamique (n. 9), p. 513.

72 Oros. Hist. VII, 9,5.

73 Hur. VII, 76.

bayt? In this passage, the Temple of Jerusalem has hitherto been called *al-bayt*, so its meaning seems to be clear. As for the term *miḥrāb*, in the mosque it denotes the niche indicating the direction of prayer, but both in the *K. Hurūshiyūsh* and in the Arabic Psalms it is used to translate the Latin words *templum* and *ara*.[74] So in this instance it may refer to an altar, or something else inside the temple.

In the next example it is evident that the word *miḥrāb* stands for something that is in the temple, which is again referred to as *bayt*. Orosius reports that after his victory against the Romans, Pyrrhus, king of Epirus (c. 318–272 B.C.), engraved an inscription in the temple of Jupiter bemoaning the heavy losses in his army[75] – hence the expression a Pyrrhic victory. The Arabic translator renders this account as follows:

> He built a *miḥrāb* in the temple (*bayt*) of the god *Yūbish*, who is the shining *Mushtarī* (on this, see *supra*), and wrote in the threshold of its door [...].[76]

However, in other cases the temple is referred to as *miḥrāb*, pl. *maḥārib*. Thus, 'the Temple of Asclepius' is rendered once as *bayt* and once as *miḥrāb*.[77] With this sense, *maḥārib* is also used in conjunction with *maqāṣīr*, plural of *maqṣūra*,[78] which in the mosque denotes a compartment for the ruler.

For *ara* or *altar* the term more often used in the *K. Hurūshiyūsh* is *madhbaḥ*, i.e. the place where sacrifices are made. For instance, 'Baal's altars' built by Manasses are referred to as *madhbaḥ al-wathan Ba'āl*.[79] *Miḥrāb* is also used with this sense. Thus, the oath against the Romans made by Hannibal as a child *ante aras* is rendered as *wa-kāna qad ḥalafa* [...] *'inda miḥrāb awthāni-him* ('he had sworn [...] at the *miḥrāb* of their gods').[80] These two terms, *miḥrāb* and *madhbaḥ*, are also found in the Arabic canons with the same meaning.[81]

Urvoy underlines the use of the word *nazala* or a derivative to designate revelation in the translation of the Psalms by Ḥafṣ.[82] For revelation, the *K. Hurūshiyūsh* uses the word in the IV form – *anzala*, *inzāl*, etc. – as well as the term *waḥy*,[83] both employed in the Quran.[84]

The third section of Urvoy's article deals with divine names. She points out that Ḥafṣ al-Qūṭī uses, to name or qualify God, the epithets *raḥmān* and *raḥīm*, which make reference to His Mercy, as well as others that refer to His power, such

---

74 URVOY: Influence islamique (n. 9), p. 514.

75 Oros. Hist. IV, 1,14.

76 Hur. IV, 9.

77 Hur. IV, 183; VI, 8.

78 Hur. I, 169; cf. Isid. Chron. (n. 20), 22: *Describunt ibi templa* [...].

79 Hur. I, 493; cf. 4 Regum 21,3: *aras Baal*.

80 Oros. Hist. IV, 14,3; Hur. IV, 91.

81 ABU-HAIDAR: A Document of Cultural Symbiosis (n. 11), p. 228.

82 URVOY: Influence islamique (n. 9), pp. 513f.

83 See e.g. Hur. I, 234; VII, 1f.

84 For the use of these two terms, see WENSINCK, Arent Jan/RIPPIN, Andrew: Wahy, in: EI², vol. 11 (2002), pp. 53–56.

as *jabbār, qādir, qahhār* or *muqtadir*,[85] all of which belong to the list of *al-asmā' al-ḥusnā*, i. e. the most beautiful names of God.[86]

In the *K. Hurūshiyūsh* only *al-raḥmān*, as a part of the *basmala* (see *supra*), is employed in reference to God. *Al-raḥīm* is also used to qualify Octavian Augustus and Antoninus Pius (*al-mulaqqab bil-raḥīm*, 'nicknamed Pius').[87] Other attributes apply to others but God: *al-jabbār* qualifies Nimrod, Nebuchadnezzar and Hercules, with the sense of 'giant' or 'strong and powerful man';[88] besides *al-raḥīm*, Octavian Augustus is given the epithets *al-qawī* – another divine attribute indicating mightiness[89] – and *al-muqtadir*.[90] In this latter paragraph are several more examples that demonstrate that the translator was doubtless familiar with the Islamic terminology concerning God's attributes: *al-khāliq, al-bāri'* and *al-mudabbir* qualify Him as creator and master of all things; God is described as *ḥayy* (living) and *ʿālim* (omniscient); other attributes such as *qadīm* and *azalī* make reference to His quality of being eternal.[91]

Conclusion

Several examples have been offered that show that the Christians of al-Andalus assimilated cultural concepts and incorporated many Islamic words and expressions into their language.[92] In *The Foreign Vocabulary of the Qur'an* (Baroda 1938) and other works, Arthur Jeffery has studied the foreign origin of many Quranic words. Jeffery argues that many of them are non-Arabic in origin (Syriac, Aramaic, Hebrew, Ethiopic); others are genuinely Arabic but in the Quran they take a meaning different from the original under the influence of Judaism and Christianity.[93] Be that as it may, Christians in al-Andalus learned certain religious vocabulary through Arabic and with Islamic connotations. They adopted words and

---

85 URVOY: Influence islamique (n. 9), pp. 514ff.
86 See GIMARET, Daniel: Les noms divins en Islam. Exégèse lexicografique et théologique, Paris 1988, index.
87 Hur. VII, 113.
88 See e. g. Hur. I, 169.194; III, 99.
89 GIMARET: Les noms divins en Islam (n. 86), pp. 237f.
90 Hur. VI, par. 2, p. 302, last line but one.
91 Ibid., pp. 301f.
92 Also the Mozarabic world history of Kairouan/Raqqada (see ROISSE, Philippe: Redécouverte d'un important manuscrit 'arabe chrétien' occidental: le ms. Raqqāda 2003/2 (*olim* Kairouan 120/829), in: Collectanea Christiana Orientalia 1 (2004), pp. 279–285), which I am currently working on, shows the linguistic islamization undergone by the Andalusi Christians. This fact has already been pointed out by LEVI DELLA VIDA, Giorgio: Un testo mozarabe d'histoire universelle, in: Études d'orientalisme dédiées à la mémoire de Lévi-Provençal, vol. 1, Paris 1962, pp. 175–183, p. 183 (repr. in: Note di storia letteraria arabo-ispanica, Rome 1971, pp. 123–192, p. 131).
93 E.g. *zabūr*, "an Arabic corruption of the Hebrew word *mizmōr*, doubtless under the influence of the genuine Arabic word *zubur*", see JEFFERY, Arthur: The Qur'ān as Scripture, New York 1952, p. 67; or *ḥawārī*, a word borrowed from the Ethiopic *ḥawāryā*, see id.: Foreign Vocabulary, pp. 115f.; WENSINCK, A. J.: Ḥawārī, in: EI², vol. 3 (1971), p. 285.

expressions that were familiar to them, and adapted them, when necessary, using them in their own way and giving them their own sense.

In sum, unlike those Christians in al-Andalus who bemoaned the loss of Latin as the sacral language, other Christians, even if they endeavoured to preserve the earlier Christian tradition, did not have any problem in resorting to Arabic, even openly defending its use, and in using religious terms and formulae they knew through this language, especially from the second half of the 9th century onwards. They even translated into Arabic their Scriptures and other books of importance to them, thus making those books available to a community more and more arabized.

Roger Wright

Language and religion in early medieval Spain

Christianity took hold in the Iberian Peninsula during the third century A.D., and touched a chord which continues to reverberate; many of the local saints who are still venerated there now were originally Christian martyrs from that period. The Roman religion shows no sign of having outlasted the Empire itself in the Peninsula, but the pre-Roman religions, Celtic or otherwise, do; when Martín de Braga in the sixth century, for example, shows signs of irritation with pre-Christian practices in his putative congregation, these seem to be pre-Roman as well. Some of the Northern areas which were never heavily Romanized were probably not fully Christianized either until the second millennium A.D., yet the use of Basque has not seriously been thought to be incompatible with Christianity, and indeed the founder of the Jesuits was a Basque. There are Basques who will tell you that their language was used in the Garden of Eden. Nonetheless, a connection between Christianity and Latin came to seem natural, in a Peninsula where probably no indigenous Christian spoke Greek, and the large Jewish communities who had once spoken Aramaic also became Romance-speakers in due course, even if they still used written Hebrew as a liturgical language.

Although the once favoured idea that Christian Latin formed a recognizable and separable dialect is now out of fashion, Michel Banniard has shown what a positive role the Latinity of the Church and the Christian texts had in preserving the linguistic unity of the Late Latin-speaking areas.[1] The Iberian Peninsula contributed its share of these texts. Prudentius, for example, was a Hispano-Roman, although it would be difficult to demonstrate this from any linguistic features of his work; and although it has proved possible to analyse Egeria as exhibiting Hispanic linguistic symptoms in her *Peregrinatio*,[2] this is really only possible because we think we know on other grounds that she was from Galicia; the linguistic evidence in itself is inconclusive.

The Visigoths took over much of the Peninsula in the fifth century, but it is now thought that they were already Latin-speaking before they came, whether or not they still also spoke Gothic, and any influence of their Gothic on the voluminous works of the Visigothic scholars in the Peninsula is invisible, except for some of the personal names. From the late sixth century, the Peninsula became a single coherent political, cultural and religious unit for the first time ever, with its border

---

1 BANNIARD, Michel: Action et réaction de la parole latinophone: démocratisation et unification (IIIe–Ve siècles), in: An Tard 9 (2001), pp. 115–129; Id.: Latinophones, romanophones, germanophones: interactions identitaires et construction langagière (VIIIe–Xe siècles), in: Médiévales 45 (2003), pp. 25–42.

2 ÁLVAREZ HUERTA, Olga: Sobre los hispanismos en el *Itinerarium Egeriae*, in: Latin vulgaire – latin tardif VI, ed. by Heikki SOLIN et al., Hildesheim 2003, pp. 83–97.

along the Pyrenees, as the rulers officially converted from Arianism to Catholicism in 589. This fact has led Mercedes Quilis to argue that the Spanish language originated as a separately identifiable language at that point.[3] This dating could hardly be argued on any linguistic evidence, and in practice the voluble seventh-century Visigothic scholars maintained the inherited written Roman tradition.

Isidore of Seville, the greatest scholar of his age in Western Europe, was well aware that the Latin language had been changing since the days of the *antiqui*, but he still regarded Latin as one single language despite the evolutions and the dialectal diversity, and he still called it Latin (*lingua latina*). Some modern Romanists (such as myself) like to call the language of that period "Early Romance",[4] but naturally the speakers did not call it that themselves. And thus we need to recognize that the various linguistic registers used in writing and in speech were still considered to form together a single monolingual variable unit, with the kind of variability that is normal in all complex and literate speech communities. We know a great deal about their written registers now, because the surviving seventh-century Visigothic production, in its modern printed form, fills several bookshelves; whereas naturally our reconstruction of their speech is at best tentative.

Isidore of Seville was a native Romance speaker, writing his own language in the only available mode;[5] yet his background still presents something of a mystery to us. His name is Greek, and his family probably came from Cartagena, a coastal area that had been under Byzantine influence in the late sixth century. His elder brother Leander travelled to Constantinople. This does not prove that they were Greek, nor that Isidore knew that language himself, but it does suggest that Isidore's cultural background may have had more to it than just what he had been taught within an Iberian context. His education may well have come partly from an African Latin tradition; Collins has recently suggested that one of the main springs for the so-called Visigothic Renaissance of the seventh century in the Iberian Peninsula was the arrival of several scholars from Africa in the later sixth century,[6] who were seeking in this way to avoid the Byzantines rather than being their cultural representatives (much as Priscian, at the start of that century, seems to have fled from Mauretania to Constantinople to avoid the Vandals).[7] The African grammarians do seem to have had an input into Isidore's own comments on Grammar and Orthography, and if he was trained within a partly African tradition of Latinity, Collins's hypothesis helps to explain why that was.

This possibility demonstrates yet again the cultural unity at that time of Latinate geographical areas which instinctively seem to later historians to be separate

---

3   Quilis Merín, Mercedes: Orígenes históricos de la lengua española, Valencia 1999.
4   Wright, Roger: Late Latin and Early Romance in Spain and Carolingian France, Liverpool 1982.
5   Wright 1982, pp. 82–95; Velázquez, Isabel: *Latine Dicitur, Vulgo Vocant*: aspectos de la lengua escrita y hablada en las obras gramaticales de Isidoro de Sevilla, Logroño 2003.
6   Collins, Roger: Visigothic Spain, Oxford 2004.
7   Ballaira, Guglielmo: Prisciano e i suoi amici, Turin 1989; Wright, Roger: A Sociophilological Study of Late Latin, Turnhout 2003, Chapter 5.

communities; that is, it seems that the Straits of Gibraltar were not the course of an important bundle of isoglosses within seventh-century Early Romance, however natural a cultural frontier they seem to be now. One consequence of this was that many, perhaps most, of the eighth-century Berbers who came from North Africa as mercenaries in the invading armies could communicate straightforwardly with the native Hispano-Romans, in the vernacular which they shared, the Early Romance (Late Latin) of their time. Berbers also spoke Berber, but there were and are some forty Berber languages, which were and are not all mutually intelligible, and their lingua franca on both sides of the Straits is likely to have been Romance.

The Visigothic state, which had come to be monolingually Early Romance-speaking apart from the Basques, received an unpleasant jolt with the Muslim invasions that began in 711. It has seemed natural to most subsequent historians to regard the invasions as totally catastrophic; as the end of an era to end all ends of eras. The Iberian Peninsula has appeared to be a model case for the Pirenne thesis that the end of the Roman cultural world happened with the Muslim expansion rather than with the earlier Germanic invasions. And there is, of course, much truth in that, not least because many people saw it that way at the time, including many Christian writers whose reactions have survived. Several Christian scholars went North before the invasions, taking some manuscripts with them; this seems, for example, to be why the so-called 'Mozarabic' prayerbook, which is actually a seventh-century Visigothic one, travelled to Verona.

But not everything changed. Not all the invaders were Arabic-speakers, even if Arabic was their official language. Neither should we assume that they were all Muslim, even if they belonged to groups which had nominally converted en masse. Historians now like to stress the continuities. Apart from anything else, at least 20% of the Peninsula was not under Muslim rule even in 750. The North resisted. Catalonia is a separate case, in that its culture had a Frankish impetus, but it is still true that considerable documentation survives there from the ninth century. There are also surviving histories and other documents written in the North-Western Christian communities between 711 and 900, most notably from the large kingdom of Asturias. But before the late ninth century there is not as much surviving in Latin from the Northern Christian realms as there is from the south.

The eighth century in the Peninsula is a culturally almost invisible time to us in some ways. Dronke's dating of the composition of the so-called *Mozarabic Preces* to the eighth century cannot be right, in view of the fact that the *Bobbio Missal* which contains them can hardly have been written later than 711,[8] but they did continue to use the Visigothic liturgy and hymns prepared by Isidore and his col-

---

8 DRONKE, Peter: The *Preces Mozarabicae*, in: Poetry of Early Medieval Europe: Manuscripts, Language and Music of the Rhythmical Latin texts, ed. by Edoardo D'ANGELO/Francesco STELLA, Florence 2003, pp. 49–62; HEN, Yitzhak/MEENS, Rob (ed.): The Bobbio Missal: liturgy and religious culture in Merovingian Gaul, Cambridge 2004.

leagues. The potential liveliness of Christian intellectual life in the eighth-century Peninsula is startlingly illuminated for us by the texts related to the so-called Adoptionist heresy, which annoyed Alcuin so much, and led to the Synod of Frankfurt of 794; the central Hispanic protagonists include Bishop Elipando of Toledo (whose writings are edited by Gil),[9] as well as Beato of Liébana (which is in the Christian-ruled Northern kingdom of Asturias) and Félix of Urgel (in Catalonia). After the Carolingian scholars tried to discipline Félix of Urgel, he fled south to join Elipando of Toledo. I mention this here because it is clear that the political border between Christian and Muslim Spain was almost incidental to the controversies; Toledo was in Al-Andalus (Muslim Spain), but it was still the head of the Peninsular Christian church in 800, a century after the initial invasion, as it had been under Isidore in 630. The ability of Christians to write complex texts in the traditional way in Toledo in the late eighth century attests to the survival of at least a part of the Visigothic cultural and educational tradition during the decades since the invasion, and although Elipando's opponents accused the supposed heretics of having been swayed by the other faiths with which they were now in daily contact, we would be hard put to see any sign of direct Arabic or Hebrew influence in the language of Elipando's writings.

One serious consequence of the Adoptionist controversy was to disconnect the Christians in Al-Andalus from the cultural and linguistic events of the Carolingian Renaissance, which were having such an effect in the North of Europe. Not, though, to cut off the Christians in Al-Andalus from those in the Christian-ruled parts of the Northern Peninsula, for they remained in contact with each other. It seems that people crossed the apparent religious and political frontier without great trouble, often just in the course of their work (including builders, decorators, merchants and other travellers). And they could communicate without trouble across the same ostensible divide. When literate Christians moved North from Al-Andalus to Galicia, as they increasingly did from the later ninth century, some of them seem to have been able to find work there in the North-West as scribes and notaries; some have Arabic names. And there is no reconstructable important or consistent difference between the Romance speech of inhabitants of Al-Andalus and of Asturias serious enough to have impeded communication; they seem to have understood each other, although regional accents are almost certain to have existed.

That is, Romanists cannot see a reason to reconstruct isoglosses along the supposed frontier. This frontier was usually no more than a no-man's land of variable width; it would be a mistake to visualize it as a kind of Berlin Wall (and it would also probably be a mistake to postulate the growth of isoglosses along the Berlin Wall). So when the scholar Eulogio of Córdoba travelled north from Córdoba to the Pyrenees in about 848, hoping to continue his journey on to Carolingian Germany, there is no sign in his account, or in that of his biographer Álvaro,

---

9   GIL, Juan: Corpus Scriptorum Muzarabicorum, Madrid 1973, pp. 67–112.

that crossing the frontier itself was awkward.[10] Travelling further North from the Pyrenees into Frankish Gaul was more difficult than crossing the religious frontier, it seems, and it was so dangerous at that time that Eulogio eventually gave up the idea, and turned back home. Travelling back south over the frontier again to Zaragoza (in Al-Andalus) was apparently no less simple. In Zaragoza, he met some merchants who had recently travelled down from Mainz, and the cross-border trade of these merchants is also presented as unsurprising in Eulogio's account. Before he turned back, Eulogio seems to have chatted at length with his hosts in the Pyrenees, particularly with the Bishop of Pamplona, without any linguistic difficulty; and the researches of recent specialists in the Ibero-Romance spoken in Muslim Spain (often misleadingly called Mozarabic) have also tended to this same conclusion, that there was no linguistic frontier within Romance corresponding to the political and religious one between Muslim and Christian rulers.

This account is probably so far uncontentious. But I feel it is also worth considering a rather more adventurous and even controversial suggestion: that on the whole there were no real linguistic distinctions within Al-Andalus corresponding to the religious distinctions either. The reason why this might seem controversial is that the instincts of many historians, from the Later Middle Ages onwards to the present day, have tended to lead us to interpret multicultural societies of the past in terms of separate competing, rather than co-operating, ethnic, religious and linguistic groups. So students and analysts of Spanish history have become used to the idea that Al-Andalus contained Romance-speaking Christians and Arabic-speaking Muslims as distinct groups in natural and continuous conflict, sometimes also remembering to mention the Jews as a third such community; thus, for example, the three chapters in Wasserstein's generally excellent *The Rise and Fall of the Party-Kings* that come under the general heading of *Taifa Society* are headed respectively *The Andalusian Muslims, The Jews in the Taifa States*, and *The Christians of Al-Andalus*.[11] Within a less sophisticated but related earlier tradition, the whole of Spanish Medieval History from 711 to 1492 came thus to be christened and represented as one continual process of *Reconquista*, of conflict between religions. Some of the early medieval historiographers to the north of the religious frontier seem also to have felt that way at the time.

But it is noticeable that in general many of the inhabitants of Al-Andalus do not seem to have shared that instinctive interpretation of their own society. And now recent scholarship is adding many nuances to this traditional view. The cultures were not neatly delimited. A large number, perhaps a majority, of the inhabitants of Al-Andalus, at least from the ninth century onwards, were probably of mixed descent; this may have been truer of the Muslims than of the Christians,

10 Eulogio's works are edited by GIL 1973, pp. 363–503; Álvaro's, pp. 143–361. See also COLBERT, Edward: The Martyrs of Córdoba (850–859): a Study of the Sources, Washington 1962; WOLF, Kenneth: Christian Martyrs in Moslem Spain, Cambridge 1988.
11 WASSERSTEIN, David: The Rise and Fall of the Party-Kings: politics and society in Islamic Spain (1002–1086), Princeton 1985, Chapters 6–8.

for the invaders had largely been male, and even those rich men who brought wives in from the East also usually took indigenous wives (since they could have as many as four). So Muslim children of ostensibly extra-peninsular descent would often be brought up by Romance-speakers. Many of the indigenous population converted to Islam, particularly after 900, although even so, it is likely that many did not. And yet religious differences may not have been as consistently psychologically salient as subsequent historians have, until recently, led us to believe. There is a strong strand of thought in the assessments of some of the latest historical analyses which claims that most of the inhabitants of Al-Andalus, with the natural exception of those employed professionally by their faith, did not see their religion as their primary identifying factor.[12] That is, we can suspect that if we had been able to ask individual inhabitants what they were, they could well have answered 'Cordoban', or 'gardener', or 'old woman', or some other category, rather than, or before, 'Christian', 'Muslim' or 'Jew'.

In support of this hypothesis, we can legitimately claim that their language was not at all a biuniquely identifying factor, since many of the inhabitants of Al-Andalus, of whatever religion, were not only of mixed descent but also bilingual in speech in Arabic and Romance. This was not only the case with Muslims and Christians, for it was also true of the large numbers of Jews, even if some of them could also read Hebrew. Only Christians would ever need to learn to read and write the old Latin way, though, so knowledge of written Latin could remain a distinguishing feature connecting their language with their religion, as written Hebrew was for the Jews.

This progressive breaking down of the boundaries is probably why Álvaro de Córdoba expressed himself so strongly in his famous lament in the 850s, in which he complained that the Christians of his time were abandoning their traditional Latin literacy and becoming happy to operate in written Arabic alone.[13] This is a specifically literate matter; it is wrong to paraphrase his lament as a complaint about Christians speaking Arabic, for there seems to have been no perceived problem or anomaly in spoken bilingualism, or even in biliteracy, since even the Christian hierarchy would need to know how to read Arabic for all sorts of practical purposes.

Álvaro's complaint has been much studied, and is obviously crucial to any assessment of the relation between language and religion in Córdoba at that time, but modern discussions of Álvaro's lament have often taken his words out of their immediate context, the year 854. So it is worth reconstructing that context briefly now. When Eulogio de Córdoba was in the Pyrenees in c. 850, he had acquired a number of manuscripts. Perhaps they were new manuscripts; but they were of

---

12 HITCHCOCK, Richard: El supuesto mozarabismo andaluz, in: Actas del I Congreso de Historia de Andalucía: Andalucía Medieval I, Córdoba 1978, pp. 149–152; CHRISTYS, Ann: Christians in Al-Andalus (711–1000), Richmond 2002.
13 GIL 1973, pp. 314f.

venerable ancient Latin texts, both Classical and Christian. It is possible that the acquisition of such texts was actually one of his reasons for wanting to go to the Frankish lands in the first place, since the Christian hierarchy in Córdoba were clearly both impressed and worried by the great cultural upsurge that Muslims in Al-Andalus were experiencing at that very period, largely because of imported contacts from Baghdad. That is to say, Eulogio wanted to acquire impressive written Latin works from both a Christian and a Classical background in order to compete with the allure of the works that kept arriving in Córdoba from the East for the attention of the young. He came back to Córdoba with these manuscripts, and indeed they made a great impression. He was able, after that, to teach colleagues the techniques of Latin metrics, for example. Writers, including himself, were encouraged to imitate the authors concerned. This must have been a live and controversial aspect of curriculum reform in 854, which is precisely when Álvaro composed his lament, probably on discovering that most of the Christians in Córdoba did not react that same way. That is, in the event these newly arrived Latin texts did not generally inspire the same desire for imitation that was felt by scholars such as Eulogio and Álvaro, largely because some of the texts were in what must have seemed to a Romance-speaker of 854 to be difficult, archaic and convoluted styles; and this disinclination must naturally have seemed gallingly ungrateful to those who had worked so hard to bring these splendid newly-rediscovered texts to their charges' attentions.

The immediately following years see a remarkable amount written by both Álvaro and Eulogio, much of it in a kind of Latin which is not easy to follow. They may have felt that the more complicated the style was, the better. I have argued elsewhere that most of the Christians found this antiquated kind of Latin too difficult to imitate, and eventually just gave it up;[14] after all, practical literacy in Arabic was enough, for most purposes, in Al-Andalus. After 880, there are a few instances of written Latin from Al-Andalus, such as on tombstones, but for most discursive purposes they seem not to have used written Latin at all any more.[15] It was also in these years that several educated Christians left for the North, accompanied by both Eulogio's body and his books (taken to Oviedo in 882).

The effect of this shift, dropping the extensive writing of Latin, was to reduce the linguistic distinctions between the religious groups even more. Even though the professional clergy must still have been able to read the Visigothic liturgical texts of the Isidorean tradition, which were not rendered into Arabic so far as we can tell, parts of the Christian Bible were indeed translated into Arabic, including the Psalms, the completion of whose translation is specifically dated to 889. It was probably the same bilingual translator who, in c. 900, also compiled the Arabic Christian History of the World based largely on Orosius and on Isidore's

---

14 WRIGHT 2003, Chapter 11.
15 WASSERSTEIN, David: The Language Situation in Al-Andalus, in: Studies on the Muwassah and the Kharja, ed. by Alan JONES/Richard HITCHCOCK, Oxford 1991, pp. 1–15.

Chronica.[16] It appears that the texts of Orosius and Isidore must have been there already in Latin, but that even so an Arabic version was thought of as being of more practical educational use in 900.

One striking consequence of the literacy shift was that when Toledo was captured by the Leonese in 1085, there was still a Christian community there, which seems to have been bilingual in speech, Arabic and Romance, but able to write, if at all, only in Arabic. This was naturally also true of the Muslims and Jews in Toledo. This explains why there are Latin manuscripts of Christian texts that were brought to Toledo after the recapture, which now have Arabic annotations written in the margins; Christians in Toledo were learning again to use written Latin after 1085, but for a long while reading and writing in Arabic remained more natural for many of them than in Latin, and legal documents continued to be written in Arabic in Toledo for another hundred years.[17]

Our modern view of the Christians living in Al-Andalus has naturally been highly coloured by the extensive writings of Álvaro and Eulogio, and by the Cordoban martyrs of the 850s. Even though Christys has made a good case for arguing that Eulogio exaggerated, and that several of the fifty martyrs he mentions as having died in Córdoba during his time had actually died earlier or elsewhere (or both), we can hardly doubt that the martyrs' movement did exist. But neither can we doubt that it fizzled out after Eulogio's own death in 859. Well over half the pages of the two large volumes of Christian writings from Muslim Spain, as edited by Juan Gil, are by these two writers, Eulogio and Álvaro, and it is difficult for us not to be impressed by them. But they are not representative of Córdoba as a whole. We have to remember that the severe views they expressed were not shared by the majority of their fellow-Christians. And although we can also read the similarly severe work of Sansón, written soon after that, in the 860s,[18] we should remember that at the time of writing Sansón was in exile outside Córdoba, and the opposing faction, who favoured being on good terms with the Muslims, had actually won the argument within the Christian community. Córdoba was not representative of all Al-Andalus, either, and Toledo, which was still the primatial see of the whole Peninsula, did not apparently participate in the martyrdoms. And beneath the hype, we can see the linguistic reality; Sansón was perhaps the last of those who felt so strongly, yet even he was not only bilingual but apparently professionally biliterate, having worked as a translator. By the 870s, any necessary link between language and religion only worked for written Latin, which was used

---

16 PENELAS, Mayte: Del latín al árabe. Una traducción 'mozárabe' del siglo IX/X, in: Actas del III Congreso Hispánico de Latín Medieval, ed. by Maurilio PÉREZ GONZÁLEZ, León 2002, pp. 423–432; Ead.: Linguistic islamization of the 'Mozarabs' as attested in a late 9th-century chronicle in this volume; KASSIS, Hanna: Arabic-speaking Christians in Al-Andalus in an age of turmoil (fifth/eleventh century until A.H. 478/A.D. 1085), in: Al-Qantara 15 (1994), pp. 401–422.

17 VAN KONINGSVELD, P. Sjoerd: The Latin-Arabic Glossary of the Leiden University Library, Leiden 1977; GONZÁLEZ PALENCIA, Ángel: Los mozárabes de Toledo en los siglos XII y XIII, Madrid 1926–1928; LINEHAN, Peter/HERNÁNDEZ, Francisco: The Mozarabic Cardinal: The Life and Times of Gonzalo Pérez Gudiel, Florence 2004.

18 GIL 1973, pp. 505–665.

only by Christians; and so once the use of written Latin had declined, and thus had also ceased to be the distinctive feature which it had been, the link between language and religion was hardly there any more outside the Church services (Banniard interprets Sansón's sociolinguistic context more directly than I do, seeing Sansón as a Latin-user and his opponents as Romance-users; but it seems improbable that such a distinction was clearly made in that context).[19]

The Jewish scholars knew already that there was no direct link between language and religion outside the sacred texts. They wrote in Arabic. It seems that they did not speak Hebrew, even if some used the Hebrew alphabet and the rabbis could read it as a liturgical language. Many of them, perhaps all of them, were in speech bilingual in Arabic and Romance. The general biliteracy involved two alphabets, and for them Hebrew added a third; but even the alphabets were not necessarily fixed to a particular language, as we can see startlingly exemplified in the best manuscripts of the kharjas, where these poems in Arabic, containing occasional Romance words, were written in the Hebrew alphabet. The alphabets may indeed even have been more identified with the relevant religion than the languages were, outside the Christian context at least; thus often Jewish writers have been content to write other languages but have preferred to do so in the Hebrew alphabet (Arabic in Spain, Judeo-Spanish in the sephardic communities, etc.), and some Muslims in later Christian Spain wrote Romance in Arabic script (aljamiado).

An even more adventurous perspective than this has been adduced in the recent book by Menocal.[20] She suggests that far from being in general conflict, in Al-Andalus most people of all backgrounds, in unmarked circumstances, felt proud of their tolerant, multilingual and multicultural society, and that this pride largely continued in New Castile after the Christian takeover in 1085, despite the approaching horrors of the Crusades elsewhere. Certainly, it is generally felt to be inappropriate to call the twelfth-century wars in the Iberian Peninsula 'Crusades'. Throughout the time of the crusades and beyond, Christian scholars of all backgrounds were fascinated by what they found in Toledo, and actively sought co-operation from those of other faiths. After the Leonese capture of Toledo in 1085, many of the educated people of all religions remained there; and then, from about 1130, the city became a magnet for scholars from further north wanting to discover for the first time all kinds of learning which might have been relatively commonplace in that context but seemed amazing to the Northerners. Thus much came to be translated into Latin, largely to fill in perceived gaps in the quadrivium,[21] and it seems fair to deduce from the evidence that many of the prime translators in the spoken mode were the Jewish scholars who could speak to all.

19 BANNIARD, Michel: Viva Voce: communication écrite et communication orale du IVᵉ au IXᵉ siècle en Occident latin, Paris 1992, Chapter 8.
20 MENOCAL, Maria: The Ornament of the World: How Muslims, Jews and Christians Created a Culture of Tolerance in Medieval Spain, New York 2002.
21 BURNETT, Charles: The coherence of the Arabic-Latin translation program in Toledo in the Twelfth Century, in: Science in Context 14 (2001), pp. 249–288.

In 1100, Ibero-Romance speakers from different areas could still understand each other without great difficulty, but it was through the twelfth century that a further linguistic complication spread in Toledo and other Christian-ruled areas of the Peninsula (as an import from France):[22] the conceptual separation of reformed normative Medieval Latin from natural spoken Romance, the separation which was to have so many unfortunate consequences in the thirteenth century, including the increasing separation of different Romance languages from each other.[23] But the early Medieval period, before the epoch-making events of the 1080s, was able to avoid that problem, and the evidence, from the Toledo translations themselves and elsewhere, suggests both that written Latin was still seen as essentially a polished up version of their Romance, rather than as a separate language entirely, and that Romance-speakers from different areas could understand each other, despite the language-internal variability that there must have been. Thus there were not in that context separated Romance-speaking groups either.

It is also becoming clear that in the Early Middle Ages, which in a Hispanic context means before the 1080s, arguments between different kinds of Christian, and between different groups of Muslims, usually tended to be more bitter than those between Christian and Muslim. In the Iberian Peninsula this even continued to be largely the case during and after the age of the Crusades, even on the whole up till the 1480s; but it may well have been essentially true throughout the whole Muslim period, even at the start. One striking example of this can be found in the Christian Church Council of Córdoba of 839, whose Acts are preserved in their original manuscript.[24] This Council, signed by eight Christian bishops with bishoprics in Al-Andalus, concerned itself exclusively with a Christian heresy apparently being practised in a cave at Cabra, which was probably an offshoot of the Adoptionist heresy that had caused such turmoil half a century before, as Colbert and Collins suggest.[25] These Acts, and thus probably the Council itself, which was held in 839 during the formative years of both Eulogio and Álvaro de Córdoba, insult the heretics cheerfully, and never mention Muslims at all, despite being held in the capital of Muslim Spain. The organizational structure of the bishoprics had survived, and the language of the Acts attests to the continuation of their educational traditions as well. Few modern scholars have worried much about the text of these Acts, and those that have commented on their language have been content to make rude remarks about it; Gil just referred to its *barbara scribendi ratio*, for example, a view since also subscribed to by Herrera Roldán.[26] But a close linguistic analysis nuances that position. Even in 839, in

---

22 WRIGHT 1982, Chapter 5.
23 WRIGHT, Roger: Early Ibero-Romance, Newark 1995; and WRIGHT 2003, especially Chapters 2 and 23.
24 GIL 1973, pp. 135–141.
25 See COLBERT 1962; and COLLINS, Roger: Early Medieval Spain: Unity in Diversity (400–1000), London ²1995, pp. 206–209.
26 GIL 1973, p. 135; HERRERA ROLDÁN, Pedro: Cultura y lengua latinas entre los mozárabes cordobeses del Siglo IX, Córdoba 1995.

the difficult years between the Adoptionists and Eulogio's visit to the Pyrenees, the tradition of teaching and learning how to write in the old traditions was still working quite well. The orthography in the *Actas* is often wrong, but rarely erratic; incorrect forms are usually explicable in terms of either contemporary phonetics, or, more often perhaps, misapplied intelligence in cases where a word's spelling is not immediately obvious. The grammar is not at all bad as far as verb-forms are concerned, and although it is considerably worse as regards some of the nominal morphology, this is a normal phenomenon in all Early Medieval Latin texts whose writers were as yet untouched by the Carolingian Renaissance. In particular, this scribe sometimes seems to lose the plot when there is a group of interconnected nouns within the same sentence, choosing the inflectional endings on an almost random basis in two or three sequences. But even there he knows what the available forms and inflections actually are; he remembers them; he is just unsure about which to use where, such that few of the actual forms produced are non-existent. And we can also tell, for example from the *Carmen Poenitentiale* of Vincentius, also of the 830s, and from some of the hymns, that competent rhythmic poetry was being composed in that context. Whatever it was that Eulogio wanted to cure ten years later, with his newly brought ancient texts, it was not total illiteracy or inability to function with the written language.

The eighth century was not a culturally thriving time in the Peninsula, either in an Arabic-Muslim context or a Latin-Christian one. Nor was it a cohesive society in Al-Andalus. But that changed. Both cultures were becoming revitalized there together in the ninth century; and perhaps, as Collins has suggested, it is fair to see the surviving Visigothic culture as one initial prime mover in the general cultural revival of Al-Andalus, as much as the imports from the East. But overall the differences were decreasing. By the end of the ninth century, the main linguistic dividing line between the religions effectively disappeared, with the loss in practice of a desire to write prose works in Latin. One possible way of interpreting developments is to follow Menocal and see the result as a relatively cohesive multicultural and multilingual society, perhaps with no obvious direct connection any more between language and religion except for the respective priesthoods whose profession necessitated relevant reading expertise. This could still have been true through the period of the Taifas; even though the number of Christians seems now to have been smaller by then, this impression could be the result of cultural assimilation (the view of Kassis) rather than because they were hardly there at all (the view of Wasserstein).[27] The historians and other intellectuals in the Christian Kingdoms of the North of the Peninsula could not have felt that way, of course, since they were monolingually speakers of what modern Hispanists tend to call Ibero-Romance, but was to them still Latin.[28] So it is worth suggesting that the linguistic divide that coincided with the political frontiers between so-called Muslim and Christian Spain did not consist of any detailed Romance-internal

---

27 Kassis 1994; Wasserstein 1985, Chapter 8.
28 Wright 1995.

isoglosses, but was instead a genuine divide between an unmarkedly monolingual and an unmarkedly multilingual culture.

Maybe then it is misleading to refer to Al-Andalus before 1086 as 'Muslim Spain' at all. We might even instead want to follow Menocal and describe Al-Andalus as 'Multicultural Spain', a multilingual society of a type which we can appreciate the nostalgia for that was felt in later times. It is a time and place which subsequent Jewish historians and intellectuals have looked back on as a highlight within their cultural history. It is, at the same time, one which subsequent Muslim historians and intellectuals still look back on with nostalgic pride. And it is one which Christian historians used to interpret as a time of darkness and repression for their culturally separate community, but which they can now appreciate too. Menocal's perspective seems to many scholars to be a rosy-spectacled and even Romantic view. Its multiculturalism may appear enhanced to us as we look back from our later age which has inherited Queen Isabel's instincts for ethnic cleansing, the same instincts that finally destroyed the splendours of Medieval Spain and ushered in the deliberately monolingual culture that Spaniards still refer to as their *Siglo de Oro* (Golden Century); but Menocal's perspective may well have been close to the ideal, even if not always to the practice, of at least some people at some times and in some places in that Multicultural and Multilingual Spain we can now glimpse as developing during the period between the failure of the Córdoba martyrs' movement after 859 and the arrival of the Almorávides in 1086 (who were invited, but were also shocked at the Spanish Muslims' cooperation with the Christians; their invitation was soon regretted). In these two centuries the religions were often able to co-operate, even if "in the likeness of a cat and a mouse", in Kassis's striking phrase,[29] or at least to refrain from persecuting each other in the absence of the more fanatical groups from each side; in a pattern not unlike that of other areas of the Muslim world of that time, but unlike most other times, both earlier and since.

---

29 KASSIS 1994, p. 421.

Charles Burnett

The astrological categorization of religions in Abū Ma'shar, the *De vetula* and Roger Bacon

In memory of Richard Lemay (1916–2004)

The discussion of a succession of six different world religions in the *Opus maius* (1267–68) of Roger Bacon (1217–92) is well known.[1] He names his source as "Albumazar in libro coniunctionum":[2] i.e. Abū Ma'shar's *Book of Religions and Dynasties*, known in Latin as *De magnis coniunctionibus*. But he also uses a section of Pseudo-Ovid's *De vetula*, an epic poem of unknown authorship,[3] which, in turn, relies on Abū Ma'shar's work. Other, unacknowledged, sources are Abū Ma'shar's *Great Introduction to Astrology*, and al-Qabīsī's *Introduction to Astrology*. Since the Arabic texts of the *Book of Religions and Dynasties*, as well as those of the *Great Introduction to Astrology* and the *Introduction to Astrology*, have recently

---

1 The fullest account is that of HECK, Erich: Roger Bacon: Ein Mittelalterlicher Versuch einer Historischen und Systematischen Religionswissenschaft, Bonn 1957. See also BEZOLD, F. von: Astrologische Geschichtsconstruction im Mittelalter, in: Deutsche Zeitschrift für Geschichtswissenschaft 8 (1892), pp. 29–72; THORNDIKE, L.: A History of Magic and Experimental Science, vol. 2, New York 1923, pp. 672f.; GARIN, E.: Noterelle di filosofia del Medioevo, in: Giornale critico della filosofia italiana 2 (1950), pp. 196–206; AGRIMI, J./CRISCIANI, C.: Albumazar nell'astrologia di Ruggero Bacone, in: Acme 25 (1972), pp. 315–38; eid.: L'utilitas dell'astrologia in Albumazar e Ruggero Bacone, in: Actas del V Congreso Internacional de filosofia medieval, vol. 1, Madrid 1979, pp. 489–94; SMOLLER, L. A.: History, Prophecy, and the Stars: The Christian Astrology of Pierre d'Ailly, 1350–1420, Princeton 1994, p. 62; LEMAY, R.: Roger Bacon's Attitude Toward the Latin Translations and Translators of the Twelfth and Thirteenth Centuries, in: Roger Bacon and the Sciences, ed. by J. HACKETT, Leiden 1997, pp. 25–47 (at p. 44); JUSTE, D.: Astrologie et philosophie naturelle chez Roger Bacon, in: Villers 15 (2000), pp. 10–18. The passage discussed here is BACON, Roger: Opus maius, ed. by J. H. Bridges, 2 vols., Oxford 1897, vol. 1, pp. 255–62. For other similar discussions by Bacon concerning religions, races, and planets, see Opus maius, vol. 1, pp. 262f., and vol. 2, pp. 371f., and Metaphysica (ed. R. Steele, Opera hactenus inedita, vol. 1, Oxford, 1909, pp. 43–50). I am very grateful to David Juste and Peter Pormann for their critical reading of an earlier draft of this article.

2 He concludes the passage by writing (Opus maius, I, p. 262): *Sic igitur astronomi discutiunt sectas et praecipue Albumazar in libro coniunctionum, et maxime primo et secundo libro, ut inveniantur sex sectae principales in quibus homines occupantur in hoc mundo* ("Thus, then, the astronomers discuss the sects, and above all Albumazar in the Book of Conjunctions, especially in the first and second books, so that six principal sects are found in which men are engaged in this world").

3 Pseudo-Ovidius: De vetula, Untersuchungen und Text, book III, lines 540–75, ed. by P. KLOPSCH, Leiden 1967, pp. 269f.; ed. by D. M. ROBATHAN, Amsterdam 1968, p. 128ff. The attribution to Richard of Fournival (1201–1260) is found only in the *Vaticanus*, written in 1424 by Arnold Gheyloven, and although it gives a plausible date and context to the poem, it has not been universally accepted: see KLOPSCH, pp. 84f.

been edited for the first time, together with their Latin translations,[4] it is worth looking at these sources for Pseudo-Ovid's and Roger Bacon's information. By simply placing next to each other the relevant Arabic texts, their Latin translations and the thirteenth-century interpretations, one can see to what extent information has become distorted, both through ambiguities in translation and through the deliberate manipulation of the text by the Latin authors.

The *Book of Religions and Dynasties* (*kitāb al-milal wa-l-duwal*) was written towards the end of Abū Ma'shar's long life (787–886), and translated into Latin, probably by John of Seville in the second quarter of the twelfth century (= V); John of Seville is also the translator of al-Qabīsī's *Introduction*, and of the version of Abū Ma'shar's *Great Introduction* that was used by Roger Bacon. Version V was thoroughly revised, especially in respect to its terminology, in Toledo later in the twelfth century (= C).[5] The revision was much more widely diffused than the original translation, and was printed in Augsburg in 1489 and Venice in 1515. The *Book of Religions and Dynasties* is a substantial book, in eight parts, concerning historical astrology, i. e. the genre of astrology that predicts conditions and changes affecting whole nations or religious communities. The first part sets out the theory of conjunctions of the planets with one another, and their influence over world events. Its fourth and last chapter is devoted to 'how to know (a race's) *sunna*s, *sharī'a*s, clothing and riding animals'. The Arabic terms *sunna* and *sharī'a*, which strictly refer to customary laws and laws revealed by God respectively, are translated in the Latin as 'decreta' ('decrees') and 'leges' (V: 'laws') or 'sectae' (C: 'sects'). In this chapter they are used in a loose sense and are not carefully distinguished from each other.

The most significant indication for religions is that of the 'mixing'[6] of Jupiter with each of the planets, when Jupiter is in the ninth 'place'.[7] I translate the Arabic text, and add the Latin translation, noting the variants of the revised version (C) when they are significant.

1) Abū Ma'shar, I, 4 [4], vol. 1, pp. 44–5 and vol. 2, p. 28:

If (Jupiter) mixes with Saturn, it indicates that the faith of the people of that religion is Judaism, which is similar to the quality of Saturn, since the <other> planets apply to it, but it does

---

4 Abū Ma'shar on Historical Astrology: the Book of Religions and Dynasties (On the Great Conjunctions), ed. and trans. by K. YAMAMOTO and C. BURNETT, 2 vols., Leiden/Boston/Cologne 2000; Abū Ma'shar: Liber introductorii maioris ad scientiam judiciorum astrorum, ed. by R. LEMAY, 9 vols., Naples 1995–6; al-Qabīsī (Alcabitius): The Introduction to Astrology, ed. and trans. by C. BURNETT, K. YAMAMOTO and M. YANO, London/Turin 2004.

5 See BURNETT, C.: The Strategy of Revision in the Arabic-Latin Translations from Toledo: The Case of Abū Ma'shar's *On the Great Conjunctions*, in: Les Traducteurs au travail: leurs manuscrits et leurs méthodes, ed. by J. HAMESSE, Turnhout 2002, pp. 51–113, and 529–40.

6 This term, which is never defined, appears to be a more informal way of referring to two planets being in the same sign, for which the technical term is being 'in conjunction'. The other indications in this chapter are not discussed here.

7 I.e. the ninth of twelve divisions of the sky beginning from the degree of the ecliptic circle rising in the east: the tenth place is the zenith, the ninth place is just to the west of the zenith.

not apply to any planet among them. Similarly, the people of all other faiths acknowledge Judaism, but it does not acknowledge them.

(Si fuerit complexus Saturno, significat quos fides civium eiusdem secte sit iudaismus qui congruit substantie Saturni, eo quod omnes planete iunguntur ei et ipse nemini eorum iungitur. Et similiter iudaica fides: omnes cives ceterarum sectarum (fidum C) confitentur ei et ipsa nulli confitetur.)

The Latin addition of 'all <the planets>' (in one manuscript: 'the other' (ceteri) <planets>') suggests that the Arabic archetype had 'sā'ir' ('all' or 'the other') here. 'Application' is an astronomical technical term for the approach of one planet to the same number of degrees within one sign as those of another planet; the application is 'complete' when the planets are in the same degree, though they may be in different signs.[8] The Latin translator has confused the matter by using different forms of the verb 'iungere' both for 'application' (*ittiṣāl*) and for 'conjunction' (*qirān*, for which two planets must be in the *same* sign).

Pseudo-Ovid, *De vetula*, III, vv. 527–32:[9]

Si complectatur Saturno Iupiter, ex quo
Saturnus gravior est omnibus *ipseque nulli*
Iungitur *ex aliis, omnes* iunguntur eidem,
Esse fides debet que *nullam confiteatur*
Ex aliis, omnes tamen inclinentur *ad ipsam*;
Talis erat Iudea fides et talis adhuc est.

(If Jupiter mixes with Saturn, because Saturn is heavier than them all, and is joined to none of the others, but all of them join it, the faith should be that which acknowledges none of the other faiths, but they all incline towards it. Such was the Jewish faith, and such is it still.)

Roger Bacon, *Opus maius*, I, p. 255–6:

Si complectatur Jupiter Saturno significat libros divinos et significat de sectis Judaicam, quia est antiquior aliis et prior, sicut Saturnus pater planetarum et remotior et prior in exitu planetarum et ordine in esse. Et *ipsam omnes confitentur et ipsa nullam aliam*, sicut Saturno *omnes* planetae complectuntur *et ipse nulli*, propter tarditatem sui motus. Quia quando planeta est ante eum ad orientem, nunquam ipse Saturnus consequitur aliquem, sed in tantum invalescit alius planeta quod consequitur aliquando Saturnum et conjungitur ei. Omnes quidem sectae appodiant se ad sectam Judaeorum, quia haec fuit prima et est radix aliarum, a qua omnes aliquod genus testimonii et constitutionis sectae habuerunt: unde philosophia accepit ab illa multa testimonia et multos modos constituendi sectam, sicut prius patuit.

(If Jupiter mixes with Saturn it indicates divine books and indicates of sects the Jewish one, because it is older and prior to others, just as Saturn, the father of the planets, is both further away and prior in the appearance of the planets and in their order of existing. All the other (sects) acknowledge it (Judaism) but it acknowledges no other (sect), just as all planets mix with Saturn, but it mixes with no other one, because of the slowness of its motion. For when a planet precedes it in the east, Saturn never catches up with it, but the other planet is so capable that it sometimes catches up with Saturn and conjoins with it. All sects rely on the sect of the Jews,

---

8   Abū Maʿshar: The Abbreviation of the Introduction to Astrology, 3.13–14, ed. by C. Burnett, K. Yamamoto and M. Yano, Leiden 1994, pp. 42–3; al-Qabīsī, Introduction, 3 [16], pp. 96–9.
9   Words that are the same in *De vetula* and the *Opus maius* are printed in italics.

because it was first and is the root of the others, from which all people have some kind of testimony and constitution for their sect. Hence philosophy has accepted from it many testimonies and many ways of constituting its sect, as became clear before.)

Pseudo-Ovid provides quite a faithful versification of the Latin version, keeping the ambiguous 'iungi'. Roger Bacon, other than adding the traditional statement that Saturn is the 'father of the planets',[10] simply provides a commentary on Abū Ma'shar's words. But he wrongly substitutes the terms 'complecti' ('to mix') and 'coniungi' ('to be in conjunction') for 'iungi' (= 'apply to' in this context). Abū Ma'shar's association of Jews with Saturn was corroborated by al-Qabīsī's *Introduction*, in which, moreover, most Latin manuscripts inserted a phrase from *De magnis coniunctionibus*:

Al-Qabīsī, *Introduction*, II [4], pp. 65 and 269:

Māshā'allāh said that <Saturn> indicates Judaism and black clothes.
(...et dixit Messehalla, *id est quod Deus voluit, qui fuit unus astrologus in scientia perspicuus Indus qui sic dictus est*, quod significat fidem iudaicam, *et est ex antiquioribus, et omnes confitentur eam et ipsa nullam aliam, sicut Saturnus, cui omnes iunguntur et ipse nulli,* et indumenta nigra.[11])

Al-Qabīsī is also quoted at the beginning of Bacon's passage: cf. *Introduction*, 2 [3], pp. 62–3 and 268: "si complectitur sibi Jupiter, significat opus pergameni in quo scribuntur divini libri" ("If Jupiter mixes with it (Saturn), then it indicates leather-working of the skins on which holy books are written").

2) Abū Ma'shar:

If Mars mixes with it (Jupiter), it indicates the worship of fire and the faith of Mazdaism (*majūsīya*).
(Et si complexus fuerit ei Mars, significat culturam ignium et fidem paganam.)

Abū Ma'shar is referring to Zoroastrianism, the state religion of the Persians, who had become subjugated to the Muslim caliphate. Abū Ma'shar himself was a Persian with considerable sympathy for the Persian cause.[12] The Latin translator translates '*majūsīya*' loosely as 'pagan'.[13]

---

10 For Saturn (Kronos) is the father of the father of the Gods in Classical mythology. In astrology Saturn is the indicator of fathers and grandfathers: e.g. in Abū Ma'shar: Great Introduction, VII, 9, vol. 5, p. 312: "significat...avos etiam et patres".

11 The Latin additions are printed in italics. They are found in the text of all the manuscripts consulted by the editor, but are noted as being respectively a gloss ('glossa') to, and absent ('vacat') from, the Arabic text in MS Vatican, BAV, Reg. 1285.

12 See PINGREE, D.: The Thousands of Abū Ma'shar, London 1968, pp. 13–18.

13 The translation of 'majūsī' as 'gentilis' occurs in the *Vocabulista in Arabico*, which was probably written in Spain in the late thirteenth century: Vocabulista in Arabico, ed. by C. SCHIAPARELLI, Florence 1871, pp. 178 and 407.

De vetula, III, vv. 533ff.:

Si Marti, Chaldea fides credetur, apud quam
Ignis adoratur, cui significatio Martis
Concordat.
(If Mars, the Chaldaean faith is believed, in which fire is worshipped, with which the indication of Mars agrees.)

Roger Bacon, ibid., p. 256:

Si vero Jupiter complectatur *Marti,* tunc dicunt ipsum significare super legem Chaldaicam, quae docet *adorare ignem,* cujus naturae Mars est in naturali potentia et effectu.
(If Jupiter mixes with Mars they say it then indicates the Law of the Chaldaeans, which teaches one to worship fire, to whose nature Mars belongs in its natural potency and effect.)

Pseudo-Ovid and Bacon identify the 'pagans' as 'Chaldaeans' and add to Abū Ma'shar the common knowledge that Mars' 'indication' or 'natural power and effect' is fiery, as implied *inter alios* by al-Qabīsī, *Introduction*, 2 [13], pp. 68–9 and 273: "...operatur calorem et siccitatem" ("it favours heat and dryness").[14]

3) Abū Ma'shar:

If the Sun mixes with it (Jupiter), it indicates the worship of the planets, graven images and idols.
(Et si complexus fuerit ei Sol, significat culturam stellarum et ydolorum et sculpturarum (anida i.e. eorum que ponuntur paria Creatori C).)

In the case of the word translated 'idols' the various corrupt readings in the manuscripts (*ābida/abidīya/abdā/andā/nadhra*) and C's transliteration 'anida' all suggest a broken plural form of *nidd* meaning 'equal/rival' (to God), and hence an 'idol';[15] cf. Qur'ān, 2.22: 'Do not set up rivals (*andād*) to Allah when you know better'. The Latin gloss to 'anida' is remarkably accurate and evokes the Qur'ānic phrase. In al-Qabīsī's *Introduction* and Abū Ma'shar's *Great Introduction* the Sun is portrayed as the planet that supports the true religion: cf. *Introduction*: 'Of religions <those of the Sun are> the true religion (*al-Ḥanīfiya*)[16] and what is similar to it' ("...culturam bonam et eius similia"),[17] and *Great Introduction*: 'matters of religion and worship' ("fidem et Dei cultum").[18]

---

14 Cf. also Abū Ma'shar: Great Introduction, VII, 9, vol. 5, p. 313: "Martis natura est ignea, calida, sicca...".
15 I am grateful to Peter Pormann for this suggestion.
16 This word is used in Arabic to refer to the religion of Abraham, the source of Judaism, Christianity and Islam, i.e. the pure form of monotheism to which Islam has remained faithful, but from which the other monotheistic religions have diverged: see *Ḥanīf*, in: Encyclopaedia of Islam, 2nd ed., III, Leiden, 1971, pp. 165f. (W. Montgomery Watt).
17 Al-Qabīsī, Introduction, II [18], pp. 72f. and 277.
18 Abū Ma'shar: Great Introduction, VII, 9, vol. 3, p. 554 and vol. 5, p. 314.

Pseudo-Ovid, *De vetula*, III, vv. 535–6:

sed *si Soli*, sequitur quod *adorent*
militiam celi, cuius princeps quoque *Sol est.*
(But if the Sun, it follows that they worship the celestial army, whose leader also is the Sun.)

Roger Bacon, ibid., p. 256:

Si Soli, significatur lex Aegyptia, quae ponit coli *militiam coeli, cujus princeps est Sol.*
(If the Sun, the Egyptian Law is indicated, which lays down that the celestial army should be worshipped, whose leader is the Sun.)

Bacon may be following classical tradition in regarding the prime examples of worshippers of idols and statues as being the Egyptians,[19] but, following Pseudo-Ovid, he singles out the worship of the planets, the item mentioned first by Abū Ma'shar.[20]

4) Abū Ma'shar:

If Venus mixes with it (Jupiter), it indicates revealed (*ẓāhira*) religion and monotheism (*tawḥīd*), like Islam and the like.
(Et si complexa fuerit ei Venus, significat fidem mundam (*ṭāhira*) et unitatem, ut fides Sarracenorum et eius simile.)

Venus was the Muslims' planet, as is indicated by the fact that they worship on her day (Friday). The Latin translator misread 'revealed' as 'pure', but has not cast any slur against the Muslims here. 'Unitas' is a literal translation of 'tawḥīd' and bears the connotation of the 'oneness' of God, just as 'trinitas' is used for the 'threeness' of the Persons.

Pseudo-Ovid, *De vetula*, III, vv. 537–9:

Si Veneri, iam nostra fides convincitur esse,
In qua, si libeat, quodcumque licere putatur,
Scripta licet super hoc nondum lex inveniatur.
Scholium: *postea longo* tempore *scripsit eam Mohametus in libro qui dicitur Alchoran.*[21]
(If Venus, now it is proved to be our faith, in which anything whatsoever is thought to be allowed, as long as it is pleasurable, although a written Law concerning this is not to be found. *Gloss*: Muḥammad wrote this down a long time afterwards in the book that is called the Qur'ān.)

---

19 See BURNETT, C.: Images of Ancient Egypt in the Latin Middle Ages, in: The Wisdom of Egypt, ed. by P. UCKO and T. CHAMPION, London 2003, pp. 65–99.
20 Note that in *Opus Maius*, II, p. 371, he refers to the 'sectam...Aegyptiacam, quae est secta colens Solem, qui est dux militiae coelestis...et colunt creaturam pro creatore' ("the Egyptian sect, which is the sect worshipping the Sun, which is the leader of the celestial army...and they worship the creature instead of the Creator").
21 Pseudo-Ovid: De vetula, ed. Robathan, p. 161. According to Robathan, pp. 30–31, there is a common core of scholia that is found in some of the best manuscripts of the *De vetula*.

Roger Bacon, ibid., p. 256:

Si Veneri, significare dicitur super legem Saracenorum, quae est tota voluptuosa et venerea, quam licet in scriptis Mahometus redegit, ipsa tamen per longa tempora in usu vitae habebatur a suis cultoribus; unde in libro qui ascribitur Ovidio de vitae suae mutatione cum loqueretur de secta venerea, quam hominibus sui temporis legem dixit esse, dicit in metro suo '*In qua, si libeat, quodcumque licere putatur, / Scripta licet super hoc nondum lex inveniatur*'. *Quam postea per sexcentos annos et amplius scripsit Mahometus in libro qui dicitur Alcoran.*

(If Venus, it is said to indicate the Law of the Saracens, which is completely given over to indulgence and lasciviousness. Although Muḥammad committed this (Law) to writing, nevertheless it had been upheld by its followers in their manner of life for a long time. Hence, in the book which is ascribed to Ovid *Concerning the Changing Fortunes of his Own Life* (i.e. the *De vetula*), when the author speaks of the lascivious sect, which he said was the (religious) Law for the people of his time, he says (in verse) "In this Law, anything whatsoever is thought to be allowed, as long as it is pleasurable, although a written Law concerning this is not to be found". Muḥammad wrote this down 600 years and more afterwards in the book that is called the Qur'ān.)

The author of the *De vetula*, maintaining the fiction that the poem was written in the time of Ovid, claims Venus's Law as that of the pagan Roman empire.[22] Bacon interprets this as meaning that it was the Law practised by the Saracens long before Muḥammad arrived to put it into a written form. Pseudo-Ovid and Bacon interpret 'Venus' in a thoroughly negative sense. They fail to mention the 'pure' or 'revealed' religion, and refer only to over-indulgence in sexual activity, which is the most common attack levelled against Muḥammad and his followers.[23] Nevertheless, they have some support from al-Qabīsī who, after detailing the varieties of physical indulgence and sexual profligacy that are indicated by Venus, states that: 'of religions <those of Venus> are taking idols and religions in which much sexual intercourse, eating and drinking is used' (whether out of prudishness, or by a sheer oversight, 'sexual intercourse' is left out of the Latin translation: "...culturam idolorum et eas in quibus maxime exercentur comestiones atque potationes").[24]

5) Abū Ma'shar:

If Mercury mixes with it (Jupiter), it indicates Christianity and every faith containing antipathy (*jafā'*), doubt (*shakk*) and trouble.
(Et si complexus fuerit ei Mercurius, significat fidem Christianam et omnem fidem in qua fuerit occultatio (= *khafā'*) et gravitas (= *shidda*) et labor.)

---

22 The association of the Romans with Venus is, however, classical: Venus was Aeneas's mother, and Julius Caesar's titulary planet: cf. Hermann of Carinthia: De essentiis, ed. by C. BURNETT, Leiden 1982, p. 172: "Veneris...cuius etiam cognatione gloriantur Romani" ('Venus...whom the Romans are proud to be related to').
23 KEDAR, B. Z.: Crusade and Mission, Princeton 1984; and VANDECASTEELE, M.: Étude comparative de deux versions latines médiévales d'une apologie arabo-chrétienne: Pierre le Vénérable et le "Rapport Grégorien", in: Mededelingen van de Koninklijke Academie voor Wetenschappen, Letteren en Schone Monsten van België 53 (1991), pp. 79–134.
24 Al-Qabīsī: Introduction, 2 [26], pp. 76f. and 281.

As a gloss C gives a translation of the last two terms that reflects a different reading of the Arabic manuscript: "dubietas (*shakk*) et pena". Al-Qabīsī attributes to Mercury, as he also did to the Sun, the true religion (*al-Ḥanīfīya*), and religions based on rational precepts, but, like Abū Ma'shar, also refers to the element of secrecy: 'the true religion and what is like it of secret monotheism and rational precepts' ("...culturam unitatis et horum similia, et hoc de secreto cum ypocrisia et simulatione").[25]

Pseudo-Ovid, *De vetula*, III, vv. 555–69:

Sed propter Mercurii tot
Circuitus et *tot inflexus atque reflexus*
Difficilis credi super omnes lex erit illa
Et multum gravitatis habens multumque laboris,
Obvia nature supponens plurima sola
Concipienda fide. Quare dubitatio multa
Surget apud multos nodosaque questio multa.
Sed quia *Mercurius scripture est significator*
Et numeri, per que lex omnis habet stabiliri,
Et quia precipue non que sunt temporis huius
Mira, sed eterne promittet commoda vite,
Tot defendetur subtilibus argumentis,
Quod semper *stabit* in firmo *robore*, donec
Tollat eam Lune lex ultima sicut et omnes
Vel saltem *suspendat* eam...

(But because Mercury has so many orbits and so many forwards and backwards movements, that Law will be more difficult to believe than all of them, being very onerous and burdensome, laying down very many precepts which fly in the face of nature, but can only be conceived by faith. Therefore much doubt and many a knotty question will arise among many people. But because Mercury is the indicator of writing and calculation, through which every Law has to be established, and especially because it will promise not marvels in the present time, but the conveniences of eternal life, it will be defended by so many very subtle arguments that it will always stand firmly and strongly until the last Law of the Moon destroys it along with the others, or at least suspends it.)

Roger Bacon, ibid., p. 256f.:

Si vero complectatur Mercurio, tunc est lex Mercurialis. Mercurius enim habet respectum, ut dicunt, ad Deitatem et oracula prophetarum et credulitatem et orationem, et maxime quando conjungitur ei Jupiter; quoniam tunc significat numerum psallendi et numerum librorum divinorum. Et dicunt quod lex Mercurialis est *difficilior* ad credendum quam aliae, et habet multas difficultates supra humanum intellectum. Et hoc convenit propter motus Mercurii *difficiles*, cujus *circuitus* est in epiciclo et eccentrico et aequante, in quibus considerantur sui motus longitudinis et *inflexus* et *reflexus* in motibus latitudinis, per declinationem eccentrici ab orbe signorum ad septentrionem et meridiem, et epicicli ab eccentrico in partem septentrionis et meridiei, et sunt mirabiliores et difficiliores omnibus motibus planetarum, sicut patet ex dictis Ptolemaei, et planius ex sententiis Albategni, Thebit, et Archaselis, et probabiliter ex dictis Alfragani. Et propter hoc significat, ut dicunt, super legem quae habe[n]t difficiles articulos et occultas veritates, cujusmodi est lex Christiana. *Sed quia Mercurius est significator scripturae* et scriptorum

---

25 Al-Qabīsī: Introduction, 2 [32], pp. 78f. and 284. The annotator in MS Vatican, BAV, Reg. 1285 has restored a correct translation of the last term, but has omitted 'secret monotheism': "unitatis vere et legum rationabilium".

et profunditatis scientiae in libris profundis atque facunditatis sive dulcedinis locutionis et linguae et rhetoricae et velocitatis ejus et explanationis sententiarum, significat quod tam authenticis scripturis et tot profundis scientiis et tanta potestate eloquentiae defendetur *quod stabit semper in robore* suo *donec ultima lex Lunae* perturbet eam ad tempus.

(If it mixes with Mercury, then it is the Mercurial Law. For Mercury is related, as they say, to the Deity and the oracles of prophets and to having beliefs and praying, especially when it is conjoined with Jupiter, since it then signifies the number of (times one) sings the psalms and the number of divine books. And they say that the Mercurial Law is more difficult to believe than others, and it contains more difficulties than the human intellect can bear. This makes sense, because the movements of Mercury are difficult, since its orbit is on an epicycle, an eccentric and an equant, in all of which its movements in longitude, and its forward and backwards movements in latitude should be considered, according to the incline of the eccentric away from the zodiac towards the north and south, and of the epicycle away from the eccentric in a northerly and southerly direction. These movements are more remarkable and difficult than all the movements of the planets, as is clear from the statements of Ptolemy, and clearer from the opinions of Albategni, Thebit and Archaselis, and backed up by proofs in the statements of Alfragani. And because of this it indicates, as they say, a Law which has difficult clauses and hidden truths, such as the Christian Law. But because Mercury is the indicator of writing and writers and the profundity of knowledge in profound books and eloquence or sweetness of diction and speech, and rhetoric and its swiftness and explanation of ideas, it indicates that it will be defended by such authentic writings, so many profound sciences and such a potency of eloquence that it will always stand firm in its own strength until the last Law of the Moon disturbs it for a time.)

In Pseudo-Ovid the coming of Christianity is predicted in hidden terms; Bacon preserves the mystery until nearly the end of his passage, where he at last identifies the Mercurial Law with the Christian Law. Both Pseudo-Ovid and Bacon try to turn Abū Ma'shar's criticism of Christianity as a faith full of hiddenness and difficulty into a positive direction: it is its hiddenness and profundity that make the Christian faith superior to the rest. Pseudo-Ovid takes, perhaps from al-Qabīsī, the statement that Mercury is the indicator of writing and calculation,[26] while Bacon quotes al-Qabīsī *verbatim*: cf. *Introduction*, 2 [31], p. 283: "(Mercurius) significat deitatem et oracula prophetarum et credulitatem et orationem,"[27] and ibid., 2 [32], p. 283: "Si complectitur ei (Mercurio) Iupiter, significat numerum psallendi et numerum librorum divinorum". In addition, Bacon quotes from Abū Ma'shar's *Great Introduction*, VII, 9, vol. 5, p. 315: "Mercurius ... significat ... profunditatem scientie in libris profundis ... facunditatem sive dulcedinem locutionis ac lingue ac velocitatem eius sive explanationem sententiarum".

---

26 Al-Qabīsī, Introduction, 2 [31], p. 283: "Mercurius ... significat ... scripturam ... et opus numeri maxime."

27 Most manuscripts of al-Qabīsī add 'et opus et' between 'credulitatem' and 'orationem', but this item, which makes little sense in Latin, is left out in MS London, Arundel 268. In Arabic the last two items are '*'amal* and *kalām*', literally 'deed and word'. 'Oratio' was probably meant to mean 'speaking', but in the context (and without 'opus') it would have been understood by its readers as 'prayer'. The same phrase (without 'et oratio' and with several words between 'prophetarum' and 'credulitatem') occurs in Abū Ma'shar: Great Introduction, VII, 9, vol. 5, p. 315, which also states that Mercury indicates 'the beauty (in Arabic the word also means 'goodness') of faith and the obedience to God' (pulcritudo fidei atque obedientiam Dei: ibid., vol. 3, p. 555, line 888, and vol. 5, p. 316).

6) Abū Maʿshar:

If the Moon mixes with it (Jupiter), it indicates doubts, confusion, *taʿṭīl*, apostasy (*ilḥād*) and distrust in the faith, and that is because of the quick change (*taghayyur*) of the Moon and its movement, and because of its short stay in (each of) the signs.
(Et si complexa fuerit ei Luna, significat dubitationem, volutionem, mutationem, negationem (expoliationem C) quoque et suspitionem in fide, et hoc fit propter velocitatem mutationis (corruptionis C) Lune et celeritatem motus eius et paucitatem more eius in signo.)

The theological term *taʿṭīl* means the denial of all attributes to God, and is the opposite of *tashbīh*, anthropomorphism, assimilating God to His creatures. The Latin translators came up with two different translations: 'negation' ('negatio'), which, not incorrectly, suggests the Christian 'negative' or 'kataphatic' theology, which claims that you can only say what God is *not*, and never what God *is*; and 'stripping away, making destitute' ('expoliatio'), which restores the basic sense of the Islamic word. Both Latin terms, however, unaccompanied by any explanation, would convey little of the true meaning to the reader. The word 'taghayyur' comes from a root which can have the sense both of a neutral change, and of change for the worse, or corruption. In this context the former sense is required, and is followed by V, but C gives the word its negative connotation.

Pseudo-Ovid, *De vetula*, III, vv. 542–53:

Lune postremam legem fore conicientes,
Vel quia post alios est circulus infimus eius,
Vel quia *lunaris motus corruptio* legem
Omnem significat tolli debere per ipsam.
Feda fides erit hec, quam rex in fine dierum
Sive *potens* aliquis violenter et absque colore
Est *inducturus*, qui divinum sibi cultum
Usurpare volens occidet et opprimet omnes
Contradictores; nec tanta occisio tanto
Tempore pro turpi causa precesserit unquam,
Sed *durare* parum poterit, quia Luna *figure,*
Motus et lucis est mutativa frequenter.
Scholium: corruptio motus Lune significat instabilitatem, sicut dicunt autores.[28]
((We) conjecture that the Moon's will be the last Law, either because its circle is the lowest after the others, or because the corruption of the movement of the Moon indicates that every Law will be destroyed by it. This will be a detestable Law, which a king or some potentate at the end of days will bring in violently and without colour (?); wishing to usurp divine worship for himself, he will kill and oppress all who oppose him; but such slaughter on behalf of such a base cause will never proceed for an appreciable time, but will rather be unable to last long, because the Moon is frequently changing its shape, its movement and its light. *Gloss*: The corruption of the movement of the Moon indicates instability, as the authorities say.)

Roger Bacon, ibid., p. 261f.:

Si vero complectatur Lunae, dicunt domini astronomiae quod erit lex Lunae et ultima, quia circulus Lunae est ultimus, et haec erit lex corruptionis et *foeda* quae violabit omnes alias leges

---

28 For this scholium, see Pseudo-Ovid: De vetula, ed. Robathan, p. 161.

et *suspendet*[29] eas, etiam Mercurialem ad tempus. Luna enim, ut dicunt, significat super nigro-mantiam et mendacium, et ideo lex Lunae erit nigromantica et magica et mendosa. Et prop-ter *corruptionem Lunaris motus* et figurationum Lunarium significat super corruptionem istius legis, quae in se erit corrupta et alias corrumpens. Non tamen multum durabit, ut dicunt, quia Luna velociter mutatur a *figura*tione *et luce* sua *et motu* propter brevitatem sui circuli. Et hoc, ut dicunt, statuetur ab aliquo magno et *potente* qui praevalebit aliis, et aestimant astronomi fideles tam moderni quam antiqui quod haec est lex Antichristi, quia ille ultimo in fine mundi adveni-et, et *inducet* legem corruptionis, et infatuabit mundum per artem magicam et mendacia sua.
(If it mixes with the Moon, astronomers say that it will be the Law of the Moon, which is the last one, because the sphere of the Moon is last, and this will be a Law of corruption, and a detestable Law which will destroy all other Laws and suspend them all – even that of Mercury for a time. For the Moon, as they say, indicates nigromancy and lying, and therefore the Law of the Moon will be nigromantic, magical and deceitful. And because of the corruption of the movement of the Moon and its shapes, it signifies the corruption of that Law which will be cor-rupt in itself and corrupting others. However, it will not last long, as they say, because the Moon quickly changes in its shape, light and movement because of the smallness of its sphere. And this <Law> will be set up, as they say, by a great and powerful man who will overcome others, and astronomers of the faith[30] both now and in the past think that this is the Law of Antichrist, because he will come last at the end of the world and will introduce a Law of corruption, and will stun the world through his magic art and lies.)

Pseudo-Ovid and Bacon make the most of the revised version's reading 'stripping off' ('expoliatio'), interpreting it as 'destroying' other religions, rather than hav-ing something to do with how one describes God. They follow C's erroneous 'cor-ruption of movement' (instead of 'change of movement'), which they interpret as referring to the Moon's deleterious effect. Bacon adds the nigromantic and lying character of the Moon from Abū Ma'shar's *Great Introduction*.[31] The misinterpre-tation of the words of the *Book of Religions and Dynasties* leads inevitably to the conclusion that the Moon signifies the religion of Antichrist, with whom Bacon identifies the unnamed usurper in Pseudo-Ovid.

We thus have the strange situation of a technical astrological work being used in a fictitious work purporting to predict the coming of Islam, Christianity and the final Usurper, which, in turn, is being used *ex post facto* to describe how Christian-ity and Islam have indeed followed on from each other and will inevitably lead to the reign of Antichrist. It was not Abū Ma'shar's intention to arrange the religions of the planets in chronological order, let alone suggest that each one succeeded its predecessor in a providential way. By rather artificially ascribing the religion of Muḥammad already to the Romans or ancient Saracens, Pseudo-Ovid and Bacon are able to set up a chronological order which follows the descending order of the planets: Judaism (Saturn), the religion of the Chaldaeans (Mars), the religion of the Egyptians (Sun), the religion followed by the Romans and Saracens (Venus), Christianity (Mercury), and finally the Antichrist (Moon).

---

29 This is the verb used by Pseudo-Ovid in: De vetula, III, v. 569 (see p. 134 above).

30 I. e. Christian astronomers.

31 Abū Ma'shar: Great Introduction, VII, 9, vol. 5, p. 316: 'Luna... significat... nigromanticos... men-dacium'. It should be noted that these negative characteristics are widely scattered among a host of positive characteristics, and are not mentioned by al-Qabīsī.

Roger Bacon uses Abū Maʿshar's *Book of Religions and Dynasties* and *Great Introduction* and al-Qabīsī's *Introduction* directly, to corroborate or add to what he had already found in Pseudo-Ovid's *De vetula*, whose only obvious source is the first of Bacon's Arabic sources. What is perplexing is the short time that separates the composition of the *De vetula* from that of the *Opus maius*. The discovery of the *De vetula* under the head of Ovid is said to have taken place in the time of 'Vathachius princeps', who is plausibly identified with the Byzantine emperor, Johannes III Vatatzes (1222–54), but the fact that his palace is stated as being in Byzantium, rather than Nicaea, may suggest that the story was invented after the recovery of the Byzantine capital in 1261. The *Opus maius* was sent to pope Clement IV only seven years later. It is difficult to believe that Bacon could have mistaken such a recent work for a genuine poem by Ovid. This closeness in time, together with the fact that Bacon has such an uncanny understanding of the true significance of the poem's prophecies, makes one wonder whether he himself was involved in the forgery of the *De vetula*.[32] Whatever the case, the Pseudo-Ovid and Bacon belong to the same intellectual context – a context in which Arabic sources were used with enthusiasm, but in which there was no compunction about distorting the sense of those sources when it suited the author to do so.

---

32 Also to be considered in regard to Bacon's involvement in the *De vetula* are the scholia, which, as we have seen, reproduce Bacon's phrases *verbatim*, and the 'letter of the glossator' (De vetula, ed. KLOPSCH, p. 289), who, like Bacon, explicitly mentions the Antichrist: "opus videri poterat futurum utile temporibus Antichristi" ('the work [De vetula] could seem to be useful in the times of Antichrist').

Esperanza Alfonso

The Patriarchs' behavior in Abraham's Cycle:
A moral issue in Sephardic and Provençal Jewish exegesis

It is well known that biblical commentaries were the most common literary product of the European Middle Ages. Latin commentaries written by the Church
Fathers were popularized by anthologies and *florilegia*, and made their way comfortably into the libraries of Romanesque monasteries whose catalogues record
them in great numbers. Beginning in the early Middle Ages the biblical text, in
fact, circulated more in the form of citations in exegetical works than through
manuscripts of the Bible itself. By the first half of the 12th century, the well-
established authority of exegetical works was further increased with the compilation of the gloss, which transformed Scripture with its commentary into an almost
indissoluble whole. Overall, exegetical literature played a major role in molding
education and intellectual life to the extent that changes made to its form and content serve scholars today as a guide to map the intellectual history of the Christian
Middle Ages.[1]

Biblical exegesis is even more relevant for the study of Jewish society and culture in the same medieval period, given the dissimilar degrees of literacy and
familiarity with the contents of the Bible found among Jews and Christians at
this time. Although the degree of literacy (both in Latin and in the vernaculars)
among medieval Christians is still debatable, there is no doubt that it was strikingly poor when compared to the knowledge of Hebrew among contemporary
Jews.[2] As for the contents of the Bible, the Psalms and Paul's Epistles seem to have
been the most widely known books among Christians. They were also the earliest biblical texts to be glossed. In contrast, the Torah had absolute priority in the
Jewish world, standing at the center of both the educational and cultic systems.
As one of the most important tasks of Jewish schools was to prepare children for
the synagogue service, at an early age every male student began to memorize the
Torah, which was read in public in its entirety over the liturgical year. The acces-

---

1   See SMALLEY, Beryl: The Bible in the Medieval Schools, in: The Cambridge History of the Bible.
    Vol. 2: The West from the Fathers to the Reformation, Cambridge 1969, pp. 197–220; also Id.: The
    Study of the Bible in the Middle Ages, Oxford ³1983, pp. VII–XXXIII.
2   On the differences in literacy between Christians and Jews in medieval Europe, cf. KANARFOGEL,
    Ephraim: Jewish Education and Society in the High Middle Ages, Detroit 1992, pp. 16f. BASKIN,
    Judith R.: Some Parallels in the Education of Medieval Jewish and Christian Women, in: Jewish
    History 5,1 (1991), pp. 41–51; BEDOS-RAZAK, Brigitte: The Confrontation of Orality and Tex-
    tuality: Jewish and Christian Literacy in Eleventh- and Twelfth-Century Northern France, in:
    SED-RAJNA, Gabrielle (ed.): Rashi 1040–1990: Hommage à Ephraïm E. Urbach (Congrès Euro-
    péen des Études Juives), Paris 1993, pp. 541–58. Although these three studies are concerned with
    Ashkenaz, the case they make may be applied more broadly to Christian Spain.

sibility of the biblical text for the general reader is equally attested in both Ashkenaz and Sepharad.[3] Within the Iberian context, the focus of the present paper, it was not until the end of the 14th century that, as a result of dramatic political events, the sources began to echo a general concern for the deterioration of Bible study. Nonetheless, it is certainly significant that even at this time of political and social decline for Jewish life in the Peninsula, any attempt at communal reconstruction would be first and foremost based on education in the Torah.[4]

Whereas within Christianity many accessible channels for the transmission of Scripture to the believer were developed over time, such as liturgical plays, illumination of manuscripts, depiction of biblical scenes in stained-glass windows, sculpture and reliefs, the contents of the Bible were familiar enough to Jews not to depend on visual aids. Knowledge of the Bible and its commentaries was not restricted or confined to the scholarly arena, but constituted the core of the general curriculum. In this sense, Hebrew running commentaries provided the main tool to mediate access to the text. They were instrumental in making the biblical content relevant to contemporary concerns, and had a key role in the transmission and popularization of religious ideas within Judaism. Written in Arabic, Hebrew and eventually in the local vernaculars, commentaries were a bridge between the elite and the less educated. As many commentators were also preachers, their contents, in turn, were further popularized in oral public or private sermons.

There were times when biblical passages became of special concern to exegetes for varied reasons. This seems to have been the case with certain objectionable episodes relating to the Patriarchal cycles in Genesis.[5] The reason may be seen as twofold: first, the behavior of the patriarchs conflicted with current moral standards. Second, as these episodes were an object of contention between Jews, Christians and Muslims, they became a recurrent locus for apologetics in Jewish exegesis.

---

3   For a recent evaluation of medieval Jewish education, cf. Roth, Norman: Education, in: Medieval Jewish Civilization: An Encyclopedia, New York 2003, pp. 229–35. On literacy and Bible study in the Sephardic context, see Goitein, Shelomo D.: A Mediterranean Society: The Jewish Communities of the World as Portrayed in the Documents of the Cairo Geniza, Berkeley/Los Angeles/London 1977, vol. 2, pp. 171–211; Kaplan, Lawrence: Moses Maimonides' Laws of the Study of Torah, in: Fine, Lawrence (ed.): Judaism in Practice: From the Middle Ages through the Early Modern Period, Princeton, NJ 2001, pp. 171–85. On the Sephardic educational system, cf. Gross, Abraham: Centers of Study and Yeshivot in Spain, in: Beinart, Haim (ed.): Moreshet Sepharad, Jerusalem 1992, vol. 1, pp. 399–410, and Gross, Abraham: A Sketch of the History of Yeshivot in Castile in the 15th Century (in Hebrew), in: Pe'amim 31 (1987), pp. 3–21. For a comparative survey of the role of the Bible in the medieval Sephardi and Ashkenazi curricula, see Talmage, Frank: Keep Your Sons from Scripture: The Bible in Medieval Jewish Scholarship and Spirituality, in: Thoma, Clemens/Wyschogrod, Michael (eds.): Understanding Scripture: Explorations of Jewish and Christian Traditions of Interpretation, Mahwah, NJ 1987, pp. 81–101.

4   Baer, Yizhak: A History of the Jews in Christian Spain, Philadelphia/Jerusalem 1992, vol. 2, pp. 26ff.

5   For a general assessment of the Patriarchs' behavior, see Berger, David: On the Morality of the Patriarchs in Jewish Polemic and Exegesis, in: Thoma, Clemens/Wyschogrod, Michael (eds.): Understanding Scripture: Explorations of Jewish and Christian Traditions of Interpretation, Mahwah, NJ 1987, pp. 49–62.

Among these controversial narratives, the relationship established between Sarah, Abraham, Hagar and ultimately Keturah, in Genesis 16, 21 and 25, is one of the most prominent, as it is a focal point at which the three religions' conflicting claims intersect. In what follows, I will analyze the evolution of Jewish religious ideas concerning ethics in several medieval commentaries written in Sepharad and Provence between the 12th and the 15th centuries in relation to these chapters in Genesis.[6] In doing so, I will reflect on the key role of commentaries as agents in the transmission and popularization of religious ideas, taking always into consideration their surrounding Christian and occasionally Islamic exegetical traditions.

The biblical story unfolds as follows. In Genesis 16:1–14, considered today as a product of the Yahvist, Sarah, who has not had children after having lived in the land of Israel for 10 years, gives Hagar, her maidservant, to Abraham *le-ishah* ("as a wife"?).[7] After having conceived from him, Hagar's esteem for Sarah goes down and Sarah, as a result, mistreats her. Hagar flees to the desert from Sarah's harsh treatment, and encounters an angel who tells her to return and submit to her mistress, as he announces to her the birth of her son Ishmael. In Genesis 21:8–21, an Elohist narrative, on the day that Isaac was weaned, Sarah sees Ishmael *metsahheq* ("playing"?),[8] and finding it disturbing, causes Abraham to cast out Ishmael and his mother. According to the biblical account, Abraham gave them bread and water and sent them away. Finally, in Genesis 25:1–15, Abraham, after Sarah's death, takes a second wife (concubine?), by the name of Keturah,[9] who bears him six more children, to whom Abraham offered gifts before his death. Ishmael, who had disappeared from the narrative earlier, reappears at this point to bury his father along with Isaac.

In post-biblical times, the rabbis came to examine the behavior of the biblical characters. In doing so, they questioned Abraham's, and especially Sarah's, fairness in their treatment of Hagar and her son. They speculated on the rationale behind Hagar's and Ishmael's actions. Finally, they sought to define the precise nature of Abraham's relationship to both Hagar and Keturah, a relationship that was left undetermined in the biblical narrative.[10]

---

6 For a precise definition and contrast of Jewish ethics in biblical and post-biblical literature, cf. DAN, Joseph: Jewish Mysticism and Jewish Ethics, Seattle/London 1986, p. 12.

7 Literally "as a wife." Hagar's status as Abraham's wife or concubine, however, will be open to question in rabbinic and medieval literature (see note 17).

8 The Hebrew term *metsahheq* was to be interpreted in varied ways. For a recent reevaluation of the term in ancient and medieval Jewish sources, see SCHWARTZ, Joshua: Ishmael at Play: On Exegesis and Jewish Society, in: Hebrew Union College Annual (HUCA) 66 (1995), pp. 203–21.

9 Again, Keturah's identity and her status regarding Abraham were to be subject to speculation among commentators.

10 A comprehensive evaluation of Hagar in the Christian and Jewish tradition from ancient to modern sources is offered in THOMPSON, John L.: Writing the Wrongs: Women of the Old Testament among Biblical Commentators from Philo through the Reformation, Oxford 2001, pp. 17–99. See also PÉREZ FERNÁNDEZ, Miguel: La tradición targúmica de Agar e Ismael, in: Miscelánea de Estudios Árabes y Hebraicos (MEAH) 49 (2000), pp. 87–103.

11th –12th centuries: Abraham ibn Ezra

In the first half of the 12th century, Abraham ibn Ezra (1092–1167), born in Tudela, when that city was still under Islamic control, transmitted some social concerns over Abraham's actions. In commenting on Genesis 21:14, he wrote: "Many are amazed at Abraham's behavior. They ask: 'How could Abraham chase his son out of his house? How could he send away mother and son empty-handed? Where is his kindness?'"[11] The vagueness of Ibn Ezra's reference to the questioners does not tell us whether he is referring to contemporary oral or written discussions, or merely echoing concerns raised in rabbinic sources. In his response, Ibn Ezra exonerates Abraham, who he argued would have acted according to Sarah's wishes and God's dictates. Moreover, Ibn Ezra softens the patriarch's attitude, pointing at a number of elements: he gave Hagar and Ishmael enough water and bread to make their way to their destination safely; it is possible that he also gave them gold and silver even if the Scripture does not mention anything in this regard. If Hagar and Ishmael had to endure hardships in the desert, these hardships came as a result of Hagar losing her way in the wilderness, so that Ishmael became ill from the lack of water. Finally, in Ibn Ezra's view, Ishmael's children would get money (*mamon*) from Abraham after Sarah's death. In pointing to elements that fill in the gaps left by the biblical text, and always keeping close to the literal meaning, Ibn Ezra acquits Abraham by proving his concern for Ishmael.

Ibn Ezra's succinct vindication of Abraham follows a trend already present in rabbinic literature and in early medieval exegesis. It may be deemed mild, however, when compared to a much stronger defense of Abraham's and Sarah's conduct in Rashi's commentary, written a few decades earlier in Northern France.[12] Drawing heavily on rabbinic sources, especially on *Genesis Rabbah*, Rashi (1040–1105) described the events by selecting those elements that enhanced Sarah's image and by emphasizing Hagar's ingratitude and Ishmael's misbehavior, which according to *Genesis Rabbah* 53:11 (also *Tosefta Sota* 6 and *Siphre Deuteronomy* 31) may have involved idolatry, immorality and murder, all charges that Rashi relates to illegal claims of inheritance.[13] In Rashi's consistently exculpatory argument, there was no shadow of patriarchal misconduct whatsoever.

---

11 All quotations from medieval commentaries will follow the standard edition of Menahem KOHEN (ed.): Mikra'ot Gedolot ha-Keter, Ramat Gan 1993-, unless otherwise indicated. For an English translation of Ibn Ezra's Commentary on the Torah, see: STRICKMAN, Norman H./SILVER, Arthur M.: Ibn Ezra's Commentary on the Pentateuch: Genesis (*Bereshit*), New York 1988.

12 English transl. in: ROSENBAUM, M./SILBERMANN, A. M.: Pentateuch with Targum Onkelos, Haphtaroth, and Prayers for Sabbath, and Rashi's Commentary. Vol. 1: Genesis, New York 1946.

13 In addition to these three interpretations of Ishmael's behavior – idolatry, immorality and murder – Rashi adds a fourth one when commenting on Genesis 21:11. Following *Tanhuma Shemot* 1, he alludes to Ishmael's degenerate ways as a possible source for his father's sadness, although he seems to lean towards a contextual interpretation (*peshuto*), according to which Abraham would have felt sad because of Sarah's request to send his son away.

Contrasting with Rashi's characterization of Hagar and Ishmael, Ibn Ezra's does not have the same negativity, though he identifies the term *pere' adam* ("wild ass of a man") – the name the angel uses to describe Ishmael in Genesis 16:12 – with the fourth beast in the book of Daniel, a clear reference to Islam in Ibn Ezra's time.[14] Another connection with Islam in Ibn Ezra's commentary is his interpretation of the term *be'er lahai*, the fountain that the angel showed Hagar in the desert (Genesis 16:14). He wrote, "*Be'er lahai* means the well of him who will be alive next year.... The well was so called because the Ishmaelites held annual festivities there. It is still in existence and is called the well of *Zamzam*." This remark departs from the Jewish tradition that identified the location with another well, the one created on the sixth day of creation or the well of Miriam.[15] This allusion to the Meccan well of *Zamzam* demonstrates Ibn Ezra's familiarity with qur'anic exegesis.

Otherwise, Ibn Ezra's commentary, centered on the *peshat*, or literal-contextual explanation of the text, focuses overwhelmingly on grammatical issues. He explains grammatical rules, points to exceptions and provides biblical proofs to support his remarks. In doing so, he transmits the exegetical and philological tradition of the Sephardic school of interpretation to the Northern Jewish communities for which he wrote his commentaries.

13th century: David Kimhi (RaDaK) and Moses ben Nahman (Nahmanides/ RaMBaN) on the Patriarchs

A generation later in Provence, the concern with ethical issues, alluded to by Ibn Ezra, was openly expressed in the work of David Kimhi (1160?–1235?). Whereas Rashi had used his exegesis as a vehicle for conveying rabbinic traditions, and Ibn Ezra had turned his largely into a vehicle for the philological explanation of the text, Kimhi was mainly concerned with the ethics of the biblical characters. According to Kimhi, Sarah's misdeeds begin in Genesis 16:5, when she harshly reproaches Abraham for his passivity toward her suffering of Hagar's contempt. Kimhi reproves her reaction, because he believes that Abraham was unaware of Hagar's attitude. Furthermore, commenting on the following verse, Kimhi claims that once Hagar's fate was in Sarah's hands, she "reacted in an extreme manner,

---

14 The use of Ishmael as a symbol for Islam became common currency from early Islamic times and as such is found in the *Pirke de-Rabbi Eliezer*, probably written in 8th-century Palestine, from which many medieval authors draw. See MILLAR, Fergus: Hagar, Ishmael, Josephus and the Origins of Islam, in: Journal of Jewish Studies 44 (1993), pp. 23–45. Also PÉREZ FERNÁNDEZ (note 10); EPH'AL, E.: 'Ishmael' and the 'Arab(s)': A Transformation of Ethnological Terms, in: Journal of Near Eastern Studies 35 (1976), pp. 225–35. Rashi, who lives in a Christian environment, gives the expression a more neutral tone, interpreting it as "one who dwelt in the wilderness and became an archer."

15 See FIRESTONE, Reuven: Journeys in Holy Lands. The Evolution of the Abraham-Ishmael Legends in Islamic Exegesis, Albany, NY 1990, pp. 65f., note 24.

[deemed] more than necessary. She forced [Hagar] into harsh servitude, and it is possible that she beat her and cursed her." Kimhi concludes, "Sarah behaved without morals or piety. [She behaved] without morals because, though Abraham had waived her duty to honor him and had told her 'Do with her as you wish,' she should have considered Abraham's honor and not Hagar's punishment. [She behaved without piety] and good consciousness [by disregarding the principle that] one does not have to act harshly with those who are subject to oneself, as the sage [Shelomoh ibn Gabirol] said: 'How excellent is forgiveness in someone with power'."[16]

Moreover, in Kimhi's opinion, the angel's advice to Hagar after her expulsion in Genesis 21:17 ("The Lord has paid heed to your suffering") hints at God's own disapproval of Sarah's action. Kimhi believes that the responsibility for Hagar's expulsion also falls on Sarah's shoulders. In contrast to her sin, Abraham's sin is lessened. Kimhi explains his passivity as being for the benefit of his family's well-being. He is aware of the misdeed and he regrets it, but he chooses not to contradict his wife (Genesis 16:6; 21:11). Kimhi also explains that it was on account of Abraham's merit that it was said that Hagar's descendants would become numerous (Genesis 16:9); it was because of him that an angel was sent to Hagar (Genesis 16:14). He further acquits Abraham by showing the good education that he gave to his son and the sadness that he felt not only for Ishmael's banishment, but also for Hagar's (Genesis 21:12). In sum, every element in the episode of Hagar's and Ishmael's expulsion vindicates Abraham's care: he gave them as much food and water as they could possibly carry along; he also gave them gold and silver (as Ibn Ezra had suggested, despite the Bible's silence in this regard); it is even possible that he accompanied them to the outskirts of the city.

In turn, and in contrast to Rashi, who, following the early rabbis, had interpreted Hagar's wandering in the desert as a return to idolatry and had cast blame on Ishmael's wrong ways, there is no charge of immorality in Kimhi's portrayal of Hagar and Ishmael. Also, unlike Ibn Ezra, who had not portrayed them in any particular light, Kimhi offers a positive description of Hagar as the submissive servant of Abraham, who gives him a child whom she cares for in the desert.

In addition to the ethical problem of Abraham's and Sarah's treatment of Hagar and Ishmael, there was another delicate issue in the patriarchal cycle. This was the fact that Abraham's decision to take Keturah as a wife (concubine?) after Sarah's death, as recounted in Genesis 25, could be misread as lust. Kimhi explains that Abraham married Keturah so that she could take care of him in his old age, and in

---

16 See Solomon ibn Gabirol. *Sefer Mivhar ha-Peninim*, ed. and transl. by B. H. ASCHER, London 1859, pp. 6ff.: "There is no happier union than that of modesty, and wisdom, and power with clemency." David Kimhi's father, Joseph, included many versified sayings taken from Ibn Gabirol's *Mivhar ha-Peninim* in his *Shekel ha-Kodesh* and translated the work into Hebrew. Another contemporary translation, by Judah ibn Tibbon, was also available to Provençal readers.

order to increase the number of his descendants. According to Kimhi, both Hagar and Keturah were Abraham's wives, not his concubines.[17]

Although Kimhi's exegesis, like that of his two predecessors, Ibn Ezra and to a lesser degree Rashi, is historical-literal, there are several instances in his commentary on Abraham's cycle where he makes use of a layer of moral exegesis. Thus he says, referring to Sarah's harsh treatment of Hagar: "This whole account is written in the Torah so that one takes from it what is good and rejects what is bad" (Genesis 16:6) and later, concerning Hagar's suffering in the desert, "All of this is written to teach that one should not be distressed when encountering difficulties and one must trust God.... It is also written to teach God's actions upon those who love His name, because the angel came to Abraham's maidservant twice, and made a miracle for her and her son" (Genesis 21:11). These instances of moral interpretation have been presented as the reemergence of a midrashic trend intended to derive religious meaning.[18] Without denying this possibility, both statements could also be seen as a consequence of Kimhi's familiarity with the techniques of Christian exegetes, among whom moral exegesis was a common tool. Therefore, just as Ibn Ezra's exegesis reveals an Islamic background, both in form and in content, Kimhi's mirrors a Christian one. This is an aspect I will revisit in what follows.

Nahmanides on the Patriarchs

Shortly after Kimhi's commentary was written, Nahmanides (1194–1270?), one of the most prominent Jewish intellectuals in 13th-century Aragon, displayed similar ethical concerns in his commentary on Genesis.[19] Nahmanides, who systematically quotes Rashi mostly to disagree with him, points to Abraham's and Sarah's noble character in several instances (Genesis 16:2 on Sarah, and Genesis 21:11 on Abraham), but he does not refrain from severely criticizing their attitudes towards Hagar and Ishmael. In commenting on Genesis 16:6, he says: "[Sarah] our mother committed sin [in doing] that and so did Abraham, who allowed her to act that way." Unlike Kimhi, Nahmanides does not make any efforts to

---

17 Rashi and Ibn Ezra had, however, taken different stances regarding Keturah's identity. The former followed R. Judah's opinion in *Genesis Rabbah* 61:4 to the letter. Taking *pilagshim*, written defectively, as *pelegesh sham*, that is "the concubine there, at the well", R. Judah had identified Hagar and Keturah as the same person. Rashi followed suit. In Rashi's view Hagar/Keturah was a concubine, as she did not get a marriage-contract (TB *Sanhedrin* 21a). Against R. Judah and Rashi's opinion, in his commentary on Genesis 25:1 Ibn Ezra claimed Keturah had to be distinguished from Sarah, as the word *pilagshim* was the plural of *pelegesh* in Genesis 25:6. In spite of its masculine plural ending, Ibn Ezra explained, the word *pilagshim* referred to female maidservants.

18 COHEN, Mordechai: The Qimhi Family, in: Hebrew Bible: Old Testament – The History of its Interpretation. Vol. 1,2: The Middle Ages, ed. by Magne SAEBO, Göttingen 2000, p. 411.

19 For Nahmanides' commentary on the Torah see: CHAVEL, Charles B. (ed.): Perush ha-torah le-Rabbenu Moshe ben Nahman, Jerusalem 1969; English transl.: Commentary on the Torah by Ramban (Nachmanides), translated and annotated with index by Charles B. CHAVEL, New York 1971–76.

justify Abraham's good intentions, and therefore in Genesis 21:15, in reference to Hagar and Ishmael in the desert, he wrote: "All this matter has to be blamed on Abraham, since he commanded everything Sarah said, and she had asked them to leave right away. According to Sarah's wishes, Abraham did not give them gold or silver. Neither did he give them camels or slaves." In keeping his commentary close to the literal meaning of the text and turning away from midrashic elements, Nahmanides highlights Abraham's responsibility in the events.

As for Hagar's and Keturah's status with regard to Abraham, Nahmanides distances himself from Kimhi, holding what could be seen as an ambivalent attitude. In his view, Hagar was a concubine (Genesis 16:11), regardless of Sarah's intention to give her to Abraham as a wife (Genesis 16:2). Keturah, in turn, was taken as a legitimate wife by Abraham, and considered as such on her own account, yet she always retained a concubine-like status, insofar as her sons were not to receive their father's inheritance. This concubine-like status may also be related to her being a handmaid from a family of slaves or, if the Rabbis were right, to the fact that Hagar and Keturah were actually the same person (Genesis 25:6). Moreover, Nahmanides opposes Rashi's distinction between wife and concubine as being based on the existence of a *ketubbah* ("marriage-contract").[20] In Nahmanides' view, a woman is called a concubine only when there is not *kiddushin* ("betrothal" or "sanctification").[21]

Whereas Kimhi advocated a moral reading of these patriarchal events, Nahmanides chooses typology to explain them. As a consequence of patriarchal sin, "God paid heed to [Hagar's] suffering, and gave her a son who was meant to be *pere' adam*, to make the descendants of Sarah and Abraham suffer in every possible way" (Genesis 16:12). He interprets the expression *pere' adam* in this verse as "someone who would rob everyone and whom everyone would rob" and understands that Ishmael's descendants would make war with all nations and will defeat them only to be finally defeated by them. Nahmanides introduces in his narrative an explicit messianic component that uses typology for the purpose of consolation. The rarity of Nahmanides' recourse to typology has been properly noted, yet the impact of his methods on later Jewish exegesis is still an open debate.[22] As was

---

20 See note 17.
21 See TB *Sanhedrin* 21a. The Talmud distinguishes between *kiddushin* or *erusin* ("betrothal", understood as first stage of marriage) and *nissu'im* ("ceremony of nuptials" or actual act of marriage). Beginning with the 10th/11th centuries, both ceremonies fused into one, though the practice of keeping them separate did not disappear completely. See FALK, Ze'ev W.: Jewish Matrimonial Law in the Middle Ages, London 1966, pp. 35–85.
22 See FUNKENSTEIN, Amos: Perceptions of Jewish History, Berkeley/Los Angeles/Oxford 1993, pp. 98–121. SAPERSTEIN, Marc: Jewish Typological Exegesis after Nahmanides, in: Jewish Quarterly Review 1,2 (1993–1994), pp. 158–70. The theological use of the characters for the sake of consolation, rarely found in Jewish medieval exegesis, was common currency, though, in *piyyutim* since the early Middle Ages. Liturgical poets advocated a reversal of the current situation where Sarah, legitimate wife and mistress, served her own handmaiden, Hagar, conceived as a type for Islam. Within this typological pattern, the future was envisioned in terms of a return to the original status quo, and implied a strong messianic component. This is an issue that deserves more attention but goes far beyond the limits of the present study.

the case with David Kimhi's moral statements, it is likely that the use of typology comes as a result of Nahmanides' familiarity with a dominant typological Christian exegesis.

Exegesis and polemics

In the preceding section I have drawn attention, if briefly, to the fact that both Kimhi's and Nahmanides' exegetical innovations revealed their familiarity with contemporary Christian exegesis, most likely known to them through direct polemical exchanges with Christians. The polemical background of the writing of 13th-century biblical commentaries had not only an effect on exegetical techniques, but also an input into the issues discussed. It is true that ethical issues regarding the patriarchal narratives were already known from Rabbinic sources. The distinct emphasis on the patriarchs' morals that both Kimhi's and Nahmanides' works evidence, however, cannot be fully explained without reference to an active polemical context, as has been observed elsewhere. [23]

In this regard, the criticism of Sarah's morals would be better understood if considered against the typological interpretation of Hagar and Sarah in Christian literature. In Galatians 4:21–31, Paul had presented Sarah as a type for Christianity and Hagar as her counterpart: Judaism. Patristic authors and medieval commentators perpetuated these types, identifying Sarah and Hagar with the Church and the Synagogue respectively. Commentaries on Genesis by 13th-century Christian exegetes prove the polemical use of both types in Kimhi's period. [24] In turn, the nature of Keturah's relationship to Abraham displays similar apologetic efforts, as a sermon written by Kimhi's comtemporary, Jacob Anatoli, proves. In his sermon on the *parashah* "Lekh lekhah" Anatoli explains that Abraham's decision to marry Keturah was a commitment to procreation. He concludes: "This is unlike the opinion of the Christians, who set apart some of their children to be barren until

23 See BERGER (note 5), p. 3; GROSSMAN, Avraham: The Jewish Polemic and Jewish Biblical Exegesis in Twelfth-Century France: On the Attitude of R. Joseph Qara to Polemic (in Hebrew), in: Zion 51 (1986), pp. 29–60. The ethical works written in Sepharad prior to the 13th century had actually presented the Patriarchs as a model of virtue. For Bahya ibn Paquda (1040?–1100?) Abraham represented the highest stage of the love of God. See A. S. YAHUDA (ed.): Al-Hidaja 'ila Fara'id al-Qulub des Bachja ibn Josef ibn Paquda, Leiden 1912, pp. 384ff. (transl. in: The Book of Direction to the Duties of the Heart. Introduction, translation, and notes by Menahem MANSOOR, London 1973, pp. 432ff.). As Touati remarks (TOUATI, Charles: La Pensée Philosophique et Théologique de Gersonide, Paris 1973, pp. 446f., note 4), Maimonides emphasized the special providence that the patriarchs and their posterity received in a very similar way. See MUNK, Shelomoh (ed.): Dalalat al-Ha'irin, Jerusalem 1930 (transl. in: The Guide of the Perplexed, translated and with an introduction and notes by Shelomo PINES, Chicago/London 1963, part III, chapter 51, pp. 623ff.).
24 See DAHAN, Gilbert: Exégèse et polémique dans les Commentaires de la Genèse d'Étienne Langton, in: Les juifs au regard de l'histoire: Mélanges en l'Honneur de Bernhard Blumenkranz, ed. by Gilbert DAHAN, Paris 1985, pp. 129–56; and GROSSMAN: The Jewish Polemic.

their deaths, as if God hates the human race."[25] One cannot but wonder if his criticism of Sarah, unprecedented and unusually strong among 13th-century Jewish commentators, and their somewhat favorable portrayal of Hagar, might be inverting and neutralizing Christian typologizing of both characters: Sarah as Christianity and Hagar as Judaism.

Let us now turn back to Nahmanides for a second. Confirmation of the polemical use of his exegetical arguments comes from an unexpected source – a polemical treatise against Judaism written in Arabic in 14th-century Aragon. Needless to say, Nahmanides' era was a time marked by bitter polemics and religious conversion. However, while public Judeo-Christian disputations of escalating violence in 13th-century Aragon would be difficult to miss, the importance of Islam in this context is often overlooked. Although receding in the political arena, Islam was distinctively perceived as a major player in inter-confessional debates. Conversions from Judaism to Islam were not unknown and, as it seems, significant enough to raise concerns in Christian legislation.[26] Some Jewish converts actively engaged in arguments against their former coreligionists, and even came to write polemical treatises against Judaism. This is the case with *Ta'yid al-Milla* ("The Fortification of the Faith"), a work that comes to provide the Judeo-Islamic polemical background of the biblical sections under analysis.[27] The anonymous author of the treatise, most likely a convert from Judaism to Islam, reports having witnessed groups of Jews getting together and letting loose their tongues with calumnies about the prophet Muhammad. Two offenses are singled out – the Jews' claim that God has not revealed any religious law or Scripture to any of the nations except to them, and their contention that Hagar was not Abraham's wife but his concubine.[28] This said, the author proceeds with his arguments against Judaism beginning with an extensive chapter on the status of Ishmael and Hagar in the Jewish tradition. Both Hagar's condition as either wife or concubine, and her rapport with Sarah, had not been given, to the best of my knowledge, similar relevance in Islamic polemical literature written to this point by either Muslims or converts from Judaism.[29]

---

25 As quoted in SAPERSTEIN, Marc: Christians and Christianity in the Sermons of Jacob Anatoli, in: Jewish History 6 (1992), pp. 225–46.

26 See ROMANO, David: Conversión de Judíos al Islam (Corona de Aragón 1280–1284), in: Sefarad 36,1 (1976), pp. 33–37; STALLS, W. C.: Jewish Conversion to Islam: The Perspective of a Quaestio, in: Revista Española de Teología 43 (1983), pp. 235–51; GARCÍA-ARENAL, Mercedes: Rapports entre groupes dans la péninsule ibérique: La conversion des juifs à l'islam (XIIᵉ–XIIIᵉ siècles), in: Revue du Monde Musulman et de la Méditerranée (REMMM) 63–64,1 (1992), pp. 91–101.

27 See KASSIN, Leon J.: A Study of a Fourteenth-Century Polemical Treatise *Adversus Judaeos*, Doctoral Dissertation, Columbia University 1970.

28 KASSIN: A Study, p. 1 (Arabic text), p. 105 (trans.).

29 The theological concept of *'isma* ("immunity from error and sin"), a term that does not occur in the Qur'an or in canonical sunni *hadith*, was applied by later Muslim theologians to the Prophets, and eventually brought up in polemical contexts regarding the Patriarchs' behavior. On this matter, see TYAN, E.: *'Isma*, Encyclopaedia of Islam, 2nd ed., Leiden 1978, vol. 4, pp. 182–84; ZUCKER, Moshe: The Problem of 'Isma – Prophetic Immunity to Sin and Error in Islamic and Jewish Literature (in Hebrew), in: Tarbiz 35 (1965), pp. 149–73. Biblical verses from Abraham's cycle were traditionally used in Islamic polemics against Judaism as proof of the prophethood of Muhammad.

From this first chapter that quotes Genesis at length and dramatizes the claims of the disputants, the Jews' portrayal of Hagar may be inferred. The author of *Ta'yid al-Milla* counters two arguments: first, the fact that a woman is not entitled to conclude the marriage of another woman and the fact that Abraham did not marry Hagar with *taqdis* (Arabic translation of *kiddushin* or "betrothal"), both elements clearly referring back to points raised by Nahmanides in his commentary on Genesis 16. Unlike Nahmanides, the author of *Ta'yid al-Milla,* familiar enough with Rabbinic and medieval exegetical sources, identifies Keturah with Hagar and following *Genesis Rabbah* 45 (referred to as "the book of the Talmud") presents Keturah as Pharaoh's daughter.

In sum, Jewish arguments, such as Nahmanides' which arose specifically for the debate with Christian polemicists, are used in the *Ta'yid al-Milla* as weapons to be used by Aragonese Muslims in their polemics against Judaism. The status of Hagar and Ishmael vis-à-vis Sarah and Isaac was a particularly delicate issue at a time when Islam was suffering defeat and humiliation in the Kingdom of Aragon.

The aftermath

Nahmanides' harsh accusations against the Patriarchs did not find much of an echo, even among his most immediate followers. Illustrative in this regard is Bahya b. Asher's (Saragossa?, 13th century) commentary on the Torah. Bahya, who quotes Rashi, Ibn Ezra and Nahmanides, on occasion relies on the latter and briefly expands on some of his arguments. However, he uses Nahmanides' work in a remarkably selective way. Most significantly, all Nahmanides' comments on the patriarchs' misconduct are systematically omitted. Far from following Nahmanides' critical attitude, Bahya returns to Rabbinic sources (especially *Genesis Rabbah*) and Rashi. In contrast to this omission, Bahya transmits Nahmanides' use of typology with even darker undertones. The following statement on Genesis 21:14 is significant enough to be quoted at length:

> [Abraham] was supposed to have given [Hagar and Ishmael] gold and silver and camels to bear them, since [Ishmael] was the son for whom he had begged God: 'Oh that Ishmael might live for your favor' (Genesis 17:18), but as Sarah had asked him to expel him and his mother, God told Abraham: 'Do everything Sarah has told you to do.' This is the reason why [Abraham] paid heed to Sarah and expelled them only with bread and a skin of water. This is Nahmanides' interpretation. It could be further added that the fact that Abraham expelled them with no more than water and bread hints at another element and this is that Abraham saw in a prophetic vision that his descendants would be subject to Ishmael in the future and that they would be hated with intense hate, as no nation in the world hates Israel as much as Ishmael.... This is why Abraham behaved as one has to behave with those one hates, giving them not more than water

See ADANG, Camilla: Muslim Writers on Judaism and the Hebrew Bible: From Ibn Rabban to Ibn Hazm, Leiden/New York/Köln 1996, pp. 146f., 152, 196, 264f.

and bread, as it is said: 'If your enemy is hungry, give him bread to eat; if he is thirsty, give him water to drink' (Proverbs 25:21).[30]

14th century: Levi ben Gershon (Gersonides)

The question concerning the patriarchs' demeanor, raised by Kimhi and Nahmanides, is also absent a century later in Gersonides' commentary on Genesis. From an exegetical point of view, Gersonides' (Provence, 1284–1344) concise, rational, and straightforward interpretation of the text according to the *peshat*[31] rules out any typological reading. Innovatively, he divides his comments into two sections: philological interpretation and general interpretation, both supplemented by *to'aliyyot*, benefits or moral lessons that can be inferred from the weekly portion. In doing so, Gersonides systematizes an exegetical device that had been introduced and sporadically used by David Kimhi in his commentary on Genesis and that seems to mirror the Christian division between *littera/sensus* or *littera/sententia*.[32] Gersonides' strong commitment to ethics, manifest in the *to'aliyyot*, materializes in his reading of the patriarchal narratives. However, it does not translate into criticism of the biblical ancestors. In Gersonides' account, the angel who encounters Hagar in the desert (Genesis 16:9) tells Hagar to return to Sarah, her mistress, beg her for forgiveness and submit to her in order to receive instruction, as Sarah's intentions were to do well by her and not to take revenge on her. Likewise, Ishmael's banishment (Genesis 21:9) has the purpose of preventing Isaac from learning wrong ways, so that he will be able to reach perfection. In the same vein, Keturah's children, not meant to be perfect, are given presents and sent away so as not to claim Isaac's inheritance or make him depart from the right path intended for him. If Hagar and Ishmael do not die in the desert, according to Gersonides, it is because the divine providence is with them. Nonetheless, God does not answer Hagar's prayer or compensate her for any injustice suffered, but helps her exclusively on account of Abraham's virtue.

In sum, Gersonides transforms Hagar's punishment into a lesson and portrays Ishmael and Keturah's children as lacking instruction and being incapable of attaining a degree of perfection that was naturally reserved for Isaac, as Abraham's only inheritor – thus the need to keep them apart from their half-brother. Hagar,

---

30 CHAVEL, Charles D. (ed.): Be'ur 'al ha-Torah: Rabbenu Bahya, Jerusalem 1966–1968. Also see Bernard SEPTIMUS: 'Tahat edom we-lo' tahat yishma'el': Gilgulo shel ma'amar, in: Zion 47,2 (1982), pp. 103–11, and Id.: Hispano-Jewish Views of Christendom and Islam, in: In Iberia and Beyond: Hispanic Jews between Cultures; Proceedings of a Symposium to Mark the 500th Anniversary of the Expulsion of the Spanish Jewry, ed. by Bernard COOPERMAN, Newark/London 1998, pp. 43–65.

31 See FREYMAN, Eli: Le commentaire de Gersonide sur le Pentateuque, in: Gersonide en son temps: Science et philosophie médiévales, ed. by Gilbert DAHAN, Louvain/Paris 1991, pp. 117–32.

32 This division has a precedent in Ibn Ezra's Commentary on the Song of Songs. On Christian influence on Gersonides' work see SIRAT, Colette: Biblical Commentaries and Christian Influence: The Case of Gersonides, in: Hebrew Scholarship and the Medieval World, ed. by Nicholas LANGE, Cambridge 2001, pp. 210–23.

Ishmael and Keturah's children were not abused or mistreated. On the contrary, it was by virtue of their proximity to the Patriarchs that they benefited from the highest degree of perfection: the provident communication of goodness, embodied by Abraham and eventually transmitted to Isaac.[33] Sarah, and especially Abraham, far from being criticized, became role models to the reader, their level of [intellectual] perfection being proportionate to the special relationship they had to divine providence.[34]

15th century: Abraham Saba and Isaac Abravanel

The 15th century witnessed new developments and adaptations in the two trends surveyed here: accusation or exculpation of the patriarchs. Strikingly similar to Gersonides' interest in education and instruction is Abravanel's commentary, written in 1506–07.[35] In his detailed, somewhat repetitive interpretation of Genesis 16, Abravanel (1437–1508) in his most classical style, most likely influenced by the scholastic technique of *quaestiones*, raises ten *she'elot* ("questions") and supplies an answer to each.[36] Some of the questions refer to ethical issues, but all of the answers conclude in the same way – exonerating the Patriarchs. Following the lead of Gersonides, Abravanel explicitly and repeatedly contradicts Nahmanides by arguing that neither Sarah nor Abraham committed any kind of sin. Abraham's only intention was to act according to Sarah's wishes. Sarah's punishment of Hagar, in turn, was for the sake of her education. It was rather Hagar's lack of ethical sense that brought about her punishment. As in Gersonides, the angel that encounters Hagar in the desert (Genesis 16:9) advises her to return home and submit to her mistress' instruction, as it will benefit her; the promise of numerous descendants was only used to convince Hagar to return, so that she would not miscarry in the desert.

As for Hagar's and Ishmael's banishment in Genesis 21:9, according to Abravanel, Sarah does not see any reason for the boy to be living in the house, given the fact that Isaac will be Abraham's only recognized heir. Hagar is banished because had she remained in the house, she could have claimed inheritance for her own child, Ishmael. Abravanel does not see any trace of mistreatment or brutality in Sarah's behavior. She acts *be-tov da'atah* ("in good consciousness") and always according to the status of mother and child. Later on, in Genesis 25, Abraham

---

33 See DOBBS-WEINSTEIN, Idit: The Existential Dimension of Providence in the Thought of Gersonides, in: DAHAN, Gilbert (ed.): Gersonide en son temps, pp. 159–78.

34 Gersonides' views coincide with a well-established Sephardic ethical tradition. See supra, note 23.

35 SHOTLAND, Avishai (ed.): Perush 'al ha-Torah le-Rabbenu Yishak Abravanel, Jerusalem 1997.

36 On the connection between Abravanel's system and contemporary Christian exegesis, see GAON, Solomon: The Influence of the Catholic Theologian Alfonso Tostado on the Pentateuch Commentary of Isaac Abravanel, Hoboken, NJ/New York 1993; LAWEE, Eric: On the Threshold of the Renaissance: New Methods and Sensibilities in the Biblical Commentaries of Isaac Abarbanel, in: HUCA 67 (1996), pp. 107–42.

will marry Keturah in order to have more children because, among other things, this will discourage Ishmael from claiming a status similar to Isaac, or an inheritance equal to his. Both the concepts of instruction and, especially, status dominate Abravanel's reading.

Another picture emerges from *Tseror ha-Mor* ("Bundle of Myrrh"), a running commentary on Genesis written by Abravanel's contemporary, R. Abraham Saba, in Fez, between 1498 and 1501, shortly after his expulsion from Portugal.[37] Saba draws from two main sources: Midrashim and Kabbalistic literature, mainly the *Zohar*. Like Kimhi and Nahmanides before him, Saba interprets Abraham's and Sarah's actions as "sin." Sarah's sin included tormenting Hagar but, most importantly – and here Saba distances himself from earlier exegetes – Sarah sinned by giving Hagar to her husband for the sake of procreation after Abraham had already been guaranteed offspring. In Saba's opinion, this action does nothing but demonstrate how short-sighted women are. As for Abraham, he is equally responsible for having listened to Sarah and having taken Hagar and Keturah as concubines. In sum, Saba emphasizes the Patriarchs' sin, but in his view, the sin committed is radically different from the one exposed by the 13th-century exegetes.

Saba also departs from his predecessors' positions, describing the sin committed as having more drastic, far-reaching consequences. The true outcome of the sin is the birth of Ishmael and Keturah's children, both personifications of cosmic evil. Explicitly quoting the *Midrash ha-Ne'elam*, in the *Zohar*, Saba describes current events saying: "Ishmael took our land, and our Temple, and rules over the whole land of Israel" (Genesis 16:1). Two elements lead to the present status. First, Abraham's sin is what gave life to Ishmael. Within the Zoharic system, this would be a re-enactment of Adam's sin, first cause for the existence of evil in the world. Second, it is by virtue of Ishmael's circumcision that he attained the possession of the land and the Temple.[38]

Along the same lines and playing with paronomasia, Saba believes that the names of Keturah's children are testimony to their evil-doing: "Zimran, 'the singing of the tyrants' (Isaiah 25:5), Jokshan, 'the fowler's trap' (Psalms 91:3), Medan, 'trial of his people' (Psalms 50:4), Midian, 'a contentious, vexatious wife' (Proverbs 21:19), Ishback, 'a stump with its roots left in the ground' (Daniel 4:12) and Shuah, 'a deep pit' (Proverbs 21:9)." Ishmael's descendants, in turn, were twelve chieftains who "came to their end without hope" (Job 7:16), in contrast to the twelve tribes of Israel. "The one, no less than the other" – Saba concludes in commenting on Genesis 25:13 – "was God's doing to be feared."

---

37 VIKHALDER, Ya'akov M. (ed.): Perush Tseror ha-mor ha-shalem 'al-hamishah humshe Torah, Bene-Berak 1989–90; GROSS, Abraham: Iberian Jewry from Twilight to Dawn: The World of Rabbi Abraham Saba, Leiden/New York 1995.

38 Following in the footsteps of the *Zohar*, Saba's attitude to Ishmael is, at the very least, ambivalent, as exemplified by the two considerations quoted: on the one hand, Ishmael enjoys a high status that places him above all nations, by virtue of his circumcision. Notwithstanding, this status is inferior to Israel's on account of his circumcision being without *peri'ah* ("uncovering of the corona"). On the other hand, Ishmael's high status stands in opposition to him being a personification of evil.

Contrasting with most of his predecessors, who conveyed a relatively favorable picture of Hagar and Ishmael, Saba leans on the Midrash in order to associate them with impurity and idolatry, as Rashi had already done. Hence, Hagar came from an impure land and an impure people (Genesis 16:3); she is characterized as a sorceress (Genesis 21:9) and takes an Egyptian wife for Ishmael (Genesis 21:21) in order to return to her idols. Keturah's sons receive impure names from Abraham in Genesis 25:6 and are sent to "the mountains of Kedem", a location that, following Isaiah 2:6, Saba describes as a place for sorcery. However, Saba brings the midrashic interpretation one step forward and identifies impurity and idolatry with *sitra' ahra'* ("the other side, the domain of dark emanations and demonic powers"), transmitting a sefirotic symbolism that links Ishmael with demonic sources.[39] This well-established symbolism of the *Zohar* develops an ancient anti-Ishmaelite tendency present in the *Pirke de-Rabbi Eliezer*.[40] Like Gersonides and Abravanel, Saba emphasizes the fact that Ishmael and Keturah's children rejected instruction, but unlike his two predecessors, he reads this rejection as departing from the ways of God, and turning to Sama'el, a significant point because in his commentaries Saba identifies Sama'el with Christianity.[41]

Conclusion

As I argued at the outset, medieval Hebrew running commentaries mediated the reader's understanding of a well-known biblical text. Thereby they were channels for the transmission and popularization of knowledge. Thus, Ibn Ezra uses his exegetical work, all produced outside the Iberian Peninsula, to introduce his audience to the Sephardic philological tradition, in which he was trained. His commentaries probably reached a more diversified audience than his grammatical treatises ever did. Gersonides used the characters of Sarah and Abraham to convey his philosophical ideas on divine providence and human perfection, as part of his rational reading of the biblical text. Finally, Abraham Saba, writing for an audience which had suffered the hardships of the expulsion from Spain and Portugal, disseminated Kabbalah in the north of Africa. The obscure sefirotic symbolism of the *Zohar*, partially written in Aramaic, was conveyed in easier terms through his running commentary. The cosmic confrontation between good and evil that the *Zohar* portrayed seemed masterfully to describe the historical and political events he was forced to live through.

---

39 See SCHOLEM, Gershom: Kabbalah, Jerusalem 1974, pp. 122–28.
40 KIENER, Ronald C.: The Image of Islam in the Zohar, in: The Age of the Zohar: Proceedings of the Third International Conference on the History of Jewish Mysticism, ed. by Joseph DAN, Jerusalem 1989, pp. 43*–65*.
41 See GROSS (note 37), p. 133, and Id.: Satan and Christianity: The Demonization of Christianity in the Writings of Abraham Saba (in Hebrew), in: Zion 58 (1993), pp. 93–105.

The passage from Genesis examined here also help in tracing the exegetical and polemical encounter between Judaism, Islam and Christianity. Ibn Ezra's philological approach, along with his occasional references to an Islamic reading of the text, points at his familiarity with Islamic sources, written or oral. Kimhi's use of a moral exegetical mode, further developed by Gersonides in his *to'aliyyot*, and Abravanel's systematic questions and answers, belong in a Christian context. The identification of Ishmael with Islam, common in rabbinic sources, and pointed at by Abraham ibn Ezra, was significantly underlined by Nahmanides and Bahya ben Asher at a time when Islam and Christianity clashed in both Aragon and Palestine. Unlike them and in the light of later historical events, Abraham Saba reads Ishmael's wrong ways as an approach to Sama'el, a symbol for Christianity.

The criticism of the patriarchs' behavior has to be understood in the context of polemics between Judaism and Christianity. This criticism, mainly occurring in the 13th century, coincides with a new awareness of each other on the part of Jews and Christians alike, fostered by mendicant pressure and religious disputations of increasing intensity. The anonymous author of *Ta'yid al-Milla* uses those arguments, a product of a Judeo-Christian encounter, and puts them in the service of his new religion – Islam. He provides Aragonese Muslims with an anti-Jewish manual. At a time of decline of Islam in the Peninsula, when Muslims were seeing their status becoming more degraded day by day, the symbolic relationship of power between Sarah and Hagar acquired preeminence. Kimhi's and Nahmanides' criticism soon lost intensity, being ignored by subsequent generations of exegetes who, like Ben Asher, followed in the footsteps of their exegetical innovations but silenced or explicitly opposed any questioning of the morals of the biblical characters.

JONATHAN P. DECTER

Subduing Hagar: The Hebraization of Arabic writing in the thirteenth century

Translation is so far removed from being the sterile equation of two
languages that of all literary forms it is the one charged with the
special mission of watching over the maturation process of the original language and the birth pangs of its own.
Walter Benjamin, "The Task of the Translator"

In his introduction to the *Book of Tahkemoni*, a book of fictional Hebrew narratives by Judah al-Harizi, the thirteenth-century Toledan author explains his reasons for composing the book. He laments that the Hebrew language had "declined
appallingly" in his day, that it had lost its former luster, especially as Jews neglected it in order to embrace the Arabic language and its literature. In the narrative,
the Hebrew Tongue appears to the author in the form of a woman complaining
that her people had sold her out in favor of the Tongue of Hagar, Arabic: "They set
Hagar the maidservant in my place and rushed to her embrace, kissing her hand
and pressing her teat – for stolen waters are sweet. Me they have abandoned, the
Rose of Sharon, saying, Hagar is fecund and Sarah barren."[1] The *Tahkemoni* was
undertaken to revive the Hebrew language and to establish its preeminence over
Arabic as a tongue of holiness and eloquence.

Al-Harizi's assessment of Hebrew's neglect in his day is not entirely fair. It is
true that Hebrew poetry did not flourish to the same extent in Christian Iberia
as it had in al-Andalus, where between the tenth and the twelfth centuries arabized Jewish poets composed an impressive corpus of Hebrew poems.[2] However,
following the decline of Andalusian Jewry, a Jewish intellectual revolution took
place in Christian Iberia and in Provence that centered on the translation of Arabic and Judeo-Arabic texts into Hebrew.[3] In Islamic al-Andalus, Jews had been
avid students of Arabic literature and Islamic disciplines and composed works on
philosophy, science, grammar, and biblical exegesis in Arabic, usually in Hebrew
characters (what is called Judeo-Arabic).[4] Fearing that the content of the Judeo-

1 ALHARIZI, Judah: The Book of Tahkemoni: Jewish Tales from Medieval Spain, translated and
explicated by David Simha SEGAL, London 2001, p. 12.
2 See for example Ross BRANN: The Arabized Jews, in: The Literature of al-Andalus, ed. by María
Rosa MENOCAL/Raymond P. SCHEINDLIN/Michael SELLS, Cambridge 2000, pp. 435–54.
3 In general, see Alfred IVRY: Philosophical Translations from the Arabic in Hebrew during the
Middle Ages, in: Rencontres de cultures dans la philosophie médiévale, ed. by J. HAMESSE/M.
FATTORI, Louvain-la-Neuve/Cassino 1990, pp. 167–86; Irene ZWIEP: Mother of Reason and
Revelation: A Short History of Medieval Jewish Linguistic Thought, Amsterdam 1997, pp. 62ff.
4 On Judeo-Arabic literature in general, see Abraham HALKIN: Judeo-Arabic Literature, in: Encyclopaedia Judaica 10, pp. 410–23. On the Judeo-Arabic language, see Joshua BLAU: The Emergence
and Linguistic Background of Judeo-Arabic, 3rd rev. ed., Jerusalem 1999.

Arabic heritage would be lost in the Christian environment, Jewish intellectuals began the process of translating works into Hebrew. However, Hebrew did not yet possess a register sufficient for philosophical and scientific writing; terminology had to be invented as the translators went along. As much as Jews may have been attached to Hebrew as a 'language of the people', they also recognized that it required significant reinvention to accommodate their intellectual needs.

Provence and Christian Iberia were the two main centers of the translation enterprise, with each region adhering to somewhat different literary ideals. In Provence, members of the Ibn Tibbon family systematically translated classic Judeo-Arabic works and Arabic scientific and philosophical literature by non-Jewish authors into Hebrew. Judah Ibn Tibbon translated critical works of Jewish thought such as Saadia Gaon's *Book of Beliefs and Opinions,* Bahya Ibn Paquda's *Book of Directions to the Duties of the Heart,* and Judah Halevi's *Book of Indication and Refutation Concerning the Despised Faith* (the *Kuzari*). Judah's son Samuel translated Maimonides' *Guide of the Perplexed,* Aristotle's *Meteorology,* and probably an Arabic commentary on Galen's *Ars Parva* as well as treatises on the intellect by Averroes. Jews were profoundly influenced by Averroes, whose works merited numerous Hebrew paraphrases, translations, and commentaries between the thirteenth and fifteenth centuries.[5]

In Christian Iberia, a second and more modest school, if we may even call it such, emerged with such translators as Judah al-Harizi, Jacob Ben Elazar, and Abraham Ibn Hasdai. Among al-Harizi's translations from Judeo-Arabic and Arabic into Hebrew are: Moses Ibn Ezra's *Treatise of the Garden of Figurative and Literal Speech*; Maimonides' *Guide of the Perplexed*; Maimonides' Introduction to the *Commentary on the Mishnah* and the commentary on the first five tractates of *Zeraim*; Maimonides' *Epistle on Resurrection*; Ali Ibn Ridwān's *Epistle on Morals*; Hunayn Ibn Ishaq's *Sayings of the Philosophers*; Galen's *Dialogue on the Soul*; and the famous *maqāmāt* of al-Hariri of Basra.[6] With the final example, al-Harizi broke away from works of philosophical, legal, and scientific content and attempted to translate a belletristic text from Arabic. Another translator who tried his hand at belletristic translation was al-Harizi's younger contemporary from Toledo Jacob Ben Elazar, who wrote a translation of the classic book of Arabic fables *Kalila wa Dimna.*[7] Abraham Ibn Hasdai translated Isaac Israeli's *Book on the*

---

5   See Steven HARVEY: Arabic Into Hebrew: The Hebrew Translation Movement and the Influence of Averroes Upon Medieval Jewish Thought, in: The Cambridge Companion to Medieval Jewish Philosophy, ed. by Daniel H. FRANK/Oliver LEAMAN, Cambridge 2003, pp. 258–80.
6   For further references, see Rina DRORY: Literary Contacts and Where to Find Them: On Arabic Literary Models in Medieval Jewish Literature, in: Poetics Today 14,2 (1993), p. 285 and appendix.
7   The tales probably originated in India and are known in Persian, Syriac, Arabic and other languages. There are several Arabic translations, the most famous of which is by 'Abdallah Ibn al-Muqaffa'. Because of his liberal translation method it is unclear which Arabic version Ben Elazar had before him when creating his rendition. On *Kalila wa Dimna* in general, see the article by C. BROCKELMANN in: Encyclopaedia of Islam (second edition), vol. 4, pp. 503–06. Ben Elazar's translation has received relatively little attention, but see Ángeles Navarro PEIRO: La versión hebrea de

Elements and paraphrased sections of another Neoplatonic work in his Hebrew rendition of the Barlaam and Josaphat story, *The Prince and the Ascetic*.[8]

The study of these translations as translations, rather than as faithful representations of original works, is a field in its infancy. Fine studies by scholars such as Zonta, Rothschild, Shiffman, and Freudenthal have focused on the development of a Hebrew philosophical vocabulary and the merits, from the perspective of accuracy, of the various methods used by translators.[9] Schirmann and others have noted the rendering of Arabic belletristic texts in the clear diction of biblical Hebrew and argued that Jews wrote these translations in order to establish, as al-Harizi had stated, Hebrew's versatility and eloquence.[10]

In this paper I explore the theory and practice of the translation schools of Provence and Christian Iberia and consider their implications for Jews' ideological attitudes toward the Hebrew language in the thirteenth century. The aim here is not to determine which translators produced the "better" translations (history has proclaimed those of the Ibn Tibbons more useful); rather, the aim is to explore the significance of divergent translation methods during the first century of the translation enterprise. In addition to looking at theoretical formulations by medieval authors concerning translation, I study the actual texture of the Hebrew texts produced.

Translators in Provence, sometimes characterized as strict literalists, were largely at ease with importing Arabic vocabulary and syntax. Even so, they did not sacrifice Hebrew purity and eloquence with reckless abandon and favored language built on indigenous terms whenever possible. Despite a general tendency for Jews in Christian Iberia to remain more connected ideologically to a pure Hebrew, their translations reflect ambivalence toward the borrowing of Arabic words, syntax, and expressions. These translators succumbed to the reality that Hebrew, the historic and ideological language of the Jewish people, lacked the capacity for scientific and philosophical expression.

Calila y Dimna de Ya'aqob ben ELAZAR, in: Jewish Studies at the Turn of the Twentieth Century, ed. by Judit Targarona BORRÁS/Angel SÁENZ-BADILLOS, Leiden/Boston/Köln 1999, vol. 1, pp. 468–75; Girón-Negrón, Luis: How the Go-Between cut her Nose: Two Ibero-Medieval Translations of a *Kalilah wa Dimnah* Story, in: Under the Influence: Questioning the Comparative in Medieval Iberia, ed. by Leila ROUHI/Cynthia ROBINSON, Leiden 2004, pp. 231–259.

8 S. M. STERN: Ibn Hasday's Neoplatonist, in: Medieval Arabic and Hebrew Thought, London 1983, pp. 58–120; originally published in: Oriens 13–14 (1961), pp. 58–120.

9 Mauro ZONTA: La filosofia antica nel Medioevo ebraico: le traduzioni ebraiche medievali dei testi filosofici antichi, Brescia 1996; Jean-Pierre ROTHSCHILD: Motivations et méthodes des traductions en hébreu du milieu du XIIe à la fin du XVe siècle, in: Traduction et traducteurs au Moyen Âge, Paris 1989, pp. 279–302; Yair SHIFFMAN: The Differences between the translations of Maimonides' *Guide of the Perplexed* by Falaquera, Ibn Tibbon, and al-Harizi and their textual and philosophical implications, in: Journal of Semitic Studies 44 (1999), pp. 47–61; Gad FREUDENTHAL: 'Ketav ha-dat' or 'Sefer ha-sekhel ve-ha-muskalot' – The Medieval Hebrew Translations of al-Farabi's *Risalah fi'l-'aql*: A Study in Text History and the Evolution of Medieval Hebrew Philosophical Terminology, in: Jewish Quarterly Review 93 (2002), pp. 29–115.

10 Jefim SCHIRMANN: Die hebräische Übersetzung der Maqamen des Hariri, Frankfurt am Main 1930; Abraham LAVI: A Comparative Study of al-Hariri's Maqamat and Their Hebrew Translation by al-Harizi, Ann Arbor, Michigan 1979.

Theory

It is well known that translators face choices between literality and free-rendering when transposing a text from the original language to a target language. In 1813, Schleiermacher expressed this choice as follows: "Either the translator leaves the writer alone as much as possible and moves the reader toward the writer, or he leaves the reader alone as much as possible and moves the writer toward the reader."[11] The choices made by medieval Jewish translators bringing Arabic texts into Hebrew seem to be based on two main factors: 1. whether the original text was literary or scientific/philosophical in nature, and 2. regional differences in translation ideals, which may have been informed by contrasting cultural environments. This paper cuts across a boundary that is often maintained between belletristic and scientific/philosophical translations. Of course the aim of each type of translation is unique; translations of belletristic texts often try to convey or recreate the beauty of the original whereas translations of technical writings are generally less concerned with the beauty of the text produced. Given this, it is most interesting that *non-belletristic* texts were translated in Christian Iberia, at least ideally, into a register of Hebrew that tended toward purity and eloquence.

Jews in Christian Iberia and Provence were heirs to a standard of Hebrew purity that had been idealized by the Jews of al-Andalus. In competing with Muslim claims to the "inimitability of the Qur'an" (إعجاز ألقرآن) and the general perfection of the Arabic language, Jews in al-Andalus came to view the Hebrew Bible with similar regard; as Ross Brann has put it, they considered the Bible a "Jewish Qur'an".[12] In composing Hebrew texts, particularly belletristic ones, Andalusian Jews sought to emulate the standards of their holy book and avoided the use of neologisms except when building words based on roots already existing in the Bible. Thus Judah Ibn Tibbon, who had migrated from al-Andalus to Provence in the late twelfth century, advised his son concerning the composition of poetry:

> The words must be pleasant and light on the tongue. [Verbal] constructions should be limited to constructions that are extant. Do not introduce foreign constructions nor foreign words, even if they are justifiable by analogy, for the foreign word is not natural... Choose what is sweet to your palate and pleasant to him who hears it.[13]

At least in the area of poetic composition, Ibn Tibbon called for the preservation of a pure register of Hebrew, one that was free of foreign syntax and terminology. However, this founder of the most famous dynasty of Hebrew translators often

---

11 Friedrich SCHLEIERMACHER: From 'On the Different Methods of Translating', trans. by Waltraud BARTSCHT, in: Theories of Translation: An Anthology of Essays from Dryden to Derrida, ed. by Rainer SCHULTE and John BIGUENET, Chicago 1992, p. 42. The original treatise *Methoden des Übersetzens* was composed by Schleiermacher in 1813.
12 Ross BRANN: The Compunctious Poet: Cultural Ambiguity and Hebrew Poetry in Muslim Spain, Baltimore/London 1991, p. 23.
13 Israel ABRAHAMS: Hebrew Ethical Wills, Philadelphia 1926, p. 69.

allowed foreign words and new constructions in the translation of philosophical texts from Arabic into Hebrew.

The translators of Provence adopted a method of translation that aimed to leave the writer alone and move the reader toward the writer. This method, which tended toward literalism, often preserved the syntax of the original Arabic even though the translators were writing for a non-arabized audience. When existing Hebrew terminology seemed insufficient to capture philosophical ideas, the Tibbonids readily adopted calques from Arabic terminology, which might have been as unintelligible to the Hebrew reader as the Arabic original. Apparently, it was the duty of the cultured reader to master the vocabulary and style of the new Hebrew. Moreover, their Hebrew sentence structure followed the syntax of Arabic to such an extent that Tibbonid Hebrew has been called a "completely new Hebrew language".[14] While offering the strength of being very 'accurate,' this method produces a new text that can be cumbersome to the Hebrew reader, especially one who is not trained in Arabic. Indeed, testimonies from the thirteenth century indicate that readers sometimes found the Tibbonid translations difficult.[15]

This tendency toward literalism may have grown out of a certain under-confidence the translators felt about the possibilities of Hebrew for expressing ideas emanating from Greco-Arabic philosophy. Judah Ibn Tibbon wrote in his introduction to Bahya Ibn Paquda's *Duties of the Heart,* "In Hebrew, we cannot always express our thoughts effectively, in a concise and pleasant style as in Arabic. For Arabic is capacious and eloquent...Hebrew, on the other hand, does not meet all of our needs".[16] Hebrew was viewed as a language that could be expanded upon, that needed to be expanded upon, if it was to become a reliable vehicle for philosophic and scientific discourse.

The translators of Provence generally translated technical terms with consistency, a point that facilitated mastery of the new terminology. Samuel Ibn Tibbon composed an "Explanation of Rare Words"[17] to accompany his translation of Maimonides' *Guide of the Perplexed* (only a few years after the translation's original publication) precisely to aid readers in understanding foreign words and also Hebrew words being used in new ways through metaphor and analogy. The foremost category of words he sought to explain consisted of "words that translators before me originated or that I originated entirely, such as 'pole' (קוטב) and

---

14 Ch. RABIN: The Linguistics of Translation, in: Aspects of Translation, ed. by A. D. BOOTH et al., London 1958, p. 133. See also IVRY: Philosophical Translations from the Arabic in Hebrew, p. 181.

15 Bernard SEPTIMUS: Hispano-Jewish Culture in Transition: The Career and Controversies of Ramah, Cambridge, Mass. 1982 p. 53. Meir Abulafia writes: "And the translator [Ibn Tibbon] translated his [Maimonides'] Arabic into an extremely difficult Hebrew. Nevertheless, I will reproduce that portion of his language that seems clear to me while changing other parts so as to make clear the notions that the author intended to convey, to the best of my ability."

16 Quoted in Irene ZWIEP: Mother of Reason and Revelation, p. 63, n. 152.

17 פירוש המלות הזרות is printed with most Hebrew editions of the *Guide;* see the edition by J. Ibn SHMUEL, revised edition, Jerusalem 1981. I understand the word זר here as equivalent to the Arabic *gharib* which can mean "rare" as well as "foreign."

'diameter' (קוטר) and others like them, which we borrowed from the tongue of the Arabs or from other languages".[18] One wonders how the non-Arabic speaking reader could have been expected to understand Tibbonid Hebrew during the years before the glossary's appearance.

The style that the Ibn Tibbons developed tended toward literalism despite the fact that they made theoretical statements expressing reservations about aping the original text too closely. Judah Ibn Tibbon wrote in his introduction to Ibn Paquda's *Duties of the Heart*:

> If it were possible for a translator to translate word for word, the danger [of distorting contents] could be avoided, although admittedly such a literal translation would be hard to understand – except for the great scholars who know the ways of the holy tongue. The language would not be pleasant nor would it conform with general usage; it would completely obscure the subject.[19]

While some readers have taken this as an anti-literalist statement, it actually captures a deep methodological ambivalence. Despite misgivings about creating a text that was not 'pleasant,' the foremost goal of translation was to avoid the distortion of content. This would be accomplished best by literal translation were it not for the ugliness of the language produced and the likelihood of obscuring comprehension. Nevertheless, literalism remained an ideal despite the difficulties it presented. The Ibn Tibbon's imagined an ideal audience of "great scholars who know the ways of the holy tongue" who would work laboriously through a text devoid of 'pleasantness' to uncover meaning. This statement is not a condemnation of literalism but calls for a balanced approach that prioritizes the preservation of meaning so long as a text that is too unnatural can be avoided. At the very least, we can see that Judah Ibn Tibbon maintained different standards for translations of technical texts and original poetic compositions; one need not be as vehement about avoiding foreign words and constructions in non-poetic compositions.

From the Iberian Peninsula, which had been and continued to be the epicenter of Hebrew belletristic activity, there survive a number of translations of belletristic and non-belletristic works from Arabic into Hebrew. The translations of belletristic works avoid using foreign constructions and vocabulary, something

---

18 Ibid, p. 12.

19 Quoted in ZWIEP: Mother of Reason and Revelation, p. 71. See also the widely quoted warning with which Maimonides admonished Samuel Ibn Tibbon: "Whoever wishes to translate from language to language and intends to translate one word with another and preserve also the order of the words and sentences will run into trouble and his translation will be dubious and exceedingly confused [...] It is not proper to do it this way. Rather, the one who translates from language to language must first understand the sense, and then express what is understood of the sense in the target language." Quoted in Steven HARVEY: Arabic Into Hebrew, p. 264. The original can be found in I. SHAILAT: Iggerot ha-Rambam, Jerusalem 1988, pp. 532–33. As Ivry points out, Samuel Ibn Tibbon did not fully follow Maimonides' advice, IVRY: Philosophical Translations, p. 181. Before Maimonides, Moses Ibn Ezra also expressed reservations toward literalism: "If you set out to transpose a matter from Arabic into Hebrew, take hold of its opinion and sense without converting its words literally, since not all languages are similar, as I have already explained. It is best if you explain it with the best word you find in [the target] language." (Kitab al-Muhadarah wa'l-mudhakara, ed. by A. HALKIN, Jerusalem 1975, p. 176).

that we recall was also central to Judah Ibn Tibbon's instructions concerning the composition of original poetry. Translators of belletristic writings probably saw their Hebrew creations as original works and therefore sought to preserve the literary ideals of al-Andalus, where poets had boasted over biblical Hebrew's innate beauty and holy status. The aim of translation was to move the writer toward the reader and leave the target language, which was idealized on a literary level, undisturbed. This meant the preservation of existing Hebrew vocabulary and syntax. This method is stated explicitly in Jacob Ben Elazar's introduction to his translation of *Kalila wa Dimna*:

> I translated this book from the Arabic language and changed some of its words so that it would be sweet, for it is not possible or reasonable to translate from one language to another letter by letter, for the word is spoiled once it leaves its language; its splendor and tumult decline. In places I subtract from their words and in [other] places I add to their words and set in all of its themes a "word aptly spoken" (Proverbs 25:11). When a translator does not adorn [a book] when producing it in his own language, the splendor of such a book will dwindle and its color will fade, its fountain will be parched and its spring dried up (Hosea 13:15). Therefore, every translator of a book from one language to another must adorn it and maintain its glory and not break his pledge.[20]

Of course, Ben Elazar was translating a belletristic text and recognized that such a text could be represented best by rendering it as a new text that was belletristic in its own right. In addition to conveying plot, the translator sought to convey literariness. Ben Elazar argued that the translator had not only the license but also the obligation to create a text that showcased the beauties and possibilities of Hebrew.

Belletristic translations serve different goals from Hebrew renderings of Judah Halevi's *Kuzari* or Maimonides' *Guide of the Perplexed*, wherein a loss of exact meaning could lead to gross misinterpretation. However, similar ideas about translation *are* expressed even in translations of non-belletristic texts from Christian Iberia. Translators exercised significant freedom in transferring any kind of text from Arabic into Hebrew. One fascinating example is Abraham Ibn Hasdai's translation of Abu Hamid al-Ghazzali's *Mizan al-'aml* (ميزان العمل), an ethical work dedicated to the Sufi life entitled *Me'oznei sedeq* (מאזני צדק) in Hebrew.[21]

---

20 Joseph DERENBOURG: Deux versions hébraïques du livre de Kalilah et Dimnāh, Paris 1881, p. 314. One should compare this with the note on translation by Dante in the *Convivio*, "Everyone should know that nothing that is bound by musical harmonies can be translated from its own language into another, without completely disrupting its sweetness and its harmonies. And it is for this reason that Homer was never translated from Greek into Latin, as were other texts that we have from the [Greeks]. And it is for this reason that the verses of the Psalms are without sweetness and harmony, because they were translated from Hebrew into Greek, and then into Latin, and in that first translation, all that sweetness disappeared." Quoted in Maria Rosa MENOCAL: Shards of Love: Exile and the Origins of the Lyric, Durham/London 1994, pp. 156–57.

21 Abu Hamid Muhammad AL-GHAZZALI: Mizan al-'amal, Cairo 1973; Me'oznei tzedeq, ed. by Y. GOLDENTAL, Leipzig 1839 [reprinted in Jerusalem 1975]. See the Arabic study by Ahmad SAHLAN: Kitab Mizan al-'amal li-Abi Hamid al-Ghazzali – al-tarjamah al-'ibriyya: me'oznei sedeq – al-Mizan bayna al-mafahim al-islamiyya wa'l-taqalid al-yahudiyya, in: Ghazâlî. La raison et le miracle, Paris 1987, pp. 93–117.

In the translator's introduction to the text, Ibn Hasdai apologizes for potentially cumbersome locutions:

> The language from which the translator translates is often clear to the translator though the matter itself becomes cumbersome in the target language. Because the translator knows the source language and because [the matter's] secrets and stores are apparent to him, he does not sense the difficulty of the target language and its construction. He imagines that everything that is clear to him will be clear to all who see it...I therefore implore all who read this book that when he reads something difficult to understand and cumbersome to listen to that he will not hasten to disapprove of it.[22]

Ibn Hasdai was very conscious of the difficulties of translation and recognized that translators were often more literal than they necessarily intended to be. He was not espousing the virtues of literal translation but was recognizing that literality is difficult to avoid. He was more than comfortable changing the exact wording of the original text. Rhyming Arabic proverbs are replaced with rhyming proverbs in Hebrew.[23] Most conspicuously, the translator systematically tried to purge the text of Islamic sources such as Qur'an and hadith:

> Although [al-Ghazzali] was a great sage who inclined toward philosophy, he would support his proofs and demonstrations.... [with texts] of their faith and the legends (הגדות, *hadith?*) that are found among their wise men. It is from the weakness of their books and the feebleness of their writings that they bring proofs for their claims, to strengthen and support their opinions. *A fortiori* those whose words are smelted from gold, sweeter than honey, built and founded upon the line of truth, their source a spring of living water, their proofs are more pure and clean, stronger and more truthful. Therefore I decided to supply, according to my ability, words similar to the original from our holy books so that I will go in the path of the author and not depart from his course, and not veer to the right or the left.[24]

Ibn Hasdai tried to recreate *Mizan al-'amal* as a Jewish text. At stake was more than the beauty of the target text produced, although Ibn Hasdai was concerned with that as well. On an ideological level, the Jewish translator had to consider the effect of conveying an Islamic text for a Jewish audience. Translating works by non-Jewish authors presented a set of problems absent when translating works by Jews. Would conveying proof texts for arguments from "their books" not require an implicit acceptance of the Islamic texts' authority? Ibn Hasdai's formulation is not only a statement of Jewish chauvinism but also implies a curious theory of translation: fidelity to the original intent of the author ("I will go in the path of the author") is to be accomplished by *not* translating the original text literally. By substituting 'strong' sources for 'weak' ones, Ibn Hasdai claims to improve upon the work of al-Ghazzali. He supplies what al-Ghazzali would have said had he only been born into the true faith. Even though *Mizan al-'amal* was not a belle-

---

22 Me'oznei tzedeq, p. 4.
23 One proverb is translated with a verse from a poem by Samuel ha-Nagid; see SAHLAN: Kitab Mizan al-'aml, p. 103.
24 Me'oznei tzedeq, p. 4. See also my article: The Rendering of Qur'anic Quotations in Hebrew Translations of Islamic Texts, in: Jewish Quarterly Review 96,3 (2006), pp. 336–58.

tristic text per se, Ibn Hasdai recognized that it too possessed literary dimensions that presented problems for the ideologically minded translator.

Before Ibn Hasdai, Judah al-Harizi, who was a zealous champion of Hebrew's eloquence, undertook translations of Maimonides' legal and philosophical works. He prefaced his translation to the *Commentary on the Mishnah* with an exposition on translation method:

> This is the method of translation toward which I incline and the way upon which I travel. In most cases I translate word for word although I strive to comprehend the topic first; I do not cease pursuing it and its young[25] on the road until [I reach] the place where its tent had been formerly (Genesis 13:3). When I find a lone Arabic word that rebels against me,[26] taking the road of rebellion like a fleeing maidservant, the warriors of my thought pursue it to the point of collapse and all its pursuers reach it in straits. And when I encounter a difficult word in Hebrew, I say it another way; I remove it from its mistress and give its majesty to her friend who is better than she. Every Arabic word I wish to express, I come up with three or four [in Hebrew], the best of which I use; I choose their course and preside over them (Job 29:25). I glean and snatch the sweetest words from the Holy Tongue, I pick a tender twig from the tip of its crown so that the words may enter the heart of the listener and so that they will be straightforward to the one who understands. The wise men of every nation agree that one cannot translate a book until he knows three things: the secret of the language from whose borders he is translating (i.e. the language he is translating from), the secret of the language into which he is translating, and the secret of the wisdom whose words he is explaining. By these three matters the string of rhetorical language will enchant, and the threefold cord is not easily broken.[27]

This formulation, written with a high degree of literary flair, captures the attitude toward Hebrew al-Harizi expresses elsewhere, as in the introduction to his *Book of Tahkemoni*. Hebrew writing, even when rendering a foreign text, must be smooth, rich and eloquent, sweet and enchanting to the ears of the listener. Although al-Harizi gives a polite nod to the ideal of accurate, literal translation ("I translate word for word"), he is also concerned with choosing the "sweetest words" in the target language so that they might "enter the heart of the listener". Also implicit in al-Harizi's statement is a polemic concerning Hebrew's superiority over Arabic. Arabic words act rebelliously like a "fleeing maidservant", which is a veiled reference to Hagar, the matriarch of Muslims, reminding the reader of Abraham's preference for Sarah, the matriarch of the Jews. For every Arabic word, the translator can choose among "three or four" Hebrew words, implying that Hebrew is at least as rich as Arabic.

Unfortunately, al-Harizi did not leave as extensive an excursus on method in his introduction to the translation of the *Guide of the Perplexed*; one imagines that he maintained similar ideals though the philosophical content of the work may have presented unique difficulties. Al-Harizi recognized that he was repeating a function already performed by Samuel Ibn Tibbon; he states that noblemen of Provence, who probably had difficulty understanding Ibn Tibbon's Hebrew,

---

25 I.e., its details.
26 I.e., that is difficult for me to translate.
27 M.D. RABINOVITZ: Rabeinu Moshe ben Maimon: haqdamot le-ferush ha-mishnah, Jerusalem 1961, pp. 4f.

commissioned him to write a new translation in "plain and pure words" (וצחים מילים פשוטים).[28] Al-Harizi claimed not to indulge in "revealing any of the book's secrets or in interpreting its themes", which he believed to be problematic aspects of Ibn Tibbon's translation. Rather, he intended on limiting himself to "ordering [the book's] themes as one who paves a highway with stones".[29]

Before Ibn Tibbon wrote his glossary of rare terms in the *Guide*, al-Harizi included a glossary (called "The Explanation of Every Rare Word Written in This Book" פירוש כל מילה זרה הכתובה בספר הזה) along with his translation.[30] In this glossary, al-Harizi never admits that words he chooses are borrowed from Arabic, even though some of them certainly are. While al-Harizi repeatedly uses the root *gshm* (גשם, a calque of the Arabic *jsm*, جسم, "body", popular in Tibbonid translations) to mean "corporeal", he defends its usage in the glossary by explaining its "biblical" origin: "*gashmut 'o hagshama* (גשמות או הגשמה) – its meaning is to explain that the Creator does not have a body, as in '*ve-geshem yegaddel*' (וגשם ינדל, Isaiah 44:14), where it means 'body'." However, al-Harizi's interpretation of *geshem* in the biblical verse is quite forced; commentators generally agree that it means "rain". Interestingly, Ibn Tibbon identifies a real biblical root for the word, from the Aramaic of Daniel 4:30, *gishmei yistab'a* (גשמי יצטבע), "his body was drenched"), but nonetheless goes on to add: "and because it is similar to the [word in the] Arabic language, which is *jism*, I use it."[31] Thus al-Harizi uses the same word as Ibn Tibbon but suggests that he allows it on the basis of its "biblical" precedent. He implies that the word is in conformity with linguistic purity.

Al-Harizi's tendency to simplify and remain true to Hebrew purity often reveals itself. When he encountered the Arabic term for "equator" (*mu'addil al-nahar*, מערל אלנהאר,[32] literally the "equalizer of day"), Ibn Tibbon used the neologism "equalizing line" (הקו השוה), explaining the term in his glossary). In contrast, al-Harizi opted for a roundabout locution within the text: "the line that divides day into two equal parts" (הקו החולק היום לשני חלקים שוים).[33] Also, al-Harizi translates the sentence "the motions of these stars is one and the same – all of these spheres being situated on the same poles (*aqtab*, אקטאב)" as "[these stars'] motions are one and the same – all of these spheres are on the same *nails* (*masmerim*, מסמרים)", using an existing Hebrew word in an novel way.[34] The term *masmerim* is explained in al-Harizi's glossary as the "two points on either side of a circle; when it rotates, it rests on them so that it will not move [off course] or fall".[35] Translating

---

28 Moses Ben Maimon: Sefer moreh nevukhim, trans. by Judah al-Harizi, ed. by S. Sheyer and S. Munk, Jerusalem 1953, p. 9.
29 Ibid., pp. 9–10.
30 Samuel Ibn Tibbon concedes that al-Harizi preceded him in including a glossary, even though al-Harizi wrote his translation after Ibn Tibbon.
31 Under the root *guf*, see ed. Ibn Shmuel: Guide, pp. 38–9.
32 Following Maimonides' original, I use Hebrew characters.
33 Ben Maimon: Moreh nevukhim, trans. by al-Harizi, 1:423.
34 The term *masmerim* can also be found in al-Harizi's glossary.
35 Ben Maimon: Moreh nevukhim, trans. by al-Harizi, 1:17.

"poles" as "nails" has strengths and weaknesses. Nails are not poles and the reader, although perhaps getting the gist of the sentence, is missing the exact nuance of the word. On the other hand, al-Harizi is "moving the writer toward the reader", using a term the reader already knows, and following a perhaps quixotic ideal of Hebrew purity.

Why do we find different ideologies of translation espoused in Iberia and in Provence? Although a definitive answer may be far off, some ideas are worth considering. It is somewhat ironic that the more Arabic-sounding text was produced in the environment where Arabic was less well known. The Jews of Christian Iberia, especially in Toledo, existed in an environment that was still thoroughly arabized. Although Muslims were reduced to minority status in Christian Iberia, Jews remained aware of Muslim claims of Arabic's perfection and the Quran's inimitability; Hebrew remained caught in a lingering polemic with Arabic wherein the Bible competed with the Qur'an for status as God's revealed speech. Beyond mere literary preference, the ideal of Hebrew purity in Iberia was related to interreligious polemic, a point that is explicit in the writings of al-Harizi.

In Provence, where Jews were not in contact with a competing Muslim population (even if translators were aware of Islamic doctrines), the need to strip a text of its Arabic feel was less pressing. In fact, writing a register of Hebrew that seemed close to Arabic may have created the impression of having a direct encounter with the original work. The Hebrew text offered a peculiar foreignness that may have appealed to non-arabized readers because it felt as though they were getting the 'real thing.' To give a modern parallel, a German text rendered into short and noncomplex English sentences does not feel as authentic as one that preserves the syntax of the original text, however awkward in English; only through sentences that span many lines rife with subordinate clauses does the English reader feel that he is hearing the voice of the original author. In Provence, the novelty of scientific and philosophical subjects was mirrored in the novelty and complexity of Tibbonid Hebrew. A text that read easily in Hebrew might have raised suspicions of distortion and inauthenticity.

Practice

So far I have looked at theoretical statements about translation method offered by Iberian and Provençal translators and highlighted some examples of their methods in practice. Iberian translators called for Hebrew purity while the Provençal translators, despite some ambivalence, leaned toward literalism. More important than the ideological statements espoused by translators in the introductions to their books are the translation choices they actually make on the page. There is sometimes a tension between theory and practice; in fact, theoretical statements of method are often made forcefully because the mechanics of translation press translators to veer from their intended practices. Despite promises to purge al-Ghazzali of Islamic references, Abraham Ibn Hasdai leaves many intact.[36] Despite al-Harizi's dedication to Hebrew purity, we also find a deep dependence on Arabic calques. Although the Ibn Tibbons privileged meaning over style, their translations sometimes select vague Hebrew terminology when the Arabic is precise while the mimicry of Arabic syntax sometimes serves to obscure meaning rather than preserve it.

In practice, no translator is a strict literalist or a free renderer; the reader cannot be moved toward the writer entirely nor *vice versa*. Literality and free rendering are only theoretical ends of a spectrum; any real translation must fall somewhere in the middle. Juxtaposing Samuel Ibn Tibbon's and Judah al-Harizi's translations of a typical passage from Maimonides' *Guide of the Perplexed* will illustrate the actual position of each translator on the this spectrum.[37] This excerpt is from 1:31 (1:30 in al-Harizi's numbering):

Moses Maimonides[38]

Know that the human intellect has objects of apprehension (*madārik*, מדארך) within its power (*quwwa*, קוה) and its nature (*tabi'a*, טביעה) to apprehend. Yet there are in existence (*al-wujūd*, אלוגוד) existing things (*mawjūdāt*, מונ'ודראת) and matters that are not within its nature to apprehend through any means or any cause; rather (*bal*, בל), the gates of apprehending them are shut before it. There are in existence matters that it apprehends in one state (*hāla*, האלה) but is ignorant of in other states. Being something that apprehends does not require that it apprehend everything, just as the senses (*hawwās*, חואס) have apprehensions though they cannot (*laysa laha*, ליס להא) apprehend them from any distance.

Samuel Ibn Tibbon[39]

Know that the human intellect has objects of apprehension (*hasagot*, השגות) within its power (*koah*, כוח) and nature (*teva'*, בע) to apprehend. Yet there are in existence (*mesi'ut*, מציאות) existing things (*nimsa'ot*, נמצאות) and matters that are not within its nature to apprehend through any means or cause; rather (*aval*, אבל), the gates of apprehending them are shut before it. There are in existence things of which it apprehends one matter ('*inyan*, ענין) but is ignorant in other matters. Being something that apprehends does not require that it apprehend everything, just as the senses (*hushim*, חושים) have apprehensions but do not (*ve-lo*, ולא) apprehend them from any distance.

---

36 Ibn Hasdai only uses verse substitution some of the time; otherwise he simply translates Qur'an verses and hadith literally.

37 In some cases, of course, differences in terminology between the two translations are motivated by different philosophical interpretations. For example, al-Harizi translates Maimonides' term for "providence," *raqaba* as *shemira*, "guarding," whereas Ibn Tibbon translates it as *hashgaha*, "overseeing." Ibn Tibbon's choice affirms his interpretation of Maimonides' theory of providence (and his own theory) as denying divine intervention. See Dov SCHWARTZ: The Debate over Maimonides' Theory of Providence in Thirteenth-Century Jewish Philosophy, in: Jewish Studies Quarterly 2 (1995), pp. 185–96.

38 Moshe Ben MAIMON: Dalalat al-ha'irin, ed. by Solomon MUNK, Jerusalem 1929, pp. 42ff.

39 Ed. by J. Even SHMUEL: Guide, p. 56.

Judah al-Harizi[40]

Know that the human intellect has objects of apprehension (*hasagot*, השגות) that it can apprehend with its power (*koah,* כוח) and its nature (*teva',* טבע). Yet there are in the world (*ba-'olam,*
בעולם) existing things (*nimsa'ot,* נמצאות) and matters that are not within his power and nature
to apprehend through any means or any cause because (*ki,* כי) the gates of apprehending them
are shut before it. There are in the world things of which it apprehends certain matters ('*inyanim
meyuhadim,* עניינים מיוחדים) [only]. [Just] because it is something that apprehends does not
require that it apprehend everything, just as the senses (*regashim,* רגשים) have apprehensions
though it is not in their power ('*ein be-koham,* אין בכוחם) to apprehend those apprehensions
from any distance.

The general similarity between al-Harizi's and Ibn Tibbon's versions is apparent.
In many cases, al-Harizi uses the same terminology as Ibn Tibbon. Both translators translate the Arabic terms *quwwa* (קוה), "power", and *tabi'a* (טביעה), "nature",
with *koah* (כוח, which sounds somewhat like *quwwa*) and *teva'* (טבע, which is a
cognate of the Arabic *tabi'a*); *koah* is a word with Hebrew precedent while *teva'* is
a neologism.[41] In other cases, al-Harizi avoids terms of Arabic origin common in
Ibn Tibbon's translation. Ibn Tibbon translates Arabic words into Hebrew cognates based on rare precedents, such as his translation of *hawwas* (הואס) as *hushim*
(חושים), which could have been based on the usage of the root *hwsh* in Ecclesiastes 2:25. Wishing to avoid confusion, al-Harizi translates the term as *regashim*
(רגשים), a more common word for "feelings", though less precise than *hushim*
since it also means "emotions". Al-Harizi's choice can be explained in part by
his patrons' request for a translation in "pure and simple words"; otherwise, one
expects that he would have followed Ibn Tibbon's expansion of an existing root,
especially one with biblical precedent. Perhaps the best explanation is that al-
Harizi did not want his Hebrew to sound too much like Arabic. Also, whereas Ibn
Tibbon uses a Hebrew neologism for "existence" (*mesi'ut,* מציאות, from the root
ms', "to find", imitating the Arabic *wujud,* וג׳וד, from the root *wjd,* "to find"), al-
Harizi opts for the simpler term *'olam* עולם, "universe, world", following Rabbinic
usage. This seems to be consistent with al-Harizi's method. However, al-Harizi
does seem comfortable with the word *nimsa'ot* (נמצאות) for "existing things". Ultimately, he is ambivalent toward neologisms.

Ibn Tibbon is largely consistent in preserving the syntax of the Arabic original.
Although the reader can sense Arabic pulsing beneath the surface of Ibn Tibbon's
and al-Harizi's Hebrew, its presence is more pronounced in Ibn Tibbon's. Ibn Tibbon is consistent in translating Maimonides' *bal* (בל), "rather" or possibly "moreover", with the Hebrew cognate *aval* (אבל) whereas al-Harizi freely substitutes the
word *ki* (כי), "because". In the final section of the passage, Ibn Tibbon translates
the idiomatic *laysa laha* (ליס להא), "they cannot" (literally "it is not to them") with

---

40 Ben MAIMON: Moreh nevukhim, trans. Al-Harizi, 1:116.
41 In its most basic meaning, the root *tb'* means to "make an imprint" in both Hebrew and Arabic.
Arabic adopted the root to indicate "nature" early on and Ibn Tibbon adopted it in Hebrew. Al-
Harizi may have been comfortable with it because it conceivably could have been derived from the
existing Hebrew root.

the morphologically approximate *ve-lo* (ולא), even though this renders the phrase "they do not" rather than "they cannot". Al-Harizi, on the other hand, moves further from the morphology of the original and translates idiomatically, *'ein be-koham* (אין בכוחם), "it is not in their power"; in this instance, paraphrase serves as a better means of preserving meaning. Al-Harizi's translation of the last sentence, "There are in the world things of which it apprehends certain matters (*'inyanim meyuhadim*, ענינים מיוחדים) [only]", is also a loose paraphrase.

One cannot say, however, that the Ibn Tibbons were complete literalists who had no regard for the natural inflections or indigenous vocabulary of Hebrew. One can, of course, imagine a Hebrew text that is even more slavish than those produced by the Ibn Tibbon family; Arabic syntax might have been followed to such an extent that it made the Hebrew even more unnatural. Greater slavishness was the characteristic of some disfavored translations from Greek into Arabic and also of Ladino translations of the Bible.[42] Despite a certain openness toward foreign vocabulary, which guarantees accuracy provided the word is explained, we find a tendency to use existing Hebrew words whenever possible. Sometimes this occurs at the expense of meaning, as in the final sentence in the example above. Ibn Tibbon translates the Arabic "state" (*hala*, האלה) with the vague and imprecise Hebrew word "matter" (*'inyan,* ענין). One wonders why he did not employ a cognate neologism.

An interesting case surfaces in Samuel's "Explanation of Rare Words" concerning the translation of the Arabic word *kihana* (كهانة, "divination"), which the translator defines as the "power to tell the future through a means other than prophecy". When he first translated the *Guide,* Samuel originated a Hebrew cognate *kahun* (כהון) explaining:

> I took the Arabic word because I did not know a name for it in our language. About ten years after I translated the *Guide of the Perplexed* an epistle reached me that the master (i.e. Maimonides) had sent to the communities of Yemen ....And in that letter I understood the masters' intention that the word *qesem* (קסם) in our language is the name for this and the one who possesses it is a *qosem* (קוסם).[43]

Samuel urges readers to change the word in their copies of the text and explains: "when a word exists in our language, it is inappropriate to take from a foreign language, unless it is for a known reason."[44] Using existing words could not be as 'accurate' since such words were burdened with histories and associations to which the translator was bound. Neologisms offered the translator free reign in assigning meaning. Still, the existing Hebrew term was preferable in this case even though it could never be as precise as the Arabic cognate. Purity could not be sacrificed for accuracy in all instances. Ibn Tibbon recognized that if neologisms were employed too liberally, the language produced would cease to be Hebrew.

---

42 On Greek into Arabic, see HARVEY: Arabic into Hebrew, p. 264 and 276 n. 24; on Ladino, see David M. BUNIS: The Language of the Sephardim: A Historical Overview, in: The Sephardi Legacy, ed. by Haim BEINART, Jerusalem 1992, vol. 2, pp. 399–422.
43 Samuel Ibn Tibbon: Perush ha-milot ha-zarot, in J. Even SHMUEL: Guide, p. 58.
44 Ibid.

The Ibn Tibbons and their successors were constantly reworking and improving upon the new Hebrew within bounds that ultimately struck a practical balance between literalism and free rendering. It is this balance and a willingness to change that allowed Hebrew to endure as a language of science and philosophy. The Provençal translators were visionary pragmatists who did not fear that Hebrew's transformation would result in a loss of status for the Jewish people. Still, they tried to limit Hebrew's transformation to the extent that meaning could also be preserved.

Iberian translators maintained Hebrew purity as an ideal through restrained word selection and paraphrase. However, even al-Harizi did not always adhere to his ostensible dedication to Hebrew purity and often used calques from Arabic. The method of translation espoused by him was forced to break down since Hebrew simply lacked sufficient vocabulary to capture Maimonides' Arabic. Two words al-Harizi includes in his glossary are *qotev* (קוטב, "pole") and *qoter* (קוטר, "diameter"), both of which, we have seen, derive from Arabic and appear in Ibn Tibbon's translation and glossary.[45] Thus, even though al-Harizi used the term "nails" for "poles" in some instances, he used the Arabic calque in others. Al-Harizi did not mention the words' Arabic origin even though it may have been apparent to educated readers. The actual text produced by al-Harizi shows that he did, at times, opt to render the text 'accurately' at the expense of purity. In the end, al-Harizi's method was not entirely consistent, a point which partially explains why his version of the *Guide* never became a part of the Jewish canon.[46]

Over twenty years ago, Bernard Septimus raised the question: "Can we speak of a Spanish versus Provençal approach to translation?"[47] Today I believe we can. For all of our translators, Hebrew was the new vessel that could contain Arabic and Judeo-Arabic thought. Members of the Ibn Tibbon family infused Hebrew with some of the feel of Arabic and thus created the sense that Hebrew was capable of such a daunting task. Their translations offered the promise that mastery of the new vocabulary and foreign syntax was tantamount to an unmediated encounter with great works of the past. Interestingly, al-Harizi, who composed original Arabic poetry and prose and was exceedingly dedicated to Arabic as a living literary language, was less interested in letting the Arabic beneath his Hebrew show through.[48] For al-Harizi, Hebrew and Arabic were separate spheres and should remain so. His translation choices were fueled by a need for simplicity and an ideological commitment to Hebrew purity. Despite the divergence in translation

---

45 Al-Harizi: Perush kol milah zarah, in Ben Maimon: Moreh nevukhim, trans. by al-Harizi, p. 19.

46 It did, however, become the basis of the translations of the *Guide* into European languages. The first translation of the *Guide* into Latin, by Augustinus Justinianus (Paris 1520), was made from al-Harizi's translation. Ibn Tibbon's version was translated into Latin by J. Buxtorf (Basel 1629).

47 SEPTIMUS: Hispano-Jewish Culture in Transition, p. 145, n. 112.

48 On al-Harizi's Arabic compositions, see Joseph SADAN: Rabbi yehudah al-harizi ke-somet tarbuti: biografiyah 'aravit shel yoser yehudi be-'einei mizrahan, in: Pe'amim 68 (1996), pp. 18–67; BLAU, Joshua/YAHALOM, Joseph: Mas'e yehudah, hamishah pirke masa' mehurazim le-al-harizi, Jerusalem 2002.

methods that grew out of the ideologies and anxieties of the contrasting social climates of Iberia and Provence, methodological differences were sometimes subsumed beneath ambivalence and the realities of translation practice.

During the centuries of translation from Arabic and Judeo-Arabic into Hebrew, Hebrew experienced birth pangs seldom paralleled in the history of a language. Competing translation styles reflect an intellectual enterprise struggling to reach maturity. The arabization of Hebrew is deeply felt in all of the translations discussed here because of neologisms based on Arabic vocabulary and the shifting meaning of existing Hebrew roots. In Iberia, the dependence on Arabic was not admitted; in Provence, it was embraced. In both cases, it was only through the process of subduing Hagar that Sarah became so fertile.

Martha Keil

„Und wenn sie die Heilige Sprache nicht verstehen..." Versöhnungs- und Bußrituale deutscher Jüdinnen und Juden im Spätmittelalter

Dieser Beitrag sucht nach sprachlichen Schnittstellen im religiösen und, meist nicht trennbar, sozio-kulturellen Leben der aschkenasischen Jüdinnen und Juden des Spätmittelalters. Übersetzungen liturgischer Texte in die Landessprache kamen auf Grund mangelnder Hebräischkenntnisse neben Männern der Unterschicht vor allem Frauen zu Gute, selbst jenen aus Elitefamilien. Daher soll der Geschlechteraspekt sowohl im kleineren Abschnitt zum synagogalen Gottesdienst als auch im umfangreicheren über Versöhnungs- und Bußrituale immer mitbedacht werden. Ein weiterer verbindender roter Faden soll das mittelalterliche Ehrkonzept sein, das bei Juden wie bei Christen eine bedeutende Kategorie der Lebens- und Rangordnungen darstellte.[1] Auch der Eid, für dessen Leistung die Ehrbarkeit Voraussetzung war, wäre in diesen Kontext einzuordnen.[2] Wenn auch auf dieses komplexe Thema hier nicht eingegangen werden kann, ist doch festzuhalten, dass Juden prinzipiell auch in der christlichen Rangordnung der Kategorie der ‚ehrbaren Leute' angehörten.

---

1   Siehe SCHEYHING, Robert: Ehre, in: Handwörterbuch zur deutschen Rechtsgeschichte, Bd. 1 (1971), Sp. 846–849 sowie ALTHOFF, Gerd: Compositio. Wiederherstellung verletzter Ehre im Rahmen gütlicher Konfliktbeendigung, in: SCHREINER, Klaus/SCHWERHOFF, Gerd (Hg.): Verletzte Ehre. Ehrkonflikte in Gesellschaften des Mittelalters und der Frühen Neuzeit, Köln/Weimar/Wien 1995, S. 63–76, S. 63.

2   Zum Eid im jüdischen Recht siehe ZIMMER, Eric: Harmony and Discord. An Analysis of the Dicline of Jewish Self-Government in 15th Century Central Europe, New York 1970, S. 30–66. Zum Eid von Juden bei christlichen Gerichten siehe KISCH, Guido: Studien zur Geschichte des Judeneides im Mittelalter, in: KISCH, Guido: Forschungen zur Rechts- und Sozialgeschichte der Juden in Deutschland während des Mittelalters, Bd. 1, Sigmaringen 1978, S. 137–165; SCHMIDT-WIEGAND, Ruth: Eid und Gelöbnis. Formel und Formula im mittelalterlichen Recht, in: CLASSEN, Peter (Hg.): Recht und Schrift im Mittelalter (Vorträge und Forschungen 23), Sigmaringen 1977, S. 55–90; VON VOLTELINI, Hans: Der Wiener und der Kremser Judeneid (Mitteilungen des Vereins für Geschichte der Stadt Wien 12), Wien 1932, S. 64–70; RÖLL, Walter: Zu den Judeneiden an der Schwelle der Neuzeit, in: HAVERKAMP, Alfred (Hg.): Zur Geschichte der Juden in Deutschland des späten Mittelalter und der frühen Neuzeit, Stuttgart 1981, S. 163–204; TOCH, Michael: Mit der Hand auf der Tora: Disziplinierung als internes und externes Problem in den jüdischen Gemeinden des Spätmittelalters, in: JARITZ, Gerhard (Hg.): Disziplinierung und Sachkultur in Mittelalter und früher Neuzeit, Wien 1998, S. 155–168.

Heilige Sprache und Landessprache im Gottesdienst

Unangefochten war das Hebräische, die Heilige Sprache (*leschon ha-kodesch*), die Sprache der Synagoge: Toralesung, Prophetenabschnitt, Gebete und liturgische Dichtungen wie Klage- und Bußlieder wurden in Hebräisch oder Aramäisch verfasst, kommentiert und vorgetragen. Übersetzungen der Bibel in die Landessprache hatten jedoch ebenfalls eine lange Tradition, angefangen von den *Targumim* – Übersetzungen – des Onkelos ins Aramäische und des Aquila ins Griechische, beide aus dem 2. Jahrhundert. Vermutlich entwickelten sich aus diesen *Targumim*, welche eher Paraphrasen und Exegesen als Übersetzungen des biblischen Textes waren, die landessprachlichen Predigten an auserwählten Schabbatot und Feiertagen.[3] Sie dienten einerseits zur Vermittlung der Schrift an Ungebildete, Frauen und Kinder, andererseits gaben sie den Gelehrten Gelegenheit, ihre Gemeinde zu moralischem und ethischem Verhalten zu ermahnen, und – ein nicht zu unterschätzender Faktor der Ehre und des Ansehens – ihre Gelehrsamkeit öffentlich zu demonstrieren. Erhalten sind diese Predigten, *Draschot*, allerdings nur in ihrer hebräischen Niederschrift, die vermutlich von ihrer ursprünglichen mündlichen Fassung mehr oder weniger abweicht. Der Unterhaltungswert durch Gleichnisse, Lehrgeschichten und dramatische Darbietungen unter Einsatz von Stimme, Mimik und Gestik des begabten Predigers, *Darschan*, erschließt sich zu unserem Leidwesen nicht mehr. Doch die Anweisung von Rabbi Eleasar ben Jehuda von Worms (ca. 1165–1230), lässt auf einen hohen Anspruch an die Predigten im deutschen Mittelalter schließen: „Man muss am Schabbat in Worten wertvoller als Gold predigen." Jedoch hatte sich der *Darschan* in Rücksicht auf den Bildungsgrad und die intellektuellen Möglichkeiten seines Publikums verständlich zu machen, wozu auch die Verwendung der Landessprache beitrug.[4]

Frauen konnten nur in Ausnahmefällen Hebräisch verstehen und Segenssprüche und Gebete in dieser Sprache rezitieren. Dulce von Worms, die Frau des erwähnten Rabbiners Eleasar ben Jehuda – sie wurde 1196 bei einem Raubüberfall ermordet – war vermutlich eine solche hochgerühmte Ausnahme: Im Trauergedicht an seine ermordete Frau, einem gereimten Kommentar auf das „Lob der starken Frau" („Eschet Chail", Prov. 31, 10–31), pries Eleasar in euphorischer Weise die Tugenden seiner *eschet chail* und hob ihre Gelehrsamkeit hervor: „In allen Städten lehrte sie Frauen und machte ihre Gesänge lieblich. [...] Die Liturgie der Morgen- und Abendgebete befolgte sie." In welcher Sprache Dulce betete und

---

3 STEMBERGER, Günter: Das klassische Judentum. Kultur und Geschichte der rabbinischen Zeit (70 n. Chr. bis 1040 n. Chr.), München 1979, S. 102f. und ZUNZ, Leopold: Die gottesdienstlichen Vorträge der Juden historisch entwickelt. Ein Beitrag zur Altertumskunde und biblischen Kritik, zur Literatur- und Religionsgeschichte, Frankfurt a. M. 1892 (ND Hildesheim 1966), S. 439.
4 Zur Entwicklung der Predigt in der jüdischen Antike siehe STEMBERGER, ibid. (Anm. 3), S. 104–107, zum Mittelalter siehe DAN, Joseph: Homiletic Literature, in: Encyclopaedia Judaica, Bd. 8 (1971), Sp. 946–955.

ob sie landessprachliche oder hebräische Gebete unterrichtete, erläuterte Eleasar leider nicht näher.[5]

Dulce verdankte ihre Bildung ihrer privilegierten Herkunft: Ihr Vater Elieser ben Jakob war *Chasan* (Vorsänger) von Mainz, schon im Elternhaus wurde sie also mit liturgischen Texten vertraut gemacht, auch wenn sie vielleicht nur ‚passiv', ohne absichtliche Unterweisung, das Beten und Üben des Vaters hörte. Vermutlich unterrichtete ihr Vater auch in seinem Haus, sodass sie eine ähnliche Bildung, wenn auch nicht Ausbildung, wie die männlichen Schüler im Haushalt genießen konnte. Außerordentliche Frömmigkeit und Gelehrsamkeit waren in einem solchen jüdischen Elitehaus ohnehin selbstverständlich. 1180 heiratete Dulce den Rabbiner, Poeten und Mystiker Eleasar ben Jehuda, einen der berühmtesten Gelehrten seiner Zeit, der ab 1190 in Worms eine große *Jeschiwa* unterhielt.[6]

Im Allgemeinen waren sich die rabbinischen Autoritäten einig, dass Frauen des Hebräischen nicht mächtig waren: „Frauen verstehen die Heilige Sprache nicht", stellte der Wiener Rabbiner Izchak Or Sarua (gest. um 1250) lakonisch fest.[7] Frauen standen in dieser Hinsicht mit Ungebildeten auf einer Stufe, doch wurde die Unkenntnis des Hebräischen nicht unbedingt als ein Mangel an Frömmigkeit oder religiöser Hingabe aufgefasst, wie der Verfasser des *Sefer Chassidim* (1. Viertel des 13. Jahrhunderts) klarstellt:

> Wenn jemand zu mir kommt, der die hebräische Sprache nicht kann, und er ist gottesfürchtig […] oder wenn zu mir eine Frau kommt, sage ich ihnen, dass sie die Gebete in der Sprache lernen sollen, die sie verstehen, denn beim Gebet zählt nur das Herzensverständnis. Und wenn das Herz nicht weiß, was aus seinem Mund kommt, was soll das nützen? Daher ist es gut, wenn jeder in der Sprache betet, die er versteht.[8]

Diese Höherschätzung der inneren Einstellung gegenüber einem liturgisch korrekten Lippengebet ist typisch für den Pietismus der *Chasside Aschkenas*, deren elitärer Gruppe auch Eleasar von Worms angehörte. Doch dürfen solche auf den ersten Blick geschlechtsneutralen Aussagen nicht darüber hinwegtäuschen, dass das Hebräische der Kommunikationsträger nicht nur des religiösen Lebens, sondern aller damit zusammenhängenden gesellschaftlichen Aspekte war: Zur Toralesung aufgerufen zu werden, bedeutete nicht nur Zurschaustellung von Bildung und Frömmigkeit, sondern brachte Ehre und Ansehen am Ort der Öffentlichkeit

---

5 Die Elegie auf Dulce ist ediert in: HABERMAN, Abraham: Sefer Gserot Aschkenas we-Zarfat, Jerusalem 1945, S. 164–167 und ins Englische übersetzt von BASKIN, Judith: Dolce of Worms: The Lives and Deaths of an Exemplary Medieval Jewish Woman and her Daughters, in: FINE, Lawrence (Hg.): Judaism in Practice. From the Middle Ages through the Early Modern Period, Princeton 2001, S. 429–437, S. 434–437.

6 Siehe DAN, Joseph: Eleazar ben Judah of Worms, in: Encyclopaedia Judaica, Bd. 6 (1971), Sp. 592–594.

7 Izchak bar Mosche: Sefer Or Sarua, ed. von Izchak HIRSCHENSOHN, Jerusalem 1976, Teil I, S. 58, Nr. 186.

8 Sefer Chassidim (Druck Bologna), ed. von Reuven MARGALIOT, Jerusalem 1969–1970, S. 394, Nr. 588.

schlechthin, der Synagoge.[9] Der prinzipielle Ausschluss der Frauen von der Toralesung verringerte die Möglichkeit der öffentlichen Ehrung schon von vornher-
ein auf Grund ihrer Geschlechtszugehörigkeit, an der auch die Beherrschung des
Hebräischen nichts geändert hätte.[10]

Neben der Predigt wurden in manchen Gemeinden auch die *Parascha*
(Wochenabschnitt der Tora), die *Haftara* (Prophetenabschnitt) und die fünf
Megillot[11] übersetzt, wie uns ein Festtagsgebetbuch, der *Machsor Vitry* des Simcha
von Speyer aus dem 12. Jahrhundert, berichtet:

> Es gibt Leute, welche die Klagelieder am Abend lesen, und es gibt welche, die sie bis zum Mor-
> gen nach der Toralesung hinauszögern, denn nach der Tora steht einer auf und sein Haupt ist
> in Staub gehüllt, seine Kleider sind geflickt und er liest mit Weinen und Heulen. Wenn er es
> übersetzen kann, ist es gut, und wenn nicht, gibt man es jemandem, der es gut übersetzen kann,
> damit der Rest des (ungebildeten) Volkes und die Frauen und die kleinen Kinder es verstehen.
> Denn die Frauen sind verpflichtet, die Toralesung zu hören wie die Männer, und umso mehr
> die männlichen (Kinder). Daher übersetzt man sie. Und du bist verpflichtet (männliche Form)
> zum *Schema* (Glaubensbekenntnis), zur *Tefila* (18-Bittengebet), zum *Birkat ha-Mason* (Tisch-
> segen) und zur *Mesusa* (Türsegen). Und wenn niemand die heilige Sprache kann, lehrt man sie
> in der Sprache, die sie können (weibliche Form), und man übersetzt für die Frauen und seine
> kleinen Söhne jede Ordnung (*seder*) und den Propheten des Schabbat nach der Toralesung.[12]

Frauen hörten auch die Predigt, wie Rabbi Eleasar von Worms in seiner Preisung
auf Dulce hervorhebt: „Am Schabbat sitzt sie und hört der Predigt ihres Gatten
zu. Sittsam vor allen und weise und lieblich; gesegnet, wer ihr Vertrauen hat."
Möglicherweise sind seine Worte „sittsam vor allen" (צנועה מכול) dahingehend zu
interpretieren, dass sich die Frauen während der Predigt im gleichen Raum wie
die Männer, also im Hauptraum der Synagoge aufhielten. Tatsächlich war die
Frauenschule von Worms, die erste im aschkenasischen Raum, erst 1213, 23 Jahre
nach Dulces Tod, erbaut worden. Ob und wo sich Frauen vor diesem Zeitpunkt
zum Gebet trafen, entzieht sich unserer Kenntnis; möglich sind Privaträume oder
Holzanbauten an der Synagoge. Jedenfalls berichteten auch andere Rabbiner des
13. Jahrhunderts von bei der Predigt anwesenden Frauen und den dafür nötigen
Adaptierungen des Raumes:

> [...] Jede Einrichtung einer Abteilung aus Gründen der Sittsamkeit (*zniut,* צניעות) ist am Schab-
> bat erlaubt, wie die *Mechiza* (מחיצה); sie in der Stunde der Predigt zwischen den Männern und
> den Frauen zu machen, ist am Schabbat erlaubt.[13]

---

9 KEIL, Martha: Bet haKnesset, Judenschul. Die Synagoge als Gotteshaus, Amtsraum und Brenn-
   punkt sozialen Lebens, in: Wiener Jahrbuch für jüdische Geschichte, Kultur und Museumswesen
   4 (1999/2000): Über das Mittelalter, hg. v. Gerhard MILCHRAM im Auftrag des Jüdischen Muse-
   ums der Stadt Wien, S. 71–90, S. 79f.

10 Siehe SAFRAI, Hannah: Women and the Ancient Synagogue, in: GROSSMAN, Susan/HAUT, Rivka
   (Hg.): Daughters of the King. Women and the Synagogue, Philadelphia/Jerusalem 1992, S. 39–49,
   insbesondere S. 43f.

11 Die sogenannten „kleinen Rollen" (*Megillot*) der Bibel, Ruth, Hohes Lied, Kohelet, Klagelieder
   und Ester wurden jeweils zu bestimmten Feiertagen gelesen, z. B. Ruth zu *Schawuot* (Wochenfest),
   die Klagelieder zum 9. Aw (Tag der Tempelzerstörung) und Ester zu Purim.

12 Machsor Vitry, ed. v. Samuel HURWITZ, Nürnberg 1923 (ND Jerusalem 1988), Bd. 2, S. 713.

13 Sefer Mordechai, Schabbat Nr. 311 (im Kommentarteil der gängigen Talmudausgaben).

Das halachische (jüdisch-rechtliche) Problem bestand in einer eventuellen Verletzung des Arbeitsverbots am Schabbat. Doch auch Rabbi Jakob bar Mosche ha-Lewi Mulin, genannt Maharil, bis zu seinem Tod 1427 Rabbiner in Mainz, leitete die Erlaubnis, eine Raumteilung mit Gebetsmänteln (*Tallitot*) zu machen, aus dem Talmud und von den rabbinischen Autoritäten des 13. Jahrhunderts ab:

> Und es sprach Maharil: Daraus (aus bEruwin 94a) legte Ba'bia (unklar, verm. Maharam, Ende des 13. Jahrhunderts) aus, dass sie üblicherweise erlaubten, am Schabbat in der Stunde der Predigt *Tallitot* auszubreiten (Variante: wenn sie – männliche Form – in der Synagoge predigten, und sie – weibliche Form – traten ein, um die Predigt zu hören), um zwischen Männern und Frauen zum Zweck der Sittsamkeit abzutrennen (Variante: damit die Männer nicht die Frauen ansehen).[14]

Die Ehrverletzung der Frauen erfolgte zwar durch die aktiven Blicke der Männer, doch wirkte diese wieder auf die Ehre der Männer zurück. Mit der Errichtung der Frauenschulen konnten die Frauen den Übersetzungen und Predigten in einem abgesonderten Raum durch Schlitzfenster lauschen, ohne selbst gesehen zu werden, und genossen so, in Ambivalenz von fremdbestimmter Ausgrenzung und freiwilliger frommer Zurückgezogenheit, „sittsam vor allen", das Ansehen der Gemeinde.[15]

Versöhnungs- und Bußrituale (*Mechilot*)

Sprachliche Schnittstellen mit einem weitaus stärkeren Bezug zu Ehre und Ehrverletzung stellten die Versöhnungs- und Bußrituale dar.[16] Ob die öffentliche Bitte um Versöhnung, hebräisch *Mechila* (מחילה), in aschkenasischer Aussprache *Mechile*, auf Hebräisch oder auf Deutsch bzw. Jiddisch mit hebräischen Formelteilen erfolgte,[17] war, im Unterschied zur Toralesung, keine Frage von Geschlecht und auch keine von Bildung. Auch Männer, und sogar erwiesenermaßen gelehrte Männer, brachten ihre *Mechile* in der Landessprache vor, denn sie sollte im öffent-

---

14 Jakob Mulin: Sefer Maharil. Minhagim schel R., ed. von Shelomo Spitzer, Jerusalem 1989, S. 220f., Nr. 35.

15 Siehe Keil, Martha: Namhaft im Geschäft – unsichtbar in der Synagoge: Die jüdische Frau im spätmittelalterlichen Aschkenas, in: Europas Juden im Mittelalter. Beiträge des internationalen Symposiums in Speyer vom 20. bis 25. Oktober 2002, hg. von Christoph Cluse, Trier 2004, S. 344–354.

16 Zur Verwendung einiger der folgenden Quellen im Kontext von gesprochener Sprache siehe Keil, Martha: Rituals of Repentance and Testimonies at Rabbinical Courts in the 15th Century, in: Jaritz, Gerhard/Richter, Michael (Hg.): Oral History of the Middle Ages. The Spoken Word in Context (Medium Aevum Quotidianum, Sonderband 12 = CEU Medievalia 3), Krems/Budapest 2001, S. 164–176.

17 Um im Sprachenstreit zwischen Germanisten und Jiddisten eine Entscheidung zu treffen, fühle ich mich nicht kompetent. Für das 15. Jahrhundert, aus denen meine Quellen stammen, scheinen allerdings ausreichende Kriterien für die eigenständige jiddische Sprache vorhanden zu sein. Ich werde die fraglichen Textstellen in hebräischen Buchstaben laut Edition wiedergeben. Die Transkription, welche die damalige aschkenasische Aussprache zu rekonstruieren versucht, verdanke ich Yacov Guggenheim (Jerusalem).

lichen Raum der Synagoge und im öffentlichen Rahmen eines Gottesdienstes von jedem Gemeindemitglied gehört und verstanden werden, auch von den Frauen, die dieser Performanz durch die Schlitzfenster der Frauenschule folgen konnten. Das kollektive Interesse an diesen Zeremonien war äußerst groß und trug auch sicher zum ‚Entertainment' eines mittelalterlichen Juden bei.[18]

Mechilot bei Ehrenbeleidigung:

In erster Linie mussten öffentliche Verzeihungen nach einer Ehrenbeleidigung geleistet werden, und hier ist interessant, wie ähnlich der Ehrbegriff von Juden und Christen des Mittelalters war:

Für die Jahrhunderte des Mittelalters bezeichnet die Ehre einer Person die Summe all dessen, was – aus Vornehmheit, Ämtern, Besitz, persönlichen Fähigkeiten und Verbindungen gebildet – die Stellung dieser Person in den verschiedenen Lebensordnungen ausmacht, die nicht zuletzt Rangordnungen waren.[19]

Juden und Christen teilten diese Auffassungen von Lebens- und Rangordnungen in einem weit größeren Ausmaß, als es Anhänger der veralteten Sicht von „Juden als Minderheit und Außenseiter der christlichen Gesellschaft" jemals für möglich hielten.

Die Schandprozesse, *Dine boschet* (דיני בושת), des Rabbiners Menachem Merseburg, der im 14. Jahrhundert auch in Österreich wirkte, zählen folgende Ehrenbeleidigungen auf, die mit Geißelhieben, Geldstrafen, Bann und öffentlicher Verzeihung bestraft und gesühnt wurden: *Mamser* ממזר bzw. *Mamseret* ממזרת, also eine nicht der *Halacha* entsprechende Herkunft, *Sona* זונה bzw. *Pruza* פרוצה, also Hure, dementsprechend *Ben Sona* בן זונה, als deutsches Wort ‚Hurensohn' (הורינזו״ן) in hebräischen Buchstaben wiedergegeben, *Ewed* עבד oder *Kanaan* כנען, was dem deutschen Knecht oder Schalk entspricht und unehrliches Verhalten impliziert, entsprechend auch die weibliche Form *Schifcha* פחה, Magd. Ein weiteres Schimpfwort war *Rescha* רשע, Bösewicht, *Ganav* גנב, Dieb sowie *Noef* נואף, *Nawal* נבל oder *Passul* פסול, was Ehebrecher oder Unzüchtiger bedeutet.[20] Alle diese Bezeichnungen hätten auch Christen als Ehrenbeleidigung aufgefasst, wie Michael Toch aus Landesgerichtsprotokollen der Obergrafschaft Katzenelnbogen von 1415–1486 gezeigt hat. Von den 1099 quellenmäßig erfassbaren Fällen betrafen fast ein Drittel Ehrverletzungen, und zwar beinahe zur Gänze durch Schimpf-

---

18 Zur Öffentlichkeit von Ritualen siehe ALTHOFF, Gerd: Empörung, Tränen, Zerknirschung. „Emotionen" in der öffentlichen Kommunikation des Mittelalters, in: Frühmittelalterliche Studien 30 (1996), S. 60–79, vor allem S. 75f.

19 Siehe ALTHOFF, Compositio (Anm. 1), S. 63 und auch JÜTTE, Robert: Ehre und Ehrverlust im spätmittelalterlichen und frühneuzeitlichen Judentum, in: SCHREINER/SCHWERHOFF, Verletzte Ehre (Anm. 1), S. 144–165, S. 149.

20 Die *Dine Boschet* sind am Ende der Responsenedition von Rabbi Jakob Weil (gest. 1453) abgedruckt: Jakob Weil: Sche'elot u-Teschuwot, ed. von Izchak SELA, Venedig 1549 (ND Jerusalem 1988), S. 176–178, nicht nummeriert.

wörter.[21] In ihrer Zweisprachigkeit sind auch die jüdischen sprachliche Schnittstellen im sozio-kulturellen Raum, oftmals mit religiösen Implikationen.

Ehre und damit Ehrverletzung ist mit dem Stand und Ansehen der jeweiligen Person verbunden. Die Genugtuung, ob nun bei Christen oder bei Juden, richtete sich daher nach dem Rang der beteiligten Personen, der Schwere des Konflikts und dem angerichteten Schaden.[22] Jüdische Besonderheiten waren das Anzweifeln der Gelehrsamkeit eines Rabbiners, was die Ehre eines ganzen bedeutenden Berufsstandes traf,[23] die Beschimpfung als *Mosser* מוסר oder *Malschin* מלשין, Denunziant oder Verräter, also jemand, der seinen Widersacher gegen dessen Willen vor ein christliches Gericht brachte bzw. denunzierte, sowie *Ben Nida* בן נידה, ein während der Menstruation Gezeugter. Alle diese Ehrenbeleidigungen gingen über eine individuelle Beleidigung hinaus und zogen eine Gruppe, einen Berufs- oder Bildungsstand oder sogar die gesamte, sich in erster Linie über die Abstammung definierende Religionsgemeinschaft in Mitleidenschaft. Daher mussten diese Ehrverletzungen auch gesühnt werden, wenn der Beleidigte bereits verstorben war. In diesem Fall musste der Delinquent mit einem Zehnmännerquorum (*Minjan*) das Versöhnungsritual am Grab des Verstorbenen leisten: „Jeder, der seinen Genossen provoziert (מקניט), auch mit Worten, muss ihn versöhnen. Und wenn dieser stirbt, muss er zehn Männer bringen und sie auf sein Grab stellen."[24]

Die Versöhnung durfte sich also nicht auf das Aussöhnen zwischen zwei im Streit befindlichen Menschen auf persönlicher Basis beschränken; sie betraf das ganze Kollektiv und musste den Gewohnheitsrechten – ob sie nun *consuetudines* oder *Minhagim* (מנהגים) hießen – Genüge tun, damit eine ‚Heilung des Bruchs' erfolgen und ein konfliktfreies Weiterleben gelingen konnte. Aus diesem Grund mussten Beleidigungen, die bereits Verstorbene, meist verstorbene Eltern oder einen Elternteil – bei einschlägigen Schimpfwörtern die Mutter – betrafen, generationsübergreifend gesühnt werden, und zwar folgerichtig am Grab des oder der Beleidigten. Menachem Merseburg weist in mehreren seiner *Dine Boschet* auf diese Form hin, die auf Grund ihrer Öffentlichkeit – es mussten mindestens zehn Männer anwesend sein, doch können wir ein breiteres Publikum annehmen – und dem besonderen Ort, dem Friedhof, eine eindrucksvolle Performanz bot. Der Friedhof galt als Ort, an dem Bitten und Gebete besonders wirksam waren, wie Maharil schrieb:

---

21 Toch, Michael: Schimpfwörter im Dorf des Spätmittelalters, in: Mitteilungen des Instituts für Österreichische Geschichtsforschung 101,1–4 (1993), S. 311–327, S. 314f.

22 Althoff: Empörung (Anm. 18), S. 69.

23 Wie empfindlich Rabbiner auf eigene oder Ehrenbeleidigungen ihrer Schüler reagieren konnten, schildert anschaulich Minhage Maharil (Anm. 14), S. 622, Nr. 44: Der Sohn des Schamasch (Synagogen- und Amtsdiener) hatte einen der Bachurim Maharils „Sauschelm" (זויא שעלם) genannt, wurde dafür von diesem gebannt und er und sein Vater mussten sowohl den Beleidigten als auch Maharil und alle übrigen Bachurim in der *Jeschiwa* um Verzeihung bitten. Ein wichtiger Aspekt der Rangordnung war hier, dass der Schamasch aus der Schicht der „*towe ha-Ir*" (wörtlich: die Guten der Stadt, *boni viri*), also der Führungsschicht der Gemeinde stammte.

24 Menachem Merseburg: Dine Boschet (Anm. 20), S. 177, äußere Spalte, 3. Din (nicht nummeriert).

„Der Friedhof (wörtl: Haus der Gräber) ist der Ruheort der Gerechten und daher ein heiliger und reiner Ort und das Gebet wird auf dem heiligen Boden umso mehr aufgenommen."[25]

Die ‚Heiligkeit und Reinheit' – ein Begriffspaar, das sich ansonsten nur auf das Heilige Land, *Erez Israel*, bezieht – standen im krassen Gegensatz zu der in den Schmähungen implizierten Unreinheit und konnten, wie an anderen heiligen Orten, ausgleichend wirken. Das Gebet an den Gräbern der Vorfahren und frommer Persönlichkeiten war – und ist – Teil der Bußriten vor dem Neujahrsfest und dem Versöhnungstag, stellt also auch bei individuellen Vergehen das Gleichgewicht zwischen Gott und dem Sünder wieder her.

Menachem Merseburg führte als besonderes Detail das Sichhinwerfen auf dem Grab an, eine sowohl in jüdischen und christlichen Gebetsriten als auch bei christlichen Herrschaftsritualen gebräuchliche, eindrucksvolle Geste, die Reue, Zerknirschung und Unterwerfung zum Ausdruck bringen sollte:[26]

> Ruben nannte Simon *hurenson* (הורנזו״ן), das heißt *Ben Sona*, und ein Zweiter bezeugte, dass er ihn *Mamser* nannte. [...] Und für die Sache, jemanden *hurenson* zu nennen, gilt nicht dasselbe Gesetz, wie wenn er sagt: Sohn der Hure (*Ben ha-Sona*; mit bestimmtem Artikel), denn das heißt, dass es der Wahrheit entsprach, dass sie sich prostituierte und auch ledig war, aber in diesem Fall muss er sich selbst der Lüge bezichtigen und auf dem Grab von dessen Mutter niederwerfen. Aber manchmal muss man je nach Beschämer und Beschämtem erschweren, und bei der Unreinheit und einigen anderen Schmähungen gibt es kein Gesetz, sondern es obliegt dem Schmäher, sich mit seinem Genossen zu versöhnen. [...] Und was sie sagen, dass er zum Grab des Geschmähten gehen muss, trifft das nur zu, wenn er (der Geschmähte) in der Nähe begraben ist, wie der Stadt, zu der sie gehören und dorthin ihre Toten zum Begräbnis schicken, aber wenn er weit weg begraben ist, muss er das nicht, sondern es genügt, wenn er einen Abgesandten hinschickt und zwei Zeugen von der Stadt nimmt, dass das Grab dort ist, und er (der Abgesandte) geht zu dessen Grab und bittet um Verzeihung im Namen des Schmähers.

Abgesehen von dem interessanten Hinweis auf jüdische Wohnorte und ihre Zugehörigkeit zu Zentralorten mit Friedhöfen,[27] können wir diesem Rechtsentscheid entnehmen, dass bei Ehrenbeleidigungsklagen weniger feste Rechtsnormen – „*Din*" – die Grundlage für eine Beilegung des Streits bildeten, als vielmehr von beiden Parteien akzeptierte Versöhnungsrituale am geeigneten Ort, in der geeigneten Form und mit den geeigneten Menschen als Zeugen. Diese Rituale hatten zwar eine lange Tradition, wurden aber von der jeweiligen Gemeinschaft neu adaptiert und auf die Bedürfnisse zugeschnitten – „man muss je nach Beschämer und Beschämtem erschweren", also entsprechend dem Rang und Ansehen

---

25 Minhage Maharil (Anm. 14), S. 270, Nr. 18. Zitiert in Maimon, Arye/Breuer, Mordechai/Guggenheim, Yacov (Hg.): Germania Judaica, Tübingen 1963–2003, hier Bd. 3 (1995), S. 2088.

26 Menachem Merseburg: Dine Boschet (Anm. 20), S. 177, innere Spalte, 5. Din. Zum Hinwerfen auf das Grab beim Gebet siehe Minhage Maharil, ibid., S. 273, Nr. 3: „Und er (Maharil) predigte, dass jeder Mensch auf den Friedhof gehen soll, um sich am Abend von *Rosch ha-Schana* (Neujahr) auf den Gräbern der Gerechten hinzuwerfen, aber an einem gefährlichen Ort (Variante: Räuber und dergleichen) besteht keine Notwendigkeit." Zum Fußfall siehe Althoff: Empörung (Anm. 18), S. 69.

27 Germania Judaica (Anm. 25), Bd. 3,3, S. 2089.

der Beteiligten vorgehen. Die Möglichkeit, einen Stellvertreter an einen weit entfernten Friedhof zu schicken, mag eine solche Adaptierung gewesen sein, sei es aus körperlichen oder rechtlichen Einschränkungen der Mobilität oder einfach aus Bequemlichkeit. Für die dortige Öffentlichkeit, welcher der Beleidiger nicht angehörte, hatte die Versöhnung nicht dieselbe Bedeutung wie in seiner Heimatgemeinde, daher konnte er dem Versöhnungsanspruch in einer Form Genüge tun, die in seinem eigenen Kollektiv nicht ausgereicht hätte.

Der Steuerkonflikt in Ulm 1435–1440

Der folgende Fall, der weit über die jüdische Gasse hinaus die Gemüter erregte, zeigt die meisten Möglichkeiten der sozialen Schmähung eines Mitmenschen und die daraus folgende Bestrafung und Versöhnung auf:

Im Zuge eines fünfjährigen heftigen Streits in Ulm, der 1440 mit einer schweren Verurteilung endete, klagte der *Chawer* – ein Gelehrter ohne Rabbinertitel – Simlin Walch[28] beim christlichen Bürgermeister der Stadt, dass ihn einige seiner Glaubensgenossen von der *Bima* gestoßen hätten, sodass er sich die Rippen brach. Die Klage beim Stadtgericht ohne Zustimmung des Gegners stellte einen klaren Fall von Denunziation dar. Simlins Nähe zur christlichen Obrigkeit überrascht nicht: Er war als einer der reichsten Geldleiher 1438 und 1439 der Vertreter seiner Gemeinde bei den Steuerverhandlungen mit Konrad von Weinsberg, dem Kämmerer Friedrichs III. Simlin hatte sich geweigert, seinen Anteil an der kollektiven Steuer für den Kaiser beizutragen – er strebte eine für ihn günstigere individuelle Vereinbarung an – und akzeptierte die daraus folgende Verurteilung durch das Gericht des Rabbiners Selikman von Ulm, eines ebenfalls überaus vermögenden Geldleihers, nicht.[29] Darüber hinaus beleidigte Simlin den Rabbiner mit der Bezeichnung „*Mamser*“. Weiters verglich er Selikmans Gelehrsamkeit mit der eines dreijährigen Kindes und zweifelte an der Ehrlichkeit der Zeugen, der Richter und Selikmans Anhängerschaft im Gesamten. Der Prozess spaltete die Gemeinde, beide Parteien riefen das Stadtgericht an, was beim Stadtrat große Verwunderung erregte. Mehr als 170 Dokumente sind aus diesen fünf Prozessjahren erhalten, bis Simlin schließlich nach einer Gefängnishaft am 27. August 1440 Urfehde schwor.[30] Der Streit, in dem es um Vermögen, Machtanspruch und nicht zuletzt um Ehre ging, sprengte also die autonomen Regelungsmöglichkeiten der

---

28 Simlin Walchs hebräischer Name war Simon oder Samuel bar Menachem, Sohn des Menly von Mellingen. Siehe Germania Judaica (Anm. 25), Bd. 3,2, S. 1507, Nr. 26.
29 Siehe ibid., S. 1506f., Nr. 25. Selikman war 1431 in Ulm aufgenommen worden. Zuvor war er in Treviso und Konstanz tätig und in letzterem mit anderen Juden wegen einer Blutbeschuldigung inhaftiert gewesen. Er wurde nach der Zahlung eines Viertels des enormen Lösegeldes von 20.000 Gulden aus der Gefangenschaft entlassen.
30 Germania Judaica (Anm. 25), Bd. 3/2, S. 1503. Zu den Einzelheiten des Streits siehe Strassburger, Ferdinand: Zur Geschichte der Juden von Ulm nach Resp. 147 des Jacob Weil, in: Festschrift zum 70. Geburtstag von Theodor Kroner, Breslau 1917, S. 224–236.

jüdischen Gemeinde von Ulm. Beide Parteien erhofften sich durch die Beiziehung der christlichen Obrigkeiten eine Stärkung der eigenen Machtposition und Ehre und schwächten damit ihre Selbstregulierung und Eigenständigkeit, was in den jüdischen Gemeinden des 15. Jahrhunderts keine Seltenheit war und auch in Ehrkonflikten anderer Gruppen ein häufiges Phänomen darstellte.[31]

Die jüdische Rechtsprechung wurde den Rabbinern Jakob Weil und Seligman Katz von Nürnberg übertragen.[32] Ihr Urteil schöpfte sämtliche Strafsanktionen der mittelalterlichen jüdischen Rechtsprechung aus. Simlin wurde zu 40 Schlägen mit der Peitsche oder 40 Gulden an die Wohltätigkeitskasse (*Zedaka*) verurteilt. Sein *Chawer*-Titel wurde ihm aberkannt, und er musste sich zu einem Jahr Buße mit Fasten und Fernhalten von Festen verpflichten. Für die diversen Beleidigungen musste Simlin auf den *Bimot* der Synagogen von Ulm, Konstanz und Nürnberg um Verzeihung bitten und sich bei Selikmans Eltern an deren Grab in Ulm öffentlich entschuldigen. Mit der Bezeichnung „*Mamser*" hatte er ja Selikmans Mutter unterstellt, entweder Ehebruch begangen oder vor der Ehe Beziehungen mit einem Verwandten, Nichtjuden, Verheirateten oder auf sonst eine Weise verbotenen Mann gehabt zu haben, womit auch ihr Ehemann in Misskredit kam. Ehre und Ehrenbeleidigung hat, wie bereits bemerkt, immer mit dem Ansehen der Person zu tun, welches auf deren Kollektiv wirkt und Einfluss nimmt: Selikmans Vater Abraham war in der ersten Hälfte des 15. Jahrhunderts einer der reichsten Juden in Coburg und damit schon auf Grund seines Vermögens und seines daraus folgenden Steuerbeitrags ein einflussreiches, wahrscheinlich sogar führendes Mitglied seiner Gemeinde.[33]

Jakob Weil bringt in seinem hebräischen Rechtsgutachten die Versöhnungsformeln in voller Länge, in „aschkenasischer Sprache" – wie wir diese Eigenbezeichnung auch immer übersetzen wollen. Wie alle im Beitrag zitierten gesprochenen oder als solche vorgesehenen Versöhnungsformeln gebe ich die *Mechile* an den Gräbern der Eltern Abraham und Mina zuerst in hebräischen Buchstaben (aus technischen Gründen hier die gescannte Quellenedition) wieder, danach, soweit rekonstruierbar, eine Transkription (hebräische Worte kursiv) und schließlich eine verständliche Übertragung ins heutige Deutsch:

---

31 Dinges, Martin: Die Ehre als Thema der historischen Anthropologie. Bemerkungen zur Wissenschaftsgeschichte und zur Konzeptualisierung, in Schreiner/Schwerhoff: Verletzte Ehre (Anm. 1), S. 29–62, S. 49.

32 Jakob Weil: Sche'elot u-Teschuwot (Anm. 20), S. 94–100, Nr. 147. Jakob Weil, einer der berühmtesten Gelehrten seiner Zeit, wurde ca. 1390 geboren, studierte in Mainz, war Rabbiner in Nürnberg von ca. 1422 bis 1429, dann in Augsburg bis 1438, darauf vermutlich in Bamberg. Spätestens 1443 übersiedelte er nach Erfurt, wo er 1453 starb. Siehe Germania Judaica (Anm. 25), Bd. 3,1, S. 46, Nr. 12.

33 Siehe Germania Judaica (Anm. 25), Bd. 3/2, S. 1519, Anm. 240. Seine Frau Mina starb am 27. 12. 1435, ihr Grabstein ist bei Brann, Markus: Zur jüdischen Geschichte – Jüdische Grabsteine in Ulm, in: Festschrift (Anm. 30), S. 182, publiziert; er hielt sie allerdings für die Ehefrau Selikmans. Siehe Yuval, Israel Y.: Scholars in their Time (Hebr.), Jerusalem 1988, S. 223, Anm. 2.

אִיך הון מה״ר זעליקמן אִין ממז' גהײשן
דאמיט הון אִיך פוגע ונוגע גוועזן אן הנ״ר
אברהם ז״ל כבוד אונ' זײנס ווײפא מרת מינא
ז״ל חטאתי עויתי פשעתי אִיך ביט דען בורא דש
ער מירש מוחל זײא אונ' דאער נוך הנ״ר
אברהם ז״ל אונ' בור מינא ז״ל

Ich hon *moreinu ha-rov* Selikman ein *mamser* geheissn, damit hon ich *pauge we-nauge* gewesen an *ha-nikhbad rov* Avraham *s'l kowed* und seins weip *marat* Mina *s'l*. *Chatosi, owisi, poschosi*. Ich bitt den *baure jis'(borekh)*, das er mirs *moichel* sei un' daer noch *ha-nikhbad rov* Avraham *s'l* un' fur Mina *s'l*.

Ich habe Unseren Lehrer, den Meister Selikman, einen *Mamser* genannt, dadurch habe ich an der Ehre des geehrten Herrn Abraham, sein Andenken zum Segen, gerührt und sie verletzt, und an der seiner Frau, Frau Mina, ihr Andenken zum Segen. Ich habe gesündigt, gefehlt und übertreten. Ich bitte den Schöpfer, gepriesen sei Er, dass Er mir verzeihe, und danach den geehrten Herrn Abraham und Frau Mina.

Jakob Weil war sich bewusst, dass sein Rechtsgutachten auch Rabbinern nicht deutsch-sprachiger Gemeinden oder solcher mit anderem *Minhag* als Präzedenzfall dienen könnte und übersetzte die gesamte Versöhnungsformel ins Hebräische, desgleichen die längere zweite, die Simlin in den drei Synagogen vorbringen musste:

הורע לו רצותי אִיך הון מסירות
גיטון אִיך הון גברוכן די הסכמות די רבנים הון
גמאכט דא אִיך אוף גחתמת בין אִיך הון אויך
פוגע ונוגע גיוועזן אן כבוד משפחה של מה״ר
זעליקמן אִיך הון אויך מה״ר זעליקמן אן זיין
כבוד גריט דש אִיך גשפרוכן ער זײא ניט גע אײן
רב אין קינד קון מי וואן ער, דא מיט הון
אִיך אויך דען רבנים אובל גריט די מה״ר
זעליקמן גסמכ' הוט לו רב אִיך הון אויך מה״ר
זעליקמן מי אובל גריט אונ' אויך קהל אִיך

הון אויך דען דײני' אונ' אײן טײל עדיס
אובל גריט חטאתי עויתי פשעתי אִיך ביט דען
בורא ית' דש ער מירש מוחל זײא אונ' די
רבנים די מה״ר זעליקמן גסמכת הוט אונ' אויך
אויך מה״ר זעליקמן אונ' אויך קהל אונ' אויך
די עדיס אונ' אויך די דײני' אִיך ביט זי אל
מחילה

Hort zu *rabbausai*, ich hon *mesires* geton, ich hon gebrochen di *haskomes* di *rabbonim* hon gemacht da ich of *gechasem(e)t* bin, ich hon oich *pauge we-nauge* gewesen an *kowed mischpoche shel moreinu ha-rov* Selikman. Ich hon oich *moureinu ha-rov* Selikman an sein *kowed* geret das ich geschprochen, er sei nit ein *rov*, ein kind kon me wen er, da mit hon ich oich den *rabbonim* ubel geret, di (MhaR) *maureinu ha-rov rebbi* Selikman *gesamkhet* hot (sic!) zu *rov*. Ich hon oich (MhaR) *maureinu ha-rov rebbi* Selikman me ubel geret un' oich *kahl*. Ich hon oich den *dajjonim* un' ein teil *eidim* ubel geret. *Chatosi, ovisi, poschosi*. Ich bitt den *boure jis'(borekh)*, das er mirs *mochel* sei un' di *rabbonim*, die (MhaR) *Moureinu ha-Rov Rebbi* Selikman *gesamkhet* hot (sic!) un' oich (MhaR) *maureinu ha-rov rebbi* Selikman un' oich *kahl* un' oich di *eidim* un' oich di *dajjonim*, ich bitt si al *mechile*.

Hört zu, meine Herren, ich habe einen Verrat begangen, ich habe die Vereinbarungen (Betreff der Steuer) gebrochen, welche die Rabbiner getroffen haben und die auch ich unterschrieben habe, ich habe auch an die Familienehre des Lehrers und Meisters Selikman gerührt und sie verletzt. Ich habe auch die Ehre von Rabbi Selikman verletzt, als ich sagte, dass er kein Rabbiner sei, dass ein Kind mehr weiß als er, und damit habe ich auch diejenigen Rabbiner verleumdet, die ihn zum Rabbiner ordiniert haben. Ich habe auch ihn durch weitere Äußerungen verleumdet, und auch die Gemeinde, die Richter und einen Teil der Zeugen. Ich habe gefrevelt, gesündigt und eine Übertretung begangen (hebr.). Ich bitte den Schöpfer, gepriesen sei Er (hebr.), dass Er mir verzeihe (hebr.), und die Rabbiner, den Selikmann, die Gemeinde, und auch die Zeugen und Richter, ich bitte alle um Verzeihung.

Diese Versöhnungsrede ist ebenfalls auf Hebräisch zitiert. Kernstück der *Mechila* ist das dreiteilige Schuldbekenntnis *chatati, awiti, paschati*, das der Liturgie des Versöhnungstages entnommen ist und nicht ins Deutsche übersetzt wurde.

Das Ritual am Grab der Eltern hatte innerhalb der nächsten drei Tage nach Zustellung des Urteils in Ulm stattzufinden, nach weiteren drei Tagen in der Synagoge und innerhalb von 30 Tagen in den Gebetshäusern von Konstanz und Nürnberg. Ob Simlin diese Worte, im Sinne von *spoken words*, tatsächlich jemals gesprochen hat, entzieht sich unserer Kenntnis; Jakob Weil drohte jedenfalls bei Nichtbefolgung mit dem Bann (*Cherem* חרם), dem Ausschluss aus der jüdischen Gemeinschaft.

Mechila bei tätlichem Angriff oder Totschlag

Anders als bei Simlin von Ulm ordnete Jakob Weil im folgenden Fall eines Gewalttäters mit dem in Rechtsgutachten üblichen Decknamen „Schimon" die *Mechila*-Formel in hebräischer Sprache an.[34] Aus welchem Ort die beiden Fragesteller, die *Chawerim* Izchak und Mordechai, stammen, ist nicht angegeben, es scheint aber aus der Erwähnung von Rabbi Jekel von Eger und dem Hinweis auf „euer Territorium" ein Ort in Böhmen wahrscheinlich. Vermutlich überließ er es dem zuständigen Rabbiner, die *Mechila* nach örtlichem *Minhag*, Rechtsbrauch, vorzutragen. Einzelne Worte aus den Zeugenaussagen sind auf deutsch zitiert, die Beteiligten beherrschten also die deutsche Sprache:

> Ein gewisser Ruben wurde von Schimon verletzt und forderte Genugtuung, denn dieser hatte ihn mit einem Stück Holz derart auf den Kopf geschlagen, dass „das Blut von der Stirne bis zum Kinn rann". Zwei Zeugen beobachteten den Vorfall. Schimon gab seine Tat zwar zu, sagte aber aus, er habe gesehen, wie Ruben seine (Schimons) schwangere Frau schlug und sei deshalb in Zorn geraten. Aus den ausführlichen Zeugenaussagen stellte sich aber heraus, dass Schimon zuerst Ruben geschlagen hatte und dieser dann erst dessen Frau,
> [...] daher hat Schimon eine große Sünde begangen. Er hat vorsätzlich ein Stück Holz in die Hand genommen und mit ganzer Kraft auf diese gefährliche Stelle geschlagen, bis das Opfer blutüberströmt war. [...] Schimon wird zu Geißel und *Mechila* verurteilt. Am Tag des Eintretens soll er nach der Toralesung auf die Bima gehen und in dieser (der hebräischen) Sprache mit lauter Stimme sagen: Ich habe gesündigt vor dem Ewigen (wörtl.: dem Namen, *ha-Schem* השם), dem Herrn Israels, und gegen Ruben, und die Schande vergrößert, weil ich Ruben mit einem Holz geschlagen habe, bis ihm das Blut von der Stirn bis zum Kinn rann. Ich habe gesündigt, gefrevelt und gefehlt und ich bitte den Herrn, gepriesen sei Er, Er möge mir verzeihen, und auch den Herrn Ruben bitte ich, er möge mir verzeihen. Und an diesem Tag zwischen *Mincha* und

---

34 Jakob Weil: Sche'elot u-Teschuwot (Anm. 20), S. 20–23, Nr. 28.

Ma'ariv, bevor sie das *we-Hu rachum* („Und Er ist barmherzig") beten, soll er in der Synagoge geschlagen werden. [...][35]

Wir wissen nicht, ob der Delinquent tatsächlich schwer „bis aufs Blut" geschlagen wurde – bei von rabbinischen Gerichten verurteilten Mördern die übliche Strafe – oder ob er, wie meist bei Denunzianten und Beleidigern, nur öffentlich gedemütigt, aber nicht ernsthaft verletzt werden sollte.[36] In beiden Varianten erfüllte das Urteil das Kriterium der ‚Ehrenstrafen', die dem Verurteilten Schmach und Schande einbringen und ihn in seiner Ehre empfindlich treffen sollten.[37] Wortwörtlich forderte Ruben von seinem Beleidiger Schimon „Genugtuung" (*Elbon* עלבון), ein Begriff, der sein Pendant in der *satisfactio* findet. Diese implizierte eine rituelle, inszenierte Unterwerfung des Schuldigen, auf welche die Verzeihung und Wiederherstellung sowohl der Ehre des Beleidigten als auch des Ansehens des Täters folgte. Oft gingen im christlich-herrschaftlichen Bereich Verhandlungen voraus, die Einzelheiten des Rituals festlegten.[38] In der jüdischen Rechtsprechung scheint der als Schiedsrichter angerufene Rabbiner entweder ein Urteil gefällt oder einen Vorschlag gemacht zu haben, der je nach Ortsbrauch differenziert werden konnte, doch hatte sich, vergleichbar mit vorausgehenden Verhandlungen, die angeklagte Partei vorher verpflichtet, seinen Urteilsspruch anzunehmen. Im vorliegenden Fall verurteilte Jakob Weil den Übeltäter zusätzlich zur einer Geldstrafe von einer Silbermark, die, falls der Verletzte arm wäre, an das Opfer, und falls er reich wäre, an die Synagoge zur Fertigung von Toramänteln gehen sollte.

Zwar geben die Quellen relativ gute Auskunft, was der um Verzeihung Bittende zu sagen und zu tun hatte, über das Objekt seiner Bemühungen erfahren wir aber meist nichts. Der Talmud wie auch die christliche Lehre verlangen, nach dem Ebenbild des barmherzigen und verzeihenden Gottes zu handeln (bSchabb. 133b, 151b). Wenn der Beleidigte nach dreimaliger Bitte nicht verzeiht, wird er selbst als „grausam" bezeichnet und nicht als Nachkomme Abrahams betrachtet (bBeza

---

35 Jakob Weil: Sche'elot u-Teschuwot (Anm. 20), S. 20, innere Spalte. Das Gebet *we-Hu rachum* wird an Montagen und Donnerstagen zwischen dem Nachmittags- und Abendgebet (*Mincha* und *Ma'ariv*) gebetet. Der Text hat Schuld und Versöhnung zum Inhalt: „Und Er ist barmherzig, sühnt die Schuld und vertilgt nicht, wendet immer wieder seinen Zorn ab und erweckt nicht seinen ganzen Grimm. Du, Ewiger, entziehst uns dein Erbarmen nicht, deine Gnade und deine Treue bewahre uns stets [...]," in: Sidur Sefat Emet, übers. v. Selig BAMBERGER, Basel 1992, S. 50.

36 Siehe ZIMMER: Harmony and Discord (Anm. 2), S. 90–93. Zur aus der christlichen Umgebung übernommenen Selbstgeißelung vor allem am Versöhnungstag siehe BARON, Salo Wittmayer: The Jewish Community. Its History and Structure to the American Revolution, Bd. 2, Philadelphia 1945, S. 225.

37 Siehe dazu BRÜCKNER, Wolfgang: Ehrenstrafen, in: Handwörterbuch zur deutschen Rechtsgeschichte, Bd. 1 (Anm. 1), Sp. 851f. sowie SCHWERHOFF, Gerd: Verordnete Schande? Spätmittelalterliche und frühneuzeitliche Ehrenstrafen zwischen Rechtsakt und sozialer Sanktion, in: SCHWERHOFF, Gerd/BLAUERT, Andreas (Hg.): Mit den Waffen der Justiz. Zur Kriminalitätsgeschichte des Spätmittelalters und der Frühen Neuzeit, Frankfurt a. M. 1993, S. 158–188.

38 Siehe ALTHOFF, Gerd: Genugtuung (satisfactio). Zur Eigenart gütlicher Konfliktbeilegung im Mittelalter, in: HEINZLE, Joachim (Hg.): Modernes Mittelalter. Neue Bilder einer populären Epoche, Frankfurt a. M. 1994, S. 247–264 und ALTHOFF: Compositio (Anm. 1), S. 72.

32b). Dem entsprechend legte Maharil von Mainz dem Beleidigten Versöhnungs-
bereitschaft nahe:

> Und nach all dem (den Bußzahlungen und anderen Strafen) soll Herr David von Herrn Issi vor
> zehn Männern des Bundes *Mechila* erbitten, dass er sich wegen dessen Leids und dessen Scha-
> dens versöhnen will. Und Herr Issi soll nicht grausam sein, sondern soll ihm sagen ‚Ich verzeihe
> dir aus ganzem Herzen'.[39]

Für eines der schwersten Vergehen, den Totschlag, war laut Rechtsnorm die
jeweilige christliche Gerichtsbarkeit zuständig. Doch scheinen manche jüdische
Gemeinden bestrebt gewesen zu sein, bei ausreichender Reue und Unterwerfung
des Täters unter die rabbinische Gerichtsbarkeit interne Lösungen zu finden. Im
vorliegenden Fall verhängte Rabbi Israel von Brünn die schwersten Leibes- und
Ehrenstrafen. Er verurteilte Simcha aus Breslau, der unter Alkoholeinfluss einen
Mann namens Nissin totgeschlagen hatte und voll Reue um Buße bat, zu einem
Jahr Verbannung mit folgenden Auflagen:[40]

> Jeden Tag, an dem er zu einer Synagoge kommt, oder wenigstens am Montag und am Donners-
> tag, soll er sich drei eiserne Reifen machen, zwei über seine Hände, damit man an ihnen eine
> Verbindung (oder: einen Bolzen?) machen kann, und einen über seinen Körper, und bei seinem
> Eintreten in die Synagoge bindet man sie zusammen und er betet in ihnen. Und am Abend
> soll er auch in die Synagoge gehen und bevor der *Chasan* das *we-Hu rachum* spricht, öffentlich
> ausrufen und sagen: ‚Wisst, meine Herren, dass ich ein Mörder bin, denn ich habe den Nissin
> böswillig getötet, und das habe ich gesühnt. Bittet für mich um Erbarmen.' Und beim Verlassen
> der Synagoge soll er sich auf die Schwelle legen und die Leute gehen über ihn hinweg, aber sie
> sollen nicht auf ihn treten.

Weiters musste er ein Jahr fasten und auf hartem Lager liegen, durfte Haare und
Bart nicht scheren, nur einmal im Monat den Kopf waschen und einmal im Halb-
jahr seine Kleider wechseln. Er durfte weder eine Schänke besuchen, denn dort
hatte sich die Untat zugetragen, noch spielen, denn ein Spiel hatte die Mordtat
ausgelöst.[41] Wenn ihn jemand öffentlich „Mörder" rufen oder ihn verhöhnen sollte, musste er es schweigend ertragen. Er hatte den Erben Unterhalt zu zahlen, sie
und die Witwe des Opfers um Verzeihung zu bitten, an den Jahrestagen des Mordes zu fasten und sein ganzes Leben lang Wohltaten zu üben.

Mehr noch als die öffentliche Prügelstrafe stellt dieses Bußritual eine Kombination von Ehrenstrafen dar, die bis zur buchstäblichen körperlichen ‚Unter-Wer-
fung' und damit völligen Auslieferung an die Mitmenschen reichte. Eine möglichst große Öffentlichkeit verstärkte die Wirkung der Demütigung, aber auch

---

39 Sche'elot u-Teschuwot Maharil, ed. v. Izchak SATZ, Jerusalem 1979, S. 153–160, Nr. 86, S. 160.
40 Israel meBruna: Sefer Sche'elot u-Teschuwot, Stettin 1860, S. 110, Nr. 265. Kurz zitiert bei ZIM-
   MER: Harmony and Discord (Anm. 2), S. 93. Den Tathergang beschreibt Israel Bruna im voranste-
   henden Rechtsgutachten an die Gemeinde von Lemberg, ibid., S. 109a, Nr. 264.
41 Es dürfte sich also um einen der für die Frühe Neuzeit bereits gut untersuchten ritualisierten
   „Raufhändel" in einer Schenke, hier allerdings mit tödlichem Ausgang, gehandelt haben. Siehe
   MÜLLER-WIRTHMANN, Bernhard: Raufhändel. Gewalt und Ehre im Dorf, in: VAN DÜLMEN,
   Richard (Hg.): Kultur der einfachen Leute, München 1983, S. 79–111.

der Aussöhnung und Wiederherstellung. Trotz der „demonstrativen Selbstentäu-
ßerung" (Althoff) und der lebenslangen Auflagen, die auch eine Gedächtnisfunk-
tion erfüllten, konnte der Delinquent als vollwertiges Mitglied der Gesellschaft
wieder ein ehrenwertes Leben führen, wie ja auch in der christlichen Rangordnung eine schwere Buße zukünftigen Macht- und Ehrenpositionen des Gedemü-
tigten nicht schadete.[42]
    Gerade das zuletzt genannte Ritual weckt Assoziationen an alte Formen der
kanonischen Kirchenbuße, die als „Weiterführung des jüdischen Synagogen-
bannes" mit den gemeinsamen Elementen des Ausschlusses des Sünders aus der
Gemeinschaft, tätiger Buße durch Fasten, Gebete und Almosen und in manchen
schweren Fällen lebenslangen Bußauflagen beschrieben wird. In der Urform, die
im christlichen Mittelalter nicht mehr praktiziert wurde, wälzte sich der Büßer,
in Lumpen gehüllt, laut schreiend auf Sack und Asche vor den Priestern auf dem
Boden.[43] Die noch in der feierlichen Kirchenbuße (*paenitentia publica solemnis*)
des Spätmittelalters enthaltene Haft, die sogenannte Einschließung (*inclusio*),
wurde im jüdischen Bußbrauch vielleicht durch das kurzzeitige Tragen des eiser-
nen Reifens und der Kette symbolisiert. Härenes Bußgewand, Fasten, Geldbu-
ßen und Geißeln in der Öffentlichkeit, das zeitweilige ‚Umherirren' als Bußpilger
sowie schließlich die endgültige Verzeihung ohne zurückbleibenden Makel auf
der reuigen Person verbinden ebenfalls kirchliches und jüdisches Bußritual – und
nicht zuletzt die nicht unerheblichen Einnahmen der geistlichen Einrichtungen
durch die Bußgelder. Das jüdische Bußritual wurde in den jeweiligen örtlichen
Ausformungen bis zur Aufklärung geübt, während sich im christlichen Bereich
um die Mitte des 12. Jahrhunderts der Übergang zum Bußsakrament mit soforti-
ger Absolution vollzog.

Mechila bei Ehebruch

Ebenso wie gewalttätiger Angriff, der zuweilen sogar in der Synagoge erfolgen
konnte, war auch Ehebruch eine schwere Gesetzesverletzung, die besondere Versöhnung mit Gott, der Gemeinde und der Familie erforderte. Die Ehrverletzung
traf hier den Ehemann, seine Familie, die Nachkommen, die Gemeinde und,
als bereits in der Tora (Deut. 22,22) mit dem Tod bestrafte Sünde, das gesamte „Volk Israel". Eine besondere Dimension bestand in der Geschlechterdifferenz:
„Im Geschlechterverhältnis dienen Ehrkonzepte entscheidend dazu, die Identität
von Männern und Frauen zu beschreiben; sie wirken [...] vielfältig auf die Selbst-
definition und die Fremdzuschreibung von Rollen ein." Demzufolge stellt Martin Dinges als erste seiner „zehn Thesen zur Erforschung von Ehrverletzungen"
folgende auf: „Das Geschlecht ist fundamental für die Ehre und ihre Verletzung.

---

42 ALTHOFF: Compositio (Anm. 1), S. 73.
43 Ibid., S. 74. Siehe dazu SCHMITZ, Rolf u. a.: Buße (liturgisch-theologisch), in: Lexikon des Mittel-
    alters, Bd. 2 (2002), Sp. 1123–1144, insbesondere Sp. 1130–1134 sowie Sp. 1136f. (Bußübungen).

Demgegenüber sind Zivilstand und Lebensalter nachrangig."[44] Im jüdischen Recht war der Ehebruch im Geschlechterverhältnis stark asymmetrisch: während der Mann entsprechend der Tora die Frau „erwarb" – später durch die Zeremonie der „Anheiligung" religiös überhöht und verstärkt – konnte er selbst zumindest theoretisch mehrere Ehefrauen haben. Polygamie war jedoch im aschkenasischen Raum seit dem frühen 12. Jahrhundert definitiv verboten und Ehebruch wurde auch bei Männern als sittenwidrig empfunden: Wie erwähnt war *noef*, Ehebrecher, ein ehrenrühriges Schimpfwort.

Dem Mann, der mit einer verheirateten Frau Ehebruch beging, drohte laut Deut. 22,22 zwar ebenfalls die Todesstrafe, doch ermöglichte der Talmud einen Freikauf; von entehrenden Bußritualen berichten die Quellen nichts. Mit einer ehebrecherischen Frau wurde weitaus strenger verfahren. Der Ehebruch einer Frau griff anscheinend viel tiefer in das Ehrkonzept von Individuum und religiösem Kollektiv mit seinen Vorstellungen von ritueller Reinheit und Verunreinigung ein. Dementsprechend grausam war das Bußritual und dementsprechend wirksam war die innerjüdische Zensur, die nur wenige Fälle aus der mittelalterlichen Rechtspraxis überlieferte, wie zwei Rechtsgutachten von Jakob Weil und Israel Bruna, zu der Zeit schon Rabbiner in Regensburg, zum gleichen Fall:[45]

Eine Ehebrecherin, vermutlich aus Regensburg oder einem Nachbarort, erschien für ihre *teschuwa* (Buße) vor Rabbi Salman Kizingen aus Regensburg. Auf seine Anweisung hin musste sie ihre Haube (*kipa*, כיפה) abnehmen, sich in einen Schleier hüllen und in Nachahmung der *sota* (ehebrecherischen Frau) in Num. 5,18 ihr Haar lösen. Dann sollte der Ehemann ihr befehlen, das Winterhaus – die geheizte Wohn- und Lernstube (שטובא) – in Anwesenheit der Männer zu betreten, und zu ihr „in dieser Sprache" (in diesem Fall *leschon aschkenas*) sagen:

קומש״ט ד״ו פרוצה ד״ו זונה ד״ו אשת איש זונה וו׳׳ז וילשט״ו

„Kumst du *pruze*, du *soine*, du *eshet ish soine*, wos willstu?"

„Kommst du Hure, du Prostituierte, hurende Frau eines Mannes, was willst du?"

Ihre rituelle Antwort musste lauten:

אי״ך בקהע״ן מיי״ן זונד״א אי״ך בי״ן אײ״ן פרוצה איי״ן זונה אי״ך וויי״ל תשובה טו״ן אוי״ף
מיי״ן זונד״א

„Ich beken mein suend, ich bin ein *pruze*, ein *soine*, ich will *teschuwe* tun oif mein suend."

„Ich bekenne meine Sünde, ich bin eine Hure, eine Prostituierte, ich will Buße für meine Sünde tun!"

---

44 DINGES: Ehre als Thema der historischen Anthropologie (Anm. 31), S. 30 und S. 48.
45 Israel meBruna: Sche'elot u-Teschuwot, S. 93b, Nr. 225 und Jakob Weil: Sche'elot u-Teschuwot, S. 8f., Nr. 12. FALK, Ze'ev W.: Jewish Matrimonial Law in the Middle Ages, Oxford 1966, bringt

Interessant ist hier der Raum, in dem sich das Ritual abspielen sollte: Im Winterhaus oder *stub(a)*, שטובא, dem mit einem großen Kachelofen beheizten Wohnraum, beteten und lernten die Männer im Winter, wie Jossel bar Mosche, Schüler und Hausdiener Rabbi Isserleins von Wiener Neustadt, berichtet.[46] Frauen hatten zu diesen Zeiten keinen oder nur eingeschränkten Zutritt; die Sühnende erhielt dazu den ausdrücklichen Befehl von ihrem Ehemann. Damit wird die geschlechtsspezifische Dimension des Vergehens deutlich zum Ausdruck gebracht. Die ‚Zeichen' des Rituals sprachen in ihrer Anspielung auf die Ehebrecherin in der Tora, welcher die Todesstrafe droht, eine deutliche Sprache: das Abnehmen der Haube – in der mittelalterlichen Gesellschaft beider Religionen das Symbol des Ehestandes – sowie das Lösen der Haare symbolisierten die ‚losen Sitten' der Frau. Es entzieht sich unserer Kenntnis, ob Salman von Kizingen, dem Jakob Weil und Israel Bruna diese Sanktionen nahelegten, sie auch tatsächlich verhängte, daher wissen wir nicht, ob sich die bedauernswerte Frau dem von ihnen beschriebenen Ritual in seiner gesamten Grausamkeit unterwerfen musste. Demzufolge sollte sie im Winter in eiskaltem Wasser sitzen und erst bei Eintreten der Bewusstlosigkeit aus dem Wasser gezogen und gewärmt werden. Eine Glosse führt aus, dass die Richter den Gesundheitszustand der Frau berücksichtigen und die Strafe entsprechend erleichtern sollten. Schließlich durfte sie ein Jahr lang weder Fleisch noch Wein zu sich zu nehmen und war von allen feierlichen Zusammenkünften der Gemeinde ausgeschlossen.

Der zweite Rechtsgutachter, Jakob Weil, der in der Einleitung seines Rechtsentscheids beklagte, dass „die Verletzung dieser ehebrecherischen Frau groß wie das Meer ist, wer wird sie heilen?", ordnete einige andere äußerst unangenehme Details für das Ritual an, die den strengen Regeln des Rabbi Jehuda he-Chassid von Regensburg (Anfang 13. Jh.) und des Eleasar von Worms folgten.[47] Auch sie ordneten das unbekleidete Sitzen im Eis und unter Bienen an, und zwar am Montag und am Donnerstag je eine Viertelstunde. Jakob Weil argumentierte, dass dieser Fall bereits in aller Munde war, und die Sühne daher besonders sorgfältig vorbereitet werden müsse. Demnach sollte die Ehebrecherin in der *Frauenschul*

---

keinen Hinweis über Sanktion von Ehebruch im Mittelalter. Das jüngste Werk zur jüdischen Frauengeschichte im Mittelalter von Grossman, Avraham: Pious and Rebellious. Jewish Women in Europe in the Middle Ages (Hebr.), Jerusalem 2001, S. 244–251 behandelt hauptsächlich den ehebrecherischen Ehemann und die Zwangslage der Frau in Gefangenschaft, weiters einige wenige Empfehlungen des Sefer Chassidim zum Umgang mit einer Ehebrecherin, aber keine konkreten Fälle. Zur Zensur in rabbinischen Rechtsgutachten siehe Breuer, Mordechai: Die Responsenliteratur als Geschichtsquelle, in: Treml, Manfred u. a. (Hg.): Geschichte und Kultur der Juden in Bayern. Aufsätze, München/New York 1988, S. 29–38, siehe vor allem S. 32 und Anm. 22.

46 Josef bar Mosche: Leket Joscher, ed. v. Jakob Freimann, Berlin 1903 (ND Jerusalem 1964), I. Teil, S. 15 (Rabbi Isserlein betet im Winterhaus) und S. 67 (Isserleins Studienplatz).

47 Siehe Anm. 6. Grossman: Pious and Rebellious (Anm. 45) zitiert das Ehebruchritual aus dem Sefer Chassidim nicht. Auch Borchers, Susanne: Jüdisches Frauenleben im Mittelalter. Die Texte des Sefer Chasidim (Judentum und Umwelt 68), Frankfurt a.M./Berlin u. a. 1998, bringt es nicht. Es stellt sich die Frage, ob es überhaupt in die Editionen aufgenommen wurde, siehe Anm. 45 zur innerjüdischen Zensur.

– hier also im geschlechtsspezifischen Raum der Frauen –, gestehen, was sie getan hatte: „Ich habe vor dem Herrn, meinem Gott gesündigt, auf diese Weise habe ich Schande über mich gebracht und schäme mich, und so kehre ich um und tue *teschuwa*."

Diese Bußformel musste sie auch auf Deutsch (*leschon aschkenas*) wiederholen, Jakob Weil zitiert sie aber leider nicht. Er verordnete die Wiederholung des Rituals in den Synagogen von Ulm, Augsburg und Pappenheim. Weiters unterwarf er die Sünderin für ihr ganzes Leben einer äußeren Kennzeichnung: Sie durfte keinen Schmuck tragen, musste schwarze Kleider „wie eine Trauernde" anlegen und ihren Kopf nicht mit einem Schleier, sondern mit einem Stück gebrauchtem Laken verhüllen. Kopfwaschen und Körperhygiene musste sie einschränken und strenge Fastenzeiten und Enthaltsamkeit von Fleisch und Wein üben. Auch vom sozialen Leben wurde sie isoliert: Sie sollte sich von den Frauen fern halten, nur das Notwendigste mit ihnen reden, in der *Frauenschul* den abgesonderten Platz einer Trauernden einnehmen, keinen Mann ansehen und nachts nicht auf einer Matratze sondern auf dem nackten Boden, höchstens auf einem Blatt Papier, schlafen. Für den Kopf durfte sie ein Federbett benützen – wie die Erwähnung des Schmucks und des Schleiers ein Hinweis auf den gehobenen Stand der jungen Frau. Vermutlich mit Recht befürchtete Jakob Weil, „ihr Wille könnte schwach werden" und sie würde sich der schweren Buße nicht unterziehen, wenn ihr von Anfang an das volle Ausmaß der Strafe bekannt wäre. Er empfahl daher, ihr im Abstand von drei Monaten die nächsten Schritte mitzuteilen, wenn sie „wie vorgesehen standgehalten hat".

Auch dieses Bußritual für Frauen zielt auf die Ehre der betroffenen Person ab. Die Ehrminderung erfolgte hier mittels Herabsetzung der äußeren Präsentation durch Kleidung, Schmuck und Hygiene, dem minderen Platz im sozio-religiösen Raum und der Isolation von den Mitmenschen beiderlei Geschlechts. Fasten und Isolation waren Strafen auch für männliche Delinquenten; die öffentliche Züchtigung wurde bei Frauen durch weniger öffentliche Körperstrafen, die zudem ohne direkte Berührung vollzogen wurden, ersetzt. Die Buße der Frau spielte sich, zumindest nach den vorliegenden Urteilen von Jakob Weil und Israel Bruna, nicht im Hauptraum der Gemeinde ab, sondern in den jeweils geschlechtsspezifischen Räumen *Frauenschul* und Winterhaus. Mit der Rezeption der äußerst strengen Gruppe der *Chasside Aschkenas* weist sich Jakob Weil allerdings als überaus konservativer Rabbiner aus, der diesen Fall vermutlich strenger verhandelte als seine Zeitgenossen. Seine Hochhaltung der Sittsamkeit und dementsprechende Strenge gegenüber Frauen, die er auch bei anderen Gelegenheiten zum Ausdruck brachte,[48] stand wohl hinter der Anweisung, den Frauen in ihrer Synagoge ein abschreckendes Beispiel von Abweichung und Sünde vor Augen zu führen.

---

48 Beispielsweise verweigerte er einer Frau, den Eid auf die Tora im Synagogenraum zu schwören, siehe KEIL, Martha: Geschäftserfolg und Steuerschulden. Jüdische Frauen in österreichischen Städten des Spätmittelalters, in: HÖDL, Günther/MAYRHOFER, Fritz/OPLL, Ferdinand (Hg.): Frauen in der Stadt (Beiträge zur Geschichte der Städte Mitteleuropas 18 = Schriftenreihe der Akademie Friesach 7), Linz 2003, S. 37–62, S. 58f.

Zusammenfassung

Auch wenn die liturgische und die Rechtssprache der deutschen Juden des Mittelalters – nicht der Jüdinnen, sie wurden von der Heiligen Sprache weitgehend ferngehalten – eindeutig das Hebräische war, erforderte die Einheit des Profanen und Sakralen im jüdischen Recht, Rücksicht auf diejenigen zu nehmen, „welche die Heilige Sprache nicht verstehen“, wie es in mehreren Quellen des Mittelalters heißt. In der Landessprache, im Deutschland des Spätmittelalters also Jiddisch oder, nach Selbstbezeichnung der Juden, Deutsch, wurden Gebete, Teile der Tora und des Prophetenabschnitts übersetzt, die Predigt gehalten, Zeugenaussagen getätigt, der Großteil des Eides gesprochen und die hier vorgestellten Buß- und Versöhnungsrituale durchgeführt. Wie sich in den Quellen gezeigt hat, bedienen sich zwar hauptsächlich Frauen der jiddischen Sprache, aber nicht ausschließlich. Auch können wir von der Verwendung des Jiddischen nicht auf Angehörige der Unterschichten schließen; das Hebräische wurde eben, bis auf wenige hochgebildete Ausnahmen, passiv gebraucht. Die meisten mittelalterlichen Juden und einige Jüdinnen konnten es allenfalls nachsprechen oder einfache Segenssprüche, Gebete und Formeln rezitieren. Da jedoch beim Gebet „nur das Herzensverständnis zählt“, wie der Autor des *Sefer Chassidim* zu Beginn des 13. Jahrhunderts schrieb, „soll jeder in der Sprache beten, die er versteht“, und, so könnte man ergänzen, sich mit seinen Mitmenschen in der ihnen vertrauten Sprache versöhnen. Die Heiligkeit dieser Zeremonien blieb durch die hebräischen Formeln, den Synagogenraum, die Anwesenheit der Torarolle und das Beisein des *Minjan* als Repräsentanz der Gemeinde gewahrt. Die Rituale einten die Gemeinschaft, stellten mit der Ehre der Beteiligten das gestörte Gleichgewicht zwischen Abweichung und Norm wieder her, stärkten die Anerkennung der Rangordnung und wirkten auf alle Anwesenden erzieherisch und identitätsstärkend.

Michel Banniard

Langue des Vies, langue des chartes aux VIe–VIIIe siècles: questions sur la réceptibilité de l'Ecriture en Occident latin

Annoncer en direct la Bonne Nouvelle?

Quelle était en Occident la réceptibilité de l'Ecriture aux VIIe–VIIIe siècle? Cette question doit être précisée en termes proprement sociolinguistiques, autrement dit, est-ce que la masse des illettrés qui écoutaient la lecture à haute voix de passages de la Bible dans le cadre de la liturgie, pouvait comprendre le message qui lui était adressé? Reformulée ainsi, l'interrogation n'a évidemment de sens qu'en terres latinophones et est largement justiciable des méthodes appliquées à l'étude de la communication verticale (CV) en Occident Latin.[1]

Avant de me consacrer à ce domaine, je voudrais rappeler que cette problématique relève d'un champ de recherches bien plus vaste. En effet, le même questionnement peut être adressé à l'espace hellénophone: dans quelle mesure et pendant combien de temps la langue de la *Septante*, des *Vies* de saints, et des *homélies*, destinées à la pastorale de l'Empire Romain d'Orient a été efficace? Dans quelle mesure l'évolution du grec parlé tardif vers le grec dit ‹moderne› a détaché la communication commune de la CV? Les mêmes questions se posent dans le cas de l'arabe littéraire, construit au VIIe siècle à partir des parlers de l'Arabie, et maintenu comme langue sacrée exclusive au fil des siècles, alors que la parole arabe évoluait et se diffractait en dialectes. Pour traiter ces questions, une partie des linguistes s'est appuyée sur le concept de *diglossie* dont nous avons de bonnes raisons de nous défier parce qu'il masque les difficultés plutôt qu'il ne les résoud.[2] Lorsque l'évêque Athanase d'Alexandrie a composé au IVe siècle sa *Vie d'Antoine*, il a laissé un peu de côté son érudition classique pour construire un *sermo simplex* dont la morphologie et la syntaxe passaient de nombreux compromis tant avec la langue de la *Septante* qu'avec la *koinè* tardive.[3]

Ces méthodes et ces recommandations sont valides pour l'Occident Latin où les conflits et les compromis dominèrent l'histoire de la communication à partir

---

1 La bibliographie de cette discipline est désormais abondante. On en trouvera un état dans Banniard, M.: Délimitation temporelle entre le latin et les langues romanes, dans: Ernst, G./Glessgen, M. D. (dir.): Romanische Sprachgeschichte, t. 1,1, Berlin/New-York 2003, p. 544–555.

2 Pour une discussion (avec le dossier bibliographique correspondant) qui conclut à l'impropriété de ce concept dans le cas de l'Occident latin avant le VIIIe siècle: Banniard, M.: Viva voce. Communication écrite et communication orale du IVe au IXe siècle en Occident Latin, Paris 1992, p. 505–515 et Id.: Diasystème latinophone et interactions communicationnelles (IIIe–VIIIe s.), dans: François, J. (ed.): Les langues de communication: Quelles propriétés structurales préalables ou acquises? (Mémoires de la SLP), Louvain/Paris 2002, p. 47–64.

3 Bartelink, G. M. J. (ed.): Athanase d'Alexandrie. Vie d'Antoine, Paris 1994.

du IIIe siècle. La genèse du langage biblique en Occident Latin en est la base exemplaire. Les premières traductions de grec en latin qui remontent au Haut Empire présentèrent une latinité qui mit en état de choc certains des intellectuels chrétiens du IVe siècle, à l'image de Jérôme qui en trouvait le style effroyable.[4] La bibliographie surabondante de cette question a surtout permis de montrer que ce latin était fortement imprégné de calques du grec original, à un point tel que la relation de ce langage au langage latin commun n'a jamais pu être établie avec certitude.[5] En outre, la dynamique interne de la nouvelle religion a impulsé des modes de penser et donc de dire qui ont pu conduire les philologues à se demander si cette latinité n'était pas un monde langagier à part. Cette vue extrême a été récusée au profit de descriptions plus souples, le «latin chrétien» ayant pris la place dans le vocabulaire moderne du «latin des chrétiens».[6] Personnellement, je verrais assez bien ce dernier placé dans une topologie générale comme un <sous-dialecte> de la latinophonie tardive. Mais le latin biblique n'est pas resté intouché. En dépit du respect apporté au texte sacré, il a fait l'objet non seulement de révisions, mais aussi de corrections, souvent importantes pour réduire un peu son hétérogénéité à la tradition classique. C'est notamment ainsi qu'à la demande du pape Damase, le savant Jérôme (qui s'horrifiait de la rudesse de ce langage) a cherché à pousser cette latinité écrite un peu plus dans le sens de l'*elegantia*, autrement dit de la grammaticalité traditionnelle.[7]

Ainsi, le texte biblique latin a varié dans l'espace et dans le temps du IIe au Ve siècle dans des proportions que l'érudition moderne a su établir avec un degré raisonnable de certitude.[8] Quelles qu'en soient les fluctuations, il s'est fixé sous forme d'un *canon* dont les modifications dans les siècles suivants ont relevé non d'une réécriture, mais d'une variation due au travail des copistes. La régionalisation de la culture et des écritures, l'émergence et la prolifération des monastères, lieux privilégiés de la transmission des textes sacrés, ont modifié, dans les siècles qui nous concernent, la texture même de cette latinité, mais non son langage. La réforme carolingienne changea assez sensiblement cet état de faits, mais ses effets ne se firent sentir qu'après la période considérée.[9]

---

4   Meershoek, G.: Le latin biblique d'après saint Jérôme. Aspects linguistiques de la rencontre entre la Bible et le monde classique, Nimègue 1966.

5   Je me borne à rappeler les nombreuses publications de l'école de Nimègue.

6   Colot, B.: «Latin chrétien» ou «latin des chrétiens». Essai de synthèse sur une terminologie discutée, dans: Bureau, B. (ed.): Moussylanea, Paris 1998, p. 411–420.

7   Banniard, M.: Saint Jérôme et l'elegantia d'après le De optimo genere interpretandi (ep. 57), dans: Duval, Y. M. (ed.): Jérôme entre l'Orient et l'Occident, Paris 1988, p. 305–322.

8   Fontaine, J./Piétri, Ch. (dir.): Le monde latin antique et la Bible, Paris 1985, et Riché, P./ Lobrichon, G. (dir.): Le Moyen Age et la Bible, Paris 1984.

9   L'ouvrage de référence sur ces aspects demeure Vogel, C.: Introduction aux sources de l'histoire du culte chrétien au Moyen Age, Spolète 1965, à compléter par sa grande étude Les échanges liturgiques entre Rome et les pays francs jusqu'à l'époque de Charlemagne, dans: Settimana 7 (1960), p. 185–295.

Les contraintes croisées de la réceptibilité

Le néologisme *réceptibilité* présente sur le terme usuel *intelligibilité* l'avantage de ne pas limiter à des opérations intellectuelles le processus de la CV, qui n'est qu'un cas particulier de la communication générale, justiciable par conséquent d'une paramétrisation moderne.[10] On doit se convaincre d'abord que seules les machines communiquant en langage codé sont efficientes à 100%. Dans le cas des humains, il existe trois zones définissable *a priori*:

1) Une zone perdue irréductible: même en situation très favorable, il se produit toujours une certaine perte (disons de 10%).

2) Une zone de fluctuation interne: le succès se module sans cesse entre les 90% idéaux et les 50% minimaux.

3) Une zone d'effondrement accidentelle qui fait sortir le processus de la zone 2 (le cas typique en étant en Occident Latin la situation révélée à Tours en 813).

A l'intérieur de ce cadre, les facteurs négatifs et les facteurs positifs internes aux énoncés se définiront en rubriques successives:

1) Rubrique linguistique: les communicants doivent appartenir au même type de langue. Entre un russophone et un francophone, la communication spontanée verbale est nulle.

2) Rubrique diatopique: les communicants peuvent parler, à l'intérieur du même type langagier, des dialectes géographiquement différents (diatopie). Un Vénitien et un Florentin parlant chacun son dialecte se comprennent.

3) Rubrique diastratique: l'écart culturel entre les communicants peut être surmonté au prix d'accommodements stylistiques réciproques. Dans le cas de la CV latinophone, les lettrés ne doivent pas trop tendre leur langage vers une norme élevée et archaïque.

4) Rubrique dialogique: le sujet traité ne doit pas être trop hétérogène entre les communicants. Dans le cas de la CV en Occident Latin, les thèmes abordés doivent être entrés dans la chaîne transgénérationnelle du savoir (*Exempla*, proverbes, sentences, chants etc.).[11]

---

10 Banniard, M.: La réception des carmina auliques: niveaux de latinité et niveaux de réception à la fin du VIIIᵉ siècle, dans: Jarnut, J. (ed.): Am Vorabend der Kaiserkrönung, Berlin 2002, p. 35–49; Banniard, M.: Parler en l'an Mil. La communication entre insularisme et flexibilité langagiers, dans: Bonnassie, P./Toubert, P. (ed.): Hommes et Sociétés dans l'Europe de l'An Mil, Toulouse 2004, p. 333–350; Banniard, M.: Prérequis de réceptibilité du latin tardif en période de transition, dans: Kiss, S. (ed.): Hommages à J. Herman, Tübingen 2005, p. 105–113. Ces travaux, qui constituent des approches successives de cette problématique, en voie d'élaboration et de calibrage, proposent la bibliographe interdisciplinaire requise.

11 Cette règle est illustrée dans Banniard, M.: Les deux vies de saint Riquier: du latin médiatique au latin hiératique, dans: Médiévales 25 (1993), p. 45–52.

Des paramètres externes aux énoncés doivent également être repérés et explicités.

1) Paramètre sociologique: la référence à un même *corpus* de valeurs référentielles est requis. Dans le cas des chrétiens, la surdité peut frapper les partisans de dogmes divergents (Ariens//Nicéens; Donatistes//Catholiques, etc.).

2) Paramètre psychologique: entre les communicants une certaine aptitude à l'interpénétration est requise. Dans les cas de la CV en Occident Latin, l'intérêt (même rétif) pour les sujets proposés est indispensable. Que les *rustici* d'Arles écoutent avec mauvaise humeur les leçons de morale sexuelle de Césaire indique qu'ils sont entrés dans le jeu communicationnel.[12]

3) Paramètres individuels: au-delà des attendus précédents, il existe également un facteur plus personnel dépendant de la relation immédiate qui peut aller de la connivence profonde au rejet dépité ou haineux. L'écoute de la parole augustinienne *in vivo* porta la marque d'un ascendant personnel exceptionnel de l'évêque.[13] Les misères d'Eloi à Noyon signèrent l'échec de ce face-à-face.[14]

A ces éléments qui relèvent de la ‹sociolinguistique générale›, s'agrègent différents points qui relèvent plus des conditions particulières de la CV, dans le cadre de la sociolinguistique diachronique du haut Moyen Age. La CV, par définition pour les siècles qui nous concernent, met en jeu la lecture à haute voix d'un texte écrit en latin à l'intention de fidèles illettrés. Tant le corpus écrit du canon de la messe que les lectures bibliques qui y sont insérées relèvent de cette opération de médiation. Celle-ci à son tour dépend de conditions que je ne peux qu'aborder: l'état du texte disponible, la capacité du *lector* à le transformer en un message oral cohérent et compréhensible, celle des fidèles à le recevoir. Si sur ce dernier point, les paramètres précédemment indiqués viennent au premier plan, il reste que les conditions d'émission du texte sacré sont soumises à une série de contraintes que je ne peux analyser en détail.

Disons qu'elle relève de trois niveaux au moins :

1) L'état du texte écrit sur le manuscrit. On a pu montrer[15] qu'en Gaule du Nord, vers le milieu du VIIIe siècle, le latin biblique présentait toutes les caractéristiques de l'état de langue que l'on retrouve dans les chartes, les diplômes, les manuscrits des lois, etc., en d'autres termes, les traits typiques du latin mérovingien. «Le latin barbare de U (manuscrit d'Autun, vers 750), reflet sans doute de celui de l'archétype, atteste sans fard un état de culture dont les monuments ont souvent été détruits par la renaissance carolingienne».[16] Les listes d'erreurs reflètent à la fois

---

12 RICHTER, M.: The Formation of the Medieval West, Studies in the oral culture of the Barbarians, Dublin 1994, p. 34 sqq., p. 64–65.

13 MANDOUZE, A.: Saint Augustin, l'aventure de la raison et de la grâce, Paris 1968, chap. XI, Dialogues avec la foule.

14 GRAUS, F.: Volk, Herrscher und Heiliger im Reich der Merowinger, Prague 1965, p. 157 sqq.

15 GRIBOMONT, J./MALLET, J.: Le latin biblique aux mains des barbares. Les manuscrits UEST des Prophètes, dans: Romanobarbarica 4 (1979), p. 31–105.

16 GRIBOMONT/MALLET: Le latin biblique, p. 33.

l'évolution de la langue parlée commune et le relatif laxisme orthographique des copistes. Le commentateur offre comme exemple du comble de cette barbarie des énoncés comme: *locutus sum ad illus* [pour *illos*]/ *nunciare debemus rege omnes sermones istus* [pour *nuntiare...regi...istos*] /*audierunt uniuersus sermones istus loquere ad eus* [pour *uniuersus...istos...loqui...eos*].[17] L'étude nuance avec opportunité le relatif pessimisme de ses observations pointillistes en concluant que: «Le vulgarisme des manuscrits résulte en réalité d'une osmose entre la culture cléricale et la société barbare où le latin reste encore un instrument de communication.»[18] Observant qu'en dépit des précautions prises pour établir les *codices* (il y a des corrections), ce manuscrit atteste de «vulgarismes atténués (l'expression est bien venue)», les auteurs estiment qu'ils mériteraient l'attention des romanistes. Pour insister sur le caractère fonctionnel de ces rédactions, il convient de replacer ces si utiles analyses dans le cadre de la communication orale. En effet, ces fautes d'orthographe, si elles nuisent à l'élégance culturelle des manuscrits, sont de peu de conséquence pour la maîtrise orale de la langue qu'ils consignent.

2) La maîtrise de la lecture de ces manuscrits. La CV requiert une médiation vitale entre la source écrite et les destinataires qui n'ont accès qu'à l'oralité. Cette dernière est assurée par le *cantor* pour les parties chantées (autre problématique) et par le *lector* pour les parties lues, soit qu'elles le soient *recto tono* (avec les intonations de la prose) ou sous forme de *cantillatio* (chant léger qui garde les accents toniques naturels). Les fonctions du *lector* ayant été décrites à plusieurs reprises, notamment par Isidore, nous pouvons nous en faire une idée assez précise.[19] Il doit rendre par sa diction les affects du texte lu; respecter le sens littéral du texte sacré; avoir une voix correcte; ne pas se laisser entraîner à des démonstrations théâtrales. Chacune de ces exigences suppose un savoir-faire particulier.[20] La lecture requiert une préparation soigneuse qui permet notamment de couper les mots et d'intoner les phrases de manière appropriée (c'est la *praelectio*), exercice difficile en un temps où les textes étaient copiés en *scriptio continua*.[21] Il est certain que son abandon au profit de la séparation des mots a considérablement facilité l'accès à cette opération de conversion écrit/oral. Il me semble en particulier que cette facilité est singulièrement opportune pour des copistes et des lecteurs dont le latin n'était pas (celtophones, germanophones) ou plus (romanophones) la langue maternelle, comme le constate avec pertinence une belle étude consacrée récemment au sujet.[22] L'hypothèse séduisante avancée dans un très beau livre[23] du passage à la lecture individuelle silencieuse pour expliquer cette mutation me paraît moins fondée que l'explication

---

17 Gribomont/Mallet: Le latin biblique, p. 62.

18 Ibid, p. 96.

19 Banniard, M.: Le lecteur en Espagne wisigothique d'après Isidore de Séville: de ses fonctions à l'état de la langue, dans: Revue d'Etudes Augustiniennes et Patristiques 21 (1975), p. 112–144.

20 Cavallo, G.: Scrivere, leggere, memorizzare le sacre scritture, dans: Settimana 45 (1998), p. 987–1008.

21 Saenger, P.: Space Between Words. The Origins of Silent Reading, Stanford 1997, p. 6–9.

22 Cavallo: Scrivere, leggere, p. 1006.

23 Saenger: Space Between Words.

précédente, comme l'affirment à raison les spécialistes.[24] Elle est allée dans le sens d'une ‹grammaire de la lisibilité›. Cette heureuse formulation a été associée à un fait qui est peut-être un peu sous-estimé en Occident, celui de la mémorisation.[25] L'apprentissage par coeur de certains textes faisait partie de la formation intellectuelle des hommes d'Eglise et des moines. Quant on connaît les enjeux de l'oralité et de la mémoire dans les société antiques et médiévales[26] on peut être tenté d'ajouter aux moyens de maîtrise orale de la lecture, celle de la mémoire des textes. Les péricopes évangéliques en particulier, répétées dans le cycle liturgique, se prêtaient admirablement à une mémorisation (pas forcément volontaire) qui permettait au *lector* de re-connaître (c'est le sens premier du verbe lire en grec!) les lignes qu'il avait sous les yeux. Et en ce sens, la connivence mémorielle pouvait également jouer avec un public accoutumé à cet éternel retour du verbe liturgique.[27]

3) L'accès à l'oralité collective. Ce dernier critère s'ajoute et se superpose aux précédents. Il installe le lien direct entre le lecteur et l'auditoire, autrement dit, c'est à travers lui que s'active l'interface entre l'écrit (traditionnel, individuel, muet) et l'oral (évolutif, collectif, sonore). Or, le paramètre fondamental de l'interaction entre oralité lettrée et oralité illettrée est précisément la phonétique.[28] Au cas où nous aurions des doutes à ce sujet, il n'est que de nous rappeler combien la lecture de textes identiques en français et, disons, en castillan est d'accès aisé pour un lettré (surtout latiniste), alors que l'écoute (sans lecture préalable) s'avère difficile pour un locuteur qui ne s'est pas familiarisé avec la phonétique de l'autre langue, pourtant romane. Les communications interdialectales (gascon/ auvergnat; flamand/ bavarois) se brouillent également au-delà d'un certain seuil de divergence phonétique. La transmission orale collective de l'Ecriture a requis que la réalisation articulatoire, tout en étant soignée, ne soit pas trop démarquée de la parole commune du lieu où elle est dite. Cela signifie que pour les siècles qui nous concernent, la prononciation est évolutive à trois points de vues:

1) Diachronique (la parole change de génération en génération)

2) Diatopique (la prononciation sur l'espace mérovingien diffère de celle usuelle sur l'espace lombard)

3) Diastratique (les rémanences culturelles et le conservatisme des lettrés laissent place à des marques distinctives).

---

24 CAVALLO: Scrivere, leggere, p. 1003 sqq.

25 Ibid., p. 988.

26 RICHTER: The Formation of the Medieval West, p. 81 sqq.

27 La question des lectures publiques des livres saints a été magistralement traitée par VOGEL: Introduction aux sources de l'histoire, et par MARTIMORT, A. G.: Les lectures liturgiques et leurs livres (Typologie 64), Turnhout 1992.

28 Les travaux les plus pertinents sur cette question sont dûs à WRIGHT, R.: Late Latin and Early Romance in Spain and Carolingian France, Liverpool 1982; Id.: Latin and the Romance Language in the Early Middle Ages, Londres/New York 1991; Id.: A sociophilological Approach of Late Latin, Turnhout 2002.

Le degré de différence entre la prononciation des lettrés et celle des illettrés a fait l'objet de débats,[29] mais tous les signes convergent pour indiquer qu'aux siècles considérés il n'y a pas de clivage. Un des traits les plus pertinents provient justement de l'irruption des ‹fautes› d'orthographe dans les manuscrits mérovingiens, ces erreurs étant presque constamment liées à ce que nous savons de la parole commune.

Le rassemblement de *testimonia* directs sur cette situation est d'autant moins facile que, si les lettrés avaient conscience des errances éventuelles de leur graphie, ils n'avaient pas de moyen de mesurer l'évolutivité de leur phonie (en fait, il n'existait pas de véritable orthoépie). Il s'en est suivi que l'écart graphie/phonie est allé grandissant, sans doute pour le plus grand tourment des copistes (on connaît les remarques inquiètes des moines copistes de Vivarium à l'adresse de leur maître Cassiodore), mais pour le plus grand bénéfice des auditeurs illettrés.

On a cité fréquemment un passage justement célèbre datant de la fin du VIᵉ siècle en Touraine. L'évêque (Grégoire), fatigué par une maladie récente, ayant délégué le soin de célébrer la messe à un prêtre, celui-ci subit une mésaventure: «Mais comme ce prêtre avait pour dire les mots de la célébration une diction vaguement illettrée, un certain nombre d'entre nous commença à ricaner en déclarant qu'il aurait mieux valu se taire plutôt que de parler de manière si peu soignée.»[30] Grégoire, embarrassé, est ensuite rassuré par un songe. L'interprétation de cet épisode a naturellement été presque toujours orientée dans un sens diastratique: ce serait la «langue vulgaire» qui aurait indûment contaminé la parole du malheureux officiant. Et la pièce a été automatiquement versée au dossier de la ‹dégradation› du latin. Mais au moins deux autres interprétations sont possibles. La première est diatopique: ce prêtre, venu peut-être de quelque région voisine (Poitiers? Orléans?) aurait pu avoir un accent local (en tous cas légèrement différent de celui qui s'entendait à Tours), ce qui aurait suscité les quolibets. Les récits ethnographiques abondent en ce genre d'anecdotes, l'autre, même voisin à vingt kilomètres, étant stigmatisé pour de menues différences dialectales. Mais l'hypothèse qui me paraît la plus vraisemblable est que ce prêtre, pris au dépourvu,[31] n'a pas eu le temps de se préparer correctement à sa tâche et notamment que sa *praelectio* a été insuffisante. Il a donc dû commettre des mécoupures, rater des intonations, peut-être bégayer.[32]

---

29 BANNIARD, M.: Vox agrestis. Quelques problèmes d'élocution de Cassiodore à Alcuin, dans: POU-
THIER, P. (ed.): D'Hippocrate à Alcuin, Trames/Limoges 1985, p. 195–208.

30 GREG. TUR.: De uirtutibus beati Martini episcopi, Liber 2,1 (Monumenta Germaniae Historica, Scriptores Rerum Merovingicarum, t. 1, ed. KRUSCH): ... *nolens me fatigare uni presbiterorum gloriosa solemnia caelebrare praecepi. Sed cum presbiter ille nescio quid rustice festiua uerba depromeret, multi eum de nostris inridere coeperunt, dicentes: ‹Melius fuisset tacere quam sic inculte loqui›.* On notera que Grégoire qualifie les moqueurs non pas de lettrés et d'érudits, mais de *stulti et faciles* («élégants sans cervelle»).

31 Le récit le désigne par un *uni presbyterorum* qui suggère une certaine improvisation.

32 Un exemple de surinterprétation similaire a transformé en *exemplum* d'ignorance langagière la mésaventure du jeune Grégoire d'Utrecht (il n'a pas su, non pas comprendre le latin du texte qu'il lisait, mais improviser une traduction en ‹patois›). Cf. BANNIARD, M.: Credo et langage: les missions de saint Boniface, dans: DIERKENS, A. (ed.): Voyages et voyageurs en Occident au Moyen Age, Bruxelles 2000, p. 133–156.

En tous cas, il a été indigne de la maîtrise épiscopale (le charisme de Grégoire lui faisait défaut...). Ce petit désastre a donc une valeur plus culturelle que linguistique. Mais en même temps, il est à verser au dossier du bon fonctionnement de la CV: le public réagit dans un contexte qui exclut une réaction d'agacement due à l'incompréhension.

L'interaction entre la phonétique naturelle commune et la diction du lecteur s'ajustait de façon spontanée à différents niveaux. D'abord, les mécanismes intonatoires liés aux catégories (affirmation/ interrogation/ négation) étaient stables en diachronie et partagés en diastratie: seule la mesure ou l'excès dans leurs effets (*aurea mediocritas*) pouvait introduire une distinction.[33] Ensuite, les accents de mots ayant gardé dans l'ensemble la même place en latin parlé classique, puis en latin parlé tardif, et enfin en roman, le marquage accentuel est demeuré identique en parole savante et en parole commune. Quant à la nature de cet accent, il est certain qu'il était nettement tonique depuis longtemps, avec des fluctuations d'intensité selon les régions (plus fort par exemple en latin du Nord qu'en latin du Sud de la France), évolution partagée par tous les locuteurs indépendamment de la diastratie. Sur ce patron prosodique et intonatoire commun, le *lector* et l'*auditor* disposaient déjà de repères communicationnels communs importants. Les autres catégories de la phonie (syllabation avec syncope et apocope, oppositions de timbres, fusion de certaines voyelles), dont l'évolution dans la parole commune est manifestée dans les manuscrits (sous forme non d'identité, mais de reflet), étaient partagées, avec de faibles fluctuations diastratiques, par les lettrés et les illettrés. La maîtrise de l'oralité collective par le *lector* était d'autant plus probable qu'avant la réforme carolingienne, il existait moins des normes de prononciation (d'où seraient-elles sorties?) que des habitudes, soit personnelles soit sociales, de démarcation, à la fois repérables et limitées.

Niveaux et documents médiateurs

Dans certaines situations privilégiées, les documents qui nous sont parvenus indiquent clairement que le public des fidèles a écouté directement la lecture de l'Evangile et qu'il est invité à réfléchir sur son sens grâce à la médiation du prédicateur.[34] Au Vᵉ siècle en Afrique, au VIᵉ siècle à Rome, Augustin, puis Grégoire I, attestent de la réception immédiate du texte biblique. Leur commentaire renvoie constamment à celui-ci dans des conditions telles que l'interaction immédiate entre les

---

33 Isidore stigmatisait les *lectores* qui adoptaient une diction et une gestualité trop théâtrales (*miseranter dicere*). BANNIARD: Le lecteur en Espagne, p. 125 sqq.

34 Les données essentielles sur la réalité de ces lectures sont réunies en particulier dans les ouvrages cités de VOGEL et MARTIMORT. On trouve également de nombreuses indications dans JUNGMANN, J.: Missarum solemnia. Explication génétique de la messe romaine, traduction française, 3 vol., Paris 1951–1954 et de précieuses attestations dans NICKL, G.: Der Anteil des Volkes an der Messliturgie im Frankenreiche von Chlodwig bis Karl den Großen, Innsbruck 1930.

auditeurs et le lecteur est manifeste.[35] En tous cas, les difficultés de compréhension ne semblent jamais relever de la langue elle-même.

Aux siècles suivants, les nôtres, ceux où la sociolinguistique diachronique estime que s'est engagée puis accomplie la sortie de la latinophonie par la communauté des locuteurs, on ne peut raisonner que par analogie en l'absence d'une documentation aussi riche en *testimonia*.[36] Cette situation tient essentiellement au fait que nous n'avons pas l'équivalent – et de loin – des recueils d'homélies saisies *in vivo* pendant les siècles précédents. C'est donc en nous appuyant sur des déductions fondées sur la chronologie générale de la fin de la CV que nous pouvons proposer des conclusions sur la situation des VIIᵉ et VIIIᵉ siècles. Etant donné qu'il est bien établi à présent qu'en Occident Latin la CV commence d'être perturbée de manière préoccupante dans la deuxième moitié du VIIIᵉ siècle pour se déliter au IXᵉ (avec des décalages possibles selon les régions, et en particulier en Italie), il y a tout lieu de supposer que la réceptibilité des textes bibliques a perduré dans les mêmes conditions.

Il me semble toutefois qu'il faudrait introduire des différences en fonction des paramètres précédemment indiqués. En effet, le langage vétéro-testamentaire a toujours paru plus difficile à interpréter aux Pères de l'Eglise que le langage néo-testamentaire, du moins celui des Evangiles et des Actes des apôtres. Les obstacles étaient dressés par le type de style employé et surtout par le sens, lié à des états de civilisation et de mentalités fort lointains. Pour des raisons inverses, les Evangiles paraissaient d'accès plus immédiat pour une communauté chrétienne peu ou non instruite. De plus, la structure même des chapitres se prêtait admirablement à des découpages qui soulageaient l'attention. L'introduction des paraboles achevait de conférer au récit une transparence formelle immédiate. Enfin, ce sont les textes qui sont lus le plus souvent et le plus régulièrement. Si l'on fait la synthèse de tout ceci, on obtient une caractérisation positive à trois niveaux :

1) La simplicité langagière, celle du fameux *sermo piscatorius* (si souvent soulignée à juste titre par tous les commentateurs).[37]

2) L'exemplarité narrative, les récits de miracle et les paraboles ponctuent la trame textuelle de manière marquante, comme autant de repères forts pour les auditeurs.[38]

3) La familiarisation grâce à la répétition annuelle du cycle. Les récits sont attendus par les fidèles au moment des grands rendez-vous festifs.

---

35 Pour Augustin voir Madec, G.: Augustin prédicateur à la lumière des sermons découverts à Mayence, Paris 1998; pour Grégoire, Banniard: Viva voce, chap. 3.

36 Banniard: Viva voce, chap. 5; Van Uytfanghe, M.: Le latin des hagiographes mérovingiens et la protohistoire du français, dans: Romanica Gandensia 16 (1976), p. 5–89; Id.: La Bible et l'instruction des laïcs à l'époque mérovingienne: des témoignages textuels à une approche langagière de la question, dans: Sacris Erudiri 34 (1994), p. 67–123.

37 Norden, E.: Die antike Kunstprosa vom VI. Jahrhundert vor Chr. bis in die Zeit der Renaissance, 2 vol., Leipzig 1898, t. 2, p. 452–655.

38 Auerbach, E.: Literatursprache und Publikum in der lateinischen Spätantike und im Mittelalter, Berne 1958.

4) La connivence culturelle qui s'établit ainsi au fil des siècles favorise la compréhension, jusqu'à entrer en interaction avec les cultes et les légendes folkloriques.[39]

En d'autres termes, et à des niveaux différenciés, le texte biblique a pu bénéficier grâce à des séries de facteurs positifs d'une réceptibilité variable, mais efficace, par tous les auditeurs illettrés. Cela revient à dire que la mémoire langagière (le savoir collectif des locuteurs) et l'accoutumance pastorale (l'accumulation rituelle des leçons) ont été longtemps une base suffisante pour l'accueil de l'Ecriture sans médiateur autre que la voix du *lector*.

Ce travail de la mémoire et la manière dont la latinité biblique pouvait s'installer ainsi dans un savoir vivant a laissé des traces diverses. On a pu montrer l'influence du latin biblique sur certaines particularités des langues romanes.[40] La chance a fait arriver jusqu'à nous des documents étonnants qui nous offrent une occasion de saisir le travail mémoriel. Sur une des ardoises datant de l'époque wisigothique trouvées dans la région de Salamanque,[41] on a retrouvé et déchiffré un texte qui mérite notre attention dans le cadre de la question posée. Elle présente une sorte de récitation individuelle et semi-spontanée du Psaume 15 par un semi-lettré.[42] L'éditeur a émis l'hypothèse (fondée) que ce texte a été copié de mémoire, ce qui expliquerait les différentes altérations de l'original biblique. Après avoir songé à un exercice scolaire dans le cadre de la *litteratio*, elle penche à présent pour un acte de prière par écrit. Ce document a en effet toute l'allure d'un geste pieux accompli par un chrétien dans le cadre privé d'une dévotion non institutionnelle. Il représente donc un excellent accès à l'interface écrit/oral dans un mouvement proche de la spontanéité.

Nous regarderons quelques lignes :

> Conserua me Domine quoniam in te isperabi. Disi Domino: Deus meus es tum, quoniam bonorum meorum non indigi.
> Sanctis qui in terra sunt eius, merificabit omnes uoluntates suas inter illos..
> Multiplicatae sunt in infimitatem eorum pos te aceleurarunt.
> Non congregabo conuenticula de sauinibus nec memor ero nomina illorum per labia mea.
> Dominus pars ereditates meas et calicis mei: tu es qui restituisti mici ereditatem mea.
> Funis cederunt mici in preclaris etenim erditatis mea praeclara est mici.
> Benedican Domine qui mici tribuit intellectum insuper et usque a nontem inripauerunt me renes mei.
> Prouidebam Dominum in conspectu meo semper, quoniam a destiris est mici, ne commouear.
> Propter hoc delegatum est cor meum et essultabit lingua mea. Insuper et caro mea requiesces in ispe.
> Quoniam non derelinques animam meam in infernum.

---

39 Sur ces interactions voir Cocchiara, G.: Storia del folklore in Europa, Turin 1953; Graus: Volk, Herrscher und Heiliger.

40 Devoto, G.: La Bibbia e le forze di conservazione linguistica nell'alto medioevo, dans: Settimana 10 (1963), p. 55–66.

41 Velazquez, I.: Documentos de época visigoda escritos en pizarra (siglos VI–VIII), Prefacio de J. Fontaine, dans: Atsma, H./Vezin, J. (dir.): Monumenta Paleographica Medii Aeui, Series hispanica, 2 vol., León/Turnhout 1997 et 2000.

42 Doc. 29, Salamanca: Plegaria, salmo 15.

Nontas mici ficisti uias uitae.
Adimplebis me cum laetitia cum uultu tuo deletaciones tuas destra usque in finem.

Quelle est la fonction d'un tel objet? Cela ne peut guère être un exercice scolaire, car le matériau retenu ne se prête pas à la normalisation. La forme de l'écriture, la liberté de la rédaction, les fluctuations du latin invitent à penser à un geste de piété privée. Peut-être un échange affectueux entre deux moines ou prêtres (et pourquoi pas même un laïc?) qui auraient ainsi partagé des ‹billets de dévotion›. En tous cas, le savoir biblique et le savoir scolaire du rédacteur, s'ils sont assurés, laissent place à divers traits de la parole spontanée, au moins en phonétique:

* *isperabi/ispe* (épenthèse vocalique);
* *indigi/calicis/incripauerunt/ficisti* (flottement graphie/phonie);
* *disi/essultabit* (assimilation consonantique);

D'autres signaux sont d'interprétation moins assurée. La graphie *mici* n'est pas vraiment une faute. L'omission de quelques consonnes finales (*pos*) ou leur confusion (*Benedica*n) peuvent provenir du matériau employé et des conditions de rapidité de l'exécution. Il en va peut-être de même de formes comme *ini fimitatem* (pour *infirmitatem*), simple bégaiement du poinçon.

En revanche, des formes comme *aceleurarunt/nontem/Nontas* indiquent que cette incision s'écarte de la tradition psalmique. Leur interprétation en termes de communication et de compréhension doit demeurer prudente. Tout se passe en effet comme si en griffonnant ces mots, le graveur entendait en voix intérieure le véritable latin oral biblique, mais réduisait la notation écrite à une sorte de logogriphe obscur pour nous, mais suffisant pour appeler à sa mémoire intime les mots sources du texte traditionnel.

En définitive, le rapport entre cette tradition latine écrite biblique et l'oralité du graveur ne se laisse pas, pas plus là qu'ailleurs, réduire à de simples indices mécaniques fondés sur des unités isolées. Il faut considérer le phrasé de ce latin et se convaincre qu'il était entendu en voix intérieure avec ses pics accentuels, son rythme progressif, ses instances sémantiques. Les approximations du graveur indiquent une grande familiarité avec ce langage (sa présence était banale), dont la teneur pluriséculaire incessamment répétée restait en contact vivant avec ces locuteurs. Ce geste de piété était aussi un acte de *ruminatio*. La capacité du récitant à écrire fait évidemment de lui un semi-lettré, ce qui atténue dans une certaine mesure l'information qu'il nous apporte sur la situation des véritables illettrés.[43] Mais sa latinité est suffisamment modeste (par rapport évidemment à la norme écrite traditionnelle)[44] pour que nous admettions que son témoignage révèle avec une bonne approximation la manière dont était pendant ces siècles intériorisé le latin biblique par les voies de l'oralité.

---

43 BANNIARD: Viva voce, chap. 4.
44 VELAZQUEZ, I.: ‹Latine dicitur. Vulgo vocant›. Aspectos de la lengua escrita y hablada en las obras gramaticales de Isidoro de Sevilla, Logrono 2003.

Certains passages des Vies de saints mérovingiennes, elles-mêmes imprégnées de latin biblique[45] offrent exactement les mêmes traits langagiers avec les conséquences communicationnelles que nous savons.[46] Je n'y reviens pas ici, en renvoyant à de nombreux autres travaux, mais je me contente d'insister sur la cohérence des données. Puisque le latin mérovingien des *Vitae* était, comme c'est établi, compris lors des lectures publiques, peut-être quelque peu dramatisées, le latin biblique, surtout évangélique, ne pouvait que l'être aussi. Convergeant avec ces données, d'autres textes plaident en ce sens: les diplômes originaux des rois mérovingiens qui nous sont parvenus et ont fait l'objet d'une édition soignée nous donnent à lire une latinité du même aloi. Les nombreuses fautes de graphie qui les émaillent rappellent celle que nous avons vues sur l'ardoise wisigothique. L'extrait donné ci-dessous manifeste cette équivalence.[47]

> Theuderici rex Francorum, uir inluster.
>
> Cum ante dies X in nostri uel procerum nostrorum presencia, Compendio, in palacio nostro, ibique ueniens fimena, nomene
> Achildis, Amalgario interpellauit dum dicerit, eo quod porcione sua, in uilla noncobanti Bactilionevalle, quem de parti genetrici suae Bertrane, quondam, ligebus obuenire debuerat, post se malo ordene retinerit.
> Qui ipse Amalgarius taliter dedit in respunsis, eo quod ipas terra in predicto loco Bactilionevalle, de annus triginta et uno, inter ipsp Amalgario uel genetore suo Gaeltramno, quondam semper tenuerant et possiderant.

On peut interpréter les graphies innovantes comme le signe d'une ‹barbarisation› due à l'incurie (c'est une attitude assez répandue chez les philologues). On peut aussi voir en elle le signe d'une langue écrite adaptée aux fonctions qui lui sont dévolues, celle d'une communication orale en style élevé.[48] Car il me semble que ces diplômes doivent être moins lus qu'écoutés: c'est pour cela qu'ils ont été rédigés dans des actes de justice royale semi-publique. Si on se donne alors la peine d'entendre le phrasé de cet acrolecte latin, on perçoit le *continuum* langagier avec le ‹latin barbare› des manuscrits bibliques précédemment analysés. L'étude *in situ* des lectionnaires qui nous sont parvenus dans des manuscrits pré-carolingiens

---

45 VAN UYTFANGHE, M.: Stylisation biblique et condition humaine dans l'hagiographie mérovingienne, 600–750, Bruxelles 1987; Id.: La formation du langage hagiographique en Occident Latin, dans: Cassiodorus 5 (1999), p. 143–169; Id.: La saveur biblique du latin mérovingien. L'exemple de la ‹Vie de sainte Rusticule›, abbesse à Arles (VIIe s.), dans: MARTINEZ, F. G./LUTTIKHUIZEN, G. P. (ed.): Jerusalem, Alexandria, Rome. Studies in Ancient Cultural Interaction in Honour of A. Hilhorst, Leyde/Boston 2003, p. 341–357.

46 BANNIARD: Viva voce, chap. 5.

47 Plaid de Thierry III 30/6/679, Palais de Luzarches. Codices Latini Antiquiores, t. XIII, Rome 1928; ATSMA, Hartmut/VEZIN, Jean (ed.): Chartae Latinae Antiquiores, France 1 (Facsimile edition of the Latin Charters prior to the ninth century 13), Zurich 1981.

48 Sur la qualité de la production manuscrite de ces siècles, BISCHOFF, B.: Manuscripts and Librairies in the Age of Charlemagne, Cambridge 1994, p. 1–19.

conduit aux mêmes conclusions.[49] Les interactions entre le texte biblique original et les modifications observables de cette langue dans sa pratique, soit mémorielle[50] (le sujet lettré ou semi-lettré pense ce texte en voix intérieure), soit communicationnelle (le même sujet[51] exporte ce texte en voix extérieure), rejoignent pleinement les descriptions des domaines en proximité immédiate de l'hagiographie et de la juridiction. L'interaction entre l'écriture traditionnelle et l'oralité commune s'y trouve pleinement confirmée.

Historiciser la réception

Il serait vain de prétendre retracer ici dans le détail cette histoire. De nombreux autres travaux seront nécessaires pour affiner nos connaissances, et, même ainsi, ces siècles garderont des zones inaccessibles à nos questions. Toutefois, à la lumière des considérations précédentes, il paraît raisonnable de soutenir que le texte latin de la Bible, lorsque sa communication était faite oralement à l'intention des fidèles illettrés de l'Occident latin dans les conditions requises énoncées plus haut, a pendant plusieurs siècles bénéficié d'un haut niveau de réceptibilité qui ne s'est vraiment abaissé en dessous d'un seuil d'efficacité suffisant qu'à partir de la seconde moitié du viiie siècle. Des raisons tant internes qu'analogiques ont conduit à cette conclusion.

Sous cette formulation globale, il conviendrait d'introduire des distinctions tant par niveaux que par époques. D'abord, il est évident que seule une partie du texte biblique (certains Psaumes, certains passages exemplaires de l'Ancien Testament, les Evangiles sans doute dans leur totalité) a pu être vraiment accessible à la communauté des locuteurs. Et même à l'intérieur de ces espaces communicationnels, la compréhension a dû beaucoup fluctuer (mais ceci ne relève plus tellement de questions langagières). Tout cela pose des questions délicates qui ont été traitées notamment sur le thème de la «démocratisation de la culture».[52] Ensuite, il paraît nécessaire de moduler l'efficacité de cette réceptibilité en fonction du temps. J'aurai tendance à calquer l'évolution de cette réception sur celle de la CV latino-

---

49 Salmon, P.: Le lectionnaire de Luxeuil, 2 vol., Rome 1944 et 1953. Cette édition critique d'un texte copié sans doute vers 700 à Paris, accompagnée de fac-similés, permet de suivre les mêmes fluctuations graphie/phonie que les manuscrits étudiés par Gribomont/Mallet: Le latin biblique. Cf. aussi Salmon, P.: Le texte biblique des lectionnaires mérovingiens, dans: Settimana 10 (1963), p. 491–519. Je pense consacrer une étude spécifique d'un point de vue sociolinguistique à ce lectionnaire célèbre.

50 Sur l'efficacité de l'apprentissage de ce type, Heinzelmann, M.: Studia sanctorum. Education, milieux d'instruction et valeurs éducatives dans l'hagiographie en Gaule jusqu'à la fin de l'époque mérovingienne, dans: Sot, M. (ed.): Haut Moyen Age. Culture, éducation, société, Paris 1990, p. 105–138.

51 Même si le copiste n'est pas aussi le lector, je veux dire que ces opérations sont caractéristiques d'individus passés au même moule.

52 Carrié, J. M./Duval, N./Cantino-Wataghin, G. (ed.): Antiquité Tardive et «démocratisation de la culture», mise à l'épreuve du paradigme, dans: Antiquité Tardive 9 (2001).

phone globale. Juqu'au VIᵉ siècle inclus, le texte biblique a été médiatisé sans difficulté autre que la qualité religieuse de son contenu. Rien ne nous empêche de penser que les Germains acculturés aient participé de cet accueil direct.[53] Ensuite, le VIIᵉ siècle et sans doute le début du VIIIᵉ ont constitué un stade de conservatisme encore efficace.[54]

Puis est venue la débâcle de la CV, due à des facteurs externes (réforme carolingienne, réaction classicisante à Cordoue), mais aussi internes (cristallisation des langues romanes). Là s'est installée une période d'instabilité où la réception directe du message latin était tout à fait aléatoire.

Cela pose la question des décisions prises par la hiérarchie ecclésiastique. A Tours en 813, il n'est question de traduire que les homélies. Rien n'est dit des péricopes bibliques. Nous savons pourtant que dans les pays germanophones ce travail de traduction était engagé. Ceux des pasteurs qui, sur un sol anciennement latinophone, étaient confrontés à des auditeurs qui ne comprenaient plus guère les textes fondamentaux de leur foi, ont dû adapter leur technique de lecture. Le temps des traductions était là aussi venu. Mais pour que cette oralité (en fait savante) d'illettrés (cette fois au sens strict) accédât à la langue écrite, un travail de quelques générations serait encore nécessaire.

Cette contribution pourrait donner l'impression que les destinataires de la CV latinophone furent de simples réceptacles dans lesquels, forte de sa maîtrise de la parole officielle, l'Eglise aurait déversé un savoir passivement assimilé. Ce n'est nullement mon point de vue. Ecouter et éventuellement comprendre ne signifie pas approuver: tous les exemples pris à l'histoire longue, mais aussi à l'anthropologie et à la dialectologie, montrent que les consciences collectives sont toujours le résultat d'actions et de réactions. Parfois, dans des documents bien plus tardifs, nous avons accès à la pensée réelle d'un de ces destinataires obscurs des messages religieux. Le résultat peut-être tout à fait surprenant.[55] Il reste à imaginer comment des Menocchio du VIIᵉ siècle purent construire à partir de ces messages martelés leur représentation de l'univers.[56]

53　FLOBERT, P.: Latin-Frankish Bilingualism in Sixth-Century Gaul: the Latin of Clovis, dans: ADAMS, J. N. (ed.): Bilingualism in Ancient Society, Oxford 2002, p. 420–430.

54　Un exposé détaillé de cette chronologie est établi dans BANNIARD, M.: The Transition from Latin to the Romance Languages, dans: VINCENT, N. (ed.): The Cambridge History of the Romance Languages, Cambridge, à paraître. Pour des mises au point plus brèves, mais convergentes, je cite, entre autres, deux belles études de J. HERMAN: The End of the History of Latin, dans: Romance Philology 44 (1991), p. 364–381, et La disparition du passif synthétique latin: nouvel essai sur l'écrit et le parlé en latin mérovingien, dans: Estudis romanics 24 (2002), p. 31–44.

55　GINZBURG, C.: Le fromage et les vers. L'univers d'un meunier du XVIᵉ siècle, Paris 1978.

56　C'était un des objets du beau livre de M. RICHTER, justement sous-titré Oral culture of the Barbarians.

MICHELE C. FERRARI

Language and communication in the Latin west

In 1782, the schoolmaster Karl Philipp Moritz (1756–1793), later a distinguished German author, set out on what would have been described at that time as an educational journey. But whereas most of his contemporaries tended to go south in order to enjoy the "soft, balmy air" that Goethe speaks of so enthusiastically in his *Italian Journey*, this independent-minded pedagogue and enlightened thinker decided to go in the opposite direction, to England. Unlike those aristocratic or well-to-do courtiers who were able to travel everywhere comfortably by coach, Moritz had to make his journey on foot; and when he found himself somewhere near Oxford, he met someone who also happened to be travelling on foot and who claimed to be a clergyman. As Moritz recalls:

> Nun fing er an, einige Worte Latein zu reden, und da ich ihm nach der Englischen Aussprache wieder Lateinisch antwortete, gab er mir seinen Beifall über meine richtige Pronunciation des Lateinischen zu erkennen. Denn, sagte er, vor einigen Jahren sei ihm einmal, auch in der Nacht, fast auf eben dem Fleck, ein Deutscher begegnet, der ihn auch auf Latein angeredet, aber es so abscheulich ausgesprochen habe, daß er nur wenige Worte davon verstanden hätte.[1]

> After he had said a few words to me in Latin and I had answered him likewise in Latin with a sort of English accent, he congratulated me on my correct pronunciation. He said that only a few years earlier, also by night and almost at the same place, he had met a German who had addressed him in Latin, but whose pronunciation was so awful that he could barely understand what he was saying.

This anecdote is a reminder that only a few years before the French Revolution the language of the ancient Romans was still very much the medium in which highly cultured Europeans communicated with one another and a foremost means of cultural transmission in Europe and elsewhere. And that is how it was to be for some time to come. Indeed, as late as the nineteenth century it was quite normal for scholars to write their doctoral dissertations in Latin, especially if the topic was a purely scientific one. Even Romain Rolland (1866–1944) had to write his thesis in that language. And we should not forget that most important scientific books before 1850 were written in Latin, such as Isaac Newton's *Philosophiae naturalis principia mathematica* (1687) or Carl Friedrich Gauss' *Disquisitiones arithmeticae* (1801).

But Latin also continued to maintain its function as a literary language long after the Roman Empire had ceased to exist. The Middle Ages was the era that produced – or at least preserved, since most Latin texts up to the third century have been lost – infinitely more Latin literature than the whole of classical antiquity had ever done. In the late Middle Ages for instance, thousands of poems,

---

1 MORITZ, Karl Philipp: Reisen eines Deutschen in England im Jahr 1782. Mit einem Nachwort von Heide Hollmer, Frankfurt a. M. 2000, p. 108.

sermons and treatises were produced – a number that was scarcely surpassed by
the writings of the Humanists.

Although the seventeenth century was the last to see Latin as the main medium of written communication, it is worth noting that Latin poetry flourished
even in the nineteenth century. Thus the French poet Charles Baudelaire (1821–
1867) occasionally wrote Latin poetry, and included a *carmen* in *Les fleurs du mal*
(1857):[2]

FRANCISCAE MEAE LAUDES
Vers composés pour une modiste érudite et dévote

Novis te cantabo chordis,
o novelletum quod ludis
in solitudine cordis.

Esto sertis implicata,
o femina delicata
per quam solvuntur peccata!
(...)

Even in our, so to speak, un-Latin era, you will occasionally come across the odd
high school teacher or retired university professor ready to put a handful of readers past all patience with their Latin poems.

During the Middle Ages and the Early Modern Period (that is up to 1800),
Latin, though no longer used in everyday life, nevertheless proved useful in its
dual role as an instrument of oral and written communication and as a literary
language.

As a means of communication, Latin proved useful as an international language, similar to French or English as used nowadays, say, in diplomacy. On his
journey through Germany in 1507, for instance, the Florentine ambassador Francesco Vettori (1474–1539) was relieved to meet people with whom he could communicate in Latin, though it must be said that he wrote his *Journey to Germany* in
his mother tongue:

> Era alloggiato nella medesima casa uno ambasciatore del conte di Traietto in Frigia (...)
> Era stato in Italia, ma non sapeva parlare in italiano, ma benissimo latino e tutte le cose che
> io volevo sapere da lui, volentieri me le diceva.[3]

> In the same house I met a legate of the count-bishop of Utrecht in the Netherlands (...) He had
> been in Italy, but was not able to speak Italian. However, he spoke perfect Latin, in which he
> was ready to tell everything I asked him about.

At an earlier period, there could be no alternative means of communication
among the learned. This applies for instance to the Carolingian period. Peter of

---

2   Baudelaire, Charles: Œuvres complètes. Texte établi, présenté et annoté par Claude Pichois,
    vol. 1, Paris 1975 (Bibliothèque de la Pléiade), pp. 61–62.
3   Vettori, Francesco/Machiavelli, Niccolò: Viaggio in Germania. A cura di Marcello Simonetta
    (L'Italia 25), Palermo 2003, p. 116.

Pisa, Theodulf of Orléans († 821), Alcuin of York († 804), who resided at Charlemagne's court and had constant discussions with him, taught in Latin and wrote
poems and treatises in Latin. They had little choice but to communicate with
one another in this language, since they each came from quite different linguistic
backgrounds. Charlemagne's court was made up of Italians, Spaniards, French-
men, Englishmen, Irishmen and Germans, all of whom perforce had to use Latin
in order to understand one another.

Yet all this was much more than a matter of mere communication. At that
time and, indeed, in later periods, Latin represented the common Roman heritage
which was of immense significance for the Carolingians and for many of their
successors. Charlemagne was a shining example of someone who showed the way
on behalf of Latin culture. In a well-known passage of the *Vita Karoli*, Einhard
speaks of Charlemagne's sound knowledge of Latin and Greek, and relates how
the latter had St. Augustine's *Civitas Dei* read aloud to him during meals, thereby
imitating a practice that was common in monastic refectories. As Einhard says:

> Erat eloquentia copiosus et exuberans poteratque quicquid vellet apertissime exprimere. Nec
> patrio tanto sermone contentus etiam peregrinis linguis ediscendis operam impendit. In quibus
> latinam ita didicit ut aeque illa ac patria lingua orare sit solitus. Grecam vero melius intel-
> legere quam pronuntiare poterat. Adeo quidem facundus erat ut etiam didascalus appareret.[4]

> Charlemagne was an outstandingly eloquent speaker, with a gift for articulating his thoughts
> most rigorously. Nor was he content to speak his mother tongue [which in Latin is called *patrius
> sermo* or "father tongue"], but undertook to learn various other foreign languages. In this way
> he acquired such a good knowledge of Latin that he was able to speak it as fluently as he spoke
> his native language. Greek, on the other hand, he could understand better than he could speak
> it. At any rate, he was clever enough at languages to be mistaken now and again for a language
> teacher.

Charlemagne was especially concerned with preserving the purity of Latin, and
that not for scholarly or cultural reasons. His efforts in that respect were directed quite specifically at improving the *cultus divinus*, or divine worship. Indeed,
it is owing to him that the liturgy was later sung in a linguistically more correct,
and hence worthier, form than ever before. Charlemagne's endeavours on behalf
of Latin grammar and against the kind of Latin used in oral contexts marked the
beginning of a new phase in the history of Latin and European languages in general.

At a time when the various vernacular languages were going their own way in
areas that had once been occupied by the Romans, and were basically breaking
away from the different types of Latin that were spoken, the Carolingian reforms
led to the cutting of that fine thread which until then had bound the Latin as spoken in everyday life with the Latin as used by the educated classes. That all this
happened in Europe at varying rates (most rapidly in northern France, and most

---

4   Einh. Karol. 25 – Einhardi Vita Karoli Magni. Post G. H. Pertz recensuit G. Waitz. Editio
    Sexta. Curavit O. Holder-Egger (Monumenta Germaniae historica: Scriptores rerum Germani-
    carum in usum scholarum ex MGH separatim editi 25), Hannover 1911, p. 30.

slowly in Italy) has been demonstrated by Michel Banniard in an excellent study published in 1992.[5]

Nevertheless, Latin continued to be a vital medium of communication, even if in relatively limited circles, not only for the Carolingian scholars and poets at Charlemagne's court whom I have already mentioned but also for a number of highly educated figures who flourished at a later period. For example, Gerbert of Rheims, later to become Pope Sylvester II († 1003), had a school in Rheims that consisted of a large number of pupils drawn from all parts of Europe. The same is true of later *scholastici*, e. g. for Lanfranc of Pavia († 1089), who taught in Normandy before becoming Archbishop of Canterbury in 1070. A contemporary tells us that even German students undertook arduous journeys from their native country in order to attend his classes.[6]

Yet it was not only in such scholarly circles that Latin continued to flourish. Indeed, from the viewpoint of quantity Latin was first and foremost a means of imparting knowledge, because it was spoken in schools at all levels and, from the twelfth and thirteenth century, at the new high schools that we today call universities. And astonishing as it may seem, Latin was being used as a medium of learning in educational contexts such as elementary schools and was predominant there for several centuries. Thus we know from accounts of late medieval classrooms that pupils were even compelled to speak Latin to each other, and threatened with corporal punishment if they failed to do so. Whether or not a pupil was punished for uttering a German or French word is uncertain. Generally speaking, however, one may assume that Latin was, at least in some measure, the teaching language in European schools well into the Early Modern Period.

The growth in literacy both north and south of the Alps from the thirteenth and fourteenth centuries onwards meant that an even greater number of people came into contact with Latin, which continued to assert itself effortlessly as a means of education. The same has been found to be true of the universities, as I have already argued above.

To be sure, there were sporadic attempts, especially in Germany, to liberate people from the constraints of a none too easily accessible language, as was done, for example, in Rostock in 1501, when one law professor decided to lecture to his students in German. But such attempts were considered eccentric at that time and did not go down well. Even in the late eighteenth century Heinrich Jung-Stilling (1740–1817) came into conflict with the authorities of his *alma mater* at Heidelberg because he had held some lectures in German. It was not till about 1800 that German became universal at Protestant universities, nor till the nineteenth cen-

---

5 BANNIARD, Michel: *Viva voce*. Communication écrite et communication orale du IVᵉ au IXᵉ siècle en Occident latin (Collection des Etudes augustiniennes, Série Moyen-Age et Temps modernes 25), Paris 1992.

6 BARTELMEZ, Erminnie Hollis (ed.): The *Expositio in Cantica Canticorum* of Williram abbot of Ebersberg 1048–1085. A critical edition, Philadelphia 1967, p. 1.

tury was well underway that it became the same at Catholic universities (in Turin Latin as an academic language was abolished only as late as in 1852).

It was thanks to the universities that Latin underwent a monumental revolution, for in the late twelfth century the notorious scholastic Latin was born:

> Quicumque enim peccat agit contra rationem rectam, quae est prudentia. Sed imprudentia consistit in hoc quod aliquis agit contra prudentiam, ut dictum est. Ergo imprudentia non est speciale peccatum.

Such passages are enough to make any honest Ciceronian's hair stand on end – and what I have just quoted is, linguistically speaking, but a mild passage from Thomas Aquinas's *Summa*.[7]

If the Latin used by medieval scholars, lawyers, philosophers and theologians in Bologna, Oxford and Paris had been the favourite target of criticism of all those humanistically-minded philologists, so too was the entire Latin culture of the Middle Ages, and somewhat unjustly so.

In this context, let me draw attention to a couple of matters. The Latin that was ridiculed with savage irony by Johannes Reuchlin (1455–1522) and his fellow campaigners in their *Letters of the Dark Men*, was first and foremost a jargon with a peculiar vocabulary and a simplified syntax. It was a swift and (within the framework of discussions) highly formal and precise means of communication. This kind of Latin in some sense resembles those scanty remains of the otherwise solid language of English which create such linguistic mischief in the everyday life of the scientific community. That is why comparisons between the formal Latin of the Scholastics and the Latin of Caesar or Virgil are somewhat out of place.

It should, however, be added that the dreadful Latin idiom used by the Scholastics was livelier than many a servile imitation of antique texts to be found in the writings of the Humanists. Erasmus of Rotterdam (1466/1469–1536) satirised those all too eager imitators of Cicero in a witty dialogue written in 1528, the *Ciceronianus*.

The Humanists of the fifteenth and sixteenth centuries have sometimes been considered murderers of the Latin language. Until that supposed philological crime was committed – a crime intended as a means of reviving a supposedly dying language – Latin was able to develop and adapt to contemporary trends, and, indeed, play a central role in literary as well as intellectual discourse. In a word, Latin was still the hub of cultural life. For, on the one hand, it still had a mighty heritage from classical antiquity at its disposal, whereby there was scarcely a writer who could afford to neglect the *auctoritates* of ancient Rome, regardless of whether they wrote in Latin, Greek, French or Italian.

On the other hand, Latin had a solid, well-ordered structure such as no other European language could yet boast; which is why the vernacular language had

---

7 Summa IIa IIae, qu. 53, a. 2 § 1 – Thomae de Aquino Summa theologiae, Cinisello Balsamo 1988, p. 1316.

to strive hard to achieve the one thing that Latin had long been conspicuous for, namely, grammar.

As far as literary standards and especially poetry are concerned, the heritage of classical antiquity was to remain *the* measure of all things throughout the Middle Ages, and even well beyond. During the many so-called Renaissance periods that followed, people were constantly harking back to that ancient classical tradition, notably in the ninth, twelfth, fourteenth and fifteenth and sixteenth centuries. Indeed, literary writers were constantly being evaluated by the standards of the Roman *auctoritates*. Even when the primacy of literatures in the vernacular was being asserted, such literatures were, nevertheless, judged by the criteria of that antique reservoir. The fact that in France there were disputes in the mid-sixteenth century and, again, towards the end of the seventeenth century over the question whether Latin literature was superior to French literature, or vice versa, is enough to indicate the importance of the heritage of classical antiquity in the post-medieval era.

Models or counter-models for most genres of literature were thus furnished by classical antiquity. There could be no epic poem without Virgil or (from the sixteenth century) without Homer, no poetry without Horace, no satire without Juvenal.

It was not by chance that the vernacular literature of the West at first depended heavily on that tradition. Antique subject-matter was re-worked in each vernacular (in that respect the word 'translation' is an inadequate concept), with content, plots and characters also being borrowed from classical texts.

This is also true of those countless authors who wrote Latin texts in which one can see the overwhelming and continuous presence of classical antiquity. All this entailed a conflict of values that should not be underrated. Certainly there were difficulties in this involvement with ancient classical authors – difficulties that had much to do with religion and that dated from Late Antiquity.

The early Christians in the West spoke Greek at first. However, when they turned to Latin, they found themselves confronted with two main problems. In the second and third centuries A.D., the Holy Scriptures had to be translated into the language of the pagans in heavy – and if I may put it thus – 'unlatin' dependence on the widespread Greek version of the Bible of the Septuagint. Then, during a second phase, the Word of God in Latin had to be made palatable for the upper classes as well as for the commonality. The latter of these tasks may have been easier to perform since the earliest translations were couched in simple language such as sometimes belies the difficulties of translation. But, with its many borrowings from Greek and its hair-raising syntactical complexities, the Bible was probably quite indigestible, even for a readership which, though uneducated, nevertheless spoke Latin.

Cultured people could, of course, only shake their heads over the *sermo piscatorius* ("the tongue of fishermen") that confronted them. Many Christian writers belonged to such circles, and for all that people marvelled at the peculiar language of the Bible, it is certain that in the words of, say, St. Jerome, St. Augustine (who had been himself a rhetorician) or Cassiodorus the classical culture is evident. In fact, the Christians were unable to replace pagan culture with their own and, indeed, they were only too painfully aware that they were using a language that had been created and used by pagans, and that it was imbued with values that went against the spirit of Christianity.

There is no need for me at this point to go into the intensive polemics that all this gave rise to and that occupied the attention of the Church Fathers. It was a problem of language as well as of content, a confrontation with one's own roots and their linguistic expression. In the end, as Christian Gnilka and others have shown, they settled for an *usus iustus* of the antique heritage, which was to make it possible to undertake a much sought after and greatly needed adaptation of those values.

The core of the conflict nevertheless persisted. The Middle Ages are rightly seen as an era whose character was stamped by a combination of Christianity and Latinity. All the same, a certain unease with the culture of 'the others', namely, the writings of the Roman predecessors, the despised pagans, continued to prevail. Thus in a letter dated around 384 A.D. one reads the following account:

> Interim parabantur exsequiae et vitalis animae calor toto frigente iam corpore in solo tam tepente pectusculo palpitabat, cum subito raptus in spiritu ad tribunal iudicis pertrahor, ubi tantum luminis et tantum erat ex circumstantium claritate fulgoris ut proiectus in terram sursum aspicere non auderem. Interrogatus condicionem Christianum me esse respondi. Et ille qui presidebat: "Mentiris", ait, "Ciceronianus es, non Christianus: *ubi thesaurus tuus, ibi et cor tuum* (Ps. 6,5)".[8]

> Meantime preparations were made for my funeral: my whole body grew gradually cold, and life's vital warmth only lingered faintly in my poor throbbing breast. Suddenly I was caught up in the spirit and dragged before the Judge's judgement seat: and here light was so dazzling, and the brightness shining from those who stood around so radiant, that I flung myself upon the ground and did not dare to look up. I was asked to state my condition and replied that I was a Christian. But He who presided said: "Thou liest; thou art a Ciceronian, not a Christian: *for where thy treasure is there will be thy heart also*".

The uncomfortable dreamer who thus related his nocturnal vision was St. Jerome († 420). He goes on to say that he was severely beaten and had to promise never again to touch a pagan text; whereupon he was released, and then woke up from his dream. Yet all this was no mere fantasy, as Jerome explained to his female correspondent, for he found himself covered with the most painful marks and bruises.

The reality of Jerome's dream is not a matter for debate here. What is important is that the dream articulated a truth that was recognised in late classical antiquity and the Middle Ages. The dream world at that time was the context in which not only were unspoken things concretely manifested, but communication could take place between heaven and earth. And the Highest Deity was for centuries angered by the fact that Christians devoted themselves to the study of pagan writers.

---

8 Hier. epist. 22, 30. English translation: Jerome, Select letters. With an English translation by F. A. WRIGHT (Loeb Classical Library), Cambridge, Mass. 1933, p. 127.

This forbidding message was the content of many a dream dreamt by monks, priests and bishops. For example, Bishop Herbert of Norwich († 1119), who had been a monk at the abbey of Fécamp, relates around 1100 that when Christ appeared to him in a dream and asked him about his *dignitas*, he immediately replied with the following fervent words: "Ego Christianus, inquam, sum, Vestrae Sanctitatis servus", "But I am a Christian, the servant of Your Holiness!".[9] But it was pointed out to the Bishop that he had, in fact, been asked a different question. And when he found he had to face criticism, he tells us that at once he recalled the thrashing that his dreaming predecessor Jerome had received, and so said he was sorry.

One should, however, not overrate the importance of these dream anecdotes, of which there are considerably more than I have space to write about here. It would be wrong to deduce from all this that every schoolmaster who picked up a text-book or seized a cane in order to drum the fundamentals of Latin into his pupils was stricken by qualms of conscience. But such texts show that people in the Middle Ages never forgot the origins of the language which they used and which they could not afford to abandon. And some of them at least wondered how they could cope with its pagan values.

The fact that Latin was indispensable had to do not merely with its illustrious literary history or its function as a supranational means of communication in a Europe that was divided into several linguistic groups. As I said above, it was for a long time the only language with fixed rules, to the extent that one did not refer to it as 'Latin' but, quite simply, as 'grammar'.

The Carolingians were already conscious of this and tried to develop late antique grammar. The status of the vernacular languages was too low for anyone to be concerned with their basic structures, and that even when, as in early medieval German, a vernacular literature had already begun to develop.

With the eventual breakthrough of the continental vernaculars as literary languages from the twelfth century onwards, the difference between the two kinds of idioms became even more glaring. Attempts to deal with this problem were at first hesitant, and discussion on the subject for the most part did not go beyond well-meaning intentions. That is why it is one of Dante's merits that he brought into the foreground, and even tried to answer, the question of the relationship between the language of the people and the language of the scholastics in two of his works: *The Banquet (Convivio)*[10] and the tract *On Vernacular Rhetoric (De vulgari eloquentia)*.[11]

---

9 Epistolae Herberti de Losinga, primi Episcopi Norwicensis, Osberti de Clara et Elmeri Prioris Cantuariensis. Nunc primum e codicibus mss. editae a Roberto ANSTRUTHER, Brussels/London 1846, p. 127.

10 Convivio: Dante Alighieri, Opere minori, vol. 1, 2. A cura di Cesare VASOLI e di Domenico DE ROBERTIS (La letteratura italiana, Storia e testi 5, 1/2), Milano/Napoli 1988, pp. 3–885.

11 De vulgari eloquentia: Dante Alighieri, Opere minori, vol. 2. A cura di Pier Vincenzo MENGALDO [et al.] (La letteratura italiana, Storia e testi 5, 2), Milano/Napoli 1979, pp. 26–237.

That there was, to be sure, no doubt in Dante's mind at first as to the supremacy of Latin can be seen especially in the *Convivio*, even though it was in Italian, because it was written as a means of imparting the antique philosophical heritage to those strata of society that did not know Latin. The *Convivio*, which was incomplete and was to have comprised fifteen tracts, only four of which have survived, was originally conceived as a series of scholarly commentaries on the *canzoni* Dante had composed himself, in which he endeavoured to popularise the Aristotelianism of his time. For instance, at the beginning of the second Book the mention of the Third Heaven in the first verse of his *canzone* ("Voi che 'ntendendo il terzo ciel movete") provides him with an opportunity to discuss Aristotelian cosmology in some detail.[12]

It is in the first book of this work that Dante examines the relationship between Latin and the vernacular languages. Thus he asserts that the *volgare*, that is, the vernacular language, obeyed custom, not art, with the result that it is as inferior to Latin, which is "perpetuo e non corruttibile" ("perpetual and not corruptible"). There were several subjects that could be treated only in Latin,[13] which had to be seen as the master of its servant, the vernacular.

In Dante's later work, *De vulgari eloquentia*, however, this viewpoint is completely turned on its head. It is because they are natural, unaffected forms of human expression that the vernacular languages are nobler than and superior to artificial Latin:

> Harum quoque duarum [*that is* linguarum] nobilior est vulgaris: tum quia prima fuit humano generi usitata; tum quia totus orbis ipsa perfruitur, licet in diversas prolationes [*pronunciations*] et vocabula sint divisa; tum quia naturalis est nobis, cum illa potius artificialis existat.[14]

In a bold and – in its detail and depth – unique undertaking, Dante sketched a history of human language in the first part of his text. Thus he tells us that primitive peoples had spoken Hebrew, that the first word they used was *El*, that is 'God', which was an expression of their joy at the Creation. He then goes on to say that, after the collapse of the infamous Tower of Babel, three linguistic groups were formed – Germanic, Anglo-Saxon and early Romance. This division developed further into three Romance traditions – *oc*, *oil* and *si* – and into countless varieties thereof. Dante devoted himself to the linguistic geography of Italy in his search for the *volgare illustre*, that is, for a supraregional form of Italian that might be suitable for literary purposes.

It is almost breathtaking to observe Dante making these linguistic comparisons and evaluating them seven hundred years ago. According to him, there can be no doubt that the origin of the vernacular languages may be traced back to that pro-

---

12 Convivio 1, 1, 1ff., as in note 10, pp. 108ff.
13 "E con ciò sia cosa che lo latino molte cose manifesta concepute ne la mente che lo volgare far non può, sì come sanno queli che hanno l'uno e l'altro sermone, più è la sua vertù che quella del volgare" (Convivio 1, 5, 12, as in note 10, p. 36).
14 De vulgari eloquentia 1, 1, 4, as in note 11, p. 32.

cess of moral corruption which was the reason for their variety, too, but he casts no aspersions upon their dignity as mother tongues and as the original medium of expression for human beings, even though, as he also suggests, nobody had ever set up rules for these languages. This was the very aim that Dante sought to achieve. However, the surviving parts of his text suggest that it was to have been concerned with questions of stylistics and poetics, whereby, among other things, he contends that poetry is superior to prose. However, he never completed the project, and so *De vulgari eloquentia* has remained but a fragment.

What, it may now be asked, is Dante's aim in his concern with Latin, or, rather, with grammar, as he calls it? Latin he regarded as a kind of conventional language which had been invented as a means of facilitating communication and which as such was not subject to any modification.

Que quidem gramatica nichil aliud est quam quedam inalterabilis locutionis ydemptitas diversibus temporibus atque locis. Haec cum de comuni consensu multarum gentium fuerit regulata, nulli singulari arbitrio videtur obnoxia, et per consequens nec variabilis esse potest. Adinvenerunt ergo illam ne propter sermonis arbitrio singularium fluitantis vel nullo modo vel saltim imperfecte antiquorum actingeremus auctoritates et gesta sive illorum quos a nobis locorum diversitas facit esse diversos.[15]

Latin is some sort of immutable language that remains true to itself regardless of time or place. Several nations have fixed its rules by mutual consent which is why it is not subject to the discretion of individuals and cannot be changed. It was invented so that it would not have to adapt itself to the arbitrary changes in human speech, and so that we might experience, however imperfectly, the thoughts and deeds of the ancients, that is, of those who, through their remote setting, are so different from ourselves.

Dante and his successors, including Humanists such as Leonardo Bruni (ca. 1370–1444), regarded Latin as an ingenious invention, as a perfectly suitable medium of communication that was designed as a service both for the future (diachrony) and for the present (synchrony). Moreover, Dante scrupulously avoids going into the question whether Latin is of divine origin or of a sacred nature. Indeed, in the *Convivio* he goes so far as to suggest that Latin translations of the Psalms, which was the best known and most popular book of the Old Testament, were a third-hand version, and hence utterly devoid of the poetic and musical qualities of the original text.[16]

It goes without saying, of course, that Latin in European Christendom was not only the language of scholarly and literary communication at all levels, from university Aristotelians to elementary school pupils, that is to say, of cultural transmission, but, above all, the language of the Bible and the liturgy. In such contexts the language of the ancient Romans was able to exert an abiding influence; it was

---

15 De vulgari eloquentia 1, 1, 4, as in note 11, pp. 78–80.
16 "E questa è la cagione per che li versi del Salterio sono sanza dolcezza di musica e d'armonia; ché essi furono transmutati d'ebreo in greco e di greco in latino, e ne la prima trasmutazione tutta quella dolcezza venne meno" (Convivio 1, 7, 15, as in note 10, pp. 48f.).

in some cases subject to a process of sacralization that put it on the same level as Hebrew and Greek, as Michael Richter has pointed out elsewhere.

What is especially significant for us here is that the Church was the context in which those who had little or no Latin had to come to terms with that foreign tongue. This was certainly true of Catholic countries until the middle of the twentieth century. Now, we might suppose that this was a one-sided process of communication that one could liken to the soil of a number of pious, though witless, illiterates being watered by a few educated people. This process of communication was, however, one-sided only inasmuch as churchgoers obviously had no influence on the Latin texts that were read aloud to them. Readings from the Bible and the liturgy remained fixed to the extent that they were maintained by the celebrants, whose level of education was sometimes extremely low.

There were, of course, sermons in the Middle Ages that were preached in the vernacular, and such sermons became more frequent from the 12th century onwards. Yet it is difficult for us to gauge the modalities and effect of those sermons, since sermons were by their very nature oral performances.

Latin was, however, also the language in which the Gospel was revealed and with which appropriate rituals were carried out week after week, month after month, year after year. Prayers and liturgical *formulae* were thus heard countless times over, and uttered countless times.

Scholarly studies have been devoted to the powerful impact of Biblical and liturgical language on the literature of the Middle Ages, especially Latin literature. Liturgical Latin, at any rate, became a constituent part of non-Latin everyday speech. At least in the Romance countries the language of ordinary people contained a considerable number of Latinisms that had been largely borrowed from the liturgy.

In a learned and witty book, Gian Luigi Beccaria has showed that in Veneto one designated the opening of doors and windows as the *far dominus vobiscum* because the celebrating priest held his arms wide open when uttering those words. *Domino vobisco*, on the other hand, meant "Good luck!" in and around Verona.

There are hundreds of such examples to be found throughout Italy, especially from the liturgy for the dead. From the *Miserere* that was sung at the end of a funeral mass, there arose expressions such as *essere al Miserere* ("to be at the Miserere") meaning "to be bankrupt", or *avere il male del Miserere* ("to be Miserere ill"), meaning "to be fatally ill". Again, *omnes iniquitates meas dele* from the same psalm became in Veneto *xe in dele* ("to be *in dele*"), meaning "to be in a hopeless situation", for which one also said *de diesila*, an obvious quotation from the mass for the dead (*Dies irae, dies illa*). An arrogantly authoritarian person was referred to as a *potente de sede* (on the basis of the verse *Deposuit potentes de sede* in the Magnificat). Again, someone who considered himself a god was referred to as an *egosum*, which is an obvious echo of the New Testament words *Ego sum resurrectio et vita*.

One can find traces of such borrowings in texts from the fifteenth century onwards and more or less deduce that they did not originate only in the Early Modern Period but earlier, even if, generally speaking, one cannot date such borrowings. In some cases, they arose from misunderstandings. For example, in Rome "Signor Nocchilia", a combination of Enoch and Elias, was the nickname of someone who was rather a grim character. Nor was the Lord's Prayer spared in this respect. Thus a *donna Bissodia* ("a Madame Bissodia") can be traced back to the request *panem nostrum quotidiam da nobis hodie* as made in the Lord's Prayer.

It is legitimate to regard the disrespectfulness of all such expressions as a perversion of liturgical language, just as it is easy to assume that the misunderstandings arising from them were for the most part intentional. But that is beside the point here. What is of interest to me in this context is something altogether different. The intentional or unintentional irony that one senses here, far from having an alienating effect, manages to bridge the gap existing between Latin and the vernacular, that is to say, between the language of religion and the language of the people. In other words, what we find expressed here is an affective value that might be described as an almost emotional approach to Latin, which turned a medium, that is, a very important, but temporally and spatially limited and highly formulated realm, that of liturgy, into a real language, that is to say into an idiom whose nature transcends the pure function of a means of exchanging information and has the effect of creating a sense of identity. Victor Klemperer (1881–1960) described in his impressive book LTI (*Lingua tertii imperii*, "The Language of the Third Reich") – significantly enough an ironizing Latin title – the cultural origins of language in a totalitarian system. In one passage, he points to those emotional values I have been speaking about:

> Aber Sprache dichtet und denkt nicht nur für mich, sie lenkt auch mein Gefühl, sie steuert mein ganzes seelisches Wesen, je selbstverständlicher, je unbewußter ich mich ihr überlasse.[17]

> Language, however, does not only create poetry or do my thinking for me, it also determines my feelings, it governs my entire spiritual being, and that more obviously, nay, more unconsciously than I allow it to do.

I have tried here to show why Latin stood at the very heart of European languages in the Middle Ages and the Early Modern Period. Latin was fed by many linguistic sources, just as it became itself the source of many languages. And though Latin was still spoken, one no longer spoke it as if one were a member of a particular linguistic community. But in all its registers and varieties Latin was not simply a neutral means of formal and technical communication, it also tirelessly provided models for literature and for everyday speech, bearing as it also did all the characteristics of a living language – and one that people thought about and could even get angry about, because it was felt to be part of one's very identity.[18]

---

17 Klemperer, Victor: LTI. Notizbuch eines Philologen, Leipzig 1996, pp. 24f.
18 I should like to thank my teacher and friend, Dr Graeme Tytler (Oxford), who translated the original public lecture held (in German) at the Kaiserpfalz in Paderborn on March 8th 2003 and kindly checked this slightly revised version of it.

Selected Bibliography

AUERBACH, Erich: Literatursprache und Publikum in der lateinischen Spätantike und im Mittelalter, Bern 1958 (English translation: Literary language & its public in late Latin antiquity and in the Middle Ages. Translated from German by Ralph MANHEIM, New York 1965, Princeton 1993).

BANNIARD, Michel (ed.): Langages et peuples d'Europe. Cristallisations des identités romanes et germaniques (VIIIᵉ–XIᵉ siècle). Colloque international (...) Toulouse-Conques, juillet 1997, Toulouse 2002.

BANNIARD, Michel: *Viva voce*. Communication écrite et communication orale du IVᵉ au IXᵉ siècle en Occident latin (Collection des Etudes augustiniennes, Série Moyen-Age et Temps modernes 25), Paris 1992.

BECCARIA Gian Luigi: *Sicuterat*. Il latino di chi non lo sa. Bibbia e liturgia nell'italiano e nei dialetti (Saggi blu), Milano 1999.

BLACK, Robert: Humanism and education in medieval and Renaissance Italy. Tradition and innovation in Latin schools from the twelfth to the fifteenth century, Cambridge 2001.

CALBOLI, Gualtiero: Latino volgare e latino classico, in: CAVALLO, Guglielmo/LEONARDI, Claudio/MENESTÒ, Enrico (eds.): Lo spazio letterario del medioevo, vol. 2: La circolazione del testo, Rome 1994, pp. 11–62.

COLISH, Marcia: The mirror of language. A study in the medieval theory of knowledge, Lincoln ²1983.

CURTIUS, Ernst Robert: Europäische Literatur und lateinisches Mittelalter, Bern/München ¹1948, ¹⁰1984 (English translation: European literature and the Latin Middle Ages. Translated from German by Willard R. TRASK, New York 1953).

GNILKA, Christian: Der Begriff des "rechten Gebrauchs" (Chrêsis 1), Basel 1984.

IJSEWIJN, Jozef: Companion to Neo-Latin Studies. Second, Entirely Rewritten Edition, 2 vols. (Humanistica Lovaniensia, Supplementa), Leuven 1990–98.

KÜHLMANN, Wilhelm: Apologie und Kritik des Lateins im Schrifttum des deutschen Späthumanismus. Argumentationsmuster und sozialgeschichtliche Zusammenhänge, in: Daphnis 9 (1980), pp. 33–63.

MANTELLO, F.A.C./RIGG, A.G. (EDS.): Medieval Latin. An Introduction and Bibliographical Guide, Washington, D.C. 1999.

MOHRMANN, Christine: Études sur le latin des chrétiens, 4 vols. (Storia e letteratura 65, 87, 103, 143), Roma 1961–77.

PERUGI, Maurizio: Dal latino alle lingue romanze. Diglossia e bilinguismo nei testi letterari delle origini, in: CAVALLO, Guglielmo/LEONARDI, Claudio/MENESTÒ, Enrico (eds.): Lo spazio letterario del medioevo, vol. 2: La circolazione del testo, Rome 1994, pp. 63–111.

PITTALUGA, Stefano: La restaurazione umanistica, in: CAVALLO, Guglielmo/LEONARDI, Claudio/MENESTÒ, Enrico (eds.): Lo spazio letterario del medioevo, vol. 2: La circolazione del testo, Rome 1994, pp. 191–217.

RICHTER, Michael: Sprache und Gesellschaft im Mittelalter. Untersuchungen zur mündlichen Kommunikation in England vom 11. bis zum frühen 14. Jahrhundert (Monographien zur Geschichte des Mittelalters 19), Stuttgart 1979.

RICHTER, Michael: Studies in medieval languages and culture, Dublin 1995.

RIZZO, Silvia: Ricerche sul latino umanistico, vol. 1 (Storia e letteratura 213), Roma 2002.

Significare e comunicare nell'alto medioevo (Settimane di studio del Centro italiano di studi sull'alto medioevo 52), 2 vols., Spoleto 2005.

STOTZ, Peter: Handbuch zur lateinischen Sprache des Mittelalters, 5 vols. (Handbuch der Altertumswissenschaft, II. 5. 1–5), München 1996–2004.

STOTZ, Peter: Le sorti del latino nel medioevo, in: CAVALLO, Guglielmo/LEONARDI, Claudio/MENESTÒ, Enrico (eds.): Lo spazio letterario del medioevo, vol. 2: La circolazione del testo, Rome 1994, pp. 153–190.

ZINK, Michel: La prédication en langue romane avant 1300 (Nouvelle bibliothèque du moyen âge 4), Paris 1982.

Hermann Moisl

Language, literacy and cultural development in early medieval England and Ireland

Introduction

There is a striking difference in the relative roles of vernacular literacy in early medieval England and Ireland. To judge from the distribution of texts that have survived from both areas[1] Latin was, in England, the dominant language of literacy and written Old English had a circumscribed role, whereas in Ireland the vernacular became an increasingly important language of literacy across a wide range of applications from the later seventh century onwards. The language of religion and the language of the people were, therefore, broadly different in Anglo-Saxon England in the sense that the primary language of the Christian establishment was Latin, but in Ireland Latin had to share its status as the language of religion with the vernacular. The aim of this paper is to suggest how this situation came about, and to attempt to assess its implications for cultural development in these areas.

1. The vernacular and the Christian establishment in early medieval England and Ireland

Throughout early medieval Western Europe, including England and Ireland, the default language of Christian ecclesiastical literacy was Latin. In England, the vernacular was used as a literary language for communication of Christian ideology to the laity, and was used for other purposes, albeit reluctantly, only when the Viking raids of the late 8th century onwards had severely compromised the educational institutions on which the Church's Latin literacy was based. In Ireland, however, a wide range of texts which, elsewhere in Europe, would have been writ-

---

1 Baumgarten, R.: Bibliography of Irish linguistics and literature 1942–1971, Dublin 1986; Best, R. I.: Bibliography of Irish philology and of printed Irish literature, 2 vols., Dublin 1913–1942; Cameron, A.: A List of Old English Texts, in: R. Frank/A. Cameron (eds.): Plan for the Dictionary of Old English, Toronto 1973, pp. 25–306; Esposito, M.: Latin learning in mediaeval Ireland, ed. by M. Lapidge, London 1988; Kenney, J.: Sources for the early history of Ireland: ecclesiastical, New York 1929; Kerr, N. R.: Catalogue of Manuscripts containing Anglo-Saxon, Oxford 1957; Lapidge, M./Sharpe, R.: A bibliography of Celtic-Latin literature 400–1200, Dublin 1985; Lapidge, M./Gneuss, H. (eds.): Learning and Literature in Anglo-Saxon England, Cambridge 1985; Richter, M.: Ireland and Her Neighbours in the Seventh Century, Dublin 1999; Sharpe, R.: A handlist of the Latin writers of Great Britain and Ireland before 1540 (Publications of the Journal of Medieval Latin 1), Turnhout 1997.

ten in Latin, if at all, were written in the vernacular; these included such texts as secular laws, annals, genealogies, dynastic and world histories.

One plausible explanation for this situation was the degree to which pre-Christian priesthoods that maintained orally -transmitted cultural knowledge in the vernacular survived in post-Conversion England and Ireland.

· In pre-Christian Ireland, the druidical order maintained a broad range of cultural knowledge, the main aspects of which were mythology, national and dynastic history, and law.[2] By virtue of this knowledge, the order was politically and socially influential. Its members were, for example, typically attached to royal courts, where they serviced the cult of sacral kingship, influenced the king's conduct by prophetic and magical powers, advised the king on his legal affairs, and maintained and publicized the history of the dynasty to which the king belonged.

The druidical order survived the Christian conversion largely intact, having lost its sacral functions but retaining the rest. A key development in the early Christian centuries was the rise of a learned élite that was an amalgam of the Christianized druidical order and Christian monastic culture.[3]

· The Anglo-Saxons, like the Germanic peoples of western Europe more generally, are also known to have had priesthoods with pretty much the same functions as the druids, but the evidence for them is much sparser than for the Irish, and one gets the impression that they were not as politically and socially entrenched as their Irish counterparts. The prime examples here are Bede's account of the priest Coifi at the court of Edwin of Northumbria in the mid-seventh century[4] and Eddius' reference to the pagan priests in seventh-century Sussex;[5] the few other examples come from different times and places in the Germanic world in, for example, Tacitus' *Germania*,[6] Jordanes' *Getica*,[7] and Willibald's *Life of St. Boniface*.[8] What is certain is that, throughout Germanic Western Europe, these priesthoods were gradually supplanted by the Christian ecclesiastical establishment. In some areas at least, court poets whose main role was the maintenance of royal dynastic tradition survived, but as a group these remained secular. Unlike in Ireland, therefore, there was no general amalgamation of pre-Christian and Christian orders.[9]

---

2   MOISL, H.: Lordship and tradition in barbarian Europe, Lewiston 1999.
3   MC CONE, K.: Pagan past and Christian present in early Irish literature (Maynooth Monographs 3), Maynooth 1990.
4   COLGRAVE, B./Mynors, R. A. B. (eds.): Bede's Ecclesiastical History of the English People, Oxford 1969, II/13.
5   COLGRAVE, B. (ed.): The Life of Bishop Wilfrid by Eddius Stephanus, Cambridge 1927, pp. 26ff.
6   MUCH, R.: Die Germania des Tacitus, Heidelberg 31967, ch. 11–12.
7   MOMMSEN, T. (ed.): Iordanis Romana et Getica (MGH AA 5,1), Berlin 1882, p. 73.
8   LEVISON, W. (ed): Vitae Sancti Bonifatii archiepiscopi moguntini (MGH Scriptores rerum germanicorum 57), Hannover 1905, ch. 6.
9   RICHTER, M.: The Formation of the Medieval West, Dublin 1994; MOISL 1999.

The proposed explanation for the difference in dominant literacies in England and Ireland is therefore that, in Ireland, the learned élite used ecclesiastical literacy to commit its traditional learning to writing in the vernacular, whereas in England there was no motivation for the Christian establishment to do so.

2. Cultural implications of the differential status of the vernacular in early medieval England and Ireland

The cultural implications of the relative status of Latin and the vernacular as a literary language in England and Ireland will be assessed in terms of the claim that the language which a population group uses significantly affects the way it conceptualizes the world, and consequently its cultural development. This implies that the Anglo-Saxon Church, whose primary language was Latin, conceptualized the world differently from the Irish hybrid learned élite whose primary language was the vernacular. As a result, Anglo-Saxon cultural development can be expected to have converged on institutions for which expressions exist in Latin, while Irish cultural development can be expected to have converged on traditional institutions articulated by the vernacular.

The remainder of this section is in two parts. The first part develops the argument using ideas about linguistic communication from contemporary cognitive science, and the second applies these ideas to a specific example.

2. 1. Linguistic communication

In the Western tradition, the study of the human mind is continuously documented from classical antiquity, but it is with the emergence of cognitive science in the second half of the twentieth century that major advances have been and continue to be made. Cognitive science is a general term used to describe a range of disciplines concerned with understanding the mind and its implementation in the brain, including subdisciplines of philosophy, psychology, linguistics, computer science, and neuroscience.[10] In what follows, we look at ideas from cognitive science about linguistic communication for spoken and written language separately.

2. 1. 1. Spoken communication
Because language is one of the main cognitive functions that distinguish humans from animals, the relationship between thought and language has been a longstanding issue in the study of the mind, and remains so in contemporary cognitive

---

10 WILSON, R./Keil, F. (eds.): The MIT encyclopedia of the cognitive sciences (MITECS), London 2001.

science.[11] The central question is whether or not thought and language are independent: is language a necessary component in the mechanism of thought, or is it just a way of encoding and communicating the individual's independently-formulated thoughts to the world, and of decoding the linguistically-encoded, independently-formulated thoughts of others? For ease of reference, these alternatives will be referred to as the cognitive and the communicative views, respectively, of the relationship between thought and language.[12]

Proponents of the cognitive view have included Wilhelm von Humboldt,[13] Vygotsky,[14] Wittgenstein,[15] and Daniel Dennett.[16] The idea that thought and language are causally interrelated is, however, primarily associated with the American linguists Edward Sapir and his pupil Benjamin Whorf, whose stance on this idea is best summed up by a much-cited quotation from Whorf:[17]

> We dissect nature along lines laid down by our native languages. The categories and types that we isolate from the world of phenomena we do not find there because they stare every observer in the face; on the contrary, the world is presented in a kaleidoscopic flux of impressions which has to be organized by our minds – and this means largely by the linguistic systems in our minds. We cut nature up, organize it into concepts, and ascribe significances as we do, largely because we are parties to an agreement to organize it in this way – an agreement that holds throughout our speech community and is codified in the patterns of our language. The agreement is, of course, an implicit and unstated one, but its terms are absolutely obligatory; we cannot talk at all except by subscribing to the organization and classification of data which the agreement decrees.

On the basis of this and other passages in the various writings of Sapir and Whorf,[18] the linguistics research community has constructed the Sapir-Whorf hypothesis, which proposes two associated principles:

· linguistic determinism, whereby thinking is determined by language – the language that a person speaks determines the way he or she interprets the world.
· linguistic relativity, whereby people who speak different languages perceive and think about the world differently.

The communicative view – that language is purely a mechanism for the communication of independently-existing thought – was held by, among others, John

11 Pinker, S.: The language instinct: the new science of language and mind, London 1994; Carruthers, P.: Language, Thought, and Consciousness: An Essay in Philosophical Psychology, Cambridge 1996.
12 Carruthers 1996.
13 Brown, R.: Wilhelm von Humboldt's conception of linguistic relativity, Paris 1968.
14 Vygotsky, L.: Thought and language (trans. by A. Kozulin), Cambridge/Mass. 1986.
15 Wittgenstein, L.: Tractatus logico-philosophicus, London 1922; Wittgenstein, L.: Philosophical investigations, Oxford 1953.
16 Dennett, D.: Consciousness explained, Boston 1991.
17 Whorf, B.: Science and Linguistics, in: Technology Review 42,6 (1940), pp. 229ff., 247f.
18 Carroll, J. (ed.): Language, thought, and reality: Selected writings of Benjamin Lee Whorf, Cambridge/Mass. 1967.

Locke[19] and Bertrand Russell,[20] and has been standard in cognitive science in the second half of the twentieth century, an accessible account of which is given in Pinker.[21] It is based on the computational model of the mind; because the remainder of the discussion presupposes understanding of that model, its essentials are briefly presented here.

In the early part of the 20th century, mathematicians were interested in the question of computability – whether all conceivable mathematical functions could be solved, and, if not, which ones could be. This rather abstruse research question became very relevant to real-world concerns during the Second World War, when the developing theory of computation was successfully applied to breaking German secret codes, thereby contributing greatly to the Allied victory. Alan Turing was one of the mathematicians interested in computability, and was involved in the team that broke the German codes using the world's first computer.[22] His formulation of what a computer is underlies present-day computer science and technology as well as the computational model of mind, and is called the 'Turing Machine'. Its fundamental concepts are:[23]

· Symbols and symbol systems: a symbol is any physical thing that represents – in other words, that humans agree to interpret as standing for something else: a flag with stars and stripes is universally recognized as a symbol for the USA. A symbol system is a collection of related symbols, like the flags of the world's countries, or the letters of the western alphabet, which are symbols that represent the phonemes of a language.
· Strings: a string is a sequence of symbols taken from a symbol system. Using the alphabet as an example, the following are strings: *aaabbb, xdghjfdsahjll, computer.*
· Algorithms: an algorithm is a sequence of instructions which, if followed, is guaranteed to result in some desired state of affairs. A cooking recipe is an example of an algorithm, as are computer programs.
· Computation: computation on Turing's model is string transformation. Specifically, given some string S1, a computer is used to transform that string into S2. For example, a computer would transform the string S1 = *(2 x 2) / 3* into the string S2 = *1.333*, or the string S1 = *the red book* into S2 = *das rote Buch*. How does a computer know what to transform a given string S1 into? It follows an algorithm.

19 LOCKE, J.: An Essay concerning human understanding, London 1690.
20 RUSSELL, B.: The analysis of mind, London 1921.
21 PINKER 1994.
22 HODGES, A: Alan Turing: The Enigma, New York 2000.
23 HAUGELAND, J: Artificial intelligence: The very idea, Cambridge/Mass. 1985; HOPCROFT, J./ MOTWANI, R./ULLMAN, J.: Introduction to automata theory, languages and computation, Harlow ²2000.

A Turing machine can be visualized like this:

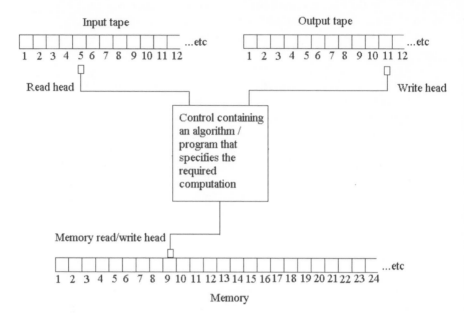

S1, the string to be transformed, is called the 'input string', and is written onto the input tape, one symbol per square; note that the input tape can be as long as required. The transformed string S2 will appear on the output tape, also one symbol per square, and as long as needed. The transformation is accomplished by the control mechanism, which contains an algorithm to accomplish the transformation. These instructions tell the control mechanism when and what to read from the input, when and what to write to the output, and how to use the memory for intermediate calculations; the memory is just a place for 'rough work' such as humans use when doing calculations. The algorithm in the control part of the machine is called a 'program'.

Turing himself proposed that the human mind was a computer.[24] This suggestion was enthusiastically taken up by the nascent cognitive science of the 1950s and has been dominant ever since, as noted.

The philosopher Jerry Fodor has been highly influential in computational cognitive science.[25] Two of his most important contributions to it have been:

---

24 Turing, A.: Computing machinery and intelligence, in: Mind 49 (1950), pp. 433–460.
25 Fodor, J.: The language of thought, New York 1975; Fodor, J.: The modularity of mind, Cambridge/Mass. 1983; Fodor, J.: The elm and the expert: mentalese and its semantics, Cambridge/Mass. 1995; Fodor, J.: The mind doesn't work that way: The scope and limits of computational psychology, Cambridge/Mass. 2001.

· Modularity: the mind is not a single computer with a hugely complex program in the control mechanism determining all aspects of cognition, but an interconnected and communicating collection of computers, each responsible for a specific cognitive function such as vision, logic, or language. Each module contains a computer with a program that carries out the function for which it is responsible, getting its input from the external environment or other modules, and communicating its output to other modules.

· Language of thought: The symbols used by central cognitive modules such as those for memory and logic are different from those used by the peripheral input/output modules like audition and vision; the symbols in central cognition constitute a language that has come to be known as 'mentalese'. Each of the input / output computational systems translates the symbols that it uses into and out of mentalese when communicating with central systems.

Modularity and mentalese are what underlies the current standard view in cognitive science that thought is independent of language. Thinking is what happens in mentalese in the central modules; the language module translates strings of mentalese into natural language strings that are communicated to the environment via speech, and natural language strings from the environment into mentalese.

The standard communicative view of the relationship between thought and language is now being challenged, most recently by Dennet[26] and Carruthers.[27] Both argue that the cognitive view is no less inherently plausible than the communicative one, and that, like the latter, it has substantial empirical support. Carruthers goes on to propose that language is only involved in a specific type of thought – conscious thought. This, of course, begs the question of what a conscious thought might be, but a rough approximation is that it includes the traditionally 'higher' functions like reasoning, planning, and memory, and excludes 'lower' ones like perceptual and motor functions. On this view, framing a coherent argument on some subject is not a matter of thinking about it in mentalese and then translating and transmitting it in, say, English, but involves the use of English sentences in formulating the argument. In other words, such thinking is done in or, more cautiously, in a way involving English.

Carruthers's argument is far from conclusive and requires extensive theoretical and empirical development, as he himself is at pains to point out. At the very least, however, his argument is persuasive to the extent that it rehabilitates the cognitive view as a reasonable hypothesis about the relationship between thought and language.

2.1.2. Written communication
One of the features of the standard computational model of mind is that it operates on mental representations of the external world. The basic idea here is that

26 Dennet 1991.
27 Carruthers 1996.

· the input modules translate physical stimuli from the environment into symbolic representations of the external world.

· these representations are sent to the relevant central cognitive modules, where they are stored as symbolic mentalese sequences in their memories.

· the central modules operate algorithmically on these sequences, thereby generating thought.

· where appropriate, the results from these central operations are sent to output modules which translate them into physical action that can affect the real-world environment, such as speech or movement.

In this way, the cognitive agent perceives and acts in the world.

While the above mechanism seems plausible enough in theory, it was found to be unworkable in practice. During its heyday in the 1970s and 1980s, the discipline of artificial intelligence attempted to use cognitive theory as the blueprint for design and construction of physical systems that emulate human cognition, or at least aspects of it. Hopes were high, but hardly any were realized, and many researchers now see little prospect of developing artificially intelligent devices on the basis of standard computational cognitive theory.[28] The problem is that maintaining an up-to-date symbolic representation of the world appears to be an insuperable task. One problem is computational load. Any cognitive agent, animal as well as human, has to survive in an environment that is constantly in flux, which means that the content of the central module memories has to be constantly updated; as the agent grows older, the quantity of stored representation grows, and with it the computational effort of updating it. At present, not even the fastest computer has come anywhere near human levels of response to the environment. One might, of course, argue that the fastest computers are simply not fast enough, but that they will be one day. There is, however, an even more serious problem: relevance. What is stored in memory is not simply sense impressions – how the world looks, smells, and feels at any given moment. Rather, knowledge is stored, that is, causal sequences that have been experienced: if there are heavy clouds, it will probably rain; if there is a car coming towards me I had better move or I will suffer and die; and so on. But this stored knowledge has to be updated in response to current sensory input if an up-to-date representation of the world is to be maintained, which means that the relevance of each sensory input to the existing knowledge base has to be assessed and changes made where necessary. But assessing relevance is easier said than done. Let's say I read that average rainfall worldwide has decreased by 18% over the past decade. What is the relevance of this to everything I know? Is it relevant to what I think I know about global warming? Probably. Is it relevant to what I know about the properties of glass? Probably not. Is it relevant to what my cat eats for dinner? Possibly. And what about all the other things I know? Without going into technicalities, it is not difficult to appreciate the complexity of what is involved here, and many believe that this complexity will always

---

28 For example Dorffner, G.: Neural networks and a new artificial intelligence, London 1997.

defeat attempts to maintain an up-to-date representation of the world in a computational system.

To address this problem, a new line of thought in cognitive science has developed a way radically to decrease the computational load associated with maintaining an up-to-date symbolic representation of the world by means of a commensurate radical decrease in how much of the world needs to be represented in the mind. This is accomplished by a reconceptualization of the relationship between the mind and its environment. The standard cognitive model described above makes a clear distinction between the abstract, non-physical, computational mind and the physical world in which it exists. This distinction is in direct line of descent from the dualism of Descartes and, ultimately, of Plato, which has generated the mind/body problem, and whose long-running resistance to philosophical resolution is a good sign that it was misconceived in the first place. Replacing it is a view of cognition, known as 'situated' or 'embedded' cognition,[29] in which the rigid ontological distinction between mind and physical world is broken down: mind, body, and environment are seen as a single, tightly-coupled system in constant, complex, dynamic interaction. The mind is primarily a mechanism that directly controls the body in its environment without necessary recourse to symbolic representation; computation on symbolic representations remains an aspect of cognition, but not the totality of it as in the standard model – in Carruthers's terms, that aspect would be coterminous with conscious thought. Because a large part of cognition is thereby accomplished without symbolic representation, the computational model of mind is rescued from implausibility.

Now, one of the implications of this revised computational model of mind is that the environment is not the object of cognition, but an intrinsic part of it. How the environment is structured determines how the body can relate to it, and this in turn constrains how the mind can control the body in its environment. This process is, however, not purely reactive. Far more than any other animal, humans shape their environment; once the environment is altered, the possibilities for subsequent cognitive action within it change. And so on throughout the individual's life. Over time and across societies, such cognitive activity generates human culture.

How does all this relate to written communication? To say that the dynamic structuring of the environment is part of the cognitive process is to say that each human uses environmental structures in the course of cognitive activity. Use of such structures not only reduces the computational load on the representational aspect of the mind, but actually augments cognitive capacity. To see this, take an example from Clark 1996:

---

29 Varela, F./Thompson, E./Rosch, E.: The embodied mind. Cognitive science and human experience, London 1992; Clark, A.: Being there: putting brain, body, and world together again, Cambridge/Mass. 1997; Kirshner, D./Whitson, J.(eds.): Situated cognition: social, semiotic, and psychological perspectives, London 1997.

> Most of us can answer simple questions like 7 x 7 at a glance [...] But longer multiplications present a different kind of problem. Asked to multiply 7554 x 4567 most of us resort to pen and paper. What we achieve with pen and paper is a reduction of the complex problem to a sequence of simpler problems beginning with 7 x 4. We use the external medium (paper) to store the results of these simple problems, and by an interrelated series of simple pattern completions coupled with external storage we arrive at a solution.

Restructuring of the environment, that is, putting physical marks on the piece of paper, allows a problem that the representational component of the integrated mind / body / environment system cannot solve on its own: the external environment extends its capabilities. Writing fulfils a function analogous to that of this arithmetical example. How much of a spoken lecture on some technical subject can a human remember verbatim? Judging from personal experience, very little. What about the gist of the lecture, that is, its propositional content? Rather more. How accurately? Again from personal experience, not very. How long does such memory last? The simple fact is that human memories are very limited in terms both of capacity and of accuracy of recall. What writing offers is a way of extending that capacity essentially without limit because it allows arbitrary amounts of linguistically encoded knowledge to be stored in the physical environment to an arbitrary degree of accuracy for as long as necessary; whenever some knowledge is required, it is only necessary to read the relevant book. Writing is, in other words, a hugely powerful way of using the external environment to augment human cognitive capacity because it provides a creature with very limited memory with an essentially unlimited one.

2.1.3. Evaluation

We have looked at two ideas from cognitive science to support the claim that the language which a population group uses significantly affects the way it conceptualizes the world, and consequently its cultural development:

· That language and thought are interdependent
· That written language extends cognitive capacity by providing it with an essentially unlimited memory

The degree to which these support the claim depends crucially on how one sees the nature of the interdependence between language and thought. At one extreme is the standard view that there is no interdependence: the claim is simply wrong, and there is nothing more to say. At the other is the Sapir-Whorf hypothesis, in which case the claim amounts to this: written language makes permanent the interpretation of the world characteristic of a given language L, and that interpretation thereby affects the culture in which L is embedded over more or less arbitrary lengths of time.

One might object that both the ideas from cognitive science are hypothetical, and that any claim based on them must therefore also be hypothetical. This is true, but it cannot be a criticism. All one has in history, as in science generally, are hypotheses whose usefulness is judged on the degree to which they are supported by empirical evidence.[30] It is to such empirical evidence that we now turn.

2.2. Application

The claim that the language which a population group uses significantly affects the way it conceptualizes the world, and consequently its cultural development, predicts that early medieval England and Ireland developed differently because their primary languages of literacy were different. The evidence used to support this prediction is the way in which the early medieval western Church's theory of Christian kingship transformed Anglo-Saxon lordship, but failed to do so in Ireland.

2.2.1. The early medieval theory of Christian lordship
The growth of the Church in and later beyond the confines of the old Roman Empire in late antiquity and the early Middle Ages was accompanied by the formulation of a political theory founded on Christian principles.[31] Based on St Paul's ideas on the relationship between secular and divine authority, the popes Leo I (440–461) and Gelasius (492–496) synthesized a set of principles according to which secular lordship was regarded as an office within the politically-conceived body of the faithful which God has instituted for the enforcement of His law in the world, and whose functions could legitimately be influenced by the ecclesiastical hierarchy that stood between the ruler and the source of his power in God. In its fullest form, this theory was captured by the motto *rex Dei gratia*.

2.2.2. The dissemination of the theory of Christian lordship in early medieval western Europe
In the West the collapse of the Empire meant that the Church was faced with the very real power of barbarian kings ruling newly conquered territories as personal kingdoms, and it was on their patronage that it depended for its continued survival and expansion. The development of a Christian theory of kingship represents an attempt to harness that royal power. Its dissemination in early medieval continental Europe is documented by Ewig.[32] By the early eighth century it had found its way to Anglo-Saxon England – Bede refers to it[33] – and to Ireland, where

---

30 CHALMERS, A: What is this thing called science?, Indianapolis [3]2002.
31 ULLMANN, W.: Medieval political thought, Harmondsworth 1975; MC DONALD, L.: Western political theory, part 1: Ancient and medieval, London 1997.
32 EWIG, E.: Zum christlichen Königsgedanken im Frühmittelalter, in: Das Königtum. Seine geistigen und rechtlichen Grundlagen (Vorträge und Forschungen 3), Lindau/Konstanz 1954.
33 COLGRAVE/MYNORS 1969, I/32.

it appears in texts like Adomnán's *Life of Columba*,[34] the *Collectio Canonum Hibernensis*,[35] and *De Duodecim Abusivis Saeculi*.[36]

2.2.3. The effects of the theory of Christian lordship in early medieval England and Ireland

The mere formulation of the theory of Christian kingship could not automatically be expected to condition the adherence of kings to their unilaterally assigned role, but that the ploy worked is attested not only for medieval and early modern Europe but even – in Britain – to the present day. Its crucial success came with Charlemagne's acclamation as emperor: it represents a full acceptance of the Church's political programme, and with it a rejection of the earlier Germanic ideas of kingship. This happened also in Anglo-Saxon England, where it is seen most clearly in the coronation of Edgar by the Archbishop of Canterbury in 973.[37] There is, however, no indication that the theory of Christian kingship, though known by the Irish Church, was ever adopted in the English and Frankish sense. Just the opposite, in fact: compare Edgar's coronation with Giraldus Cambrensis' late twelfth-century account of a royal inauguration in Ulster,[38] a ceremony deeply embedded in the totemism of pre-Christian kingship mythology.[39]

2.2.4. Interpretation

Seen in terms of the Sapir-Whorf hypothesis and of situated cognition, the difference in the effect of the theory of Christian kingship in early medieval England and Ireland is a consequence of the difference in their languages of literacy. In England, as in continental Europe, the language of literacy was overwhelmingly Latin, and the Church was consequently predisposed to think in terms of linguistically-expressed categories characteristic of Rome in Late Antiquity. In Ireland, however, law tracts that were based on the teaching of the preliterate druidical schools and that explicitly articulated the ideology and structures of lordship, as well as royal dynastic genealogies and histories which exemplified these things,[40] were written in the vernacular, and thus defined a thought-world that the Irish Church and Irish society more generally accepted.

---

34 ANDERSON, A. O./ANDERSON, M. O. (eds.): Adomnan's Life of Columba, London 1961, pp. 200, 236, 280.
35 WASSERSCHLEBEN, H. (Ed): Die irische Kanonensammlung, Leipzig ²1885, chs. 24, 25.
36 HELLMANN, S. (ed.): Pseudo-Cyprianus, De XII Abusivis Saeculi, in: Texte und Untersuchungen zur Geschichte der altchristlichen Literatur 34 (1910), pp. 44f.
37 SAWYER, P. H.: From Roman Britain to Norman England, London ²1998, p. 184.
38 O'MEARA, J. (Trans.): Gerald of Wales, The History and Topography of Ireland, Harmondsworth 1983, pp. 93f.
39 BYRNE, F. J.: Irish kings and high kings, London 1973, pp. 17f.
40 MOISL 1999.

Conclusion

This discussion has been too brief for it to be conclusive or even convincing, but that was not the aim. The aim, rather, was to suggest a way in which current thinking in cognitive science might provide a theoretical framework for historiography of the early medieval period, at least with respect to the particular topic in question here. Much of the work in early medieval history is descriptive – essentially, it attempts to reconstruct what happened in the past as reliably as possible. What cognitive science offers is a theoretical framework, using principles of human cognition to explain why what happened did happen.

PRÓINSÉAS NÍ CHATHÁIN

Some aspects of the vernacular vocabulary of Christianity in early Ireland

Irish Christianity is first mentioned in the Chronicle of Prosper of Aquitaine for the year 431 where he writes: *Ad Scottos in Christo credentes ordinatus a papa Caelestino Palladius primus episcopus mittitur.* It may be inferred from this statement that there must have been some communities of Christians in Ireland before this time when Rome sent Palladius as their first bishop. The British missionary Patrick, whose exact dates are not as yet ascertained, was active in the fifth century and is venerated as the apostle of Ireland. There has always been a tradition that there had been early Christian foundations, in places along the east and south coasts, thought to be separate from the Palladian and the Patrician communities. The Patrician church was an episcopal institution but in the sixth century there is a great flowering of monasticism.[1]

Irish is the historical language of Ireland, a branch of the Celtic family of Indo-European, which is attested archaeologically in Central Europe in the Late Bronze Age. Irish first appears in inscriptions written in an alphabet or cipher known as Ogham on memorial stones based overwhelmingly in the southwest of Ireland with some in Wales. A small number of bilingual stones occur in Wales, which are inscribed in Latin as well as primitive Irish.

The religious vocabulary of the early Irish church is comprised of native and borrowed elements and combinations of both. It has been noted that non-Greek speaking churches without comparable philosophic or rhetorical registers were obliged to resort to direct borrowing and literal calques e.g. Coptic. We shall note similar situations in the early Irish material.

The French IndoEuropeanist Émile Benveniste points out that there are no common terms from the parent culture for religion, cult, priest, or even for any of the "dieux personels". The only exception is *deiwos* meaning 'luminous' and 'celestial', the celestial being who is contrasted with the terrestrial human inhabitants. Here the Old Irish *Día* a native word is used of the God of the Christians cognate with, but not borrowed from Latin *Deus*.[2]

The OI *féda* 'lord'< *weid-ont-s* 'knower' came to be used of The Lord and it occurs in the genetive locution *ar Fédot* 'of Our Lord' in the archaic Irish Cambrai Homily. Another word, which is found in conjunction with Latin *dominus* is *Coimdiu* 'lord or governor'. Its most frequent usage appears to be in reference to

---

1 KENNEY, J. F.: The sources for the Early History of Ireland: Eclesiastical, New York 1929, p. 164f. BINCHY, D. A.: Patrick and his Biographers Ancient and Modern in: Studia Hibernica 2 (1962), pp. 7–173.
2 BENÉVISTE, Émile: Le Vocabulaire des Indo-Européens, 2 vols., Paris 1969, vol. 2, p. 180.

God. It can be construed as a reflex of *kom-med-wot-s, and thus a perfect participle of OI con-midethar 'governs' with a possible conflation with midithir 'judges' based on the root *med.[3]

Dúil, OI for 'creature', is the base-word for a formation Dúlem 'Creator' with agent- suffix *-iamon (already obsolescent in the OI period), does not appear to be found in the earliest texts. A derivative adjective dúilech is commonly found with Día referring to God as the Creator.

At first sight the OI creitid 'believes, comes to believe' and creitem its verbal noun appear to be borrowed from Latin credo but this is not so. Crē-do corresponds exactly in form to Sanskrit śrad-dhā >*kred-dhē and the tertium quid in this instance is the cognate OI creit- ; OI creitim is the parallel of śrad dadhāmi 'I place my trust'. The Welsh equivalent is credaf. The meaning of *kred < *krezd < *kredd is obscure, although it has been suggested that it could be a magic or mystic power endemic in an object. The usage in the Rig Veda implies restitution given by the god in the form of a divine favour for this act of trust. Benvéniste observes that this complex IE notion reappears without religious connotation in Latin credo "confier une chose avec certitude de la récupérer".[4] In early Irish sources we find creitem denoting the Christian faith e.g.: hiris creitme Iesu Christi 'the faith of belief in Jesus Christ', Wb 2 b 8.[5]

In this eighth-century gloss we note the use of another native word denoting 'faith': OI ires(s) < *iri-sess-a (possibly containing a lost prefix *peri, (Skt. pari, Gk.peri). The verbal stem *siss- derives from a reduplication of the IE root *stā- and perhaps there may be a semantic connection between the word iress and erissem 'staying, standing firm' the verbal noun of ar-sissedar.[6]

The earliest loan words derive from Christian Latin usage in early Britain and possibly Gaul. At the phonological level Latin and Welsh p were nativised as q: Celtic had lost p long before, but Welsh had acquired p once more through the phonological historical evolution of labio-velar *kw > p. We may note the very early substitution of Irish q [< *kw] for p in Cásc 'Easter' from Latin Pascha and in the Ogham inscription form QRIMITIR alongside MS. cruimther modelled on OW premter 'priest' ultimately from Latin presbyter. Similarly the earlier name for St. Patrick in OI was Cothrige < *qatrikias < *patrikios < Patricius, but when Welsh had voiced the internal consonants the word was pronounced *pádrigios which on being re-borrowed re-entered Old Irish as Pádr(a)ic when p was adopted without any adjustment.[7]

A calque is a word created by an exact substitution of native elements of words for the new word coming in, in order to express the same meaning or concept. A

---

3 Benéviste: Le Vocabulaire des Indo-Européens, vol. 2, pp. 123–132.
4 Ibid., vol. 1, p. 171–174.
5 Stokes,Whitley/Strachan, John (ed.): Thesaurus Palaeohibernicus. A collection of Old-Irish glosses scholia prose and verse, 2 vols., Cambridge 1903, vol. 1, pp. 499–712, the source for this and all the Wb (Würzburg) glosses quoted in this paper.
6 Thurneysen, Rudolf: A grammar of Old Irish Dublin 1946, p. 69 and p. 499.
7 Ibid., pp. 565–576.

classic example is OI *soscéle* coined to translate L. *euangelium* comprising the prefix *so-* 'good' and *scéle* 'tidings, news', a calque on the Greek rather than the Latin which is simply a nativisation of the Greek in Latin. English 'gospel' is of course also a calque.

However, Latin *credo* 'I believe', the first word of the creed, was taken straight into OI as a noun, *crēdo,* which appears in early Irish as *créda* and is still in use today in modern *Cré* 'Creed' in the sense of the Apostles' or the Nicene Creed. Another derivative from the same Latin root, the adjective *credulus,* is the OI *credal* 'a believer, a righteous one, hence a holy person'. An important Celtic inherited word denoting piety, devotion and more particularly asceticism is OI *crábud* with its Welsh cognate *crefydd.*

The work entitled *Apgitir Chrábaid* 'An Alphabet of Piety', attributed to Colmán maccu Béognae († 611), is a short prose tract concerning "the ideal state of Christian conduct and the rewards that ensue therefrom". In this treatise we read that one of the components of holiness is *crésine cen sechtai* 'piety without simulation'.[8] This abstract noun signifying religion or piety is derived from an adjective *crésen* < Late Latin *Chrēstianus.* It occurs in the law tracts e.g. *fri cuibsena cresion* 'the confessions of believers'. That this is an early borrowing is also borne out by its appearance in glossaries where it is variously explained as *cráibhtech .i. sen a chré,* 'a devout i.e. old his clay', O'Davoren 447, and *crésean .i. creadhal no craibhtheach,* O'Clery.[9] We can recognise here the adjective from *crábud* and the later form of *credal.* Evidently *crésen* and *crésine* were already generalised in meaning, since the terms we find in the classical Old Irish period are *críst(a)ide* 'Christian', Wb 7 d 1, and *crístaidecht* 'Christianity', both formed in a linguistically orthodox manner from *Críst* 'Christ'.

We have already noted substitution of *q* < **kw* for Latin *p* in the Ogham inscription form *QRIMITIR* beside manuscript *cruimther* modelled on OW *premter* 'priest' < *presbiter* < *presbyter,* itself a borrowing from Greek. The early loanword has survived in the names of some ancient foundations. It was superseded by later *sacart* from Latin *sacerdos;* the word *sagart* denoting a priest is still in use in the modern language.

The word *flaith* is both abstract and concrete: authority, rule, and the person who exercises such authority or rule. It may refer to a king, a noble, a lord over clients. The *grád fhlatha* the noble grades are distinguished from the commoners, above all, by the possession of *céli* or clients. It is a function of this *flaith-céle* relationship that the eighth-century monastic reformers styled themselves *Céli Dé* 'God's Clients', a name familiar to monastic studies as Culdees, a Scottish popular form of their indigenous name. The clients received a fief or *rath* from their lord or *flaith. Rath* is the verbal noun of *ernaid* 'to grant, to bestow' and it included the

---

8   Ed. by Vernam HULL in: Celtica 8 (1969), pp. 44–89 at p. 58 line 7.
9   STOKES, Whitley (ed.): O'Davoren's Glossary, in: Archiv für Celtische Lexikographie, vol. 2, Halle 1903–04, pp. 197–504, entries referred to by number; MILLER, A. W. K. (ed.): O'Clery's Irish Glossary, in: Revue Celtique 4 (1880), pp. 349–428, 5 (1881), pp. 1–69, s.v. *crésean.*

concept of good fortune, prosperity and power. It was the word applied to denote the grace of God in OI *rad nDé,* Wb 7 b 3. The 'grace of performing miracles' is *rath denma ferte,* Wb 12 b 21, where the last word is *fert,* a borrowing of Latin *virtus. Mac raith* was a 'son of grace'; his Welsh counterpart *yr mab rat.* We may note its use in *Ce notad maic-si raith* 'though ye are sons of grace' Wb 33 b 8. The word *rath* still retains its meaning of good fortune and good luck in the Irish language but the theological concept has been superseded by *grás, grása* and *grásta* derived directly or indirectly from the Latin *gratia.* This process of substitution has already begun in the Late Middle Irish period.[10]

In the Alphabet of Piety we read the words *flaith nime* 'kingdom of heaven' literally the 'lordship of heaven' where *flaith* corresponds to Welsh *gwlad* 'land, country'. In later Irish *flaithius,* with an added abstract suffix, is frequently found as the equivalent of Latin *imperium,* denoting the kingdom of heaven. Heaven in the Lord's Prayer is *nem* 'sky'; its affiliations have been suggested as Skt. *nábhah* 'cloud' or alternatively Skt. *námah* 'bow' from **nem-* 'bend', hence the sky as the vault of heaven. The Welsh equivalent is *nef.*[11]

The compound noun *ríched* <**rigo-sedo-n* 'royal seat' is sometimes used of the firmament, e.g. *ríched rindach* 'the starry firmament', in the Martyrology of Óengus in the entry for May 22, where it is cited as the ultimate destination of a soul. It is greatly favoured in religious poetry and no doubt it reflects the imagery of the Throne of God.[12] In a Middle Irish homily we read: *isin domnach dorónta ríched cona ainglib* 'on Sunday Heaven with its angels was created'.[13]

Pardus from Latin *paradisus,* itself a borrowing of Gk. *Parádeisos,* and ultimately of Iranian origin with the meaning of a walled garden, in OI reflects a terrestrial pleasure-ground; it is used to describe the Garden of Eden and equally the celestial realms of the blessed in heaven. It is perhaps a more poetic word than *flaithius,* but it is still widely used in current Irish *parthas.*[14]

The words for prayer are difficult to analyse; we find several Latin words being glossed with their seeming Old Irish semantic correspondance. Benveniste discussed at some length the root **prek-* which gives Latin *precor* and with the infix *-ske-, posco.* He observes: "Tel est le trait distinctif de *prek-,* c'est une demande orale, adressée a une autorité supérieure et qui ne comporte pas d'autres moyens que la parole".[15] The enlarged form of this root **prkske/o,* reflected in Latin *posco,* occurs in Welsh *archaf* 'I ask' and in the Old Irish petrified expression *arcu fuin* explained as Latin *posco veniam* 'I beg pardon (of God)'; a saying found in religious verse. It is probable that we are presented here with an old calque surviving from the earlier Christian period when the simplex **arcid* 'asks' was still current in

---

10 Lexique Etymologique de l'Irlandais Ancien (LEIA), ed. by J. VENDRYES/E. BACHELLERY/P. Y. LAMBERT, Paris/Dublin 1959–, RS 1974, p. R-8.
11 Ibid., MNOP 1969, p. N-8.
12 Ibid., pp. R–28f. See STOKES, Whitley (ed.): Félire Óengusso céli Dé, London 1905, p. 125.
13 ATKINSON, Robert (ed.): Passions and homilies from the Leabhar Breac, Dublin 1887, line 3530.
14 LEIA, MNOP, p. P-4.
15 BENÉVISTE: Le Vocabulaire des Indo-Européens, vol. 2, p. 159.

the speech. There are several compounds from this root in both branches of Celtic which do not appear to be immediately relevant for our purposes.[16]

The terms most commonly occurring in Irish for prayer and praying derive from the root *ghwedh- 'pray, wish', which the Celtic languages share with Greek and Iranian, [OP jadiya-, Avest. jadya- 'ask the god in prayer' and Gk. pothéo 'desire', théssasthai 'implore']. The OI forms are guidid 'prays' and guide 'a prayer'; Welsh has the cognate in gweddio 'praying'. Guide is paired with a Latin lemma, in many instances with a different Latin word: the nouns oratio, supplicatio, prex, alligatio and their corresponding verbs, both simple and compound, with their participles. The modern language has retained this word, guí, which has both verbal and nominal function.

The word for a prayer-book in Irish to day is leabhar urnaithe, made up of the Latin borrowing from liber, leabhar being the modern descendant of OI lebor. The second element is a plural of urnaí, the modern reflex of airnigde, which was originally the verbal noun of an old compound ar-neget < *air-ni-guid 'prays'. This is a comparatively rare verb in our sources but the verbal noun has stood the test of time. Apart from the root guid which we have just discussed, the prefixes are of interest: air <*are 'before' and ni 'down, low' which we have in English 'nether, nether regions.' The semantics envisage praying low before God. A directive from the reform movement tells us of the unlettered cleric maini lega arnegat ina c[h]ridiu 'if he cannot read [his Latin]] he prays in his heart'.[17]

The modern paidir 'prayer', is easily recognised as a generalisation of the term for the Pater noster 'the Lord's Prayer' whose first word was borrowed as paiter in the older language.

The Holy Spirit is named in Spirut Nóib, the noun, a borrowing from Latin Spiritus combined with a native adjective from the IE root *noibho. This word, according to Meillet, originally denotes an active force before it comes to mean 'holy'. Such an evolution in meaning would not inhibit the loan shift required when noíb was said of the Holy Spirit; Meillet also associated OI noeb with Old Persian naiba 'good, beautiful'. The Welsh denote the Holy Spirit as yrYspryd Lan 'The Pure Spirit'. There may have been a corresponding spirut glan in Old Irish, but it does not appear to occur in the main texts.[18]

The seven-day week was incorporated in to the Irish year by the Christian church and Latin septimana was taken into the language as sechtmon. It is an index of the influence of the Christian ethos on early Irish society that four of the seven weekdays are named from Christian cult and practice. Sunday in common with the Romance languages is the Lord's Day, Dies Dominicus, Domnach or Dé Domnaig. Wednesday is named Cétaín gl. quarta sabati, or Dia Cétaíne, the first

---

16 THURNEYSEN: A grammar of Old Irish, p. 465 and 523; LEIA, p. A-96.

17 BINCHY, D. A. (ed.): The Old Irish Table of Penitential Commutations, in: Ériu 19 (1962) pp. 47–72, at p. 64, line 26.

18 MEILLET, A.: Irlandais Nóib – Níabh, in: Zeitschrift für Celtische Philologie 10 (1915) p. 309; LEIA, p. N-20.

fast day, Thursday was designated the day between the two fasts *Dé Dardaín* (a syncopated form of *Dé-eter-dá- aín*), and Friday is *Aíne* or *Dé Aíne dídine* day of the last fast.[19]

These designations for the days of the week provide us with interesting aspects of early Irish society. Not surprisingly the fasting in these instances is a nativisation of Latin *ieiunium* > OI *aíne, aín*, and it denotes the ascetic practice of the early church which observed a fast *on quarta feria* and *sexta feria*. There was however a pre-Christian practice of ritual fasting in early Ireland which was not used in the Christian context. This is the word *troscud* which is a an extreme legal remedy in Old Irish Law where the plaintiff fasts outside the house of a very high-status person – a king, a chief poet, perhaps – and the person fasted against must fast too, or else agree to a just solution. In the event of the noble defendant holding out against the fasting, and the ensuing death of the lower-status plaintiff, the higher personage was then seen to have been polluted by the presence of the corpse and thereby lost his high eminence. All this of course was based on pre-Christian practice and belief and repugnant to early Irish Christianity. *Abstanait* < L. *abstinentia* makes a brief appearance as a learned borrowing but once Christianity was firmly rooted the indigenous *troscad* regains its place in Irish. In the Middle Irish Tripartite Life of Patrick *abstanait* is glossed by *troscad*. In native hagiography, Saint Patrick is engaged in *troscad* against God on top of the mountain, to persuade God by the old juridical system to squeeze huge numbers of the Irish race into heaven on Judgment Day. *Troscadh* is still our word for the exiguous fasts prescribed by the church today and were it not for the days of the week the old *aíne* would have long gone into oblivion with *abstanait*.

In regard to the spiritual quest for sanctity Irish monks, who were actively engaged in living the *vita actualis* were named the *oís achtáil* while their contemplative brethren who pursued the inner life were the *óis teoáir* 'the people of *theoria*', Greek in Latin dress. Individual contemplatives were given the name *oíbell teoir* 'a spark or flame of the theoric life'. The laws define a *fer co rath De .i. aibillteoir no deorad De* 'a man with God's grace, namely a flame of contemplative life or a stranger for God', in other words a hermit, or a pilgrim; a *deorad* has alienated himself from his rights as an *urrad* or freeman. Such a hermit would undergo *bánmartre* 'white martyrdom' and *glasmartre* 'blue martyrdom' by virtue of cutting himself off from everything dear to him in the first instance, and in the second, suffer the hardships and labours of mortification and repentance in the casting off of this world's desires. Irish monasteries had anchorites attached to them who lived at some distance from them, on occasion. The Latin *anachoreta* became the Old Irish *ancharae*, who may have been associated with a *reclés* 'an oratory or small monastic cell' taken to be named from *reclusum,* a Late Latin word for an enclosure.

---

19 This and following paragraphs are based on the interpretation of the words under discussion as put forward in the Dictionary of the Irish Language, compact edition, Royal Irish Academy, Dublin 1998.

Vendryes suggests that *anmcharae* 'confessor, spiritual director' composed of *ainim* plus *carae,* literally soul-friend, was a volks etymologie for the anchorite or *ancharae*. However that may be, *anmchairde* 'soul-friendship' describes both the function of a confessor and the relation of a penitent to his confessor. Early Irish law of speaks of *clérig is caillecha fri heclais fo réir anmcarat* 'clerics and nuns in the church under the guidance of spitual directors'.[20] The *anmcharae* appears comparatively often in legal contexts in the function of a character witness.

---

20 ALI, vol. 3, p. 14, line 13.

JEAN-MICHEL PICARD

The colour purple: cultural cross-fertilisation and translation in early medieval Ireland

The introduction of Christianity in Ireland in the fifth century corresponds to the spread of literacy there, first in Latin, but soon after in the vernacular language. By the seventh and eighth centuries Ireland had produced a rich literature in Old Irish, both lay and ecclesiastical in content, and reflecting the interests of the aristocracy and the native learned classes but also those of the Church. As the largest and oldest vernacular literature in Europe, it has been the object of studies from linguists and historians for nearly two centuries. Until recently it was seen mostly as a monument for the study of the Iron Age Celts and it was used as a tool for shaping and defining the modern idea of a pure Celtic culture on the ground that, unlike the continental Celts, the Irish were never subjected to the rule of the Roman Empire. Nowadays, scholars are aware that Irish culture is not monolithic and that the influence of Christian and Latin culture in the vernacular texts written in the seventh and eighth centuries cannot be ignored. Awareness of cross-cultural expression is especially pertinent in the cases of ecclesiastical texts written in the vernacular. Because of their nature, these texts necessarily borrow, adapt or translate Latin, Greek or Hebrew originals. This is the case of the oldest manuscript containing a continuous text in Old Irish, written between 763 and 790 and now preserved in the town library of Cambrai in France.[1] Known as the 'Cambrai Homily', this well known text has been studied extensively by scholars of the Old Irish language both for its linguistic interest and for its spiritual content, especially with regard to martyrdom.[2] In particular, the Cambrai Homily is the source for the definition of a form of asceticism referred to as 'Green Martyrdom' (*glasmartre*) in text books dealing with the early Irish Church. I propose to revisit this text with a view to show how the process of translation from Latin to the vernacular was understood and practised in early medieval Ireland.

---

1 Cambrai, Bibliothèque Municipale, ms. 679; description in LOWE, Elias Avery: Codices Latini Antiquiores, 12 vols, London 1934-1972, vol. 6, pp. 12–13.

2 O'CURRY, Eugene/TARDIF, André: Fragment d'homélie en langue celtique, in: Bibliothèque de l'École des Chartes 3 (1852), pp. 193–202; ZEUSS, Johann Kaspar: Grammatica Celtica, Leipzig 1871, pp. 1004–1007; ZIMMER, Heinrich: Glossae Hibernicae, Berlin 1881, pp. 213–215; STOKES, Whitley/STRACHAN, John: Thesaurus Palaeohibernicus II, Cambridge 1903, pp. 244–247; THURNEYSEN, Rudolf: Old Irish Reader, Dublin 1949, pp. 35–36; GOUGAUD, Louis: Les conceptions du martyre chez les Irlandais, in: Revue Bénédictine 24 (1907) pp. 360–373; GOUGAUD, Louis: Devotional and ascetic practices in the Middle Ages, London 1927, pp. 205–223; RYAN, John: Irish Monasticism, Dublin 1931, pp. 197–198; Ó NÉILL, Pádraig: The background to the Cambrai Homily, in: Ériu 32 (1981) pp. 137–147; STANCLIFFE, Clare: Red, white and blue martyrdom, in: Ireland in Early Medieval Europe, ed. by Dorothy WHITELOCK et al., Cambridge 1982, pp. 21–46.

The Cambrai homily begins with a Latin quotation from the Gospel of Matthew, immediately followed by a commentary in Old Irish:

In nomine Dei Summi
Si quis uult post me uenire, abneget semetipsum et tollat crucem suam, et sequatur me.[3] Insce inso asber ar féda Ísu fri cach n-oein din chenélu dóine are n-indarbe anal-chi óod ocus a pecthu ocus ara tinóla soalchi ocus are n-airema futhu ocus airde cruche ar Chríst, céin bes i commus coirp ocus anme, aire sechethar slictu ar fédot i n-dagnímrat-ib.

In the name of God most High
'If someone wants to come after me, let him deny himself and take up his cross and fol-low me!' This is the word which our Lord Jesus says to everyone of the human race, that he banish from him his vices and his sins and that he gather virtues and receive lacerations and the signs of the Cross for Christ's sake as long as he is in power of body and soul, in order to follow the tracks of our Lord in good thoughts.

The text of Matthew is quoted again to explain the words *abneget semetipsum* and *tollat crucem suam*:

Isaire asber: *Si quis uult post me uenire, abneget semetipsum et tollat crucem suam,* ocuis ticsath a chruich, *et sequatur me,* ocuis numsechethse. Isée ar ndiltuth dúnn fanis-sin mani cometsam de ar tolaib ocuis ma fristossam de ar pecthib. Issí ticsál ar cruche dúnn furnn ma arfóimam dammint ocus martri ocus coicsath ar Chriist.

Therefore He says: '*If someone wants to come after me, let him deny himself and take up his cross* and take up his cross, '*and let him follow me!*' and let him follow me! The deni-al of ourselves is when we do not indulge our desires and if we abjure our sins. Taking up our cross is if we receive loss and martyrdom and suffering for Christ's sake.

At this point in the discourse, one may be tempted to think that the homily is aimed at a public that does not understand Latin since the author takes care to give literal translations into Irish of words as simple as *et tollat crucem suam* and *et sequatur me*. It may seems strange therefore to discover in the following sentence a long quotation in Latin, commenting on the same words *et tollat crucem suam*:

Amail assindber alaile *et nomen crux quippe a cruciatu dicitur, et duobus modis crucem Domini baiulamus, cum aut per abstinentiam carnem afficiamus, aut per conpassionem proximi necessitatem illius nostram esse putamus; qui enim dolorem exhibet in aliena necessitate crucem portat in mente. Ut Paulus ait: portate onera uestra inuicem, sic adimplebitis legem Christi.*[4] Ocus asbeir daniu ind apostol: *flete cum flentibus, gaudete cum gaudentibus.*[5] *Si patiatur unum membrum, compatientur omnia membra.*[6]

As someone else says, the word 'cross' comes from 'suffering' and we carry the cross of our Lord in two ways, either when we weak-en the flesh through abstinence or when we make our own our neighbour's misfor-tune through compassion for him. For he who shows pain for someone else's misfor-tune carries the cross in spirit. As Paul says: 'Bear one another's burdens and so fulfil the law of Christ'. And then the Apostle says: 'Weep with them that weep, rejoice with them that do rejoice. If one member suffers, all the members suffer with it'.

---

3   Mt 16,24; cf. Mc 8,34 and Lc 9,23.
4   Gal 6,2.
5   Rom 12,15.
6   I Cor 12,26.

In sharp contrast with the last two sentences which are clearly attributed to Saint Paul the first sentence is introduced by an enigmatic 'As someone else says'. In fact, it is a straight quotation from the *Homily on the Gospels* 37 of Pope Gregory the Great.

> 5. [...] *Crux quippe a cruciatu dicitur. Et duobus modis crucem Domini baiulamus, cum aut per abstinentiam carnem afficimus, aut per compassionem proximi necessitatem illius nostram putamus. Qui enim dolorem exhibet in aliena necessitate, crucem portat in mente.*[7]

The same idea is also found in Homily 32:

> 3. *Sed qui iam se a uitiis abnegat, exquirendae ei uirtutes sunt in quibus crescat. Nam cum dictum est:* Qui uult post me uenire, abneget semetipsum, *protinus additur:* Et tollat crucem suam quotidie, et sequatur me. *Duobus etenim modis crux tollitur, cum aut per abstinentiam afficitur corpus, aut per compassionem proximi affligitur animus.*[8]

Could it be, as Padraig O'Néill has suggested, that the Pope's name was deliberately omitted because the homily was written for 'an unlettered audience unfamiliar with Gregory's work'? Yet the many exhortations to a life of asceticism seem to be addressed to a monastic audience. The paradox can be resolved if we consider that this quotation of Gregory had become a set piece of exegesis in insular monastic circles by the end of the seventh century. It is found in the Irish *Liber de Numeris*:

> *Duobus modis crux portatur, id est, cum per abstinentiam afficitur corpus, aut per compassionem proximi affligitur animus.*[9]

Bede uses it both in his commentary on Luke and in his commentary on Mark:

> *Duobus etenim modis crux tollitur, cum aut per abstinentiam afficitur corpus, aut per conpassionem proximi affligitur animus.*[10]

On the continent, before the Carolingian period, it is found in Defensor of Ligugé in the chapter about compassion included in his *Liber Scintillarum* written about the year 700:

> *crux quippe a cruciatu dicitur, et duobus modis crux tollitur, cum aut per abstinentiam crucem Domini baiulamus, aut per conpassionem proximi necessitatem illius nostram esse putamus. [...] Duobus enim modis crux tollitur, cum aut per abstinentiam affligitur corpus, aut per conpassionem proximi affligitur animus.*[11]

---

7 Gregorius Magnus: Homiliae in Evangelia, 37,5 in: MIGNE, Jean-Paul: Patrologia Latina, 221 vols., Paris 1844–1864, vol. 76, col. 1277.

8 Greg. Mag.: Homeliae in Evangelia, 32,3 in: MIGNE: Patrologia Latina, vol. 76, col. 1234.

9 Liber de numeris, in: MIGNE: Patrologia Latina 83, col. 1300. For the date of this work see McNALLY, Robert E.: Der irische Liber de numeris, München 1957.

10 Bede: In Lucae Evangelium Expositio, ed. by HURST, D.: Bedae Opera, Corpus Christianorum Series Latina 120, Turnhout 1960, p. 02; Bede: In Marci Evangelium Expositio ed. by HURST, D.: Bedae Opera, CCSL 120, Turnhout 1960, p. 539.

11 Defensor: Liber Scintillarum, 15, ed. by ROCHAIS, H.-M.: Defensor de Ligugé, Livre d'étincelles, Paris 1962, p. 82.

Incidentally, Defensor is the earliest continental author to use the Irish *Liber de ordine creaturarum* written in the second half of the 7th century.[12]

In the Cambrai Homily, the author makes a clever use of both homilies 32 and 37, using the same biblical quotations and developing the same logical arguments as Pope Gregory. For example, in the first paragraph quoted above the words *indárbe analchi óod* 'that he banish from him his vices' and *tinóla soalchi* 'that he gather virtues' are not straight translations from the Latin but follow closely the original ideas found in Homily 32 in the expressions *se a uitiis abnegat* 'he fully renounces his vices' and *exquirendae ei virtutes sunt* 'he must seek virtues'. In this respect it is a good example of the fusion of Latin and vernacular cultures in a bilingual environment. The authoritative text is written in Latin and the vernacular is introduced, not because the monastic audience does not understand Latin (as the use of long Latin quotations shows), but as a tool of exegesis, in order to elucidate and clarify concepts expressed in the sacred text. Bilingual exegesis seems to have been the norm in Irish schools. This is the approach found in the Milan and Würzburg glose commentaries, where Latin and Irish cannot be dissociated and are used together to express a coherent line of argument.

This brings us to the most famous passage of the Cambrai Homily, which deals with different types of martyrdoms and raises the problem of perception of colours across cultures and across the ages (I use here the text and English translation by Whitley Stokes and John Strachan).

Filus trechenélæ martre daneu adrímiter ar chruich du duiniu, ma desgre báanmartre ocus glasmartre ocus dercmartre. Issí in bánmartre du duiniu intain scaras ar Dea fri cach réet caras, cení césa áini na laubir n-oco. Issí ind glasmartre dó intain scaras fria thola leó nó céssas sáithor i ppennit ocus aithrigi. Issí in dercmartre dó foditu chruche ocus diorcne ar Chríst amail tond-ecomnucuir dundaib abstolaib oc ingrimmin inna clóen ocuis oc forcetul recto Dée.

Now there are three kinds of martyrdom which are counted as a cross to man, that is to say, white martyrdom and green martyrdom and red martyrdom. This is the white martyrdom to man when he separates for the sake of God from everything he loves, although he suffer fasting or labour thereat. This is the green martyrdom to him when by means of them [= fasting and labour], he separates from his desires and suffers toil in penance and repentance. This is the red martyrdom to him, endurance of a cross or destruction for Christ's sake as has happened to the Apostles in the persecution of the wicked and in teaching the law of God.[13]

The concepts of red martyrdom (violent death) and white martyrdom (ascetic life) are well attested in early Christian literature. The latter especially was promoted in

---

12 See DÍAZ Y DÍAZ, Manuel C.: Review of edition of Liber Scintillarum, CCSL 117, in: Hispania Sacra 11 (1958) p. 483 and DÍAZ Y DÍAZ, Manuel C.: Liber de ordine creaturarum: un anónimo irlandés del siglo vii, Santiago de Compostela 1972.

13 STOKES, Whitley/STRACHAN, John: Thesaurus Palaeohibernicus II, Cambridge 1903, pp. 246–247.

monastic circles.[14] The meaning of *glasmartre* is less obvious and has been under-stood in two different ways by modern scholars. The traditional rendering is 'green martyrdom' while a more modern suggestion by Pádraig O'Néill and Clare Stan-cliffe has been 'blue martyrdom'.[15] The discrepancy comes from the well-known fact that the perception of colours has changed since the middle ages. For exam-ple, in modern French, *bleu* means 'blue' but in Medieval French texts *bloi* could also mean 'greenish', 'grey', 'pale' or even 'blond'. *Glas* generally means 'green' in Modern Irish but it had a wider semantic spectrum in Old Irish and could express the green of leaves and grass, the blue of the sky, the inky colour of the sea, the greyish colour of wolves, the livid colour of the sick and dying.[16] In fact, it would be impossible to determine the colour of *glasmartre* were it not for the fact that Irish scholars also wrote in Latin. Ó Néill and Stancliffe have already identified a number of Latin texts where the tripartite division of colours found in the Cam-brai Homily is matched by Latin terms. *Derg* corresponds to *ruber* or *rubicundus*, *bán* to *albus* or *candidus* and *glas* to *hyacinthinus*. For example, commenting on Genesis 9, 13-16, the Irish author of the *De operibus sex Dierum* writes:

In arco autem III colores sunt: albus color, qui martyrium cotidianum indicat; rubicundus color, sanguinis effusionem in martyrio; iacentinus penitentiam.[17]	Now, there are three colours in the rainbow: the colour white which means daily martyr-dom, the colour red which means bloodshed through martyrdom, the colour of hyacinth which means penance.

Similarly, in the collection of homilies known as *Catachesis Celtica*, the colours of the Three Kings' clothes are interpreted thus:

Item colores uestimentorum illorum moraliter nobis proficiunt. Color albus castitatem nobis indicat; color iacinthinus ieiunium nobis indicat [...] color rubicundus rubicundum martirium nobis indicat.[18]	Similarly, the colours of their clothes are of help to us on an allegorical level. The colour white points us towards chastity; the col-our of hyacinth points us towards fasting [...] the colour red points us towards the red martyrdom.

The association of *hyacinthinus* and *glas* is confirmed in the vernacular language since the Irish word for hyacinth, *buga*, is defined as *gorm no glas*.[19] In Old Irish

14 See FONTAINE, Jacques: Sulpice Sévère, Vie de saint Martin, 3 vols., Sources Chrétiennes 133–135, Paris 1967–1969, vol. 3, pp. 1214–1241; STANCLIFFE: Red, white and blue martyrdom, pp. 29–32.
15 See above, note 2.
16 See Dictionary of the Irish language based mainly on Old and Middle Irish materials, Dublin 1913–1975, Letter G, cols. 95–96.
17 Munich, CLM 6302 (saec. VIII2) < Freising, fol. 59r; cf. B. BISCHOFF: Wendepunkte in der Geschichte der lateinischen Exegese im Frühmittelalter, in: Sacris Erudiri 6 (1954) pp. 189–281, at pp. 230–31.
18 Vatican, Reg. Lat. 49 (saec. IX) fol. 55r, ed. by WILMART, André: Analecta Reginensia. Extraits de manuscrits latins de la reine Christine conservés au Vatican, Vatican 1933, pp. 29–112, p. 78.
19 Dictionary of the Irish language, Letter B, col. 232. I owe this reference to Dr Patricia Kelly, Department of Early and Medieval Irish, University College, Dublin.

literature, *buga* is often used as a term of comparison to describe the colour of the eyes of the hero[20] and it would be fair to assume that *glas*, like *hyacinthinus* in classical Latin, means 'blue'. But the context of the Cambrai Homily and of the Latin texts quoted above is different. The sources of the Irish exegetes are Biblical and Patristic and, in that context, *hyacinthinus* referred to a different colour. In the Vulgate *hyacinthinus* is one of the sacred colours stipulated in the making of priestly vestments and for the various draperies of the Tabernacle.

1. The veil of the Tabernacle (Exodus 26, 30–31)
   26:30 *et eriges tabernaculum iuxta exemplum quod tibi in monte monstratum est*
   26:31 *facies et uelum de hyacintho et purpura coccoque bis tincto et bysso retorta*

2. The ephod and robe of Aaron (Exodus 28, 6 and 31)
   28:6 *facient autem superumerale de auro et hyacintho ac purpura coccoque bis tincto et bysso retorta*
   [...]
   28:31 *facies et tunicam superumeralis totam hyacinthinam*

In his translation Jerome followed the Septuagint, who translated Hebrew *tekêleth* by Greek *huákinthos* and *'argamân* by *porphúra*. These two words refer to the two types of purple extracted from the *murex* shellfish. In the chemical process of manufacturing the purple dye, two hues were produced, red and violet purple. The medieval west was aware of the two colours of purple. Thus *purpureus* was used not only to designate the crimson purple of the emperors, but also the violet colour in the rainbow (see plate 1).

The link between *hyacintinus* and *purpureus* is clearly expressed in Isidore of Seville's *Etymologiae*: *Hyacinthus herba est habens florem purpureum* 'The hyacinth is a plant which has a purple flower' (see plate 2).[21]

The symbolism of the colour of hyacinth was already linked to penance, fasting and suffering in the fifth century. For example it is found in Quotvultdeus's *Liber promissionum et praedictorum Dei*, where the mystical interpretation of the colours of the veil of the tabernacle is explained:

In hyacinthino colore pallor quidam est cum splendore, concordans ieiuniis elemosinisque conueniens [...] *In ieiuniis pallor, in elemosinis splendor refulget : quae hyacinthinam figuram ostendunt.*[22]	In the colour of hyacinth, there is a kind of pallor mixed with splendour, thus agreeing with fasts and suited to alms [...] Pallor radiates in the fasts, so does splendour in the alms: both are represented in the colour purple.

One may compare Quotvultdeus's interpretation to that of the anonymous Irish author of the homily on the parable of the pearl (Mt. 13,45–46) found in the *Catachesis Celtica*:

---

20 For example in Togail Bruidne Da Derga, 24: *Batar glasithir buga na dí súil* and in Fled Bricrend 7326, Lebor na Huidre, fol. 90b: *Is glasidir buga indala suil.*

21 Isidore, Etymologiae, 17, 9, 15.

22 Quotvultdeus: Liber promissionum, 2, 2, 3, ed. by BRAUN, René: Quodvultdeus: Livre des promesses et des prédictions de Dieu (Sources Chrétiennes 101), Paris 1964, p. 294.

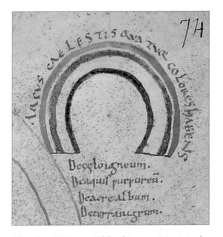

Plate 1: Dijon, Bibliothèque Municipale, ms. 448 (saec. XI) < Lotharingia, fol. 74r.

Plate 2: Hyacinthus orientalis (common hyacinth).

[Margarita] est etiam multicolor, quia aliquando rubicunda est, quando martirum passiones narrat, qui rubrum suum sanguinem pro Christo fuderunt, aliquando iacinthina est ... quando abstinentiam quae iacinthinas et pallidas efficit facies in aeclesiis docet ... aliquando item est candida, quando corporis castitatem et cordis munditiam cunctis docet.[23]

The pearl is also multicoloured. For it is red when it tells of the deaths of the martyrs who have spilled their red blood for Christ's sake. It is purple when it teaches abstinence which causes people's faces to be pale and livid in the churches. Also, it is white when it teaches to all chastity of body and purity of mind.

A later passage in the *Catachesis Celtica* leaves no doubt about the colour of penance:

Ornatur enim aeclesia auro apostolorum, argento profetarum, gemmis uirginum, coco martirium, purpura penitentium (For the Church is adorned with the gold of the apostles, the silver of the prophets, the precious stones of the virgins, the red of the martyrs and the violet purple of the penitents).[24]

In subsequent centuries, violet purple, symbolising sorrow and penance, would become the colour of the priestly vestments for Advent, Lent and Septuagesima. However, while Patristic exegesis was based on a fourfold system (violet purple, red purple, crimson and white), Irish exegetes merged the two shades of red to produce a threefold division more akin to the triads favoured by the Celtic mind. The threefold division was already established in the 670s when the Irish Pseudo-Hilary wrote his *Commentary on the seven Catholic Epistles.*

---

23 Vatican, Reg. Lat. 49, fol. 31r (= WILMART, p. 88).
24 Vatican, Reg. Lat. 49, fol. 36v (passage not edited by Wilmart).

Nuntii autem qui domum defenderunt Raab per inposita signa coloris uarii, id est rubri et iacinctini et bissini, qui castitatem et martyrium <et> offensa membra in laboribus significant, doctores sunt aecclaesiae, qui tria haec genera bonorum aecclaesiae commendant, a uero Iesu saluatore missi.[25]	Now the messengers who protected Rahab's house by placing signs of various colours – that is red, purple and white, which mean chastity, martyrdom and members hurting from toils – are the doctors of the Church who were sent by Jesus, the true Saviour, to recommend to the Christian community three kinds of perfections.

The author of the Cambrai Homily belongs to the same tradition of exegetical teaching as Pseudo-Hilary. In addition to the mention of toil and suffering in connection with the colour purple, they both use the same string of Pauline quotations when commenting on the notion of compassion. One can compare the two quotations at the end of the long Latin passage in the Cambrai Homily with Pseudo-Hilary's *Commentary on the First Epistle of Peter*:

> *Compatientes: id est 'onera uestra inuicem portate' et aliter 'si patitur unum membrum compatiuntur omnia membra.*[26]

In spite of the use of the vernacular, the Cambrai Homily is not a work written for the uneducated plebs. Not only the long Latin quotation, but also the intricate web of allusions and intertextual references to earlier exegesis seems to point towards a learned ecclesiastical audience. But in that case, why the use of the vernacular? The fact that this homily survived only by chance, mistakenly inserted in a codex of law texts, leads me to surmise that there might have been many other similar examples in early Christian Ireland. There are numerous references to the three sacred languages in Hiberno-Latin texts and the Irish were well aware of the vernacular nature of their native tongue.[27] However, they were proud of their own language and viewed it as a tool of communication in no way inferior to the other languages spoken by other people, including Latin in so far as it was a medium of communication as well as one of the sacred languages. Writing shortly before 700, Adomnán, abbot of Iona, clearly voices the idea that the Irish language was equal to any other in the world and could be used to relate facts showing the power of God.[28] I mentioned earlier the Milan and Würzburg glosses. The latter include long quotations in Latin from Pelagius, Cassiodorus, pseudo-Primasius and sometimes Origen in a Latin translation. Origen's commentary on the Pauline Epistles is the most sophisticated and the most complex of the commentaries used by Irish exegetes. It may be significant that in the Würzburg codex the more substantial glosses written in Irish are often clear and concise renderings of some diffi-

---

25 Ps. Hilarius: Tractatus in septem epistolas canonicas, ed. by McNALLY, Robert E.: Scriptores Hiberniae minores I, CCSL 108B, Turnhout 1973, p. 68.

26 McNALLY, CCSL 108B, p. 88.

27 See McNALLY, Robert E.: The 'tres linguae sacrae' in early Irish Bible exegesis, in: Theological Studies 19 (1958) pp. 395–403.

28 See PICARD, Jean-Michel: Tailoring the sources: The Irish hagiographer at work, in: Irland und Europa im früheren Mittelalter, ed. by Próinséas Ní CHATHÁIN und Michael RICHTER, Stuttgart 1996.

cult development in Origen's commentary. The evidence of the glosses shows that, indeed, Irish was used in ecclesiastical schools, not just at the elementary stage when students are beginning to learn Latin, but at the advanced level too. As in modern universities, translation and textual analysis in the vernacular language were probably used to clarify and elucidate the more difficult concepts. The transposition to their first tongue usually helps second-language learners to reconstruct a given train of thought according to the patterns of their own native language. It is also a way to remove all ambiguity and make sure that the message is clearly understood. Given that general context, it seems unlikely that the Cambrai Homily was written in Irish to suit the needs of an uneducated audience. Furthermore, the register of language chosen by the author is patently literary, with the use of stylistic devices such as *uariatio*.[29] If I may borrow from Michael Richter his archipelago metaphor,[30] we have here one of the remaining islands left after the disappearance of a large continent where the language of religion was undoubtedly Latin, but where Irish was commonly used as the language of the learned classes for the purpose of teaching and exegesis, leading to a better understanding of the sacred text.

---

29 For example, in the passage quoted above (note 13), use of the synonyms *saethar*, which is the proper Celtic term, and *laubir*, which is the corresponding Latin borrowing. On the use of the technique of *uariatio* by Hiberno-Latin authors, see PICARD, Jean-Michel: Eloquentiae exuberantia: words and forms in Adomnán's *Vita Columbae*, in: Peritia 6/7 (1987/88) pp. 141–157, at p. 144.

30 RICHTER, Michael: Ireland and her neighbours in the seventh century, Dublin 1999, p. 235.

Morfydd E. Owen

Some Welsh words: language and religion in early Wales

Students of language have emphasised the contribution that studies of native and borrowed words can make to our understanding of the history of institutions. The work of Christine Mohrmann in analysing the vocabulary of the Western Church is well known.[1] This paper is concerned with the light which vernacular words can throw on our understanding of the use of Latin and the early history of the language of Christianity in Britain. The nature of the language of the Christian religion in early Wales was determined by a series of historical accidents. Wales was part of the Roman Empire; Ireland was not. Christianity came to Britain in Roman times. We know this first from historical references to Christianity in the work of Tertullian, Origen, the *Vita Germani* of Constantius, and the work of Sulpicius Severus and Jerome.[2] Secondly we have some reflection of the extent of that Christianity from the archaeological evidence of contemporary Roman villas, Christian signs such as Chi-Ro symbols, possible baptisteries and other material remains. This evidence suggests that in Roman times Christianity was most prevalent in east and south-east Britain.[3] A little evidence shows the Christian religion penetrating into the Severn basin and into what is today south-east Wales. Two martyrdoms from the early period caught the imagination of the chroniclers and writers: those of St Alban at Verulamium, now St Albans, and of Julius and Aaron at Caerleon in present day Gwent.[4]

The language of Western Christendom was Latin, which was also the language of the Roman conquerors, and which was adopted by a proportion of the population of Britain. Before the advent of Christianity the British had already borrowed words from Latin.[5] Kenneth Jackson thought that the Latin which was borrowed

---

1 MOHRMANN, Ch.: Études sur le Latin des Chrétiens, 3 vols., Roma 1961–1965.

2 For what remains the best survey of these sources, see WILLIAMS, H.: Christianity in Early Britain, Oxford 1912, pp. 96–100. For more recent comment, see particularly SHARPE, R.: Martyrs and Local Saints in the Early Medieval West, in: SHARPE, R./THACKER, A. (eds.): Local Saints and local churches in Late Antique Britain, Oxford 2002, pp. 114–121.

3 THOMAS, Ch.: Christianity in Roman Britain to A. D. 500, London 1981, and for a recent review, SHARPE: Martyrs and Local Saints (n. 2), pp. 119–130.

4 Gildas: De Excidio, ch. 10, ed. by H. WILLIAMS, 2 vols., London 1899/1901.

5 JACKSON, K.: Language and History in Early Britain, Edinburgh 1953, p. 99 et passim. For the Latin loanwords in Welsh, see LEWIS, H.: Yr Elfen Ladin yn yr iaith Gymraeg, Cardiff 1943; LOTH, J.: Les mots latins dans les langues brittoniques (gallois, armoricain, cornique), phonétique et commentaire, Paris 1892; HAARMAN, H.: Der lateinische Lehnwortschatz im Kymrischen, Bonn 1970 and HAARMAN, H.: Der lateinische Lehnwortschatz im Bretonischen, Hamburg 1973. For language contact: EVANS, E.: Language Contact in Pre-Roman and Roman Britain, in: HAASE, W. (ed.): Aufstieg und Niedergang der römischen Welt, Part 2: Principat, vol. 29: Sprache und Literatur, Berlin 1983, gives an excellent survey. The Irish loans are dealt with by VENDRYES, J.: De Hibernicis Vocabulis quae a Latina Lingua Originem Duxerunt, Paris 1902; and more

was high class, taught by masters who deliberately followed classical pronunciation of the language. Eric Hamp, followed by Charles Thomas, on the other hand,
considered the language to have been absorbed in five degrees of intensity reflecting the social gradience of British-spoken Latin. These degrees of Latin Hamp
classified as: Literary Standard, Colloquial Standard Language, Provincial Standard Language, Substandard and Local Dialect.[6]

These different standards are thought to be reflected in the pattern of borrowings from Latin into Welsh as Thomas showed: for instance: a colloquial form
santus (< Classical Latin *sanctus,* 'saint') gave *sant,* whereas *sactus,* another colloquial form of *sanctus,* gave another Welsh form *saith,* also meaning 'saint'; from
other colloquial borrowings, *scrittura* (<*scriptura*) gave (*y*)*sgrythur* 'scripture' and
*precetta (<**precepta* < *praecepta*) gave *pregeth* 'sermon'. The morphological standard of Latin of the words borrowed by the Brittonic peoples was thus variable.

We know very little of the history of the Britons in the period after the *Excursus
Romanorum*[7] at the end of the fourth century so that the early story of the insular
church must be largely based on speculation. Apart fom the sixth-century reports
of Gildas and a few penitential texts[8] our evidence is almost entirely archaeological. The chief archaeological evidence for Wales is 150-plus inscriptions on stone
belonging to the period from the fifth to the tenth centuries; these belonged primarily to west Wales.[9] The earliest of these inscriptions are written in the Ogham
alphabet. Some are bilingual, with the Goidelic forms of the Ogham paralleled in
the texts written in debased Brythonic-Latin. Some of the inscribed stones bear
the symbol of the cross, some have words on them such as *sacerdos* or *presbyter*[10]
and by the end of the first millennium A.D. some of the stones have artistically
sophisticated crosses. The main series of the inscriptions are written in Latin and
use formulae which derive from fifth-century Gaul. There are but few in south
east Wales. There presumably Christianity either carried on steadily in its traditional Roman way or was wiped out for a period by the invading Saxons.

The fifth and sixth centuries A.D. have been called the 'Age of the Saints'.[11] This
title specifies an age when local good and holy people were regarded as spiritual

---

    recently in Mc Manus, D.: The Latin Loan-words in Irish. PhD Dissertation, Trinity College,
    Dublin 1982.

6 Hamp, E.: Social Gradience in British Spoken Latin, in: Britannia 6 (1975), pp. 150-161; Tho-
    mas, Ch.: Christianity in Roman Britain to A.D. 500, pp. 61-79. There is a plethora of later litera-
    ture: for a review of some of it see Russell, P.: Recent work on British Latin, in: Cambridge Medi-
    eval Celtic Studies 9 (1985), pp. 19-31.

7 See Lapidge, M./Dumville, D.: Gildas. New Approaches, Woodbridge 1984, pp. 1-25; James,
    Edward: Britain in the First Millennium, London 2001, pp. 90-97.

8 The Irish Penitentials, ed. and transl. by L. Bieler/D. A. Binchy, Dublin 1963, pp. 61-73.

9 Nash-Williams, V. E.: The Early Christian Monuments of Wales, Cardiff 1950; Sims-Williams,
    P.: The Celtic Inscriptions of Britain. Phonology and chronology (c. 400–1200), Oxford 2003.

10 Nash-Williams: The Early Christian Monuments of Wales (n. 9), p. 14.

11 See for instance, Chadwick, N. K.: The Age of the Saints in the Early Celtic Church, London
    1961 (repr. 1963), and for a sensible review of 'The Cult of saints' see Davies, W.: Wales in the
    Early Middle Ages, Leicester 1982, pp. 173–178, and again Sharpe: Martyrs and Local Saints
    (n. 2), pp. 133f.

leaders and intermediaries with God in a fairly barbaric world. Such a period is not a purely Celtic phenomenon. As far as we can see the churches established by these men developed into centres of religion, culture and literacy. It is these centres that provided us with the earliest manuscript records of the Welsh language.[12]

At this time the speech of the vast majority of the people was some form of British. The British language at the time of the Roman Conquest was at a similar stage of development to Latin, that is, it was a synthetic language with case endings. During a period roughly between the fourth and sixth centuries this language, complete with loanwords derived from Latin, developed into a language without case endings and one that had undergone other phonetic changes.[13] The largest number of Latin loanwords are concerned with religion. Many of these had already been borrowed into Latin from Greek, such as *ecclesia*.[14] They had been absorbed initially to fulfil the linguistic needs of a small group of people who were being converted to Christianity. The written records are our main witness to the language of the period. How does the language used by the scribes of these records contribute to the history of the language of religion?

Our fragmentary written records are:

1) Place-names associated with religious settlements and churches, preserved particularly in the twelfth century *Liber Landavensis*, whose documents derive from a much earlier period.[15]

2) Glossed texts stemming from a learned literary milieu which sometimes contain words with a religious connotation.[16]

3) Poetry which derives both from oral secular sources and a learned milieu. The secular poetry may contain incidental references to Christian practices: an example is the line from the poems of the Gododdin corpus, which derive from the sixth century: *Cyd elwynt lanneu i benydyaw,* "Although they may go to churches to do penance".[17] Poetry may be specifically religious in its nature. Much

---

12 The earliest records of the Welsh language take the form of glosses on Latin texts, macaronic texts such as an essay on the Computus and a number of three-lined stanzas called *englynion*. FALILEYEV, A.: Etymological Glossary of Old Welsh, Tübingen 2000, cites some 24 sources in all. These are the sole contemporary records of the common parts of speech of the Welsh language before 1200. We have of course other sources in the forms of place-names and proper names found in the *Liber Landavensis* and the Harleian genealogies and saints' lives.

13 See for instance, JACKSON: Language and History in Early Britain; SIMS-WILLIAMS, P.: Dating the Transition to Neo-brittonic. Phonology and History (400-600), in: BAMMESBERGER, A./WOLLMANN, A. (eds.): Britain 400–600. Language and History, Heidelberg 1990, pp. 217–262.

14 JACKSON: Language and History in Early Britain, pp. 78–81; GREENE, D.: Some Linguistic Evidence relating to the British Church, in: BARLEY, M. W./HANSON R. P. C. (eds.): Christianity in Britain (300–700), Leicester 1968, pp. 75–86.

15 DAVIES, W.: The Llandaff Charters, Aberystwyth 1979; DAVIES, W.: The Orthography of the Personal Names in the Charters of *Liber Landavensis*, in: Bulletin of the Board of Celtic Studies 28 (1980), pp. 553–557; SIMS-WILLIAMS, P.: The Emergence of Old Welsh, Cornish and Breton Orthography (600–800). The Evidence of Archaic Old Welsh, in: Bulletin of the Board of Celtic Studies 38 (1990), pp. 20–86.

16 See FALILEYEV: Etymological Glossary of Old Welsh.

17 WILLIAMS, I.: Canu Aneirin, Cardiff 1938, line 61.

of this poetry stems from monastic sources, such as the *Juvencus Englynion*, and the *Lorica* poems.[18] Finally, we have the religious poems of the later Court poets who used the diction of the encomium of the Court poetry in praise of secular rulers to address the Deity.[19] As regards liturgical texts, we have in Wales only scraps; the sources are minimal when we consider the extent of the written sources for the history of the Faith which are available from early Ireland.[20] Nothing survives to compare with the Antiphonary of Bangor,[21] the Springmount Bog Tablets[22] or the Stowe Missal.[23] There are many reasons for this shortage of written material. One is the plundering of the monastic libraries at the time of the Reformation. Another, though unlikely, is that Latin was more generally understood in Wales than in Ireland, so that vernacular glossing was not therefore as necessary. Let us consider the significance of these examples for the language of religion. Although the language of the liturgy was Latin, the language used to interpret the faith to the people must have been at least partly Celtic. What kinds of words were used? Which kind were borrowed? How far does the difference reflect the mentality of the people and the inheritance of concepts from a pagan Celtic past? Since relatively little is known of the church in Early Wales, what we know of the words used by the members of that church should add substantially to our understanding of its history and workings.

When I began preparing this paper I collected all the words I could find referring to the practice of Christianity from the texts of the early period, namely the period of Old Welsh, and became overwhelmed with data. I have therefore been selective and shall restrict my discussion to a consideration of words for the members of the Trinity preserved in the earlier sources, for the church and its officials, for the sacraments and for some of the abstract and theological concepts which are

---

18 HAYCOCK, M.: Blodeugerdd Barddas o Ganu Crefyddol Cynnar, Llandybie 1994, pp. 3–16, pp. 23–29.

19 Particularly those of the period between 1090 and 1282 published in: Cyfres Beirdd y Tywysogion (henceforth CBT), CAERWYN WILIAMS, J. E. et al. (eds.): Gwaith Meilyr Brydydd a'i ddisgynyddion (CBT I), Cardiff 1994; BRAMLEY, K. A. et al. (eds.): Gwaith Llywelyn Fardd ac eraill (CBT II), Cardiff 1994; JONES, N. A./PARRY-OWEN, A. (eds.): Gwaith Cynddelw Brydydd Mawr, vol. 1 (CBT III), Cardiff 1991; JONES, N. A./PARRY-OWEN, A. (eds.): Gwaith Cynddelw Brydydd Mawr, vol. 2 (CBT IV), Cardiff 1995; JONES, E. M. (ed.): Gwaith Llywarch ap Llywelyn 'Prydydd y Moch' (CBT V), Cardiff 1991; COSTIGAN N. G. et al. (eds.): Gwaith Dafydd Benfras ac eraill (CBT VI), Cardiff 1995; ANDREWS, R. M. et al. (eds.): Gwaith Bleddyn Fardd ac eraill (CBT VII), Cardiff 1996.

20 The best survey is still KENNEY, J. F.: The Sources for the Early History of Ireland: Ecclesiastical. An Introduction and Guide, New York 1929.

21 WARREN, F. E.: The Antiphonary of Bangor. An Early Irish Manuscript in the Ambrosian Library at Milan, 2 vols., Part 1: Facsimile, Part 2: Amended Text (Henry Bradshaw Society 4 and 10), London 1893–1895.

22 MCNAMARA, M.: Psalter-text and Psalter-study in the Early Irish Church (AD 600–1200), in: Proceedings of the Royal Irish Academy (73 C) 1973, pp. 201–298; reprinted in id.: The Psalms in the Early Irish Church, Sheffield 2000; pp. 1 ff.; LOWE, E. A.: Codices Latini Antiquiores, Oxford 1935–1971, Suppl. no. 1684.

23 WARNER, G. F.: The Stowe Missal (Henry Bradshaw Society 32), London 1915.

innate in the Christian religion as found in sources of the period of Old Welsh (pre-1100) but using later examples for comparison.

Names for the Trinity

Judging from the poetic references, the concept of the Trinity caught the poetic imagination in Wales as it did in Ireland.[24] The Latin word for the Trinity was borrowed into Welsh in two forms: *Trined* from *Trinitas* and *Trindod* from an oblique case such as *Trinitātem*.[25] Welsh interest in the Trinity is reflected in the fact that St Augustine's *De Trinitate* was copied at Llanbadarn Fawr in Ceredigion[26] and by the preoccupation of the poets with the concept:

Arduireau-e Tri:
I shall exalt Three
Trined in Celi
The Trinity as God
Yssyd Un a Thri
Who is one and Three
Vned un ynni
A Unity of one power, (MH 18)

or

Ry drychafom, erbyn Trindawt gwedy gwaret
We may rise up to meet the Trinity after salvation
Croes crist glae[a]r. lluryc llachar rac pop aelet
The bright cross of Christ, a shining breastplate against every pain
Rac pop efnys, poet yn dilis, dinas diffret.
In the face of every hostility let it be undisputed, a protective citadel (Based on MH 23-9)[27]

The word usually used for God is Celtic: *Duw* (OIr *Dé*), but other terms are used, particularly in the poetry:[28] these include kennings such as *dofydd* (lord), *arglwydd* (lord), *gwledig* (ruler, cf. Irish *flaith*), *rhi* (cf. OIr. *ri* = king), *rhwyf* (rudder/lord), *brenin* (king) which stem from the nomenclature of lay authority. Additional names represent very oral borrowings from words for God which were used in the liturgy of the church such as *Eloÿ, Celi* (< *caeli*), *Dews* (<*deus*).These liturgical names are also obvious in the poetry; the last extract quoted includes one of the words for the deity, *Celi: Eloÿ* is found in the following extract:

24 See for instance MURPHY, G.: Early Irish Lyrics, Oxford 1998, pp. 22f.: *In t-Athair, in Mac,/ in Nóebspirut án,/ a tréide dom din,/ ar nélaib na plág,* "The Father, the Son, the glorious Holy Spirit, may these three protect me against all plague-bearing clouds".
25 LEWIS: Yr Elfen Ladin yn yr Iaith Gymraeg, p. 47.
26 LAPIDGE, M.: The Welsh-Latin Poetry of Sulien's Family, in: Studia Celtica 8/9 (1973/1974), pp. 68–106, cf. Davies, O.: Celtic Christianity in Early Medieval Wales, Cardiff 1996, pp. 52f., 57f.
27 HAYCOCK: Blodeugerdd Barddas o Ganu Crefyddol Cynnar, p. 18, pp. 23–29.
28 COSTIGAN, N.: Defining the Divinity, Aberystwyth 2002, pp. 115–162.

Ys bud bartoni
It is profitable to sing poetry
Ar helv Eloÿ,
Under the power/protection/expense of Eloi (MH 19).

Apart from *Iesu* and *Crist* (< Jesu Christus), kennings such as *Mab Rhad* (Son of Grace) are used for Christ. The Holy Spirit is a straight calque: *yr Ysbryd* (<*Spiritus*) 'Spirit' and *Glan* (meaning clean, pure or holy). Two forms of the word *sanctus* meaning a saint, as we have seen, gave two forms in Welsh *sant* and *seith/saith*.

Religious Settlements

The words used for the religious settlements of the Church in early Wales are revealing for what they tell us about the nature of the churches and of the ecclesiastical communities who occupied them. The words can be culled from place-names and from the early poetry. The earliest of the terms used is perhaps Bassaleg from the Latin *basilica,* retained in a single place-name in Gwent, the most fertile and romanised area in Wales. The most important church of the *cantref* (hundred) of Gwynllwg in present day Gwent is in a place now known as Bassaleg (<basilica). The name probably indicates that this was the site of an early ecclesiastical settlement, although it seems unlikely to have been a Roman *basilica*. The church of Bassaleg however stands at the point where the Roman road from Caerleon (*Isca Silurum*) to Cardiff crossed the river Ebwy, probably by a bridge and close to the site of a Roman villa.[29] Like the Irish *baislec*, discussed by Charles Doherty,[30] a *basilica* was probably originally a church where the bones of its patron or some other precious relics were kept.[31] It is unlikely that any major *basilicae* were built in Britain. The word was probably used to denote, first of all, any large building, perhaps originally of basilican plan and latterly an important church. Later in the middle ages the church of Bassaleg became a minster or mother church with a large number of chapelries dependent on it. The original patron of the church of Bassaleg was Gwladus, wife of Gwynllyw and mother of Cadog. The other well-known dedication to Gwladus is Capel Gwladus (*capel* 'chapel' is a learned borrowing from *capella*) on a mountain, Cefn Gelligaer, at the side of the Roman road which ran from the Roman fortress of Brecon (*Bannium)* to Cardiff. Gwladus was

---

29 GREENE, M./HOWELL, R. (eds.): The Monmouthshire County History, vol. 1, Cardiff 2004, pp. 234f., p. 272.
30 DOHERTY, Ch.: The Basilica in Early Ireland, in: Peritia 3 (1984), pp. 305–315; SHARPE: Martyrs and Local Saints, pp. 114–121.
31 ROBERTS, T.: Welsh Ecclesiastical Place-names and Archaeology, in: EDWARDS, N./LANE, A. (eds.): The Early Church in Wales and the West, Oxford 1992, p. 42.

one of the daughters of Brychan Brycheiniog,[32] traditionally the most prolific and important progenitor of Welsh saints.[33]

With this let us consider another early term for the church, namely the word *Merthyr*. *Merthyr* (< Latin *Martyrium*), meant a shrine or a church containing the remains of a martyr (Welsh *merthyr* <*martyrus*), or, by extension, of some other person regarded as holy.[34] *Merthyr* place-names in Wales are more frequent in the romanised south-east. Cynog, a brother of Gwladus, and a son of Brychan Brycheiniog, the principal saint of Brycheiniog, had as the resting place of his bones Merthyr Cynog, whose original site was again beside a Roman road and near to a Roman camp. Many of the early *Merthyr* names have been replaced in the later literature.[35] The burial place of saints Julius and Aaron, outside the Roman cemetery in Caerleon, was initially known as the *Merthyr Jun et Aaron* or *Martyrium Iulii et Aaron*.[36] By the twelfth century the church had acquired also a relic of St Alban and so became known as the *ecclesia* of Julius, Aaron and Alban.[37]

The most frequently used name for a church today is *eglwys* (<*ecclesia*) and that word occurs frequently, although it is also less frequent in place names than in the literature. To consider the semantics of this word: *ecclesia* originally referred to the body of believers who met in one place, and this has been suggested to be the force of the word in the *Eccles-* place-names to be found in England.[38] Vestiges of the early connotations of its name may have been retained in early Welsh. The earliest written example of the word is from the *Liber Landavensis* where the privilege of the church, that is community (*eglwys*) of St Teilo is recorded.[39] The word soon lost its abstract meaning and became associated with the buildings of the Christian community. Reference to the churches of Baschurch (*eglwysseu Bassa*) being destroyed are found in one of the tenth-century (?) Llywarch Hen poems,[40] *Eccluis Guinau* (*Eglwys Gwinau*) is the place where St Teilo is said to have been born in his twelfth-century life,[41] and the thirteenth-century law codes speak of the *eglwys* (church) and its *cangell* (chancel).[42] By the sixteenth century we have evidence

32 JONES, T. T: The Daughters of Brychan – Their Importance in the History of Breconshire, in: Brycheiniog 17 (1976/1977), pp. 17–59.

33 THOMAS, Ch.: And Shall These Mute Stones Speak?, Cardiff 1994; THORNTON, D. E.: Brychan and Welsh Genealogy, University of Wales MA, Bangor 1989, p. 65; EVANS, J. D./FRANCIS, M. J.: Cynog. Spiritual Father of Brycheiniog, in: Brycheiniog 27 (1994), pp. 15–25.

34 ROBERTS: Welsh Ecclesiastical Place-names, p. 42; PIERCE, G.: The Place-names of the Dinas Powys Hundred, Cardiff 1968, pp. 133ff.

35 RICHARDS, M.: Ecclesiastical and Secular in Welsh medieval Settlement, in: Studia Celtica 3 (1968), p. 11.

36 SHARPE: Martyrs and Local Saints (n. 2), p. 121.

37 KNIGHT, J.: Britain's other Martyrs: Julius, Aaron and Alban at Caerleon, in: HENIG, M./LINDLEY, P. (eds.): Alban and St. Albans: Roman and Medieval Architecture, Art and Archaeology (British Archaeological Association Conference Proceedings 24), Leeds 2001, pp. 38–44.

38 See THOMAS, Ch.: Christianity in Roman Britain to A.D. 500, London 1981, pp. 262–266 for a summary of the scholarship on *eccles* also < *ecclesia*.

39 DAVIES, W.: Braint Teilo, in: Bulletin of the Board of Celtic Studies 26 (1974–6), pp. 123–137.

40 WILLIAMS, I. (ed.): Canu Llywarch Hen, Cardiff 1939, p. 39.

41 EVANS, J. G. (ed.): The Text of the Book of Llandâv, Oxford 1893, p. 255.

42 E.g. WILIAM, A. R. (ed.): Llyfr Iorwerth, Cardiff 1960, p. 76.

for the word being coupled with an adjectival form of the noun, *cadair* meaning a chair, a borrowing from Latin *cathedra,* namely *cadeiriol,* to denote the *eglwys gadeiriol* (cathedral), which contained the bishop's throne. In earlier sources this church was known as an *esgopty* or bishop house.

Other Latin borrowings are used for religious establishments, though less frequently, namely *myfyr, llog* and *mwstwyr. Myfyr* 'grave' (< *memoria*) followed by the saint's name Eilian occurs in Myfyr Eilian in Anglesey.[43] *Llog* (<Latin *locus*) is used in one early text to gloss *podi*.[44] *Podum* (an elevated place) is a word commonly found for a religious settlement in the *Liber Landavensis.*[45] There are a few instances of *mwstwyr* which is a direct borrowing from *monastērium.*[46] The word *llog* combines with *mynach* (<*monachus*), 'a monk' to form one of the most common words for a monastery in early Welsh, *mynachlog.*[47] Two names reflect the eremitic element in the Welsh Church, namely *cil,* a native word meaning retreat and *diserth* (< *desertum*) meaning a hermitage.[48]

The most frequent ecclesiastical place-name element is not any of these, however, but the native word *llan.*[49] *Llan* originally meant an enclosure, later a sacred enclosure and church; it is the most productive of the ecclesiastical place-name elements and is frequently coupled with the name of a saint, for instance Llandeilo, the church of St Teilo. Its cognates are found in Brittany and Cornwall, where it is preserved in place-names such as Lanilis, Landevennec, Landewednack and Lanteglos.[50] This *llan* element perhaps reflects native concepts of the essentials of a human settlement, namely a building surrounded by some kind of wall. The names quoted all refer to religious establishments each containing a group of clergy. This has led scholars to call the early Welsh church a monastic church, although it was not monastic in the sense of Benedictine or Cistercian monasticism. By the High Middle Ages the centres which were the descendants of these early communities were called *clas* (< *classis*).[51] The earliest example of the Latin word *classis* being used in a Welsh ecclesiastical context is that of Rhigyfarch, son of Bishop Sulien, when in his late eleventh-century *Life of St David* he refers to the community at St David's as *monastica classis.*[52]

---

43 ROBERTS: Welsh Ecclesiastical Place-names, p. 42.
44 See FALILEYEV: Etymological Glossary of Welsh, p. 105 who corrects the traditional reading of *lo* to *loc.* The gloss is possibly Latin.
45 DAVIES, W.: An Early Welsh Microcosm. Studies on the Llandaff Charters, London 1978, pp. 37f., pp. 121f.
46 PIERCE, G. O.: The Evidence of Place-names, in: SAVORY, H. N. (ed.): Glamorgan County History, vol. 2: Early Glamorgan, Cardiff 1984, pp. 485–489.
47 GPC s. n. *Mynachlog.*
48 GPC s. n. *cil* and *diserth.*
49 ROBERTS: Welsh Ecclesiastical Place-names, pp. 43f.
50 See DESHAYES, A.: Dictionnaire des Noms de Lieux Bretons, Douarnenez 1998, p. 169; PADEL, O.: Cornish Place-name Elements, Nottingham 1985, pp. 142–145, s. v. **lann.*
51 See EVANS, E. W.: The survival of the clas as an institution in medieval Wales: some observations on Llanbadarn Fawr, in: EDWARDS/LANE: The Early Church in Wales, pp. 33–40.
52 JAMES, J. W. (ed.): Rhigyfarch's Life of St David, Cardiff 1967, ch. 20.

The Personnel of the Church

Gildas's Preface on Penance and his Synod of North Britain, texts argued by Bieler to date from the sixth century, assume that these communities included bishops, *episcopi*, priests, *sacerdotes* and deacons, *diaconi* as well as abbots, *abbates* and monks, *monachi*.[53] Gildas distinguishes priests and deacons who had taken monastic vows from those who had not: even at the beginning of the Middle Ages, it appears that monastic communities in Wales contained what in later centuries would have been termed both secular and monastic clergy. Four of the Latin words used by Gildas were borrowed directly into Welsh as *esgob* (<* *epscopus* <*episcopus*), *diagon* (< *diaconus*), *abad* (<*abbat-*) and *mynach* (<*monachus*). Other terms were used for believers who imposed upon themselves the stricter rules of extreme abstinence which are associated with early Welsh and Irish Christianity: namely the *meudwy*, coined from two native words, *mau* (cf. OIr *mug*) 'servant' + *dwy* (an alternative form of *Duw* 'God') 'Servant of God'; corresponding to *mug Dé* in Irish and compared with the Irish *Celi Dé*, or clients of God, and the *diofredawg* (a nominal form with a gutteral suffix < the verb *diofryd* 'abjure from') for a person 'avowed to abstinence from riding, meat and women'[54] or the *didryfwr* ('a hermit or the man from land with no *tref* or farm').[55] An example of a Welsh borrowing from Latin *presbyter* is preserved in Cormac's Glossary in the form *premter/premeter*. This is the British form which gave OIr *cruimther*.[56] There is no recorded instance of the word in Welsh sources *per se*, suggesting that the word disappeared early from use in Wales.

With the terms which we find for the priest, most probably the parish priest, we meet with some of the idiosyncrasies of the Welsh church. Unlike Irish there is no borrowing in Welsh from the Latin *sacerdos* (OIr *sacairt*). The Welsh terms reflect the liturgical *rôle* of the priest in the Welsh church. The rarest of these terms is one of the words used for the mass priest namely *periglor*. Various derivations have been suggested for this word. Its form suggests that it derives from the Latin *periculum*, 'danger', with a personal suffix equivalent to the Latin suffix *–ārius* which could mean 'the one who deals with danger' to be associated with the *periculum* of sin as reflected in the *oratio periculosa* of the mass.[57] The preoccupation of Celtic ecclesiastical writers with the word *periculum*, a fact also noticed by Professor Ní Chatháin, is reflected in the Preface of Gildas on Penance: *Si quis*

---

53 BIELER, L. (ed.): The Irish Penitentials, Dublin 1975, p. 60, p. 67.
54 PRYCE, H.: Native Law and the Church in Medieval Wales, Oxford 1993, pp. 42–46.
55 GPC s. n. *didryfwr*.
56 THURNEYSEN, R.: A Grammar of Old Irish, Dublin 1946, p. 147; GREENE, D.: Some Linguistic Evidence relating to the British Church, in: BARLEY/HANSON: Christianity in Britain, p. 80.
57 See The Stowe Missal 65v 24–66r, vol. 2, p. 40; STOKES, W.: Thesaurus Palaeohibernicus, vol. 2, p. 252 who suggested the meaning was: the priest who reads the *oratio periculosa* of the mass. This conclusion differs however from that of PRYCE, Huw: Duw yn lle Mach: Briduw yng Nghyfraith Hywel, in: CHARLES-EDWARDS, T. et al. (eds.): Lawyers and Laymen, Cardiff 1986, pp. 68f., n. 82 and n. 83, who like WILLIAMS: Christianity in Early Britain, p. 433 would derive the word from such as *paroch(l)iarius*.

errans commutauerit aliquid de uerbis ubi periculum adnotatur, triduanum aut .iii. super positiones faciat, "If anyone in error has changed any of the words [of the sacrifice], where [the word] 'danger' is noted, he shall keep three special fasts".[58] The Welsh examples of the word cited by Dr Huw Pryce suggest that the priest who was a *periglor* was the one who served mass and took confession, that is, he administered the sacraments which saved the individual soul from the dangers of sin.

The most commonly used word for the priest is *offeiriad* 'the one who offers'. Its root *offeir-* is a borrowing ultimately from the Latin verb *offerre*. The word has an agent suffix *-iad* and refers to the 'one who offers' the gifts on the altar and the sacrifice of the mass. A third word found in medieval sources is the *aberthwr* or offerer of the sacrifice.

Words used for the mass

With this we reach my third group of words, the words used for the mass. These words throw light on the liturgy of the early Welsh Church, of which we know very little. The mass has essentially two different parts which were originally distinct. The foremass, the liturgy of the word, began with biblical readings or *lectio* borrowed into Welsh as *llith* 'reading/lesson', as in the collects of the Anglican Church, interspersed with song and a sermon, *pregeth* borrowed from **precetta <praecepta*. The sacrificial mass or eucharist consisted of the offering of the bread and wine, and the immolation or partaking of the victim of the sacrifice.

The general word for the mass is *offeren* < Latin *offerenda* ('that which should be offered').[59] The same Latin word was borrowed into Irish to give the Irish *aifreann*. It was pointed out years ago that the Ambrosian rite at Milan has a prayer called the *offerenda*, which is sung while the bread and wine are brought to the altar at the offertory.[60] In the Gallican rite, according to Gregory of Tours, the offerings of bread and wine were brought to the sacristy at the very beginning of the Mass, so that perhaps is how the Welsh word offeren came to be equated with the full Mass.[61] *Offerre,* however, was also commonly used by the Latin writers of the British Isles during the early Middle Ages for the offering of the sacrifice of the mass.[62] Gildas uses *offerre* and *sacra offerre,*[63] the *Liber Davidis offerre sacrificium*[64] (*sacrificium* was borrowed as W. *segrffyg*) as does Saint Patrick's Con-

---

58 BIELER: The Irish Penitentials, p. 63, also echoed in the Penitential of Cummean, op.cit. p. 127.
59 WILLIAMS, J. E.: Caerwyn: offeren, offeiriad, in: Bulletin of the Board of Celtic Studies 26 (1974–1976), pp. 38f.
60 NÍ CHATHÁIN, P.: The Liturgical Background of the Derrynavlan Altar Service, in: Journal of the Royal Society of Antiquaries of Ireland 110 (1980), p. 130.
61 See The Dictionary of the Middle Ages, vol. 8, p. 190. I am grateful to Professor Patrick O'Neill for drawing my attention to this point.
62 WARREN, F. E.: The Liturgy and Ritual of the Celtic Church, ed. by J. STEVENSON, Woodbridge 1987, p. 95 (1st edition Oxford 1881).
63 BIELER: The Irish Penitentials, p. 62 clauses 23 and 24.
64 BIELER: The Irish Penitentials, p. 72 clause 12.

fession. Side by side with these borrowed words stood a pair of native words. *Aperth* pl. *aperthou*; 'sacrifice' in Modern Welsh, is used in the *Ars Amatoria* to gloss *muneribus* (altar bread), *sacra* (sacred host), and *victima* (host)[65] and the derivative noun *aberthwr* 'offerer, sacrificer, priest' is found in the poetry as well as in the unpublished dictionary of the sixteenth-century Catholic Syr Thomas Williams in the form *abertyhwr*. This variation in meaning from the use of *offeiriad* meaning originally 'the one who offers' but later 'the one who sacrifices', and the use of *aberthwr* (sacrificer) may reflect a development in the terminology and emphasis of the mass.[66] In Europe generally, the word *hostia* (English: host*)* which originally meant the victim of a sacrifice, from the ninth-century *Ordo Romanus* V gradually supplanted the term *oblatio* (*offering) which in previous centuries could denote altar bread (*muneribus*).[67]

Perhaps the most interesting form is a native *calque*. The bread of the offering and of the mass, as well as the bread distributed at the end of the service, is known as *bara*.[68] Wine, however, was not native and we have again a Latin borrowing *gwin* (< *vīnum*). The sacred wafer is by the end of the Middle Ages referred to as *afrllad* or *afrlladen*. This was probably a compound coined orally from common speech. The first element is a metathesised form of *bara* 'bread', *abra >afra*; the second element is *llad*.[69] *Llad* originally meant 'drink, usually alcoholic' and developed a secondary meaning of 'gift' or 'blessing'. If this analysis is correct we have in this word an example of a *dvandva* compound. Communion was originally offered to the Celtic laity in both kinds: *bara* (bread) + *llad* (drink).[70] *Afrllad,* a word which originally referred to both bread and wine, came to mean the wafer of the mass at a time when lay people took communion in one kind.

Another word was borrowed into Welsh for the communion namely *celyfrad* (< *celebratio*) referring to the celebration of the mass.[71] The same word was borrowed into Old Irish, where it is coupled with *oifreann: gan celebraid 7 oifrend* (without celebration and offering). The more frequently used word for the communion is however *cymun* (< *commūnio*). The blessing of the mass is the Latin *benedictio* borrowed into Welsh as *bendith* and into Irish as *bennacht*, while the act of blessing, *benedico*, gave the Welsh verb *bendigo*. Latin *maledictio*, 'curse' gave

---

65 Falileyev: Etymological Glossary of Old Welsh, p. 9.

66 This is open to dispute since the noun *idbairt*, a near cognate of *aberth*, is also used in Old Irish for the sacrifice and the base meaning of both the Welsh *aberth* and Irish *idbairt* was 'that which was brought', see Warren: The Liturgy and Ritual of the Celtic Church, p. 131 n. 1; Williams: Caerwyn: offeren, offeiriad, would see a similar semantic development in the use of the word *offeiriad*.

67 Vauchez, A. (ed.) in conjunction with Dobson, B./Lapidge, M.: Encyclopedia of the Middle Ages, Cambridge 2000, p. 693.

68 Pryce: Native Law and the Church in Medieval Wales, p. 58f., p. 61.

69 I am gratified to see that this derivation was also given in Davies, J.: Dictionarium Duplex, London 1632, s. n. *afrlladen*.

70 Warren: The Liturgy and Ritual of the Celtic Church, pp. 134ff.

71 There are examples of the word in the poetry, for instance praising the community of Cadfan's church in CBT II p. 14, line 97: *Molidor y chor ae chelyfrad*; 'Its choir and celebration of mass is praised'.

Welsh *melltith*. The kiss of peace was *pog* in Welsh, known from a late attestation, a development from *(osculum) pācis* and borrowed from the British into the Irish *pog*. We have a reflection of the impact which some of the words of the Church ritual made on the people in a triad of loan words, *pader, bwyeid* and *credo* found in two religious poems.[72]

> *Pader a bwyeid a bendigeid Creto*
> Pader and Beati and the blessed Creed
> *a'e cano rac eneid*
> Whosoever may sing them for the sake of [their] soul
> *Hyd braud, goreu gortywneid:*
> Until [the Day of] Judgement, that is the best practice [73]

The *Pader* < *Pater [Noster]* refers to the Lord's Prayer, the *Bwyeid* < *Bēati* (Irish *bíait*) refers to Psalm 119 (Vulgate 118), known to be used as a ritual form of prayer and intercession in the early Irish Church,[74] and the *Credo* referring to the opening words of the Creeds.

The church, accoutrements and sacraments

What of the shape of the church and the furniture of the mass? Again we have Latin borrowings for parts of the church building and vestments. Both *cor* (< *chorus*)[75] for choir and *cangell* (<*cancellus*) 'chancel' are Latin borrowings. Latin *casula*, 'chasuble' gave Welsh *casul*, OIr *casal*. An extended form survives in an Old Welsh gloss *casulheticc*, gl. *penulata* from the Martianus Capella glosses, meaning "one who wears a chasuble".[76] *Allor*, an altar, is from Latin *altāria*. Altars might be large stone or wooden structures or small portable objects.[77] The fact that altars might be small plate-like objects may explain one Old Welsh gloss where words for both paten and altar are used to gloss the same Latin word. This leads us to the terms used for the paten and chalice in early Welsh. The word used for the paten in early Welsh was *mwys* from Latin *mensa*. Borrowings from Latin *mensa* 'table' are found in all the Celtic languages. The word gave *muiss/moys* in early Welsh, which later became Welsh *mwys*, usually translated as a 'basket/plate'. It gave Cornish *moys* 'table', Middle Breton *meux*, meaning 'dish/plate'[78] and was borrowed into Irish as *mías* 'table' or '[altar]stone'. The Welsh forms *muiss/moys* occur in two glosses, *moys* vel *altaur* gl. *catenum* from a Priscian grammar and *muiss* gl. *disci*

---

72 HAYCOCK: Blodeugerdd Barddas o Ganu Crefyddol Cynnar, poems 28 and 29, pp. 288 and 293.
73 Based on HAYCOCK: Blodeugerdd Barddas o Ganu Crefyddol Cynnar, p. 288.
74 MCNAMARA, M.: The Psalter in Early Irish Monastic Spirituality, in: The Psalms in the Early Irish Church, pp. 357f.
75 Pace GPC s. n. *côr*[1].
76 See FALILEYEV: Etymological Glossary of Old Welsh, p. 23.
77 STEVENSON, J.: Introduction, in: WARREN: The Liturgy and Ritual of the Celtic Church, pp. XCVf..
78 FLEURIOT, L.: Dictionnaire des Gloses en vieux Breton, Paris 1964, p. 260.

from the Martianus Capella corpus. This second text might be Old Breton but according to recent authority shows the characteristics of Old Welsh.[79] In the first gloss *moys* is coupled with *altaur* 'altar' in a gloss on *catenum*. *Catenum* (classical Latin, *catinum*) means a dish or a bowl; in this double gloss *altar* and *paten* seem to have been confused.[80] In the second gloss the form *muiss* glosses *disci*. In Hiberno-Latin sources *discus* is a word used for the paten of the mass; thus, in this second gloss the word seems to mean 'paten'.[81] The Welsh word for a chalice, *kerygyl* (< *caliculum)* is first recorded in a twelfth-century Welsh poem, but occurs earlier in an Old Cornish form *kelegel* gl. *calix*.[82]

The eucharist was only one of the sacraments of the church. A late medieval list of the seven sacraments in Welsh is entitled *Saith Rhinwedd yr Eglwys,* 'the Seven Sacraments of the Church'.[83] The word used for a sacrament is *rhinwedd,* a Welsh word whose meaning is closer to that of the word 'mystery' (Latin *mysterium* borrowed from Greek μυστήριον) than of the word sacrament.[84] *Sacramentum* superseded *mysterium* in Latin but this very usage loses much of the meaning of the original; to quote Mohrmann: "One continually notices that *sacramentum* is used as the Latin equivalent of μυστήριον but often it is forgotten that this <equivalence> conceals a great mystery."[85] *Sacramentum* was borrowed into Welsh in the form *sagrafen* which later superseded *rhinwedd*. The text *Saith Rhinwedd yr Eglwys* lists the sacraments as: *bedydd* (baptism), *bedydd esgob* (confirmation, literally 'bishop's baptism'), *segrffyg/kymmyn* (communion), *penyd* (penance), *angennu neu olew* (extreme unction), *urdeu* (ordinations) and *priodas* (marriage). *Bedydd* (< *baptizio*), 'baptism' was administered to the people from at least the sixth century. According to the Breton Life of St Samson the sixth-century saint converted and baptised an adult in Cornwall on his way from South Wales to Brittany[86] and is therefore likely to have done the same in Wales after receiving episcopal status, while Bede reported that the British clergy's form of baptism was together with their reckoning of Easter a point of dispute with Augustine of Canterbury.[87] The Welsh word *bedydd* was also used to denote the world in the sense of the baptised and the form *bydysawd* (< *baptizātī)* was used to denote the whole of the universe.

79 FALILEYEV: Etymological Glossary of Old Welsh, p. 115.
80 LATHAM, R. E./HOWLETT, D. (eds.): Dictionary of Medieval Latin from British Sources, Oxford 1975, s. v. *catinum*.
81 WARREN: The Liturgy and Ritual of the Celtic Church, p. 143.
82 GPC s. v. *caregl*.
83 JONES, J. M./RHYS, J. (eds.): The Elucidarium and other tracts in Welsh from Llyvyr Agkyr Llandewivrevi A.D. 1346, Oxford, 1884, p. 145; GRUFFYDD, R. G.: Yny lhyvyr hwnn (1546): the earliest Welsh printed book, in: Bulletin of the Board of Celtic Studies 23 (1967), pp. 105–116.
84 *Rhinwedd* glosses *mysterium* in: JONES, J. M./RHYS, J. (eds.): The Elucidarium and other tracts in Welsh from Llyvyr Agkyr Llandewivrevi A.D. 1346, p. 24. The first element in the word, *rhin,* is cognate with Irish *rún,* Old English *rún,* words which mean 'something secret'.
85 MOHRMANN: Études sur le Latin des Chrétiens, vol. 3, p. 181 and referring to Études, vol. 1, pp. 144ff.
86 FAWTIER, R. (ed.): La Vie de saint Samson, vol. 1, Paris 1890, p. 50.
87 Bede: Historia Ecclesiastica, ed. by Ch. PLUMMER, in: Venerabilis Baedae Opera Historica, vol. 2, Oxford 1896, pp. 75f.

In the earliest days of the Christian church confirmation, *bedydd esgob* (bishop's baptism) and baptism were often administered at the same time. The next sacrament, *segrffyg* (<*sacrificium*) or *kymmyn* (< *commūnio,* 'communion') we have already dealt with. The poetry of the North British poet Aneirin, purported to derive from the sixth century, speaks of the warriors going to *cymun* (line 781) and *penyd* (line 290), 'penance' (< Latin *penitio*), before setting out for battle. One line of a gnomic poem speaks of *Atwyn rin rypenyt yryred,* "Fine also is the miracle of great penance [making recompense] for arrogance".[88] What the nature of such penances was we can only gauge from the two early penitential texts.[89]

The next of the *saith rhinwedd* is *angennu neu olew,* literally 'anointing or oil'. The phrase, which refers to extreme unction, is tautological. The rite involved anointing with the sacred oil while uttering in Latin the words *ungo te oleo.* The Welsh form *angennu* (a verbal noun meaning 'to administer extreme unction') or *angen* (a noun meaning 'extreme unction') is regarded as a borrowing from Latin *unguen.* The vowel of the borrowing has been changed under the influence of the native word *angen* 'need'. *Olew* (<*oleum*) is a borrowing. The phrase occurs in several different forms, for instance: *angen ac olew a llen,* literally 'anointing with/ and oil and a veil'. The phrase is glossed in the fourteenth-century Book of the Anchorite of Llanddewi Brefi as *pymhet rinwedd yw aghennu. Sef yw hynny dodi olew kyssegredic ar ddyn yny gleuyt periglus,* 'the fifth mystery is *angennu,* that is to place the sacred oil on a man in his mortal illness'. The sixth sacrament, *urdeu,* is the plural of *urdd* (< *ōrdō*) and probably refers to the seven different stages of ordination to holy orders from the porter through deacon to priest.[90] The last-listed, *priod*[*as*] (< *privātus*) referred originally to someone who was the special property of another. The word has a complicated linguistic and legal history and probably derives from a purely secular milieu. In the Welsh laws *priodas* is the most dignified type of sexual union recognised.[91] The Welsh law of marriage, as preserved in the native lawbooks, is amazingly non-ecclesiastical. By the time of the list the word had acquired a sacramental meaning.

Relics and concepts

Let us turn now to terms used in the practice of the faith and relics. The terms for the chief festivals of the Christian Church, with which Professor Ní Chatháin deals in greater detail, are borrowed in both Irish and Welsh: *Pasg,* Easter (< *Pascha,* OIr *Cásc*), *Nadolig,* Christmas (< *Natalicia,* MidIr *Notlaic*), *Y Grawys,* Lent(< *Quadragesima,* OIr *Corgus*); *Gŵyl,* Feast day (< *vigilia,* OIr *Féil*); OW *Gueleri,* a church calendar (*vigilarium< *vigiliārium,* OB *guileri,* OIr *Félire*).

---

88 HAYCOCK: Blodeugerdd Barddas o Ganu Crefyddol Cynnar, p. 32.
89 BIELER/BINCHY: The Irish Penitentials, pp. 61–73.
90 New Catholic Encyclopedia, vol. 7, p. 85.
91 JENKINS, D./OWEN, M. E. (ed.): The Welsh Law of Women, Cardiff 1980, s. v. *priodas.*

One of the noteworthy features of the church in Celtic lands, as Julia Smith has pointed out, was the emphasis placed on relics.[92] The relic was also an important feature used in the swearing of oaths in secular law. The words for relic, Welsh *crair*, Irish *cretair*, derive from the same root as the verbs, Welsh *credu*, Irish *cretaid*, which mean 'to believe' in both languages and despite their resemblance to Latin *credo* and related words are native.[93] Many relics were the ecclesiastical accoutrements of local saints, such as the *bagl* (<*baculus*), originally the saint's crozier of authority. An *englyn* to St Padarn's crozier, which was known by the pet name Cyrwen, was preserved as a *marginalium* in one of the eleventh-century manuscripts of the Llanbadarn family of Bishop Sulien:

> *Amdinnit trynit trylenn*
> Sparkling bright, much loved, it gives protection
> *Am trybann teirbann treisguenn,*
> Its holy power reaching the limits of three continents,
> *Amcen creireu gurth Cyrrguenn,*
> Other relics are different from Cyrwen,
> *Amdifuys daul bacl Patern*
> Padarn's staff is a wonderful portion.[94]

The saint's bell was a *cloch* (<*clocca*, OIr *clocc*), a word which occurs in Late Latin but which was probably of Celtic origin. Like Cyrwen the bell sometimes had a pet name; St David's bell was called *Bangu* 'the high sweet one'.[95] The saint's *Llyfr Efengylau*, 'his gospel book' (< *Liber Evangeliorum*) was also important. Some relics have a more secular association, such as Cynog's *armilla* (? 'armband') which "from its weight, texture and colour one would think was gold".[96]

Most of the words for the objects used as relics then are borrowed from Latin and paralleled in Irish.[97] The objects were used as part of native legal practices for the taking of legal oaths. The terms for the process of oath taking are on the whole Celtic; they stem from a Celtic past and derive from a legal milieu. *Tyngu*, the verb which means 'to swear', has its parallel in Irish *tongid* and *llw*, 'an oath' in Irish

---

92 SMITH, J. M. H.: Oral and Written: Saints, Miracles and Relics in Brittany, c. 850–1250, in: Speculum 65 (2000), pp. 309–343; also PRYCE: Native Law and the Church in Medieval Wales, p. 41.

93 VENDRYES, J.: A propos du Verbe 'Croire' et de la 'Croyance', in: Revue Celtique 44 (1927), pp. 90–96.

94 The text and translation are based on those of WILLIAMS, I.: The Beginnings of Welsh Poetry, ed. by R. BROMWICH, Cardiff 21980, pp. 186f. and HAYCOCK: Blodeugerdd Barddas o Ganu Crefyddol Cynnar, p. 243. The text has now been excised from the manuscript.

95 For Welsh Bells, see FISHER, J. L.: The Welsh Celtic Bells, in: Archaeologia Cambrensis 81 (1926), pp. 324–334; KNIGHT, J. K.: Sources for the Early History of Morgannwg, in: SAVORY: Glamorgan County History, pp. 370f.

96 Gerald of Wales: The Journey through Wales, ed. and transl. by L. THORPE, Harmondsworth 1978, p. 86. The Latin reads *armilla*.

97 PRYCE: Native Law and the Church in Medieval Wales, p. 41; LUCAS, A. T.: The Social Role of Relics and Reliquaries in Ancient Ireland, in: Proceedings of the Royal Irish Academy 116 (1986), pp. 21–27.

luige. The word *briduw* 'God's power' used for a particularly sacred kind of oath sworn over seven altars is also composed of the native words *bri* 'power' and *duw* 'God'.[98] The word for grace, *rhad*, judging from its Old Irish cognate form *rath,* the verbal noun of *ernaid*, 'he pays', was also originally a term with legal associations, meaning 'a fief of base clientship' given by a lord.[99] The words for praying, *gweddïo*, and believing, *credu*, as we have seen, are also native. The word for faith, *ffydd*, is however a borrowing from Latin *fides*. A native legal term is used for judgement, namely *brawd*, which is preserved in one of the two earliest Christian formulae which are recorded in Welsh in the eighth-century *Surexit Memorandum* found in the Lichfield Gospels. The first is *hit did braut* ('until the Day of Judgement'); the second is *i ois oisou*; translating *saecula saeculorum*.[100]

A formulaic reference to the God of Judgement is also preserved in the oath attributed to St Patrick and probably wrongly interpreted in Cormac's Glossary:

[...] *mo debroth ol Patraic quod Scotici dicunt corrupte, sic hoc dici debet. i. muin doíu braut i. muin didiu is meus. in díu is deus, in braut is Judex. i meus deus judex.*

The *muin* is in fact more likely to represent Modern Welsh *myn,* as used at the beginning of oaths before the name of the person or object in whose name the oath is made, *braut* means 'judgement' rather than 'judge' and what St Patrick actually meant to say was, 'By the God of Judgement'.[101]

Most words which were used for concrete things or for parts of the liturgy were thus borrowed from Latin. This was the case throughout Latin Christendom. Words for concepts on the other hand were largely native. Some of these words are technical legal terms which were used in the native Welsh laws. Although the word for sin (a concept especially Christian rather than pagan) is a borrowing: *pechaud/pechod < peccātum*, the word used for atoning for a sin by penance is *difwyn, diwygiaf,* (the verbal noun *difwyn* being replaced by the form *diwygio* in later Welsh) as in:[102]

O treinc mab din heb ymdiwin a duv
If the son of man dies without making recompense to God
Am a wnel o pechaud
For whatever sin he may [have] done.(Based on MH 284–5)[103]

or

Diwyccom ne a digonhom o gamuet
Let us atone for whatever wrongdoing we have committed

98 Pryce: Duw yn lle Mach, pp. 47–71.
99 Kelly, F.: A Guide to Early Irish Law, Dublin 1988, p. 27 *et passim.*
100 Jenkins, D./Owen, M. E.: The *Surexit* Memorandum, in: Cambridge Medieval Celtic Studies 7 (1984), pp. 106f.
101 Dictionary of the Irish Language and Contributions to a Dictionary of the Irish Language, Dublin 1913–75, s.v. *debroth.* Ct. GPC s.v. *mwyn*[3].
102 Jenkins/Owen: The Welsh Law of Women, p. 68.
103 Haycock: Blodeugerdd Barddas o Ganu Crefyddol Cynnar, pp. 284–5.

Kin myned im gwerid im iruet
Before going to my earth, to my fresh grave.[104]

This word is used in the laws of compensation found in the native law tracts for making reparation and is cognate with Irish *do-fich* 'to fight' whose verbal noun is *digal,* Welsh *dial* which means 'avenge'. In Welsh law the verb *difwyn* has the meaning to remove the heat of the feud by paying compensation. A native word is also used for salvation, *gwaredigaeth,* an abstract noun from *gwared,* the cognate of OIr *foreth,* whose components correspond semantically with those of the Latin *succurro.* Other words used in the secular laws show the conflation of ecclesiastical and secular law. Two such words which stem from native legal concepts, and which have been discussed at length by Dr Huw Pryce as showing such conflation of ecclesiastical and secular legal concepts, are the words *braint* and *nawdd.*

In secular law *braint* means the privilege of enjoying full legal status or privilege.[105] In the case of a church, the privilege is generally associated with a royal grant or royal protection. The early poetry illustrates how a church's *braint* was conditional on the power of a secular ruler,[106] but the most explicit source for understanding the implications of the *braint* of a church is the document known as *Braint Teilo,* preserved in the *Liber Landavensis,* which specifies the *braint* of Teilo's church at Llandaff.[107] *Braint Teilo* claimed for Teilo's church immunity from secular interference, an immunity upheld by the sanctity of native law. The *Braint* claimed the same competence for the Llandaff lawcourt as for the lawcourt of the secular lord. This privilege was conferred by the local lord, in the case of Teilo by the king of Morgannwg. Three twelfth-century poems to St Cadfan, St Tysilio and St David (Dewi) respectively are concerned with the *braint* or rights of the communities of their principal churches. The Cadfan poem speaks of the *braint* of Tywyn, probably conferred by the ruler of Meirionnydd, the Tysilio poem of the *braint* of Meifod, conferred by the ruler of Powys, the Dewi poem of the *braint* of Llanddewibrefi, conferred by the lord of Deheubarth.[108]

One of the rights which formed part of the *braint* or privilege of the church, according to *Braint Teilo,* was the right to give *nawdd.*[109] *Nawdd,* an ancient con-

---

104 JARMAN, A. O. H.: Llyfr Du Caerfyrddin, Cardiff 1982, p. 13.
105 PRYCE: Native Law and the Church in Medieval Wales, pp. 235-239, cf. JENKINS/OWEN: The Welsh Law of Women, pp. 49f. and CHARLES-EDWARDS, T. M. et al. (eds.): The Welsh King and His Court. History and Law Committee of the Board of Celtic Studies, Cardiff 2000, p. 562 s. v. *braint.*
106 See, for instance, 'Canu Heledd' where it is mentioned that the churches of Baschurch lost their *braint* after the defeat of Cynddylan and Elfan of Powys by the English (WILLIAMS: Canu Llywarch Hen, p. 39 stanza 49; ROWLAND, J.: Early Welsh Saga Poetry. A Study and Edition of the Englynion, Cambridge 1990, p. 435, stanza 49), and the tenth-century poem, *Armes Prydain,* which asks why the enemies of the Welsh trampled on the *braint* of their saints (WILLIAMS, I. [ed.]: Armes Prydein, Cardiff 1955, p. 5, line 139).
107 See DAVIES: Braint Teilo, pp. 123–137.
108 JONES N. A./OWEN, M. E.: Twelfth-century hagiography: the Gogynfeirdd poems to Saints, in: CARTWRIGHT, J. (ed.): Celtic Hagiography, Cardiff 2003, pp. 55ff.
109 PRYCE: Native Law and the Church in Medieval Wales, pp. 165–274.

cept of the secular law texts, and cognate with the Irish *snádud*, was originally
connected with the right of individuals to afford protection within specific tem-
poral and geographical limits. By the thirteenth century this right *eo nomine* is
only recorded for the king and his court and for churches and saints' relics where
the term is equated with the Latin *refugium*. This right was equated in territo-
rial terms with a specific territory or *noddfa*, meaning sanctuary place or field.
Giraldus Cambrensis in the late twelfth century emphasised the importance of
these sanctuaries "which extended as far from the church as cattle could travel
grazing during the day and where criminals could flee from the wrath of the local
lord",[110] using a *topos* common in hagiography. We have a definite historical record
of the importance of the sanctuary offered by Llanddewibrefi, since in 1109 the
chronicle records the fact that after a conflict, the partisans of a local nobleman,
Cadwgan, and his son Ithel fled to the sanctuary of the church of Llanddewibrefi.[111] Gwynfardd Brycheiniog, a court poet of the twelfth century, speaks of fleeing to the *nawdd* of Dewi (St David),[112] and in a series of lines offers what may be
a definition of the wide geographical extent of the *noddfa* of Llanddewibrefi, from
Carawn to Tywi, from the Llyndu to Twrch,[113]

> *Diogel ei nawdd i'r neb a'i cyrcho ...*
> His sanctuary is secure for those who seek it ...
> *O Garawn gan iawn, gan ehöeg,*
> from Caron with its fair rule, with its purple hue,
> *Hyd ar Dywi, afon firain a theg,*
> as far as Tywi, a fine fair river,
> *O'r Llyndu, lle'd fu llid gyhydreg,*
> from Llyn Du, broader was the roused tumult,
> *'Hyd ar Dwrch, terfyn tir â charreg.*
> as far as Twrch, where the land is bounded by a stone.

Dr Huw Pryce has pointed out that the key to this territorialisation of *nawdd* lies
in the standard equivalent for the term found in the Latin texts of the Welsh Laws,
namely *refugium*. According to Pryce, *refugium* was an unusual term for sanctuary
in medieval Europe and is attested mainly in Irish and Welsh sources. The eighth-
century *Collectio Canonum Hibernensis* devotes an entire book to the topic and
shows that sanctuary was modelled on the Levitical cities of refuge to which those
who had killed by accident or in ignorance might flee.[114] The *Hibernensis* envisages that sanctuary should apply solely to homicide, protecting the killer from the
avenging kinsmen of the victim, cutting through the code of the bloodfeud which
was, as in Israel, general in early medieval Ireland and Wales. The *Hibernensis* text

---

110 Gerald of Wales: The Journey through Wales, p. 254.
111 JONES, T.: Brut y Tywysogion (Red Book Version), Cardiff 1952, p. 60; PRYCE: Native Law and
     the Church in Medieval Wales, p. 173.
112 OWEN, M. E.: Canu i Ddewi, in: CBT II, p. 450, line 76.
113 OWEN: Canu i Ddewi, p. 452, line 140, lines 144–148.
114 PRYCE: Native Law and the Church in Medieval Wales, p. 170 referring to WASSERSCHLEBEN,
     F. W. H. (ed.): Collectio Canonum Hibernensis: Die Irische Kanonensammlung, Leipzig ²1885,
     pp. 174–179.

seems to have adapted the ancient Irish institution of *maigen digona* 'the place of not slaying', which featured around all freemen's houses. Another *Hibernensis* canon distinguishes between a church's central holiest place containing the relics of bishop and martyrs and an outer area reserved for fleeing criminals. In this both Ireland and Wales adapted a native legal concept to ecclesiastical usage.

Other concepts show a duality in the nature of their borrowings. The word for hell is a Latin borrowing, *uffern* (< *infernum*), the word for heaven, *nef*, is native. Does this mean that the native concept of the other world was close to the Christian concept of heaven and the concept of hell was alien to the pre-Christian, pagan British?

Christianity, as Mohrmann pointed out, was a language of signs. The Latin word *signum* meaning a 'standard or sign' in classical Latin was borrowed into Welsh as *swyn* and later developed the additional meaning of a charm.[115] *Signum* in medieval Latin meant among other things a 'miraculous sign of supernatural power or sign of the cross'. This meaning is retained in early Welsh, *Gwedi gwyth omedd senedd swynau* 'after furiously rejecting the assemblies of blessings or ceremonies';[116] *dwfr swyn* meant 'water which had been blessed' presumably by making a sign of the cross over it. The derivative verb *swyno*, like Latin *signare*, means 'to make a sign of the cross, bless (a meal)' as in the line *Duw o nef ry'th swynas* 'God from heaven has blessed you'.[117]

Another derivitive of *signum/signare* has also left its mark on the Medieval Welsh legal vocabulary: *cyswyn* (< *consigno*). *Consigno* is given the meanings: 'confirmare/signare/notare', *apud christianos: confirmare aliquem sacramento, consecrare, signo crucis notare* in Medieval Latin dictionaries.[118] One of the meanings of the compound *consigno* is to make the sign of the the cross over something and thereby designate a certain status or function to the object. The Welsh derivitive *cyswyn* is used in the Law texts as an adjective for a child concerning whose paternity the mother has sworn a declaration of affiliation on the altar and relics of the church where lay the paternal family's grave; the affiliation had legally neither been confirmed nor rejected.[119]

My last words are concerned with the two Welsh terms for the cross, the central symbol of the Christian religion. These Welsh words are again borrowings from two cases of the same Latin word: *crwys* or *croes* (cf. Ir. *cros*) comes from the nom-

115 Cf. DAVIES, J.: Dictionarium [sic] Duplex, London 1632, s. n. *Swyn* + *Incantatio, incantamentum, fascinum, Item Remedium, medela, pharmacum.*

116 CAERWYN WILIAMS, J. E. et al. (eds.): Gwaith Meilyr Brydydd a'i ddisgynyddion, CBT I, p. 461, line 79.

117 Cf. *Duw o nef ry'th swynas* CBT V, p. 172. (My translation follows that of John Davies in his Dictionarium [sic] Duplex (1632) s. v. *swyno*, who used the word *benedixit* to translate *swynas*; this differs from the translation of the modern edition.)

118 E. g. Thesaurus Linguae Latinae, editus auctoritate et consilio academicarum quinque germanicarum Berolinensis, Gottingensis, Lipsiaensis, vol. 2, Lipsiae 1906, s. v. *consigno.*

119 JENKINS, D.: Property Interests in the Classical Welsh Law of Women, in: JENKINS/OWEN: The Welsh Law of Women, pp. 91f. For the rite of rejection which also involved swearing on relics, see PRYCE: Native Law and the Church in Medieval Wales, p. 42.

inative form *crux* and *crog* (cf. Irish *croch/cruiche*) from an oblique form of the same word,: *cruc-*.[120] These double forms are a linguistic curiosity: could the forms deriving from the nominatives be learned borrowings and the others oral?

This survey of some of the key words for the Christian religion used in early Welsh may be considered to demonstrate several features. First, despite the regular use of Latin for the liturgy, early Welsh was developing a rich Christian vocabulary. Many of the words have their correspondences, not only in Cornish and Breton, but also in Irish (see Appendix) suggesting that perhaps much of the terminology of Christianity in Ireland came to Ireland through the medium of the British church. Secondly, this vocabulary consisted largely of words borrowed from Latin, some of which in turn had originally been borrowed from the Greek of the early Christians; these were sometimes borrowed as doublets. Most of the borrowed words denote tangible objects, institutions or people. Thirdly, the substitution of these borrowed words by native words as in the case of *aberthwr* and *offeiriad,* as well as the semantic development of the form *afrlladen* may illustrate changes in liturgical practice. Fourthly terms used for abstract concepts are often native legal terms adopted for a Christian usage. This pattern, as Mohrmann has shown in words which express the implications of the phenomenon more eloquently than do the words of this paper, is paralleled in the ecclesiastical vocabulary of the Latin-speaking areas of Christendom, where Greek words were borrowed for material objects, but indigenous Latin terminology was used to convey concepts:

> Les noms d'institutions ecclésiastiques, de la hiérarchie et en général des <choses> plus ou moins concrètes, qui ont été importées en occident avec christianisme, sont le plus souvent d'origine grecque et jamais on ne les a remplacés par les mots indigènes. C'est un procédé tout naturel: le peuple ne fait pas de distinction entre la <chose> et le nom: en adoptant la chose il emprunte le nom. Et la chose devenue une fois d'un usage courant, on ne sent pas le besoin de remplacer le nom par une expression de la langue maternelle.
>
> Mais il y a certaines catégories d'idées qui, dès le commencement, ont été interprétées par des mots indigènes et il vaut la peine de se rendre compte quelles sont les notions qui ont trouvé une expression adéquate dans la langue maternelle [...] nous pouvons constater que les notions qui sont en relation étroite avec la doctrine chrétienne, qui désignent des éléments essentiels de l'idéologie chrétienne, ainsi que celles qui avaient une valeur affective, ont obtenu le plus souvent une interprétation latine. Un mot étranger suffisait pour désigner des choses plus ou moins concrètes, mais dès le moment qu'il y est question des vérités de la foi, de la doctrine chrétienne et de choses touchant le cœur, la langue étrangère reste en défaut et c'est la langue maternelle qui entre en scène.[121]

---

120 See LEWIS: Yr Elfen Ladin yn yr Iaith Gymraeg, p. 35 who deals with some of the linguistic problems of the form *crog.*

121 MOHRMANN: Études sur le Latin des Chrétiens, vol. 1, pp. 126f.

Appendix

Abbreviations used in the list: OB. = Old Breton; B. = Middle or Modern Breton; OC. = Old Cornish; C. = Middle or Modern Cornish; OIr. = Old Irish; Ir = Middle or Modern Irish

A) Welsh loan words from Latin quoted in the text together with equivalents from other Celtic languages. The derivations given are standard.

abad < *abbat- <abbāt-, cf. OC. **abat,** OIr. **ab** < abbas, abbot
allor < altāria, cf. OC. **altor** MB. **aoter,** Ir. **altóir,** altar
angen < unguen-, cf. Ir. **oingid** (anoint), extreme unction
bagl < *bac'lus < baculus, cf. Ir. **bachall,** crozier
Basaleg < basilica, cf. OIr. **baislec,** church
bedydd < *batidio < baptidio, cf. B. **badez,** baptism
bendigo < benedīco, cf. C. **benyga,** B. **bennig,** OIr. **bendachad,** bless
bendigaid <bendig- + aid, C. **beneges,** B. **beniguet,** blessed
bendith < benedictio, cf. C. **bennath, B.** bennoes, **Ir. bendacht,** blessing
bwyaid, bwyeid < béati, cf. OIr. **bíait,** the Beati, Psalm 119
cadair < cathedra, cf. C. **cadar,** B. **cadoer,** Ir. **cathair,** chair
cangell < cancellus, B. **cancell** 'locus', Ir. **caingel,** chancel.
capel < Late Latin cappella, chapel
caregl < calicula, cf. OC. **kelegel** gl calix, chalice
casul < casula, cf. OB. **kasul,** OIr. **casal,** chasuble, cf. **casulhetic** gl. penulata
celi < coeli, Lord/God (of heaven)
celyfrad < celebratio, cf. OIr. **celebrad,** celebration of the Mass
clas < classis, cf. OIr. **class** (choir), ecclesiastical community
cloch < Celt.Latin clocca, cf. C. **cloch,** B. **cloch,** Ir. **clog,** bell
cor < chorus, choir
credo <credo, creed
croes < **crux,** cf. OC. **crois, B. croes,** OIr **cros(s),** cross
crog <croc- cf. C. **crog,** B. **croug** , OIr. **croch**
cymun, cymmyn, kymmyn < commūnio, communion
cyswyn < consignum, consigno, designated
Dews < Deus, God
diagon < diaconus, deacon
diserth < disertum <dēsertum, cf. B. **desers,** OIr. **desert,** hermitage
Efengyl(au) < evangelium, Gospel
eglwys < ecclēsia, cf. C **eglos,** B. **iliz,** OIr. **eclais,** church; cf. **eglwys gadeiriol,** cathedral
Eloÿ, < Hebrew Eloi, name for God
esgob < episcopus, cf. C. **escop,** B. **eskop,** OIr. **epscop,** bishop; cf. **esgopty,** bishop-house
ffydd < fides, cf. C. **fedh,** B **feiz,** faith
Y Grawys < quadragēsima, cf.B. **koraiz,** Ir. **corgus, corgas,** Lent

gwin < vīnum, cf. OC. **guin**, C. **guyn, gwyn**, B. **guin, gwyn, gwin**, OIr. **fín**, wine

gweleri. gwyleri < *vigilarium < vigiliārum, cf. OB **guileri** OIr. **félire**, ecclesiastical calendar

gŵyl < vigilia, cf. OB. **guil**, Ir. **féil**, festival

llith < lectio, cf. OIr. **lechtain**, lection

llog < locus, cf. B. **loc**, OIr. **loc** monastery, place

llyfr < liber, cf. OC. **liuer** gl. liber uel codex, OB. **libr(ou)**, OIr. **lebor**, book

melltith < maledictio, cf. C. **mollath**, B. **malloez**, OIr. **maldacht**, curse

merthyr < martyrium, cf. Ir. **martre**, church

merthyr < **martyrus**, cf. B. merzer, OIr. **martir/martar**, martyr

muis/moys < mensa, cf. OC. **muis** gl. mensa, OB. **moys** gl catenum, Ir. **mías**, plate, basket, altar

mwstwyr < monastērium, cf. Ir. **mainistir/muinter**, monastery

myfyr < memoria, cf. OB. **memor**, OIr. **mebair**, grave, church

mynach < monachus, cf. OC. **manach** gl. monachus, B. **manach**, OIr. **manach**, monk

cf. **mynachlog** < mynach+llog < locus, monastery

Nadolig < Natālicia, cf. C. **Nadelik**, OB. **Natolic**, Ir. **Notlaic**, Christmas

offeiriad < offerre +iad, cf. OC. **oferiat** gl. presbyter, priest (who made the offering)

offeren < offerenda, cf. C. **oferen**, B. **offeren**, OIr. **oifrend**, mass

olew < oleuum < oleum, cf. OC. **oleu** gl. oleum, B. **oleo** Ir. **olae**, oil

pader < Pater (Noster), cf. **C. pader**, the Lord's prayer

Pasg < Pascha, cf. C. **Pask**, B.**Pasc**, OIr. **Cásc**, Easter

pechod <peccātum, cf. C. **peghes, pehas**, B. **peched**, OIr. **peccad**, sin

penyd < penitio, C. **penys**, B. **penet**, Ir. **pennait**, penance

periglor < *periculārius <periculum, priest (who took confession etc.)

pog < (osculum) pācis-, cf. OC. **poccuil**, B. **pok**, OIr. **poc**, kiss (of peace)

premter (pryfder) < presbyter, cf. OIr. **cruimther**, priest

pregeth < praecepta, cf. C. **pregoth, OIr. precept**, sermon

priodas < privātus+as, marriage

saith < **sacti** < **sancti**, saint

sant, < santus < sanctus, cf. **C. sans, B. sant,** saint

segrffyg < sacrificium, cf. Ir. **sacerbaic**, sacrifice (of the mass)

swyn, swynau < segnum < signum, cf. Ir. **sén**, sign (of the cross)

Trindod < Trinitātem, cf. C. **Drensys**, B. **Trindet**, OIr. **Trindoit**, Trinity

Trined < Trinitas, Trinity

uffern < infernum, cf. OB. **iffern**, OIr. **ifern**, hell

urd(eu) < ōrdō, cf. B. **urz**, holy orders

Ysbryd (Glân) < Spiritus, cf. OC. **spirit** gl. spiritus, B. **speret**, OIr. **spiurt/spirut**, (Holy) Spirit

ysgrythur < scrittūra < scriptūra, cf. Ir. **scriptuir, scripture**

B) Native Terms quoted in the text

aberth, cf. OIr. **idbairt,** sacrifice
aberthwr, sacrificer, priest
afrllad(en), sacred host
arglwydd, cf. C. **arluth,** B. **arluz,** lord
braint, status, privilege
brawd, cf. C. **bres,** B. **breut,** Ir. **bráth,** judgement
brenin, cf. C. **brentyn,** king
briduw, God's power, sacred oath
cil, OC. **chil** gl. cervix, B. **kil,** Ir. **cúl**
crair, cf. B, **krer(iu),** OIr. **cretar,** relic
credu, cf. C. **cresy,** B. **kridi,** OIr. **creteid,** believe
dial cf. C. **dyal,** Ir. **digal,** revenge
Did Braut, cf. Ir. **Dia Brátha,** Judgement Day
difwyn, diwygiaf, cf. Ir. **dofich,** atone, make reparation
diofredawg, cf. B. **diouerat,** abjured from
dofydd, lord
didryfwr, hermit, anchorite
Duw, cf. OC. **Duy,** B. **Doe,** OIr. **Día,** God
gwared[igaeth] cf. Ir. **foreth,** salvation
gweddio cf. Ir. **guidid,** pray
gwledig cf. OB. **guletic,** Ir. **fláith,** lord
llan cf. C. **lan,** B. **lann,** church settlement
llw cf. Ir. **luige,** oath
meudwy < **mau+dwy,** cf. OIr. **mug Dé,** hermit
nawdd, cf. Ir. **snádud,** protection
nef, cf. OC. **nef,** OB. **nem,** OIr. **nem,** heaven
ois oisou, cf. OC. **uis** gl. saecula, for ever and ever
rhad, cf. C. **ras,** OB. **Rad**(uuelen) Ir. **rath,** grace
rhi cf. C. **ri,** Ir. **rí,** king
rhin(wedd), cf. Ir. **rún** (secret, mystery), mystery, sacrament
rhwyf, rhwy, cf. OC. **ruy** gl. rex, **ruif** gl.edictum, B. **roue,** lord, king
tyngu, cf. Ir. **tongid,** swear (an oath)

ECKHARD HAUSWALD

Quellenrezeption und sprachliche Dynamik in Pirmins *Scarapsus*

Zur Einführung

Der folgende Beitrag bietet einen Zwischenbericht zum Projekt einer Neuedition des *Scarapsus*[1] genannten Kurzkatechismus von Pirmin „in der Form einer großen Predigt".[2] Neben Überlegungen zu Besonderheiten der Quellenrezeption, die über die Diskussion ausgewählter lexikalischer Einzelphänomene im Text des *Scarapsus* zur Klärung der Frage nach dem Entstehungsraum beitragen können, sollen des Weiteren besonders gesamtsprachliche Erscheinungen behandelt werden, die den pragmatisch-dynamischen Umgang des Autors mit der lateinischen Sprache seiner eigenen Zeit und der Sprache und Intention seiner Quellen betreffen. Sprachliche Dynamik zeigt sich:

1. im gestaltenden Umgang des Autors mit seinen heterogenen Ausgangstexten wie dem Bibeltext, patristischer Literatur und zeitgenössischen Gebrauchstexten. Auch die Rezeptionsebene des *Scarapsus*, und hier die Veränderung des Textes im Verlauf der Rezeption durch die Benutzer, können unter diesem Punkt subsumiert werden.

2. im Wechsel sprachlicher Ebenen innerhalb des Werkes selbst. Im Wesentlichen betrifft dies den Wechsel der eingesetzten sprachlichen Register beziehungsweise deren Zusammenspiel im Text.

---

1 *Scarapsus = Excarpsus*: „Exzerpt, Auszug". Die Forschungen am Text wurden durch ein Stipendium der Gerda Henkel Stiftung (Düsseldorf) ermöglicht, der an dieser Stelle herzlich gedankt sei. Die Neuedition wird den Text auf der Basis der nordfranzösischen Überlieferung bieten und die in JECKER, Gall: Die Heimat des heiligen Pirmin, des Apostels der Alemannen (Beiträge zur Geschichte des alten Mönchtums und des Benediktinerordens 13), Münster 1927, S. 34–73 ersetzen. Zur Überlieferung des *Scarapsus* siehe HAUSWALD, Eckhard: Die handschriftliche Überlieferung des Scarapsus, in: Ní CHATHÁIN, Próinséas/RICHTER, Michael (Hg.): Ireland and Europe in the Early Middle Ages. Texts and Transmission, Dublin 2002, S. 103–122. Es werden im Folgenden nur die stark von der bisherigen Edition bzw. der Übersetzung von ENGELMANN, Ursmar: Der heilige Pirmin und sein Pastoralbüchlein, Sigmaringen ²1976 abweichenden Textstellen übersetzt.

2 MILLEMANN, Honoratus: Caesarius von Arles und die frühmittelalterliche Missionspredigt, in: Zeitschrift für Missionswissenschaft und Religionswissenschaft 23 (1933), S. 12–27, S. 21; die weitere Literatur zum Textumfeld ist zusammengefasst in HAUSWALD: Handschriftliche Überlieferung, S. 103.

1. Zu Autor, Werk und Überlieferung

Pirmin († um 750/753?) war der letzte merowingerzeitliche Vertreter der irisch geprägten *peregrini*, der der asketischen Heimatlosigkeit in der konsequenten Nachfolge Christi verpflichteten Mönche, Missionare und auch Seelsorger.[3] Pirmin war Abt und Organisator des monastischen Lebens mindestens der Klöster Reichenau 724, Murbach 727 und Hornbach „kurz vor 742",[4] vermutlich jedoch auch wenigstens spirritueller Mitorganisator oder Vorbereiter einiger anderer mehr.[5] Er lebte und wirkte in der formal bereits christianisierten *Alamannia* links von Hoch- und Oberrhein, im Elsass, in der Südwestpfalz, in Regionen, in denen sich bereits spätantikes Christentum nachweisen lässt und, was die in dieser Hinsicht besonders dunklen Verhältnisse an Hochrhein und Bodensee betrifft, auch über die Völkerwanderungszeit hinaus kleinräumig erhalten hat, so namentlich im Siedlungssaum südlich des Hochrheins, in und um die alten Kastellorte.[6]

Pirmin war nach seinen bekannten Stationen ein Vertreter der inneren Mission im frühen 8. Jahrhundert,[7] nicht die räumliche Ausdehnung der *christianitas*

---

3 Zur monastischen Spiritualität Pirmins siehe ANGENENDT, Arnold: Monachi Peregrini. Studien zu Pirmin und den monastischen Vorstellungen des frühen Mittelalters (Münstersche Mittelalter-Schriften 10), München 1972, S. 124–229, zur im Zuge der Klostergründungen angestrebten Seelsorge über klostereigene Kirchen siehe ibid., S. 164.

4 HERRMANN, Hans-Walter: Hornbach, in: Lexikon des Mittelalters (LexMA, Studienausgabe), Bd. 5 (1999), Sp. 126f. Zu Pirmins Leben und Werk siehe SEMMLER, Josef: Pirminius, in: Mitteilungen des Historischen Vereins der Pfalz 87 (1989), S. 91–114. Zur merowingisch-alemannischen Gründungsgeschichte der Reichenau siehe RICHTER, Michael: Neues zu den Anfängen des Klosters Reichenau, in: Zeitschrift für die Geschichte des Oberrheins 144 (1996), S. 1–18.

5 Die Vita Pirminii c. 8, zitiert nach: Leben und Taten des Bischofs Pirmin. Die karolingische Vita, ed. v. Richard ANTONI (Reichenauer Texte und Bilder 9), Stuttgart 2002, S. 78; c. 5, Vita Perminii, ed. v. Oswald HOLDER-EGGER (Monumenta Germaniae Historica [MGH] SS 15,1) Hannover 1887, S. 26,4f., nennt noch Niederaltaich, Schuttern, Gengenbach, Schwarzach, Maursmünster, Neuweiler. Einige Hss. fügen noch Pfäfers hinzu. Der Reichenauer Chronist Gall Öhem weiß um 1500 noch von einer frühen, der Reichenau vorangegangenen Klostergründung in Pfungen bei Winterthur: Die Chronik des Gallus Öhem, ed. v. Karl BRANDI (Quellen und Forschungen zur Geschichte der Abtei Reichenau 2), Heidelberg 1893, S. 8.

6 Zu den religiösen Verhältnissen im Wirkungsraum Pirmins siehe jetzt: BERSCHIN, Walter/GEUENICH, Dieter/STEUER, Heiko (Hg.): Mission und Christianisierung am Hoch- und Oberrhein, 6.–8. Jahrhundert, (Archäologie und Geschichte. Freiburger Forschungen zum ersten Jahrtausend in Südwestdeutschland 10), Stuttgart 2000; LORENZ, Sönke/SCHOLKMANN, Barbara (Hg.): Die Alemannen und das Christentum. Zeugnisse eines kulturellen Umbruchs (Schriften zur südwestdeutschen Landeskunde 48,2), Leinfelden-Echterdingen 2003. Als archäologischen Niederschlag dieser Verhältnisse ungleicher Prägung, Intensität und Ausrichtung von Christentum im alemannischen Siedlungsraum sieht man heute die Tatsache, dass in der Zentralalamannia am Neckar und auf der Schwäbischen Alb der norditalienisch-langobardische Bestattungsbrauch, den Toten Goldblattkreuze beizugeben, reichlich belegt ist, sich jedoch in der linksrheinischen Region dazwischen, d. h. in der Nordschweiz, und auch nicht (bis auf eine Ausnahme) im Elsass.

7 Darunter ist hier die „auf das moralische Verhalten des einzelnen Christen, sowohl des Laien wie auch des Klerikers" zielende, mit den „Stichwörter(n) [...] corrigere und emendare" verbundene Form der Christianisierung im frühen 8. Jh. zu verstehen, REUTER, Timothy: „Kirchenreform" und „Kirchenpolitik" im Zeitalter Karl Martells, in: JARNUT, Jörg/NONN, Ulrich/RICHTER, Michael (Hg.): Karl Martell in seiner Zeit, Sigmaringen 1994, S. 41. Auf das Individuum

durch Bekehrung war sein Anliegen, sondern die inhaltliche, qualitative Anhebung des Christentums innerhalb der bereits christlichen Gebiete.[8]

Diesem nach den erhaltenen Quellen – insbesondere den echten wie auch den verfälschten Urkunden – für einige der Pirminklöster[9] noch hinreichend nachvollziehbaren Werk entspricht der in einer Handschrift des ausgehenden 8. oder beginnenden 9. Jahrhunderts ihm zugeschriebene Text der *Dicta Priminii*, des sogenannten *Scarapsus*, der mit derzeit zehn bekannten direkten Textzeugen[10] im Mittelalter erstaunlich weit verbreitet war und überdies auch oft indirekt überliefert beziehungsweise inhaltlich rezipiert worden ist. Dies unterstreicht seine Bedeutung für die pastorale Praxis.[11]

---

in der o. g. Weise zielt der *Scarapsus* häufig ab, am eindringlichsten am Ende des c. 13 (entspricht JECKER, Heimat, S. 44, 24–45,2): *Ideo, karissimi, rogamus karitate vestra, ut intenti aures cordis vestrae audiatis, quid vobis de haec vitia superscripta dominus per semetipsum vel per sancta scriptura prohibet, ut nuncquam ea faciatis, et qui fecerit, quomodo debet* (*debeat* Hss.) *emendare* (= „deshalb, Geliebte, bitten wir euch bei eurer Liebe, dass ihr mit euren angespannten Herzensohren zuhört, was euch über die oben erwähnten Fehler der Herr selbst oder durch die Heilige Schrift gebietet, damit ihr sie niemals macht, und wer sie macht [od. gemacht hat], wie er sich bessern muss [od. möge]").

8 Diese selbstgesetzte räumliche Beschränkung unterscheidet ihn von seinen angelsächsischen Zeitgenossen Willibrord und Bonifatius, in deren Vorstellungen von Mission die Bekehrung der *gentes*/Heidenvölker gemäß der frühmittelalterlichen Lesart des Missionsaufrufs Matth. 28,19 noch die maßgebliche Rolle spielte (hierzu grundlegend FRITZE, Wolfgang H.: Universalis gentium confessio. Formeln, Träger und Wege universalmissionarischen Denkens im 7. Jahrhundert, in: Frühmittelalterliche Studien 3 (1969), S. 78–130. Zu den unterschiedlichen Vorstellungen der drei Missionare siehe ANGENENDT, Arnold: Pirmin und Bonifatius. Ihr Verhältnis zu Mönchtum, Bischofsamt und Adel, in: BORST, Arno (Hg.): Mönchtum, Episkopat und Adel zur Gründungszeit des Klosters Reichenau, Sigmaringen 1974, S. 251–304 sowie LÖWE, Heinz: Pirmin, Willibrord und Bonifatius, in: Settimane di Studio del Centro Italiano di Studi sull'Alto Medievo 14 (1967), S. 217–261, mit Diskussion S. 517–526.

9 Siehe die Quellendiskussion zu Reichenau, Murbach und Hornbach bei ANGENENDT: Monachi, S. 81–102.

10 Die Hss. und ihre Siglen sind **A**: Paris, BnF, Lat. 1603 [saec. VIIIex.; nordostfranzösisch, „Umkreis des Hofes"; St. Amand], ff. 163r–192r: anonym, titellos. **B**: Oxford, Bodleian Library, Ms. Bodley 572 [Teil D: saec. IX1/3; (nord)französisch; Provenienz ungeklärt], ff. 91r–106v: anonym, titellos, Fragment: cc. 1–23(24). **R**: Albi, Bibl. Mun., Ms. 40 [saec. IX1; süd(west)französisch; Albi], ff. 18v–42r: *Sentencia sancti Agustini*. Auszug. **C**: Paris, BnF, Lat. 13408 [saec. IX1, nordostfranzösisch, „nicht fern von Reims"; Corbie], ff. 105r–121r: *Incipit admonitio beati Gregorii urbis Rome ad plebem*. Auszug. **D**: Paris, BnF, Lat. 1008 [saec. IX/X; französisch; St. Denis], ff. 54r–81v: anonym, titellos. **N**: Chicago, Newberry Library, Ms. 1 (ehemals *Cheltenham 1326*) [saec. XII; südwestfranzösisch; wohl Moissac], ff. 121r–135r: *Incipit homelia sancti Agustini episcopi*. Auszug, Fragment: cc. 1–29(30). **O**: Paris, BnF, Lat. 1207 [saec. XII; nordfranzösisch; wohl Orléans], f. 9v: *Incipit omelia | sancti Agustini episcopi deinde die iudicii* [...]. Fragment: cc. 1–2. **H**: London, British Library, Ms. Harley 3072 [saec. XI/XII; Schriftheimat und Provenienz ungeklärt], ff. 89r–90r: *Incipit omelia utilis ad populum praedicandum* + ff. 87r–89r. Auszug: cc. 1–7 + cc. 28a–34. **T**: Turin, Bibl. Nazionale Universitaria, F.II.20 [saec. X/XI; norditalienisch; Bobbio], ff. 188v–202v: *Item admonicio ista ex(c)e(rp)ta de libris sanctorum et antiquorum patrum | ut qui se crimine capitalia fecisse cognoscit ad penitentie medicamenta | confugiat*. **E**: Einsiedeln, Stiftsbibl., Cod. 199 [saec. VIII/IX; (chur-)rätisch; Einsiedeln], pp. 461–510: *Incipit dicta abbates Priminii: de singulis libris cannonnicis scarapsus*.

11 Dass der *Scarapsus* nicht nur im literaturgeschichtlichen Sinne benutzt worden ist, sondern auch praktisch durch häufiges Heranziehen, Aufschlagen und Vorlesen, zeigt auch der schlechte Erhal-

Als wichtigste indirekte Textzeugen[12] sind vorläufig zu nennen:

1. Die Aufnahme des Credo mit Apostelrahmen in den süddeutschen Zweig der *Collectio Vetus Gallica*.[13]

2. Der Text einer verlorenen, ca. 800 entstandenen nordfranzösischen Kirchenrechtssammlung, der in die Privatarbeit des Benedictus Levita und auch in die Sammlung der sogenannten *Capitula Vesulensia* der Hs. Vesoul, BM 79 (73) sowie in die verwandten *Statuta Bonifatii* eingegangen ist.[14]

3. Das sogenannte *Paenitentiale Oxoniense I* in der Hs. Oxford, Bodl. 311, das den Abschnitt c. 19 des *Scarapsus* über das Verbot unreiner Speisen enthält.[15]

4. Eine unter dem Titel *Homilia sacra* bekannte, stark bearbeitete Kurzfassung, die in einer südfranzösischen Handschrift aus dem 9. Jahrhundert überliefert ist.[16]

5. Ein später vom sogenannten Augustinus Belgicus zusammengestellter Predigttext *Sermo ad fratres in eremo* 64, Teil 3, der den Schlussteil des *Scarapsus* fast wörtlich wiedergibt.[17]

6. Eine in Norditalien kursierende, wohl im 13./14. Jahrhundert in Bobbio auf Grundlage der Hs. T entstandene Predigt *De charitate Dei ac proximi*, die das

---

tungszustand einiger der Hss., vor allem der Fragmente B und N, vgl. HAUSWALD: Handschriftliche Überlieferung, S. 108f..

12 Dies ergänzt die genannten Rezeptionsspuren in HAUSWALD: Handschriftliche Überlieferung, S. 121.

13 Ediert in: MORDEK, Hubert: Kirchenrecht und Reform im Frankenreich. Die Collectio Vetus Gallica, die älteste systematische Kanonessammlung des fränkischen Gallien. Studien und Edition, Berlin/New York 1975, S. 359f.

14 Capitula Vesulensia, ed. v. Rudolf POKORNY (MGH Capit. episcoporum 3), Hannover 1990, S. 346–353, 360–366; vgl. die Diskussion der Entstehungsgeschichte der *Capitula Vesulensia* ibid., S. 339–345, bes. 343: Dass der *Scarapsus* entgegen der von Pokorny vertretenen Ansicht der Ausgangstext ist und nicht aus einer gemeinsamen Zwischenüberlieferung schöpft, ergibt sich dadurch, dass er allein direkt auf Martin von Braga: De correctione rusticorum (= DCR) und auf Isidor von Sevilla: De ecclesiasticis officiis (= DEO) zugreift; vgl. hierzu vorläufig die Stellen Scarapsus c. 23, JECKER: Heimat, S. 57,1–5 + 15–18 mit dem Text der direkten Vorlagen Martin v. Braga: DCR, c. 18, Martini episcopi Bracarensis opera omnia, ed. v. Claude W. BARLOW, New Haven 1950, S. 183–203, S. 202, S. 11–16 und Isidor: DEO, I, XXIIII (1), (Corpus Christianorum – Series Latina [CCSL] 113), S. 27,4–6 und der adaptierten Form der Capitula Vesulensia, c. 16,5–8, ed. v. Rudolf POKORNY (MGH Capit. episcoporum 3), S. 349.

15 Ediert in: CCSL 156, S. 87–93, der betr. Abschnitt S. 93, S. 191–199.

16 Ediert in: Gennadii Massiliensis Presbyteri Liber De Ecclesiasticis Dogmatibus, Veteris cuiusdam Theologi Homilia Sacra [...], ed. v. Geverhard ELMENHORST, Hamburg 1614, S. 47–55, mit Anm. S. 189–201; zur Hs. Kopenhagen, Kongelige Bibliotek, Gl. Kgl. Saml. 1943. 4o siehe MORDEK, Hubert (Hg.): Bibliotheca capitularium regum Francorum manuscripta. Überlieferung und Traditionszusammenhang der fränkischen Herrscherlasse (MGH Hilfsmittel 15), München 1995, S. 192–195.

17 Ediert in: Patrologia (Series) Latina (PL) 40, Sp. 1347–1350, das *Scarapsus*-Exzerpt PL 40, Sp. 1349f. Zum belgischen Augustinus siehe die aktuellen Daten im Cetedoc Library of Christian Latin Texts (CLCLT) sowie FREDE, Hermann J.: Kirchenschriftsteller (Vetus Latina 1,1), Freiburg 1995, S. 291f.: „Die Sammlung entstand nicht vor dem 11. Jh. [...] 64 wohl späte Kompilation."

Anfangskapitel des *Scarapsus* wörtlich, weitere Abschnitte, wie solche aus c. 13, inhaltlich ausschreibt.[18]

So, wie sich Pirmins Nachfolger und Schüler fast umgehend unter den Exponenten der kirchlichen Erneuerung finden – zum Beispiel Pirmins Abts-Nachfolger auf der Reichenau Heddo zugleich als Klostergründer, Bischof von Straßburg und Teilnehmer am *Concilium Germanicum*[19] –, so ist auch der *Scarapsus* selbst in der zweiten Hälfte des Jahrhunderts bereits Teil dieser Bestrebungen.[20]

Er wird, was ja gerade seine Rezeption in den kanonistischen Sammlungen bestätigt, zu einem Zentraltext der einsetzenden Reform der fränkischen Kirche. Die nach Bernhard Bischoff hofnah entstandene Hs. A,[21] Trägerin der nordfranzösischen Hauptüberlieferung der Corbie-Redaktion der *Coll. Vet. Gall.*, die diese Kirchenrechtssammlung mit dem *Scarapsus* direkt verbindet und zudem noch mit dem *Paenitentiale Remense* und den *Canones Theodori* Versionen zweier wichtiger Gebrauchstexte der Vorlagenebene bringt, ist ein Reflex dieser Bedeutung. Die Hs. A gilt nach dem Arrangement ihres Inhalts als für die praktischen Bedürfnisse der Seelsorge zusammengestellt.[22]

Wie konnte der *Scarapsus* diese Bedeutung vornehmlich im 8. und 9. Jahrhundert gewinnen? Was sind seine Stärken?

Zur Beantwortung dieser Fragen sei auf folgende Merkmale hingewiesen:

1. Der *Scarapsus* ist allgemein anwendbar, weil er von der christlichen Lehre aus normativ operierend nur allgemeingültige Inhalte transportiert. Letztere werden konsequent mit mindestens einem Bibelzitat unterlegt und somit allgemein verbindlich untermauert. Er hat dementsprechend nur sehr wenig Regionalbezug.

2. Er hat einen ebenso konsequent nach didaktischen Erwägungen konzipierten Aufbau, der bei der Vermittlung der Inhalte unterstützend wirksam wird, was seinen Gebrauchswert gegenüber einer primär einzelne moralische Instruktionen aneinanderreihenden Langpredigt, wie der sogenannten Eligius-Kompilation, das ist die in die Eligius-Vita eingeschaltete Musterpredigt,[23] erheblich steigert.

---

18 Ediert und kommentiert von NUVOLONE, Flavio G.: Il Sermone de Charitate Dei ac proximi e il contesto ospedaliero Bobbiese. Edizione e spunti analitici (II), in: Archivum Bobiense 5 (1983), S. 99–167.

19 Zu Heddo siehe ANGENENDT: Monachi, S. 224–229; ANGENENDT: Mönchtum, S. 284–290.

20 Dies ergibt sich aus dem Umstand, dass auch der wichtigste indirekte Textzeuge des *Scarapsus*, die Hs. S1 der *Coll. Vet. Gall.*, noch dem 8. Jh. zuzurechnen ist. Siehe MORDEK: Kirchenrecht, S. 294f. Mit A und E sind zwei Hss. der direkten Überlieferung ebenfalls mindestens saec. VIII/IX zu datieren und keine dieser wie auch aller übrigen Hss. ist die direkte Abschrift einer anderen. Mordek rechnet damit, dass der *Scarapsus* bereits Teil der Hs. war, die auch den Archetypus der redigierten *Coll. Vet. Gall.* enthielt; daraus ergibt sich, dass der *Scarapsus* im 2. Viertel des 8. Jh. in Corbie vorgelegen haben muss. Vgl. MORDEK: Kirchenrecht, S. 86 und S. 359 App.

21 MORDEK: Bibliotheca, S. 420f.

22 MEENS, Rob: Het tripartite boeteboek, Hilversum 1994, S. 239.

23 Der Text ist vollständig ediert in: Vita Eligii, II, c. 15, PL 87, Sp. 524-550 bzw. PL 40, Sp. 1169–1190. Die Musterpredigt übertrifft in ihrer Länge mit 26 PL-Spalten noch die des *Scarapsus* mit, PL

3. Er ist in den erklärenden und unterweisenden Abschnitten, die die Rezipienten direkt ansprechen, in einer bewusst einfachen, leicht verständlichen und deshalb auch leicht paraphrasier- beziehungsweise übersetzbaren Sprache gehalten. Als Predigttext gesehen ist er ein geradezu idealtypischer *Sermo humilis* oder *Sermo rusticus* im Sinne der allgemeinen Verkehrssprache,[24] einfacher noch als die Sprache *Ad usum vulgi* der merowingischen Heiligenvita.[25] Der *Scarapsus* als Hilfsmittel zur Predigtgestaltung[26] wird den beiden Forderungen von c. 17 des Konzils von Tours 813, sowohl was den Inhalt als auch was die sprachliche Darbietung des Inhalts betrifft, in jeder Beziehung gerecht.[27] Der *Scarapsus* ist keineswegs ein „chaotische(r) Normenkatalog".[28]

2. Zur Quellenrezeption

Der *Scarapsus* besteht aus drei Textteilen unterschiedlicher Art. Der erste (cc. 2–11), der auf das Einleitungskapitel folgt, ist narrativ-rekapitulierend und dogmatisch-instruierend, der zweite (cc. 12–27) sittlich-belehrend, der dritte (cc. 28a–34) rekapituliert sowohl den Inhalt des ersten wie auch den des zweiten Teils. Im ersten Teil dominieren Texte aus dem iberischen Raum und der südlichen *Gallia*, im zweiten werden diese Texte mit solchen, die im nördlicheren Frankenreich entstanden sind oder dort kursierten, frei kombiniert.

89, Sp. 1029–1059, fast 20 vollen PL-Spalten. Zur Eligius-Kompilation siehe MILLEMANN: Missionspredigt, S. 15–17; Zur *Vita Eligii*, vgl. Clavis Patrum Latinorum (CPL) Nr. 2094: Danach ist sie wohl ein anonymes Produkt der ersten Hälfte des 8. Jh. und Audoenus/Dado von Rouen zu Unrecht zugeschrieben.

24 Ich übernehme die Terminologie von BANNIARD, Michel: Language and Communication in Carolingian Europe, in: McKITTERICK, Rosamond (Hg.): The New Cambridge Medieval History, Bd. 2, Cambridge 1995, S. 695-708, S. 698.

25 Die Vita Richarii primigenia, die BANNIARD, Michel: Seuils et frontières langagières dans la Francia romane du VIIIe siècle, in: JARNUT/NONN/RICHTER (Hg.): Karl Martell, S. 171–191, S. 175–181 als Beispiel für einen *Sermo simplex*, einen in einem allgemeinverständlichen Basisniveau gehaltenen Text, analysiert, leistet sich immerhin c. 2 *ad suum perduxit domicilium*; Vita Richarii sacerdotis Centulensis primigenia, ed. v. Bruno KRUSCH (MGH SS rer. Merov. 7), Hannover/Leipzig 1919–1920, S. 438–453, S. 445, Z. 7f., eine inversive Stellung des Prädikats, die man im frei formulierten Scarapsustext nicht findet.

26 Siehe HAUSWALD: Handschriftliche Überlieferung, S. 110–112 zu den Textbearbeitungen des *Scarapsus* in den einzelnen Hss.

27 Concilium Turonense a. 813, ed. v. Albert WERMINGHOFF (MGH Concilia 2. Conc. aevi Karolini 1), Hannover 1908, c. 17, S. 288; BANNIARD: Language and Communication, S. 699f.; BANNIARD, Michel: Viva voce. Communication écrite et communication orale du IVe au IXe siècle en Occident latin, Paris 1992, S. 410f.; RICHTER, Michael: Kommunikationsprobleme im lateinischen Mittelalter, in: RICHTER, Michael (Hg.): Studies in Medieval Language and Culture, Dublin 1995, S. 24–53, S. 27ff. [= Historische Zeitschrift 222 (1976), S. 43–80].

28 So SCHEIBELREITER, Georg: Der Missionar im Frankenreich im siebten und achten Jahrhundert. Typus und Individuum, in: BANGE, Petty/WEILER, A.G. (Hg.): Willibrord, zijn wereld en zijn werk, Nijmegen 1990, S. 328–347, S. 341.

Den formalen Rahmen für die Konzeption des ersten Teils liefert Martins von Braga DCR.[29] Wie bei Martin wird die Heilsgeschichte nach ihren markanten Stationen wie Sündenfall und Sintflut entwickelt, und zwar mit dem Ziel, über die Sendung Christi und das christliche Erlösungsversprechen die Verbindung zur Gegenwart der Rezipienten und zu ihren (vertraglichen) Verpflichtungen als Christen herzustellen. Kulminationspunkt ist demgemäß die Rekapitulation des Taufgelöbnisses nach der Martin-Vorlage, ergänzt durch das Isidor-Zitat aus *Etym.*, VII, 14,1: *A christo enim Christiani sunt nominati* (*cognominati* Isidor).[30] Der so abgesteckte Rahmen wird durch volkstümlich adaptierte Entnahmen aus der Bibel wie der Präsentation des Dekalogs als dem mit dem Zeigefinger Gottes auf zwei steinerne Tafeln eingeschriebenen Gesetz (nach Bibeltext und Augustinus), der Darbietung des Vaterunser (nach der kanonischen Form des Textes Matth. 6,9–13) und des Apostolischen Glaubensbekenntnisses im vollen Wortlaut[31] sowie Elementen aus der beziehungsweise Allusionen an die Liturgie angefüllt. Weitere Texte aus Patristik und Gebrauchsliteratur wie Volkspredigten werden ergänzend herangezogen.[32]

Mit der Taufe und der Definition dessen, was einen wahren Christen ausmacht, einer nahtlosen Fortsetzung des Isidor-Exzerptes, *Etym.* VII,14,3 (c. 13: ***Non se autem glorietur Christianus*** (*Christianum* Hss.)***, que nomen habet et facta non habet. Christianus ille est,*** *que* (*qui* Hss.) ***Christum in omnium imitatur et sequitur*** [...]), beginnt der zweite inhaltliche Hauptteil des *Scarapsus*, der Teil, der der ethischen Belehrung der Bevölkerung gewidmet ist. In c. 13 wird erstmals im Überblick die Systematik der acht Hauptsünden geboten, die im nächsten Kapitel, c. 14, noch etwas verfeinert wird. Pirmin folgt hier der in monastischen Kreisen rezipierten Cassianschen Acht-Laster-Lehre.[33] Es ist allein, wie die Wiederaufnahme c. 14 zeigt, unter dem Eindruck der Apostelstelle 1. Tim. 6,10 *radix enim omnium malorum est cupiditas* und der Exegese des Caesarius[34] die *cupiditas* an die Spitze des Sündenkatalogs gerückt. Pirmins Version weist in Aufbau und einbettender Wortwahl engste Verbindungen zum Text der *Instructio* 17 *Columbani* auf.[35]

---

29 Neben der Edition von BARLOW: Martini opera, ist jetzt wegen der neuen, gründlichen Diskussion der Überlieferungsverhältnisse und der ausführlichen Bibliographie nützlich: Martini Bracarensis Pro castigatione rusticorum, ed. v. Gennaro LOPEZ, Rom 1998.

30 Vgl. hier und im Folgenden LINDSAY, Wallace M.: Isidori Hispalensis episcopi Etymologiarum sive originum libri XX, Bd. 1, Oxford 1911.

31 Zu diesen drei aus didaktischen Erwägungen eingeflochtenen Textabschnitten s. u. S. 290f.

32 Als wichtigster Ergänzungstext ist die in vielen Caesarius-Hss. überlieferte sog. Doctrina cuiusdam sancti viri (= Homilia XVII Ps.-Caesarii, in: PL 67, Sp. 1079–81) zu nennen, siehe FREDE: Kirchenschriftsteller, S. 348; zum Titel siehe CCSL 103 S. XLVIII. Einen ähnlichen Aufbau zeigt auch der irische Ps.-Isidor: De ortu et obitu patriarcharum, c. 42,8–10 (CCSL 108E), S. 53–56.

33 Vgl. ANGENENDT: Monachi, S. 63; die Vorlage ist Cassian, Inst. V, 1 (Corpus Scriptorum Ecclesiasticorum Latinorum [CSEL] 17,1), S. 81 bzw. Coll., V, 2 (CSEL 13), S. 121.

34 Vgl. Sermo 23,1 (CCSL 103) S. 98: 104,19–99: 104,1.

35 Sancti Columbani opera, ed. v. George S. M. WALKER (Scriptores Latini Hiberniae 2), Dublin ²1970, S. 210–213. Die Frage der Echtheit der *Instructio* 17 kann hier nicht diskutiert werden, sie ist jedoch sicher mindestens dem Umkreis Columbans zuzurechnen. Siehe hierzu: LAPIDGE, Michael (Hg.): Columbanus. Studies on the Latin Writings, Woodbridge 1997.

Instructio 17:	*Scarapsus:*
Octo sunt vitia principalia, quae mergunt hominem in interitum:	c. 13: *Mala ergo sunt octo principalia vitia,* QUI (*que* Hss.) DEMERGUNT HOMINES IN INTERITO ET PERDITIONEM:
gula, fornicatio, cupiditas, ira, tristitia, accedia, vana gloria, superbia.	*Cupiditas, gula, fornicatio, ira, tristitia, accidia* (*adsidia* A), *vana gloria, superbia.* [...]
De gula castiganda dicitur: *Nolite seduci in saturitate ventris.* [...]	c. 14: *De gula vero dicit: Cavete autem gula* [...], *quia scriptum est: Nolite seduci in sacietate ventris.*
De cupiditate autem legitur: *Radix omnium malorum cupiditas est.* (WALKER: Columbani Opera, S. 210,15–18)	c. 14: *De cupiditatem* (*-tate* Hss.) *autem Dominus in lege dicit:* NON CONCUPISCERE [...] *Et per apostolum:* RADIX ENIM OMNIUM MALORUM EST CUPIDITAS. (entspricht JECKER: Heimat, S. 44,18–21 + 45,3–8, die Abschnitte aus c. 14 umgestellt)

Eine zusätzliche Verbindung der hier behandelten Texte stiftet die Allusion an Prov. 23,20 (eher als an Luk. 21,34, wie Walker S. 210 App. zur Stelle meint): *Nolite seduci in sacietate ventris.* Dieser Spruch, mit der dem *Scarapsus* entsprechenden Lesart *satietate*, findet sich auch im *Sermo de poenitentia Joannis*, einem dem Prolog des *Paenitentiale Merseburgense* A vorgeschalteten Kurztraktat, der sowohl Cassian als auch die *Instructio* 17 direkt verwendet.[36] Pirmins im gesamten Werk feststellbare Bestrebungen, einen möglichst bibelnahen Text zu bieten, zeigen sich in der Fortführung des ersten Satzes nach dem Wortlaut der Bibelstelle 1. Tim. 6,9.

Die Parallele zur *Instructio* 17 ist nicht das einzige auf einen kontinentalirisch beeinflussten, also irofränkischen Entstehungshintergrund weisende Merkmal:

Drei im *Scarapsus* versprengte Textparallelen finden sich in relativer Nähe zueinander im ersten Teil des *Excarpsus Cummeani*[37] beziehungsweise *Paenitentiale Remense.*[38]

---

36 Der *Sermo Joannis* fährt nach *ventris* mit *et grapula* fort, vgl. WASSERSCHLEBEN, Friedrich W. H.: Die Bußordnungen der abendländischen Kirche, Halle 1851 (Neudruck Graz 1958), S. 387.

37 Einstweilen noch zitiert nach WASSERSCHLEBEN: Bußordnungen, S. 460-493. Eine Neuedition durch Ludger KÖRNTGEN für das Corpus Christianorum ist in Vorbereitung. Die inhaltlichen Parallelen bes. im Bereich des von Pirmin bekämpften vorchristlichen Brauchtums zwischen den Bußbüchern und dem *Scarapsus* sind bekannt, wenn auch JECKER: Heimat, S. 134f. daraus wegen der von ihm vertretenen späten Datierung der Bußbücher frühestens in die zweite Hälfte des 8. Jh. für die Entstehung des *Scarapsus* keine Konsequenzen zog. Der *Exc. Cumm.* ist spätestens im 2. Viertel des 8. Jh. entstanden. Vgl. KOTTJE, Raymund: Excarpsus Cummeani, in: LexMA, Bd. 4 (1989), Sp. 155.

38 ASBACH, Franz B.: Das Poenitentiale Remense und der sogenannte Excarpsus Cummeani, Diss. Regensburg 1975, S. 1–77, mit Edition im Anhang.

Exc. Cumm. / Paen. Remense:	*Scarapsus:*
Vetus namque proverbium est: contraria contrariis sanantur. (WASSERSCHLEBEN: Bußordnungen, S. 462; ASBACH: Remense, S. 9,6f.)	c. 26: *Igitur, karissimi, consideremus, quod scriptum est: Contraria contrariis sanantur.* (entspricht JECKER: Heimat, S. 59,14f.)
Unde quidam sapiens ait: cui plus creditur plus ab eo exigitur. (WASSERSCHLEBEN: Bußordnungen, S. 462; ASBACH: Remense, S. 9,19f.)	c. 29: [...] *ut scriptum est: Cui plus creditur plus ab eo exigitur (exceditur* A).[39] (entspricht JECKER: Heimat, S. 68,24–69,1)
Legitur quoniam Christus ieiunavit, qui nullum peccatum commisit, similiter et apostoli post donum spiritus sancti. (WASSERSCHLEBEN: Bußordnungen, S. 464; ASBACH: Remense, S. 13,19–14,1)	c. 27: *Et apostulus in ieiuniis frequenter. Et Christus ieiunavit, qui peccatum non fecit.* (entspricht JECKER: Heimat, S. 61,27–29)

Die *doctores*, die als Schrift-Gelehrte zugleich Ärtzte sind, die über das Wissen verfügen, wie die Sünden durch ihr Gegenteil geheilt werden können, finden sich nach Art des *Scarapsus*[40] auch in der *Vita Fursei*, der Lebensbeschreibung desjenigen, zu dessen Gedenken das picardische Kloster Péronne gegründet wurde.[41] Durch die auffallend mit dem *Scarapsus*-Beginn übereinstimmende Anfangssequenz der *Homilia 16 Ps.-Eligii*[42] ergibt sich zudem auch eine Verbindung mit dem nordfranzösisch-südbelgischen Eligius-Kreis.

Caesarius von Arles, aus dem eine große Anzahl von Abschnitten und Einzelsätzen meist wörtlich stammt, zitiert den alten medizinischen Grundsatz hingegen weniger schlagwortartig,[43] und die ältere irische Bußliteratur zitiert ihn in abweichendem Wortlaut.[44]

Der *Scarapsus* steht über die Parallelen auch zu diesen kleineren Textstücken aus der pastoralen Gebrauchsliteratur fest auf der spirituellen und textlichen Grundlage der späteren Vertreter der irisch-fränkischen Mission, dies auch bezüglich der räumlichen Herkunft dieser Texte.

Die schon von Kottje angeführten deutlichen Verbindungen des *Scarapsus* zum irischen Schrifttum hinsichtlich Rezeption und Exegese der normativen Teile des

---

39 Hieronymus, Epist. 14,9 (CSEL 54), S. 58; Regula Magistri, c. 2,32 (Sources Chrétiennes [SC] 105), S. 358; die *Regula Benedicti* hat hier c. 2,32: *cui plus conmittitur* (CSEL 75), S. 26.

40 Das Thema wird c. 27, am Ende des zweiten Hauptteils, wieder aufgenommen: *Sic et contra singula vicia vel peccata* [...] *contrariis virtutibus et bonis operibus* [...] *est pugnando (-dum* Hss.). Entspricht JECKER: Heimat, S. 64,13–16.

41 Siehe RICHTER, Michael: Ireland and her Neighbours in the Seventh Century, Dublin 1999, S. 127. Vgl. Vita Fursei, c. 18, in: Vitae Sanctorum Hiberniae, ed. v. William W. HEIST, Brüssel 1965, S. 37–50, 45: *Omnis ergo doctor singulis viciis congrua debet opponere medicamenta.* [...] *Contraria enim vicia contrariis virtutibus sanantur.*

42 *Fratres Charissimi, Spiritus sanctus per Isaiam prophetam, sacerdotibus et levitis omnibusque doctoribus Ecclesiae praecipit dicens: Clama* [...], siehe hierzu MILLEMANN: Missionspredigt, S. 19, der Text ist ediert in: PL 87, Sp. 650–654.

43 Caesarius, Sermo 23,1 (CCSL 103), S. 104: 98,23f.: *Et quia contrariis solent sanari contraria* [...].

44 Vgl. Penitentialis Vinniani, c. 28 und c. 29, in: The Irish Penitentials, ed. v. Ludwig BIELER/Daniel A. BINCHY, Dublin 1963, S. 82 und S. 84: *Haec est penitentia huius criminis, ut e contrariis contraria curet et emendet.* (c. 29) [...] *Sed e contrariis, ut diximus, festinemus curare contraria* [...].

AT, wie sie insbesondere der *Liber ex lege Moysis*[45] aufweist, lassen sich somit um wichtige weitere Punkte ergänzen.[46]

Wenn Pirmin textextern zu Recht als später Exponent der irofränkischen Mission gilt, so gilt gleiches zweifelsohne textintern auch für den *Scarapsus*.

Nachdem im Vorübergehen bereits einige Merkmale angesprochen worden sind, die den *Scarapsus* mit dem nordfranzösisch-belgischen Raum im weiteren Sinne verknüpfen, soll dies durch die Diskussion einer besonders problematischen Textstelle vertieft werden.

Gegen die Tendenz, nur Allgemeingültiges, wenig Regionaltypisches zu transportieren, was den *Scarapsus* für die regionale Brauchtumsforschung unergiebig macht,[47] weist eine vereinzelte Stelle an der Textoberfläche sprachlich-terminologisch einen engeren Bezug zum nordfranzösischen, insbesondere dem picardischen Raum auf.

In c. 22 des *Scarapsus*, der der Bekämpfung von vorchristlichem Brauchtum beziehungsweise Aberglauben gewidmet ist, findet sich auf handschriftlich ausreichend breiter Basis der besonders markante und bisher unbefriedigend erklärte Ausdruck *maones* im Satz *nec aliquid pro hoc eis dare, qui dicunt, quod maones fructa tollere possint* (= und nicht irgendetwas dafür denen geben, die sagen, dass die *maones* Erntefrüchte/Ertrag bringen könnten).[48]

Zwei weitere Texte enthalten diesen ungewöhnlichen Beleg für einen vorchristlichen agrarischen Vermehrungszauber. Die *maones* entsprechen den *mavonis/ mavones* im erweiterten Text der predigtartigen Gebrauchsschrift *Excarpsum de diversis auctoribus*.[49] Den vermutlich frühesten Beleg und die Ausgangsform die-

---

45 Ich danke Herrn Prof. Raymund Kottje (Bonn) für die Überlassung seines Manuskripts und der Fotografien der *Liber*-Hss. Die Durchsicht des Inhalts des *Liber* hat ein deutlich erkennbares gemeinsames Interesse bezüglich der als relevant erachteten Bibelpassagen gezeigt, textkritisch bestehen jedoch keine engeren Verbindungen zwischen den Texten.

46 KOTTJE, Raymund: Studien zum Einfluss des Alten Testamentes auf Recht und Liturgie des frühen Mittelalters (6.–8. Jahrhundert) (Bonner historische Forschungen 23), Bonn ²1970, S. 51, S. 67, S. 80. Vgl. ANGENENDT: Monachi, S. 71f.

47 FEHRLE, Eugen: Inwieweit können die Predigtanweisungen des hl. Pirmin als Quelle für alemannischen und fränkischen Volksglauben angesehen werden?, in: Oberdeutsche Zeitschrift für Volkskunde 1 (1927), S. 97–109.

48 Die Stelle ist bei JECKER: Heimat, S. 55,3f., der der hier verderbten Lesart der Hs. A *manus* folgt und zu *manes* konjiziert, und somit auch in der Übersetzung ENGELMANN: Pastoralbüchlein, S. 55 mit „die Seelen der Verstorbenen" sinnentstellt wiedergegeben. Ob es sich um echten Vermehrungszauber handelt, oder aber um Schadenszauber im Sinne des Herüberziehens der Ernte eines anderen auf das eigene Feld, ist für die Diskussion der Stelle nicht entscheidend.

49 Der betreffende Abschnitt ist nur in der Hs. British Library, Cotton MS. Nero A II, „entstanden um 778, wahrscheinlich in Frankreich, vielleicht auch in Norditalien [Verona]" (so nach ANGENENDT: Monachi, S. 71) enthalten und ediert in: LEVISON, Wilhelm: England and the Continent in the Eighth Century, Oxford ²1949, S. 307–312, hier S. 310f.; Nach LEVISON: England, S. 303 ist die Hs. an einem Ort „connected with an Irish circle" entstanden. Auf diesem Text beruht auch der Eintrag *mavones* in: DUCANGE, Charles: Glossarium mediae et infimae Latinitatis, Bd. IV–V (G–N), 1883–1887, S. 312 und danach auch: *mavo, -nis m.* [orig. incert.] *démon* in: BLATT, Franz (Hg.): Novum Glossarium Mediae Latinitatis, Bd. M–N, Kopenhagen 1959–1969, Sp. 184.

ses Begriffs findet man in der älteren, anonymen *Vita Richarii*.[50]
Dass jeweils inhaltlich dieselben Sachverhalte vorliegen, zeigt die Gegenüberstellung der drei Textabschnitte:

Vita Richarii primigenia:	*Excarpsum de diversis auct.:*	*Scarapsus:*
Malefacere adfirmabant stulti, quod essent dusi (dusie 2*); hemaones (manes* 2*) vocitabant, qui deum non credebant; eis reputabant, quod segetes tollebant.*[51] (ed. B. KRUSCH, S. 445,4f.)	*et mavonis, quasi messis et vindemia portari possint.*[52] (LEVISON: England, S. 311)	c. 22: *nec aliquid pro hoc eis dare, qui dicunt, quod maones (manus* A*) fructa tollere possint.*[53] (entspricht JECKER: Heimat, S. 55,3f.)

Der gemeinsame Terminus *maones/mavonis* (*-es*) entspricht den handschriftlich überlieferten Lesarten *hemaones/*(*dusi*)*e manes*, die in der älteren *Vita Richarii* aus dem Ende des 7. Jahrhundert mit *dusi* verbunden werden und die im *Excarpsum* zuvor schon leicht abgewandelt als *dusiolus* erscheinen. Unter *dusii* sind die schon bei Augustinus, *De Civitate Dei*, XV, 23[54] und danach bei Isidor, *Etym.* VIII,11,103 erwähnten gallischen *incubi*, regionale (Wald-)Geister zu verstehen: *Vnde et Incubi dicuntur ab incumbendo, hoc est stuprando. Saepe enim inprobi existunt etiam mulieribus, et earum peragunt concubitum: quos daemones Galli Dusios vocant, quia adsidue hanc peragunt inmunditiam.*[55] Die *Vita Richarii* rezipiert nicht mehr den ursprünglichen Sinn der Isidor-Stelle, sondern vielmehr nur noch den Wortlaut der Erklärung von *dusii: quos daemones Galli dusios vocant.*

Da eine romanische Etymologie für *maones/hemaones* nach dem Stand der Dinge ausgeschlossen bleibt,[56] bietet sich eine rein paläographisch zu erklärende Entstehung und eine rein literarische Verbreitung dieses neu geprägten Begriffes an: *daemones > haemones ≥ hemaones > h*(*oc*) *e*(*st*) *maones > maones ≥ mauones.*[57]

Der Anlaut h kann durch die spiegelverkehrte Anfügung des halbkreisförmigen d-Bogens bereits im Archetypus der Vita zu h verschrieben sein. Über die

50 Vita Richarii, S. 4. Von den beiden verwendeten Hss. ist die Haupt-Hs. 1 eine ehemals Salzburger, jetzt Wiener Hs. des 9., die Hs. 2 eine aus dem Kloster Mont St.-Michel stammende des 13. Jh.
51 Etwa: „Böses zu tun versicherten die Törichten, dass sie dusii seien; hemaones nannte man sie gewöhnlich, die nicht an Gott glaubten, denen man zurechnete, dass sie Feld(-Ertrag) brächten".
52 „[...] und die *mavones* als ob sie (Feld-)Ernte(ertrag) und Wein(ernte) bringen könnten".
53 „[...] und nicht irgendetwas dafür denen geben, die sagen, dass die *maones* Erntefrüchte/(-Ertrag) bringen könnten".
54 Vgl. LEVISON: England, S. 310, Anm. 4; KRUSCH: Vita Richarii, S. 445 Anm. 5.
55 LINDSAY: Isidori Etymologiae.
56 BANNIARD: Seuils et frontières, S. 176 hat diesen Ausdruck in seiner sprachlichen Analyse der Vita dem Sinn der verwendeten Vorlage entsprechend, jedoch gegen die handschriftliche Überlieferung, zu *daemones* konjiziert. *Maones* lässt sich entweder an die Kette *Maiorica, Mallorca, Mayonnaise* (so Roger WRIGHT, mündlich) anschließen, einer Richtung, der die Lesart *maiores fructus* der Hs. T folgt, oder aber an den Eintrag des Novum Glossarium, BLATT, Sp. 184: *mao, -nis* v. *madonus*, ital. *mattone* (Ziegel, Langeweiler).
57 Zu *uo* diphthongiertes *o* tritt vorübergehend auch im Altfranzösischen auf. Siehe STOTZ, Peter: Handbuch zur lateinischen Sprache des Mittelalters, Bd. 3, München 1996, S. 59f., § 46.

Interpretation von *he* als *hoc est* wird *maones* zum eigenständigen Begriff. Letzteres wird der Anlass für das Fehlen dieser ersten Silbe des entstandenen neuen Wortes bei Pirmin, im *Excarpsum* und der Hs. 2 der Vita gewesen sein. Dass sich nach Ansicht der christlichen Autoren hinter vorchristlichen Göttern Dämonen und Magier, letztlich betrügerische Menschen verbergen,[58] kann die Akzeptanz des neuen Terminus gefördert haben; er steht lautlich und orthographisch deutlich in der Nähe der umgangsprachlichen Betrüger schlechthin, der *mangones*, der antiken betrügerischen (Sklaven-)Händler, denen in Quellen des Mittelalters nach Sinn und Verwendung – und selbst noch im Neuhochdeutschen – die sprichwörtlichen Rosstäuscher entsprechen.[59]

Die ältere Vita des Lokalheiligen von Centula-St. Riquier (Bistum Amiens) ist in der westlichen Picardie (Grafschaft Ponthieu) angesiedelt und auch dort – zum lokalen Gebrauch – entstanden. Die Verehrung des Heiligen erstreckte sich von hier aus entlang der Kanalküste Richtung Seinemündung und nach Flandern.[60] Sie ist der älteste der Texte, steht zeitlich dem *Scarapsus* jedoch schon recht nahe. Der *Scarapsus* und das *Excarpsum* stehen in keinem direkten Abhängigkeitsverhältnis zueinander, sie schöpfen jedoch, wie gerade die diskutierte Stelle zeigt, aus einem gemeinsamen regionalen, vielleicht sogar konkreter aus einem bibliotheksinternen Fundus an gesammelten vorchristlichen religiösen Vorstellungen und Brauchtumstermini respektive dessen philologisch-literarischem, teilweise wenigstens auch verderbtem Niederschlag. Letztere Annahme wird auch durch die unterschiedliche Einbettung der zweiten gemeinsamen terminologischen Besonderheit, den *inpurias* (= Feuerschauerinnen) im *Excarpsum* und im *Scarapsus* deutlich. Das *Excarpsum* bietet mit *inpurias quod mensas conponunt* eine Kontamination zweier aufeinander folgender Stellen der Eligius-Kompilation[61] und entspricht nicht dem Gebrauch des Terminus bei Pirmin c. 22, wo es heißt, dass die *inpuriae* „Menschen auf die Dächer setzen, um ihnen irgendetwas ankündigen zu können, was ihnen an Gutem oder Schlechtem geschehen wird".[62]

---

58 Dies wird ausführlich behandelt bei Martin von Braga, DCR, cc. 7-9, ed. v. BARLOW: Martini opera, S. 188f.

59 Vgl. Lexicon Latinitatis Nederlandicae Mediae Aevi, Bd. 5, Leiden 1994, S. 2905 mit einschlägigen Belegen, auch in der Schreibvariante *magonibus*; vgl. aus dem weiteren Textumfeld des *Scarapsus* bes.: Admonitio generalis, c. 79, ed. v. Alfred BORETIUS (MGH LL Capit. reg. Francorum 1), Hannover 1883, S. 52–62, S. 60, Z. 40 mit Anm. 16.

60 Zur Entstehung und Datierung der Vita sowie zur Verbreitung des Heiligenkultes vgl.: POULIN, Joseph-Claude: Richarius, in: LexMA, Bd. 7 (1999), Sp. 828f.

61 [...] *neque mensas super noctem conponat neque strenas aut bibitiones superfluas exerceat. Nullus christianus inpuras credat neque in cantu sedeat* [...]. Vita Eligii, II, 16, ed. v. Bruno KRUSCH (MGH SS rer. Merov. 4), Hannover/Leipzig 1902, S. 705–708, S. 705,14f.; Vita Eligii, II, c. 15, PL 87, Sp. 528C. Die *Vita Eligii* schöpft, was das „Tische bereiten" betrifft, direkt aus Caesarius von Arles, Sermo 192 (CCSL 104), S. 781:740,10–12: *Aliqui etiam rustici mensulas suas in ista nocte, quae praeteriit, plenas multis rebus,* [...] *conponentes, tota nocte sic conpositas esse volunt,* [...].

62 [...] <ne>*que in inpurias, qui dicunt hominis super tectus mittere, ut aliqua possent eis denunciare, quod eis bona aut mala adveniat*; entspricht JECKER: Heimat, S. 55,5–7. Die Eligius-Kompilation (Anm. 51) gibt keine Auskunft darüber, was *inpuriae* sind oder machen.

Die Unklarheit, die seitens der Autoren über Bezeichnung und Funktion der Dämonen/Personen wie *maones* und *inpuriae* besteht, zeigt aber auch eine gewisse Distanz zu der sie umgebenden Welt der Laien. Das *Excarpsum* erweist sich als wichtiges Bindeglied zwischen dem *Scarapsus* und der Eligiuskompilation. *Excarpsum* und *Scarapsus* sind zudem auf das engste mit der älteren *Vita Richarii* verbunden.

Noch einmal erinnert sei an die handschriftliche Verbreitung des *Scarapsus* im nunmehr auf die Picardie und benachbarte nördlichere Gebiete eingegrenzten Raum: Der *Scarapsus* ist in der Haupt-Hs. der Corbi-Redaktion der *Coll. Vet. Gall.* enthalten (=A), deren mittelalterliche Bibliotheksheimat St. Amand war. Die Präsenz des Werkes im Raum zeigt auch die „nicht fern von Reims"[63] entstandene Hs. C des *Scarapsus*, deren mittelalterliche Bibliotheksheimat Corbie war. Wenn Pirmin seine Ausbildung und mit ihr sein literarisches Material – gegebenenfalls über selbst angelegte Exzerptsammlungen – aus dem umrissenen Raum bezogen hat, dann ist es auch nicht mehr ganz unplausibel, das ominöse *Melcis castellum* der Pirmin-Vita, den Ort, von dem aus Pirmin an den Bodensee eingeladen worden sein soll, in dieser Richtung zu suchen: Es bietet sich heute wieder das südlich von Brüssel gelegene, mittelalterlich bezeugte Meltburch an.[64] Und auch personale beziehungsweise persönliche Bezüge zur angelsächsischen Mission im betreffenden Raum sind zeitlich und räumlich naheliegend. Vorrangig ist hier der Friesenapostel Willibrord zu nennen, der – wegen der Seltenheit des Namens – sehr wahrscheinlich auch derjenige ist, der das sogenannte Widegern-Privileg für das Pirminkloster Murbach „im Namen Gottes" mitunterzeichnete.[65]

3. Zum sprachlichen Hintergrund des Scarapsus

Sprachlich markant sind neben allerlei Einschränkungen im Formengebrauch[66] insbesondere die negierten Imperative vom Typ non + Imp. I (*non facite*), die meist gemischt mit anderen Formen des Verbotes gebraucht werden.

---

63 Bernhard BISCHOFF zitiert nach ANGENENDT: Monachi, S. 57.
64 Vita Pirminii, c. 1, ed. v. ANTONI: Leben und Taten, S. 56, der in der Einleitung S. 9f. allerdings der Deutung ‚Meaux' folgt; ed. v. HOLDER-EGGER (Anm. 5), S. 21f.; MORIN, Germain: Le Meltis castellum des chorévêques Pirmin et Landri, Meltburch en Brabant?, in: Revue Bénédictine 29 (1912), S. 262–273; MORIN, Germain: Saint Pirmin en Brabant, in: Revue d'histoire ecclésiastique 36 (1940), S. 8–18, 14; vgl. hierzu ANGENENDT: Monachi, S. 41.
65 Regesta Alsatiae aevi Merovingici et Karolini (496–918), Bd. 1, ed. v. Albert BRUCKNER, Straßburg/Zürich 1949, Nr. 113, S. 53–57, hier S. 56; Chartae latinae antiquiores 19, ed. v. Hartmut ATSMA/Jean VEZIN/Robert MARICHAL, Zürich 1987, S. [5-7] Nr. 671; LÖWE: Pirmin, S. 226f., diskutiert bei ANGENENDT: Monachi, S. 45; vgl. METZNER, Ernst: Der heilige Pirminus. Namen und Herkunft, Klosterheimat und Wirkungskreis (Protokolle des Konstanzer Arbeitskreises für mittelalterliche Geschichte 293), Konstanz 1987, S. 1–19, hier S. 6. Für METZNER ist Pirmin auf Grund seines Namens ein Niederrheinfranke oder Reichsfriese aus dem Raum zwischen Köln und Utrecht (s. hierzu ibid., S. 4–6).
66 Der *Scarapsus* entspricht bezüglich der Nominalflexion dem sprachlichen Befund der *Vita Richarii*. Siehe BANNIARD: Seuils et frontières, S. 177f.

Auf der Basis der Orthographie der ältesten Hs. A illustriert dies der folgende Abschnitt aus c. 28b:

> *Nullus ex vobis homicidium faciat, non adulteratae, fornicationem et libidinem* [*et*] *inmunditiam et inpudicitiam fugite. Furtum non facite, non concupiscite rem proximi vestri, falsum testimonium non dicite, iram non perficite* (*preficite* A) *iracundiam usque ad noctem non servate* (*res-*Hss.)*, sed ante solis occaso in pace reddite. Dolum et malitiam in cordibus vestris non tenete; falsam pacem inter vos non facite; non mentire* (*mentite* CD, *mentites* E, *mentimini* HT) *invicem. Nolite iurare nec periurare; malum pro malum non reddite; iniuste iniuriam* <*vel*> *male ordine nulle homine* [*ne*] *faciatis; sed si aliquis vobis iniuriam fecerit, propter deum pacienter sustinete. Inimicus* ⌜*vestros*⌝ *dilegite et pro ipsus orate. Non maledicite, et siquis vos* ⌜*maledixerit*⌝*, non remaledicite, sed amplius benedicite, et persecutionem propter iustitiam sustinete.* [...] *multum loqui et verba vana non amate* (*amaretis* E) [...]*.*
> (entspricht JECKER: Heimat, S. 66,14–67,10)

Die Formen weisen auf eine Varietät des gesprochenen beziehungsweise nicht-literarischen Lateins hin,[67] die zwar insgesamt alt ist, jedoch üblicherweise mit *ne* statt *non* gebildet wird, und seit Ciceros Zeiten in der Prosa überhaupt vermieden wird.[68] Belege für diesen Verbotstyp sind demnach selten, wenn sie auch seit dem 6. Jahrhundert etwas weniger rar zu sein scheinen.[69]

Der *Scarapsus* gehört diachron einer Sprachstufe an, die die Akzeptanz dieser Formen durch die Hörer voraussetzt. Diese Sprachstufe muss zeitlich dem Altfranzösischen vorausgehen, weil der Autor sonst den Typ *non facitis, non dicitis* gewählt hätte.[70] Morphologisch ist der Übergang zur altfranzösichen Sprachstufe – die man im Norden mit Banniard in die zweite Hälfte des 8. Jahrhundert setzen darf[71] – also noch nicht vollständig vollzogen, der *Scarapsus* ist ein Text der Umbruchzeit. Das passt zu der aus den verwendeten Vorlagen rekonstruierten Abfassungszeit, zur handschriftlichen Überlieferung und zur zeitlichen Einordnung des Autors; als Schluss aus diesem Merkmalsbündel ist jetzt besonders hervorzuheben:

Der Autor schreibt in seinen eigenformulierten Abschnitten im rezipientenorientierten Register des *Sermo rusticus* seiner Gegenwartssprache.

Ein entsprechender Abschnitt wie der aus dem c. 28b des *Scarapsus* findet sich auch in der langen Eligius-Kompilation beziehungsweise in deren Hauptquelle, der sogenannten *Praedicatio Eligii*. Die angebliche Eligius-Predigt und der *Scarapsus*

---

67 Zum Folgenden vgl. LÖFSTEDT, Leena: Les expressions du commandement et de la défense en latin et leur survie dans les langues romanes (Mémoires de la Société néophilologique de Helsinki 29), Helsinki 1966.

68 LÖFSTEDT: Expressions, S. 208.

69 Siehe LÖFSTEDT: Expressions, S. 63–66 mit den bekannten Belegen, zu denen immerhin auch ein vereinzeltes Vorkommen bei Augustinus (Epist. 105,15: *immo vos non recedite, sed accedite*) zählt. Auch im italienischen Raum, in dem diese Verbotsform einzelsprachlich fortgesetzt wird, erscheint der Typ in den Quellen selten. Aus dem Text- und Zeitumfeld des *Scarapsus* findet man noch in der Admonitio generalis, c. 72, ed. v. BORETIUS (Anm. 59), S. 60,5f.: *Et pueros vestros non sinite eos vel legendo vel scribendo corrumpere.*

70 Siehe RHEINFELDER, Hans: Altfranzösische Grammatik, Bd. 2, München 1967, S. 201: Der Imperativ 2. Pers. Pl. wird durch den Indikativ ersetzt: *cantatis = chantez*! „singet".

71 BANNIARD: Viva voce, S. 488f., S. 492.

passen jeweils eine weithin bekannte Vorlage – die *Instrumenta bonorum operum* beziehungsweise c. 4 der *Regula Benedicti*[72] – um einige Zusätze erweitert an den neuen Kontext an, der *Scarapsus* allerdings unter minimalster Veränderung, Ps.-Eligius unter sparsamster Verwendung des Verbotstyps.[73] Am gewählten Ausdruck stört sich der Schreiber saec. VIII/IX der Hs. E: Er fügt meist an das Vorgefundene einfach ein -s an und überliefert somit *non facites, non dicites* usw.

4. Sprachliche Dynamik textintern: Zum didaktischen Aufbau und den sprachlichen Ebenen des *Scarapsus*

Ziel des Autors ist es, die christlich getauften Menschen mit Wissen über ihren Glauben und die daraus resultierenden Verhaltensregeln zu versorgen und sie so von aktuellen, oft beklagten Zuständen in der merowingerzeitlichen Kirche unabhängig zu machen. Sie sollen gemäß Matth. 23,3 selbst entscheiden können, was gut und was schlecht ist.[74] Grundlage der individuellen Entscheidung zur Besserung ist der Text der Heiligen Schrift,[75] motiviert ist die Abfassung des Traktates durch das Wissen um die nicht immer verlässliche Umsetzung der ethischen Normen seitens der in apostolischer Nachfolge eingesetzten Bischöfe, ein Thema, das ausführlich in c. 11 behandelt wird.

Aus diesem Grund wird der Dekalog bereits in die Heilsgeschichte eingeflochten.

Die Zehn Gebote werden hier – wohl primär nach Augustinus,[76] der Rahmen aber unter Benutzung auch des Bibeltextes[77] – als die auf zwei Steintafeln mit dem Zeigefinger Gottes eingeschriebenen und Moses übergebenen Gesetze überaus plastisch und somit anschaulich präsentiert:

C. 5: *Cum vidisset deus tanta malicia hominum, DEDIT per famulum suum MOYSEN LEGEM in DUAS TABULAS LAPIDIAS DIGITO DEI SCRIPTAS. In prima tabula: AUDI, ISRAEL, DOMINUS DEUS TUUS DEUS UNUS EST. NON ADSUMES NOMEN DEI TUI IN VANUM. ⌜MEMENTO⌝*

---

72 Siehe CSEL 75, S. 31–37, der Nachweis der Abhängigkeit des *Scarapsus* hiervon ist bereits erbracht von: HAUTKAPPE, Franz: Über die altdeutschen Beichten und ihre Beziehungen zu Cäsarius von Arles, Münster 1917, S. 100–102.

73 Vgl. Praedicatio Eligii (6), ed. v. KRUSCH (Anm. 61), S. 753,24: *falsum testimonium non dicite, furtum non facite* (= PL 87, Sp. 527B). Statt wie der *Scarapsus non mentire/mentite* hat Ps.-Eligius z. B. die positive Formulierung: *mendacium fugite* (ed. v. KRUSCH (Anm. 61), S. 753,23; PL 87, Sp. 527B).

74 C. 11, entspricht JECKER: Heimat, S. 42,13f.: *Qui* (ACD, *quae* Hss., *quod* E.) *dicunt vobis bona facere, facite, et, quod absit, si illi mala faciunt, facere nolite* (< Matth. 23,3, bearbeitet).

75 C. 1, entspricht JECKER: Heimat, S. 34,15–18: *Petimus ergo, karissimi, caritatem vestre* (*vestram* E), *ut que* (*quem* A) *pro salute vestra dicuntur, adtentius audiatis. Longus* (*longius* A) *quidem per* (*pro* A) *devinis scripturis ordo degeritur, sed vel* (*volo* A) *ut aliquantulum in memoria teneatis, pauca vobis de plurebus conmendamus* (< Martin v. Braga, DCR, c. 2,3–6, ed. v. BARLOW: Martini opera, S. 184.

76 Vgl. Augustinus, Sermo 9,7 (CCSL 41), S. 121; Sermo 248,4 (PL 38), Sp. 1160.

77 Vgl. Exod. 31,18: *Dedit quoque Mosi [...] duas tabulas testimonii lapideas scriptas digito Dei.*

(-*TOTE* A), *UT DIEM SABBATI SANCTIFICIS. SEX DIEBUS OPERAVERIS ET FACIES OMNIA OPE-RA TUA; SEPTIMUS AUTEM DIES SABBATUM EST DOMINI DEI TUI; NON FACIES OMNE OPUS. In secunda tabula: HONORA PATREM TUUM ET MATREM TUAM. NON MOECHABERIS. NON OCCI-DES. NON FURTUM FACIES. NON FALSUM TESTIMONIUM DICIS. NON CONCUPISCERE UXOREM PROXIMI TUI. Et iterum: NON CONCUPISCERE REM PROXIMI TUI.*
(entspricht JECKER: Heimat, S. 36,14–23)

Vorgestellt und eingeübt werden durch die Verteilung der Gebote auf die beiden Tafeln die christlichen Gebote der Gottesliebe (erste Tafel) und die der Nächsten-liebe (zweite Tafel).[78]

Nach der erstmaligen Aufzählung der Apostel folgt der Text des Vaterunser, so wie „der Herr sie es zu beten gelehrt hat":

C.7: *Et sic illis dominus docuit orare: PATER NOSTER, QUI IN CAELIS ES, SANCTIFICETUR NOMEN TUUM. VENIAT REGNUM TUUM. FIAT VOLUNTAS TUA SICUT IN CAELO ET IN TERRA. PANEM NOSTRUM SUPERSUBSTANCIALE (COTIDIANUM RD) DA NOBIS HODIE. ET DEMITTE NOBIS DEBITA NOSTRA, SICUT ET NOS DEMITTEMUS DEBITORIBUS NOSTRIS; ET NE INDUCAS NOS IN TEMPTATIONE, SED LIBERA NOS A MALO.*
(entspricht JECKER: Heimat, S. 38,1–6)

Der Text enthält die Lesart *panem supersubstantialem*, streng nach Matth. 6,11, nicht das „tägliche Brot", das Eingang in die volkssprachlichen Versionen – und als Variante auch in den *Scarapsus* – gefunden hat. Dem Autor geht es hier ersicht-lich um Authentizität in einem für Ritus und Dogma zentralen Text.

Den bereits eingeführten Aposteln als den verbindlichen, die Kirche begrün-denden Authoritäten (s. o. zu c. 11) obliegt es, den wichtigsten der dogmatischen Zentraltexte darzubieten – das Glaubensbekenntnis:

Das Credo wird – wie zum Beispiel auch im *Missale* von Bobbio[79] – in der seit alters beliebten Form des Apostelrahmens[80] geboten. Wie beim Vaterunser so steht auch hier im Text des Credo die Authentizität des Wortlautes des zu vermit-telnden Dogmas im Vordergrund:

C. 10: [...] *et cumposuerunt symbulum, hoc est: Petrus dixit: Credo in deum patrem omnipotentem, creatorem celi et terrae. Iohannes <ait>: Et in Iesum Christum, filium eius unicum dominum nostrum. Iacobus <dixit>: Que conceptus est de spiritu sancto, natus ex Maria virgine. Andreas <ait> Passus sub Pontio Pilato, crucifixus, mortuos et sepultus. Filippus <dixit>: Discendit ad inferna. Thomas <ait>: Tertia die resurrexit a mortuis. Bartholomeus <dixit>: Ascendit ad*

---

78 Vgl. den darauf rekurrierenden Abschnitt c.28b, entspricht JECKER: Heimat, S.66,10–13: *Credite ergo, karissimi, patrem et filium et spiritum sanctum unum deum in trignitate* (trin-Hss.), *et trignitatem* (trin- Hss.) *in unitatem, ET DELEGITE eum EX TOTO CORDE ET EX TOTA MENTE, <ET> EX TOTA VIRTUTA* (-TE Hss.), *et deligite prosximus* (prox-Hss.) *vestros sicut vosmetipsos* sowie ANGENENDT: Monachi, S. 73 zu den monastischen Parallelen.

79 Vgl. LOWE, Elias A. (Hg.): The Bobbio Missal. A Gallican Mass-Book, MS. Paris. Lat. 13246, (Henry Bradshaw Society 58), London 1920, S. 181.

80 Siehe hierzu JECKER: Heimat, S.99–102. Der Rahmentext ist nach der vollständigen Version der Hs. B ergänzt, einen jeweils an unterschiedlichen Stellen durch Vertauschung von *dixit* und *ait* defekten Rahmen bieten die Hss. E und T des *Scarapsus* sowie die Hs. S1 der *Coll. Vet. Gall.* Vgl. MORDEK: Kirchenrecht, S. 359f.

celos, sedit ad dexteram dei, patris omnipotentis. Matheus <ait>: Inde venturus iudicare vivus et mortuus. Item Iacobus Alfei <dixit>: Credo in spiritum sanctum. Simon Zelothis <ait>: Sanctam ecclesiam catholicam. Iudas Iacobi <dixit>: Sanctorum communionem, remissionem peccatorum. Item Thomas <ait>: Carnis resurrectionem, [in] vitam aeternam. Amen.

(entspricht JECKER: Heimat, S. 41,14–26)

Es gibt keinen zweiten Text, der diese Version des Apostelrahmens so stringent durchkomponiert bietet wie der *Scarapsus*. Je zwei Apostel treten hier jeweils gemeinsam auf und tragen ihren Teil des Credo vor.[81] Die vom Autor gewählte Form und ihre sprachliche Repräsentation durch den abwechselnden Gebrauch der Verben *dixit* und *ait* erinnert nicht zufällig an liturgischen Wechselgesang. Dass auch die Benutzer des Textes dies so interpretiert haben, zeigt die Version der Hs. N, die im ersten Paar nach *dixit* die Variante *respondit* folgen lässt.

Der Text entspricht dem *Textus receptus* des Apostolischen Glaubensbekenntnisses ohne jegliches eigenständig Pirminische oder sonstiges regionales Kolorit.[82]

Weil Wiederholung dem Ziel des *Scarapsus* dienlich ist, wird das Credo noch zwei weitere Male, selbstverständlich in exakt demselben Wortlaut, geboten. Ein Mal im dritten, dem Wiederholungsteil des *Scarapsus* c. 28b, ein Mal wie in der Vorlage Martins von Braga, DCR, c. 15[83] abschnittsweise eingebettet in die Wort-für-Wort gebotene Taufliturgie des c. 12, die auch die liturgischen Regieanweisungen enthält und die rituellen Handlungen erklärt und vor allem mit dem den Textabschnitt einleitenden Vollzitat der liturgischen Stelle Ezech. 36, 25f.: *Effundam super vos aquam munda* (-*am* Hss.) [...][84] die religiöse Grundstimmung der Taufe erneut evoziert und nachvollziehbar macht.

Der *Scarapsus* bietet in beiden Versionen des Credo handlungsorientierte religiöse Dramaturgie. Ein Gespür für wirksame Präsentation zeigt auch das Arrangement des Dekalogs. Allen präsentierten glaubensrelevanten Texten gemein – dies gilt auch für das Vaterunser – ist die Bestrebung, einen gesicherten, authentischen Text zu bieten.

Neben diesen offen am korrekten Ritus orientierten Abschnitten findet sich eine subtil dies unterfütternde zweite Ebene:

Die heilsgeschichtliche Erzählung von Leben, Passion und Auferstehung Christi wird zugleich zur Vorstellung und Erklärung der wichtigsten Stationen des Kirchenjahres benutzt, der kirchliche Jahreszyklus mit der (linearen, eschatologischen) Heilsgeschichte synchronisiert.

---

81 Da die Zwölfzahl durch das Ausscheiden des Judas Ischarioth nicht erreicht wird, darf Thomas, der Zweifler an der leiblichen Auferstehung Christi, zwei Mal sprechen. CASPARI, Carl P.: Ungedruckte, unbeachtete und wenig beachtete Quellen zur Geschichte des Taufsymbols und der Glaubensregel, Bd. 3, Christiania 1875, S. 252f., Anm. 435.

82 Insofern ist neben JECKER: Heimat, S. 102 auch der Text bei DENZINGER, Heinrich/HÜHNERBACH, Peter (Hg.): Kompendium der Glaubensbekenntnisse und kirchlichen Lehrentscheidungen, Freiburg 1999, S. 28 und S. 32 zu korrigieren.

83 BARLOW: Martini opera, S. 196f.

84 Entspricht JECKER: Heimat, S. 42,23–43,1; vgl. ANDRIEU, Michel: Les Ordines Romani du Haut Moyen Age, Louvain 1931–1961, Bd. 2, Ordo Romanus XI,28, S. 424; ANGENENDT, Arnold: Geschichte der Religiosität im Mittelalter, Darmstadt 1997, S. 464.

Ein Beispiel aus den cc. 8 und 9 illustriert das Verfahren:

C. 8: [...] *venit ad cenam quinta (quinque A) feria, que vocatur die (dies T) Iovis et cena domini.*
C. 9: *Et hoc actum est quinta feria, que vocatur dies Iovis, quod est ascensio domini.*
(entspricht JECKER: Heimat, S. 39,7f. und 41,4f.)

Zwar werden die Wochentage nach dem kirchlich gewünschten Muster der schlichten Durchzählung eingeführt und geübt, auf die rezipientenbezogen nachgereichte Erwähnung der vorchristlichen Namen kann und will der Autor jedoch nicht verzichten.

Der *Scarapsus*-Autor ist – wie das letzte Beispiel gezeigt hat – durchaus Realist und knüpft an den Wissensstand und den Erwartungshorizont seiner Rezipienten an. Aus diesem Grund füllt er den Abschnitt über das Leben Jesu mit dem Inhalt an, von dem er sich den größten Anklang bei den Rezipienten verspricht: Das sind die Wundertaten Jesu, geboten in Form eines biblischen *Cento*:

C. 7: *Et ipse Christus, filius dei, de aqua vinum fecit, et de quinque panis et duos pisces quinque milia populo saciavit, et super mare pedibus ambulavit, et leprosus mundavit, et demonia eiecit, ET SURDUS FECIT AUDIRE ET MUTUS LOQUE, et paraliticus sanavit, et cecus inluminavit, et mortuus suscitavit, ET OMNEM INFIRMITATEM ET LANGUORE IN POPULO SANAVIT.*
(entspricht JECKER: Heimat, S. 38,6-11)

Heiligkeit ist zugleich die Fähigkeit Wunder zu wirken, in Zeiten primär agrarischer Subsistenzwirtschaft – erinnert sei an das oben S. 284 behandelte *maones*-Problem – bietet sich der Einstieg über die Mehrungswunder an, gefolgt von Wundern, die die heilenden Kräfte Jesu thematisieren. Die Argumente des *Cento* sind die der frühmittelalterlichen Volkspredigt insgesamt, deren bildliche Entsprechungen beispielsweise auf den (nach neuerer Forschungsmeinung) spätkarolingischen Wandbildern von St. Georg auf der Insel Reichenau noch heute zu betrachten sind.[85]

Dynamik ist hier also der subtile Wechsel von der Ebene der Bedürfnisse und Erfahrungswelt der Rezipienten (Mangel und Mehrung, Krankheit und Heilung) zur Ebene des den Glauben und seine Inhalte vermittelnden Katecheten, der auf diesem Weg den Heiland volkstümlich einführen kann. Aber dies durchaus im biblischen Wortlaut (bzw. Register), den er (oder das er), der unmittelbar verstanden werden will, gerade noch benutzen darf.[86]

---

85 Man vergleiche den Text des *Scarapsus-Cento* mit der Bilderthematik von Sankt Georg: Wasser zu Wein machen, mit fünf Broten und zwei Fischen 5000 Menschen sättigen, über das Wasser gehen, Aussätzige heilen (= Bild 5, Südwand Nr. 1), Dämonen austreiben (= Bild 1, Nordwand Nr. 1), Tote auferwecken (= Bilder 6–8, Südwand Nr. 2–4), Taube hören und Stumme sprechen machen, Gelähmte heilen und Blinden das Licht geben (= Bild 4, Nordwand Nr. 4), jedes Gebrechen und jede Krankheit des Volkes heilen (= summarisch Bild 2, Nordwand Nr. 2), vgl. ERDMANN, Wolfgang: Die acht ottonischen Wandbilder der Wunder Jesu in St. Georg zu Reichenau-Oberzell, Sigmaringen 1983.

86 Vgl. BANNIARD: Viva voce, S. 489 zur Verständlichkeit biblisch-liturgischer Textstellen im hier relevanten Zeitraum S. 650–750.

5. Textauthentizität im *Scarapsus* – Ergänzendes zum Titelvermerk: *De singulis libris cannonnicis scarapsus.*

Der erweiterte Titel des *Scarapsus* in E, für den Autor eigentlich eine Art kirchliche Approbation in Gestalt eines bibliographischen Nebeneintrags, verweist bereits auf ein bestimmtes Merkmal, das von frühmittelalterlichen Benutzern auch als solches erkannt und gewürdigt wurde: die angestrebte Authentizität bei der Wiedergabe wichtiger Glaubenssätze.

De singulis libris cannonnicis scarapsus heißt, er ist aus einzelnen theologisch zuverlässigen Büchern ganz im Sinne von c. 72 der *Admonitio generalis*[87] zusammengestellt und somit für die Unterweisung der Kleriker wie auch der Laien geeignet.

Dieses Streben nach einem authentischen Text beziehungsweise dessen zuverlässiger Wiedergabe zeigt sich auch in der oft sehr exakten Darbietung biblischer Textstellen wie der langen Perikope Matth. 4,2–11 in c. 7 über die Versuchung Jesu,[88] teils sogar in Form von Wiederherstellung des genauen biblischen Wortlautes gegen den Wortlaut der verwendeten literarischen Vorlage:

Das gekürzte Jesaia-Zitat in c. 1 (Isai. 58,1): *CLAMA, NE CESSIS, QUASI TUBA EXALTA VOCEM TUAM ET ADNUNTIA POPULO MEO SCELERA EORUM* ist (indirekt?) Caesarius, *Sermo* 183,1[89] entnommen, der jedoch statt *scelera* – hier wie sonst auch – die Lesart *peccata* (< der Fortsetzung [...] *et domui Iacob peccata eorum*) überliefert (entspricht JECKER: Heimat, S. 34,5f.).

In c. 3 wird Martin v. Braga, DCR, c. 4,[90] nach dem Bibeltext Gen. 2,7 korrigiert:

Post istam ruinam angelorum FORMAVIT DEUS HOMINEM DE LIMO TERRE (entspricht JECKER: Heimat, S. 35,13f.).

Texte von unsicherer Qualität und Provenienz werden kritisch-emendatorisch an Hand der erschlossenen patristischen Vorlagen ausgerichtet:

Die sogenannte *Doctrina cuiusdam sancti viri* (= Ps.-Caesarius, *Homilia* 17) korrigiert und ergänzt er in c. 33 nach der dort ausgeschriebenen Vorlage Isidor, *Sententiae* III,1,3, nach einem Werk, das ihm bestens bekannt war:[91]

---

87 BORETIUS: Admonitio generalis, S. 60,3f.: [...] *et libros catholicos bene emendate*; zu den engen Verbindungen zwischen weltlicher *Admonitio* und kirchlicher *Praedicatio* in den Kapitularien siehe jetzt BUCK, Thomas M.: Admonitio und Praedicatio. Zur religiös-pastoralen Dimension von Kapitularien und kapitulariennahen Texten (507–814) (Freiburger Beiträge zur mittelalterlichen Geschichte 9), Frankfurt a. M. 1997.

88 Der Text ist reine *Vulgata*, die in der Edition JECKER: Heimat, S. 38,11–21 anklingenden *Vetus-Latina* Lesarten, namentlich *procidens* statt *cadens* in Matth. 4,9, sind durchweg Sonderlesarten der Hs. E. Vgl. zu den Varianten HAUSWALD: Handschriftliche Überlieferung, S. 114–116.

89 CCSL 104, S. 744: 703,18f.

90 BARLOW: Martini opera, S. 185, c. 4,1f.: *Post istam ruinam angelicam placuit deo de limo terrae hominem plasmare.*

91 Aus den *Sententiae* schöpft Pirmin auch an anderen Stellen, vgl. JECKER: Heimat, S. 111 u. 115. Der Text der *Doctrina* ist mittels der oft besseren Hs. München, Bayerische Staatsbibliothek, Clm 6430 [saec. IX/X; Freising], fol. 86r (ehem. 66r) ergänzt.

Doctrina (= Homilia 17 Ps.- Caesarii):	Scarapsus:	Isidor:
Proinde beatus Ysidorus dicit: Nequaquam (nunquam PL) deus delinquentibus parcit (parcet PL), quoniam peccatores ideo (PL, fehlt Mü) flagello temporali per purgationem non ferit (per-ferit Mü, non castigat PL), ut iudicio aeterno poniendos relinquat;	c. 33: Proinde scriptum est: Nequaquam deus delinquentibus [non] parcit, quoniam peccatore aut[em] flagellum temporale ad purgationem ferit, aut aeternum iudicium poniendo relinquet, aut ipsi in se homo, quod male admiserit, puniendo ponit.	Nequaquam Deus delinquenti parcit, quoniam peccatorem aut flagello temporali ad purgationem ferit, aut iudicio aeterno puniendum relinquit, aut ipse in se homo paenitendo punit quod male admisit (q. m. ad. pa. ponet Hs. A v. Korr., - ponit Hs. A n. Korr.).
ac proinde est, quod Deus (Dominus PL) delinquentibus non parcet. (Mü = München, Clm 6430/PL 67, Sp. 1080D)	Ac proinde est, quod deus delinquente (-ti Hss.) non parcit (-et Hss.). (entspricht JECKER: Heimat, S. 72,2–6)	Ac proinde est quod Deus delinquenti non parcit. (Isidor: Sent. III, 1,3 [CCSL 111], S. 194,14–18)

Vom Autor angestrebt wurde der jeweils bestmögliche, der authentische Text: Biblisch – liturgisch – patristisch – nachpatristisch/pastoral und, wie die bisher vorgestellten Beispiele zeigen, auch in dieser hierarchischen Reihenfolge.

Diesem Phänomen, das der verständlichen vertikalen Kommunikation wegen der unterschiedlichen sprachlichen Zeitstufen der rezipierten Textabschnitte nicht unbedingt immer förderlich ist, steht polar die leicht verständliche, rezipientenorientierte Ausdrucksweise gegenüber.

So folgt auf den biblischen Lasterkatalog Gal 5,20f. in c. 28b unmittelbar:

[...] nolite talia facere, quia apostolus contestat, ut hoc non faciatis. Omnia, que deus per scriptura sancta iussit, ut non facerit homo, nullus Christianus presumat hoc facere, et quicumque contra dei precepta fecit, cito per puram confessionem et veram penitentiam cum operibus bonis et elymosinis iustis se emendet, antequam mors illum subeto rapiat. Omnia, que per sancta scriptura deus precepit facere, in omnibus custodite.
(entspricht JECKER: Heimat, S. 67,16–23).

(= gekürzt) Solches tut nicht, da ja der Apostel eindringlich mahnt, dass ihr solches nicht tut. Alles, was Gott durch die Heilige Schrift befohlen hat, dass es der Mensch nicht tue, das soll auch kein Christ zu tun wagen. Wer aber gegen Gottes Gesetze handelt, der soll sich sogleich [...] bessern [...]. Alles, was Gott durch die Heiligen Schriften zu tun geboten hat, das haltet in allem.

Sicherlich kennt der Autor mehr Verben für das Wortfeld tun/machen als nur *facere* – er benutzt sie aber nicht.

Der Autor verzichtet an zweifelsfrei eigenformulierten Stellen selbst auf minimalste Ausflüge in das Repertoire der lateinischen Stilistik wie etwa Hyperbaton oder rhythmische Satzschlüsse: Solcherlei findet sich nur ganz selten und mit einer Ausnahme ausschließlich in direkten Väterzitaten; sie sind wohl eher als mitgezogene und unbearbeitet stehen gelassene stilistische Fremdkörper denn als ein bewusster Zugriff auf das patristische Register zu bewerten.

Folgende Verstöße gegen die konsequente lineare Reihung der Satzglieder ohne Umstellung oder Aufsprengung einzelner Teile (Hyperbaton) können – ohne Anspruch auf Vollständigkeit – genannt werden:

C. 23 (JECKER: Heimat, S. 57,6): [...] *pro exquoquendo* (*-da* A) *pertinet cibo* < Martin v. Braga: DCR, c. 18,16f. (ed. BARLOW: Martini opera, S. 202).

C. 23 (JECKER: Heimat, S. 57,16): [...] *super apostulus* (*apostolos* Hss.) *sanctus discendit spiritus* < Isidor v. Sevilla: DEO, I,25,(3),19f. (CCSL 113, S. 28).

C. 26 (JECKER: Heimat, S. 60,14f.): [...] *dum in nostra sunt potestate remedia* < Caesarius v. Arles: Sermo 13,1 (CCSL 103, S. 65:63, 23f.).

Der selbstauferlegte Verzicht ist berechtigt: Selbst eine einfach religiöse Formel wie c. 33 *et gloriam possidebit aeternam* (*ET*) wird in den frühen beziehungsweise nicht-emendierten Hss. unweigerlich zu *et gloriam possedebit in aeternum* (ADHv. Korr., *in eterno* R, *in aeternam* H n.Korr.) (entspricht JECKER: Heimat, S. 72,15).

Neben der literarischen Produktion steht die zeitgenössische Gebrauchstextproduktion: Sie muss auf solcherlei die Kommunikation möglicherweise behindernde Fallstricke Rücksicht nehmen, wenn sie ihren Zweck erfüllen soll.

Die im Ergebnis erkennbare erstaunliche Polarisierung der verschiedenen sprachlichen Ebenen innerhalb des Urtextes ist – von unvermeidlicher Textverderbnis einmal abgesehen – durch glättende Eingriffe innerhalb der späteren Überlieferung zum Teil zurückgenommen, der Text sprachlich-stilistisch ‚nachgebessert' worden.

Am Ende des c. 7 zum Beispiel bringt E statt *sicut noster magister Christus docuit et illum vicit* die dem Schreiber angemessener erscheinende Wortfolge *sicut noster magister docuit Christus et illum vicit* (entspricht JECKER: Heimat, S. 39,5f.).

6. Zusammenfassung

Die sprachliche Verortung des Scarapsus macht die Identität von Herkunftsraum und frühmittelalterlichem Verbreitungsraum des Textes wahrscheinlich. Das nördliche Frankreich und die anschließenden südbelgischen Gebiete im weiteren, die Gegend entlang der Somme, die Picardie im engeren Sinne, kommen hier in Frage.

Das hat Rückwirkungen auf die Fragen nach Herkunft beziehungsweise monastischer Ausbildung des Autors.

Demnach darf man in Pirmin einen in Nordfrankreich, vielleicht in der Picardie, erzogenen Mönch sehen beziehungsweise einen, der intensive Kontakte zu dieser Region pflegte, von ihr beeinflusst wurde und durch sein Werk auch wieder auf sie Einfluss ausüben konnte. Dass der *Scarapsus*-Autor den Pseudobegriff *maones* (< *daemones*) für eine bestimmte Klasse von Feldgeistern übernimmt, zeigt, dass er aus keinem direkten, tieferen Wissen um die religiösen Verhältnisse der Region und deren Brauchtum schöpfen konnte. Seine wahrscheinliche monastische Heimat im nordostfranzösischen Raum ist also eher nicht mit der gentilen Heimat gleichzusetzen.

Der Autor wechselt in seinem Werk sehr geschickt die sprachlichen Ebenen:

Was die Unterweisung im Glauben betrifft, so holt er seine Rezipienten inhaltlich und sprachlich an der Stelle ab, an der sie sich hinsichtlich ihrer Lebenswelt und natürlich auch hinsichtlich ihrer christlichen Vorbildung befinden, und flicht dann en passant den katechetischen Stoff in möglichst authentischer Form ein.

Dies macht er sehr bildlich und handlungsorientiert. Mnemotechnische Verfahren und Wiederholung stützen sein didaktisches Anliegen.

Bewusste Schlichtheit in der Sprache bei eigenformulierten, direkt an die Rezipienten gerichteten Abschnitten und größtmögliche Authentizität im Ausdruck bei der Wiedergabe der exzerpierten Schriften steht gegenüber einem klassizistisch-literarischeren Stil vieler Texte ähnlichen Inhalts und vergleichbarer Entstehungszeit (des langen Sermo Ps.-Eligii z. B.), die wegen der fehlenden Nähe zur anvisierten Rezipientenschicht, wie sie hier für den Scarapsus herausgearbeitet wurde, jedoch hinter den Scarapsus zurücktreten müssen.

Martin Fuss

Gottesbezeichnungen im Althochdeutschen und im Altsächsischen[1]

Hebräisch, Griechisch und Lateinisch sind die *tres linguae sacrae*. Lateinisch wird in der Antike die Sprache des Christentums auf dem westeuropäischen Kontinent, und es ist die Sprache der Schriftlichkeit im frühen Mittelalter.[2] In der germanischen Volkssprache, im Althochdeutschen, setzt die Schriftlichkeit im 8. Jahrhundert mit der Glossierung lateinischer Texte als Lesehilfe zu Lern- und Unterrichtszwecken im klösterlichen Lateinunterricht ein. Ein entscheidender Auslöser für die Entstehung deutschsprachiger Texte gegen Ende des 8. Jahrhunderts und im 9. Jahrhundert war die Mission. Um eine illiterate, das heißt nicht lateinisch sprechende Bevölkerung zu erreichen, mussten die wichtigsten Stücke – biblische und katechetische Texte – in der Volkssprache zur Verfügung stehen. Die Grundkenntnisse des Glaubens sollten bei allen vorhanden sein, das wurde in der *Admonitio Generalis* Karls des Großen vom 23. März 789 festgeschrieben.[3] Die aus althochdeutscher Zeit überlieferten Texte sind deshalb fast alle christlich-religiösen Inhalts. Sie reichen von Wort-für-Wort-Übersetzungen aus dem Lateinischen bis hin zu eigenständigen Nachdichtungen biblischer Vorbilder. Zunächst war es kaum möglich, theologische oder philosophische Inhalte in der germanischen Volkssprache auszudrücken, dafür fehlten meist die Lexeme (Wörter als Bestandteile des Wortschatzes). Ab dem 8. Jahrhundert mussten, um die neuen christlichen Inhalte zu transportieren, vorhandene Lexeme gefunden werden, die geeignet waren, die neuen Bedeutungen wiederzugeben (Lehnbedeutungen oder Bedeutungslehnwörter); es mussten aus vorhandenem Sprachmaterial neue Wörter nach fremdem Vorbild gebildet werden (Lehnbildungen); schließlich mussten Fremdwörter germanisiert werden (Lehnwörter).[4]

---

1   Der Vortrag und diese überarbeitete Niederschrift basieren im Wesentlichen auf meiner Dissertation: Die religiöse Lexik des Althochdeutschen und Altsächsischen, Frankfurt a. M. u. a. 2000.

2   Ursprung und Hintergründe erläutert Michael Richter in seinem Beitrag: Concept and evolution of the *tres linguae sacrae*, in diesem Band. Im frühmittelalterlichen England war die Situation ähnlich, in Irland hatte dagegen die volkssprachliche Schriftlichkeit einen höheren Stellenwert, siehe dazu den Beitrag von Hermann Moisl: Language, literacy, and cultural development in early medieval England and Ireland, in diesem Band.

3   Ehrismann, Gustav: Geschichte der deutschen Literatur bis zum Ausgang des Mittelalters, Bd. 1, München 1966, S. 291–295; Meineke, Eckhard/Schwerdt, Judith: Einführung in das Althochdeutsche, Paderborn u. a. 2001, S. 96–99. Natürlich fanden solche Texte primär auf Lateinisch Verbreitung. Ein Beispiel ist der *Scarapsus* Pirmins, den Eckhard Hauswald in seinem Beitrag in diesem Band behandelt.

4   Termini nach Betz, Werner: Lehnwörter und Lehnprägungen im Vor- und Frühdeutschen, in: Maurer, Friedrich/Rupp, Heinz (Hg.): Deutsche Wortgeschichte, Bd. 1, Berlin/New York ³1974, S. 135–163. In Irland hatte sich zuvor bei der Christianisierung die Lexik auf ähnliche Weise entwickelt. Zu Erbwörtern und Lehngut im altirischen und walisischen christlichen Wortschatz

Die althochdeutsche Lexik umfasst ca. 28.000 Lexeme. Etwa 10% davon sind religiös; ‚religiös‘ als semantisches Merkmal eines Lexems bedeutet: Das Denotat oder Konnotat ist Bestandteil einer Ideologie mit überweltlichem Bezug, das heißt hier: der jüdisch-christlichen Glaubens- und Vorstellungswelt.

Gottesbezeichnungen haben in den Sprachen aller theistischen Religionen einen zentralen Platz. Beispielhaft für die religiöse Lexik des Althochdeutschen und Altsächsischen werden hier einige Gottesbezeichnungen behandelt. Zunächst das Wort *Gott*:

Ahd. *got*, as., altenglisch *god*, gotisch *guþ*, altnordisch *goð, guð*, gehen auf germ. **guða-*‚Gott, Gottheit‘, Pl. ‚Schicksalsmächte‘ zurück. **guða-* ist N., ein substantiviertes Partizip II. Die Anknüpfung an eine ie. Wurzel ist unsicher. Es könnte als Part. II ie. **ghuto-* ‚angerufen‘ zur Wurzel ie. **ghau-* ‚rufen, anrufen‘ gehören. Die substantivierte Form ie. **ghutom* bedeutete dann ‚das (durch Zauberwort) angerufene Wesen‘. Eine Anknüpfung an die Wurzel ie. **gheu-* ‚gießen‘ würde für germ. **guða-* auf die Bedeutung ‚das Wesen, dem ein Trank- oder Gussopfer dargebracht wird, dem geopfert wird‘ führen. Die Deutung des Partizips als ‚das (in Erz) Gegossene‘ ist weniger plausibel, denn dass der Gott der Juden und Christen mit einem Wort für ein Standbild bezeichnet worden wäre, ist schwer nachzuvollziehen (vgl. Ex 20,4, Deut 5,8 und besonders Leviticus 26,1). Shields führt urgermanisch **guðom* auf spätindoeuropäisch **gho-ut-óm* zurück. Ie. **gho-* ist deiktische Partikel, **-ut-* ist adverbiales Element mit der Bedeutung ‚upwards, outside‘; die Gesamtbedeutung sei ‚that one above, beyond‘. Das tabuierte Numinose wäre demnach mit einer Lokalisierung als Hüllwort bezeichnet worden. Durch gotisch *guþ* N. und ahd. *abgot* st. M. und N. ist bezeugt, dass das ursprüngliche Genus Neutrum ist. Dies lässt vermuten, germ. **guða-* habe zunächst eine hinter oder über den Göttern stehende Schicksalsmacht bezeichnet (Eggers). Der Übergang vom N. zum M. vollzog sich mit der Übernahme von *got* zur Bezeichnung des christlichen männlichen Schöpfergottes, *got* M. ist ein Wort mit einer christlichen Lehnbedeutung.[5]

---

siehe die Beiträge von Morfydd Owen (Some welsh words: language and religion in early Wales) und Próinséas Ní Chatháin (Some aspects of the vernacular vocabulary of Christianity in early Ireland), in diesem Band.

5   Die in den Fußnoten genannte Literatur stellt eine Auswahl dar. Sie wird im Folgenden meist stillschweigend herangezogen. Pfeifer, Wolfgang u.a.: Etymologisches Wörterbuch des Deutschen, Berlin ²1993; Kluge, Friedrich: Etymologisches Wörterbuch der deutschen Sprache, bearbeitet von Elmar Seebold, Berlin u.a. ²³1995. Dasselbe, bearbeitet von Walther Mitzka, Berlin u.a. ²¹1975, Artikel *Gott*. Die Schreibweise der Formen richtet sich nach Pfeifer oder Kluge/Seebold. Die dort verwendeten diakritischen Zeichen können hier aber aus technischen Gründen nicht wiedergegeben werden. Zur exakten Schreibweise sei daher auf diese Wörterbücher verwiesen. Grimm, Jacob/Grimm, Wilhelm: Deutsches Wörterbuch, Leipzig 1854–1971 (Neudruck München 1984), Art. *Gott*; Shields, Kenneth: A Proposal Regarding the Etymology of the Word God, in: Leuvense bijdragen 85 (1996), S. 69–74; Eggers, Hans: Deutsche Sprachgeschichte, Bd. 1, Hamburg 1986, S. 112; Wiens, Gerhard L.: Die frühchristlichen Gottesbezeichnungen im Germanisch-Althochdeutschen, Berlin 1935, S. 11f.; Berr, Samuel: An Etymological Glossary to the Old Saxon Heliand, Bern/Frankfurt a.M. 1971; Bosworth, Joseph/Toller, T. Northcote: An Anglo-Saxon Dictionary, mit Supplement, reprinted Oxford 1976; Feist,

got steht ganz überwiegend für *deus* der lat. Vorlage (meist der Vulgata), gibt aber auch vereinzelt *dominus* und *deitas, divinitas* wieder. Umgekehrt wird lat. *deus* allermeist durch *got* wiedergegeben, auch durch Ableitungen von und Komposita mit *got*.[6] In der ahd. Überlieferung ist *got* ca. 3900 mal belegt. Dazu kommen ca. 540 Belege aus dem altsächsischen Heliand (Sigle Hel) und der Altsächsischen Genesis (AGs).[7] Alle Belege sind religiös, das heißt sie beziehen sich auf das Denotat: ‚über den Menschen stehendes Wesen'. *got* bezeichnet ganz überwiegend (mit ca. 3800 Belegen) den christlichen Gott, daneben auch nichtchristliche Gottheiten. Im Fränkischen Taufgelöbnis (rheinfränkisch oder ostfränkisch, Anfang des 9. Jhs.) heißt es: *Forsahhistu allem them bluostrum indi den gelton indi den gotum, thie im heidene man zi bluostrum indi zi geldom enti zi gotum habent? Ih fursahhu.* (Schwörst du all den Opfergaben, den Opfern und den Göttern ab, die bei den Heiden als Opfergaben, Opfer und Götter gelten? Ich schwöre ab.)[8]

Das Nomen *got* ist ein Appellativum, eine Gattungsbezeichnung, es wird aber in der Regel, wie in der jüdisch-christlichen Religion überhaupt, als Personeneigenname (des Schöpfergottes und Gottvaters) verwendet. Ausnahmen liegen vor, wenn ahd. *got* mit Artikel oder Possessivpronomen steht, aber auch dann ist nicht immer klar, ob es sich um das Appellativum oder den Eigennamen handelt.

Der Artikel *got* im Leipziger Althochdeutschen Wörterbuch bietet eine Gliederung des Belegmaterials nach semantischen Kriterien. Die Lexik von Heliand und Altsächsischer Genesis ist durch das Wörterbuch von Sehrt erschlossen, aber nicht in semantischer Differenzierung.[9] Ordnet man die as. Belege dem semantischen Gliederungsschema des Leipziger Ahd. Wörterbuchs zu, so ergibt sich, dass viele semantische Kontexte des Lexems *got* – das heißt welche Eigenschaft

Sigmund: Vergleichendes Wörterbuch der gotischen Sprache, Leiden [3]1939; FISCHER, Bonifatius: Novae concordantiae bibliorum sacrorum iuxta vulgatam versionem, Bde. 1–5, Stuttgart 1977; GEORGES, Heinrich: Ausführliches lateinisch-deutsches Handwörterbuch, 2 Bde., Basel [11]1962; HEIDERMANNS, Frank: Etymologisches Wörterbuch der germanischen Primäradjektive, Berlin/New York 1993; LEHMANN, Winfred P.: A Gothic Etymological Dictionary, Leiden 1986; LLOYD, Albert L./SPRINGER, Otto: Etymologisches Wörterbuch des Althochdeutschen, Bd. 1, dazu: Wörterverzeichnisse, Göttingen/Zürich 1988; SCHÜTZEICHEL, Rudolf: Althochdeutsches Wörterbuch, Tübingen [5]1995; SLEUMER, Albert: Kirchenlateinisches Wörterbuch, Limburg a. d. Lahn 1926 (Neudruck Hildesheim 1990); SPLETT, Jochen: Althochdeutsches Wörterbuch. Analyse der Wortfamilienstrukturen des Althochdeutschen, Bde. I,1, I,2, II, Berlin/New York 1993.

6 KÖBLER, Gerhard: Wörterbuch des althochdeutschen Sprachschatzes, Paderborn u.a. 1993, Art. *got*; KÖBLER, Gerhard: Lateinisch-althochdeutsches Wörterbuch, Göttingen u.a. 1971, Art. *deus*, siehe auch G. Köblers Verzeichnisse zu den Übersetzungsgleichungen ahd. Texte in Einzelbänden.

7 Textausgabe: Heliand und Genesis, ed. v. Otto BEHAGHEL und bearb. v. Burkhard TAEGER, Tübingen [9]1984.

8 Die kleineren althochdeutschen Sprachdenkmäler, ed. v. Elias von STEINMEYER: Sigle S, Dublin/Zürich [3]1971, hier S 23,3–5. Übersetzung: Althochdeutsche Literatur. Ausgewählte Texte mit Übertragungen, hg. und übersetzt von Horst Dieter SCHLOSSER, Neuausgabe, Frankfurt a.M. 1989, S. 213.

9 KARG-GASTERSTÄDT, Elisabeth/FRINGS, Theodor (Begründer): Althochdeutsches Wörterbuch, hg. im Auftrag der Sächsischen Akademie der Wissenschaften zu Leipzig, Berlin (Ost) 1952ff., Art. *Gott*. Wird im Folgenden stillschweigend herangezogen. SEHRT, Edward H.: Vollständiges Wörterbuch zum Heliand und zur Altsächsischen Genesis, Göttingen [2]1966.

Gottes jeweils aktuell hervorgehoben wird – sowohl im Ahd. als auch im As. vor-
kommen. Das kann nicht überraschen, es gibt keinen inhaltlichen oder formalen
Unterschied zwischen ahd. und as. Literatur. Es sind aber nicht alle semantischen
Kontexte, die im Ahd. belegt sind, auch in Hel und AGs belegt, und umgekehrt
kommen in Hel und AGs Kontexte vor, die es in der ahd. Überlieferung nicht gibt.
Vergleicht man die im Ahd. belegten Kontexte mit den in Hel und AGs belegten
Kontexten danach, wie oft sie aktualisiert werden, so ergibt sich unter Berücksichtigung der stark unterschiedlichen Belegzahlen – ca. 3900 ahd. Belege stehen 540
as. gegenüber, das heißt, das Mengenverhältnis der ahd. Belege zu den as. Belegen beträgt ungefähr 7:1 –, dass folgende Kontexte im As. im Vergleich zum Ahd.
deutlich stärker repräsentiert sind:

- Gottes Allmacht, Stärke und Größe
- Gottes Herrlichkeit, Glanz und Glorie
- Gott der Herr, der Herrscher
- das Reich Gottes
- Gottes Recht, Gesetz, Gebot
- sowie die Formel ‚in Gottes Namen‘

Im As. im Vergleich zum Ahd. unterrepräsentiert sind die Kontexte:

- Gott als Beschützer, Erhalter, Helfer und Erlöser, Gottvater
- Gottes Gnade, Erhörung durch Gott
- Gott als Rächer, Richter, Strafender
- Gott loben, preisen, rühmen

Solch ein (quantitativer) Vergleich der semantischen Kontexte von ahd. *got* und
as. *god* deutet darauf hin, dass den Sachsen Gott als allmächtiger, starker und
glanzvoller, ruhmreicher Herrscher und die Forderung, Gottes Gebote zu halten,
leichter nahe zu bringen waren als die Botschaft vom gnädigen Gott, dem Helfer
und Erlöser, und die Forderung nach Lobpreisung Gottes. Das heißt nicht, dass
im as. Heliand ein anderes Gottesbild vermittelt wird als in der ahd. Literatur.[10]
Aber die Entstehungsbedingungen der ahd. und der as. Texte sind unterschiedlich, und dadurch sind auch ihre Zielsetzungen verschieden. Die ahd. Überlieferung setzt in einer Zeit und an Orten und in Räumen ein, in denen das Christentum unangefochten und gefestigt ist. Ahd. Literatur entsteht im Kloster für eine
christliche Gesellschaft. Die Texte können bei Lesern oder Hörern auf vorhande-
nes Basiswissen oder die Bereitschaft, sich mit christlicher Thematik zu beschäf-
tigen, aufbauen. Otfrid von Weißenburg kann deshalb in den Mysticé- und Spi-

---

10 Der Begriff ‚Germanisierung des Christentums‘ (A. Bonus), der in diesem Zusammenhang oft
   gefallen ist, trifft den Sachverhalt nicht, und er ist ideologisch geprägt, siehe dazu SCHÄFERDIEK,
   Knut: Germanisierung des Christentums, in: Theologische Realenzyklopädie, Bd. 12, Berlin
   u. a. 1983, S. 521–524.

ritaliter-Kapiteln seines *liber evangeliorum* (fertiggestellt zwischen 863 und 871, Sigle O) theologische Auslegungen nach der Methode des vierfachen Schriftsinns anbieten.[11] Der Heliand ist um 830 entstanden, zu einer Zeit, als die Erstmission der Sachsen noch nicht abgeschlossen war, und er dient erkennbar diesem Zweck: Die Sachsen sollen durch die epische Dichtung, abgefasst in dem ihnen vertrauten Metrum des germanischen Stabreims, an den noch kaum bekannten christlichen Glauben herangeführt werden. Christi Leben, seine Lehre und sein Erlösungshandeln müssen erst bekannt gemacht und erklärt werden. Das ist das Ziel des Helianddichters. Theologische Reflexion steht hier noch nicht im Vordergrund.

Komposita zu *got/god* sind as. *thiodgod* und *waldandgod* und ahd. *irmingot.* Ahd. *thiot* < germ. **þeuðô* bedeutet ,Volk', darauf geht auch das Adj. ahd. *thiutisk* ,zum (eigenen) Volk gehörig', nhd. *deutsch* zurück. Das Substantiv ist noch mhd. nicht selten belegt: als *diet* st. F. M. N. ,Volk, Leute', etwa in *diu varnde diet* ,Spielleute, fahrendes Volk' und in einigen Komposita, und es hält sich bis heute in Personennamen wie *Dietrich, Dietlinde.*[12] *thiodgod* ist im Hel einmal Appellativum, sonst ist das Lexem als Eigenname zu werten. Die wörtliche Bedeutung, ,Gott des Volkes', wird nicht aktualisiert. Das Erstglied des Kompositums as. *Waldandgod,* ahd. *waltant got,* ist Part. I zu as. *waldan,* ahd. *waltan,* mhd. *walten* ,herrschen'. Artikel fehlen, daher ist *waldandgod* im Hel als Eigenname aufzufassen. Beide Bildungen, *thiodgod* und *waldandgod,* betonen Gottes Herrscherrolle, ohne dass die biblische Vorlage an den jeweiligen Stellen dies nahe legt. Sie haben als Ehrentitel weniger wortsemantische als pragmatische Funktion.[13] Der Heliand ist reich an solchen Schmuckformen: Komposita, aber auch Simplicia, als Gottesbezeichnungen. Sie dienen dazu, das mit christlichen Glaubensinhalten noch nicht vertraute Publikum für den neuen Gott einzunehmen, denn Bezeichnungen, die die Herrschertugenden Gottes vorstellen, sind den Sachsen als Fürstenpreis aus ihrer Dichtung vertraut. Wie viele Schmuckformen steht *thiodgod* außerdem aus verstechnischen Gründen, um des Stabreims Willen. Der Stabreimvers ist die poetische Form der mündlich tradierten germanischen Heldendichtung. Gleiche anlautende Konsonanten innerhalb eines Verses staben miteinander, mit einem Hauptstab im Abvers korrespondieren ein bis zwei Nebenstäbe im Anvers:

[...]
Thiu bium ic theotgodes. Nu ik theses thinges gitrûon;
uuerðe mi aftar thinun uuordun, al sô is uuilleo sî,
hêrron mînes; nis mi hûgi tuîfli,
ne uuord ne uuîsa.'

---

11 Dazu OHLY, Friedrich: Vom geistigen Sinn des Wortes im Mittelalter, in: Zeitschrift für deutsches Altertum und deutsche Literatur 89 (1958), S. 1–23, wieder abgedruckt in OHLY, Friedrich: Schriften zur mittelalterlichen Bedeutungsforschung, Darmstadt 1977, S. 1–31.
12 PFEIFER: Wörterbuch (Anm. 5), Art. *deutsch,* Sp. 219f.; BENECKE, Georg Friedrich/MÜLLER, Wilhelm/ZARNCKE, Friedrich: Mittelhochdeutsches Wörterbuch, 3 Bde., Leipzig 1854–1866; LEXER, Matthias: Mittelhochdeutsches Handwörterbuch, 3 Bde., Leipzig 1872–1878, Art. *diet.*
13 Zu solchen Bildungen siehe ILKOW, Peter: Die Nominalkomposita der altsächsischen Bibeldichtung, Göttingen 1968, wird im Folgenden auch stillschweigend herangezogen.

Hel 285–288, nach *ecce ancilla Domini fiat mihi secundum verbum tuum* Lk 1,38.

(Ich bin die Magd Gottes. Nun vertraue ich dieser Sache;
es werde mir nach deinen Worten, ganz so wie es sein Wille sei,
meines Herrn; mein Gemüt ist nicht zweifelnd,
nicht am Wort, nicht an der Weise.)[14]

Nicht im Hel, sondern im Hildebrandslied (ostfränkisch oder bairisch, um 770)
findet sich die Anrufung *wettu irmingot [quad Hiltibrant] obane ab heuane*
(„Ich rufe Gott vom Himmel", sprach Hildebrand da, „zum Zeugen an, [...]").
Das urgermanische Adj. **erm(a)na-* bedeutet nach Braune ‚gewaltig, ungeheuer',
irmin- bezeichnet das Universelle, Unbegrenzte. *Irmingot* übersetzte er mit ‚deus
universalis, Allgott'. Nach Lühr ist *Irmin* möglicherweise ein vorchristlicher Got-
tesname.[15] Im Hildebrandslied gibt es zwei Anrufungen Gottes: *wettu irmingot*
und *welaga nu, waltant got, [quad Hiltibrant] wewurt skihit* („O waltender Gott",
fuhr Hildebrand fort, „das Schicksal will seinen Lauf!").[16] Es handelt sich um
Anrufungen des christlichen Gottes, ohne dass das Lied dadurch zu einer christlichen Dichtung würde. Hildebrand und Hadubrand handeln wie germanische
Krieger, nicht wie christliche Ritter.

Die Gottesbezeichnungen *thiodgod* und *irmingot* kommen im Mittelhochdeut-
schen nicht mehr vor, obgleich neben dem Simplex *diet* auch *irmin-* (in *irmensûl*)
mhd. belegt ist. *waldender,* auch *waldendiger* und *waldendinger got* sind mittel-
hochdeutsch. Zwischen ahd. und mhd. Literatur gibt es kaum Kontinuität. Mhd.
Literatur ist ein Neubeginn mit anderen Ursprüngen, anderen Autoren, Textsor-
ten und Entstehungssituationen. Für den Wortschatz besagt das zwar zunächst
nichts, aber der Anteil der Lexik, die aus der ahd. Überlieferung ungebrochen in
die mhd. hineinreicht, wird im Rahmen der Arbeit an einer neuen mhd. Grammatik gegenwärtig ermittelt; es erweist sich, dass er mit vermutlich ca. 35 % über-
raschend klein ist.

Die zahlreichen Umschreibungen für Gott im Hel, aber auch in der ahd.
Literatur kann man semantisch gliedern: Gott ist unter anderem der Schöpfer,
der Herrscher, der König, der Beschützer und Belohner.[17] Hier seien beispielhaft Bezeichnungen für den Schöpfergott und Gott, den Herrscher vorgestellt:
Die Vulgata hat für das Semem ‚Gott, der Schöpfer' hauptsächlich *creator*, sonst
auctor und einmal *conditor*. Diese bibellateinischen Vorlagen werden im Ahd.

---

14 Kennzeichnung der Stäbe und wörtliche Übersetzung von mir. Zur germanischen Heldendichtung
siehe SCARDIGLI, Piergiuseppe: Der Weg zur deutschen Sprache, Bern u. a. 1994, S. 214–224.

15 BRAUNE, Wilhelm: *irmindeot* und *irmingot*, in: Beiträge zur Geschichte der deutschen Sprache
und Literatur 21 (1896), S. 2–5; LÜHR, Rosemarie: Studien zur Sprache des Hildebrandsliedes,
Teile 1 und 2, Frankfurt a. M./Bern 1982, 2, S. 551f.

16 Zitate aus STEINMEYER: Denkmäler (Anm. 8), S 4,30 und 6,49. Übersetzungen von SCHLOSSER:
Althochdeutsche Literatur (Anm. 8), S. 265 und S. 267.

17 Eine ähnliche Vielfalt von Rollenbezeichnungen Gottes zeigt das Walisische, siehe dazu CORTZ-
GAN, Nora: Divining the Divinity, Aberystwyth 2002, dort die Aufstellung im Appendix. Morfydd Owen danke ich für den freundlichen Hinweis auf der Tagung. Zwischen den Religionen
liegt ein Vergleich mit den hundert Namen Gottes im Islam nahe.

durch Lehnbildungen wiedergegeben. Am produktivsten ist hier die Wurzel ie. *skap- ‚schneiden, spalten'. Daraus entsteht germ. *skap-ja-, gotisch ga-skapjan, ahd. skephen, as. skeppian als starkes und als schwaches Verb mit den Bedeutungen ‚erschaffen, bewirken' und ‚(Wasser) schöpfen'. St. und sw. V. und die Bedeutungen ‚creare' und ‚haurire' vermischen sich in ahd. Zeit.[18] Es gibt im Ahd. eine Reihe unterschiedlicher *nomina agentis* zum Verb *scephen: scepfo* sw. M. mit dem alten Tätersuffix *-o* hat der Weißenburger Katechismus (WK, südrheinfränkisch, entstanden nach der *Admonitio Generalis* 789) für *creatorem* im Credo. Außerdem gibt es den Glossenbeleg *scaffo*; die ahd. Übersetzung des lat. Isidortraktats (I, alem., nach 802) hat *scheffidh* st. M.; die Murbacher Hymnen (MH, alem., Anfang 9. Jh.) haben *scepfant*, substantiviertes Part. I; die ahd. Benediktinerregel (B, alem., Anfang 9. Jh.) und wiederum die MH haben *sceffanto* sw. M., und O (südrheinfränkisch, 863–871) und der ahd. Physiologus haben *scepheri* mit dem Wortbildungs-Lehnsuffix *-âri* aus lat. *-arius,* das sich ab dem 9. Jahrhundert gegenüber den anderen durchsetzt und als *-er* bis heute produktiv ist. Diese Entwicklung ist in ahd. Zeit noch nicht abzusehen, keine der Bildungen ist wesentlich häufiger belegt als die anderen. Im Mhd. findet sich neben *schepfære, schephære, scheffære* ‚Schöpfer, Bildner' zu mhd. *schaffen* st. V. auch *schaffære* ‚Schöpfer' mit einen Beleg für ‚Gott' im Jüngeren Titurel. Dieses Nebeneinander von ungefähr im selben Zeitraum, aber an verschiedenen Orten entstandenen *creator*-Übersetzungen zeigt, dass man unabhängig voneinander nach Übersetzungsgleichungen für wichtige Programmwörter suchte.

Bezeichnungen für den Schöpfergott wurden auch zu anderen Stämmen gebildet. Hier seien noch vorgestellt: *ortfrumo* sw. M., Kompositum aus *ort* ‚Spitze' und einer Substantivierung zu germ. *fruma-* ‚erster' aus ie. *per* ‚vorne, früh, erster', das die MH für *auctor* haben. Dazu bietet der Hel die Erweiterung *aðalordfrumo*; das Erstglied bedeutet ‚edel, adlig', die ganze Bildung übersetzt Sehrt mit ‚der hochgeborene Schöpfer'. Der Vers Hel 31 lautet *aðalordfrumo alomahtig*. Die Stelle scheint der einzige Beleg für das Semem ‚Schöpfergott' im As. überhaupt zu sein, und sie zeigt, mit welchen Gestaltungsmitteln der Helianddichter sein Publikum gewinnen wollte. Der Hel ist ein Beispiel für frühes adressatenspezifisches Schreiben. *ortvrümaere* st. M. ‚Urheber' ist mhd. (belegt in Walthers von Reinau Marienleben).

Von den Bezeichnungen für Gott, den Herrn, die weiter unten behandelt werden, sind die Bezeichnungen für Gott, den Herrscher zu unterscheiden. Ein paar davon seien hier vorgestellt. Die Rolle Gottes als Herrscher betont besonders der Helianddichter. Neben den genannten Komposita mit *-god* hat der Hel *thiodan*, wiederum eine Bildung zu as. *thiod* ‚Volk', zu vergleichen sind gotisch *þiudans* für griech. *basileus* ‚König' und ags. *þeoden* ‚Prinz, König'. *thiodan*, eigentlich also ‚Herr der Volksmenge', ist die Bezeichnung für Christus als Herr der Gefolgschaft.

---

18 Die Ansätze im Ahd. bei GRAFF, E[berhard] G[ottlieb]: Althochdeutscher Sprachschatz, Teile I–VI, Berlin 1834–1842, mit Index von H. F. MASSMANN, Berlin 1846 (Neudruck Hildesheim 1963), hier: VI,442–449.

Ohne Christus zum germanischen Heros umzudeuten und damit die christliche Botschaft zu verfälschen, konnte der Helianddichter ihm Attribute verleihen, die ihn für sein Publikum als Gott und Herrn glaubwürdiger und damit attraktiver machten (siehe auch oben Anmerkung 10).

Die wichtigste, weitaus häufigste as. Bezeichnung für Gott, den Herrscher ist *waldand*, substantiviertes Part. I von *waldan* red. V. ‚walten, herrschen über‘. Es kommt in Hel und AGs 213 mal vor und steht immer für ‚Gott‘. In 50 Fällen ist *waldand* Bestandteil einer festen Verbindung: *hebanes, landes, weroldes waldand*. Steht es allein, ist es als Substantiv aufzufassen. *waldand* ist überwiegend Prädikator. Im Mhd. kommt das substantivierte Partizip als Gottesbezeichnung nicht mehr vor. Das Marienleben Walthers von Reinau hat *waltære, walter* ‚Walter, Herrscher, Fürsorger‘.

Für das Semem ‚Christus, der Herrscher‘ hat der Hel auch *râdgebo*, eigentlich ‚der, der Hilfe, Unterstützung gibt‘ (Sehrt), was in die Bedeutung ‚Befehlshaber, Herrscher‘ übergehen kann (Ilkow). Mhd. sind *râtgeber* und, zahlreicher, *râtgebe* sw. M ‚consiliarius‘. Die ehrende Bezeichnung eines Herrn als Geber liegt nahe, denn die Freigebigkeit, ahd. *milti*, ist eine Herrschertugend, und die Bezeichnung Gottes als Geber hat kirchenlateinische Vorbilder: *dator, largitor*. Das *Carmen ad deum* (bairisch, Anfang 9. Jh.) nennt Gott *largus dator. milter kepo* S 290,2. Der Hel hat *mêdgebo, mêdomgibo*, zu as. *mêdom* st. M. ‚Kleinod, Kostbarkeit‘; *côs im the cuninges thegn Crist te hêrran, milderan mêdomgebon* (der Dienstmann des Königs wählte sich Christus zum Herren, einen milderen Kleinodgeber) heißt es im Hel 1199f. von Matthäus, dem Zöllner: Christus ist ein freigebigerer, das heißt besserer Herr als der König. Das Lexem hat keine Vorlage bei Mt 9,9 oder Lk 5,28. *mêdom* ist mhd. als *mêdeme* M. ‚auf Grundstücken haftende Abgabe‘ belegt.

Die Bezeichnung für Gottvater ist *fatar/fader*. Zwei mal ist im Hel *godfader* für Gott als den Vater Christi belegt. Ob wirklich ein Kompositum vorliegt, ist nicht sicher zu entscheiden, die Graphie (Getrenntschreibung) ist nicht maßgeblich. *fader* könnte auch ein Attribut zu *god* sein. *himilfadar* steht für ‚Vater der Menschen‘, weil Gott als dieser im Himmel gedacht wird und die Bildung als Kompositum mit dem weltumspannenden *himil-* ein Konnotat von Universalität vermittelt. *himelvater* ist mhd. einmal belegt, *gotvater* als Kompositum nicht, *vater* als Attribut von *got* wohl (Heinrich der Teichner).

Gott der Herr

Für lat *dominus* < griech. *kyrios* (in der Vulgata ca. 1.300 Belege) gibt es in voralthochdeutscher Zeit und im Ahd./As. in zeitlicher Abfolge drei Übersetzungen: *frô, truhtîn* und *hêrro*.[19]

---

19 EHRISMANN, Gustav: Die Wörter für ‚Herr‘ im Althochdeutschen, in: Zeitschrift für deutsche Wortforschung 7 (1905/06), S. 173–202; EGGERS, Hans: Die Annahme des Christentums im Spiegel der deutschen Sprachgeschichte, in: SCHÄFERDIEK, Knut (Hg.): Die Kirche des früheren Mittelalters (Kirchengeschichte als Missionsgeschichte 2,1), München 1978, S. 466–504.

Die älteste, *frô* < germ. **frawan-* (*n*-Stamm), und germ. **fraujan-* (*jan*-Stamm; gotisch *frauja*, as. *frôio*) gehen zurück auf ie. **prô* ‚vorwärts, vorn, voran‘. Gotisch *frauja* schreibt Wulfila für *dominus*. Möglicherweise ist *frô* schon vorchristlich Appellativum gewesen. *frô* bedeutet undifferenziert ‚Herrscher, Machthaber‘.

Von 34 Belegen im Ahd. und As. insgesamt sind 23 mit Sicherheit Anreden oder Bezeichnungen Gottes beziehungsweise Christi, alle finden sich in Hel und AGs. Mögliche ahd. Belege für ‚Gott, der Herr‘ sind unsicher (etwa O V,7,49 nach J 20,15: Maria spricht den auferstandenen Christus mit *frô mîn* an, hält ihn aber für den Gärtner). Während also im Ahd. *frô* als Bezeichnung für Gott, den Herrn schon nicht mehr vorkommt, das Lexem als Grußformel in die weltliche Sphäre abgedrängt ist, ist es im konservativeren As. in seiner älteren Verwendung als Gottesbezeichnung noch in Gebrauch. Mhd. ist *vrô* ‚milder, gnädiger Herr‘ noch einmal belegt (im Renner Hugos von Trimberg).

truhtîn, as. *drohtin*, ist eine Ableitung von ahd. *truht* ‚populus, familia‘ aus urgermanisch **ðruhtiz-* ‚Menge, (Kriegs-)Schar‘; vgl. gotisch *gadrauhts* ‚Soldat‘. *truhtîn* bedeutet zunächst ‚Herr der Gefolgschaft‘. Möglicherweise hat *truhtîn* *frô* als Gottesbezeichnung verdrängen können, weil die Germanen sich als freie Gefolgsleute ihrer irdischen Herren und dann auch Gottes verstanden. *dominus* war auch die Anrede des weströmischen Kaisers, des obersten Kriegsherrn. Germanische Soldaten im römischen Heer können ihren *dominus* in ihrer Sprache *truhtîn* genannt haben (Eggers). In anderer Herleitung bringt Dick die Wurzel westgermanisch **druht-* mit vorchristlichen Vorstellungen von Wachstumsheil in Verbindung. Altenglisch *dryht* steht ursprünglich für eine Kultgemeinschaft, die dem *dryhten*, einer Fruchtbarkeitsgottheit, huldigt.[20] Von einem solchen vorchristlichen Kontext ist aber im Ahd./As. nichts zu bemerken.

Im Ahd./As. gibt es 1542 Belege, fast alle beziehen sich auf Gott oder Christus. Nach *got* ist *truhtîn* die häufigste Gottesbezeichnung. *truhtîn* ist eigentlich Appellativum, wird aber mehr als Eigenname für Gott, speziell für Christus verwendet. Besonders Otfrid verwendet *druhtîn* als Eigennamen für Christus (ohne Artikel), öfter noch als *Krist*. Auch im Hel ist *drohtin* die meistverwendete Bezeichnung für Gott, den Herrn; mit einer Ausnahme beziehen sich hier alle Belege auf Gott beziehungsweise Christus. Im Mhd. ist das Lexem, ausschließlich als Gottesbezeichnung, noch oft belegt, meist als *trehtîn*, aber ab dem 11. Jahrhundert wird es verdrängt von *hêriro*.

hêriro, hêrôro, hêrro, Komparativ zu ahd./as. *hêr* ‚alt, ehrwürdig‘, ist Analogiebildung zu lat. *senior*. Im Ahd./As. ist das Lexem ca. 420 mal belegt, ca. 300 Belege beziehen sich auf Gott oder Christus, davon stammen aber nur ca. 50 aus der Zeit vor dem 11. Jahrhundert. Vor Notker III. († 1022) wird *hêriro/hêrro* erst zögernd für Gott gebraucht. Der ahd. Isidor hat nur *truhtîn*. Der Verfasser der ahd. Tatianbilingue (T, ostfränkisch, um 830) und Otfrid trennen zwischen *truhtîn/ druhtîn* für Gott einerseits und *hêrero/hêrro* für weltliche Herren andererseits. Im

---

20 EGGERS: Annahme (Anm. 19), S. 483ff.; DICK, Ernst S.: Ae. *dryht* und seine Sippe, Münster 1965, S. 384–395.

Fränkischen des 8./9. Jahrhunderts war *hêriro* als Komparativ noch erkennbar. Otfrid verwendet zwar *hêrero* auch für Christus, zur Herausstellung des Rangunterschieds zu den Jüngern (IV,11,21f.), eine Gottesbezeichnung ist *hêrero* bei Otfrid damit jedoch nicht. Der Hel hat zwar überwiegend *drohtîn* für ,Gott', aber daneben auch *hêrro*. Im sächsischen Missionsgebiet gibt es noch keine verbindliche Terminologie einer gefestigten Kirchensprache, wie schon am Festhalten an *frô* als Gottesbezeichnung in Hel und AGs zu sehen war. Im Mhd. sind *hêrre* und *herre* die Normalformen. Warum sich *hêrro* seit spätalthochdeutscher Zeit gegen *truhtîn* durchsetzte, ist unklar. *truhtîn* ist heute ganz verschwunden, *frô* M. ebenfalls. Das F. dazu, *Frau*, mhd. *frouwe*, ahd. *frouwa* ,Herrin' < germ. **frawjô*, und *Herr* halten sich seit ihrem Aufkommen bis in die Gegenwart.

Bezeichnungen für Jesus

Der hebräische Name *Jeschu'a, Joschu'a > Jesus* bedeutet ,Gott rettet' oder ,Heil, Rettung' (vgl. lat. *salvator* ,Heiland, Erlöser').[21] Der Eigenname Christi ist in der Vulgata 889 mal belegt, im Ahd./As. nur 22 mal, davon noch am meisten im Isidor und in den Monseer Fragmenten (MF). O hat *Jesus* nur in den lat. Kapitelüberschriften. Der Eigenname *Jesus* wird also im Ahd. nicht völlig unterdrückt, er wird aber merklich gemieden, während biblische Vornamen sonst ohne Scheu ins Deutsche übernommen werden.[22] Antijüdische Tendenzen sind nicht der Grund; sie sind in der ahd. Literatur nirgends erkennbar. Dass Jesus Jude ist, wird weder verschwiegen, noch thematisiert. Für die Zurückhaltung ist wohl eher religiöse Scheu die Ursache. Die Furcht, gegen das Gebot, den Namen Gottes nicht zu missbrauchen, (Ex 20,7; Deut 5,11) zu verstoßen, wird dazu geführt haben, den Eigennamen überhaupt zu meiden. Anstelle von *Jesus* wird im Ahd./As. *Krist* als Eigenname Jesu verwendet. Einzelne Übersetzer kannten zwar die Bedeutung des griech. Part. II *christós* – substantiviert ,Gesalbter' – im Allgemeinen war sie aber nicht bekannt. Warum man *Krist Jesus* vorgezogen hat, ist nicht klar. Die Erklärung, *Krist* klinge germanischer, ist spekulativ.

Nach *Krist* ist *heilant* die gebräuchlichste Bezeichnung für den Sohn Gottes. Das westgermanische Substantiv ist eigentlich Part. I zu *heilen* ,wiederherstellen, erlösen, (er)retten'. Im Ags. erhielt es die Bedeutung ,zum Heil führend'. Ags. *hêlend* ist Lehnübersetzung (die exakteste Form der Lehnbildung) von *salvator*, dieses wiederum ist Übersetzung von griech. *sotér*, zu griech. *sózein* ,retten'. Für das Adj. *heil* ist bereits von einer vorchristlich-religiösen Bedeutung ,Heil bringend, heilvoll' auszugehen, dasselbe könnte von *heilant* auch gelten.[23] Das zu Grunde liegende *heilen* steht also für ,salvare', nicht für ,sanare: gesund machen nach Krankheit'.

---

21 SLEUMER: Kirchenlateinisches Wörterbuch (Anm. 5), Art. *Jesus*.
22 Anders KLEIBER, Wolfgang: Otfrid von Weißenburg, Bern/München 1971, S. 72f.
23 BAETKE, Walter: Das Heilige im Germanischen, Tübingen 1942, S. 1–46.

Die angelsächsische Mission auf dem Kontinent im 7./8. Jahrhundert hatte die Einrichtung der römischen Diözesanverfassung und Gründungen bedeutender Klöster zur Folge. In Fulda, einer Gründung des Winfried Bonifatius, entstand die ahd. Tatianbilingue. Der Erfolg der ags. Mission lässt sich in sprachlicher Hinsicht nur an wenigen, dafür prägnanten Bildungen ablesen: Im Süden der Germania herrscht als *salvator*-Übersetzung ahd. *nerrend(e)o* vor, Part. I zu ahd. *nerien* ,retten, erlösen, ernähren, heilen'. Möglicherweise besteht ein gotischer Einfluss, gotisch *nasjands*, Part. I zu *nasjan* ,retten', ist Lehnübersetzung von griech. *sotér*. Mit der ags. Mission tritt *heiland* auf und drängt *nerrend(e)o* zurück. Vielleicht ist die schon vorchristlich-religiöse Bedeutung von *heil* ein Grund für den Erfolg.

Isidor, alem., nach 802, hat 10 *Jesus*, 65 *Christ* und 5 *nerrend(e)o*, kein *heilant;*
die MF, bairisch, Anfang 9. Jh., haben 6 *Jesus*, 4 *nerrend(e)o*, kein *heilant;*
die B, alem., Anfang 9. Jh., hat 5 *Christ*, kein *heilant* und kein *nerrend(e)o;*
die MH, alem., Anfang 9. Jh., haben 30 *Christ*, 5 *heilant;* kein *nerrend(e)o;*
der as. Hel, um 830, hat 5 *Jesus*, 254 *Crist* und je 24 *hêliand* und *neriand;*
der ostfränkische T, um 830, hat 1 *Jesus*, 43 *Crist*, 271 *heilant*, kein *nerrend(e)o*
und O, südrheinfränkisch, um 863–871, hat 169 *Krist*, 15 *heilant*, 1 *heilâri*,
kein *nerrend(e)o*.

Die Übersicht spiegelt das räumlich/zeitliche Zurückgehen von *nerrend(e)o/ neriand* einerseits und das Vordringen von *heilant* andererseits in einigen der größeren Texte punktuell wider. Zu Beginn des 9. Jahrhunderts haben die oberdeutschen Texte Isidor und MF *nerrend(e)o*, nicht aber *heilant*, die B hat keines der beiden Lexeme, die alem. MH haben aber schon umgekehrt *heilant* und kein *nerrend(e)o*. Der Hel, um 830, hat beides gleich oft, im As. und im Altostniederfränkischen ist *neriand* (neben *hêliand*) noch stark vertreten. Der fuldische T hat sehr oft *heilant*, aber *nerrend(e)o* gar nicht, und O aus den 60er Jahren des 9. Jahrhunderts hat *heilant* und ebenfalls kein *nerrend(e)o* mehr.

Es ist allerdings nicht zwingend, in *heilant* einen ags. Import zu sehen; nach Kolb hätte die *salvator*: *heilant*-Gleichung auch anderswo entstehen können.[24] Die beschriebene geographische Verbreitung von *heilant* und die Dominanz im T ist aber so am plausibelsten zu erklären: *heilant* tritt im Verbreitungsgebiet der ags. Mission zuerst auf. Erst später dringt das Lexem von da aus in Gebiete vor, die von der ags. Mission zunächst nicht erfasst sind. *heilant* ist nicht die einzige zu *heil* gebildete *salvator*-Übersetzung. Ein sw. M. *heilanto* mit dem älteren Wortbildungssuffix *-o* wurde durch das bloße Part. verdrängt, und die Bildung *heilâri*, mit dem zukunftsweisenden Suffix *-âri* > nhd. *-er* zur Bildung von *nomina agentis*, kam zu spät auf, um dem bereits fest etablierten *heilant* noch Konkurrenz machen zu können.

---

24 KOLB, Herbert: Über *Heilant* als Eigennamen in der althochdeutschen Literatur, in: BERGMANN, Rolf u. a.(Hg.): Althochdeutsch, Bd. 2, Heidelberg 1987, S. 1234–1249.

Der T ist der einzige der genannten Texte, in denen *heilant* die vorherrschende Christusbezeichnung ist. Isidor, MH und besonders Hel und O haben für Jesus Christus *Krist/Crist*. Mhd. sind *heilant, heilent* ‚Heiland, Erlöser, Erretter‘ und *heilære, heiler* ‚Heiler, Arzt‘, bezogen auf Jesus. Das sw. V. *nern, neren, nerigen, nergen* ist mhd. noch unter anderem mit den Bedeutungen ‚genesen machen, heilen, retten, erretten‘ belegt, das substantivierte Part. I als Christusbezeichnung kommt nicht mehr vor.

Der Heilige Geist

Griech. *hágion pnéuma* übersetzt Wulfila mit *ahma sa weiha*. *ahma* bedeutet ‚Verstand‘. Gotisch *weihs* < germ. **wîhaz* trägt vermutlich schon von seinem Ursprung her die Bedeutung ‚heilig‘, eine angenommene Bedeutung ‚gebunden, abgesondert‘ ist sekundär (Baetke). In lautlicher Anlehnung an die gotische Bildung hat der Süden der Germania *ther wîho âtum* zur Übersetzung von *spiritus sanctus*. Das Lexem *âtum* trägt primär das physikalische Semem ‚Lufthauch‘.

Die ags. Übersetzung von *spiritus sanctus* ist *sê hâlga gâst*, auf das die ahd. Bildung *ther heilago geist*, zunächst verbreitet im Gebiet der ags. Mission, erkennbar zurückgeht. Ahd. *heilag* ist eine Ableitung von *heil* und wie dieses bereits vorchristlich religiös. *Heil* Subst. bedeutet ursprünglich ‚magisch bedingtes Glück, Segen‘, *heil* Adj. und auch *heilig* bedeuteten ‚Heil bringend, heilvoll‘; *heilig* enthielt vielleicht gegenüber *heil* ein intensivierendes Element.[25] Heiligkeit ist die besondere Kennzeichnung des Göttlichen und daher einer Zugehörigkeit zu Gott.

Geist, aus der erweiterten Wurzel germ. **gheis-d-* ‚in Schrecken versetzen‘ bedeutet im Germ. ursprünglich etwa ‚inneres Erregtsein, Extase‘, auch ‚Schreckgespenst‘. Dieser schon vorchristlich religiösen Grundbedeutungen wegen ist *geist* als heidnisches Wort identifiziert und zur Übersetzung von *spiritus* im Süden erst gemieden worden (Betz), man hielt hier zunächst an *âtum* fest. Andererseits machten gerade diese Vorbedeutungen *geist* zur Übersetzung von *spiritus sanctus* geeignet, und sie dürften auch der ags. Prägung zum Erfolg über das *wîho âtum* des Südens verholfen haben: Die wörtliche Bedeutung ‚geweihter Lufthauch‘ war zu blass gegenüber dem, was bei *geist* noch konnotativ an religiösem Vorstellungspotential mitschwang. Dass diese Konnotate vorchristlichen und damit heidnischen Ursprungs waren, hat den Erfolg der Übersetzung also vielleicht zunächst verzögert, aber nicht behindert, sondern dann sogar befördert.[26]

---

25 Baetke: Das Heilige (Anm. 23), S. 1–46, S. 55ff.
26 Betz, Werner: Die frühdeutschen *spiritus*-Übersetzungen und die Anfänge des Wortes „Geist“, in: Liturgie und Mönchtum 20 (1957), S. 48–55; Lutze, Ernst: Die germanischen Übersetzungen von *spiritus* und *pneuma*, Bonn 1960; Neunheuser, Burkhard: Gnade, Geistesgaben, Heiliger Geist in mittelalterlicher und neutestamentlicher Sicht, in: Liturgie und Mönchtum 20 (1957), S. 34–47.

geist ist im Ahd. und As. zusammen ca. 330 mal belegt, davon beziehen sich ca. 260 Belege auf Gott. Die Kombination *geist* und *heilag* kommt im Ahd. und As. ca. 140 mal vor. *geist* + *wîh* ist im Ahd. nur dreimal belegt, nach dem ersten Viertel des 9. Jahrhunderts kommt diese Kombination in ahd. Zeit nicht mehr vor. Mhd. sind *der heilige, heilig geist*, auch *heilegeist, der hêre geist, der vrône*, auch *der gotes geist*.

âtum für den Heiligen Geist ist im Ahd. 29 mal belegt, oft mit *wîh*. Im Ahd. tritt *âtum* mit dieser Bedeutung nur in oberdeutschen Texten und nur bis zum Ende des ersten Viertels des 9. Jahrhunderts auf, danach wird es auch im Süden von *geist* verdrängt. Die Kombination *hêlag* und *âðom* kommt nur zweimal und nur im As. vor. Beide Male ist nicht der Heilige Geist, sondern der Lebensgeist Christi gemeint. Im Mhd. kehrt *âtem* mit der Bedeutung ‚spiritus sanctus‘ zurück: *ze dem heiligen âteme*. Mhd. belegt ist auch *der godes âtem*.

Die Kombinationen *heilag* und *geist* und *wîh* und *âtum* sind in ahd. Zeit sehr fest. Ein Zurückgehen von *wîho âtum* in ahd. Zeit kann auch damit zusammenhängen, dass *wîh* als gotisch identifiziert und wegen des arianischen Hintergrundes gemieden wurde.[27]

Im Vorangehenden wurden einige ahd. und as. Gottesbezeichnungen im Hinblick auf ihre Semantik und Verwendung vorgestellt: Das Lexem *got* in seiner semantischen Bandbreite im Ahd. im Vergleich zum As.; Komposita mit *-got* in ihrer pragmatischen Funktion als Schmuckformen im Hel; die Vielfalt der Bezeichnungen für Gott, den Schöpfer, besonders aus der Wurzel **skap-*; as. Wörter für ‚Gott, der Herrscher‘, die konnotativ unterschiedliche Aspekte des göttlichen Herrschens betonen: Gott ist ‚Herr der Volksmenge‘, ‚Waltender‘, ‚Helfer‘, ‚der Freigebige‘; es wurden vorgestellt die Bezeichnungen für Gott, den Herrn in ihrer zeitlichen Abfolge; schließlich Benennungen Jesu, hier die in frühalthochdeutscher Zeit konkurrierenden *salvator*-Übersetzungen, und die ebenfalls konkurrierenden *spiritus-sanctus*-Übersetzungen. Anhand dieser Beispiele wurden verschiedene Möglichkeiten des Sprechens von Gott, unter denen die Autoren der ahd. Zeit nach ihren Zielsetzungen auswählen konnten, gezeigt. Einige der behandelten Lexeme sind als Gottesbezeichnungen noch heute gebräuchlich, andere sind untergegangen. Ihre Entstehung und ihre Durchsetzung gegen andere Bildungen oder ihr Misserfolg sollten schlaglichtartig beleuchtet werden.

---

27 BRAUNE, Wilhelm: Althochdeutsch und Angelsächsisch, in: Beiträge zur Geschichte der deutschen Sprache und Literatur 43 (1918), S. 361–445, hier S. 404–408; EGGERS: Annahme (Anm. 19), S. 497f.; SCARDIGLI, Piergiuseppe: Die Goten, München 1973, S. 58–62, S. 219–223; SCARDIGLI: Der Weg (Anm. 14), S. 127f.

Anna Kuznetsova

New religion, new letters.
Invention of alphabets in the lives of holy missionaries

It is a commonplace that Christian mission has been closely connected to literacy. Christianity, like Judaism and Islam, is a 'religion of the book' (by which I imply not only their Scriptures but also liturgical books, prayer books, etc.). Yet it is still worth asking: how important was the use of literacy during the process of Christianisation? This question is, if I see it correctly, less frequently asked in the relevant scholarship than the more general one about the use of the vernacular by 'the agents of conversion' in Michael Richter's words.[1] Or, in other words: what was the weight of the spoken word in relation to the written in bringing people to Christianity?[2] How far from each other were the two steps of addressing pagans: talking to them so that they understood the preacher – and writing down basic formulae that are to be heard by them? And was it always necessary to design a new alphabet in order to write those formulae down and to be a successful teacher of Christianity?

This last question is answered positively in regard to the three saints I propose to discuss here. The authors of the Lives of the saints Mesrop/Mashtots, who created an alphabet for the Armenians, Constantine/Cyril, who created what is known as the Glagolitic alphabet for the Slavs, and Stephen of Perm, who was the father of an alphabet for the Fenno-Ugric people, the Komi/Zyrien, glorify them for their invention of alphabets for the newly converted people.

Let me begin by suggesting that the refined use of the vernacular and, under certain circumstances, translations and a new alphabet, seem to be more important in the later stages of Christianisation. In the initial confrontation with pagans and paganism, when the superiority of the new religion has to be proven, actions and visible signs appear to have been crucial. Idolatry was for a missionary the kind of enemy that had to be defeated first of all by actual destruction. As for pagans, the inability of their gods to defend themselves demonstrated their weak-

---

1   RICHTER, Michael: Practical aspects of the conversion of the Anglo-Saxons, in: Irland und die Christenheit. Bibelstudien und Mission, ed. by Próinséas Ní CHATÁIN/Michael RICHTER, Stuttgart 1987, p. 363. See also e.g.: LUISELLI FADDA, Anna Maria: The vernacular and propagation of the faith in Anglo-Saxon Missionary Activity, in: Missions and Missionaries, ed. by Pieter N. HOLTROP/Hugh McLEOD, London 2000, pp. 1-15.
2   For all these issues see e.g. WOOD, Ian: The Missionary Life. Saints and the Evangelisation of Europe 400–1050, London 2001; VON PADBERG, Lutz: Mission und Christianisierung. Formen und Folgen bei Angelsachsen und Franken im 7. und 8. Jahrhundert, Stuttgart 1995; ŠEVČENKO, Ihor: Religious Missions seen from Byzantium: The Imperial Pattern and its Local Variants, in: ŠEVČENKO, Ihor: Ukraine Between East and West. Essays on Cultural History to the Early Eighteenth Century, Edmonton 1996.

ness most vividly.[3] The best of the examples is probably the one from the Life of St. Stephen of Perm. His (verbal) 'debate' with the shaman Pam on the advantages of the beliefs they represented may have been extensive, but the audience's decision occurred when Stephen won out in an ordeal of fire and water.[4] In contrast to that in two other Vitae (that of St. Mesrop/Mashtots and St. Constantine/Cyril), whose heroes met people who were already formal Christians, education and not confrontation is characteristic. Their activity was not connected with the initial 'conversion' but was aimed at enhancing the religiosity of already baptised peoples.

Still, it is obvious that Christian missionaries, when encountering people to be converted, had to be able to communicate in the language of the 'pagans' and convey to them the notions of the Christian religion. This issue goes back to the Biblical event of the Pentecost, when the apostles were sent out to preach the Word and were given the ability to speak in tongues.[5] The task was then taken up by the successors of the apostles, missionaries and teachers: they, too, needed tongues to convey the Christian message. Sometimes their predicament was solved by miracles, as reported by John of Ephesus about Mar Symeon, the bishop. His *Vita* tells us: "The good and merciful God [...] seeing the man's purpose of mind and his zeal [...] bestowed on him His gift that was given to the apostles [...]. For whatever people's country he entered, on the third day he would speak with them in their own tongue."[6] But not all the teachers of the newly converted experienced such divine favour.

As the teachers usually came from a different cultural context and were speaking, writing, and reading a language that had its own Christian vocabulary and alphabet (even if it was not one of the 'three holy languages', but, for example, Anglo-Saxon or Irish), they needed to bridge the gap. For this they had, first of all, to be familiar with the given language – let us call it vernacular – or at least, for a start, to acquire helpers who were. Moreover, they had to 'make up' words and phrases for the divine beings, for the crucial terms of Christianity, for God and the Devil, from Creation to Passion, and for the rituals of their religion, in the language of the people they were addressing. And in many cases they found it necessary to design an alphabet appropriate for the given language.

The monk Boso (later Bishop of Merseburg) wanted to use Slavic in his activity. In Thietmar's *Chronicle* we read that he knew some Slavic and wanted to apply

---

3   More on that see Кузнецова А. М.: Миссии латинской церкви: Опыт христианского Запада и Центральная и Юго-Восточная Европа на рубеже второго тысячелетия [KUZNETSOVA, Anna: Missions of the Latin Church: the Christian West and the countries of Central and South-Eastern Europe on the border of the second millenium], in: Христианство в странах Восточной, Юго-Восточной и Центральной Европы на пороге второго тысячелетия [Christianity in the countries of Eastern, South-Eastern and Central Europe on the border of the second millenium] Moscow 2002, pp. 56–58.

4   See note 32.

5   Acts, 2: 1–4.

6   John of Ephesus: Lives of the Eastern Saints, ed. by E. W. BROOKS, in: Patrologia Orientalis, vol. 17, Paris 1923, pp. 155f.

it to his missionary work. However, Thietmar also tells us that hearing the words *kyrie eleison* his flock burst out in laughter since they understood it in a totally wrong way.[7] The sacred formula remained incomprehensible to them because in their language it meant something entirely different – and funny. This example suggests that the mere basic knowledge of language did not always guarantee success. Attempts of the Western missionaries to translate the essential Christian notions are known from as early as the Carolingian times. The so-called Freising Monuments, for example, contain prayers in Slavic written in Latin letters.[8] It is also known that bishop Werner of Merseburg (second half of the 12th c.) asked for books in Slavic to be brought to him to work for Christianity among the Lusatian Serbs.[9]

However, the topic of knowing the local language is not emphasised as much in writings about the Western missionaries as in the Eastern Church. Latin missionaries had of course also considered the issue important. One of the best-known examples is Gregory the Great's recommendation to Augustine of Canterbury that if he goes to England, he should have the support of locals, familiar with the vernacular.[10] We read in Bede that King Oswald acted as interpreter for St. Aidan.[11] The legends of St. Gerhard of Csanád mention that he did not know Hungarian and used translators in his activities. His *Legenda maior* contains a passage reporting that Gerhard selected from among his ten monks those seven who knew Magyar to be archdeacons (and even lists their names).[12] However, major linguistic projects were apparently not pursued. The translation of the main Christian notions and formulae into the languages of the people did not seem to be a central issue in the western part of Europe. A new alphabetisation of the vernacular did not come up as a major enterprise either.

In contrast to the Western Church, where Latin was essentially unchallenged – with the exception of Irish and Anglo-Saxon and later the other vernaculars, at least for those parts of the service that were to be understood by all believers, mainly the sermon – the oriental church was much more open to 'vernacular' variations of scriptural and liturgical use. As we know, in the Syrian and Coptic churches Christians used their own languages extensively in the church, as well

---

7 Thietmari Merseburgensis Episcopi Chronicon. L.II. Cap. 37, ed. by R. Holtzmann/W. Trill-mich, Darmstadt 1957, p. 74.

8 See, e.g. Čapkova, Vera: The Freising Monuments, in: Irland und die Christenheit, Stuttgart 1987, pp. 461–470.

9 Vita Werneheri episcopi Merseburgensis, in: MGH SS, Scriptores in folio, vol. 2, Hanover 1856, p. 246.

10 Wood, Ian: Pagans and Holy Men, 600–800, in: Irland und die Christenheit, pp. 352–354.

11 Bede's Ecclesiastical History of the English People, ed. by Bertram Colgrave/R. A. B. Mynors, Oxford 1991, p. 21.

12 Madzsar, Emericus (ed.): Legenda S. Gerardi episcopi, in: Szentpétery, Emericus (ed.): Scriptores rerum Hungaricarum tempore ducum regumque stirpis Arpadianae gestarum, Budapest 1938, vol. 2, p. 494, ch. 9; for more on this, see Kuznetsova, Anna: Signs of Conversion in *Vitae sanctorum*, in: Armstrong, G./Wood, I. N. (ed.): Christianizing Peoples and Converting Individuals, Turhout 2000 (International Medieval Research 7), pp. 125–32.

as their traditional alphabets, although the Coptic one was a mixture of Greek and local demotic characters. This kind of procedure was also followed by Bishop Ulfila of the Goths, who added some characters from the Latin alphabet and even some runic signs.

An entirely new method was chosen around 400 AD by the Armenian monk Mesrop (or Mashtots), who, when he made an ecclesiastical language of his mother tongue, decided to use a wholly new set of signs. Gottfried Schramm in his study of this invention as well as of the alphabets made by St. Constantine and St. Stephen called those "radikale Neuschrift[en]."[13]

Mesrop/Mashtots (361/2–440) is known to us as the inventor of the Armenian alphabet and literary language from the works of his disciple Koriun as well as from a work of the fifth-century author Lazar Parbeci.[14] The most extensive account of Mesrop's/Mashtots' life is preserved in the hagiographic writing of Koriun.[15] Unlike the Lives of Saints Constantine/Cyril and Stephen of Perm the work by Koriun is mainly focused on the saint's activities as the inventor of the alphabet and as a teacher. According to the Vita, Mesrop/Mashtots was born in the family of a saintly man by the name of Vardan and was educated in a Greek school. He studied literature and languages as well as military disciplines. He served at the court of the Arsacids and became known there as a wise statesman. But he soon left office and became a monk and later a preacher.[16]

The Vita tells us that the idea of inventing the alphabet came to Mashtots while he was still at the court. But it was at the time when he was preaching to Armenians, who, a century after the country's Christianisation, were still 'weak in the faith', that he realised how the business of spreading the word of God would benefit from the use of the vernacular. The idea was supported by the patriarch and by the tsar of Armenia.[17] The latter informed Mesrop/Mashtots that there is a certain Syrian by the name of Daniel, who had letters for the Armenian language. Mesrop/Mashtots took those and taught children in schools with them for a few years. After a while, however, he realised that those were "not sufficient to properly reflect all the complications of the Armenian language".[18] So he sent half of his disciples to study Syriac and another half to study Greek. After many efforts they

---

13 SCHRAMM, Gottfried: Drei Schöpfer neuer Alphabete für den Ostrand der Christenheit (im 5., 9. und 14. Jahrhundert), in: Universalgeschichte und Nationalgeschichten, ed. by Gangolf HÜBINGER/Jürgen OSTERHAMMEL/Erich PELZER, Rombach 1994, pp. 73–103.

14 WINKLER, Gabriele: Koriwns Biographie des Mesrop Mastoc. Übersetzung und Kommentar, in: Orientalia Christiana Analecta 245 (1994); THOMSON, Robert: Mission, Conversion, and Christianization: The Armenian example, in: Studies in Armenian Literature and Christianity, Aldershot 1994, pp. 28–45.

15 I am going to use the following edition of this text: Корюн: Житие Маштоца. Перевод Ш.В.Смбатян и К. А. Мелик-Оганджанян, Erevan 1962 [Koriun: The Life of Mashtots].

16 Koriun, pp. 85–86.

17 Koriun, pp. 87–89.

18 Koriun, p. 90.

were given the revelation of the new script. And he started to translate the Old Testament with them.[19]

Following that, Mesrop/Mashtots started to teach his alphabet first of all to the court and later to the rest of the country. Koriun emphasises that teaching literacy went hand in hand with evangelisation of the country. In those parts of it where Christianity was not around at all, he set up churches, monasteries and many schools.[20] Later he went to other Caucasian people, called 'still barbarian' by Koriun, to establish alphabets for them as well. He is reported to have kept an eye on the process of learning and returned to the places he had visited before to be sure the alphabet was known well. He and his disciples continued work in translating the Gospels and the Christian liturgy. The hagiographer stresses that these activities again went hand in hand with further development of church organisation. It was absolutely clear for him that only with the new alphabet could his country become truly Christian.[21] To stress the authenticity of his work, Koriun underlines that he wrote about the events he had witnessed himself, not relying on oral tradition, but on his own eyes and ears.[22]

The Armenian alphabet consists almost entirely of freely invented signs, even though some minor influence from Greek can be detected. It is thus comparable to secret 'chiffres', which Mashtots may have known from his work in the chancellery. He seems to have been anxious to differ from both the Byzantine and the Syriac literacy systems and to delineate forms that were not only most suitable for the phonemes of Armenian, but also special and independent. As I have mentioned, according to the Vita, the new script was very well received by the tsar. It has been suggested that the uniqueness of the Armenian letters should be seen as an expression of the wish for independence. In those times, half of the country was under the jurisdiction of Syria while the western part of it was under the control of Byzantium. So it might very well have been the wish of Mashtots to create letters that would look neither like those of the Syrians nor like those of the Byzantines.[23]

But regardless of the role of the specially designed letters in building the identity of the Armenians, in the work of Koriun it is presented as absolutely crucial for success in bringing the Caucasian people to Christianity.

Four hundred years later another alphabet was invented for a newly converted people. The creation of a Slavonic alphabet by St. Constantine/Cyril in the mid-ninth-century is maybe the most 'politicised' of the stories of this kind. It reflects the competition between Latin clergy and the Byzantine newcomers, Constan-

---

19 Koriun, pp. 91–92.
20 Koriun, pp. 95–100.
21 Koriun, pp. 101–122.
22 Koriun, pp. 122.
23 Севак Гурген: Месроп Маштоц. Создание армянской письменности и словестности, Erevan 1962 [SEVAK, Gurgen: Mesrop Mashtots. Creation of the Armenian script and literacy]. See also SCHRAMM 1994, pp. 73–103.

tine and Methodius, for superiority over the newly converted Slavs of Moravia and Pannonia. Here the alphabet was the 'apple of contest'.

We learn about the invention of Slavonic script mainly from hagiographic sources. The one that is regarded as being contemporary with the events is the *Life of Constantine*, considered to have been written soon after the death of the saint (in 869) by one or more of his disciples.[24] It tells us the following: It was prince Rostislav (Rastislav) of Moravia who urged the saint to create the alphabet. In ch. 14 of this work we read that Rostislav wrote to the Byzantine Emperor Michael (the Third) that "though Moravians have rejected idolatry and become Christian" they need a teacher (and later in the text he adds: a bishop) who would explain them the basics of the Christian faith.[25]

This request was appreciated by the emperor and he ordered Constantine to invent Slavonic letters. Here again, as in the Life of Mashtots, we read about many unsuccessful efforts by predecessors of the saint to invent a suitable alphabet. After many prayers, Constantine finally received a revelation with the letters and started translating the Gospel using them.[26]

Later he went to Moravia, founded schools, and worked educating the locals. There he faced severe criticism from German and Frankish clergy, whose major argument was that one can glorify the Lord only in Hebrew, Greek and Latin. The author of the Vita calls those clerics three-linguals or Pilatians. He also suggests that Constantine had spent forty months in Moravia and went there to consecrate his disciples. He was in Venice debating with "Latin bishops and monks" for a Slavonic alphabet's right to exist when an invitation from Rome arrived. The appearance of Constantine at the Apostolic See was very welcome, since "it was known that he carried the relics of St. Clement, martyr and Roman pope". It was allowed that a liturgy in Slavonic be conducted in several churches in Rome starting with St. Peter's. That is how a Slavic liturgy (and by implication the new alphabet) was 'officially' approved.[27]

That the argument with Latin clergy really did take place we know also from letters and bulls of the popes. The bull *Industriae tuae* by Pope John VIII written in 880 agreed with the existence and use of "the Slavonic alphabet invented by Constantine the Philosopher". It refers to the Pentecost in its approval of the necessity to glorify the Lord in all languages (not only in the three main ones) and suggests that the Gospel was to be read in Latin first and later in Slavonic.[28]

---

24 Edited by: Лавров, Пётр А.: Материалы по истории возникновения древнейшей славянской письменности, Leningrad 1930, pp. 1–39 [LAVROV, Petr A.: Materials on the history of old Slavic literacy]. I am going to use the most recent translation with commentaries in: Флоря Борис Н.: Сказания о начале славянской письменности, St. Petersburg 2000 [FLORIA, B. N.: The legends on the beginnings of Slavic literacy].

25 Житие Константина (ЖК), p. 14; Сказания, p. 167.

26 Ibid.

27 ЖК pp. 15–17, pp. 168–175.

28 Сказания, p. 383.

Here too, for the author of the Vita the role of the alphabet in the popularisation of Christianity was understood as its central function. As we have seen, those in power approved this merit of the new script. The possible political implications of this approval as well as Constantine's and Methodius' probable ideas on that matter are extensively discussed in the literature.[29]

The problem of invention of a new type of signs for the alphabet which is believed to have been the one now known as Glagolitic, is most convincingly explained in the so-called "Legend of the invention of the Slavic letters by the monk Khrabr". Written most likely at the beginning of the 10th century, it maintains that letters of the Greek alphabet were insufficient for the proper transcription of all the sounds of Slavic speech. That is why it was so important to dream up completely new letters.[30] Whether they were designed as in case of Armenian alphabet, to be something absolutely unique for the needs of the self-identity of the Slavs, is difficult to judge. I believe it must have been rather the personal choice of the scholar Constantine with the aim of designing letters so that they might best serve the purpose of Slavic literacy. No doubt those who worked on this alphabet wanted it to be suitable for writing down Slavic texts so that the language should be perfectly reflected in it. But we should keep in mind that all this was done primarily for the sake of evangelisation of the newly converted, for making their language the language of the religion. It could have been used by different authorities as a tool in political games, but essentially and originally it was meant for the sake of a proper understanding of Christianity.

St. Stephen of Perm lived in the second half of the fourteenth century. He was born in the town of Ustjug to a Russian family. While still very young, he became a monk in one of the monasteries near Rostov. There he studied languages and decided to set out for the land of the Permians (Zyrians, Komi) on a mission for which he obtained the approval of Bishop Gerasim of Kolomna. He converted the Komi to Christianity, translated the liturgy and the Gospels into their vernacular for which he designed an alphabet, and became the first bishop of Perm. He died in 1396. Unfortunately, almost nothing of St. Stephen's translations into old Zyrian has survived.[31]

Stephen of Perm's Vita was written soon after his death, at the end of the fourteenth or the beginning of the fifteenth century, by Epiphanius the Most Wise, a friend of the saint, author of other hagiographic and theological works. There are about 50 known copies of the *Life,* half of which contain shorter versions of it.

29 VAVŘÍNEK, Vladimír: Staroslověnské životy Konstantina a Metoděje [Old Slavonic Lives of Constantine and Methodius], in: Rozpravy Československé Akademie Věd – Řada společenských věd 73,7 (1963); WOOD 2001, pp. 168–86.
30 Сказания, pp. 197–201.
31 More on St. Stephen see KUZNETSOVA, Anna: St. Stephen of Perm: Missionary and Popular Saint, in: The Man of Many Devices, Who Wandered Full Many Ways, Festschrift in honour of János M. Bak, ed. by B. NAGY and M. SEBŐK, Budapest 1999, pp. 222–29.

This is the major source on St. Stephen, but we can also learn about him from other hagiographic works, contemporary and later chronicles, and popular legends.[32]

At the end of the eighteenth century, academician Ivan Lepexin went on an expedition to various parts of the Ural region. He managed to collect materials among which were the letters of St. Stephen's alphabet and a fragment of his translation of the liturgy of St. John Chrysostom. These fragments of the translations and of the alphabet designed by St. Stephen suggest that he had recourse partly to Greek, partly to Slavic (i.e. Cyrillic) letters, but selected a good number of signs from the ideograms used by the Komi before Christianization. In this sense, his method was somewhat closer to that of Ulfila than to that of Mashtots and the Thessalonian brothers.

The hagiographer of the saint stresses that one of the most effective insights of Stephen of Perm was his realisation of the importance of the use of the vernacular for the conversion of the Komi. He was successful in his mission largely because he addressed pagans in their own language, for the people of the Ural region had been forced to pay tribute to Novgorod and later to Moscow, and had a long history of unfriendly relations with Slavic speakers.

St. Stephen's approach to the translation of the names of important Komi deities was very sophisticated. He did not insist on introducing calques from Greek or Russian to indicate the Father, the Son and the Holy Spirit, but rather used the words that already existed in Zyrian for venerated spirits. For example, it seems that the supreme god of the Komi, who created the entire universe, was called "Jen". Stephen accepted this name for the Christian "God" and used variations of it for the Son and the Holy Spirit. He did the same with the identification of the evil spirit of the Zyrians, who lived under the earth and was called "Kul'." St. Stephen introduced the usage for the Christian Komi that the word "Kul'" should mean "Devil." Clearly, by retaining the names of the main local deities, the saint made the changes of belief less sharp and thus easier to follow for his new Christians.

Let me come back now to the importance of the visual demonstration of a divinity's superiority in contrast to the effects of oral disputations on learned subjects for which the knowledge of the language was so important.

In the work of Epiphanius, St. Stephen's ability to win in debates with pagans is stressed several times. The most extensive description of a debate, including the arguments on both sides, is contained in the chapter "On the victory over the shaman." First, the hagiographer informs us that the shaman Pam and St. Stephen argued for a long time with no result. An important part of the contest was Pam's formulation of three major arguments against Christianity. The first was that the numerous pagan gods are patrons of different types of hunting, which makes the Permians very successful at collecting the furs of many different animals, which

---

32 The edition of St. Stephen's Life used here: Прохоров, Гелиан М.: Святитель Стефан Пермский. К 600-летию со дня преставления, St. Petersburg 1995 [PROKHOROV, Gelian M.: Bishop Stephen of Perm. On the 600th anniversary of his assumption].

can then be sold to Constantinople, Germany and Lithuania. The second argument was that his traditional faith helps the bear-hunter: the shaman maintains that even one or two of their men can kill a bear, while hundreds of Christians could not hunt down even one. Finally, Pam appears to refer to clairvoyance among shamans: he argues that the Permian faith is better because news is rapidly disseminated, and that "whatever happens in a far-off country, in a foreign town – the complete news of it reaches us at the same hour. And you Christians cannot learn this."[33] Even though we are reading a Christian author's Vita written for Christians and presumably reflecting the Christian perception of the heathen Zyrian faith, the three arguments give us a hint of what pagans may have considered the main strengths of their religion. This is quite rare for Vitae in general, as hagiographers were mainly interested in their saints and in Christian values and not in the ideas of pagans.

The description of the 'practical' part of the contest between Pam and Stephen, an ordeal by fire and water, came after the debate. Epiphanius does not tell us who initiated this ordeal. Although later Stephen asked Pam why he proposed what he could not accomplish, it was Stephen himself who made a burning hut to pass through and had an opening made in the ice on the Vychegda River to jump into. Such trials by fire and water are well known in challenges between shamans, and Stephen of Perm must have been aware of that and known exactly what would convince the heathens of Christian superiority. At first Pam agreed to the challenge, but then he lost courage, and when Stephen dragged him by the hand into the fire, he acknowledged defeat. He was convinced that the Christian had learned from childhood how to conjure fire and water, whereas he, Pam, did not possess this gift. The people demanded Pam's death according to their custom, but the saint rescued him. He condemned Pam to exile and forbade the shaman to eat and drink with the newly converted Christians.

This story of a competition between the shaman and St. Stephen illustrates the same pattern of missionary methods as the other ones. As before he was replacing names and objects of the pagan deities, so now he presented himself to the heathens as a kind of replacement of the mediator between them and the powers above. This competition, in the form of traditional shaman competitions, presented for the people in visual form the victory of a new and stronger 'shaman', St. Stephen, bishop of Perm. As such he was remembered for many centuries afterwards.

The different methods of confronting, transforming and incorporating elements of pagan beliefs into the Christian code of values had been a problem of missionaries at least since the times of Gregory the Great. The Vita of St. Stephen of Perm offers examples for these tactics in all possible spheres. According to the Vita and the folk tradition recorded elsewhere, the missionary not only replaced the meaning of numinous pagan names with that of *nomina sacra*, sanctuaries

33 I am quoting the translation of this passage in: Fedotov, George: The Russian Religious Mind, 2 vols., Cambridge, MA 1966, vol. II, pp. 238–240.

with churches, and Zyrian sacred trees with Biblical ones, but even succeeded in usurping the place of the old shamans of the Komi in popular memory.

The three examples of missionary alphabet-makers were far from each other in time and space alike. Sts. Constantine/Cyril and Methodius may have known about Mesrop/Mashtots, but it is unlikely; St. Stephen of Perm's hagiographer of course, knew about the Thessalonians, but was writing at a time when alphabets seemed to be all firmly established. I believe, though, that the three saints still resemble each other in so far as they – more or less consciously – recognised not only the importance of the vernacular for Christianization, but the value of designing a new alphabet for the newly converted. That not only gave them a feeling of what in modern (surely anachronistic) terms we should call self-identity or cultural independence, but gave them a better chance of obtaining their own language as a language of religion new to them: Christianity.

DUŠAN TŘEŠTÍK

Slawische Liturgie und Schrifttum im Böhmen des 10. Jahrhunderts.
Vorstellungen und Wirklichkeit

Die Frage des slawischen Schrifttums und der damit zusammenhängenden slawischen Liturgie im Böhmen des 10.–11. Jahrhunderts gehörte noch vor kurzem zu den Schlüsselfragen des Konzeptes der böhmischen Geschichte. Für eine einflussreiche Gruppe von Philologen und einigen Historikern soll das auf der Tradition der Heiligen Kyrill und Method fußende slawische Schrifttum die Hauptachse der älteren Nationalgeschichte gewesen sein, um die herum sich die Eigenart der durch ihre Sprache und Kultur definierten Nation herausgebildet hatte. Während dieser ganzen Jahrhunderte verlief in Böhmen angeblich ein Kampf zwischen der fremden, lateinischen (,deutschen') Kultur und der einheimischen slawischen Kultur, zwischen der West- und der Ostorientierung der werdenden Nation, ein zwar verlorener, aber doch tief die eigentlichen Wurzeln der tschechischen Kultur und Volkszugehörigkeit beeinflussender Kampf.

Die Geschichte dieser offen ideologischen Konstruktionen, deren ganz offensichtliche Zusammenhänge zunächst mit dem katholisch konservativen Flügel des nationalen Kampfes des 19. Jahrhunderts und zuletzt insbesondere mit dem Neoslawismus als Stütze von Benešs Politik des Seiltanzes zwischen Stalin und den westlichen Aliierten, mit Dank von den kommunistischen Ideologen übernommen, ist zwar faszinierend, deren Schilderung ist aber hier nicht unsere Aufgabe.[1] Sie überlebt übrigens als politische Ideologie heute nur noch an der äußersten Peripherie des gesellschaftlichen Lebens in verschiedenen obskuren Vereinen sowohl auf der extremen Rechten als auch auf der extremen Linken. Sie lebt allerdings auch noch als eine wissenschaftliche Theorie nach, heute selbstverständlich bereits ausschließlich an den Lehrstühlen der Slawistik, die immer noch durch ihren Rücktritt vom Ruhm nach 1989 desorientiert sind. Das Wesen dieser Theo-

---

1 Darüber HAUNER, Milan: Von der Verteidigung der „kleinen Völker" zum neuen Slawismus. Edvard Beneš und der Slawenmythos, in: Geschichtliche Mythen in den Literaturen und Kulturen Ostmittel- und Südosteuropas, hg. von E. BEHRING/L. RICHTER/W. F. SCHWARZ (Forschungen zur Geschichte und Kultur des östlichen Mitteleuropa 6), Stuttgart 1999, S. 293–309 und auch HADLER, Frank: Der Magna-Moravia-Mythos zwischen der Geschichtsschreibung und Politik im 19. und 20. Jahrhundert, in: Geschichtliche Mythen, S. 275–291. Aufmerksamkeit verdient in diesem Zusammenhang auch das unvollendete polemische Essay von ČERNY, Václav: Vývoj a zločiny panslavismu, Prag 1995. Zum Versuch Roman Jakobsons, auf der Kyrillo-Methodschen Kulturtradition ein neues, hart nationalistisches, das Traditionskonzept Palackýs ersetzende Konzept der tschechischen Geschichte aufzubauen (insbesondere im Buch Moudrost starých Čechů, New York 1943) vgl. LEHÁR, Jan: Roman Jakobson: Moudrost starých Čechů (Nedokončená polemika o smysl českých dějin), in: Česká literatura 43 (1995), S. 39–56.

rie besteht in der Überzeugung von einer ununterbrochenen Kontinuität des altkirchenslawischen Schrifttums und auch der Liturgie von Großmähren bis zum
přemyslidischen Böhmen des 10. und 11. Jahrhunderts, die zahlreiche altkirchenslawische literarische Denkmäler böhmischer Herkunft belegen sollen. Ihre
Anzahl und ihr Gattungsreichtum zwingen zur Vorstellung mehrerer Kulturzen-
tren,[2] in denen dieses Schrifttum in Böhmen gepflegt wurde und legen auch die
Vorstellung nahe, es hätte eine Art ‚slawische‘ Gruppe innerhalb der Landeskirche
des sich formierenden böhmischen Staates gegeben, die sich nicht nur durch die
Schrift, sondern selbstverständlich auch durch die Liturgie unterschied und mit
der vorherrschenden lateinischen Gruppe einen Konkurrenzkampf führte.[3] Im

---

2   In Wirklichkeit gab es in Böhmen vor der Entstehung Sazawas drei Klöster – Břewnow (bald Nie-
    dergang und dann Belegung mit bayrischen Mönchen aus Niederaltaich), Ostrov/Insula (aus Nie-
    deraltaich belegt) und das Frauenkloster St. Georg auf der Prager Burg – ein Bistum und dann nur
    noch etwa zwanzig Kirchen auf Verwaltungsburgen, die man jedoch auch beim besten Willen
    nicht als ‚Kulturzentren‘ betrachten kann.
3   Ältere Literatur verzeichnet ausführlich VEČERKA, Radoslav: Slovanské počátky české knižní
    vzdělanosti, Prag 1963. Ferner VEČERKA, R.: Velkomoravská literatura v přemyslovských Čechách,
    Slavia 32 (1963), S. 398–416; KADLEC, Jaroslav: Osudy slovanské bohoslužby v českých zemích od
    smrti sv. Metoděje do založení kláštera sázavského, in: KADLEC, J.: Svatý Prokop, Rom 1968, S. 22–
    34; VEČERKA, R.: Problematika staroslověnského písemnictví v přemyslovských Čechách, in: Sla-
    via 39 (1970), S. 223–237; MAREŠ, František V.: Die slawische Liturgie in Böhmen zur Zeit der
    Gründung des Prager Bistums, in: Millenium dioeceseos Pragensis 973–1973, Wien/Köln/Graz
    1974, S. 95–134. (auch in MAREŠ, F. V.: Cyrilometodějská tradice a slavistika, Prag 2000, S. 477–
    486); MAREŠ, F. V.: Církevně-slovanské písemnictví v Čechách, in: Id.: Cyrilometodějská tradice,
    S. 256–326; BLÁHOVÁ, Emilie: Staroslověnské písemnictví v Čechách 10. století, in: REICHER-
    TOVÁ, K./BLÁHOVÁ, E./HUŇÁČEK, V.: Sázava – památník staroslověnské kultury v Čechách,
    Prag 1988, S. 55–69; BLÁHOVÁ, E.: Staroslověnská literární činnost Sázavského kláštera, in: ibid.,
    S. 104–116; HAUPTOVÁ, Zoe: Církevněslovanské písemnictví v přemyslovských Čechách, in:
    Jazyk a literatura v historické perspektivě, Ústí nad Labem 1998, S. 5–42. Zuallerletzt versucht
    KONZAL, Václav: Církevněslovanská literatura – slepá ulička na prahu české kultury? in: Specu-
    lum medii aevi, Prag 1998, S. 150–158, die traditionellen Vorstellungen von einem Kampf zwi-
    schen der slawischen und der lateinischen Liturgie abzumildern und behauptet, dass es sich eigent-
    lich um keinen Streit handelte, dass beide Riten friedlich koexistierten bis zur Zeit Gregors VII.,
    der erst eine Vereinheitlichung und Zentralisierung des Ritus innerhalb der Kirche mit Nachdruck
    betrieb. Dies gilt sicher allgemein für Sazawa in den Jahren 1032–1096 (von anderen ‚Zentren‘ der
    slawischen Liturgie weiß man nichts, sie sind eine reine Annahme der Philologen), das als Kloster
    kein ernst zu nehmender Konkurrent des außerklösterlichen Priestertums war (auch wenn man
    die slawischen Mönche von hier im Jahre 1056 vorübergehend vertrieb); für das 10. Jahrhundert
    könnte man dies aber selbstverständlich nur dann in Betracht ziehen, wenn die slawische Litur-
    gie damals in Böhmen tatsächlich existiert hätte. Ablehnend diesen Mutmaßungen gegenüber
    stand insbesondere GRAUS, František: Slovanská liturgie a písemnictví v přemyslovských Čechách
    10. stoleti, in: Český časopis historický 14 (1966), S. 473–495 und unlängst CLIFTON-EVEREST,
    John M.: Slawisches Schrifttum im 10. und 11. Jahrhundert in Böhmen, in: Bohemia 37 (1996),
    S. 257–270. Einen besonderen Standpunkt vertritt Králík, der zwar die Kontinuität der slawischen
    Liturgie und des slawischen Schrifttums zwischen Großmähren und dem přemyslidischen Böhmen
    ablehnte, jedoch ihr Wiederaufleben unter Adalbert annahm: KRÁLÍK, Oldřich: Josef Dobrovský
    a bádání o počátcích českých dějin, in: Pocta Zdeňku Nejedlému, Olomouc 1959, S. 73–140; Id.:
    K počátkům literatury v přemyslovských Čechách (Rozpravy ČSAV, Reihe SV, 70, Heft 6) Prag
    1960; Id.: Kosmova kronika a předchozí tradice, Prag 1976; Id.: Kržeščenije Borživoja i vopros
    o nepreryvnosti staroslavjanskoj literatury v Čechii, in: Trudy Otdela drevnerusskoj literatury 19
    (1963), S. 148–168; Id.: Labyrint dávných dějin českých, Prag 1970; Id.: Nejstarší rodokmen české

Hintergrund dieser Vorstellung steht eine Kirche russischen Typs, eine zwar universale (byzantinische), aber mit eigener Schrift und Liturgie, also ‚nationale' Kirche. Der Rahmen aller dieser Betrachtungen ist slawistisch, die Frage wird als ein Überleben des Erbes der Hll. Kyrill und Method im Bereich der *Slavia orthodoxa* behandelt. Das Ergebnis, zu dem Böhmen allerdings – zum großen Bedauern der Philologen – nicht gelangte, hätte das Herausbilden einer einheimischen Kultur auf byzantinischer Grundlage sein sollen. In Wirklichkeit handelt es sich aus der Sicht der böhmischen Entwicklung um das genau entgegengesetzte Phänomen, um die verschiedensten, aber doch überall im wesentlichen die gleichen Versuche, in den neu entstehenden und sich etablierenden Landeskirchen des lateinischen Europa aus praktischen Gründen die einheimische Sprache zu benutzen, wobei alle, mit Ausnahme des angelsächsischen Englands, Irlands und später auch Norwegens, scheiterten und Latein siegte. Die in die Gemeinschaft des christlichen Europa im 10. Jahrhundert eintretenden Staaten in Mitteleuropa Polen, Ungarn bzw. in Skandinavien Dänemark und Schweden, machten diese Etappe des Versuchs ihrer einheimischen Sprache für ihr Christentum überhaupt nicht durch, nur Böhmen hatte offenbar so etwas versucht, wenn auch nur vorübergehend und offensichtlich ohne Nachdruck. Aus dieser Sicht ist allerdings das Ergebnis, das Böhmen erreichte, gleich wie anderswo in diesem westlichen Bereich: die Annahme der universalen lateinischen Bildung. Würden wir eine solche teleologische Sicht akzeptieren, müssten wir sagen, dass es kein Scheitern, sondern die Erfüllung war.

Die positive bzw. negative Wertung, mit der wir eine solche oder andere gezielte (teleologische) ‚Entwicklung' belegen, ist natürlich nicht in ihr selbst enthalten, sondern in uns, es sind unsere Werte und keine Geschichtswerte. Sie werden jedoch zu einem beträchtlichen Teil vom Rahmen bestimmt, in dem wir geschichtliche Ereignisse erzählen. Die Slawisten können es noch heute bedauern, dass wir uns nicht an die mächtige Eiche der slawischen Kultur im Osten angeschlossen hatten, sie können jedoch nicht die Augen verschließen vor der Tatsache, dass es darum ging, wie und nicht ob sich der přemyslidische Staat in den lateinischen Kulturkreis eingliedern wird. Vor so einer einigermaßen realistischen Alternative der Wahl zwischen Ost und West stand vielleicht die Rus in der Zeit Wladimirs[4] und teilweise auch Ungarn vor Stephan,[5] aber nicht Böhmen in der Zeit der ers-

literatury, Prag 1971; Id.: Nová fáze sporů o slovanskou kulturu v přemyslovských Čechách, in: Slavia 37 (1968), S. 474–494; Id.: Od Radima ke Kosmovi (Acta Universitatis Palackianae Olomucensis, Facultas Philosophica 48, Philologica XXVI), Prag 1968; Id.: Sázavské písemnictví XI. století (Rozpravy ČSAV, Reihe SV, 71, Heft 12), Prag 1961; Id.: V příšeří české protohistorie (Acta Universitatis Palackianae Olomucensis, Fac. Philos. 56, Philologica 28), Prag 1969; Id.: Vozniknovenije 1go staroslovjanskogo „Žitija Vjačeslava", in: Byzantinoslavica 27 (1966), S. 131–163.

4 Zu Wladimirs berühmter ‚Glaubenswahl' gibt die letzte Übersicht W. J. PETRUCHIN in: Christianstvo v stranach vostočnoj, jugo-vostočnoj i central'noj Evropy na poroge vtorogo tysjačletija, hg. von B. N. FLORJA, Moskau 2002, S. 69–91.

5 ERSZEGI, Géza: Die Christianisierung Ungarns anhand der Quellen, in: Europas Mitte um 1000. Beiträge zur Geschichte, Kunst und Archäologie, Bd. 2, hg. von A. WIECZOREK/H.-M. HINZ, Stuttgart 2000, S. 600–607; GYÖRFFY, Gy.: La christianisation de l'Hongrie, in: Harvard

ten Boleslaws. Vor einer Wahl zwischen ‚West und Ost', die eine so große Rolle in den ideologischen Konstruktionen der Neoslawisten·spielt, stand sogar nicht einmal Großmähren im 9. Jahrhundert. Es genügt, sich die unbestrittenen Fakten zu vergegenwärtigen: Die ursprüngliche Mission der beiden Brüder von Thessaloniki in den Jahren 863–867 hatte keinen machtpolitischen Hintergrund, es ging dabei nicht um Schließung eines Bündnisses Rostislaws mit Byzanz gegen das Ostfränkische Reich und die Bulgaren, wie es offensichtlich irrtümlich mehrere Historiker vermuteten.[6] Das spätere Erzbistum des hl. Method der Jahre 873–885 stützte sich gegen die Ansprüche der ostfränkischen Kirche voll und vorbehaltlos auf Rom und nicht auf Konstantinopel. Erneuert wurde es im Jahre 899 ebenfalls von Rom aus. Methods Streit mit dem Bischof von Neutra (Nitra) Wiching um die slawische Liturgie spielte sich vor Päpsten ab und hatte auf Methods Seite weder unter dem Aspekt der Rechtsprechung noch unter dem der Glaubenslehre etwas mit Byzanz zu tun. Als Streit zwischen dem westlich-lateinischen und dem orthodox-byzantinischen Christentum wird er, ganz im Stil der zeitgenössischen Polemiken gegen die ‚Lateiner', erst in Theophylaktos' Vita des hl. Kliment aus dem Ende des 11. Jahrhunderts dargestellt,[7] d. h. aus der Zeit nach dem Schisma. Realistisch konnte Großmähren zwischen der fränkischen Kirche und Rom wählen. Da die Franken als unabdingbare Bedingung der Eingliederung in ihre Kirche die politische Unterwerfung stellten,[8] wählten die Mährer und dann ihr Erzbischof Rom. Im 10. Jahrhundert war aber keine dieser Alternativen mehr aktuell, besonders nicht für das neue Regnum der Přemysliden. Diese Alternativen existierten nur in den Köpfen der Slawisten und einiger Historiker.

Versuchen wir also unsere Frage soweit möglich ohne diese ideologischen Vorurteile zu untersuchen. Wir beginnen mit einer Frage an die Hauptquellen und

---

Ukrainian Studies 12-13 (1988-89), S. 75-86; MARSINA, Richard: Kristianizácia Maďarov a Uhorska medzi východom a západom, in: Historický časopis 40 (1992), S. 409-421; GYÖRFFY, Gy.: Zu den Anfängen der ungarischen Kirchenorganisation auf Grund quellenkritischer Ergebnisse, in: Archivum Historiae Pontificae 7 (1969), S. 79–113. Die slawische Liturgie in Polen (eine Übersicht aus der Sicht deren Anhänger gibt beispielsweise DVORNIK, František: Byzantské misie u Slovanů, Prag 1971, S. 204–214 [DVORNIK, Francis: Byzantine missions among the Slavs, New Brunswick 1970]) ist – bekanntermaßen – eine historische Legende, die sich auf eine Reihe waghalsiger Mutmaßungen und nicht auf Fakten stützt. Vgl. die vernichtende Kritik dieser Hypothesen von LABUDA, Gerard: O obrządku słowiańskim w Polsce południowej, czyli krakowscy biskupi przed rokiem 1000, in: LABUDA, G.: Studia nad początkami państwa polskiego II, Poznań 1988, S. 83–166.

6 Vgl. TŘEŠTÍK, Dušan: Vznik Velké Moravy. Moravané, Čechové a střední Evropa v letech 791–871, Prag 2001, S. 184ff.

7 Siehe Anm. 133.

8 Klar formulierte das der Salzburger Erzbischof Theotmar in seinem Schreiben an Papst Johann IX. im Jahre 900. Darin sagt er, dass die Mährer die Taufe aus dem Reich empfingen und deshalb müssen sie diesem – ob sie wollen oder nicht – sowohl in geistigen als auch in weltlichen Dingen untertan sein, LOŠEK, F.: Die Conversio Bagoariorum et Carantanorum und der Brief des Erzbischofs Theotmar von Salzburg (MGH Studien und Texte 15), Hannover 1997, S. 140: ... *in terram Sclauorum, qui Maraui dicitur, quae regibus nostris et populo nostro, nobis cum habitatoribus suis subacta fuerat tam in cultu christianae religionis quam in tributo substantiae secularis quia exinde primum imbuti et ex paganis christianes sunt facti.* Und weiter (S. 146): *sive velint, sive nolint, regno nostro subacti erunt.*

werden nach dem tatsächlichen Gewicht des slawischen Schrifttums im entstehenden přemyslidischen Staat fragen. Da es sich großenteils um Legenden über
die ersten böhmischen Heiligen, den hl. Wenzel und seine Großmutter Ludmila handelt, kommen wir dadurch zu der sehr komplizierten Frage des gegenseiti-
gen Verhältnisses und der Datierung der einzelnen lateinischen und altkirchenslawischen Schriften. Wir können diese Frage hier nicht in ihrer ganzen Breite
erörtern, werden jedoch versuchen, immer vom neuesten Stand der hundert Jahre alten Diskussion[9] auszugehen und zumindest die sachlichen Hintergründe der
einzelnen Probleme kurz darzustellen.

Wir müssen vor allem das mit der Tätigkeit des frühestens im Jahre 1032 gegründeten und als slawisch bis zum Jahre 1096–1097 bestehenden Sazawer Klosters verbundene Schrifttum sorgfältig vom vorangehenden Zeitraum trennen. Die
Frage kann man auch so stellen, ob der slawische Charakter von Prokops Kloster Sazawa der einheimischen böhmischen Umgebung des 10. und Anfang des
11. Jahrhunderts entstammte, oder ob er ein Import aus dem Ausland war. Um
die Annahme der ersten Möglichkeit durchzusetzen, datieren die Slawisten eine
lange Reihe literarischer Werke in die Zeit vor dem Sazawa-Kloster. F.V. Mareš
zählt in seiner kritischen Übersicht insgesamt 26 hypothetisch in die Zeit vor der
Entstehung dieses Klosters[10] datierte Schriften angeblich böhmischer Herkunft
auf, er selbst beschränkt jedoch sofort die Zahl auf drei, die laut ihm unbestritten
sind: I. Altkirchenslawische St.Wenzelslegende,[11] II. Altkirchenslawische Legen-

---

9 Übersichten: PEKAŘ, Josef: Die Wenzels- und Ludmila-Legenden und die Echtheit Christians,
   Prag 1906, S. 262–280; URBÁNEK, Rudolf: Legenda tzv. Kristiána ve vývoji předhusitských legend
   václavských a ludmilských a její autor, Bd. 1, Prag 1947, S. 7–31; LUDÍKONVSKÝ, Jaroslav: Crescente
   fide, Gumpold a Kristián. (Příspěvek k datování legendy Kristiánovy s dodatkem o dnešním stavu
   této otázky), in: Sborník prací filosofické fakulty Brněnské university D 4 (1955), S. 53–63; JILEK,
   H.: Die Wenzels- und Ludmila-Legenden des 10. und 11. Jahrhunderts (Forschungsbericht), in:
   Zeitschrift fúr Ostforschung 24 (1975), S.101–121; LUDÍKONVSKÝ, Jaroslav: Latinské legendy
   českého středověku, in: Sborník prací filosofické fakulty Brněnské univerzity E 18/19 (1973/74),
   S.99–148; TŘEŠTÍK, Dušan: Počátky Přemyslovců. Vstup Čechů do dějin (530–935), Prag 1997,
   S. 117–122. In Bezug auf die altkirchenslawischen Legenden: KONZAL Václav, in: Staroslověnské
   legendy českého původu, Prag 1976.
10 MAREŠ: Slovanská liturgie v Čechách, S. 483. Ähnlich auch BLÁHOVÁ: Staroslověnské písemnictví v Čechách 10. století, S. 55–69. Viel vorsichtiger ist HAUPTOVÁ: Církevněslovanské písemnictví, die das Vorhaben aufgibt, bestimmte Werke eindeutig der Zeit vor Sazawa zuzuordnen. Die
   böhmische Herkunft einer Reihe dieser Werke stellt grundsätzlich in Frage THOMSON, Francis J.:
   A Survey of the vitae allegedly translated from Latin into Slavonic in Bohemia in the tenth and eleventh centuries, in: Popoli e paesi nella cultura altomedievale (Settimane di studio del Centro italiano di studi sull' alto medioevo 29), Spoleto 1983, S. 331–348, der zeigt, dass sie aus dem Griechischen und nicht aus dem Lateinischen übersetzt wurden, daher nicht in Böhmen (vgl. auch ders.:
   Early Slavonic translations – an Italo-Greek connection?, in: Slavica Gandensia 12 (1985), S. 221–
   234).
11 Die Legende ist in drei Fassungen bekannt, von denen sich eine in Kroatien und zwei in Russland
   erhalten haben. Die kroatisch-glagolitische Fassung veröffentlichte VAJS, J., in: Sborník starosla-
   vanských literárních památek o sv. Václavu a sv. Lidmile, hg. Von J. VAJS, Prag 1929, S. 31–43; die
   russischen Fassungen, die sog. Wostokowsche und die Menologien-Fassung, gab N. J. SEREBRJANS-
   KIJ heraus in: Sborník, S. 11–28 (kommentierte Übersetzung ins Tschechische siehe V. KONZAL in:
   Staroslověnské legendy, S. 55–140). Ein neues Manuskript der Wostokowschen Fassung entdeckte

de über denselben Heiligen[12] (d. h. eine nicht allzu gelungene slawische, aus anderen Quellen ergänzte Übersetzung der Gumpoldslegende)[13] sowie das Lied Hospodine pomiluj ny (Herr, erbarme dich unser).[14] Dazu ordnet er noch, als teilweise hypothetisch, die nicht erhaltene altkirchenslawische St. Ludmilalegende, deren Überrest der in der Rus angefertigte Auszug für den Prolog[15] ist, d. h. eine Art kurze ‚Brevierlesungen' aus den in vollem Wortlaut in den Menologien enthaltenen Legenden.

Auch diese minimalistische Aufzählung ist jedoch ebenfalls mehr als übertrieben. Die Datierung der II. Altkirchenslawischen Legende in die Zeit kurz nach dem Jahr 1000, die Mareš als gesichert benutzt,[16] stützt sich auf nichts außer dem vagen Eindruck von J. Vašica,[17] die Legende müsse bald nach der Predigt am Feiertag der Translation des hl. Wenzel *Licet plura* entstanden sein,[18] deren Autor angeblich der hl. Adalbert war.[19] Die Homilie kommt in den Manuskrip-

---

A. N. TURILOV: Novyj spisok Vostokovskoj legendy, in: Litterae slavicae medii aevi Francisco Venceslao Mareš sexageario ... oblatae (Sagners Slawistische Sammlung 8), München 1985, S. 104–109. Zur Orientierung eines des Altkirchenslawischen bzw. des Tschechischen unkundigen Lesers dient die lateinische Übersetzung von M. WEINGART: První česko-církevněslovanská legenda o sv. Václavu, in: Svatováclavský sborník, Bd. 1, Prag 1934, S. 974–983. Es handelt sich allerdings um Weingarts hypothetische ‚Rekonstruktion' des ursprünglichen Textes (die Übersetzungen von KANTOR, Marvin: The Origins of Christianity in Bohemia: Sources and Commentary, Evanston 1990, waren mir nicht zugänglich).

Allgemein nahm man stets an, dass die kroatisch-glagolitische Fassung dem Archetyp am nächsten steht und dass die Wostokowsche Fassung deren spätere Bearbeitung darstellt, wobei die allerletzte, sicher die in der Rus entstandene Umarbeitung der Menologien-Fassung sein sollte. Tkadlčík und Konzal versuchen hingegen zu beweisen, dass die ursprüngliche Fassung die Wostokowsche ist; TKADLČÍK, V.: První staroslověnská legenda o sv. Václavu a Besedy sv. Řehoře Velikého, in: Litterae slavicae medii aevi Francisco Venceslao Mareš sexagenario ... oblatae (Sagners Slawistische Sammlung 8), München 1985, S. 329–334; KONZAL, V.: První staroslovanská legenda václavská a její „Sitz im Leben", in: Studia Medievalia Pragensia 1 (1988), S. 113–127. Ihre Argumente sind jedoch kaum überzeugend, vgl. TŘEŠTÍK: Počátky Přemyslovců, S. 220–223. Einmalig – und völlig unmöglich – ist der Versuch, die Menologien-Fassung für die ursprüngliche zu halten; PODHORNÝ, J.: Sporné otázky dvou staroslověnských legend václavských, in: Slavia 45 (1978), S. 159–174.

12 Herausgegeben von J. VAŠICA in: Sborník, S. 69–135 (kommentierte Übersetzung ins Tschechische von KONZAL in: Staroslověnské legendy, S. 141–189).

13 Gumpoldi: Mantuani episcopi, Vita Venceslai, hg. von J. EMLER, in: Fontes Rerum Bohemicarum (FRB), Bd. 1, Prag 1878, S. 146–166. Über Gumpolds rhetorischen Stil zuletzt KALIVODA, Jan: Semper laus eius in ore meo, in: Acta Universitatis Carolinae – Philologica 3 (Graecolatina Pragensia XIX), 2002, S. 95–105.

14 Edition aufgrund aller Manuskripte und eine detaillierte Analyse: MAREŠ, F. V.: Hospodine pomiluj ny, in: Id.: Cyrilometodějská tradice, S. 403–476; hier ältere Literatur. Neuere Edition LEHÁR, J.: Česká středověká lyrika, Prag 1990, S. 15–29.

15 Hg. von N. J. SEREBRJANSKIJ in: Sborník staroslovanských, S. 64f. (kommentierte Übersetzung ins Tschechische: KONZAL, V. in: Staroslověnké legendy, S. 261–286).

16 Vgl. MAREŠ: Cyrilometodějská písemnictví, S. 294.

17 VAŠICA in: Sborník staroslovanských, S. 79.

18 Hg. von J. PEKAŘ: Die Wenzels- und Ludmila-Legenden und die Echtheit Christians, Prag 1906, S. 385–388.

19 Dies versuchte H. G. VOIGT zu beweisen, ohne dass er jedoch irgendwelche gewichtigeren Argumente hätte anführen können: Der Sermon von der Übertragung des hl. Wenzels. Věstník Královské české společnosti nauk, třída filosoficko-historická, 1906, Bd. 4, S. 1–7. Die letzte Analyse der

ten regelmäßig in Verbindung mit der Gumpoldslegende vor und es verwundert daher nicht, dass der Autor der II. Altkirchenslawischen Legende, der Gumpold übersetzte, diese zur Verfügung hatte und sie zitierte. Die Homilie spricht von den „bisher überlebenden" Zeugen des Wunders bei St. Wenzels Translation[20] und Pekař datierte sie deshalb an das genaue Ende des 10. Jahrhunderts.[21] Auch wenn man diesem in der Hagiographie üblichen Hinweis auf die Zeugen Glauben schenken und die *Licet plura* etwa ans Ende des 10. Jahrhunderts datieren sollte, würde es noch nicht bedeuten, dass der die Homilie zitierende Übersetzer Gumpolds kurz nach deren Entstehung arbeiten musste. Er kann sie doch jederzeit nachher kennengelernt haben. Die Legende wurde offenbar erst im Sazawer Kloster übersetzt,[22] frühestens vor dem Jahr 1050, als sie schon in der Rus bekannt war. Sehr wahrscheinlich zitierte sie[23] nämlich der Metropolit Ilarion in seinem „Slovo o zakone i blagodati" („Wort über das Gesetz und die Gnade"),[24] das er in Anwesenheit des Fürsten Jaroslaws des Weisen irgendwann in den Jahren 1037–1050 vortrug.[25]

Im Sazawer Kloster wurde sicher auch die Übersetzung der ursprünglichen nicht erhaltenen lateinischen St. Ludmilalegende *Fuit in Provincia Bohemorum* verfasst. Diese gelangte gemeinsam mit weiteren Böhmischen Legenden nach der Rus, wo sie für den Prolog aufbereitet wurde.[26] Die Paralleltexte zu der lateinischen Legende *Fuit in provincia Bohemorum*[27] sind die betreffenden Kapitel der Christianslegende[28] und den Handlungsfaden bewahrt auch der altkirchenslawi-

---

Frage von Adalberts ‚literarischem Nachlass', dargestellt von H. FROS: Czy biskup męczennik pozostawił po sobie spuściznę literacką?, in: Tropami świętego Wojciecha, hg. von Z. KURNA-TOWSKA, Poznań 1999, S. 133–145, kommt zu dem Schluss, dass man Adalbert mit einer gewissen Wahrscheinlichkeit vielleicht nur die Homilie über den Heiligen Alexius zuschreiben kann, alle übrigen Zuschreibungen sind unmöglich (genauso LABUDA, G.: Święty Wojciech biskup – męczennik, patron Polski, Czech i Węgier, Wrocław 2000, S. 151ff.). Fast sicher ist aber Adalberts Urheberschaft einer bisher unbekannten bischöflichen Predigt für Priester in einer Heiligenkreuz-Handschrift (hierzu siehe Anm. 141). Vgl. ZACHOVA, Jana/TŘEŠTÍK, D.: Adhortace De ammonitione ad presbyteros a biskup Vojtěch, in: Český časopis historický 99 (2001), S. 279–293.

20 PEKAŘ: Die Wenzels- und Ludmila-Legenden, S. 385: *ut plures adhuc visi miraculi superstites referunt testes.*

21 PEKAŘ: Die Wenzels- und Ludmila-Legenden, S. 380 und 38f.

22 Dies bewies überzeugend KRÁLÍK, Oldřich: Prameny II. staroslověnské legendy václavské, in: Slavia 31 (1962), S. 578–598. Hierzu neigt auch KONZAL in: Staroslověnské legendy, S. 143.

23 Vgl. ROZOW, N. N.: Iz istorii russko-češskich literaturnych svjazej drevnejšego perioda, in: Trudy otdela drevnerusskoj literatury 23 (1968), S. 75f.

24 Hg. von L. MÜLLER: Des Metropoliten Ilarion Lobrede auf Wladimir den Heiligen und Glaubensbekenntnis, Wiesbaden ²1962.

25 JAKUBOWSKI, W.: Ilarion, in: Słownik Starożytności Słowiańskich 2 (1964), S. 250–251; ROZOW, N. N.: Ilarion, in: Slovar' knižnikov i knižnosti Drevnej Rusi, Moskau 1987, S. 198–204.

26 Zur Entwicklung der Ludmila-Legende vgl. TŘEŠTÍK: Počátky Přemyslovců, S. 138–174.

27 Hg. von Václav CHALOUPECKY: Prameny X. století legendy Kristiánovy o svatém Václavu a svaté Ludmile (Svatováclavský sborník 2,2), Prag 1939, S. 459–481. Der eigentliche Text endet in der Edition allerdings mit Kapitel 7 auf S. 476, den Rest hat Chaloupecký irrtümlich hinzugefügt. Es handelt sich um Auszüge aus der Christian-Legende, in einigen Manuskripten an Fuit angefügt.

28 Hg. von J. LUDÍKOVSKÝ: Kristiánova legenda – Legenda Christiani, Prag 1978. Über die Legende und die Streitigkeiten um sie TŘEŠTÍK: Počátky Přemyslovců, S. 117–137 mit älterer Literatur.

che Prologsauszug aus der nicht erhaltenen altkirchenslawischen Legende.[29] Diese
betrachtete man als Vorlage der Fuit- und Christianslegende, offenbar jedoch zu
Unrecht. Diese Vorlage wurde nämlich offenbar vom gleichen Autor verfasst wie
die St.Wenzelslegende *Crescente fide christiana*, also vom in Prag kurz nach dem
Jahre 975 wirkenden Regensburger Mönch oder zumindest von einem Autor, der
in der gleichen Umgebung des Prager Archipresbyteriats wirkte. Es war also zweifellos eine lateinische Legende. Die Filiation ist daher wie folgt:[30]

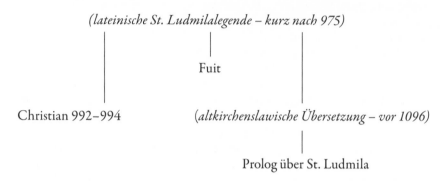

(lateinische St. Ludmilalegende – kurz nach 975)

Fuit

Christian 992–994   *(altkirchenslawische Übersetzung – vor 1096)*

Prolog über St. Ludmila

Die altkirchenslawische Legende, die Vorlage für den Prolog-Auszug, war offensichtlich eine Übersetzung der ursprünglichen lateinischen Legende (grob der
Fuit-Legende entsprechend), die nach dem Jahr 975 und vor dem Jahr 1096 entstand, denn allein in dieser Zeit konnte sie aus Sazawa nach der Rus gelangen.
Auch wenn wir damit eine ziemlich breite Datierung bekommen, kann man kaum
bezweifeln, dass die Übersetzung im Kloster Sazawa entstand.

Das Lied *Hospodine pomiluj ny* ist aus Aufzeichnungen im 14. Jahrhundert
bekannt und nichts in seinem Text ermöglicht dessen Datierung. Es wird zwar
am häufigsten ins 10. Jahrhundert datiert, vor allem aufgrund der Tradition
über Adalberts Urheberschaft, die bereits im 13. Jahrhundert belegt[31] und dann
besonders in diesem Lied gewidmeten Traktat Johanns von Holleschau (Jan z
Holešova) dargestellt ist,[32] wirkliche Stützen für dessen Datierung fehlen jedoch.
Einige Worte des sehr kurzen Textes betrachtet man als „altkirchenslawisch",

---

Neuere Stellungnahmen: FLORA, Boris N.: Kirillomefodievskie tradicii v „Legende Kristiana",
in: Byzantinoslavica 56 (1995), S.571–577; KØLLN, Hermann: Die Wenzelslegende des Mönchs
Christian (Den Kongelige Danske Videskabernes Selskab, Historisk-filosofiske Meddelelser 73),
Kopenhagen 1996; KALIVODA, Jan: Historiographie oder Legende? „Christianus monachus"
und sein Werk im Kontext der mitteleuropäischen Literatur des 10. Jahrhunderts, in: Beiträge zur
Altertumskunde, Bd.141, München/Leipzig 2001, S.136–155.

29 Siehe Anm. 30.

30 TŘEŠTÍK: Počátky Přemyslovců, S.174.

31 II. Fortsetzung von Cosmas zum Jahr 1260 (FRB, Bd.2, S.319): *canentes hymnum a sancto Adalberto editum.*

32 NEJEDLY, Zdeněk: Dějiny předhusitského zpěvu I, Prag ²1954, S.425: *in Libic hoc canticum
composuit, populum informavit et cum populo illud cantavit ad Dominum Deum ut fames et gwerras
averteret et necessitam pacem in terra daret.*

die übrigen als „tschechisch", für die Datierung hat es jedoch keine Bedeutung.[33]
Sofern die Annahme richtig wäre, dass das Lied wirklich altkirchenslawisch und
nicht einfach allgemein slawisch („prototschechisch') mit einigen altkirchenslawischen Elementen des kirchlichen Wortschatzes ist, könnten wir es genauso gut in
die Sazawa-Zeit datieren.

Es bleibt also wirklich nur die I. Altkirchenslawische Legende. Man kann wohl
nicht ernsthaft bezweifeln, dass sie in Böhmen geschrieben wurde,[34] umstritten
kann nur deren Datierung sein. Wenn sie bald nach Wenzels Ermordung entstanden wäre, irgendwann um das Jahr 940, wie es sich die meisten Slawisten vorstellen,[35] könnte man annehmen, dass sie von einem in der altkirchenslawischen
Schrift noch in Mähren gebildeten Priester verfasst wurde,[36] der dann nach Böhmen ging und hier die Legende zu Ehren eines neuen böhmischen Heiligen verfasste. Sie müsste also nicht notwendigerweise das lebendige altkirchenslawische
Schrifttum und die Kontinuität dessen Tradition in Böhmen belegen. Aber die
Legende ist offenkundig ein nicht allzu sorgfältiger Auszug aus der ursprünglichen lateinischen St. Wenzelslegende, der Grundlage der ganzen weiteren hagio-
graphischen Tradition.[37] Diese verlorene lateinische Legende entstand noch vor
der Zeit um das Jahr 975, aus der die älteste zuverlässig datierbare St. Wenzelslegende *Crescente fide* stammt, und selbstverständlich nach Wenzels Ermordung im
Jahre 935. Sie muss für die Bedürfnisse des bereits gefestigten St. Wenzelskultes
geschrieben worden sein, wohl frühestens nach Wenzels Translation aus Altbunzlau (Stará Boleslav) nach Prag, die sein Brudermörder Boleslaw I. veranstaltete.

Der Sinn dieser moralisch und politisch sehr heiklen Tat, mit der sich Boleslav doch zur Ermordung nicht nur seines Bruders, sondern auch eines Heiligen
bekannte, kann nichts anderes als Wenzels Kanonisation gewesen sein.[38] Zu der

---

33 Zur Datierung MAREŠ: Hospodine, S. 446ff. Er stützt sich ausschließlich auf unsichere sprachliche Phänomene, vor allem auf den Untergang der schwachen weichen und harten Zeichen (*jers*),
   die es im Lied noch gibt. Deren Vokalisierung legt er – allerdings hypothetisch – an das Ende des
   10. bis an den Anfang des 11. Jh. Ferner stützt er sich auf das Wort Hospodin mit der Bedeutung
   „Herrgott", von dem es ihm „scheint", dass man in der zweiten Hälfte des 10. Jh. begann, es in diesem Sinne zu verwenden. Als Beleg dient ihm jedoch die II. altkirchenslawische Legende, die er in
   das Jahr 1000 datiert – allerdings irrtümlich, in Wirklichkeit ist es eine im Sazawa-Kloster entstandene Schrift.
34 Nur KRÁLÍK: Vozniknovenie, S. 158ff. lokalisierte die Entstehung der Legende nach Kroatien.
   Die Textfakten sprechen aber eindeutig für deren böhmische Herkunft, auch wenn der Autor der
   Legende (oder deren Vorlage, der Legende X?) offensichtlich die Akten der berühmten kroatischen
   Synode in Split im Jahr 925 kannte (vgl. TŘEŠTÍK, D.: Miscellanea k I. staroslověnské legendě o sv.
   Václavu: „Každý, kdo povstává proti pánu svému, podoben jest Jidáši", in: Československý časopis
   historický 15 (1967), S. 337–343).
35 So z. B. VAJS in: Sborník, S. 34f.; WEINGART: První česko-církevněslovanská legenda, S. 124 (laut
   ihm entstand die Legende sogar in ihrem Passionsabschnitt, ohne einige Sätze über die Translation, „an der Wende von den zwanziger zu den dreißiger Jahren des X. Jahrhunderts", d. h. über dem
   kaum kalt gewordenen Leichnam Wenzels).
36 Über die mährischen Priester im frühpřemyslidischen Böhmen siehe unten.
37 Meine Annahme dieser verlorenen Legende (Legende X) ist die Grundlage meiner Filiation der
   Wenzels- und Ludmila-Legenden. Vgl. TŘEŠTÍK: Počátky Přemyslovců, S. 239ff.
38 Siehe CIBULKA, Josef: Václavova rotunda sv. Víta, in: Svatováclavský sborník, Bd. 1, Prag 1934,
   S. 386ff.

war damals keine päpstliche Genehmigung notwendig, es reichte lediglich die Zustimmung und die Teilnahme des zuständigen Diözesanbischofs.[39] Das Datum des Ereignisses ist dabei bei weitem nicht so klar, wie man oft annahm. Die Legende *Crescente fide* (und die von ihr abgeleiteten Legenden) behauptet, dass es zur Translation drei Jahre nach dem Mord kam,[40] d.h. akzeptiert man 935 als das Mordjahr,[41] im Jahre 938. Die von der ursprünglichen, nichterhaltenen St. Wenzelslegende direkt abgeleiteten Legenden, d.h. die I. Altkirchenslawische und die Laurentius-Legende wissen aber nichts von den drei Jahren und datieren die Translation nicht. Es ist daher offensichtlich ein selbständiger Zusatz des Autors der *Crescente*-Legende zur älteren Legendentradition. Die schematische Zahl drei (drei Tage zur Auferstehung Christi – drei Jahre zur Translation Wenzels) verrät klar seinen künstlichen Ursprung. Josef Pekař hat also Recht, wenn er bemerkt, dass die „Angabe über das dreijährige Bestehen von Wenzels Grab in Altbunzlau nur durch die Legende *Crescente fide* belegt ist und dass man, vermute ich, deren Richtigkeit bezweifeln kann".[42] Cosmas führt das Jahr 932 an,[43] das hat er aber selbst oder seine annalistische Vorlage[44] berechnet aufgrund der Angabe von den drei Jahren und des in das Jahr 929 datierten Tages von Wenzels Ermordung. Auch dieses Datum, das die Christian-Legenden und die russischen Fassungen der I. Altkirchenslawischen Legende anführen, wurde jedoch errechnet aufgrund der Angabe der ältesten Legende, dass der Mord am Montag, den 28. September verübt wurde.[45] Zur Translation schritt Boleslaw wohl nicht drei Jahre nach dem Mord, sondern offenbar erst wenn es für ihn politisch vorteilhaft war, die Heiligkeit seines Bruders – und selbstverständlich auch die eigene Schuld – einzugestehen. Falls die Translation eine Kanonisation sein sollte, war die Teilnahme des Diözesanbischofs daran mindestens geignet, wenn nicht unerlässlich. Dies hatte

---

39 Klauser, Renate: Zur Entwicklung des Heiligensprechensverfahrens bis zum 13. Jahrhundert. Zeitschrift für Rechtsgeschichte, Kanonistische Abteilung 40 (1954), S. 85–101; Vauchez, A.: La sainteté en occident aux derniers siècles du moyen âge, Rom ²1988, S. 25–67.

40 Crescente fide, in: FRB, Bd. 1, S. 188: *Requievitque corpus eius in eodem loco tres annos ...*; Gumpold c. 23, in: FRB, Bd. 1, S. 161: *Quiescente ibidem per tria spacia annorum venerando corpore ...*; Christian c. 8, hg. von J. Ludvíkovský, S. 78: *Requievit corpus beati martyris in ecclesia sanctorum Cosmae et Damiani humatum per tres annos.*

41 Dies beweise ich ausführlich in Třeštík: Počátky Přemyslovců, S. 209–248. Zum Morddatum in der I. altkirchenslawischen Legende zuletzt Tkadlčík, V.: Číslovky v První staroslověnské legendě o sv. Václavu, in: Sborník prací filozoficko-přírodovědecké fakulty Slezské univerzity v Opavě. Řada jazykovědná D1 (2001), S. 36–42. Der Autor beweist erneut und überzeugend, dass in den russischen Fassungen der I. altkirchenslawischen Legende tatsächlich das Datum 929 stand. Daraus ergibt sich jedoch keineswegs, dass dieses auch in deren ursprünglichen Fassung gestanden hatte. Es handelt sich um einen offensichtlichen Zusatz des Kopisten von Sazawa.

42 Pekař, Josef: Svatý Václav, in: Svatováclavský sborník, Bd. 1, Prag 1934, S. 66, Anm. 78.

43 Cosmas, Chronik der Böhmen I, 19, hg. von Bretholz: Die Chronik der Böhmen des Cosmas von Prag (MGH SS rer. Germ. NS 2), Berlin 1923, S. 38: *Anno dominicae incarnationis DCCCCXX-XII quarta Non. Martii translatum est corpus S. Wenceslai martyris de Bolezlau oppido in urbem Pragam invidi fratris odio.*

44 Über diese Třeštík, D.: Anfänge der böhmischen Geschichtsschreibung. Die ältesten Prager Annalen, in: Studia Źródłoznawcze 23 (1978), S. 1–37.

45 Vgl. Třeštík: Počátky Přemyslovců, S. 112ff.

jedoch Boleslaw offenbar nicht erreicht, weil alle Legenden über die Teilnahme des Bischofs an der Translation – sicher nicht zufällig – schweigen. Die Anwesenheit des Bischofs bei der Translation wäre in allen Fällen angebracht gewesen, selbst wenn deren Zweck nicht direkt die Kanonisation gewesen wäre. Laurentius von Monte Cassino kennt zwar bei der Translation einen Bischof, setzt ihn aber dem zweiten Prager Bischof Adalbert gleich.[46]

Von diesem Versuch sprach zweifellos auch Widukind, der einen deutlichen Abstand zu Wenzels Heiligkeit bewahrte, offensichtlich identisch mit der Zurückhaltung des Regensburger Bischofs.[47] Widukind schrieb in den Jahren 967–968,[48] vor diese Zeit muss man daher Wenzels feierliche Translation datieren. Das ist aber eben die Zeit, wo Boleslaw I. – offenbar unter Mitwirkung des polnischen Mieszko I. – Verhandlungen mit dem Papst über ein Bistum für Prag und Mähren anknüpfte. Man kann sich also kaum eine passendere Gelegenheit vorstellen, die Legende über einen neuen Heiligen zu schreiben, als das Bemühen um seine feierliche Kanonisation, auch wenn offenbar nicht ganz gelungen, ein Bemühen, das zweifellos mit dem Streben nach gleich zwei Bistümern für Boleslaws Länder zusammenhing. Diese nicht erhaltene Schrift wurde zur Grundlage jeglicher weiteren St. Wenzelshagiographie.

Diese Schrift enthielt noch nicht eine lange Aufzählung von Wundern wie die späteren Legenden, daher fehlen detaillierte Wunder auch in ihren unmittelbaren Ableitungen, sowohl in der lateinischen Legende des Laurentius von Monte Cassino,[49] als auch in der altkirchenslawischen Bearbeitung, wie sie die I. Altkirchenslawischen Legende darstellt. Die I. Altkirchenslawische Legende führt nur das Wunder mit Wenzels Blut an, das man von den Wänden der Kirche nicht abwaschen konnte.[50] Dieses Wunder enthalten auch die *Crescente*,[51] die Gumpold-[52]

---

46 Laurentius von Monte Cascsino, Vita Venczlai c. 12, hg. von F. NEWTON: Laurentius, monachus Cassinensis, archiepiscopus Amalfitanus, Opera (MGH, Quellen zur Geistesgeschichte des Mittelalters 17), Weimar 1973, S. 38–39. Er stützt sich hier offensichtlich auf Erzählungen der aus Böhmen nach Monte Cassino gekommenen Kleriker, die ziemlich ungenau aus dem Gedächtnis die Translatioslegende im Wesentlichen in der Crescente-Fassung wiedergaben (wo es auch der Kern des Wunders ist, dass man den den Körper überführenden Wagen nicht bewegen konnte, obwohl die Umstände anders als bei Laurentius sind) und den Bischof entsprechend der geltenden kanonischen Praxis in diese einfügten.

47 Widu F. NEWTON (Anm. 46), S. 23–42. Zur Datierung TŘEŠTÍK, D.: Miscellanea zu den St. Wenzelslegenden II: Laurentius aus Monte Cassino und Laurentius aus Amalfi, in: Medievalia Bohemica 1 (1969), S. 73–91 und NEWTON, F. in Medievalia Bohemica 1 (1969), S. 2ff. KRÁLÍK, O.: La leggenda di Laurentius di Monte Cassino sul S. Venceslao ed il suo modello, in: Ricerche Slavistiche 7 (1959), S. 24–47 und Id.: Kosmova kronika a předchozí tradice, S. 56ff. versuchte, die Legende in die Zeit Adalberts zu datieren, eine entsprechende Begründung ist jedoch nicht überzeugend.

50 I. altkirchenslawische Legende (kroatisch-glagolitische Fassung), hg. von J. VAJS, Sborník, S. 42. Zur Interpretation MAREŠ, F. V.: Crkvi vzide nad nim, in: Id.: Cyrilometodějská tradice a slavistika, S. 342–346, der eine Emendation vorschlägt, anstelle „die Kirche ging über ihm auf" „Blut floss auf der Wand über ihm", d. h. entsprechend dem Wortlaut der lateinischen Legenden.

51 Crescente, in: FRB, Bd. 1, S. 187. LUDÍKOVSKÝ, Jaroslav: Crescente fide, Gumpold a Kristián. (Anm. 9).

52 Gumpold c. 21, in: FRB, Bd. 1, S. 161. Gumpoldi, Mantuani episcopi, Vita Venceslai, hg. von J. EMLER in: FRB, Bd. 1, Prag 1878 (Anm. 10).

und die Christianslegende.[53] Christian und Laurentius[54] führen darüber hinaus das Wunder mit Wenzels abgehauenem Fingerglied an, das an seinen Körper wundersam anwuchs. Das Wunder hat sein Vorbild in der Erzählung Gregors des Großen über den Bischof Herculan von Perugia, das in seinen Dialogen[55] enthalten ist. Es fehlt in der *Crescente*-Legende und deren übrigen Ableitungen mit Ausnahme Christians. Bei Christian tritt jedoch das „Öhrchen" (*auriculum*) auf, während es bei Laurentius ein Fingerglied ist – *articulum*, offenbar richtig, denn es handelt sich um Wenzels Finger, der durch einen Schwerthieb im Kampf mit dem Bruder beim Mord abgehauen wurde.[56] Christian hat hier offensichtlich seine schriftliche Vorlage entstellt, die nur die Legende X sein konnte.[57] Die beiden übrigen Wunder von Laurentius stammen nicht aus der schriftlichen Vorlage, sondern aus den Erzählungen der Pilger aus Böhmen, die in den ersten Jahrzehnten des 11. Jahrhunderts Monte Cassino besuchten. So wurde das Wunder mit den Ketten, die auf St. Wenzels Fürsprache hin von den Gefangenen abgefallen waren, angeblich von „dem sächsischen Volk entstammenden Herrn Benedict erzählt, der in Monte Cassino ein gottesfürchtiges Leben führend, andächtig sein ganzes Leben lang ein Bruchstück dieser Ketten bei sich trug und erzählte, dass jenes große Wunder in seiner Anwesenheit geschah".[58] Der gleichen Herkunft ist wohl auch das Wunder mit dem Heilen des gelähmten Armes einer an Sonntagen arbeitenden Frau.[59] Beide entsprechen dabei in etwa den neuen Wundern, die der *Crescente*-Autor lieferte. Das Kettenwunder ist in der Crescente gleich das erste in der Reihenfolge und das Wunder mit der geheilten Frau das sechste.[60] Die Frau ist hier „bitterarm", erblindet und mit einem gelähmten Arm. Bei Laurentius ist sie „arm" in dem Sin-

---

53 Christian c. 8, hg. von J. LUDVÍKOVSKÝ, S. 74. LUDÍKOVSKÝ, J. (Hg.): Kristiánova legenda – Legenda Christiani, Prag 1978.

54 Christian c. 8, hg. von J. LUDVÍKOVSKÝ, S. 82, Laurentius c. 11, hg. von F. NEWTON, S. 37. Dazu WOSTRY, Wilhelm: Die Ursprünge der Primysliden, in: Prager Festgabe für Theodor Mayer, Freilassing/Salzburg 1953, S. 201, BLASCHKA, A.: Die St. Wenzelslegende Kaiser Karls IV., Prag 1934, S. 128ff.; KRÁLÍK, O.: K počátkům literatury, S. 42, die darauf hinwiesen, dass das abgehauene Ohr von der Passion Christi stammt und dass Christian daher den ursprünglichen Text bewahrte. VESELSKÝ, Jiří: Diskuse k tajemstvím Laurentiovy legendy. Pribislava, ava nomine Pribizl, mulier aevi plena, in: Listy filologické 107 (1984), S. 77–84 zeigte jedoch, dass die I. altkirchenslawische Legende von der verletzten Hand Wenzels spricht und dass das abgehauene Fingerglied bei Laurentius daher ursprünglich sein kann.

55 Gregorii Magni, Dialogi III. 13, hg. von U. MORICA, Rom 1924, S. 161ff. Vgl. TŘEŠTÍK, D.: Diskuse k předloze václavské legendy Laurentia z Monte Cassina, in: Listy filologické 107 (1984), S. 85–89. Das Wunder hat also nichts zu tun mit dem Ohr, das Simon Petrus dem Hohenpriesterdiener Malchus abgehauen hatte (Johannes 18, 10).

56 Außer der I. altkirchenslawischen Legende weiß auch Christian von diesem (c. 7, hg. von LUDVÍKOVSKÝ, S. 72), es stammt daher aus deren gemeinsamer Vorlage.

57 TŘEŠTÍK, D.: Diskuse, S. 89.

58 Laurentius, c. 12, hg. von F. NEWTON, S. 41f.: *Hoc ita factum esse, viva, ut aiunt, voce testari solitus est dominus Benedictus, Saxonum gente progenitus, qui religiosissimam in Cassinensi coenobio ducens vitam, partem fragminis earundem catenarum omni quod vixit tempore secum devote gestare consueverat, referens se presente tam ingens fuisse patratum miraculum.*

59 Laurentius, c. 12, hg. von F. NEWTON, S. 39f. (vgl. Anm. 51–53)

60 Crescente, in: FRB, Bd. 1, S. 189.

ne, dass sie Sklavin ist, die am Sonntag auf ihrem Feld mit der Sichel arbeitete, weil sie an Werktagen auf dem Feld ihres Herrn arbeiten musste. Es traf sie deshalb die Strafe für Nichtheiligung der Feiertage, ihr Arm erlahmte. Sie erblindete jedoch nicht. Das alles ist sicher eine mündlich erzählte Ergänzung, sie fehlte in Laurentius' schriftlicher Vorlage, der Legende X, genauso wie das Translationswunder.[61] Diese Legende führte offensichtlich nur zwei Wunder an: das Wunder mit dem nicht abwaschbaren Blut und das Wunder mit dem abgehauenen Finger. Die Erste Altkirchenslawische Legende ließ dieses zweite Wunder weg (genauso wie ihn der *Crescente*-Autor wegließ), vergaß aber nicht zu bemerken: „[...] wir hoffen jedoch auf Gott, dass er auf die Fürsprache des frommen und guten Mannes Wenzel ein noch größeres Wunder zeigt."[62] Ein umfangreiches Wunderverzeichnis bot erst die irgendwann kurz nach dem Jahr 975 entstandene Fassung, eines Mönchs des Prager Archipresbyteriats des Priesters Paul, d.h. die Legende *Crescente fide christiana*. Aus der übernahm Gumpold die Wunder und ergänzte sie mit weiteren, genauso wie nach den beiden Legenden Christian. Dadurch fällt das einzige wirkliche Argument für die frühe Datierung der I. Altkirchenslawischen Legende, es gilt nämlich für deren Vorlage und nicht für die Legende selbst. Die Altkirchenslawische Legende kann praktisch jederzeit vor dem Ende des slawischen Sazawa geschrieben worden sein. Nach der Rus konnte sie nämlich nur durch die Vermittlung dieses Klosters gelangen. Die erste Fassung der Altkirchenslawischen Legende wurde jedoch noch in Sazawa überarbeitet und diese Neufassung wurde dann zur Vorlage der beiden russischen Fassungen.[63] Dies deutet auch darauf hin, dass die I. Altkirchenslawische Legende wohl außerhalb Sazawas frühestens im 10 Jahrhundert verfasst wurde. Die Filation ist wie folgt:[64]

---

61 Über dieses siehe Anm. 46.
62 I. altkirchenslawische Legende (sog. kroatisch-glagolitische Fassung), hg. von J. VAJS, S. 42. Eine der Handschriften schreibt jedoch: „[...] ein größeres Wunder wird er *dort* wirken", d.h. in Altbunzlau, auf das sich das Wunder mit dem unabwaschbaren Blut bezieht. Es ginge daher nicht um Wenzels Wunder als solche, sondern nur um diejenigen an der Stelle seiner Ermordung. In den russischen Fassungen fehlt das Wort *dort* allerdings.
63 Dies ist eine insbesondere von O. KRÁLÍK überzeugend begründete Lösung: K historii textu I. staroslověnské legendy václavské, in: Slavia 29 (1960), S. 434–452 und Id.: K počátkům literatury, S. 41–62. Králík stellte sich allerdings vor, dass man in Sazawa Christian benutzte, um die I. altkirchenslawische Legende abzuwandeln. Dies ist nicht notwendig, viel eher diente hier direkt die Legende X, genauso wie man diese nicht erhaltene Legende in Sazawa benutzte, um die II. altkirchenslawische Legende abzuwandeln.
64 TŘEŠTÍK, D.: Počátky Přemyslovců, S. 248 (hier vereinfacht).

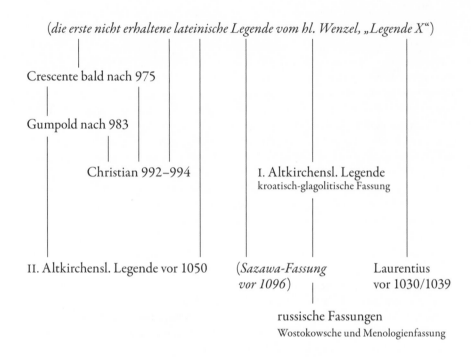

(die erste nicht erhaltene lateinische Legende vom hl. Wenzel, „Legende X")

Crescente bald nach 975

Gumpold nach 983

Christian 992–994

I. Altkirchensl. Legende
kroatisch-glagolitische Fassung

II. Altkirchensl. Legende vor 1050

(Sazawa-Fassung
vor 1096)

Laurentius
vor 1030/1039

russische Fassungen
Wostokowsche und Menologienfassung

Aber gerade deshalb wird die I. Altkirchenslawische Legende zu einem zwar relativ späten, aber doch genug überzeugenden Zeugnis der Existenz eines slawischen Schrifttums im Böhmen des 10. Jahrhunderts. Sie setzt nämlich ein breiteres Publikum voraus, das in der slawischen Schrift kommuniziert. Es ergibt sich aus ihr jedoch nicht zwangsläufig die Existenz einer in einer slawischen Sprache zelebrierten Liturgie. Die Legende zitiert zwar das Gebet des Bischofs bei der ersten feierlichen Haarschur[65] des hl. Wenzel,[66] von dem einige vermuteten, es sei östlicher Herkunft[67] gewesen, dies ist jedoch bei weitem nicht sicher. Die Schwierigkeit besteht darin, dass die Episode mit der Haarschur einschließlich des bischöflichen Gebets ganz gewiss bereits in der ursprünglichen lateinischen Legende

---

65 Über dieses Ritual Gąsiorowski, Antoni: Postrzyżyny, in: Słownik Starożytności Słowiańskich 4 (1970), S. 250f.

66 I. altkirchenslawische Legende (kroatisch-glagolitische Fassung), hg. von J. Vajs, S. 37: „Herre Jesu, segne diesen Knaben wie Du alle Deine Gerechten gesegnet hast"; die Wostokowsche Fassung (Sborník, S. 14): „Herre Jesu Christe, segne diesen Knaben mit dem Segen, mit dem Du alle Deine Gerechten gesegnet hast"; die Menologien-Fassung (Sborník, S. 20): „Großer Gott Jesu Christe, segne diesen Knaben, wie Du alle Deine Gerechten Abraham, Isaak und Jakob gesegnet und die rechtgläubigen, den Aposteln gleichen Kaiser, Konstantin und Helena, gekrönt hast."

67 Frček, J.: Byl sv. Václav pokřtěn podle ritu východního či západního? in: Slovanské studie, Prag 1948, S. 144–158; Avenarius, Alexander: Prvá slovanská václavská legenda a slovanská kultúra v Čechách 10. storočí, in: Typologie raně feudálních slovanských států, Prag 1987, S. 277–282.

(Legende X) enthalten war, sodass das Gebet hier lateinisch gewesen sein muss.[68] Ganz sicher östlich ist auch dieses Gebet nur in der späten russischen Bearbeitung der I. Altkirchenslawischen Legende. Im ursprünglichen Text der kroatisch-glagolitischen Fassung könnte man für ‚östlich‘ vielleicht nur die Zweiteiligkeit des Gebets halten, das in seinem zweiten Teil auf eine analoge Lage oder Situation aus der Bibel verwies.[69] Dieser Verweis ist hier jedoch, zum Unterschied von der russischen Bearbeitung, ganz unkonkret. Lateinische Benediktionen zur ersten feierlichen Haarschur sind außerdem nur unzureichend bekannt, daher ist es verfrüht, zu dieser Frage einigermaßen bestimmte Meinungen zu äußern. Höchstens kann man das als eine unsichere Spur betrachten, dass der Autor der I. Altkirchenslawischen Legende den östlichen Ritus kannte, aber auf keinen Fall als einen Beleg einer lebendigen, praktizierten slawischen Liturgie.

Ein solcher Beleg könnten die Kiewer Blätter sein, ein in einer Abschrift aus dem 9. Jahrhundert oder eher dem 10.–11. Jahrhundert erhaltener *libellus missae*, eine Übersetzung des lateinischen Messeoffiziums ins Altkirchenslawische.[70] Man datiert ihn manchmal nach dem Böhmen des 10. Jahrhunderts, mit gleicher Berechtigung aber auch anderswohin, nach dem Mähren des 9. Jahrhunderts und vor allem in die südslawische Umgebung.[71] Rechnen kann man also nicht mit ihm. Genauso kommt ein weiterer, durch seine Herkunft zweifelsohne böhmischer liturgischer Text in Frage, diesmal ein rein östlicher, ein Kanon zu Ehren des hl. Wenzel.[72] Der ist zwar in einer russischen Handschrift aus den Jahren 1095-1096 erhalten, d. h. sehr früh, sein Autor kannte aber zweifelsohne die II. Altkirchenslawische St. Wenzelslegende,[73] wirkte also sicher in Sazawa. Direkt das Offizium der hll. Kyrill und Method betreffen die altkirchenslawischen Gebete an die beiden,[74] welche einst R. Večerka für den entscheidenden Beleg eines (sonst durch nichts belegten)[75] Kultes der hll. Kyrill und Method hielt sowie der Existenz eines

---

68 Es taucht nämlich bei Laurentius auf (c. 3–4, hg. von F. NEWTON, S. 28f.), auch wenn Laurentius die ihm unbekannte feierliche Haarschur in Anwesenheit des Bischofs als eine durch diesen gespendete Taufe begriff.

69 AVENARIUS, A.: Prvá slovanská legenda, S. 278.

70 Hg. (als Phototypie) von NIMČUK, V.V.: Kievski glygoličny listky I, II, Kiew 1983; dort auch eine vollständige Literaturübersicht. Dazu neuerdings insbesondere SCHAEFKEN, J.: Die Kiewer Blätter, Amsterdam 1987.

71 Vgl. HAUPTOVÁ Z.: Církevněslovanské písemnictví, S. 26ff. HAMM, J.: Das glagolitische Missal von Kiew, Wien 1979, betrachtete diesen sogar als Falsum des bekannten Fälschers Václav Hanka.

72 Hg. von J. VAŠICA in Sborník, S. 137–145. PRAŽAK, E.: K otázce původu a geneze slovanského václavského kánonu, in: Listy filologické 95 (1972), S. 215–219 nimmt an, dass es in Böhmen ursprünglich zwei Kanons gab, einen zum Fest des Martyriums (28. September) und den zweiten zum Fest der Translation (4. März), die man zur gegenwärtigen Form erst in der Rus zusammenlegte.

73 KONZAL, V. in: Staroslověnské legendy, S. 221ff.

74 BERČIČ, I. (Hg.): Dvie službe rimskogo obreda za svetkovim Čirila i Metuda, Zagreb 1870.

75 GRAUS, F.: Slovanská liturgie, S. 486–491; Id.: Böhmen zwischen Bayern und Sachsen. Zur böhmischen Kirchengeschichte des 10. Jahrhunderts, in: Historica 17 (1969), S. 13; Id.: Die Entwicklung der Legenden der sogenannten Slawenapostel Konstantin und Method in Böhmen und Mähren, in: Jahrbücher für Geschichte Osteuropas N. F. 19 (1971), S. 161–211.

slawischen Gottesdienstes im vorsazawer Böhmen überhaupt;[76] V. Tkadlčík wies
jedoch nachher überzeugend nach, dass diese Gebete erst im 14. Jahrhundert
im von Karl IV. im Jahre 1347 gegründeten Prager Emmaus-Kloster entstanden
sind.[77]

Das Ergebnis, zu dem man gelangt, ist aber nur teilweise negativ. Das Vorhan-
densein der I. Altkirchenslawischen Legende im 10. Jahrhundert reicht vollkom-
men aus, damit man mit der Existenz eines Schrifttums in der altkirchenslawischen Schrift rechnen muss, auch wenn bei weitem nicht in dem von den Slawisten
angenommenen Umfang. Gleichzeitig stellt man jedoch fest, dass die Verwendung der slawischen Schrift noch lange nicht auch eine Verwendung der slawischen Sprache bei der Messe und im Offizium, d. h. die Verwendung der slawischen Liturgie bedeutete. Diese beiden Angelegenheiten hingen wohl miteinander
nicht so selbstverständlich zusammen, wie man sich das unter dem Eindruck der
Kämpfe zwischen Method und Wiching angewöhnte vorzustellen, obwohl Papst
Stephan V. sie in seinem „Abschlusswort" zu Methods Streit aus dem Jahr 895
sehr genau unterschied, als er die Benutzung der slawischen Sprache bei der Messe
und im Offizium untersagte, jedoch andererseits deren Benutzung bei der Apos-
tel- und Evangeliumsauslegung sowie in der Seelsorge überhaupt nachdrücklich
empfahl,[78] wie es übrigens Papst Johannes VIII. bereits einige Jahre zuvor deutlich
zum Ausdruck brachte, der die „von Konstantin dem Philosophen erfundenen
slawischen Buchstaben" direkt anordnete.[79] Die Päpste hießen somit die Benutzung von Konstantins slawischer Schrift „durch Gebildete" immer willkommen
und förderten diese, sie zögerten nur in der Frage der Liturgie. Diesen wesentlichen Unterschied zwischen der slawischen Schrift und Schrifttum und der slawischen Liturgie wurde aber in der ganzen bisherigen Forschung wirklich konsequent eigentlich nur von Gerard Labuda verstanden.[80]

---

76 VEČERKA, R.: Velkomoravská literatura, S. 400ff.; Id.: Cyrilometodějský kult v české středověké
   tradici, in: Československý časopis historický 12 (1964), S. 40–43. TUREK, R.: „Národy české"
   lublaňského breviáře, in: Slavia 32 (1963), S. 458–463 suchte in ihnen sogar einen Beleg für die
   Existenz zahlreicher Stämme im Böhmen des 10. Jahrhunderts.
77 TKADLČÍK, V.: K datování hlaholských služeb o sv. Cyrilu a Metoději, in: Slovo 27 (1977), S. 85–
   128.
78 Schreiben Papst Stephans V. an Swatopluk vom J. 885, Magnae Moraviae Fontes historici
   (MMFH), Bd. 3, Brno 1969, S. 224f.: *Divina autem officia et sacra mysteria ac missarum sollemnia,
   quae idem Methodius Sclavorum lingua celebrare praesumpsit, quod, ne ulterius fueret, super
   sacrastissimum beati Petri corpus iuramento firmaverat, sui periurii reatum pehorrescentes nullo
   modo deinceps a quolibet praesumatur, Dei namque nostraque apostolica auctoritate sub anathematis
   vinculo interdicimus, excepto quod ad simplicis populi et non intelligentis aedificationem attinet, si
   evangelii vel apostoli expositio ab eruditis eadem lingua annuntietur, et largimur et exhortamur et ut
   frequentissime fiat monemus, ut omnis lingua laudet Deum et confiteatur ei.*
79 Schreiben Johanns VIII. an Swatopluk (MMFH, Bd. 3, S. 224): *Litteras denique Sclaviniscas a
   Constantino quondam philosopho repertas, quibus Deo laudes debite resonent, iure laudamus et in
   eadem lingua Christi domini nostri et opera ennarantur, iubemus.*
80 LABUDA, G.: Ze spuścizny kulturowej misji arcybiskupa Metodego na pograniczu słowiańsko-ger-
   mańskim, in: Etnolingwistyczne i kulturowe związki Słowian s Germanami, Wrocław u. a. 1987, S.
   83–90.

Man sollte davon ausgehen, dass die slawische Schrift und die darin geschriebene Literatur eine praktische Angelegenheit waren und dass die Päpste deren Vorzüge für ein neu christianisiertes Land anerkannten und begrüßten sie so wie in allen übrigen Fällen neu christianisierter Länder. Sie hatten auch mit dem Dogma nichts gemeinsam. Lediglich Konstantin und Method versuchten, den Streit um Liturgie in slawischer Sprache dogmatisch zuzuspitzen, als sie ganz im byzantinischen streitsüchtigen Stil ihre Gegner der „dreisprachigen" Häresie bezichtigten, obwohl sie gut wissen mussten, dass die Lehre über die drei heiligen Sprachen nur eine Theorie einiger Theologen ist über eine das Dogma überhaupt nicht berührende Frage, und daher keine Häresie sein kann.[81] Man sollte also unterscheiden und fragen, was die Benutzung der slawischen Schrift und Sprache für die werdende böhmische Kirche der ersten Přemysliden wohl bedeutete? Die Antwort ist durch die tatsächliche Lage dieser Kirche gegeben, dadurch, dass sie eigentlich nur eine große Improvisation Boleslaws I. war, die vom Regensburger Diözesanbistum nur sehr schwach unterstützt wurde.

Alles lag hier wirklich auf den Schultern Boleslaws I. Er konnte sich nur auf die Tradition seiner mittelböhmischen ‚Minikirche' stützen, die von Bořiwoj bei seiner Taufe im Jahre 884 gegründet wurde. Die Zugehörigkeit Bořiwojs mittelböhmischer Domäne zu Methods Diözese in den Jahren 884–895 hatte jedoch offensichtlich unter dem Aspekt der organisatorischen Festigung des Christentums in der mittelböhmischen přemyslidischen Herrschaft keine größere Bedeutung. Bořiwoj bekam nach seiner Taufe den Priester Kaich,[82] der für die geistigen Bedürfnisse des Proselyten sorgen sollte, und wahrscheinlich wurden ein oder einige Priester aus Mähren an die Kirchen St. Klemens in Levý Hradec und St. Maria in Prag entsandt, die Bořiwoj erbauen ließ. Über deren Beziehung zur slawischen Liturgie kann man nichts sagen; man muss nämlich berücksichtigen, dass die slawische Liturgie in Methods Diözese nur eine vorübergehend tolerierte Ausnahme war, bestimmt keine Regel. Sofern Bořiwojs Priester zu deren Anhängern gehört hätten, wären sie im Jahre 886 gemeinsam mit den übrigen, das Zelebrieren einer lateinischen Messe ablehnenden Priestern Methods gezwungen gewesen, auf Swatopluks Anordnung dessen Domäne zu verlassen, zu der doch Böhmen gehörte.[83] Wahrscheinlicher scheint es, dass diese Priester in der slawischen Schrift gebildet waren, denn das hätte schon eher ein mährischer Standard sein können, der durch die von Konstantin eingeführte Art der Ausbildung der einheimischen, mährischen Priester bedingt war. Diese wenigen Priester konnten jedoch auf kei-

---

81 THOMSON, Francis J.: SS. Cyril and Methodius and a Mythical Western Heresy: Trilinguism. A Contribution to the Study of Patristic and Mediaeval Theories of Sacred Languages, in: Annalecta Bolandiana 110 (1992), 67–122.

82 Christian, c. 2, hg. von J. LUDVÍKOVSKÝ, S. 20. (Anm. 53).

83 Zur Frage der Vertreibung von Methods Anhängern vgl. GRIVEC, F.: Konstantin und Method, Lehrer der Slawen, Wiesbaden 1960, S. 148ff.; DITTRICH, Z. R.: Christianity, S. 282ff.; DVOR-NÍK, F.: Byzantské misie, S. 202ff. Gewöhnlich zieht man nur das eigentliche Mähren in Betracht, man muss jedoch das ganze Reich Swatopluks berücksichtigen, dessen Bestandteil auch Böhmen war; Swatopluks Maßnahme musste daher auch Böhmen betreffen.

ne wesentliche Weise die tatsächliche Christianisierung des přemyslidischen Regnums beeinflussen. Über die innere Lage der mährischen Kirche in den zwei Jahrzehnten zwischen Methods Tod und dem Untergang Großmährens weiss man de facto nichts, sie konnte jedoch nicht schlecht sein, wenn der Papst im Jahre 889 mit der Wiederherstellung des mährischen Erzbistums einverstanden war. Vom Erbe Methods konnte hier ganz gut manches überleben, das nicht direkt die slawische Liturgie betraf, insbesondere der Unterricht für Priester in der einheimischen Sprache unter Verwendung von Konstantins Schrift. Man darf doch nicht vergessen, dass Stephan V. im Jahre 885 eben diese Bildungs- und Seelsorgepraxis nachdrücklich empfahl.

Auf Böhmen übte aber die mährische Kirche in den Jahren 885–895 kaum Einfluss aus. Entscheidend war hier die Zeit Spytihnievs I. (Spytihněvs), der erst die Gründertat seines Vaters vollendete, indem er die Grundlagen einer auf Burgen gestützten Territorialverwaltung Mittelböhmens legte.[84] Sein Vorbild dabei war zweifelsohne Mähren, weil sich die fränkische Verwaltung nie auf Burgen stützte; die böhmische burgengestützte Verwaltung, wie man sie aus dem 11. und 12. Jahrhundert kennt, war jedoch ohne Zweifel überwiegend eine heimische Schöpfung, zu der Mähren nur das Grundprinzip geliefert hatte.[85] Dieses bestand in der Delegierung der fürstlichen Vollmachten auf die mehr oder weniger regelmäßig über das besiedelte Gebiet verteilten Burgen. Die Burgen wurden im přemyslidischen Regnum zu örtlichen Zentren nicht nur der Verwaltung, sondern eigentlich des gesamten öffentlichen, rechtlichen, militärischen, wirtschaftlichen und kulturellen Lebens der Region. Unterhalb von ihnen fanden Gerichte und Märkte statt, in deren Verband zog man, aufgefordert von Boten mit dem Zeichen *viti*, ins Feld, hierher zahlte man Abgaben und Steuern, von hier aus leistete man „öffentliche"(= fürstliche) Arbeiten wie den Brückenbau, die Reparaturen von Burgmauern und Wegen.[86]

Dieses Prinzip wurde aber bereits in Mähren und sofort vom Anfang an in Böhmen umgesetzt als ein Organisationsschema dessen, was man mit einer gewissen Übertreibung Kirchenverwaltung nennen könnte. Die Übertreibung besteht hier darin, dass es nicht die Kirche war, die ihre territoriale Organisationsstruktur schuf, sondern der Herrscher, der die Priester in seiner ‚weltlichen' Verwaltung einsetzte. Im 11. und teilweise noch im 12. Jahrhundert sah es so aus, dass auf jeder Burg eine Kirche stand, an der ein Archipresbyter mit seinem Priesterkollegium wirkte. Die Kirche hatte volle ‚Pfarrrechte', der Archipresbyter hatte jedoch

---

84 Das bewies Sláma, J.: K počátkům hradské organizace v Čechách, in: Typologie raně feudálních slovanských států, Prag 1987, S. 175–190; Id.: Střední Čechy v raném středověku III: Archeologie o počátcích přemyslovského státu, Prag 1988, S. 71ff.

85 Zu den Unterschieden zwischen der böhmischen und der großmährischen Burgorganisation Třeštík, D.: Pád Velké Moravy, S. 39ff. Staňa, Č.: Staré Město a velkomoravská hradiště, in: Staroměstská výročí, hg. von L. Galuška, Brno 1990, S. 72 bezeichnet dies als einen „großen Irrtum", seine Einwände sind jedoch kaum überzeugend.

86 Eine Übersicht gibt Žemlička, Josef: Čechy v době knížecí (1034–1198), Prag 1997, S. 149ff. (mit Literatur).

auch umfassende Vorrechte in Bezug auf die Gläubigen seines Burgbezirkes. Er belangte auch strafrechtlich deren Sünden, wie beispielsweise Verletzungen des Arbeitsverbotes an Feiertagen. Dabei unterstand er jedoch nicht dem Bischof, sondern dem örtlichen Kastellan.[87] Auch dieses organisatorische Prinzip einer engen Verbindung zwischen der Burg und der Kirche (das übrigens offenbar auch in der Etymologie des Wortes *kostel/castellum* = „Kirche" anklingt)[88] wurde von Mähren übernommen, wo doch Swatopluk laut Methods Vita dem neu bestellten Bischof im Jahre 874 seine „Landeskirche" so übergab, dass er ihm „alle Kirchen und alle Kleriker auf allen Burgen" übergab.[89] Dieses Prinzip wurde bereits in der ‚Burgorganisation' des přemyslidischen Regnums unter Spytihniew I. umgesetzt. Auf allen diesen Burgen standen nämlich Kirchen, offensichtlich mit der Funktion der späteren „Großpfarreien".[90]

Als sich Spytihniew im Jahre 895 in Regensburg König Arnulf unterwarf, wurde sein Regnum in kirchlicher Hinsicht Bestandteil des Bistums Regensburg.[91] In den St. Wenzelslegenden taucht dann der höhere Priester (*maior presbyter*) Paul auf,[92] als Vorsteher des Priesterkollegiums. Die Bezeichnung seiner Funktion *maior presbyter* ist nur der latinisierte Name der gut bekannten Funktion des Archipresbyters, eines Bischofsstellvertreters, der mit der Ausübung einiger bischöflicher Vollmachten beauftragt war, vor allem mit der Spendung der Taufe und einiger anderer Sakramente. Diese Archipresbyteriate des Passauer Bischofs kennt man aus dem zeitgenössischen Mähren,[93] man braucht daher nicht zu bezweifeln, dass auch das Prager Archipresbyteriat des Priesters Paul eine in Prag vom Regensburger Bischof Tuto errichtete Institution war. Seine Priester stammten sicherlich vor allem aus dem Regensburger St. Emmeramskloster, wo der Bischof gleichzeitig Abt war.

Es waren aber weder diese, noch ihr Bischof, die die Christianisierungsaktion von Bořiwojs Söhnen in deren mittelböhmischem Regnum leiteten. Es waren eben diese Fürsten selbst, die die Kirchen auf den Burgen bauten,[94] an sie Priester bestellten, diesen den Lebensunterhalt sicherten und offenbar auch dafür sorg-

---

87 ŽEMLIČKA, J.: Čechy v době knížecí, S. 180.

88 NĚMEC, Igor: Nejstarší české názvy kostela, in: Slavia 61 (1992), S. 61–65.

89 Vita Methodii c. 10, in: MMFH, Bd. 2, S. 154.

90 Über „Großpfarreien" HRUBÝ, František: Církevní zřízení v Čechách a na Moravě od X. do konce XII. století a jeho poměr ke státu, in: Český časopis historický 22 (1916), S. 257 f.

91 Es ist zwar nirgendwo ausdrücklich belegt, es ergibt sich aber eindeutig aus der Lage. Vgl. GRAUS, F.: Böhmen zwischen Bayern und Sachsen S. 17 und auch WOSTRY, Wilhelm: Drei St. Wenzel-Studien, in: Jahrbuch des Vereines für Geschichte der Deutschen in Böhmen 3 (1933), S. 5ff.

92 Crescente fide (die bayrische Fassung), in: FRB, Bd. 1, S. 184.

93 Vita Constantini c. 15, in: MMFH, Bd. 2, S. 102 spricht von „lateinischen und fränkischen" Archipresbytern, Priestern und Klerikern, gegen die Konstantin in Mähren kämpfte. Die Organisation eines solchen Archipresbyteriats kennt man gut aus Pribinas Fürstentum von Moosburg/Zalavár. Vgl. VAVRINEK, Vladimír: Die Christianisierung und Kirchenorganisation Großmährens, in: Historica 7 (1963), S. 25ff. und HAVLÍK, L. E.: Morava v 9.–10. století. K problematice politického postavení, sociální a vládní struktury a organizace, Prag 1978, S. 84.

94 Kirchenbauten werden in den St. Wenzelslegenden, insbesondere in der *Crescente*, sorgfältig als Verdienste der einzelnen Fürsten aufgezählt.

ten, was sonst dem Bischof zustehen sollte; die Fürsten besorgten für die Kirchen nicht nur Priester, sondern auch liturgische Geräte, die zur Hinterlegung im Altar erforderlichen Heiligenreliquien und die liturgischen Bücher. Die Legende Crescente fide sagt, dass Priester aus Bayern, Schwaben und anderswoher zu Wenzel „mit Heiligenreliquien und Büchern" kamen.[95] Darin spiegelt sich sicher Wenzels Sorge um die notwendige Ausstattung seiner Kirchen wieder. Es handelt sich nämlich keineswegs um eine einfache Angelegenheit. Genug Priester zu gewinnen war sehr schwer, da die außerhalb der Klöster wirkenden Priester in der Umgebung, besonders im erwähnten Bayern und Schwaben, ihre Familien hatten und daher fest niedergelassen waren und die Mönche verpflichtete wiederum ihre Regel zur Anwesenheit im Kloster. Die Salzburger Erzdiözese litt beispielsweise an chronischem Priestermangel und eine Reihe von Kirchen war ganz unbesetzt.[96] In dieser Lage, die sogar zum Einkauf von Priestern auf dem Sklavenmarkt zwang,[97] kam der Untergang Großmährens im Jahre 906 den Prager Přemysliden sehr gelegen. Unter den Flüchtlingen aus dem Lande gab es nämlich Priester, die auch in Böhmen Zuflucht suchten. Die *Crescente* spricht zwar von bayrischen und schwäbischen Priestern im Regnum der Přemysliden, die mit Namen bekannten sind jedoch, außer dem oben erwähnten Priester Paul, Slawen. Slawe war zweifelsohne der von Method Bořiwoj zugeteilte Priester Kaich.[98] Außerdem kennt man den Burgpriester von Altbunzlau (Stará Boleslav), der der offensichtliche Sla-

---

95 Crescente fide (die bayrische Fassung), in: FRB, Bd. 1, S. 185: *In tempore autem illo multi sacerdotes de provincia Bavariorum et de Svevia audientes famam de eo confluebant cum reliquiis sanctorum et libris ad eum.*

96 KOLLER, H.: Die Salzburger Missionsmethode der Karolingerzeit, in: Österreich in Geschichte und Literatur 14 (1970), S. 277.

97 Die Erste altkirchenslawische Legende vom hl. Wenzel sagt in ihrer ersten (kroatisch-glagolitischen) Fassung (hg. von J. VAJS, S. 38–39), dass Wenzel „diejenigen, die verkauft waren" loskaufte; die russischen Fassungen sprechen hier jedoch übereinstimmend davon, dass Wenzel Priester loskaufte, also nicht jeden Sklaven (Wostokowsche Fassung, S. 16; Menologien-Fassung, S. 23). Dies entstammt deren gemeinsamer, im 11. Jh. in Sazawa aufgeschriebenen Vorlage (dazu TŘEŠTÍK, D.: Počátky Přemyslovců, S. 199ff. mit Literatur), es spiegeln sich hier daher böhmische Verhältnisse wieder. Es ist übrigens nicht ausgeschlossen, dass bereits der Autor der ursprünglichen Fassung gerade Priester meinte. Es ging eigentlich nicht ums Loskaufen, sondern ums Einkaufen, wie es Christian schildert (c. 7, hg. von J. LUDVÍKOVSKÝ, S. 66ff.), der sagt, dass sich Wenzel so sehr um die richtige Ausübung kirchlicher Zeremonien sorgte, dass – wenn es zu den vorgeschriebenen Terminen nicht genug zu taufende Kinder gab – Wenzel Boten auf den Prager Markt schickte und dort Knaben einkaufen ließ, die ebendort zum Verkauf ausgestellt waren. Vgl. dazu TŘEŠTÍK, D.: Kristián a václavské legendy 13. století, in: Acta Universitatis Carolinae, Philosophica et historica 2 (1981), S. = Problémy dějin historiografie 1), S. 60–67. Dass Priester unter den Sklavenwaren auf dem Prager Markt nicht fehlten, bezeugt der Sazawer Verfasser der Fortsetzung von Cosmas' Chronik aus dem 12. Jahrhundert, dessen Vorfahr einer der Priester war, die auf den Prager Markt gemeinsam mit den Gefangenen des polnischen Kriegszuges Břetislaws I. im Jahre 1039 gebracht wurden (Cosmas II. 5, hg. von B. BRETHOLZ, S. 90: *adductus est meus attavus, consors in clero, presbyter officio.* Vgl. TŘEŠTÍK, D.: Kosmova kronika, S. 38ff. mit Literatur).

98 Der Name ist rein slawisch, gebildet durch das Suffix *-ch* vom Verb *kajati se* (bereuen). Vgl. HAUPTOVÁ, Z.: Církevněslovanské písemnictví, S. 10.

we Krastej war.[99] Der Burgpriester in Budeč hieß direkt Učen, d. h. „Gelehrter".[100] Heimischer Herkunft können diese Priester kaum gewesen sein; man weiß nichts von einer von einheimischen Priesters gebildeten Schule (die ‚Schule' in Budeč, wo der hl. Wenzel ‚studiert' haben soll, ist ein Missverständnis),[101] es muss sich daher um Priester aus Mähren handeln. Sie waren es, die nach Böhmen nicht nur das slawische Schrifttum, sondern auch einige Gewohnheiten der mährischen Kirche brachten, die dann Adalbert als „verkehrte Religion" vergeblich auszuroten versuchte.[102] So bildete sich, bereits seit der Wende vom 9. zum 10. Jahrhundert, selbständig und ohne einen wesentlichen Einfluss aus Regensburg, die eigene böhmische ‚Landeskirche' heraus, in ihren organisatorischen Prinzipien und auch in ihrem Leben von der Kirche der ‚standardmäßigen' Reichsbistümer unterschiedlich.[103]

Es war damals allerdings nur die „mittelböhmische Kirche", auf das přemyslidische Fürstentum beschränkt. Die übrigen böhmischen Fürsten, und selbstverständlich auch das Volk deren Fürstentümer, waren keine Christen. Böhmen galt zwar als ein christliches Land; dies rührte aber daher, dass die Fürsten irgendwann ab Spytihniews Zeiten eine (formale) Oberherrschaft der christlichen Přemysliden anerkannten.[104] In Wirklichkeit waren sie jedoch weder von den Přemysliden abhängig noch waren sie wirkliche Christen. Diese Situation deutet Christians Geschichte über den Fürsten von Kauřim (Kouřim), der sich zwar gegen Wenzel empörte und militärisch besiegt, aber doch auf seiner Burg belassen wurde.[105] Es

---

99 FLAJŠHANS, Václav: Jména osob a míst v legendách svatováclavských, in: Svatováclavský sborník, Bd. 1, Prag 1934, S. 829.

100 FLAJŠHANS, V.: Jména osob, S. 828. Die Lesart der Namen in den Handschriften der Crescente ist allerdings nicht sicher, man könnte diesen Namen auch als Weno lesen, dann würde es sich um einen Bayern handeln. Vgl. TŘEŠTÍK, D.: Počátky Přemyslovců, S. 364, Anm. 114.

101 SPUNAR, Pavel: La plus ancienne école en Bohème, in: Cahiers de la civilisation médievale 17 (1974), S. 125–127; SLÁMA, Jiří: Příspěvek ke kulturním dějinám raně středověkých Čech, in: Sborník Kruhu přátel Muzea hlavního města Prahy 1 (1988), S. 65–75; TŘEŠTÍK, D.: Počátky Přemyslovců, S. 365ff.

102 Bruno von Querfurt, Vita S. Adalberti c. 11, hg. von J. KARWASIŃSKA, in: Św. Wojciecha biskupa i męczennika Żywot drugi napisany przez Brunona z Kwerfurtu (Monumenta Poloniae Historica Series nova, Bd. 4,2), Warschau 1969, S. 12: *Populus autem durae cervicis ... dies festos confusa religione observant, dies vero ieuniorum voluptatibus vacantes omnino non curant.*

103 Für die spätere böhmische Kirche stellt dies GRAUS, F.: Böhmen zwischen Bayern und Sachsen, S. 31–37 mit Recht fest.

104 Zum letzten Mal treten die böhmischen Fürsten als eine politische Gemeinschaft in Beziehung zum Ausland im Jahre 897 auf (Annales Fuldenses, cont. Ratisbon. zum Jahr 911, hg. von F. KURZE, S. 131) und bereits im Jahre 929 wird Wenzel von Widukind (Widukind I. 35, hg. von H.-E. LOHMANN/P. HIRSCH, S. 50f.) für den Herrn über ganz Böhmen gehalten. Es ist nicht ausgeschlossen, dass es irgendwann in dieser Zeit zum ‚Umsturz' kam, durch den sich Spytihniew die übrigen böhmischen Fürsten unterwarf. Nach den letzten dendrochronologischen Daten würde nämlich der Bau der Prager Burg an der Stelle eines alten Kultbezirkes und an der von Bořiwoj kurz nach 884 gestifteten Marienkirche in diese Zeit gehören.

105 Christian c. 10, hg. von J. LUDVÍKOVSKÝ, S. 100–102. Dass dieser Text kein Zusatz zur Legende, sondern Bestandteil deren ursprünglichen Textes ist, bewies LUDÍKOVSKÝ, J.: Souboj sv. Václava s vévodou kouřimským v podání václavských legend, in: Studie o rukopisech 12 (1973), S. 89–100.

ist darin nicht gesagt, dass dieser Fürst, Dalimils Radslaw, Heide war,[106] aber es ist sicher kein Zufall, dass es bisher nicht gelang, trotz relativ intensiver Grabungen, auf einem der Burgwälle, die man diesen nichtpřemyslidischen Fürsten zuschreiben kann, eine Kirche zu finden, obwohl Kirchen auf praktisch allen Burgwällen den Přemysliden jener Zeit standen und bis heute stehen. Diese Fürsten tolerierten zwar das Christentum, genauso wie sie die Oberhoheit der Přemysliden anerkannten, trotzdem ließen sie sich – aus begründeten Befürchtungen vor ihrem Volk – nicht taufen.[107]

All das änderte sich nach dem Altbunzlauer Mord im Jahre 935. Die erste Tat Boleslaws I. war die Vernichtung der böhmischen Fürstentümer. Ihre Burgen wurden entweder zerstört wie die Burg jenes „Unterkönigs", den er als ersten angriff,[108] oder sie gingen unter und Boleslaw baute in ihrer Nähe seine eigenen, neuen Burgen,[109] die er mit seinen Leuten besetzte und deren Verwalter er aus den Reihen seines Gefolges ernannte. Nur in Ostböhmen wählte er eine etwas andere Lösung; hier ernannte er zum Verwalter seinen Verwandten Slawnik und unterstellte ihm ein relativ ausgedehntes Gebiet, größer als den übrigen Burgen.[110] Im Grunde ging es um nichts anderes als um die Ausdehnung der Burgorganisation des Prager Fürstentums auf ganz Böhmen – einschließlich deren kirchlicher Komponente. Wenn dies bereits ein Problem für das kleine mittelböhmische Fürstentum war, vergrößerte es sich jetzt um mehrere Größenordnungen.

Nach dem von Cosmas zitierten „St. Georgsprivileg" baute Boleslaw I. (nicht der Zweite, wie Cosmas behauptet) 20 Kirchen,[111] zweifelsohne gerade auf seinen neuen Verwaltungsburgen. Sofern er an jeder Kirche ein von einem Archipresbyter geleitetes Priesterkollegium hätte stiften wollen, wie wir es auf den Burgen im 11. Jahrhundert finden, hätte er um hundert Priester, viele liturgische Geräte, Bücher und Reliquien gebraucht. Dies war ein fast unüberwindliches Problem auch für eine alte und eingeführte Diözese, geschweige denn für ein Land, das durch diese Aktion eigentlich erst wirklich christlich wurde. Vom Regensburger Bischof Michael konnte dabei Boleslaw so gut wie nichts erwarten. Auch die uner-

---

106 Třeštík, D.: Kristián a václavské legendy 13. století, S. 63. Es scheint jedoch, dass Wenzels Zweikampf und hauptsächlich das Wunder mit dem strahlenden Kreuz auf seiner Stirn einen wirklichen Sinn nur dann hat, wenn der Gegner Heide war. Einen analogen Zweikampf trug laut Vita Mathildae reginae antiquior (MG SS 10, S. 574) Karl der Große gegen den Anführer der heidnischen Sachsen Widukind aus, und das Wunderergebnis war Widukinds Taufe durch Karls Erzbischof Bonifatius (!), der hier eine Analogie zu Swatopluks Method in der Geschichte von Bořiwojs Taufe ist.

107 Bořiwojs Taufe rief, eigentlich automatisch, einen Aufstand gegen ihn hervor. Zu seiner möglichen ‚Absicherung', die darin bestand, dass er Spytihniew nicht taufen ließ, um ihm – als einem ‚Heiden' – die Nachfolge zu sichern für den Fall, dass er selbst gestürzt würde, vgl. Třeštík, D.: Počátky Přemyslovců, S. 323.

108 Widukind II. 3, hg. von H.-E. Lohmann/P. Hirsch, S. 67–80. Vgl. Třeštík, D.: Počátky Přemyslovců, S. 435ff. mit Literatur.

109 Sláma, J.: Střední Čechy III, S. 80ff.; Id.: K počátkům hradské organizace, S. 182ff.

110 Sláma, J.: Slavníkovci – významná či okrajová záležitost českých dějin 10. století? in: Archeologické rozhledy 47 (1995), S. 197.

111 Cosmas I. 22, S. 42.

lässliche Weihe dieser Kirchen musste für Michael sehr beschwerlich sein, insbesondere falls man dabei die bayrische Sitte großer, mehrtägiger Feste einhielt.[112] Nachdem der erste Prager Bischof Thietmar nach dem Jahre 976 sein Amt übernahm, weihte er vor allem zahlreiche, offensichtlich schon vor längerer Zeit gebaute Kirchen, die ohne Weihe da standen.[113] Mindestens am Anfang mussten viele dieser Kirchen auch unbesetzt bleiben und auch bei den besetzten bildeten sich die Archipresbyteriate erst heraus. Eine willkommene Priesterquelle muss daher vor allem das zerstörte Mähren gewesen sein. Man kann mit vollem Recht voraussetzen, dass manche der mährischen Priester nach dem Jahr 906 und dann insbesondere unter der Herrschaft Boleslaws I. Zuflucht in Böhmen fanden.

Dabei handelt es sich jedoch nicht um einen allmählichen Vorgang, sondern sicher um eine einmalige, vom Fürsten selbst geleitete Christianisierungsaktion. Davon zeugt auch die Tatsache, dass Boleslaw die Märkte an die Burgen verlegte und den Markttag auf den Sonntag legte, um so das Burgbezirksvolk zu zwingen, mindestens am Sonntag an der Messe teilzunehmen.[114] Diese pragmatische Maßnahme, die deutlich gegen das Gebot der Sonntagsheiligung verstieß, empörte Adalbert so sehr, dass er das für einen ausreichenden Grund hielt, Böhmen zum zweiten Mal zuverlassen.[115] Auch die Qualität der Priester, die es Boleslaw gelang zu beschaffen, muss notwendigerweise unterschiedlich gewesen sein und ihre zweifellos bunte Herkunft brachte ähnliche Schwierigkeiten, mit denen ein Jahrhundert früher Rostislaw in Mähren zu kämpfen hatte, der sich in seinem, den byzantinischen Kaiser um Entsendung von „Lehrern" ersuchenden Brief beklagte, dass verschiedene Priester unterschiedlicher Herkunft „unterschiedlich lehren"[116]

---

112 Ausführliches Material dazu sammelte aus den Freisinger Traditionsbüchern STUTZ, Ulrich: Das Eigenkirchenvermögen, in: Festschrift für Otto Gierke, Weimar 1911, S. 1187–1268. In Böhmen scheint es ähnlich gewesen zu sein. Es gibt zwar keine direkten Berichte darüber, man weiß aber, dass bereits unter Wenzel der Jahrestag der Kirchweihe mit großen Festlichkeiten begangen wurde, um die sich die Geschichte des Altbunzlauer Mordes dreht (am 22. September fand die Kirchweih bei St. Veit in Prag statt und am 27. September dann bei St. Kosmas und Damian in Altbunzlau). Die Erste altkirchenslawische St. Wenzelslegende spricht von Kirchweihen als von einer allgemeinen Sitte; sie sagt, dass Wenzel sie zu besuchen pflegte (hg. von J. VAJS, S. 39). In Mähren ist das Kirchweihfeiern durch die Vita Methods belegt (c. 11, in: MMFH, Bd. 2, S. 156; zur Auslegung dieser Stelle RATKOŠ, Peter: Die Sankt-Petrus-Kirmes in Großmähren gemäß der Vita Methodii, in: Byzantinoslavica 45 (1985), S. 61–66). Auf die große Schwierigkeit für Tuto, auch wenn er wohl krank war, nach Prag zur Kirchenweihe zu kommen, deutet die komplizierte Geschichte der Weihe von Wenzels St. Veit hin (darüber TŘEŠTÍK, D.: Počátky Přemyslovců, S. 254ff.).

113 Cosmas 24, hg. von B. BRETHOLZ, S. 46: *Post haec praesul Diethmarus ecclesias a fidelibus in multis locis ad Dei laudem constructas consecrat … .* Auf die Bedeutung dieser Worte verwies J. SLÁMA: Slavníkovci, S. 194 (Anm. 110).

114 LALIK, Tadeusz: Targ, in: Słownik Starożytności Słowiańskich 6 (1977), S. 25.

115 Bruno von Querfurt, Vita S. Adalberti c. 15, hg. von J. KARWASIŃSKA, S. 18.

116 Vita Constantini c. 14, in: MMFH, Bd. 2, S. 98f.; Vita Methodii c. 5, in: MMFH, Bd. 2, S. 144. Zu Rostislaws Schreiben vgl. MAREČKOVÁ, D.: Rostislavovo poselství v Životech Konstantinově a Metodějově ve světle středověkých řeckých listin a listů in: Listy filologické 91 (1968), S. 401–414; Ead.: Moravské posleství do Cařihradu jako řecký dokument in: Slovo 18–19 (1969), S. 109–139.

und dass dadurch Unordnung in der kirchlichen (liturgischen, epistemischen u. a.) Praxis entsteht, die für das damalige ritualbetonte Christentum am wesentlichsten war. Als daher der Regensburger Bischof Wolfgang um das Jahr 974 in einer angeblich von ihm selbst verfassten Urkunde schrieb, dass die Tschechen, die sich erst vor kurzem vom Heidentum abwandten, „nicht gut genug wissen, wie die rechtgläubige Religion praktiziert wird", hatte er Recht und Recht hatte er auch mit seinem Hinweis auf die Ursache dieses Zustandes: die Lage ist deshalb so, weil die Tschechen keinen eigenen Bischof haben.[117] Ohne einen Bischof konnte nämlich Boleslaws Christianisierungsaktion wirklich nicht mehr weitergehen.

Die Christianisierung des neuen Regnums Boleslaws war eine große Improvisation, auch wenn zuletzt erfolgreich. Boleslaw schöpfte deren Quellen wo es ging und das Ergebnis war offenbar eine ziemliche Buntheit der Priester verschiedenster Herkunft und Ausbildung und selbstverständlich auch dessen, was sie lehrten. Man ist nicht in der Lage zu beurteilen, wie groß dabei die Rolle der slawischen Schrift und der slawischen Bücher war; man weiß nur, dass man sie in Böhmen benutzte, auch wenn nicht in dem Umfang, den die Slawisten voraussetzen. Dass einige der Priester Boleslaws auch slawische Liturgie benutzt hätten, ist zwar in den ungeordneten Verhältnissen jener Zeit vorstellbar, Belege dafür gibt es jedoch keine. Wenn man daher nicht mit leeren Mutmaßungen arbeiten will, muss man die Existenz der slawischen Liturgie im Böhmen der Zeit Boleslaws ablehnen. Um so mehr überrascht es, dass die slawische Liturgie – nicht Schrift – plötzlich begann, in dem großen Bemühen um die Errichtung eines Bistums, das das Christianisierungswerk Boleslaws krönen sollte, eine bedeutende Rolle zu spielen.

Auf das plötzlich erwachte Interesse für die slawische Liturgie weist sowohl das Verbot der slawischen Liturgie im die Gründung des Prager Bistums bewilligenden Brief des Papstes Johanns XIII. etwa vom Jahr 968, als auch die Verteidigung der slawischen Liturgie durch den in den Jahren 992–994 schreibenden Christian. In beiden Fällen jedoch – und das ist das Wesentliche – spricht man von der slawischen Liturgie wie von etwas, was in Bulgarien üblich ist, aber nicht in Böhmen. Diese Angaben kann man also nicht als Belege für die Existenz der slawischen Liturgie im přemyslidischen Regnum der ersten Boleslaws werten; sie belegen lediglich, dass diese hier aus irgendwelchen Gründen Interesse weckte als etwas, was im fernen und damals noch bedeutenden Bulgarien lebendig ist.

Christian, Bruder des regierenden Fürsten Boleslaws II.,[118] Verwandter und naher Mitarbeiter des Bischofs Adalbert (also kein unbedeutender Mönch aus einem entfernten Kloster) führt bekanntermaßen das böhmische Christentum auf Mähren zurück, durch die Taufe des Fürsten Bořiwoj. Dabei polemisiert er indirekt mit der St. Wenzelslegende *Crescente fide*. Deren Autor, Mitglied des Prager Archipresbyteriats des Priesters Paul, erklärte zum ersten christlichen Fürs-

---

117 Othloni, Vita Wolfgangi c. 29, hg. von G. Waitz, MGH SS 4., S. 538.
118 Třeštík, D.: Přemyslovec Kristián, in: Archeologické rozhledy 51 (1999), S. 602–613.

ten in Böhmen Spytihniew, Bořiwojs Sohn.[119] Er sagte zwar nicht, von wem und wo der böhmische Fürst die Taufe empfing, die Absicht war jedoch auch so klar. Spytihniew unterstellte nämlich im Jahre 895, nachdem er sich von Mähren getrennt hatte,[120] seine mittelböhmische Herrschaft der Obödienz des Regensburger Bischofs Tuto.[121] Böhmen sollte zwar möglicherweise bereits im Jahre 845 Bestandteil der Regensburger Diözese werden, als die böhmischen Fürsten in Regensburg getauft wurden;[122] diese kurze, einige Monate dauernde Episode des böhmischen Christentums[123] war jedoch in der zweiten Hälfte des 10. Jahrhunderts bereits vergessen, daher argumentierte Regensburg erst mit Spytihniews Unterwerfung. Regensburg erkannte Methods mährisches Erzbistum nicht an, betrachtete es, in Übereinstimmung mit dem auf der Synode von 900 zum Ausdruck gebrachten Standpunkt der bayrischen Bischöfe,[124] als vom Papst widerrechtlich errichtet. Dies bedeutet zwar nicht, dass auch die Bořiwoj von Method gespendete Taufe ungültig sein sollte, verdächtig war jedoch die Taufe des Landes, ein politischer, nicht liturgischer Akt. Diese Taufe jedoch, für Regensburg unrechtmäßig, für Prag konstitutiv, war sowohl in Prag als auch in Regensburg gut bekannt. Christian erzählt darüber eine zusammenhängende und kompakte Geschichte, deren ‚folkloristische‘ Elemente klar zeigen, dass es sich um eine lebendige, in die Form einer ‚Sage‘ gestaltete Tradition nicht nur der böhmischen ‚Minilandeskirche‘, sondern vor allem der Familie Christians selbst handelte.[125]

---

119 Crescente fide, in: FRB, Bd. 1, S. 183: Crescente fide christiana in illis diebus Dei nutu et ammonitione sponte dux Boemorum nomine Zpitigneus una cum exercitu nec non omni populo suo sordes idolorum abiciens baptizatus est.

120 Annales Fuldenses (cont. Ratisbon.) zum Jahr 895 (hg. von F. KURZE, MGH SS rer. Germ., Hannover 1891), S. 126. Vgl. TŘEŠTÍK, D.: Počátky Přemyslovců, S. 188ff. Über den anderen hier genannten Anführer der böhmischen Fürsten SLÁMA, Jiří: Vitislav (UI UTIZLA), in: Seminář a jeho hosté. Sborník prací k 60. narozeninám doc. Dr. Rostislava Nového, Prag 1992, S. 11–19.

121 Siehe Anm. 91.

122 Annales Fuldenses zum Jahr 845 (hg. von F. KURZE, S. 85).

123 Über diese TŘEŠTÍK, D.: Počátky Přemyslovců, S. 74–98 und Id.: Vznik Velké Moravy, S. 147–152; Id.: The Baptizm of the Czech Princes in 845 and the Christianization of the Slavs, in: Historica 2, Nova series, 1995 (erschienen 1997), S. 7–59.

124 Schreiben des Salzburger Erzbischofs Theotmar an Papst Johann IX. vom Jahre 900. Hg. von LOŠEK, F.: Die Conversio Bagoariorum et Carantanorum und der Brief des Erzbischofs Theotmar von Salzburg, Hannover 1997 (Monumenta Germaniae Historica, Studien und Texte Bd. 15), S. 138–157. Zu den Zweifeln an der Echtheit des Schreibens, die BOSHOF, Egon: Das Schreiben der bayerischen Bischöfe an einen Papst Johannes – eine Fälschung Pilgrims? in: Papstgeschichte und Landesgeschichte. Festschrift für Hermann Jakobs zum 65. Geburtstag, hg. von J. DAHLHAUS/A. KOHNLE (Beihefte zum Archiv für Kulturgeschichte, Bd. 39), Weimar/Wien 1995, S. 37–67, äußerte, vgl. TŘEŠTÍK, D.: Großmähren, Passau und die Ungarn um das Jahr 900, in: Byzantinoslavica 59 (1998), S. 137–160.

125 Christian c. 2, hg. von J. LUDVÍKOVSKÝ, S. 16–24. Zur Interpretation vgl. TŘEŠTÍK, D.: Počátky Přemyslovců, S. 312–347 (auch Id.: Bořivoj a Svatopluk. Vznik českého státu a Velká Morava, in: J. POULÍK/B. CHROPOVSKÝ et al.: Velká Morava a počátky československé státnosti, Prag 1985, S. 273–301; Id.: Die Entstehung des böhmischen Staates und Großmähren, in: Großmähren und die Anfänge der tschechoslowakischen Staatlichkeit, hg. von J. POULÍK/B. CHROPOVSKÝ et al., Prag 1986, S. 311–344).

Über Swatopluks und Methods Mähren selbst wusste man jedoch im Böhmen des 10. Jahrhunderts nur sehr wenig. In der ‚Sage' von der Taufe Bořiwojs sind Method und Swatopluk einträchtig zusammenarbeitende gute Herren über Böhmen und Bořiwoj ist deren treuer geistiger und weltlicher Untertan. In Christians Mähren und dessen Christentum schildernder Einleitung zu Bořiwojs Geschichte erscheint jedoch unerwartet ein ganz anderer Swatopluk. Er versuchte seinen frommen Onkel Rostislaw zu vergiften, hörte nicht auf Method und erlaubte seinem Volk, teilweise *dem Teufel zu dienen.* Deshalb verhängte Method einen schweren Bann über Mähren, das von vielen Katastrophen heimgesucht wurde, *sodass es bis heute deshalb jammert.*[126] Die spätere böhmische, durchweg auf Christians Legende und deren Echos gegründete Tradition, begriff dies so, dass es sich eigentlich um zwei Swatopluks handelte, einen guten Vater und seinen bösen Sohn.[127]

Das, was Christian schildert, ist weder eine böhmische[128] noch eine örtliche mährische[129] Tradition, es ist offensichtlich eine ‚importierte' Tradition. Christian sagt selbst sehr klar, wo er sie her hatte, nämlich aus Bulgarien.[130] Von dort

---

126 Christian c.1, hg. von J. LUDVÍKOVSKÝ, S.12: *Moravia, regio Sclavorum, antiquis temporibus fama memorante creditur et noscitur Christi fidem percepisse, Augustini, magnifici doctoris, ut aiunt, temporibus. Bulgri vel Bulgarii, attamen longe ante eadem potiti fore referentur gratia. Siquidem Quirillus quidam, natione Graecus, tam Latinis quam ipsis Graecorum apicibus instructus, postquam Bulgri crediderunt, aggressus est in nomine sanctae Trinitatis et individuae Unitatis etiam supradictae genti, Moraviae degenti, fidem domini nostri Iesu Christi praedicare. Et cooperanti divina gratia, postquam illos Christo lucratus erat, etiam apices vel caracteres novas comperit et vetus novumque testamentum pluraque alia de Graeco seu Latino sermone Sclavonicam in linguam transtulit. Missas praeterea ceterasque canonicas horas in ecclesia publica voce resonari statuit, quod et usque hodie in partibus Sclavorum a pluribus agitur, maxime in Bulgariis, multeque ex hoc animae Christo domino acquiruntur.*

127 Dazu GRAUS, F.: Velkomoravská říše v české středověké tradici, in: Československý časopis historický 14 (1966), S.289–305 (= Das Grossmährische Reich in der böhmischen mittelalterlichen Tradition, in: Das östliche Mitteleuropa in Geschichte und Gegenwart, Wiesbaden 1966, S.129–139).

128 Die böhmische Tradition ist doch durch die Geschichte der Taufe Bořiwojs repräsentiert.

129 Tatsache ist, dass man über die Kirche in Mähren in den Jahren 906–976 nichts weiß. Alle mehr oder weniger ausgeklügelten Mutmaßungen über deren Schicksal stützen sich auf eine einzige Quelle, den Katalog der Bischöfe von Olomouc, das sog. *Granum Catalogi praesulum Moraviae* (hg. von LOSERTH, J.: Das Granum Catalogi praesulum Moraviae, in: Archiv für österreichische Geschichte 78 (1892), S.41–48), eine wertlose Kompilation aus dem 15. Jahrhundert (vgl. BREITENBACH, A.: Über die Quellen und die Glaubwürdigkeit des Granum Catalogi praesulum Moraviae, in: Zeitschrift des Vereines für die Geschichte Mährens und Schlesiens 6 (1902), S.274–300). Den Gipfel stellt hier der Versuch L.E. Havlíks dar, aufgrund des Granums altkirchenslawisch geschriebene mährische Annalen aus dem 11. Jahrhundert zu ‚rekonstruieren', die aus noch älteren „Alten großmährischen Annalen" bestehen (HAVLÍK, Lubomír E.: On the Dating of the Old Slav Literary Monuments and on the Primary Slav Chronography, in: Studia Źródłoznawcze 30 (1987), S.1–38; über Havlíks phantastische Methode TŘEŠTÍK, D.: Kdy zanikla Velká Morava? in: Studia Medievalia Pragensia 2 (1991), S.16ff.). Über das altkirchenslawische Schrifttum im Mähren des 10. Jahrhunderts dachte – ohne Stütze in den Quellen – KYAS, Vladimír: Ke kulturním poměrům na Moravě v 10. a 11. století, in: Slavia 49 (1981), S.1–7, nach.

130 Die Bedeutung dieser Tatsache unterstrich VEČERKA, R.: Slavistický příspěvek k latinské legendě Kristiánově in: Slavia 45 (1976), S.132–136: Christians Hinweis auf die slawische Liturgie und

kam, nachdem er die Bulgaren bekehrt hatte, der Grieche Kyrill, der viele Bücher aus dem Lateinischen und Griechischen in die slawische Sprache übersetzte und „bestimmte, dass die Messe und die übrigen kanonischen Stundengebete in der Kirche in der gemeinen Sprache zu singen sind, wie es bis heute in den slawischen Ländern häufig geschieht, hauptsächlich in Bulgarien".[131] Auch die Auffassung der Geschicke der Kyrillo-Methodschen Mission in Mähren, wie man sie bei Christian findet, entspricht genau dem, was man ausschließlich in den bulgarischen Quellen der ersten Hälfte des 10. Jahrhunderts findet.[132] Eine systematische und umfassende Schilderung bietet hier erst die griechische Vita eines von Methods Schülern, Kliment, der nach seiner Vertreibung aus Mähren Bischof im bulgarischen Ochrid wurde und deren Autor der Ochrider Erzbischof Theophylaktos war (1094–1107).[133] Es gab jedoch eine ältere altkirchenslawische Kliment-Legende, die eine der Hauptquellen Theophylaktos' war. Auf diese bezieht sich bereits die altkirchenslawische I. Vita eines weiteren Schülers Methods, der Zuflucht in Ochrid fand, Naum,[134] die am Anfang des 10. Jahrhunderts aufgeschrieben wurde; es ist daher evident, dass das, was Theophylaktos erzählt, auf der Ochrider, schriftlich etwa in der Mitte des 10. Jahrhunderts aufgezeichneten Tradition basiert.

Vor allem erscheint hier der böse, Lastern verfallene Swatopluk.[135] Bei Christian vergiftet er darüber hinaus Rostislaw und erlaubt seinem Volk, teilweise im Christentum, teilweise im Heidentum zu Leben.[136] In der bulgarischen Tradition steht an der Stelle der Heiden die ‚lateinische Ketzerei' Wichings und seiner Anhänger,

---

das slawische Schrifttum, das „hauptsächlich in Bulgarien" gepflegt wurde, ist nur in der Zeit vor dem Untergang des Ersten bulgarischen Zarenreiches im zweiten Jahrzehnt des 11. Jahrhunderts möglich. Irgendwann im 11. Jahrhundert wird Russland im böhmischen Bewusstsein zum Land der slawischen Liturgie, und Bulgarien wird vergessen. VEČERKA (S. 134ff.) weist auch richtig darauf hin, dass sich diese Veränderung im Wortlaut des die Gründung des Prager Bistums betreffenden Schreibens Johanns XIII. in Cosmas' Chronik wiederspiegelt (s. unten Anm. 149). Über das slawische Schrifttum und die slawische Liturgie im Ersten bulgarischen Zarenreich FLORJA, B. N./ TURILOW, A. A./IWANOW, S. A.: Suďby kirillo-mefodievskoj tradicii posle Kirilla i Mefodija, Sankt Petersburg 2000 (war mir nicht zugänglich) und LITAWRIN, G. G.: Christianstvo v Bolgarii v 927–1018 gg, in: Christianstvo v stranach vostočnoj, jugo-vostočnoj i central'noj Evropy na poroge vtorogo tysjačletija, Moskau 2002, S. 133–189.

131 Christian c. 1, hg. von J. LUDVÍKOVSKÝ, S. 12: *Missas praeterea ceterasque canonicas horas in ecclesia publica voce resonari statuit, quod et usque hodie in partibus Sclavorum a pluribus agitur, maxime in Bulgariis, multeque ex hoc anime Christo domino acquiruntur.*

132 Dazu und zum Nachfolgenden insbesondere FLORJA, B. N.: Kirillo-mefodievskie tradicii v „Legende Kristiana", in: Byzantinoslavica 56 (1995), S. 571–577.

133 Hg. von A. MILEW: Gräckiete žitija na Kliment Ochridski, Sofia 1966. Auszug in MMFH, Bd. 2, Brno 1967, S. 200–234.

134 J. IWANOW (Hg.): Bälgarski starini, 2. Ausg., Sofia 1931, S. 306f. Auszug in MMFH, Bd. 2, S. 177ff. Zu den Naum-Legenden vgl. Z. HAUPTOVÁ, Les légendes slavonnes rela tives à Naum, in: Slovo 36, 1986, S. 77–86.

135 Theophylaktos, Vita Klimenti, c. 18–19, in: MMFH, Bd. 2, S. 213ff.

136 Christian c. 2, hg. von J. LUDVÍKOVSKÝ, S. 16: *Dehinc Zuentepulc tyrannide suscepta, fastu arrogantiae inflammatus, coům sibi militantibus sodalibus pontificis Metudii praedicationem mellifluam quasi respuit monitaque sacrastissima non pleniter recepit, verum membra sua, scilicet plebem populumque suum, partim Christo, partim diabolo servire exhibuit.*

denen Swatopluk Gehör schenkt, ja sogar voll unter deren Einfluss steht. Die bulgarische Tradition schilderte die Geschicke der von Swatopluk aus Mähren vertriebenen Schüler Methods, daher musste der Konflikt zwischen Method und den ,Lateinern' verständlicherweise den Kern der Erzählung bilden. Dieser Konflikt interessierte Christian nicht und deshalb sprach er von Heiden.

Nach der bulgarischen Fassung wurde Swatopluk und sein ganzes Land für seine Verachtung Method gegenüber mit der Zerstörung des Landes durch den Angriff der Ungarn bestraft. Method soll diese Zerstörung vorausgesagt haben,[137] laut Christian hat er sie jedoch sogar verursacht dadurch, dass er das Land mit dem Bann belegte.[138] Christian konnte von Methods Bann aus dem Schreiben des Papstes Stephans V. an Swatopluk vom Jahre 885 erfahren haben, wo der Kontext die irrtümliche Auffassung erlaubt, das sich der Bann auf Swatopluk und sein ganzes Volk bezog,[139] obwohl er in Wirklichkeit offenbar nur Wiching galt.[140] Das Schreiben kannte Christian gut, es wurde nämlich im Archiv des Prager Bistums aufbewahrt und es hat sich gemeinsam mit anderen vorwiegend dem Bischof Adalbert gehörenden Schriftstücken im aus Prag stammenden Manuskript des Heiligkreuz-Klosters aus dem 11. Jahrhundert erhalten.[141]

---

137 Theophylaktos, Vita Klimenti, c. 19, in: MMFH, Bd. 2, S. 215: Method „machte Swatopluk Angst, dass – wenn er sich den Ketzern anschließt – sowohl sich selbst als auch alle seine Untertanen vernichten wird, den Feinden ermöglichend, ihn leicht anzugreifen und leicht zu bezwingen. Gottlosigkeit nämlich, auch wenn sie eine kurze Zeit blüht, verwelkt doch nach einer gewisen Zeit von sich selbst, damit die Gottlosen das Böse nicht erlernen. Und dies, sagte er, wird den Fürsten nach seinem (Methods) Tod treffen, was auch tatsächlich gemäß den Voraussagen des Heiligen geschah". I. Vita Naumi, in: MMFH, Bd. 2, S. 178f.: „Aber das Land Mähren, wie der heilige Erzbischof Methodius prophezeit hatte, traf bald die Vergeltung Gottes für die Gesetzlosigkeit der Landestaten, für die Ketzerei und die Vertreibung der rechtgläubigen Väter, denen sie (die Mährer) glaubten. Nach wenigen Jahren kamen die Ungarn, ein pannonisches Volk, und plünderten und verheerten deren Land; und diejenigen, welche die Ungarn nicht gefangen genommen hatten, flohen nach Bulgarien. Und deren Land blieb wüst in der Gewalt der Ungarn".

138 Christian c. 2, hg. von J. Ludvíkovský, S. 16: *Quapropter a pontifice beatae memoriae supra notato pagus eius cum habitantibus incolis anathemate percussa cum sulcis suis et fructibus diversis cladibus attrita usque in hodiernum diem deflet. Data est enim in direptionem et captivitatem et praedam et derisum et desolationem et in sibilum universe carni gradienti per eam, quoniam non est societas luci ad tenebras nec conventio Christi cum Belial.*

139 Schreiben des Papstes Stephan V. an Swatopluk vom Jahr 885, in: MMFH, Bd. 3, S. 224: *Anathema vero pro contemnenda catholica fide qui indixit, in caput renundabit eius. Tu autem et populus tuus sancti Spiritus iudicio eritis innoxii, si tamen fidem, quam Romana praedicat ecclesia teneritis inviolabiliter.*

140 Marsina, Richard: Metodov boj, Bratislava 1985, S. 97.

141 Es handelt sich um ein Manuskript des Klosters Heiligenkreuz Nr. 217. Hier erhielt sich das sog. Edikt Boleslaws II. aus dem Jahr 992, durch das er Adalbert erlaubt, nicht kanonische Ehen zwischen Verwandten zu scheiden, an geeigneten Orten Kirchen zu bauen und den Zehnten zu erheben (CDB I n. 37, p. 43). Offensichtlich war das eine Aufzeichnung der Vereinbarungen zwischen Adalbert und dem Fürsten bei den Verhandlungen nach der Rückkehr des Bischofs nach Böhmen im Jahre 992 (Novotný, V.: České dějiny I/1, Prag 1913, S. 635). Im Manuskript wurden jedoch, ähnlich wie dieses Edikt, auch weitere Texte hinzugefügt (diese wurden – sehr oberflächlich – von Zagiba, Franz: Der Kodex 217 der Stiftsbibliothek Heiligenkreuz in Niederösterreich, in: Millenium dioceseos Pragensis 973–1973 (Annales Instituti Slavici, Bd. 8), Köln/Graz 1974, S. 64–72 herausgegeben). Das Schreiben ist nur hier erhalten und seine Echtheit wurde daher öfter

Es ist möglich, dass diese Information schriftlich war, es konnte ein Text sein, der insbesondere Konstantins berühmte Verteidigung der slawischen Schrift und Liturgie beinhaltete, die er in Venedig vorgetragen haben soll. Jedenfalls ergibt sich daraus, dass man sich in Prag am Ende des 10. Jahrhunderts stolz zur Kyrillo-Methodschen Mission in Mähren bekannte und sein Christentum von ihr ablei-tete, wusste aber von ihr nichts Genaueres. Ihr Andenken war offenbar erloschen und man musste sich um einschlägige Informationen nach Bulgarien wenden. Dies stimmt ganz sicher nicht mit der Vorstellung eines umfangreichen, blühen-den, fließend an Großmähren anknüpfenden slawischen Schrifttums in Böh-men überein, und schon gar nicht mit der mutmaßlichen Existenz der slawischen Liturgie.

Aber gerade um diese Liturgie ging es. In Prag fragte man nicht nach den Ge-schicken Kyrills und Methods in Mähren, man interessierte sich auch nicht für die slawische Schrift und Literatur, man fragte nach der Liturgie in slawischer Spra-che. Christians Schilderung gipfelte eben durch die Verteidigung dieser Liturgie, so wie sie Konstantins Vita beschreibt im Streitgespräch, das Konstantin-Kyrill mit den fränkischen Bischöfen in Venedig führte.[142] Christian legt dieses jedoch nach Rom und vor den Papst.[143] In Venedig soll es vor allem um die Schrift (und das Schrifttum) und erst in zweiter Linie um die Liturgie gegangen sein,[144] Chris-tian spricht aber nur über die Liturgie und erwähnt ferner nur das Übersetzen aus dem Lateinischen oder Griechischen in die slawische Sprache.[145] In Venedig hatte

---

angezweifelt, heute sind sich die Forscher jedoch über seine Echtheit einig (Eine Übersicht geben HAVLÍK, L. E. in MMFH, Bd. 3, S. 215–217 und MARSINA, R.: Štúdie k slovenskému diplomatáru I., in: Historické štúdie 16 (1971), S. 50–61). Von den Texten literarischer Gattung ist es ein – gewöhnliches – Pönitentiale (ZAGIBA, F.: Der Kodex, S. 66ff.) und insbesondere eine (schlecht abgeschriebene, stellenweise unleserliche und unverständliche) synodale Predigt des Bischofs an die Priester seiner Diözese (hg. von Jana ZACHOVÁ in: ZACHOVÁ, J./ TŘEŠTÍK, D.: Adhortace De ammonitione ad presbyteros a biskup Vojtěch, in: Český časopis historický 99 (2001), S. 279–293). Man kann kaum bezweifeln, dass der Autor der den Priestern deren Ehen vorwerfenden Predigt Adalbert selbst war. Jedenfalls war die Predigt Bestandteil von Adalberts Schriftstücken, genauso wie das Edikt Boleslaws II. und letzten Endes auch das Schreiben Stephans. Es scheint, dass uns ein Fragment von Adalberts Akten, seines kirchlich-politischen Dossiers, im Heiligen-kreuzer Manuskript erhalten blieb.

142 Vita Constantini c. 16, in: MMFH, Bd. 2, S. 105–110.

143 Christian c. 2, hg. von J. LUDVÍKOVSKÝ, S. 12: *Cumque quodam tempore memoratus Quirillus Romam causa orationis adisset, a summo pontifice vel a reliquis sapientibus et rectoribus ecclesiae redarguitur, ut quid contra statuta canonum ausus fuerit missarum sollemnia instituere canere Sclavonica lingua.*

144 Vita Constantini c. 16, in: MMFH, Bd. 2, S. 105: „Lateinische Bischöfe, Priester und Mönche stürzten sich auf ihn wie die Raben auf einen Falken, die Dreisprachenketzerei mit folgenden Worten vertretend: ‚Sage uns, Mensch, wieso hast du nun für die Slawen Buchstaben geschaffen und lehrst diese, und niemand anders hat sie vorher erfunden, weder ein Apostel, noch ein römi-scher Papst, noch Gregor der Theologe, noch Hieronymus, noch Augustinus? Wir kennen jedoch nur drei Sprachen, mit denen es sich ziemt, Gott in Büchern zu rühmen: Hebräisch, Griechisch und Lateinisch'".

145 Christian c. 2, hg. von J. LUDVÍKOVSKÝ, S. 12: *cur me, patres electi, prohibetis missarum celebritatem modulare Sclavonice seu alia queque de Latino vel Graeco verbo eorum vertere in sermonem?*

Konstantin verloren,[146] in Rom jedoch gewonnen und der Papst erkannte die slawische Liturgie an.[147] In Venedig argumentierte Konstantin mit dem Recht aller Völker, Gott in der eigenen Sprache zu preisen, in Christians Rom jedoch mit der Notwendigkeit, die slawische Liturgie in der Missionspraxis bei einem ungebildeten „hartnäckigen" Volk anzuwenden.[148] All das hatte Christian nicht aus Bulgarien, dort gab man – sofern man weiß – die Fassung der Vita Konstantins der weiteren großmährischen Texte über das Venediger Streitgespräch weiter. Die Situation hatte sich wesentlich geändert: Christian wollte nicht die slawische Schrift vor den Reichs-, vor allem den bayrischen Bischöfen verteidigen, wie es Konstantin darum ging; er wollte die slawische Liturgie vor dem Papst verteidigen. Der Ausgangspunkt war hier ganz sicher die letzte gültige Entscheidung der Kurie in der Sache, enthalten im oben erwähnten Schreiben des Papstes Stephans V. vom Jahre 885, wo der Papst hier streng verbietet, die Messe in der slawischen Sprache zu zelebrieren, empfiehlt jedoch nachdrücklich die slawische Schrift als Missions- und Seelsorgemittel. Eben dieses Argument benutzte Christian, er übertrug es lediglich von der Schrift auf die Liturgie und verteidigte die letztere als Mittel zur ‚Erweichung' des ‚harten Nackens' des Volkes.

Christian wollte also die slawische Liturgie verteidigen und benutzte dazu einen Text bulgarischer oder wohl genauer Ochrider Herkunft, den er jedoch seinen eigenen Bedürfnissen anpasste. Er hatte dabei aber offensichtlich das alte Mähren betreffende Verbot Stephans V. im Sinn, und nicht das neuere Verbot Johanns XIII., das direkt seine Diözese traf. Dieses zitiert Cosmas als Schreiben des Papstes Johanns XIII., mit dem dieser Boleslaw I. auf Ersuchen seiner Tochter Mlada-Marie die Gründung eines Bistums und des St. Georgsklosters in Prag bewilligte.[149] Cosmas vermutete, dass das Schreiben an Boleslaw II. geschickt wur-

---

146 Die Disputation führte zu nichts, Konstantin „beschämte nur" seine Gegner und „verließ sie" (vita Constantini c. 16, in: MMFH, Bd. 2, S. 110). Erst in Rom genehmigte Papst Hadrian II. die slawischen Bücher, die der Streit betraf, und anschließend zelebrierte man in einigen Kirchen die Messe in slawischer Sprache, welche die Disputation in Venedig nicht betraf. (Vita Constantini c. 17, in: MMFH, Bd. 2, S. 110f.).
147 Christian c. 2, hg. von J. LUDVÍKOVSKÝ, S. 14: *Ac illi ... auctoritate sua statuerunt et firmant suprascripto sermone partibus in illis missarum sollemnia ceterasque canonicas horas hymnizari.*
148 Christian c. 2, hg. von J. LUDVÍKOVSKÝ, S. 14.
149 Cosmas I. 22, hg. von B. BRETHOLZ, S. 43–44: *Iohannes, servus servorum Dei, Bolezlao catholice fidei alumno apostolicam benedictionem. Iustum est benivolas aures iustis acco- modare petitionibus; quia Deus est iustitia et, qui diligunt eum, iustificabuntur et omnia diligentibus Dei iustitiam cooperantur in bonum. Filia nostra, tua relativa, nomine Mlada, quae et Maria, inter ceteras haud abnegandas petitiones cordi nostro dulces intulit ex parte tui praeces, scilicet ut nostro assensu in tuo pricipatu ad laudem et gloriam Dei ecclesiae liceret fieri episcopatum. Quod nos utique leto animo suscipientes, Deo grates retulimus, qui suam ecclesiam semper et ubique dilatat et magnificat in omnibus nationibus. Unde apostolica auctoritate et sancti Petri principis apostolorum potestate, cuius, licet indigni, tamen sumus vicarii annuimus et collaudamus atque incanonizamus, quo ad ecclesiam sancti Viti et sancti Wenczlai martyrum fiat sedes episcopalis, ad ecclesiam vero sancti Georgii martyris, sub regula sancti Benedicti et obedientia filiae nostrae, abatissae Mariae constituatur congregatio sanctimonialium. Verumtamen non secundum ritus aut sectam Bulgariae gentis vel Ruziae, aut Sclavonicae linguae, sed magis sequens instituta et decreta apostolica unum potiorem totius ecclesiae ad placitum* eligas in hoc opus clericum *Latinis adprime* litteris eruditum, *qui*

de, aus dem Text geht jedoch eindeutig hervor, dass der Adressat Boleslaw I. war,[150]

<u>verbi vomere</u> *novalia cordis gentilium* <u>scindere</u> *et triticum bonae operationis serere atque manipulos frugum vestrae fidei Christo reportare sufficiat, Vale.* Unterstrichen sind Cosmas' Entlehnungen aus den St. Adalbertslegenden hervorgehoben (Bruno c. 15, Canaparius c. 22, Versus de passione S. Adalberti v. 939–940). Vgl. TŘEŠTÍK, D.: Kosmova kronika. Studie k počátkům českého dějepisectví a politického myšlení, Prag 1968, S. 128.

Zur Frage der Gründung eines Bistums in Prag und in Mähren: eine Übersicht der älteren Literatur gibt NAEGLE, August: Kirchengeschichte Böhmens I/2, Wien-Leipzig 1918, S. 385–517. Daraus sind wichtig insbesondere SPANGENBERG, Hans: Die Gründung des Bistums Prag, in: Historisches Jahrbuch 21 (1900), S. 758–775; SCHULTE, Wilhelm: Die Gründung des Bistums Prag, in: Historisches Jahrbuch 22 (1901), S. 285–297; HOLTZMANN, Robert: Die Urkunde Heinrichs IV. Für Prag vom Jahre 1086, in: Archiv für Urkundenforschung 6 (1918), S. 177–193. Siehe ferner auch NOVOTNÝ, Václav: České dějiny I/1, Prag 1913, S. 583–592 und S. 609–611; DVORNIK, Francis: The Making of Central and Eastern Europe, London 1949, S. 75–83. Neuerdings untersuchte die ganze Frage FIALA, Zdeněk: Dva kritické příspěvky ke starým dějinám českým, in: Sborník historický 9 (1962), S. 53ff. Mit der Problematik befassten sich ferner BÜTTNER, Heinrich: Erzbischof Willigis von Mainz und das Papsttum bei der Bistumserrichtung in Böhmen und Mähren im 10. Jh., in: Rheinische Vierteljahrsblätter 30 (1965), S. 1–22 (kennt die tschechische Literatur nicht); KADLEC, Jaroslav: Auf dem Wege zum Prager Bistum. Zur Vorgeschichte seiner Gründung, Geschichte der Ost- und Westkirche in ihren wechselseitigen Beziehungen (= Annales Instituti Slavici 1,3), 1967, S. 29–45; KRÁLÍK, Oldřich: Od Radima ke Kosmovi. K nejstarším dějinám české vzdělanosti (Acta Universitatis Palackianae Olomucensis, Facultas Philosophica 48, Philologica XXVI), Prag 1968, S. 25–69; GRAUS, František: Böhmen zwischen Bayern, S. 5–42; ŁOWMIAŃSKI, Henryk: Początki Polski IV, Warszawa 1970, S. 433ff.; KRÁLÍK, Oldřich: Kosmova chronologie počátků pražského biskupství, in: Strahovská knihovna 5/6 (1970/71), S. 51–57; HILSCH, Peter: Der Bischof von Prag und das Reich in sächsischer Zeit, in: Deutsches Archiv 28 (1972), S. 6–16; ZIMMERMANN, Gerd: Wolfgang von Regensburg und die Gründung des Bistums Prag, in: Beiträge zur Tausendjahrfeier des Bistums Prag, Bd. 2, München 1973, S. 38–60; KADLEC, Jaroslav (unter dem Pseudonym V. A. Kaiser): Die Gründung des Bistums Prag, in: Archiv für Kirchengeschichte von Böhmen-Mähren-Schlesien 3 (1973), S. 9–23; Id.: (unter dem gleichen Pseudonym): Das Millenium des Prager Bistums im Spiegel der historischen Literatur, in: Archiv für Kirchengeschichte von Böhmen-Mähren-Schlesien 4 (1976), S. 194–204; GRAUS, F.: Tausend Jahre Prager Bistum (Ein Literaturbericht), in: Jahrbücher für Geschichte Osteuropas 23 (1975), S. 525–635; KRÁLÍK, Oldřich: Kosmova kronika a předchozí tradice, Prag 1976, S. 157–168; NOVÝ, Rostislav: K zakládací listině pražského biskupství, in: Traditio et cultus. Miscellanea historica bohemica Miloslao Vlk archiepiscopo Pragensi ... dedicata, Prag 1993, S. 13–19; LABUDA, Gerard: Czeskie chrześciaństwo na Śląsku i w Małopolsce w X i XI wieku, in: Chrystianizacja Polski południowej, Krakau 1994, S. 94–961. TŘEŠTÍK, D.: Moravský biskup roku 976, in: Ad vitam et honorem. Profesoru Jaroslavu Mezníkovi přátelé a žáci k pětasedmdesátým narozeninám, Brno 2003, S. 197–200; Id.: Die Gründung des Prager und des mährischen Bistums, in: Europas Mitte um 1000. Beiträge zur Geschichte, Kunst und Archäologie, Bd. 1, hg. von A. WIECZOREK/ H.-M. HINZ, Stuttgart 2000, S. 407–410; Id.: K založení pražského biskupství v letech 968–976: pražská a řezenská tradice, in: Vlast a rodný kraj v díle historika, Prag 2004, S. 179–196; KALHOUS, David: Záhadné počátky pražského biskupství, in: Evropa a Čechy na konci středověku, Prag 2004, S. 195–208.

Zum Schreiben Johanns XIII. vgl. SPANGENBERG, H.: Die Gründung, S. 763–766; DVOŘAK, Max: O listině papeže Jana XIII. v Kosmově kronice, in: Věstník Král. Čes. Spol. Nauk 1899/1900, Bd. 13, S. 1–5; HRUBÝ, Václav: Původní hranice biskupství pražského, in: Časopis Matice moravské 50 (1926), S. 144–146; FIALA, Z.: Dva kritické, S. 56–63; KADLEC, J.: Die Gründung, S. 12–15; VESELSKÝ, Jiří: K pravosti listu Jana XIII. v Kosmově kronice, in: Listy filologické 111 (1988), S. 76–82; NOVÝ, R.: K zakládací listině, S. 13–19, DVOŘÁK/TŘEŠTÍK, D.: K založení, S. 179–196.

150 Cosmas I. 22, hg. von B. BRETHOLZ, S. 43: (Mlada) *fratri suo refert, insuper litteras ex parte apostolici sibi directas obtulit.* Mlada übergab also laut Cosmas das Schreiben ihrem Bruder, d. h. Boleslaw II., das Schreiben selbst spricht aber von ihr als von *filia nostra, tua relativa,* der Adressat

was bestätigt, dass der Chronist das Schreiben nicht erfunden hatte wie einige weitere, die in seiner Chronik enthalten sind,[151] sondern dass er es fertig vorgefunden hatte. Das Schreiben hatte er allerdings stilistisch ausgeschmückt – wie es bei den fremde Texte zitierenden Geschichtsschreibern üblich war – besonders mit Entlehnungen aus den St. Adalbertslegenden.

Der von Cosmas benutzte Text war jedoch kaum identisch mit dem vorausgesetzten Originalschreiben Johanns XIII. Ganz offensichtlich konnte dieses Original kein Verbot der slawischen Liturgie „nach dem Ritus und der Sekte des bulgarischen oder russischen Volkes" enthalten, besonders nicht in Bezug auf Russland, das damals noch nicht getauft war. Daher betrachtete man dieses Schreiben als gefälscht. Die Bezeichnung des slawischen Ritus als ‚Sekte' deutet auf die Lage nach dem Schisma des Jahres 1054 hin und der Hinweis auf Russland ist im 10. Jahrhundert selbstverständlich auch unmöglich; dies bedeutet aber nicht, dass auch der Hinweis auf Bulgarien in dieser Zeit genauso unmöglich wäre. Christian ist hierfür der unwiderlegbare Zeuge. Außerdem muss man sich vergegenwärtigen, dass man im 11. Jahrhundert von der ehemals führenden Rolle Bulgariens in der slawischen Liturgie und im slawischen Schrifttum nichts mehr wusste und dass Russland zum ‚Modellland' in dieser Hinsicht wurde.[152] Diese Situation spiegelt auch Cosmas' Text des Schreibens Johanns XIII. wieder mit seinem Hinweis auf *ritus aut sectam Bulgariae gentis vel Ruziae*, wo *Ruziae* als Ergänzung zum ursprünglichen *Bulgariae* aus dem 10. Jahrhundert erscheint. Dies würde bedeuten, dass das Schreiben Johanns XIII. tatsächlich ein Verbot der slawischen Liturgie nach dem Vorbild Bulgariens enthielt und dass es sich daher nicht um ein Echo des Streits um die slawische Liturgie unter Wratislaw II. handelt, der bekanntermaßen den Papst um deren Bewilligung ersuchte.

---

ist daher ihr Vater, nicht ihr Bruder. Bereits Gelasius DOBNER: Wenceslai Hajek a Liboczan, Annales Bohemorum 4, Prag 1772, S. 171 interpretierte *filia nostra spiritualis, tua relativa* als „unsere geistige, deine eigene, leibliche Tochter". Vgl. SPANGENBERG, H.: Die Gründung, S. 765; NOVOTNÝ, V.: České dějiny 1,1, S. 585; NAEGLE, A.: Kirchengeschichte Böhmens 1,1, S. 399ff., dort auch über den irrtümlichen Versuch von VACEK, František: Církevní dějiny české 1, Prag 1890, S. 391, *relativa* als „diejenige, die Nachrichten gebracht hat (*relata est*)" zu übersetzen; FIALA, Z.: Dva kritické, S. 57.

Will man sich um jeden Preis an Cosmas' Text halten, kann man diese Situation so auslegen, dass Mlada zwar ein an Boleslaw I. adressiertes Schreiben nach Prag brachte, übergab es jedoch bereits an Boleslaw II., weil ihr Vater inzwischen, während ihres Aufenthaltes in Rom, gestorben war (so FIALA, Z.: Dva kritické, S. 59); dies ist jedoch ziemlich an den Haaren herbeigezogen. Der jegliche Teilnahme des Brudermörders an der Gründung seines Bistums bestreitende Cosmas hätte so etwas wissentlich nicht geschrieben. Es hat eine Bedeutung für die Chronologie der Ereignisse, da Mladas Botschaft im ersteren Fall in die Jahre 970–972 datiert wäre, während man diese im letzteren Fall eigentlich nur in das Pontifikat Johanns XIII. datieren könnte (er trat sein Amt im Jahr 965 an und starb am 6. September 972, kurz nach Boleslaw I., der am 15. Juli desselben Jahres starb), am ehesten in die Jahre 966/967 bis Mitte 972.

151 Diese behandelt HLAVÁČEK, Ivan: Diplomatisches Material in den narrativen Quellen des böhmischen Mittelalters bis zum Anfang des 13. Jahrhunderts, in: Palaeographica diplomatica et archivistica. Studi in onore di Giulio Battelli, Rom 1979, S. 73–96.

152 Siehe Anm. 130.

Warum sollte der Papst aber die slawische Liturgie im künftigen Prager Bistum verbieten? Dies würde bedeuten, dass die Kurie die Lage des Christentums in Prag am Ende der 60er Jahre des 10. Jahrhunderts als der in Bulgarien ähnlich einstufte und befürchtete, dass hier durch die Bistumsgründung ein Zentrum slawischer Liturgie entstehen könnte. Dafür gab es aber bestimmt keine ernsthaften Gründe. Man weiß, dass hier sicher der slawischen *Schrift* kundige Priester wirkten, aber wir haben ziemlich klar gezeigt, dass im damaligen Böhmen keine aktive slawische *Liturgie* existierte. Dass Boleslaw selbst um die slawische Liturgie für das neue Bistum ersucht hätte und dass gerade dies Gegenstand des abgelehnten Gesuchs gewesen wäre, das das Schreiben Johanns XIII. erwähnt, ist genauso wenig wahrscheinlich. Boleslaws Gesuch musste etwas anderes betreffen, etwas, das die Bedenken des Papstes eher indirekt weckte.

Man muss berücksichtigen, dass Boleslaw nicht nur ein Bistum für Prag, sondern auch für Mähren wollte. So war nämlich das Ergebnis aller Verhandlungen im Jahre 976; damals entstanden zwei Bistümer und nicht nur eines, das Prager Bistum. Die Antwort des Papstes – einschließlich des Verbots der slawischen Liturgie – betraf daher beide, auch wenn sie nicht notwendigerweise hätte in einem Schreiben enthalten sein müssen. In diesem Falle werden allerdings die Bedenken des Papstes, dass diese neuen Bistümer die von Rom verbotene slawische Liturgie benutzen könnten, voll verständlich. Das Hauptargument für das mährische Bistum, das Boleslaw ganz sicher einsetzte, war die Tatsache, dass es in Mähren bereits ein Bistum gegeben hatte und dass man es nur zu erneuern braucht. Es ging selbstverständlich um das mährische Bistum Methods. Die Verknüpfung dieses Bistums mit der slawischen Liturgie war einerseits in Rom sicher bekannt, andererseits hatte Boleslaws Gesuch selbst zweifellos daran erinnert.

Man könnte daher erwägen, dass Christians auf einer ‚Nachfrage' in Bulgarien basierende Schilderung der Geschicke der mährischen Kirche einschließlich der Verteidigung der slawischen Liturgie eigentlich bereits aus dem Jahre 968 stammt und dass sie daher ein angepasstes „Weißes Buch" – am ehesten in Form eines Schreibens – darstellt, das damals Boleslaw aufgrund der Informationen aus Bulgarien in Rom vorlegte. Sofern sie jedoch ein eigenes Werk Christians aus dem Ende des 10. Jahrhunderts sein sollte, würde sie durch ihre Betonung der Nützlichkeit der slawischen Liturgie und des slawischen Schrifttums bei der Mission auf eine veränderte Lage hinweisen, als Adalbert nach dem Tode des hiesigen Bischofs zum Administrator der neu errichteten Mährischen Diözese wurde und gleichzeitig ausgedehnte neu eroberte heidnische Gebiete im Osten und Norden unter seine Verwaltung kamen, wo Missionierung notwendig war. Hier ging es jedoch wahrscheinlich nicht mehr um das Mährische Bistum, sondern um ein Erzbistum, jenes sagenhafte Erzbistum Christians „mit sieben Suffraganen", um das sich bereits um das Jahr 974 Pilgrim in Passau bemühte und das nachher eine

Rolle spielte auch beim Planen dessen, was dann mit dem „Akt von Gnesen" des Jahres 1000 endete.[153]

Eine Verfolgung dieser ‚bulgarischen Spur' mit allen diesen Folgen würde uns aber zu weit von unserem Thema weg führen. Erwähnenswert ist es aber jedenfalls, dass gerade diese Spur am besten die Frage nach der Herkunft der slawischen Liturgie im Kloster Sazawa beantworten könnte. Wo erwarb dessen Gründer Prokop seine Bildung und selbstverständlich auch seinen typisch östlichen Namen?

Sicherlich nicht in Ungarn und nach dem, was wir gesagt haben, wohl auch nicht in Böhmen. Dies muss in einem Kloster geschehen sein, daher ist die ‚bulgarische Spur' auch in dieser Hinsicht aktuell. Die einzigen slawischen Klöster und insbesondere die mit ihnen verbundenen Schulen gab es doch am Ende des 10. Jahrhunderts in Bulgarien[154] und die Beziehungen Böhmens zu ihnen sind unter anderem auch durch die ‚bulgarische Information' belegt. Es gab hier das slawische Schrifttum und auch wenn die slawische Liturgie nicht benutzt wurde, so weckte sie doch – aus politischen Gründen – lebhaftes Interesse. Das alles lenkte die Aufmerksamkeit auf Bulgarien. Über Bulgarien (vor allem das Ochridsche) führten die Pilgerwege ins Heilige Land[155] – ist es so schwer sich vorzustellen, dass Prokop als Pilger nach Bulgarien kam, der sich offenbar bereits zu Hause für die bulgarische Bildung interessierte?

Dies sind gewiss nur Vermutungen; für uns ist vor allem wichtig, dass man im Böhmen der zweiten Hälfte des 10. Jahrhunderts vom mährischen Kyrillo-Methodschen Christentum nichts Bestimmtes mehr wusste. Als die Frage der Erneuerung des Mährischen Bistums auftauchte, musste man einschlägige Informationen darüber in Bulgarien suchen. Am Mährischen Bistum des 9. Jahrhunderts haftete ein ernster Makel in Form der slawischen Liturgie; die ‚bulgarische Information' sollte daher Argumente für die Verteidigung der slawischen Liturgie liefern, nicht aber der aktuell existierenden, sondern der längst untergegangenen. Die böhmische Argumentation nutzte dabei die päpstliche Empfehlung eines slawischen Schrifttums, das – zum Unterschied von der Liturgie – in Böhmen wirklich existierte, auch wenn in bescheidenem Umfang und sie versuchte zu beweisen, dass die Liturgie für die Mission und die Christianisierung insgesamt genauso hilfreich ist wie die Schrift. Inwieweit dies ein Programm sein sollte und nicht nur ein Bemühen, das Mährische Bistum von möglicher Verleumdung rein zu waschen, ist schwer zu sagen. Sicher ist nur, dass so ein Programm nicht umge-

---

153 Diese Möglichkeiten untersuche ich in: TŘEŠTÍK, D.: Svatý Vojtěch a formování střední Evropy, in: Svatý Vojtěch, Čechové a Evropa, hg. von. D. TŘEŠTÍK/J. ZEMLICKA, Prag 1998, S. 81–108 und Id.: Die Entstehung Mitteleuropas aus der Kraft des Tatsächlichen und aus einer Idee, in: The Neighbours of Poland in the 10th century, hg. von P. URBAŃCZYK, Warszawa 2000, S. 111–145.

154 Über die Klöster in Bulgarien LITARWIN, G.G.: Christianstvo v Bolgarii v 927–1018 gg, in: Christianstvo v stranach vostočnoj, jugo-vostočnoj i central'noj Evropy na poroge vtorogo tysjačletija, Moskau 2002, S. 149ff.

155 Cosmas I. 37, hg. von B. BRETHOLZ, S. 67, verzeichnet anlässlich der Thronbesteigung Heinrichs II. im Jahr 1002 die Geschichte vom Kelch aus Bamberg, den ein frommer Pilger nach Jerusalem trug. Er kehrte aus Konstantinopel über Bulgarien zurück, offenbar auf der üblichen Pilgerstraße.

setzt, die slawische Liturgie von Johannes XIII. verboten wurde und dass man das Verbot in Böhmen offenbar befolgte.

Das slawische Schrifttum war hier offensichtlich nicht nur Jagičs „zarte Zimmerpflanze"[156] aber auch nicht die blühende, mit der lateinischen Kultur erfolgreich konkurrierende Kultur ‚vieler Zentren', wie es die Slawisten ausmalen. Es war mehr eine Frage als Tatsache, mehr Suche als Programm – übrigens analog zu allen ähnlichen Versuchen, das Problem der Benutzung der Nationalsprache in der Praxis der entstehenden Landeskirchen zu lösen. Der Unterschied bestand darin, dass es in Böhmen gleichzeitig (und wohl vor allem) eine politische Frage war, da sie mit dem umstrittenen Erbe Großmährens, mit seinem Bistum (und Erzbistum) zusammenhing, das die ersten Boleslaws versuchten zu erneuern.

---

156 JAGIČ, Vatroslav: Entstehungsgeschichte der Kirchenslawischen Sprache, Berlin 1913, S. 108.

Roman Michałowski

Die ‚nationale' Interpretation des Christentums im frühmittelalterlichen Polen

Die Entscheidung des Herzogs von Polen ebnete den Weg, auf dem das Christentum nach Polen gelangte. Im Jahre 966 nahm Mieszko I. die Taufe an, und seitdem vollzog sich die Christianisierung des Landes unter der Schirmherrschaft und der Aufsicht polnischer politischer Behörden.[1] Wir sind nicht im Stande, festzustellen, ob und inwieweit die Einführung der neuen Religion auf Widerstand der einheimischen Bevölkerung stieß. Die unzureichende Zahl der Quellen macht es nicht möglich. Wenn es jedoch einen Widerstand gab, dann wurde er sehr rasch gebrochen.

Die wichtigsten und interessantesten Informationen über Polen in den ersten zwei Jahrzehnten des 11. Jahrhunderts verdanken wir dem Merseburger Bischof Thietmar. Dieser Geschichtsschreiber wusste nichts über irgendwelche gegen das Christentum gerichtete Rebellionen, er schrieb auch nichts über die Existenz und die Aktivitäten von Zentren des heidnischen Kults. Thietmar beurteilte den damals in Polen herrschenden Herzog, Bolesław Chrobry, sehr kritisch und hatte ihm vieles vorzuwerfen. Im langen Katalog der Schulden, die er dem Herzog anlastete, gab es jedoch nichts, was Chrobrys Nachsicht gegenüber den Gegnern des Christentums und den Anhängern alter Götter suggerieren könnte. Das Schweigen Thietmars diesbezüglich ist markant. Wenn das Heidentum in Polen damals existierte, und es ist doch kaum vorstellbar, dass es gänzlich in Vergessenheit geriet, dann wurde es zu einem heimischen Kult herabgestuft, der nur in engen Kreisen und heimlich betrieben wurde. Als er über das große heidnische Sanktuarium auf dem Berg Zobten schrieb, bezog der Merseburger Bischof die dort zelebrierten Bräuche auf die Vergangenheit.[2] Im Jahre 1017, zu Zeiten, als

---

1 Zur Christianisierung Polens im Mittelalter siehe vor allem die Arbeiten von GIEYSZTOR, Aleksander: Les paliers de la pénétration du christianisme en Pologne au Xe–XIe siècle, in: Studi in onore di Amintore Fanfani, Bd. 1, Mailand 1962, S. 329–367; Id.: La religion populaire en Pologne et en Bohême, in: DELUMEAU, Jean (Hg.): Histoire Vécue du Peuple Chrétien, Bd. 1, Toulouse 1979, S. 315–334; Id.: Le fonctionnement des institutions ecclésiastiques rurales en Bohême, en Pologne et en Hongrie aux Xe et XIe siècles, in: Cristianizzazione ed organizzazione ecclesiastica delle campagne nell'alto medioevo (Settimane di studio del centro italiano di studi sull'alto medioevo 28), Spoleto 1982, S. 925–954; Id.: La chrétienté et le pouvoir princier en Europe du centre-est des origines jusqu'à la fin du XIIe siècle, in: La cristianità dei secoli XI e XII in occidente: Coscienza e strutture di una società. Atti della Ottava Settimana Internazionale di Studio (Miscellanea del Centro di studi Medioevali 10), Mailand 1983, S. 123–145; überdies ŁOWMIAŃSKI, Henryk: Religia Słowian i jej upadek, Warschau 1979. Vgl. dazu auch MICHAŁOWSKI, Roman: La christianisation de la Pologne aux Xe–XIIe siècles, in: ROUCHE, Michel (Hg.): Clovis. Histoire et mémoire, Bd. 2: Le Baptême de Clovis, son écho à travers l'histoire, Paris 1997, S. 419–434.
2 Thietmari Merseburgensis episcopi Chronicon, hg. v. Robert HOLTZMANN (MGH Scriptores rerum Germanicarum, nova series 9), Berlin 1935, lib. VII, c. 59, S. 472. Zur heidnischen Kultstätte

deutsche Truppen unweit von diesem Berg vorbeizogen, wurde die Kultstätte von niemandem aufgesucht, es sei denn heimlich.

In den dreißiger Jahren des 11. Jahrhunderts änderte sich die Lage. Es erfolgte eine heidnische Reaktion.[3] In manchen Quellen ist die Rede von der Verfolgung des christlichen Klerus, die damals stattfand; es ist auch bekannt, dass die Bistümer, deren Netz von den Piasten mit großem Aufwand in den Jahren 966–1000 aufgebaut wurde, ihre Tätigkeit einstellten, wohl mit Ausnahme des Krakauer Bistums.[4] Archäologische Funde scheinen auf die Tatsache zu verweisen, dass man auf manchen Gebieten zum heidnischen Kult zurückkehrte.[5] Der Untergang des von Mieszko I. und Bolesław Chrobry aufgebauten Staates wurde von diesen Ereignissen begleitet. Die königliche Macht brach zusammen und der einzige Vertreter der Dynastie, Kasimir der Erneuerer, wurde aus dem Land verbannt. Zweifellos war die religiöse Krise die Folge einer politischen Krise. Solange eine starke Piastenmonarchie bestand, erfreute sich das von ihr eingeführte Christentum einer Autorität. Ihre Erfolge zeugten von dem Wert der neuen Religion und die Militär- sowie die Polizeimacht des Herzogs vermochten es, die Unzufriedenen und Ungläubigen zum Schweigen zu zwingen. Gemäß dieser Denkweise wurden die Niederlagen, die Polen nach dem Tode Chrobrys seitens der Nachbarn erlitten, sowie das Chaos im Lande als eine Bloßstellung des Christentums angesehen. Es bedurfte der Rückkehr Kasimirs des Erneuerers aus der Verbannung und eines mühsamen Wiederaufbaus der Staatsstrukturen, damit Bedingungen geschaffen wurden, die die Restitution der kirchlichen Organisation und die erneute Evangelisierung ermöglichten.

Die Bedeutung, die öffentliche Institutionen für die Christianisierung Polens hatten, resultierte unter anderem daraus, dass die Religion im Frühmittelalter eine rechtliche Angelegenheit war. Anders gesagt, es war der Gesetzgeber, der sich zur Einführung des Christentums äußern musste. In Polen waren es die Piasten, die ihren Untertanen die Annahme der Taufe geboten. Sie fühlten sich auch dazu verpflichtet, eine Reihe von Normen aufzuheben, die den Kult sowie die Bräuche betrafen, die von dem alten Glauben herrührten oder mit ihnen übereinstimmten. Thietmar gab an, dass im heidnischen Polen nach dem Hinscheiden des Gatten die Frau enthauptet wurde, damit sie den Tod mit ihm teilte.[6] Zu der Zeit, als der Merseburger Bischof sein Werk verfasste, galt dieser Brauch nicht mehr. Er wurde von Mieszko I. verboten, da er im Widerspruch zu der neu angenommenen Religion stand.

---

auf dem Berg Zobten siehe SŁUPECKI, Leszek: Slavonic Pagan Sanctuaries, Warschau 1994, S. 172–176.

3 GIEYSZTOR, Aleksander: Mouvements para-hérétiques en Europe centrale et orientale du 9ᵉ au 11ᵉ siècle: Apostasies, in: LE GOFF, Jacques (Hg.): Hérésies et sociétés dans l'Europe préindustrielle 11ᵉ–18ᵉ siècles, Paris 1968, S. 159–167.

4 JUREK, Tomasz: Losy arcybiskupstwa gnieźnieńskiego w XI wieku, in: STRZELCZYK, Jerzy/GÓRNY, Janusz (Hg.): 1000 lat Archidiecezji Gnieźnieńskiej, Gniezno 2000, S. 49–72.

5 MOŹDZIOCH, Sławomir: Schlesien im 10. Jahrhundert, in: SOMMER, Petr (Hg.): Boleslav II. Der tschechische Staat um das Jahr 1000 (Colloquia mediaevalia Pragensia 2), Prag 2001, S. 427f.

6 Thietmari Merseburgensis episcopi Chronicon (Anm. 2), lib. VIII, c. 3, S. 494.

Anstelle der alten Normen mussten neue eingeführt werden. Thietmars Chronik enthält interessante Informationen diesbezüglich. Wir erfahren, dass Menschen, die Fleisch nach der Septuagesima verzehrten, die Zähne ausgebrochen wurden.[7] Das Verbot, Fleischgerichte in der Fastenzeit zu essen, resultierte aus dem kirchlichen Gebot; es war jedoch im Mittelalter üblich, dass die weltliche Macht über die kirchlichen Gebote wachte. Karl der Große sowie viele andere Herrscher im Westen verstanden ihre Pflichten eben auf diese Art und Weise. Die Herrscher der Länder Mittel-Osteuropas, solche wie Boleslaw Chrobry oder der ungarische heilige Stephan, verfuhren gemäß demselben Grundsatz, nur mit dem Unterschied, dass die von ihnen angewandten Sanktionen von einer weitgehenden Brutalität gekennzeichnet waren.[8] Der heilige Stephan ordnete z. B. jenen gegenüber die Prügelstrafe an, die am Sonntag nicht in die Kirche gingen.[9] Über Strafmaßnahmen, die in Polen für Überschreitungen auf religiösem und sittlichem Gebiet drohten, erfahren wir aus Thietmars Bericht. Die Beschreibung ist so drastisch, dass sie hier nicht angeführt werden kann. Das, was wir über die Repressalien sagten, die jene trafen, die die Fastenzeit nicht beachteten, sollte genügen.

Der Gegenstand unserer Betrachtungen wird jedoch nicht die Tatsache sein, dass die weltliche Macht die Überschreitungen der kirchlichen Norm äußerst streng bestrafte, sondern vielmehr die Tatsache, dass mindestens in einem Fall die Norm selbst sehr streng zu sein scheint. Wie aus der angeführten Quelle hervorgeht, galt im Land Chrobrys das Verbot Fleisch zu essen nicht vom Aschermittwoch, sondern vom Sonntag Septuagesima an (genauer gesagt, vom Montag nach der Septuagesima). Die Fastenzeit erlegte den Gläubigen verschiedenartige Einschränkungen auf, sie betrafen allerdings nicht nur die Art der verzehrten Nahrungsmittel. Wenn man das Problem jedoch ausschließlich von diesem Standpunkt aus betrachtet, begann die Fastenzeit in Polen über zwei Wochen früher als andernorts üblich.[10] Eines ist sicher: Thietmar irrte sich nicht, denn der Brauch,

---

7   Thietmari Merseburgensis episcopi Chronicon (Anm. 2), lib. VIII, c. 2, S. 494: *Et quicumque post LXX. carnem manducasse invenitur, abscisis dentibus graviter punitus*. János M. Bak lässt die Möglichkeit zu, dass bereits im heidnischen Polen denjenigen die Zähne ausgestoßen wurden, die gegen die Fastenzeit verstießen (es ist anzunehmen, dass das mit einem heidnischen Tabu im Zusammenhang stand), und dass in dem hier interessierenden Fall lediglich die Anpassung eines alten Brauches an die neuen Bedingungen erfolgte. Siehe Bak, János M.: Signs of Conversion in Central European Laws, in: Armstrong, Guyda/Wood, Ian W. (Hg.): Christanizing Peoples and Converting Individuals (International Medieval Research 7), Turnhout 2000, S. 115–124, S. 117, (Anm. 8). Auch wenn es tatsächlich so war, wobei es hier keine bestätigenden Angaben gibt, musste das Verbot doch, nach der Septuagesima Fleisch zu essen, von einem schon christlichen Herrscher verordnet worden sein.

8   Zur Gesetzgebung der mitteleuropäischen Herrscher im Frühmittelalter unter besonderer Berücksichtigung Ungarns, siehe Bak: Signs of Conversion (Anm. 7).

9   Sancti Stephani Decretorum Liber Primus, cap. 9, zitiert nach Györffy, György: Wirtschaft und Gesellschaft der Ungarn um die Jahrtausendwende (Academia Scientiarum Hungarica 186), Wien/Köln/Graz 1983, S. 266.

10 Zur neunwöchigen Fastenzeit in Polen siehe Modelski, Teofil E.: Post dziewięciotygodniowy w Polsce, in: Przegląd Historyczny 15 (1912), S. 1–12 und 127–138; Krasiński, Andrzej: Posty w dawnej Polsce, in: Przegląd Teologiczny 12 (1931), S. 190–235, insbesondere S. 197–214; vgl.

die Fastenzeit am Sonntag Septuagesima zu beginnen, wurde in späteren Quellen bestätigt. Die wichtigsten von ihnen werden hier aufgeführt.

Unter diesen Umständen stellt sich die folgende Frage: Gab es im christlichen Westen Länder, in denen die Fastenzeit an dem genannten Sonntag begann? Wenn es solche Länder nicht gab oder wenn sie eine Ausnahme bildeten, aus welchen Gründen wählte dann die polnische Kirche diese strengere Norm bzw. legte selbst eine solche Norm fest?

An der Schwelle des Mittelalters bildete sich im lateinischen Christentum die Fastenzeit heraus, die sechs Wochen vor Ostern begann. Da man sich darüber einig war, dass die für die genannte Zeit charakteristischen Verschärfungen an den Sonntagen nicht galten, nahm man an, dass die Fastenzeit im Grunde genommen 36 Tage dauerte. Manche Vertreter der Kirche hielten diese Zahl für unzureichend. Sie meinten, dass die Fastenzeit an das Fasten Christi anknüpfen sollte und Christus hielt sich in der Wüste nicht 36, sondern 40 Tage auf.

Aus diesem Grunde wurde in der zweiten Hälfte des 5. Jahrhunderts der Begriff der Quinquagesima geprägt, der sowohl den siebenten Sonntag vor Ostern als auch die an diesem Sonntag beginnende Fastenzeit bezeichnet.[11] Weit verbreitet war die Überzeugung, dass Karfreitag und Karsamstag, obwohl sie mit nicht minderer Buße erfüllt waren, nicht in die Fastenzeit gehörten. Bei einer solchen Berechnung betrug die siebenwöchige Fastenzeit genau 40 Tage. Bald darauf, in der zweiten Hälfte des 6. Jahrhunderts, legte man den achten Sonntag vor Ostern als Sexuagesima fest. Dieser Sonntag verlängerte die Zeit der Entsagungen und der Buße noch. Seine Einführung war wohl mit der im Osten weit und im Westen vereinzelt verbreiteten Ansicht verbunden, dass man am Samstag nicht fasten sollte. Bei der Berücksichtigung dieses Prinzips betrug die Zahl der für die Buße bestimmten Tage von der Sexuagesima bis exklusive Karfreitag 40 Tage. Im Laufe des 7. Jahrhunderts wurde schließlich in den liturgischen Kalendern der Sonntag Septuagesima eingeführt, das heißt der neunte Sonntag vor dem Pascha. Während die Sonntage Quinquagesima und die Sexuagesima festgelegt wurden, um die Zahl der realen Fastentage auf 40 zu bringen, ist ein solcher Zusammenhang im Falle der Septuagesima nicht ersichtlich und es ist überhaupt nicht sicher, inwieweit die nach ihm folgende Woche in den frühesten Zeiten für Verzichtleistungen, die an die Fastenpraxis erinnerten, bestimmt war.

---

hierzu auch MICHAŁOWSKI, Roman: Post dziewięciotygodniowy w Polsce Chrobrego. Studium z dziejów polityki religijnej pierwszych Piastów, in: Kwartalnik Historyczny 109,1 (2002), S. 5–40 (englische Fassung: MICHAŁOWSKI, Roman: The Nine-Week Lent in Boleslaus the Brave's Poland. A Study of the First Piasts' Religious Policy, in: Acta Poloniae Historica 89 (2004), S. 5–50).

11 Zur Herausbildung der Vorfastenzeit siehe SIFFRIN, Petrus: Zwei Blätter eines Sakramentars in irischer Schrift des 8. Jahrhunderts aus Regensburg, in: Jahrbuch für Liturgiewissenschaft 10 (1930), S. 19–29; FROGER, Jacques: Les anticipations du jeûne quadragésimal, in: Mélanges de science religieuse 3 (1946), S. 207–234; CHAVASSE, Antoine: La structure du Carême et les lectures des messes quadragésimales dans la liturgie romaine, in: La Maison-Dieu 31 (1952), S. 76–119, vor allem S. 86–93; CHAVASSE, Antoine: A propos d'une anticipation du jeûne quadragésimal, in: Revue des sciences religieuses 52 (1978), S. 3–13; TALLEY, Thomas J.: Les origines de l'année liturgique, Paris 1990 (Übersetzung aus dem englischen Original von 1986), vor allem S. 239–242.

Die beschriebenen Änderungen in der Liturgie und in der asketischen Disziplin vollzogen sich zunächst in Italien, vor allem in Capua, Rom und Turin und
wenn wir die Provence ausschließen, musste man bis zum Ende des 7. Jahrhunderts warten, bevor sie sich auf andere Länder auszuwirken begannen. Ein echter
Durchbruch erfolgte jedoch in der karolingischen Epoche. Die Romanisierung
der fränkischen Liturgie, die auf Anordnung der Könige aus der neuen Dynastie durchgeführt wurde, trug zur Verbreitung des römischen Kirchenkalenders
bei. Im Endeffekt wurden die Sonntage der Septuagesima, der Sexuagesima und
der Quinquagesima bekannt und zunächst in vielen und dann schließlich in allen
Ländern des lateinischen Christentums begangen.

Es stellt sich jedoch folgende Frage: War die Vorfastenzeit in der Epoche der
Karolinger und der Ottonen mit der Pflicht besonderer Verzichtsleistungen verbunden? Vor allem jedoch, denn das ist für uns von Bedeutung, waren die Gläubigen in der Woche der Septuagesima zu besonderen Verzichtleistungen verpflichtet?

Sogar ein flüchtiger Blick auf die Quellen führt zur Überzeugung, dass im
8.–9. Jahrhundert das westliche Christentum eine solche Fastenzeit, die in der
genannten Zeitspanne gültig und die als Rechtsnorm verstanden worden wäre,
nicht kannte.[12] Entgegen diesem Sachverhalt jedoch unterlag es für die Theologen
und sogar für manche Weltliche keinem Zweifel, dass die liturgische Zeitspanne,
die mit der Septuagesima begann, in Zusammenhang mit der Buße und der Entsagung gestanden haben muss. Diese Überzeugung stützte sich auf zwei Annah-
men: Einerseits sei die Septuagesima der erste der Sonntage gewesen, die die Kirche auf das Osterfest vorbereiteten, und andererseits sei die Macht des Bösen und
der Sünde, mit der sich der Mensch mit Hilfe Gottes messen konnte und sollte,
das Leitmotiv ihres Messmusters gewesen.

Erhalten geblieben ist der Briefwechsel zwischen Alkuin und Karl dem Großen, der Einblick in den Stand der Diskussion über das uns interessierende Problem gewährt. Wie aus den erwähnten Briefen hervorgeht, waren der König
und viele seiner Zeitgenossen davon überzeugt, dass die Christen die Fastenzeit
irgendwo, höchstwahrscheinlich im Nahen Osten, mit der Septuagesima begannen.[13] Ein Vierteljahrhundert später vertrat Amalarius von Metz die Ansicht, dass
auch die Kirche im Westen sich von diesem Sonntag an der Entsagung hingeben
solle. Bis zu einem gewissen Grad tat sie dies bereits, wenn in der Vorfastenzeit in
der Liturgie die Hymne Gloria ausgelassen und das Halleluja nicht gesungen wur-

---

12 Das Problem der Fastenzeit nach der Septuagesima, die tatsächlich für die lateinische Kirche galt
oder zumindest postuliert wurde, ist eine Frage, die bis jetzt nicht bearbeitet wurde. Was die Karolingerzeit und die Zeit der Ottonen betrifft, vgl. Michałowski: Post dziewięciotygodniowy
(Anm. 11); nachstehend werden die Thesen dieses Artikels angeführt.
13 Alcuini sive Albini Epistolae, hg. v. Ernst Dümmler u. a. (MGH Epistolae 4: Epistolae Karolini
aevi 2), Berlin 1895 (Neudruck 1994), Nr. 143, S. 224–227, vor allem S. 225–226; Nr. 144 und
S. 228ff.

den.[14] Dies sei jedoch zu wenig, da die Christen im Westen zu größeren Verzicht-leistungen verpflichtet seien. Zu dieser Schlussfolgerung kam Amalarius, indem er sich der allegorischen Methode bediente, in der er ein Meister war.

Die Ansichten von Amalarius wurden zwar gern in der Karolinger- und Otto-nenzeit wiederholt, sie fanden jedoch lange Zeit keine Widerspiegelung im kano-nischen Recht. Möglicherweise begannen manche klösterlichen Kreise in der zweiten Hälfte des 9. Jahrhunderts die Fastenzeit nach der Septuagesima. In einem solchen Fall hätten wir es eher mit einem Reflex der privaten Frömmigkeit als mit einer Rechtsnorm zu tun.[15]

Der Durchbruch erfolgte in der zweiten Hälfte des 10. Jahrhunderts. In man-chen klösterlichen *consuetudines* erschienen damals Verschärfungen, die sich auf die Art der in der Vorfastenzeit verzehrten Nahrungsmittel bezogen. Sie betra-fen nicht das Fleisch, sondern tierisches Fett, genauer gesagt Speisen, die mit tieri-schem Fett zubereitet wurden.[16] Die Mönche aßen, wie bekannt, überhaupt kein Fleisch. Auch die karolingischen *consuetudines* verbaten den Konsum von Fett, das Verbot jedoch trat an der Quinquagesima in Kraft, also an dem Tag, an dem die Mönche die Fastenzeit begannen. In manchen Klöstern begann das Verbot nun, zwei Wochen früher gültig zu sein, an der Septuagesima.

Die Einschränkungen galten auch für Weltliche, mit dem Unterschied jedoch, dass sie das Eherecht betrafen. Im Frühmittelalter galt das aus dem Altertum über-nommene Prinzip, nach dem die Eheschließung an bestimmten Tagen des Jahres verboten war. Dies galt für Sonn- und Feiertage, vor allem jedoch für jene Tage, an denen die Pflicht der ehelichen Enthaltsamkeit geübt werden musste. Eheschlie-ßungen durften nicht in der Fastenzeit vorgenommen werden, manchmal auch nicht im Advent, an den Quartalstagen und an den Vorabenden der Feiertage. Von der Vorfastenzeit war in diesem Kontext nicht die Rede. Dies änderte sich erst gegen Ende des 10. und im ersten Viertel des 11. Jahrhunderts.[17] Die Synode, die 992 in Aachen zusammentrat, erkannte an, dass das besprochene Verbot von

---

14 Amalarii Epistolae, hg. v. Ernst DÜMMLER u. a. (MGH Epistolae 5: Epistolae Karolini aevi 3), Ber-lin 1898 (Neudruck 1995), Nr. 6, S. 248–250; Liber officialis, hg. v. Johannes M. HANSSENS (Ama-larii episcopi opera liturgica omnia 2), Vatikanstadt 1948, lib. I, c. 1: De septuagesima, S. 26–36.

15 Siehe dazu die *homilie* für den Sonntag Septuagesima, geschrieben im 9. Jh. in Auxerre: QUADRO, Riccardo: L'omelario di Eirico di Auxerre, in: IOGNAT-PRAT, Dominique/JEUDY, Colette/LOB-RICHON, Guy (Hg.): L'école carolingienne d'Auxerre de Muretach à Remi 830-908, Paris 1991, S. 285ff.

16 Siehe z. B. Cluniacensium antiquorum Redactiones principales, hg. v. Kassius HALLINGER in: Consuetudines Cluniacensium antiquiores cum redactionibus derivatis (Corpus consuetudinum monasticarum 7/2), Siegburg 1983, c. 29, S. 46 (Manuskript *B*); Redactio sancti Emmerami dicta Einsidlensis, in: ibid., c. 67, S. 245.

17 FREISEN, J.: Geschichte des canonischen Eherechts bis zum Verfall der Glossenliteratur, Pader-born ²1893, S. 644–646; RITZER, Korbinian: Formen, Riten und religiöses Brauchtum der Ehe-schließung in den christlichen Kirchen des ersten Jahrtausends (Liturgiewissenschaftliche Quellen und Forschungen 38), Münster 1962, S. 292ff.; AMIET, Andreas: Die liturgische Gesetzgebung der deutschen Reichskirche in der Zeit der sächsischen Kaiser 922–1023, in: Zeitschrift für Schweize-rische Kirchengeschichte 70 (1976), S. 257–261.

dem Sonntag der Septuagesima an gelten sollte[18] und die Synode in Seligenstadt im August bestätigte diesen Grundsatz.[19] Ein identisches Dekret nahm die angelsächsische Synode an, die im Jahre 1009 in Enham tagte.[20] Das neue Verbot wurde in Burchards Dekret eingeführt.[21] Es ist auch bemerkenswert, dass Boleslaw Chrobry deswegen von Thietmar kritisiert wurde, weil er seine vierte Frau, Oda, nach dem Sonntag Septuagesima ehelichte, ohne dafür die kanonische Erlaubnis zu haben.[22]

Erwähnt werden sollten schließlich auch Einschränkungen, die sich auf das öffentliche Leben bezogen. In der Karolingerzeit begann sich der Brauch herauszubilden, Gerichtssitzungen und andere öffentliche amtliche Versammlungen nicht in der Fastenzeit abzuhalten. Dann wurden allmählich verschiedene andere Tage hinzugefügt, an denen die Pflicht der Enthaltsamkeit galt, bis schließlich erst um die Wende des 10. zum 11. Jahrhunderts die Vorfastenzeit hinzugezählt wurde. Die oben erwähnten Synoden in Aachen und Enham verbaten es Ordalien zu fällen sowie *placita saecularia* vor Ostern, von der Septuagesima an, abzuhalten.[23]

Wir kommen somit zur folgenden Schlussfolgerung: Die Überzeugung, dass die Fastenzeit in der Zeit der Ottonendynastie neun Wochen dauern sollte, fand ihre Widerspiegelung im positiven Recht. Andererseits bleibt festzustellen, dass nicht einmal zu dieser Zeit der Konsum von Fleisch in der Zeit der Septuagesima verboten wurde. Es wurden auch keine anderen Einschränkungen hinsichtlich der Mahlzeiten für die Laien und den weltliche Klerus eingeführt. Es gab selbstverständlich auch solche, die bereits am Sonntag Septuagesima auf den Verzehr von Fleisch verzichteten (z. B. Heinrich II.),[24] dies ergab sich jedoch aus ihrer privaten Frömmigkeit und nicht aus einem gesetzlichen Verbot.

Das Quellenmaterial, das wir gesammelt haben, gestattet es, die polnische Gesetzgebung in einen breiteren Kontext einzubetten. Es ist uns gelungen festzustellen, dass in keinem Land des frühmittelalterlichen Europas, außer Polen, das neunwöchige Verbot des Fleischkonsums galt. Es scheint also, dass die polnische Gesetzgebung im europäischen Kontext eine Anomalie darstellte. Andererseits jedoch war das erwähnte Verbot den im damaligen Westen herrschenden Tenden-

---

18 Pertz, Georg H. (Hg.): Bernoldi Chronicon (MGH SS 5), Hannover 1844, S. 423.

19 Weiland, Ludwig (Hg.): Constitutiones et acta publica imperatorum et regum (MGH Legum sectio 4,1), Hannover 1893, Nr. 437, c. 3, S. 637.; siehe Wolter, Heinz: Die Synoden im Reichsgebiet und in Reichsitalien von 916 bis 1056, Paderborn 1988, S. 300f.

20 Sacrorum Conciliorum nova et amplissima Collectio, Bd. 19, hg. v. Iohannes Dominicus Mansi, Venetiis 1774, col. 301.

21 Migne, Jacques-Paul (Hg.): Burchardi Wormaciensis Ecclesiae episcopi decretorum libri viginti (Patrologiae cursus completus, Series latina 140), Paris 1880, lib. IX, c. 4, Sp. 816. Siehe den Kommentar zu diesem Kanon von Hoffmann, Hartmut/Pokorny, Rudolf: Das Dekret des Bischofs Burchard von Worms. Textstufen – Verbreitung – Vorlagen (MGH Hilfsmittel 12), München 1991, S. 53 i 212.

22 Thietmari Merseburgensis episcopi Chronicon (Anm. 2), lib. VIII, c. 1, S. 494.

23 Wie Anm. 18 und 20; siehe Amiet: Die liturgische Gesetzgebung (Anm. 17), S. 49ff.

24 Thietmari Merseburgensis episcopi Chronicon (Anm. 2), lib. VII, c. 52, S. 462.

zen ausgezeichnet angepasst. Dort war man auch bemüht, die Fastenzeit früher beginnen zu lassen und zu verlängern – bis zur Septuagesima einschließlich. Der Unterschied beruhte jedoch darauf, dass die in Deutschland und England eingeführten Rechtsnormen viel milder waren als die in Polen vorgenommenen Modifizierungen. Sie betrafen ja nicht das Wichtigste: den Verzehr von Nahrungsmitteln. Das Verbot Gerichtssitzungen zu halten oder Ehen zu schließen, war für die Individuen lästig, doch das Verbot des Fleischkonsums war eine Belastung für alle.

Wir kennen die Umstände nicht, unter denen man sich in Polen dafür entschied, das kanonische Recht in diesem Punkte zu verschärfen. Es liegt jedoch nahe, dass dieses Ereignis unter der Herrschaft Boleslaw Chrobrys und nicht unter der seines Vaters Mieszkos I. († 992) stattfand, denn in Westeuropa begann sich die Überzeugung von der Notwendigkeit, die Verlängerung der Fastenzeit auch für weltliche Personen zur geltenden Rechtsnorm zu erheben, erst in den neunziger Jahren auszubreiten. Es ist kaum vorstellbar, dass die Piastenmonarchie diese Modifizierung vornahm, ohne Inspiration aus den Ländern des alten Christentums.

Wir können ferner annehmen, dass diese Verschärfung des kanonischen Rechts von der Synode der polnischen Kirchenprovinz beschlossen wurde. Dies erfolgte demnach nicht früher als im März des Jahres 1000, als die Provinz gegründet wurde. Wir haben auch Grund zu vermuten, dass die Synode von Boleslaw Chrobry geleitet wurde – einem Herzog, der in Bezug auf die polnische Kirche über alle Rechte verfügte, die in Deutschland dem König zustanden. Analogien aus den damaligen Verhältnissen zeugen davon, dass der König formal und auch tatsächlich dafür verantwortlich war, Synodalbeschlüsse zu fassen und zu vollstrecken. Das war z. B. in Deutschland der Fall, wo das Episkopat durch die Kirchenpolitik Heinrichs II.[25] auch in der politischen Struktur eine herausragende Stellung hatte. So muss es in Polen, das erst seit einigen Jahrzehnten christlich und in dem die Stellung der Bischöfe dem Herrscher gegenüber notgedrungen schwach war, *a fortiori* gewesen sein.

In Boleslaw sollte man daher den Mann sehen, der es entgegen dem überall geltenden kanonischen Recht angeordnet hatte, sich in der Vorfastenzeit des Verzehrs von Fleischspeisen zu enthalten. Der König richtete sich sicherlich nach dem religiösen Eifer. Wir wissen aus anderen Quellen, dass er religiöse Angelegenheiten sehr ernst nahm.[26] Dieser Eifer gebot ihm, praktische Konsequenzen aus den Ansichten mancher Theologen zu ziehen, die behaupteten, dass die Fastenzeit bereits am neunten Sonntag vor Ostern beginnen sollte.

Chrobrys Entscheidung wurde jedoch wohl auch von politischen Umständen beeinflusst. Die Verlängerung der Fastenzeit um über zwei Wochen war eine dermaßen radikale Verschärfung der Prinzipien, dass man darin eine Manifesta-

---

25 Siehe z. B. HOFFMANN, Hartmut: Mönchskönig und rex idiota. Studien zur Kirchenpolitik Heinrichs II. und Konrads II. (MGH Studien und Texte 8), Hannover 1993, S. 50–60.
26 Zur Herrschaft Bolesław Chrobrys siehe STRZELCZYK, Jerzy: Bolesław Chrobry, Poznań 1999.

tion sehen sollte. Was war ihr Ziel? Zwei Hypothesen drängen sich hierbei auf. Im März des Jahres 1000 wurde dem polnischen Herzog von Otto III. in Gnesen das Amt des Mitarbeiters des Kaiserreiches verliehen (*cooperator imperii*).[27] Dieser Titel, der keine Analogie im Mittelalter hatte, wurde höchstwahrscheinlich *ad hoc* geschaffen, um die Aufgaben zu umreißen, die Boleslaw zu Gunsten des Imperiums erfüllen sollte. Es muss dies eine sehr hohe Würde gewesen sein, wenn der Herrscher, dem sie verliehen wurde, die Kopie der Heiligen Lanze geschenkt bekam. Zu den Aufgaben des Amtes gehörten an erster Stelle die Verbreitung des Christentums in heidnischen Ländern und seine Festigung in Polen selbst.[28] Die Stellung, die Boleslaw im Kaiserreich von Otto III. verliehen bekam, wurde von dem Nachfolger des Letzteren in Frage gestellt.[29] Es drängt sich nun folgende Vermutung auf: Indem der polnische Herrscher die kanonische Norm dermaßen verschärfte, wollte er betonen, dass er entgegen der Ansicht Heinrichs II. ein Mitarbeiter des Kaiserreichs war und dies auch verdiente. Es ist zwar nicht leicht, sich ein Bild von den wahren Zielen zu machen, die Boleslaw Chrobry anstrebte, es besteht jedoch kein Zweifel, dass die Mitwirkung an der Expansion des Imperiums eine Rolle war, die ihm entsprach. Er stellte jedoch eine Bedingung: Er wollte in diesem Imperium einen hohen Rang haben.[30]

Erwägenswert ist auch eine andere Möglichkeit. Wir müssen uns darüber im Klaren sein, dass der polnische Staat um das Jahr 1000 ein ganz neues Gebilde war. Er entstand in den vorhergehenden Jahrzehnten auf dem Wege der Eroberungen. Der Stamm der Polanen, der ein verhältnismäßig kleines Territorium um

---

27 Die Information hierzu verdankt man Gallus Anonymus. Siehe Galli Anonymi Chronicae et Gesta ducum sive principum Polonorum, hg. v. Karol Maleczyński (Monumenta Poloniae Historica, series nova 2), Krakau 1952, lib. I, c. 6, S. 19f. Dieser Geschichtsschreiber schrieb seine Chronik zwar erst im 12. Jahrhundert, er bediente sich jedoch einer Quelle, die hundert Jahre früher verfasst worden war. Bei aller Kritik, die man bei der Analyse der Informationen von Gallus über das Treffen Ottos III. mit Boleslaw Chrobry in Gnesen in Betracht ziehen sollte, sollte man die Nachricht darüber, dass der Pole mit dem Amt eines Mitarbeiters des Kaiserreiches beschenkt wurde, als zuverlässig ansehen; siehe Michałowski, Roman: Polen und Europa um das Jahr 1000, mit dem Anhang: Zur Glaubwürdigkeit des Berichts von Gallus Anonymus über das Treffen in Gnesen, in: Ranft, Andreas (Hg.): Von den Wurzeln zum Neuen Europa. Hoftag in Quedlinburg 973 (im Druck). Von der sehr umfangreichen Fachliteratur, die das Treffen in Gnesen betrifft, siehe zwei neue Arbeiten: Labuda, Gerard: Der „Akt von Gnesen" vom Jahre 1000. Bericht über die Forschungsvorhaben und Ergebnisse, in: Quaestines Medii Aevi Novae 5 (2000), S. 145–188; Strzelczyk, Jerzy: Zjazd Gnieźnieński, Poznań 2000; siehe auch Michałowski, Roman: Zjazd gnieźnieński. Religijne przesłanki powstania arcybiskupstwa gnieźnieńskiego, Wrocław 2005.

28 Jasiński, Tomasz: Tytulatura Bolesława Chrobrego na Zjeździe Gnieźnieńskim, in: Memorie amici et magistri. Studia historyczne poświęcone pamięci Prof. Wacława Korty (1919–1999), Wrocław 2001, S. 23–31.

29 Görich, Knut: Eine Wende im Osten? Heinrich II. und Boleslaw Chrobry, in: Schneidmüller, Bernd/Weinfurter, Stefan (Hg.): Otto III. – Heinrich II.: eine Wende? (Mittelalter Forschungen 1), Sigmaringen 1997, S. 95–167.

30 Kętrzyński, Stanisław: Karol Wielki I Bolesław Chrobry, in: Przegląd Historyczny 36 (1946), S. 19–25; Ludat, Herbert: An Elbe und Oder um das Jahr 1000. Skizzen zur Politik des Ottonenreiches und der slavischen Mächte in Mitteleuropa, Köln/Wien 1971, S. 67–92, insbesondere S. 85–92.

Gnesen und Posen bewohnte, eroberte ein von verschiedenen Stämmen und Völkern bewohntes Gebiet, das erheblich größer als ihr ursprüngliches Siedlungsgebiet war. Es musste die Frage gestellt werden, wie dieser Staat und die Untertanen seines Herrschers genannt werden sollten, da die Polanen doch eine Minderheit in der Bevölkerung bildeten. Trotz der geringen Zahl der Quellen wissen wir, dass verschiedene Versuche in dieser Hinsicht unternommen wurden. Ibrahim ibn Jakub wählte die einfachste Lösung: Er nannte das Reich der Polanen nach dem Namen seines Herrschers Mieszko. Mieszko I. selbst, als er die *oblatio* seines Hoheitsgebiets zu Gunsten des heiligen Petrus vornahm, nannte es die *civitas* von Gnesen. Er verzichtete somit auf jegliche ethnische Bezüge und wählte eine andere Lösung: Den Namen des geschenkten Herzogtums bestimmte er mit Hilfe des Namens seiner Hauptstadt. Ein Vierteljahrhundert früher bezeichnete der sächsische Geschichtsschreiber Widukind Mieszko I. als einen Monarchen, der über „Slawen, die sich Licikaviki nennen", regierte.[31] Diese Bezeichnung ist eine echte *crux interpretum*. Gemäß der wahrscheinlichsten Interpretation sollte man den erwähnten Begriff als „die Menschen von Lestek" auslegen, wobei Lestek der Vorfahr von Mieszko I. gewesen sein soll, der aus späteren polnischen Chroniken bekannt ist.[32] Erneut haben wir es nicht mit einem ethnischen Begriff zu tun, der die Untertanen des polnischen Herzogs bezeichnen würde. Ähnlich wie in den zwei vorhergehenden Fällen wurden also die Abhängigkeitsbande als definierender Faktor gewählt. Es gab zwar ethnische Bezeichnungen, beziehungsweise solche, die sich auf das Ethnische bezogen, sie waren jedoch unscharf, da zu allgemein. Es ging um die Bezeichnungen *sclavenus*, *sclavi*, *sclavania* usw.

Und doch wurde schließlich ein präziser ethnischer Begriff geprägt, der alle anderen Bezeichnungen verdrängte. Es war die Bezeichnung „Polanen" als Bezeichnung für ein Volk und die von ihm stammende Bezeichnung „Polen", die das Land und das Reich meinte.[33] Man kehrte also zur Bezeichnung des Stammes zurück, der dieses Reich gegründet hatte, zugleich jedoch verlieh man ihr eine neue, allgemeinere Bedeutung. Die alte Bezeichnung verschwand jedoch nicht sofort, und infolgedessen wurden die beiden Begriffe bis zum Spätmittelalter parallel in enger Bedeutungsverwandtschaft benutzt, wobei sie das ehemalige Territorium des Polanenstammes und seine Einwohner ebenso bezeichneten wie auch dessen Erweiterung.

Es ist bemerkenswert, dass der Begriff *poloni*, *polonia* usw. um das Jahr 1000 aufzutauchen begann, und zwar in verschiedenartigen Schriftdenkmälern, wie

---

31 Dies sind gut bekannte Tatsachen, die in diesem Kontext mehrmals zusammengestellt wurden. Siehe z. B. ŁOWMIAŃSKI, Henryk: Początki Polski, Bd. 6, Teil 1, Warszawa 1985, S. 21.

32 ŁOWMIAŃSKI: Początki Polski (Anm. 31), Bd. 5, Warszawa 1973, S. 481–488, mit einer Zusammenstellung der früheren Fachliteratur zu diesem Thema; GOŁĄB, Zbigniew: Jak sąsiedzi zachodni nazywali Polaków w połowie X wieku? in: Slavia Occidentalis 48/49 (1991/92), S. 85–92. Diese Interpretation, die Aleksander Brückner als erster darlegte, stößt bei manchem Forscher auf entschiedenen Widerstand.

33 ŁOWMIAŃSKI: Początki Polski (Anm. 31), S. 21–23; LABUDA, Gerard: Studia nad początkami państwa polskiego, Bd. 2 (Uniwersytet Adama Mickiewicza w Poznaniu, Reihe: Historia 140), Poznań 1988, S. 461 ff.

z. B. in der *Vita s. Adalberti*, die gegen 999 verfasst wurde, in den seit 1007 ge-schriebenen Quedlinburger Annalen oder auf polnischen königlichen Münzen.[34] Es scheint, dass Boleslaw Chrobry damals eine Entscheidung traf, die sich auf die ideellen Grundlagen seines Reiches bezog und die darauf abzielte, ihn in Anleh-nung an die ethnische Gemeinschaft zu integrieren. Zweifelsohne knüpfte er dabei an den bereits entstehenden Brauch an.[35]

In diesem Kontext sollte man die Modifizierung des kanonischen Rechts betrachten, die Boleslaw Chrobry vornahm. Vom objektiven Standpunkt aus verlieh die neue Norm allen seinen Untertanen ein gemeinsames Merkmal und zugleich unterschied sie sie von allen anderen christlichen Völkern. Es ist daher möglich, dass der Herrscher die Fastenzeit verlängerte, um die Untertanen zu einem Volk zu vereinen, unabhängig von ihrer tatsächlichen ethnischen Herkunft. Wenn diese Hypothese stimmen sollte, dann hätten wir es hier mit einer Aufwer-tung der Nation zu tun, denn von diesem Zeitpunkt an konnten sich die Polen für frömmere Menschen halten, also für besser als andere Völker und Stämme.

Dies ist natürlich lediglich eine Vermutung, sie ist jedoch hochwahrscheinlich. Um sich davon zu überzeugen, reicht es, Quellen aus dem 12.–13. Jahrhundert

---

34 Jüngst wurden diese Angaben von FRIED, Johannes: Der Hl. Adalbert und Gnesen, in: Archiv für mittelrheinische Kirchengeschichte 50 (1998), S. 50f. zusammengestellt.

35 FRIED: Der Hl. Adalbert (Anm. 34), verbindet die Entstehung der Bezeichnung „Polen" mit dem Tod des heiligen Adalbert und mit dem Treffen in Gnesen. Er tut das jedoch auf eine selt-same Art und Weise. Vor allem bestreitet Fried die Existenz des Stammes der Polanen, indem er bemerkt, dass keine Quelle von dieser Existenz berichtet. Er stellt die Behauptung auf, dass die Bezeichnung „Polen" eine biblische Genese hatte (er beruft sich an dieser Stelle auf die Prophezei-ungen von Isaiah und Daniel) und ein aufblühendes Land (also eben „pole" – Feld) im mystischen Sinne, dank dem Märtyrertum des Prager Bischofs, bedeutete. Man darf keine neue Interpretati-on von Fakten und Tatsachen aus dem Frühmittelalter *a limine* ablehnen. Wir haben zu wenige Quellen zu dieser Epoche, um im Voraus über die Falschheit der einen oder der anderen These zu entscheiden. Die Ansicht Frieds sollte auch in Erwägung gezogen werden. Man kann sich jedoch des Eindrucks nicht erwehren, dass die Hypothese des deutschen Forschers nicht aufrecht-erhalten lässt, und zwar aus mindestens zwei Gründen. Erstens verweisen wir auf den Umstand, dass Frieds Konzeption die Dualität der Bezeichnung „Polen" im Mittelalter nicht erklärt, dass sie sowohl Großpolen als auch das ganze Polen bedeuten konnte. Die Konzeption hingegen, welche annimmt, dass es den Stamm der Polanen gab, der andere Stämme, die die Gebiete zwischen der Oder und der Weichsel bewohnten, eroberte, belegt diese Dualität ausreichend. Zweitens kommt in der von Otto III. in Gnesen ausgestellten Urkunde in der Datierung die Bezeichnung Sclavania vor: Ottonis III. Diplomata, hg. v. Theodor SICKEL (MGH Diplomatum regum et imperatorum Germaniae 2, 2), Hannover 1893, Nr. 349, S. 779, dazu WOJTECKI, Dietrich: Slavica beim Anna-listen von Quedlinburg, in: Zeitschrift für Ostforschung 30 (1981), S. 161–194, S. 173. Wenn der Kaiser tatsächlich *polonia* der ‚Pate' der Bezeichnung gewesen wäre und wenn sie tatsächlich im Zusammenhang mit dem Gnesener Treffen geschaffen worden wäre, könnten wir erwarten, dass man sich dieser Bezeichnung eben in der kaiserlichen Urkunde bedient hätte, die am Grab des hei-ligen Adalbert ausgestellt wurde. In der polnischen Fassung des Artikels lässt der Autor die Exis-tenz eines Stammes der Polanen zu: FRIED, Johannes: Święty Wojciech i Polska (Instytut Historii Uniwersytetu im. Adama Mickiewicza w Poznaniu, Wykłady 5), Poznań 2001, S. 35 (Anm. 68). Somit lässt er jedoch die Hauptprämisse seiner These aus. Wenn die Bezeichnungen „Polanen" und „Polen" früher existierten, dann besteht kein Grund, um zu einer ‚mystischen' Interpretation zu greifen. Es ist einfacher anzunehmen, dass der erwähnte kleine Stamm seine Bezeichnung auf die eroberten Gebiete der umliegenden Stämme und Völker übertrug.

anzuführen, in denen von der neunwöchigen Fastenzeit die Rede ist. Ihre Autoren wussten zwar nichts davon, dass Boleslaw Chrobry eine Verschärfung der sich auf die Fastenzeit beziehenden Vorschriften eingeführt hatte – im Gegenteil, manche verbanden diese Tatsache mit einer anderen Person –, auffallend ist jedoch die aus den Texten ersichtliche Denkweise.

Die interessanteste von diesen Quellen ist die *Vita s. Adalberti*, genannt *Legende Tempore illo*, die höchstwahrscheinlich im 12. Jahrhundert in Polen, jedenfalls nicht später als 1248 verfasst wurde.[36] Die Faktographie des Werks stützt sich im Grunde genommen auf die Lebensbeschreibungen des heiligen Adalberts, die gegen Ende des 10. und zu Beginn des 11. Jahrhunderts entstanden sind. Es gibt jedoch eine große Textpartie, die keine Entsprechungen in früheren Quellen hat. Die dort dargestellten Ereignisse sind eine Schöpfung der reinen Imagination, es sind jedoch eben diese, die unsere Aufmerksamkeit auf sich ziehen.[37]

Der heilige Adalbert fragte die Einheimischen, die er auf seiner Wanderung in Polen traf, nach dem Weg nach Gnesen. Diese jedoch, anstatt dem ehrwürdigen Reisenden ausführliche Informationen zu geben, begannen, sich wegen der Sprache, die er sprach (er war ein Tscheche) sowie wegen der Mönchskutte, die er trug, über ihn lustig zu machen. Die Polen kannten damals ein solches Gewand nicht. Daraufhin wurden die Spötter hart bestraft: Auf Befehl des Missionars wurden sie sprachlos. Trotz der Hindernisse, auf die er stieß, kam der heilige Adalbert in die Hauptstadt des Landes und wurde dort durch die Wunder, die er vollbrachte, und das Verkünden des Wortes Gottes berühmt. Davon erfuhren die bestraften Einwohner der Dörfer, durch die der Missionar ging. Sie schämten sich ihrer Tat und begaben sich zum Bischof, um reuevoll um Vergebung zu bitten. Der Missionar erbarmte sich ihrer, bewirkte, dass sie ihr Sprechvermögen wieder erlangten und spendete ihnen das Sakrament der Taufe. Daraufhin begannen die Polen, die voll Freude und Bewunderung für den heiligen Mann waren, ihn um eine besondere Buße für ihre frevelhafte Tat zu bitten. Adalbert erfüllte ihre Bitte und verordnete, dass die Fastenzeit in Polen nicht am Aschermittwoch begann, wie das allgemein üblich war, sondern am Sonntag Septuagesima, also über zwei Wochen früher. Seitdem, stellte der Hagiograph fest, beachtete man in ganz Polen eine längere

36 De sancto Adalberto episcopo, hg. v. Wojciech Kętrzyński (Monumenta Poloniae Historica 4), Lwów 1884, S. 206–221. Zu demselben Werk u. a. Gromadzki, Grzegorz: Legenda de sancto Adalberto episcopo oraz Miracula sancti Adalberti. Studium źródłoznawcze, in: Roczniki Humanistyczne 37,2 (1989), S. 5–76; Labuda, Gerard: Nad legendą o św. Wojciechu „Tempore illo". Analiza źródłoznawcza, in: Ecclesia Posnanensis. Opuscula Mariano Banaszak Septuagenario dedicata, Poznań 1996, S. 11–31; Grzesik, Ryszard: Uwagi o legendzie De sancto Adalberto episcopo, Roczniki Historyczne 63 (1997), S. 139–148; Labuda, Gerard: Święty Wojciech biskup – męczennik, patron Polski, Czech i Węgier, Wrocław 2000, S. 274–284.
37 Labuda: Nad legendą (Anm. 36), behauptet, dass die Fragmente eine spätere Interpolation sind. Dies ist möglich, es ist jedoch entgegen der Meinung des Autors anzunehmen, dass sie vor 1248 entstanden sind.

Fastenzeit als in anderen Länder, nur dass das Fasten in den ersten zwei Wochen auf dem Verzicht von Fleischkonsum beruhte.[38]

Wir sehen also, dass die neunwöchige Fastenzeit in Polen tatsächlich galt und Thietmar uns nicht getäuscht hat. Unsere Aufmerksamkeit richtet sich jedoch auch auf einen anderen Umstand. Die Neuigkeit, die Boleslaw Chrobry in die polnischen Kirchenbräuche einführte, wurde von dem Hagiographen mit dem heiligen Adalbert in Zusammenhang gebracht und mit Hilfe einer umfangreich erzählten Anekdote erklärt.[39] Was waren die Gründe hierfür?

Der Hagiograph sah die Geschichte seiner Heimat von einem recht originellen Standpunkt aus. Er war der Überzeugung, dass Polen in der Zeit, in der der Prager Bischof dorthin kam, noch ein heidnisches Land war. Dies ist eine irrtümliche Meinung. Sie ermöglichte es jedoch, dem Heiligen eine herausragende Rolle in der Geschichte des Landes und des Volkes zuzuschreiben. Nach Ansicht des Autors war es eine Doppelrolle: Polen erhielt aus den Händen Adalberts das christliche Recht und überdies nahm es mit Ehre die von dem Heiligen festgelegten Bräuche an und wurde dank dieser Umstände auf einen Felsen gegründet.[40] Der Hagiograph präzisierte nicht, was er unter den Bräuchen verstand, aber es ist kaum zu bezweifeln, dass unter ihnen womöglich an erster Stelle die neunwöchige Fastenzeit stand. Es stellt sich also heraus, dass in den Augen des Betrachters aus dem 12. Jahrhundert (oder aus der ersten Hälfte des 13. Jahrhunderts) die Verlängerung der Fastenzeit in den Rang eines epochalen Ereignisses erhoben wurde, das über das Schicksal Polens entschied.[41]

Die Denkweise, die zu einer solchen Schlussfolgerung führte, war, wie es scheint, folgende: Man war sich sehr wohl der Tatsache bewusst, dass der Beginn

---

38 De sancto Adalberto (Anm. 36), c. 10, S. 217: *Precepit itaque illis vir dei, ut nouem septimanas ante pascha uno quoque anno ita custodiant, sicut ceteri fideles Christiani generali abstinentia septem ebdomadas rite obseruant. Quod illi preceptum desiderantissime suscipientes et in uita libenter custodierint et posteritati custodiendum tradere curauerunt. Nec frustra namque et in presens usque tempus eadem abstinentia per uniuersam Poloniam deuotissime obseruatur et quasi ab apostolis id traditum sit, inuiolabiliter colitur et tenetur, ita tamen ut per duas ebdomadas precedentes ab esu duntaxat carnium se abstineant.*

39 Über den Kult des Heiligen Adalbert in Polen im 12. und 13. Jh.: GIEYSZTOR, Aleksander: Drzwi Gnieźnieńskie jako wyraz polskiej świadomości narodowościowej XII wieku, in: WALICKI, Michał (Hg.): Drzwi Gnieźnieńskie, Bd. 1, Wrocław 1956, S. 1–18; GIEYSZTOR, Aleksander: Politische Heilige im hochmittelalterlichen Polen und Böhmen, in: PETERSOHN, Jürgen (Hg.): Politik und Heiligenverehrung im Hochmittelalter (Vorträge und Forschungen 42), Sigmaringen 1994, S. 331–336; LABUDA: Święty Wojciech (Anm. 36), S. 271–284; GAWLAS, Sławomir: Der Hl. Adalbert als Landespatron und die frühe Nationenbildung bei den Polen, in: BORGOLTE, Michael (Hg.): Polen und Deutschland vor 1000 Jahren. Die Berliner Tagung über den „Akt von Gnesen" (Europa im Mittelalter. Abhandlungen und Beiträge zur historischen Komparatistik 5), Berlin 2002, S. 193–233, vor allem S. 231ff.

40 De sancto Adalberto (Anm. 36), c. 11, S. 217: *Sancto igitur spiritu per famulum suum predicante multaque illic signa mirabiliter faciente, christianam legem Polonia gratanter uniuersa suscipit sanctique instituta uiri ouanter amplectens supra firmam petram fundari meruit.*

41 Über die Herausbildung des polnischen Nationalbewusstseins im Mittelalter siehe GIEYSZTOR, Aleksander: Gens Polonica: aux origines d'une conscience nationale, in: Etudes de civilisation médiévale. Mélanges offerts à Edmond-René Labande, Poitiers 1974, S. 351–362.

der Fastenzeit am Sonntag Septuagesima eine polnische Eigentümlichkeit sei. Der Hagiograph betonte dies sehr stark. Die verlängerte Enthaltsamkeit mit Blick auf den Fleischkonsum war also eine Eigenschaft, die das polnische Volk von den anderen Völkern unterschied und damit das polnische Volk konstituierte. Dies waren jedoch schwer greifbare Eindrücke, die einer intellektuellen Vertiefung bedurften.

Den Versuch einer solchen Vertiefung unternahm der Verfasser der *Legende Tempore illo*. Vor allem bezog er die Festlegung der neunwöchigen Fastenzeit auf Zeiten, in denen seine Heimat die endgültige Gestalt annahm, also auf den Zeitpunkt der Taufe. Nur unter dieser Bedingung konnte die am Sonntag Septuagesima beginnende Periode der Enthaltsamkeit als ein das Volk konstituierendes Merkmal angesehen werden. Zweitens musste man, um die hohe Würde, die den Polen zuteil wurde, hervorzuheben, die Entstehung der Nation mit der Person eines großen Heiligen verbinden. Die einzige Gestalt, die in dieser Hinsicht in Frage kam, war der heilige Adalbert. Daher auch stellte ihn der Hagiograph, entgegen der Wahrheit, als ‚Christianisator‘ dar und deshalb auch verband er die Verlängerung der Fastenzeit – eine Tatsache, die endgültig die Existenz Polens und der Polen als eigenes Land und Volk besiegelte – mit seiner Person. Das Ergebnis dieser Denkvorgänge war die Monumentalisierung der besprochenen Rechtsnorm, die so weit ging, dass ihre Einführung die Assoziation mit einem Felsen, auf den Polen gegründet wurde, weckte.

Die nächste wichtige Quelle sind die Akten der Synode der polnischen Kirchenprovinz, die 1248 in Breslau unter dem Vorsitz des Legaten Jacques Pantaléon, des Archidiakon von Lüttich und des späteren Papstes Urban IV. stattfand. Im Kapitel 12 schildert Jacques die Klage, mit der sich deutsche Siedler an ihn wandten, die sich kurz vorher im Gebiet der Breslauer und Krakauer Diözese angesiedelt hatten. Die Bischöfe forderten von ihnen, dass sie sich in der Zeit zwischen der Septuagesima und Ostern des Fleischkonsums enthalten und den Ungehorsamen drohten sie mit dem Fluch. Sie begründeten das mit der Tatsache, dass dies für Einheimische galt.[42] Die erwähnten Deutschen aßen jedoch ebenso wie ihre Vorfahren immer bis zum Dienstag vor Aschermittwoch Fleisch und diesen Brauch brachten sie in das Land mit, in dem sie sich ansiedelten. Sie sahen also keinen Grund, auf ihr Recht zu verzichten, insbesondere da dieses nicht im Widerspruch zu dem Glauben und den Normen stand, die in der Universalkirche galten. Außerdem aßen nach der Septuagesima unter dem Einfluss der deutschen Siedler auch viele Einheimische die von den Bischöfen verbotenen Speisen. Jacques von Lüttich berücksichtigte dies und hob den dortigen Brauch, genauer gesagt seinen Pflichtcharakter auf. Sollte jemand es so wollen, dann hatte er das

---

42 Schlesisches Urkundenbuch, Bd. 2, hg. v. Winfried Irgang, Wien/Köln/Graz 1978, Nr. 346, c. 12, S. 210: *Cum nuper per Wratislauiensem et Cracouiensem dioceses transitum faceremus, accesserunt ad nos Theutonici, qui ad incolendam terram eandem de Theutonia advenerant, nobis querimoniam deponentes super hoc, quod eorum episcopi, ut dicebant, eos per excommunicationis sententiam compellebant ad hoc, ut singulis annis a Septuagesima usque ad Pascha a carnibus abstinerent pro eo, quod homines regionum illarum eisdem temporibus ab esu carnium consueverant abstinere.*

Recht, sich des Fleischkonsums zu entziehen, man durfte jedoch niemanden, der nicht einen solchen Wunsch hegte, dazu zwingen – dies war die Rechtsformel, für die sich der päpstliche Legat entschied.[43]

Bemerkenswert ist noch ein Argument, das die Deutschen angeführt hatten. Sie verwiesen auf die Tatsache, dass sie nie die Versprechung gemacht hatten, laut derer sie sich zu dem Verzicht auf Fleisch nach der Septuagesima verpflichtet hätten. Darin kann man die Entgegnung auf die Ansicht sehen, dass die neunwöchige Fastenzeit das Ergebnis eines Eids war, den die Polen einst ablegten. Auf diese Überzeugung stießen wir, als wir die *Legende Tempore illo* analysierten. Diese Ansicht war, wie man sehen kann, weiter verbreitet, als man annehmen könnte und der Kreis ihrer Bekenner war keineswegs auf eine Gruppe von Intellektuellen beschränkt. Es muss also die offizielle Stellung der polnischen Kirche gewesen sein. Und in der Tat, die späteren Quellen, die die Beschlüsse der Breslauer Synode festlegten, betonten, dass die Polen damals von dem Eid befreit wurden.[44]

Es ist jedoch nich bekannt, ob und wie lange das Beachten der verlängerten Fastenzeit in der privaten Frömmigkeit beibehalten wurde. In der polnischen Historiographie des Spätmittelalters überdauerte die Erinnerung an den volkstümlichen Brauch. Der Angelegenheit wurde weiterhin eine große Bedeutung beigemessen. Es wurde auch nach neuen Möglichkeiten gesucht, die Einführung der neunwöchigen Fastenzeit mit dem Leitfaden der Nationalgeschichte zu verbinden.[45]

Nun ist es Zeit, Schlussfolgerungen aus dem dargestellten Material zu ziehen. Nach Polen kam ein völlig herausgebildetes Christentum, das eine präzise Doktrin, verwurzelte Gebräuche und ein entwickeltes System von Instanzen hatte. In solcher Gestalt wurde es auch angenommen, obgleich der Prozess der völligen Assimilation dieses Erbes lange dauerte, so wie etwas später auch der Prozess der Aneignung der Errungenschaften der Gregorianischen Reform lange dauerte und mit Hindernissen verlief. Dies bedeutet aber nicht, dass der *genius loci* keine Spuren in dem christlichen Erbe hinterließ. In Polen wie auch in anderen Ländern

---

43 Zum Problem der Fastenzeit auf der Breslauer Synode siehe Modelski: Post dziewięciotygodniowy (Anm. 10), S. 132ff.; Pfitzner, Josef: Besiedlungs-, Verfassungs- und Verwaltungsgeschichte des Breslauer Bistumslandes (Prager Studien aus dem Gebiet der Geschichtswissenschaft 18), Reichenberd i. B. 1926, S. 76f.; Krasiński: Posty (Anm. 10), S. 204ff.; Panzram, Bernhard: Geschichtliche Grundlagen der ältesten schlesischen Pfarrorganisation, Breslau 1940, S. 17f.

44 Siehe z. B. Rocznik kapituły poznańskiej, hg. v. Brygida Kürbis in: Annales Poloniae Maioris (Monumenta Poloniae Historica, series nova 6), Warszawa 1962, S. 25, unter dem Jahr 1248.

45 Ćwikliński, Ludwik (Hg.): Kronika polska (Monumenta Poloniae Historica 3), Lwów 1878, S. 619ff. Als Kasimir der Erneuerer aus dem Land vertrieben wurde, so der in den achtziger Jahren des 13. Jh. in Schlesien schreibende Verfasser, wurde Polen von schrecklichen Katastrophen heimgesucht. Um dem entgegenzuwirken, gaben sich die großen Herren Mühe, den König zur Rückkehr auf den Thron zu bewegen. Da er jedoch in der Zwischenzeit die Ordensgelübde in Cluny abgelegt und die Diakonatsweihe angenommen hatte, baten sie um die Erlaubnis beim Papst; es war dies umso nötiger, als der König doch eine Frau ehelichen musste, die ihm einen Nachfolger gebären würde. Der Papst gab die Erlaubnis, er stellte jedoch eine Reihe von Bedingungen, wie etwa jene, dass sich die Polen schon von der Septuagesima des Fleischkonsums enthalten sollten.

unterlag die neu angenommene Religion gewissen Modifizierungen unter dem Einfluss lokaler Bedingungen.

Der Ausgangspunkt dieser Untersuchung war die Tatsache der im Vergleich mit den allgemein herrschenden Gebräuchen verlängerten Fastenzeit. Diese war keine ernsthafte Abweichung, dahinter steckte auch keine Häresie und die ausländischen Kirchenfürsten waren dieser Verschärfung gegenüber zwar zurückhaltend, jedoch im Allgemeinen wohlwollend gesinnt. Die besprochene Modifizierung resultierte aus authentischen politischen und geistigen Bedürfnissen. Sie ermöglichte zuerst Boleslaw Chrobry, dann den Eliten und womöglich breiteren Schichten der Gesellschaft, sich unter den anderen Herrschern und Völkern der christlichen Welt zurechtzufinden. Die verlängerte Fastenzeit wurde demnach als Beweis für einen besonderen christlichen Eifer angesehen; seitdem die Einführung des neuen Brauchs mit dem heiligen Adalbert in Zusammenhang gebracht wurde, war dieser Brauch gewissermaßen eine Garantie der enormen Gnade, die durch den Heiligen dem Land und dem Volk zuteil wurde.

Besonders bemerkenswert ist die Beständigkeit der zu Beginn des 11. Jahrhunderts vorgeschriebenen Rechtsnorm. Wie wir bereits erwähnten, kam es in den dreißiger Jahren des 11. Jahrhunderts zu einer heidnischen Reaktion. In großen Gebieten Polens schwand das Christentum und die kirchliche Organisation brach zusammen. In den 40er Jahren wurde die Herrschaft der Piasten restituiert und der Wiederaufbau der kirchlichen Organisation in die Wege geleitet. Ihre Rekonstruktion wurde erst in den 70er Jahren abgeschlossen. Trotz dieses Zusammenbruchs blieb die polnische Kirche dem Prinzip treu, dass die Fastenzeit am Sonntag Septuagesima beginnen sollte.

Petr Hlaváček

Die deutsch-tschechischen Streitigkeiten unter den böhmischen Franziskanern auf dem Generalkapitel in Urbino (1490)

Das böhmische Observantenvikariat der Franziskaner zeichnete sich seit seiner Gründung im Jahre 1452 durch eine große National- und Sprachverschiedenheit aus. Dieses Vikariat wurde durch den Generalvikar der Observanten Johannes Kapistran und dessen italienische Mitbrüder errichtet. Ursprünglich umfasste es nicht nur die böhmischen Länder, sondern auch Österreich, die Steiermark und das ganze polnische Königreich.[1] Die Mehrheit der Novizen war deutschsprachig. Die Anzahl der tschechischen, polnischen und ungarischen Brüder stieg jedoch stetig, so dass es zur Entstehung erster Konflikte kam. Die böhmische Problematik wurde auf dem Generalkapitel im italienischen Mantua im Jahre 1467 behandelt. Der neu gewählte Generalvikar Baptist von Levant, dem die schwierige Situation im böhmischen Vikariat persönlich gut bekannt war, bezeugte, dass eine Teilung *propter locorum distanciam, lingwarum, morum et dominorum diversitatem* nötig sei. Die Patres der Observantenkongregation waren hiermit einverstanden, und Papst Paul II. erließ am 16. Juni 1467 in Rom eine Bulle, in der er die Teilung des Vikariats genehmigte. Baptist von Levant entsandte zu den böhmischen Franziskanern seinen Generalkommissar Peter von Neapel mit dem Sozius Angelus von Chiavasso, die im selben Jahr das Provinzkapitel nach Krakau einberiefen. Der

---

1   Zum mittelalterlichen Patriotismus und Nationalismus im Mitteleuropa allgemein Macek, Josef: Jagellonský věk v českých zemích 4 [Die Jagiellonenzeit in den böhmischen Ländern 4], Prag 1999, S. 169–215; Šmahel, František: Idea národa v husitských Čechách [Die Idee der Nation im hussitischen Böhmen], Prag 2000. Zu den ostmitteleuropäischen Franziskanern vgl. Hlaváček, Petr: Národnostní a jazykové rozpory v českém vikariátě františkánů-observantů na přelomu 15. a 16. století (Příspěvek k nacionálnímu partikularismu ve středoevropském prostoru) [National- und Sprachenstreitigkeiten im böhmischen Vikariat der Franziskaner-Observanten an der Wende vom 15. bis zum 16. Jahrhundert (Ein Beitrag zum Nationalpartikularismus im mitteleuropäischen Raum)], in: In omnibus caritas. Sborník Katolické teologické fakulty Univerzity Karlovy, Sv. IV. K poctě devadesátých narozenin prof. ThDr. Jaroslava Kadlece, hg. von Milada Mikulicová/Petr Kubín, Prag 2002, S. 181–202; Minařík, Klemens: Die Provinzvikare der österreichisch-böhmisch-polnischen Observantenprovinz von 1451 bis 1467, in: Franziskanische Studien 1 (1914), S. 328–336; Teichmann, Lucius: Nationale Wirren in den mittelalterlichen Observantenklöstern, in: Archiv für schlesische Kirchengeschichte 5 (1940), S. 64–95; Teichmann, Lucius: Der deutsche Charakter der böhmischen Observantenprovinz im Mittelalter, in: Franziskanische Studien 34,1 (1952), S. 61–87; Teichmann, Lucius: Die franziskanische Observanzbewegung in Ost-Mitteleuropa und ihre politisch-nationale Komponente im böhmisch-schlesischen Raum, in: Archiv für schlesische Kirchengeschichte 49 (1991), S. 205–218; Ryschawy, Franz: Das Kommissariat der sudetendeutschen Franziskaner und seine Vorgeschichte (1935-1947), in: Archiv für Kirchengeschichte von Böhmen – Mähren – Schlesien 6 (1982), S. 184–205.

Kommissar Peter leitete die Beratungen zur Teilung ein und gründete das selbstständige österreichische und polnische Observantenvikariat. Ein ungelöstes Problem blieb jedoch die Stellung der böhmischen Länder innerhalb der Strukturen der franziskanischen Observanz, da Peter von Neapel für die Errichtung eines dritten Vikariats keine Vollmacht hatte. Für die böhmischen Länder konstituierte er daher nur ein Kommissariat, dessen weiteres Schicksal er der Entscheidung des Generalvikars überließ. Zum böhmischen Kommissar wurde Johannes von Meißen ernannt.[2]

Das neu errichtete böhmische Observantenkommissariat versank im Chaos, das durch die komplizierte kirchenpolitische Stellung des Böhmischen Königreichs noch verworrener wurde. Die verbliebenen Italiener verließen die Klöster, wie zum Beispiel im Jahre 1468 Christoph von Varese.[3] Erst auf dem Provinzkapitel in Wrocław/Breslau im Jahre 1469 wurde die Errichtung eines selbstständigen Observantenvikariats für die böhmischen Länder offiziell erklärt. Zum ersten böhmischen Provinzvikar wurde Peter von Hlohovec/Golgotz gewählt, ein Franziskaner aus Oberungarn, der kurz zuvor als Kreuzprediger nach Mähren gekommen war. Dies geschah vor allem aus politischem Opportunismus der Brüder, die die Gunst des ungarischen (und böhmischen) Königs Matthias Corvinus gewinnen wollten. Mit Unterstützung der tschechischsprachigen Brüder, die das ganze Vikariat beherrschen wollten, griff der Provinzvikar Peter jedoch unsensibel in die Konstitutionen des Vikariats ein und berief auch das Provinzkapitel nicht regelmäßig ein.[4] Dieses fand erst auf Befehl des Generalvikars Markus von Bologna im Jahre 1471 im schlesischen Koźle/Kosel statt, und Johannes von Meißen stand ihm als Generalkommissar vor. Unter den böhmischen Franziskanern herrschte damals eine ablehnende Haltung gegen den Provinzvikar Peter von Golgotz, nur die Tschechen mit dem Pilsner Guardian Thomas von Čáslav an der Spitze unterstützten ihn immer noch. Thomas von Čáslav verlas vor dem Provinzkapitel eine Erklärung, in der die Tschechen die Wiederwahl Peters von Golgotz verlangten, andernfalls würden sie der Wahl des Provinzvikars und der Definitoren nicht zustimmen. Gleichzeitig forderten sie auch, dass die Klöster in Böhmen ausschließlich mit tschechischsprachigen Brüdern besetzt würden. Was sollte jedoch mit den Deutschen geschehen? Dieser Vorschlag wurde sowieso von den Kapitularen resolut abgelehnt. Nach einer heftigen Diskussion wurde schließlich die Wahl der Definitoren vorgenommen; gewählt wurden der Znaimer Guardian Paul von Mähren, Alexander von Jauer, der Brünner Guardian Anthonius von Ungarn und der tschechische Anführer und Pilsner Guardian Thomas von Čáslav. Nach

---

2   Chronica Fratrum Minorum de Observancia Provincie Bohemie, Bibliothek des Nationalmuseums in Prag, sign. VIII F 75, S. 94–96; Memoriale Ordinis Fratrum Minorum a fr. Ioanne de Komorowo compilatum, hg. von Xawery LISKE/Antoni LORKIEWICZ (Monumenta Poloniae Historica 5), Lwów 1888, S. 95ff.; Zentralstaatsarchiv (ZSA) in Prag, Provinzarchiv der böhmischen Franziskaner (PBF), Urkunde Num. 38.
3   Chronica Fratrum, S. 96 und 169.
4   Chronica Fratrum, S. 100, passim. TEICHMANN: Die franziskanische Observanzbewegung, S. 212.

der Anrufung des Heiligen Geistes erfolgte auch die Wahl des neuen Provinz-vikars. Die Verantwortung für das böhmische Observantenvikariat wurde Paul von Mähren übertragen, der für die Ambitionen der tschechischen Minderheit kein Verständnis hatte. Als Urheber des vorherigen Konflikts wurde der ehemali-ge Provinzvikar Peter von Golgotz bezeichnet, dem eine Rückkehr nach Ungarn erlaubt wurde, was er jedoch erst im Jahre 1473 in die Tat umsetzte.[5] Die Erfah-rungen des ersten deutsch-tschechischen Streits spiegelten sich auch in den neuen Provinzstatuten wieder, die auf dem Provinzkapitel in Kosel (1471) verabschie-det wurden. Keinem der Brüder wurde gestattet, schriftlich oder mündlich von sich oder von anderen zu behaupten, er gehöre zu der böhmischen/tschechischen, deutschen, mährischen, schlesischen oder einer ähnlichen Partei, andernfalls dro-he ihm die Strafe der Buße bei Brot und Wasser. Die in den zweisprachigen Gebie-ten liegenden Klöster sollten einen tschechisch- und einen deutschsprachigen Pre-diger einsetzen.[6]

Bereits auf dem Provinzkapitel in Brünn im Jahre 1472 kam es wieder zu einem neuen Zwischenfall, der von drei tschechischen Brüdern, die eine Revision der Beschlüsse des letzten Kapitels in Kosel und die Rehabilitation Peters von Gol-gotz forderten, verursacht wurde. Sie schrieben ebenfalls eine Anklageschrift an König Matthias Corvinus und den böhmischen Adel, in der sie den Provinzvikar Paul von Mähren und andere Vorgesetzte scharf kritisierten. Dieser Brief wurde jedoch zufällig aufgehalten, wodurch die letzten Hoffnungen der Tschechen auf einen Umsturz zunichte gemacht wurden. Einer der tschechischen Brüder wur-de zwei Jahre gefangen gehalten, bis er von dem Generalkommissar Ludwig von Verona befreit wurde.[7] In der Folgezeit wurden die tschechischsprachigen Brüder durch die Gründung zweier neuer Klöster mit überwiegend tschechischer Beset-zung gestärkt: 1475 wurde das Kloster in Jindřichův Hradec/Neuhaus gegründet, dem die Tschechen Bernhardin von Prag und Bernhard von Netolitz vorstanden, und um 1480 wurde das Kloster in Horažďovice errichtet, das mit dem bekann-ten Literaten Jan Bosák Vodňanský in Verbindung gebracht wird.[8]

---

5 Chronica Fratrum, S. 109–111: *Finaliter tamen ex inductu et persuasione fratris Petri* [de Golgocz] *et quorumdam licet paucorum sibi dyademata querencium, guardianus cum discreto Plznensi nomine suo et aliorum fratrum bohemorum, quorum tamen intencio non fuerat, licet ad voluntatem illorum et inductionem se subscripsissent literam quandam appellacionis plenam iniuriis contra fratrem patrem vicarium generalem et contra statuta ordinis et provinciam legerunt, protestantes appellaverunt ad fratrem patrem vicarium generalem, qui nollent consentire in electionem diffinitorum aut vicarii nisi prefatus Petrus reeligeretur in vicarium et fratres Bohemi essent in locis Bohemie et quam plura alia gravissima, que directe divisionem pretendebant*; TEICHMANN: Die franziskanische Observanz-bewegung, S. 213.

6 Constituciones provinciales facte in Capitulo Cosslensi 1471, Nationalbibliothek in Prag, sign. XIV H 22, ff. 72r, 74v–75r; FUSSENEGGER, Gerold: Statuta observantium provinciae Bohemiae annis 1471 et 1480 condita, in: Archivum Franciscanum Historicum 47 (1954), S. 367–384, 374 und 376.

7 Chronica Fratrum, S. 113–114.

8 TRUHLÁŘ, Josef: O životě a spisech známých i domnělých bosáka Jana Vodňanského [Vom Leben und den bekanten und auch vermutlichen Schriften des Barfüßers Jan Vodňanský], in: Časopis Musea království Českého 58 (1884), S. 524–547 und 527; VLČEK, Pavel/SOMMER, Petr/FOLTÝN,

Auf dem Provinzkapitel in Kłodzko/Glatz 1480 wurden die Bestimmungen gegen den National- und Territorialpartikularismus erneuert. Sollte jemand von sich oder von anderen behaupten, er sei Tscheche oder Deutscher, sollte er vor den versammelten Brüdern im Refektorium des Klosters gebührend bestraft werden. Weiterhin behielt auch die Verordnung zur Ernennung von Predigern nach dem Nationalitätenprinzip ihre Gültigkeit.[9] Trotz dieser Maßnahmen erhob sich bald eine neue Welle der nationalen Intoleranz. Eine neue Revolte der Tschechen gegen die Patres des Vikariats begann schon auf dem Provinzkapitel in Breslau im Jahre 1481. Die tschechischen Franziskaner beantragten die geheime Wahl des Provinzvikars und der Definitoren, aber die Mehrheit der Kapitularen stellte sich grundsätzlich dagegen. Die tschechische Opposition dauerte bis zum Provinzkapitel in Brünn im Jahre 1483 an, als die Tschechen die Bereitschaft zur tschechisch-deutschen Versöhnung deklarierten. Auf diesem wurde auch Nikolaus von Böhmen zu einem der Definitoren gewählt, was für einige Zeit eine Beruhigung der tschechischen Revolte bewirkte. Briefe und Schriften der Rebellen wurden vernichtet, und die tschechischen Brüder kehrten friedlich in ihre Klöster zurück. Zu den Repräsentanten der tschechischen Partei gehörten damals nicht nur der bekannte Thomas von Čáslav, sondern auch Daniel von Litoměřice/Leitmeritz, der ehemalige Diskret in Plzeň/Pilsen und Guardian in Kosel, sowie Wenzel von Ivanovice, der ehemalige Definitor.[10]

Meldungen über die Nationalitätenkonflikte zwischen Tschechen und Deutschen im böhmischen Observantenvikariat erreichten durch den Kardinal Gabriel von Verona, den ehemaligen böhmischen Provinzvikar, auch Papst Sixtus IV. Dieser lud mit einem Brief vom 24. September 1483 Paul von Mähren nach Rom vor. Der damalige Brünner Guardian sollte dem Papst persönlich die Situation *de rebus Bohemiae* darstellen.[11] Im Jahre 1487 verzichtete Paul von Mähren, der damals schon Provinzvikar war, auf sein Amt und schickte dem Provinzkapitel in Opava/Troppau sein *sexterniculum*, das heißt eine Aufstellung der sechs Hauptprobleme, die die Entwicklung des Vikariats behinderten. An erster Stelle nannte er weder das Armutsproblem noch die falsche Frömmigkeit, sondern die nationale Verschiedenheit der Brüder (*nacionum diversitas*).[12] Der Wahrheitsgehalt dieses Schlusses zeigte sich bald am Schicksal seines Amtsnachfolgers, Jakob von Głogów/Großglogau, der ein überzeugter Gegner jeglicher Formen des Nationalpartikularismus im Ordensleben war. Als er im Jahre 1488 bei der Visitation des Klosters in Kadaň/Kaaden in Böhmen infolge eines Hirnschlag starb, kam es

Dušan: Encyklopedie českých klášterů [Die Enzyklopädie der böhmischen Klöster], Prag 1997, S. 228 und 275f.

9 Ordinaciones provinciales colecte in capitulo glacensi (1480), Nationalbibliothek in Prag, sign. XIV H 22, ff. 89v, 92r; Fussenegger: Statuta observantium provinciae Bohemiae, S. 382 und 384; Teichmann: Der deutsche Charakter, S. 82f.; Chronica Fratrum, S. 116 und 119–120.

10 Chronica Fratrum, S. 133–136 und 145.

11 Bullarium Franciscanum (Nova Series 3), hg. von Ioseph M. Pou y Marti, Florenz/Quaracchi 1949, S. 894 (n. 1780).

12 Chronica Fratrum, S. 150.

zum Skandal. Bei seiner feierlichen Bestattung bespuckten seine Opponenten, vor allem die Tschechen, sein Grab im Kirchenchor und schändeten seine Kleidung unter gleichzeitigen Beschimpfungen.[13]

Dieser Zwischenfall bedeutete jedoch nur ein Vorspiel neuer Streitigkeiten, die auf dem Provinzkapitel in Brünn im Jahre 1488 ausbrachen, dem der Generalkommissar Ludwig von Verona vorsaß. Nach Brünn kam damals eine große Zahl der Tschechen, auch älterer Patres, die zum Provinzkapitel nicht eingeladen waren. Kommissar Ludwig hörte sie dennoch an, öffentlich sowie privat, so dass es fast den Anschein erweckte, die Tschechen würden das Provinzkapitel leiten. Alle Kapitulare waren über dieses Vorgehen verwundert, da sie gar nicht ahnten, welche Angelegenheiten eigentlich verhandelt wurden. Die tschechischen Brüder bedrängten den Kommissar, ihre Forderungen noch vor der Eröffnung des Kapitels zu erfüllen. Andernfalls würden sie sich weigern, ähnlich wie einst die Polen, an der Wahl teilzunehmen. Die tschechischen Forderungen waren fundamental, und deren Erfüllung hätte eine radikale Änderung der Provinzstatuten und die Einschränkung der freien Wahl der Vorstände bedeutet. Der Provinzvikar sollte abwechselnd – einmal ein Tscheche, dann ein Deutscher – gewählt werden. Zwei von vier Definitoren sollten immer Tschechen sein. Nach dem endgültigen Verlust des Prager Klosters nach einem Utraquistenaufstand im Jahre 1483 sollte das Kloster in Pilsen die Vorrangstellung im böhmischen Observantenvikariat erhalten. Die Tschechen forderten ebenfalls, dass für die Zeit der Abwesenheit des Vikars ein bevollmächtigter Kommissar ernannt werden solle, der mit dem Provinzvikar de facto gleichrangig wäre. Ein deutschsprachiger Vikar sollte von einem Sozius aus den Reihen der tschechischen Brüder begleitet werden.[14] Der Generalkommissar Ludwig berief unter Ausschluss der Tschechen neun Patres zur Beratung, die einst eines der Ämter im böhmischen Observantenvikariat ausgeübt hatten, und teilte ihnen die tschechischen Forderungen mit. Die Patres, unter denen auch Paul von Mähren und Johannes von Meißen nicht fehlten, stellten sich entschieden gegen diese Forderungen, da sie das Recht der freien Wahl wie in anderen Provinzen und Vikariaten des Ordens des Heiligen Franziskus beibehalten wollten. Resolut verlangten sie, den ungerechten tschechischen Forderungen nicht entgegenzukommen, sogar auch dann nicht, wenn das Generalkapitel anders entscheiden sollte. Die Neuordnung der Verhältnisse im böhmischen Observantenvikariat fand also nicht statt, womit den deutschsprachigen Brüdern der maximale Einfluss auf die Leitung des Vikariats erhalten blieb. Erwähnenswert ist jedoch die Tatsache, dass die deutschsprachigen Brüder sich in der absoluten Mehrheit befanden. Die wenigen Tschechen konnten daher kein Verständnis für ihre emanzipatorischen beziehungsweise hegemonialen Bemühungen erwarten.

---

13 Chronica Fratrum, S. 150–151; Teichmann: Die franziskanische Observanzbewegung, S. 214.
14 Chronica Fratrum, S. 152: [...] *ad illud [capitulum] venerunt plures fratres Bohemi* [...] *quod alternatim esset vicarius eligendus et quod duo diffinitores essent ex Bohemis* [...] *et quod vicarius Teutunicus haberet socium Bohemum etc.*

Die Kapitulare gingen wie gewohnt zur Wahl, an der auch ein kleiner Teil der Tschechen teilnahm. Zum Provinzvikar wurde Anton von Leipzig gewählt, und im Definitorium befand sich kein einziger Vertreter der tschechischsprachigen Minderheit. Die Tschechen mussten sich vor Kommissar Ludwig unter der Androhung einer Gefängnisstrafe sogar verpflichten, sich nicht um eine Teilung des Vikariats zu bemühen. Ludwig warnte überdies die Vorstände vor einem Versuch der Tschechen, sich an das Generalkapitel in Italien zu wenden, da das deutsch-tschechische Problem so in breitere internationale Zusammenhänge geraten würde.[15]

In den Jahren 1488 und 1489 fanden in einigen Klöstern in Böhmen Versammlungen sowie geheime Sitzungen statt, und die böhmischen Franziskaner sprachen über die Unmöglichkeit des deutsch-tschechischen Zusammenlebens im gemeinsamen Vikariat. In ganz Böhmen herrschte eine sehr kritische Stimmung. Als im Jahre 1489 der Provinzvikar Anton von Leipzig das Kloster in Neuhaus visitierte, bereiteten die Tschechen eine List vor. Sie behaupteten, es würden Gerüchte verbreitet, falls aus Böhmen die Ketzer nicht verjagt würden, werde über König Wladislaus Jagello der Bann und über das Böhmische Königreich das Interdikt verhängt. Die Tschechen verlangten daher vom Provinzvikar weitere Instruktionen. Dieser durchschaute die List nicht und gab den tschechischen Brüdern zur Antwort, sie sollten nach dem Rat des päpstlichen Legaten handeln, der sich gerade in Ungarn aufhielt. Die Tschechen sandten unter diesem Vorwand und ohne Wissen des Provinzvikars zwei Mitbrüder nach Ungarn mit Briefen an den Legaten aus, um weitere Instruktionen zu holen. Von dem kranken König Matthias Corvinus, seiner Gemahlin Beatrice sowie dem päpstlichen Legaten und ortonischen Bischof Angelus erbaten sie sich ein Empfehlungsschreiben an den Papst, das zu ihren Gunsten geschrieben wurde.[16] Bei dem ungarischen (und böhmischen) König Matthias Unterstützung zu suchen, war politisch sicherlich klüger, als um die Hilfe des gewissermaßen isolierten König Wladislaus zu bitten, da dieser bei der päpstlichen Kurie bei weitem nicht die Position Matthias' hatte. Nach zehn Wochen kehrten die tschechischen franziskanischen Gesandten aus Ungarn nach Prag zurück, vor dem Provinzvikar erwähnten sie ihre Mission jedoch mit keinem Wort. Zur gleichen Zeit akzeptierte der Provinzvikar Anton von Leipzig die Forderung der Tschechen, zwei von ihnen nach Neuhaus zu schicken, um unter den dortigen Tschechen und Deutschen für Frieden und Einigkeit zu sorgen.[17] Er machte ihnen ein zweites großzügiges Angebot: Falls sie bereit sein sollten, mit den Deutschen auch weiterhin in Einigkeit zu leben, würden sie auf dem nächsten Provinzkapitel (im August 1489 in Breslau) vor allen Kapitularen angehört wer-

---

15 Chronica Fratrum, S. 151–152, 154 und 161.

16 Chronica Fratrum, S. 155–156: *Item isto anno* [1489] *et superiori in certis locis Bohemie plures concitate sunt conspiraciones et conscripciones ex utraque parte, ut qui vellent stare cum Bohemis aut qui cum patribus Almanis et fuit turbacio non modica.*

17 Chronica Fratrum, S. 156: *Supradicto eciam tempore idem pater vicarius obtulit fratribus Bohemis in Plzna misitque duos ex ipsis ad Novam Domum et propones pacem, querens unitatem, quod si adhuc vellent ad concordiam venire cum fratribus Almanis* [...].

den. Der Vikar versprach weiter, dass auf das Kapitel Vertreter der Tschechen eingeladen würden, die von den tschechischen Brüdern selbst zu wählen seien. Alle
Beschwerden und Klagen sollten auf dem Kapitel geklärt werden. Für den Provinzvikar war es jedoch undenkbar, dass die tschechische Frage auf dem Generalkapitel in Italien verhandelt würde. An dem Provinzkapitel in Breslau 1489 nahm
jedoch nur eine kleine Anzahl von Tschechen teil. Aus Neuhaus, das das Zentrum der radikalen tschechischen Opposition war, erschien lediglich der Diskret
des Klosters. Jetzt war klar, dass die Tschechen auf die italienische Karte setzten.
Auf dem Kapitel entstand daher Chaos. Zum Provinzvikar wurde erneut Anton
von Leipzig gewählt, zu Definitoren der Breslauer Guardian Alexander von Jauer,
der Znaimer Guardian Daniel von Prievidza, der Olmützer Guardian Tobias von
Žd'ár und der Liegnitzer Guardian Paulin von Löwenberg. Die neue Führung des
Vikariats ging sofort zum Gegenangriff über. Für das Generalkapitel wurde ein
Schriftstück mit der Aufforderung verfasst, dass auf die Forderungen der Tschechen bezüglich der abwechselnden Wahl des Vikars, der Diskreten, Guardiane
und anderer nach dem nationalen Prinzip nicht eingegangen werden soll, denn
die tschechischen Brüder beabsichtigten hiermit die Teilung des Vikariats. Der
Brief wurde von allen Kapitularen außer dreien, nämlich dem Pilsner Guardian
und den Gemnitzer und Neuhauser Diskreten, unterzeichnet.[18]

Auf den Weg zum Generalkapitel ins italienische Urbino begaben sich der Provinzvikar Anton von Leipzig, der Provinzdiskret Paulin von Löwenberg sowie die
offiziellen tschechischen Repräsentanten, die von den Generalvorständen vorge-
laden wurden. Das Kapitel fand im Mai 1490 statt. Die Tschechen forderten hier
die Errichtung eines selbstständigen Vikariats und legten den Vorständen zehn
Gründe vor, welche die Vorteile einer Trennung der Tschechen von den Deutschen verdeutlichen sollten.

Erstens sei es für die Erlösung der Seelen notwendig, da sich die deutschsprachigen Vorgesetzten um die tschechischen Brüder zu wenig kümmerten. Die Deutschen in den böhmischen Klöstern hätten keine Kenntnisse der tschechischen
Sprache und hätten daher für die Tschechen keinen Nutzen. Zudem sei die Teilung
auch für die Observanz nützlich, denn das Vikariat würde kleiner, und der Provinzvikar müsste zur Visitation nicht wie ein Kaufmann zu Pferde reisen, sondern
nur noch mit einem Stock und in Begleitung seines Sozius.[19] Zweitens verlange die
brüderliche Liebe eine Teilung, weil die Tschechen und die Deutschen verschiedene Nationen seien. Sie würden sich in keinem Stand vertragen, da die Deutschen
immer herrschen wollten, die Tschechen jedoch nicht so demütig seien, dass sie
dies ertragen könnten, vor allem in Böhmen. Die deutschsprachigen Brüder hass-
ten die tschechische Sprache, so dass die Tschechen sich gar nicht mehr trauten,

---

18 Chronica Fratrum, S. 155–157; Teichmann: Die franziskanische Observanzbewegung, S. 214f.
19 Chronica Fratrum, S. 161–162: *Racio prima est zelus divinus et salus animarum, quia melius et
    liberius possumus pro Dei honore et animarum salute facere, nam ipsi prelati Teutuni non multum
    curant de fratribus nostris et raro sunt nobiscum. Similiter fratres Teutuni stantes in locis Bohemie,
    quid possunt prodesse Bohemis quia ignorant nostrum ydeoma* [...].

frei Tschechisch zu sprechen. Weiterhin gäben die Deutschen den Tschechen den
schändlichen Spitznamen „Hundskopf", woraus Nörgeleien, lügenhafte Klagen an
die Vorstände und eine große Gefahr für die Seelen entstünden.[20] Drittens sei die
Teilung angesichts der Schwierigkeiten bei Visitationen angebracht, da der Provinzvikar gezwungen sei, innerhalb des Vikariats bis zu zweihundert Meilen und
unter großer Gefahr zu reisen. Der Vikar müsse daher von Burg zur Burg begleitet
werden, damit ihm sein Pferd nicht entwendet werde. Einige Klöster würden nur
sehr selten besucht, in Böhmen habe die letzte Visitation vor zwei Jahren stattgefunden. Viertens zwängen die unregelmäßigen Visitationen die Brüder, zu ihren
Vorgesetzten weit zu reisen. Aus ihrem Herumtreiben folgten dann Ärgernisse,
woraus der Hass der Bevölkerung gegen die Observanz entstehe. Fünftens sei es
sehr anstrengend zum Provinzkapitel zu reisen, da dieses außerhalb von Böhmen
stattfinde und viele Tschechen schon sehr alt und schwach seien. Zum letzten Provinzkapitel in Breslau (1489) hätten der Guardian und der Diskret von Neuhaus
hundert Meilen wandern müssen. Der Herr von Neuhaus habe um ein Kapitel in
Neuhaus gebeten, die deutschen Vorgesetzten hätten jedoch abgelehnt. Sechstens
verstünden die Tschechen den deutschsprachigen Provinzvikar während der Visitation nicht und könnten bei ihm lediglich mittels eines Dolmetschers beichten.
Ebenso wenig könnten sie die Vorgesetzten über die Situation in einem Kloster
informieren.[21] Siebtens kümmerten sich die deutschen Brüder nicht um die Ver-
mehrung der Observantenklöster in Böhmen, sie würden diese sogar verhindern,
obwohl sie notwendig für die Erhaltung des katholischen Glaubens sei. Nach der
Teilung des Vikariats würde die Zahl der Klöster sowie der Brüder in Böhmen
anwachsen, da die Tschechen sich um diese Dinge mit größerer Sorgfalt kümmern
würden. Achtens könnten durch die Teilung viele Unruhen beschwichtigt werden, da die tschechischen Brüder sich ihren Vorgesetzten eher fügten. Neuntens
würden Ärgernisse entstehen, falls auf die Forderungen der Tschechen nicht eingegangen werden sollte, und den Seelen werde die Verdammung drohen, da viele
Tschechen lieber nach Italien und Polen oder zu den Franziskaner-Konventualen
gingen. Die übrigen Tschechen, die auf Grund der nicht vorhandenen Kenntnisse
einer fremden Sprache in Böhmen bleiben würden, könnten wegen dieser Wid-
rigkeiten auf die Burgen des böhmischen Adels ausweichen und dort berichten,
dies geschehe infolge des deutschen Widerstands. Dies würde schreckliche Folgen für das Vikariat, die Observanz sowie die ganze römische Kirche in Böhmen
nach sich ziehen. Zehntens bestehe die Hoffnung auf ein friedliches Zusammen-

---

20 Chronica Fratrum, S. 162: *Secunda racio est fraterna charitas, quia sumus diverse nacionis se ad
   invicem non intelligentes, que in omni statu se male compaciuntur, videlicet Bohemi et Teutuni, nam
   Teutuni semper volunt dominari et Bohemi non sunt ita humiles, ut sustineant, maxime in Bohemia.
   Fratres denique Teutuni quam plures ex malo ad Bohemos affectu nostrum ydeoma audire non possunt,
   neque audemus iam libere loqui bohemicum, quia nos subsanant, spuunt vocant nos hundeskop, quod
   sonat caput canis* [...].
21 Chronica Fratrum, S. 162–163: [...] *quod est gravissimum quod fratres pauperes laici Bohemi
   non possunt aliquid intelligere prelatum in visitacionibus nec facta sua videlicet visitacionem aut
   confessionem si casus accideret facere, nisi per interpretem, nec credimus sub celo esse provinciam sancti
   Francisci, ubi fratres non possent suo prelato loqui sicut est nobiscum.*

leben der Tschechen und Deutschen nicht mehr, da die Deutschen behaupteten, dass auf Grund dieser Beschwerde an die italienischen Patres für die Tschechen kein Weg in irgendein Amt im böhmischen Vikariat mehr offen sei. In diesem Fall wäre es besser, sich irgendwo „in der Welt" aufzuhalten, als ein schlechtes und bitteres Leben im Orden zu führen.[22]

Den umfangreichen Brief der Tschechen nahm der Generaldefinitor und ehemalige Generalkommissar für das böhmische Observantenvikariat Ludwig von Verona entgegen und las ihn dem Definitorium vor. Die tschechischen Forderungen waren nicht systematisch aufgestellt, so dass zu erkennen war, dass sie in Eile aufgesetzt worden waren. Einige Formulierungen wirkten ein wenig verworren. Der böhmische Provinzvikar Anton von Leipzig, der von den Definitoren aufgefordert wurde, sich zu den Beschwerden zu äußern, nutzte diese Schwächen aus. Einige Behauptungen bezeichnete er direkt als unwahr, und er bezweifelte auch den Nutzen einer Teilung des Vikariats. Die Aussage über den Hass der Deutschen gegenüber den Tschechen erklärte er für eine Lüge und betonte, dass auch die Tschechen der deutschen Sprache ungern zuhörten. Die Schwierigkeiten mit der Durchführung von Visitationen und Kapiteln entschuldigte der Vikar mit dem Argument, dass böhmische Wege und Straßen nicht sicher seien. Auch nach einer Teilung des böhmischen Vikariats würde es noch Gebiete geben, in denen beide Sprachen, das Deutsche und das Tschechische, gemischt seien (*commixta ydeomata*). Rein tschechische Klöster gebe es schließlich nur in Pilsen und Neuhaus, und die dortigen Brüder wollten gerne über das gesamte böhmische Vikariat herrschen.[23]

Die italienischen Patres hörten die Reaktion des Provinzvikars aufmerksam an und entließen die Tschechen aus dem Verhandlungsraum. Danach fragten sie den Provinzvikar, wie er den Streit zur beidseitigen Zufriedenheit lösen wolle. Die zwei oder drei Varianten, die er ihnen vorschlug, gefielen den Italienern jedoch nicht. Schließlich entschieden der Generalvikar Angelus von Chiavasso und die Definitoren, dass für die tschechischsprachigen Klöster (*de lingua bohemica*) ein Kustos ernannt werden solle, welcher der Autorität des Provinzvikars völlig unterstehen würde. Dies betraf vor allem die Klöster in Pilsen und Neuhaus, die restlichen Klöster in Böhmen, das heißt Tachov/Tachau, Kaaden und andere, sollten unmittelbar dem Provinzvikar unterstellt sein. Für die Wahl des Kustoden sollten die Tschechen drei Kandidaten nominieren, aus welchen der Vikar und die Definitoren einen für das Amt auswählen würden. Falls keiner der Kandidaten den Vorstellungen des Vikars und der Definitoren entsprechen würde, hätten die Vorgesetzten das Recht, einen anderen Tschechen (*nacione Bohemus*) zum Kustos zu ernennen. Dem Kustos war allerdings nicht gestattet, Brüder aus anderen Pro-

---

22 Chronica Fratrum, S. 163: *Decima racio, quia non est spe, quod possemus simul pacifice stare, nam propter illud factum, quod ad Italicos patres detulimus et causam nostram defendimus, dicunt Teutuni patres, quod aliqui ex nobis amplius non ascendent ad officia [...].*

23 Chronica Fratrum, S. 164: *Item tantum duo sunt loca puris Bohemis, scilicet Plzne et Novedomus, que volunt regere totam provinciam.*

vinzen in die Klöster aufzunehmen – dies blieb Bestandteil der Kompetenzen des Provinzkapitels. War der Kustos nicht zugleich Guardian oder Diskret, hatte er auf dem Kapitel kein Wahlrecht. Sein Amt durfte er maximal drei Jahre ausüben, aber auch nur dann, wenn er jedes Jahr wiedergewählt wurde. Bei Visitationen durfte er vom Provinzvikar für seine Vergehen gestraft oder des Amtes enthoben werden. Den tschechischen Brüdern wurde vom Generalkapitel gestattet, dass der Provinzvikar für sie zwei neue Klöster bestimmte. Weitere Klöster konnten sie auch in Zukunft bekommen, jedoch nur mit Zustimmung des Provinzkapitels. Falls die Klöster aber nicht ausreichend belegt werden konnten, sollten sie so lange nicht vermehrt werden, bis eine ausreichende Anzahl von Brüdern bereitgestellt werden konnte.

Die tschechischen Brüder lehnten jedoch diese Bestimmung ab, und der Generalvikar Angelus von Chiavasso und die Definitoren ordneten *pro concordia, pace et unione inter fratres Teutunos et Bohemos in provincia Bohemie* folgende Punkte an: 1. Die Tschechen dürfen für sich zwei Klöster in Böhmen gründen, das eine in Bechyně/Bechin und das zweite in Dobrohostov/Ronsberg. Mit der Errichtung des Klosters in Ronsberg muss jedoch die Mehrheit der Brüder des benachbarten Klosters in Tachau einverstanden sein.[24] 2. Wenn der Provinzvikar außerhalb des Vikariats weilt, darf er ohne Begründung keinen Kommissar ernennen. Falls er es aber dennoch in einer bestimmten Situation tut, muss er den Kommissar nicht nur für Mähren und Schlesien, sondern auch für Böhmen ernennen. 3. Sollten sich die Tschechen unterdrückt fühlen, sollen sie sich mit ihren Beschwerden an das Provinzkapitel oder an den Generalvikar wenden. 4. Die Tschechen sollen die neuen Klöster *pro puris Bohemis* ohne die Mithilfe der deutschsprachigen Brüder besiedeln. In diese Klöster dürfen nur die deutschsprachigen Brüder aufgenommen werden, die selbst Interesse daran zeigen. Es bedarf dafür jedoch der Zustimmung des Provinzvikars. Auch ist es nicht die Pflicht des Provinzvikars, mit dem Provinzminister der böhmischen Franziskaner-Konventualen über die Übergabe des Klosters in Bechin zu verhandeln.[25]

Die Mehrheit der tschechischen Franziskaner fügte sich, nur einige Brüder blieben in Opposition. Zwei tschechischen Brüdern, die ohne das Wissen des Provinzvikars Anton von Leipzig zum päpstlichen Legaten nach Ungarn gereist waren, wurde ihr Vergehen verziehen. Einer der radikalsten Tschechen (Thomas von Čáslav?) ging für einige Zeit ins Heilige Land. Nach seiner Rückkehr in das böhmische Observantenvikariat versuchte er neuen Zwist zu erregen. Ein anderer bestand weiterhin darauf, dass Tschechen und Deutsche sich in den Ämtern abwechseln sollten. Die Zuspitzung der langjährigen deutsch-tschechischen Streitigkeiten auf dem Generalkapitel in Urbino im Jahre 1490 deutet darauf hin, dass

---

24 Chronica Fratrum, S. 165–166: *Primo quod fratres Bohemi possunt recipere duo loca pro Bohemis unum in Bechina, alium in Romsperg de consensu maioris partis fratrum Bohemorum* [...].

25 Chronica Fratrum, S. 166: *Quarto quod fratres Bohemi promiserunt soli velle tenere loca sua, que pro puris Bohemis receperunt nec velle molestare aliquem vicarium, ut defectum fratrum pro Teutunos suppleret* [...]

die tschechische Frage nicht marginal war. Die Tschechen zeigten klar, welches Gewicht ihre Stimme hatte und bewiesen, dass sie fähig waren, eine durchdachte kirchenpolitische Aktion durchzuführen. Wegen ihrer Hartnäckigkeit gewannen sie jedoch schließlich weniger als möglich gewesen wäre.[26]

Noch im Jahre 1490 wurde mit Hilfe Zdeslavs von Sternberg ein neues Franziskanerkloster in Bechin für die Tschechen errichtet. Nach Absicht des Generalkapitels in Urbino sollte auch ein Kloster in Ronsberg gegründet werden. Der Provinzvikar Anton von Leipzig entsandte ins benachbarte Tachau eine Delegation, die prüfen sollte, ob die Existenz eines neuen Klosters die Rechte der Tachauer Franziskaner verletzen würde. Der Objektivität der Untersuchung wegen wurden der Provinzdiskret Paulin von Löwenberg sowie Vertreter der tschechischen Brüder, Nikolaus von Böhmen und Alexander von Chrudim, nach Tachau entsandt. Zur Gründung des neuen Klosters in Ronsberg kam es allerdings nicht, da die Tachauer Franziskaner die Errichtung eines neuen Klosters in ihrer Nachbarschaft ablehnten.[27]

Die Position der tschechischen Gruppe wurde jedoch stärker, so dass die Gefahr der nationalen Streitigkeiten erneut zunahm. Nach Ostern 1491 wurde der Herr von Neuhaus von den tschechischen Brüdern zur Ausweisung des deutschen Beichtvaters aus dem Kloster in Neuhaus angestiftet, obwohl dieser vom Provinzvikar Anton von Leipzig ernannt worden war. Diese Aktion wurde auch von dem Guardian und einem tschechischen Prediger unterstützt. Dieser Prediger schlug dem Provinzvikar bei einer Visitation ernsthaft vor, alle Deutschen aus dem Kloster in Neuhaus zu vertreiben, der Vikar reagierte auf derartige Provokation jedoch nicht.[28]

Eine wichtige Stütze der tschechischsprachigen Franziskaner war der gelehrte Bischof Jan Filipec, der Administrator der Diözese Olmütz. Im Jahre 1491 erschien er in Begleitung vieler Franziskaner aus Mähren und Böhmen auf dem Provinzkapitel in Nysa/Neiße und erwirkte bei der Leitung des Vikariats die Ernennung eines tschechischen Predigers für das Kloster in Olmütz. Die dortigen Bürger wehrten sich dagegen zunächst, der bischöflichen Autorität mussten sie sich aber beugen. Das Provinzkapitel bewilligte ebenso die Gründung eines neuen

---

26 Chronica Fratrum, S. 161–167: *Fratres Bohemi* bemühten sich um die Gerechtigkeit für *totam communitatem sue nacionis*. Für die Bezeichnung der Deutschen werden in der Chronik zwei Ausdrücke genutzt. *Teutoni* bzw. *Teutuni* sind all die, die Deutsch als Muttersprache sprechen, *Almanus* ist dann der deutschsprachige Bruder, der direkt aus dem Reich stammt. Anders gesagt: der erste Terminus wird im Hinblick auf die Sprache verstanden, der zweite geographisch.

27 ZSA Prag, PBF, Urkunden Num. 76, 83, die Errichtung des Klosters Bechin *per patres et fratres Bohemos*. Chronica Fratrum, S. 165–167; Bullarium Franciscanum (Nova Series 4,2) (1489–1492), hg. von Caesar Cenci, Grottaferrata/Rom 1990, S. 671f. (n. 1796); Vlček/Sommer/Foltýn: Encyklopedie českých klášterů, S. 169f.

28 Chronica Fratrum, S. 169: *Item anno quo supra post Pasca inductus fuit dominus Novedomus per quosdam fratres Bohemos et cetera, ut confessorem Deutunorum de loco amoverat, quem pater vicarius illuc locavit. Ad aliquorum eciam peticionem videlicet guardiani et predicatoris, qui omnino ad patrem vicarium in visitacione seriose locutus est, ut omnes Teutunos amoveret [...]*; Teichmann: Der deutsche Charakter, S. 65.

Klosters in Uherské Hradiště/Ungarisch Hradisch in Mähren, das sich dank seinem Fundator, Bischof Jan Filipec, als tschechischsprachiges Kloster profilierte.[29] Jan Filipec trat auf dem Provinzkapitel in Olmütz im Jahre 1492 in den Orden ein, und damit stabilisierten sich auch die nationalen Verhältnisse im böhmischen Observantenvikariat. Wahrscheinlich mit Unterstützung von Filipec wurde der Vertreter der Tschechen, der gebildete Jurist Alexander von Chrudim, vom Provinzkapitel ins Definitorium gewählt. Das Kapitel bestimmte auch, dass die Tschechen, die nicht ruhig in den böhmischen Klöstern verharren wollten, sich in mährische und schlesische Klöster begeben konnten.[30]

Aus dem Jahre 1493 blieb eine einmalige Sammlung von Informationen erhalten, der Provinzkatalog des böhmischen Observantenvikariats, der auf dem Provinzkapitel in Brünn zusammengestellt wurde. Dieser Katalog informiert uns über die Herkunft der ungefähr 700 Franziskaner. Drei Viertel der Brüder stammten aus den böhmischen Ländern, vor allem aus Schlesien – Schlesier repräsentierten mehr als vierzig Prozent aller Franziskaner im böhmischen Vikariat. Der Rest kam aus Preußen, Meißen, Österreich, Bayern, Franken oder aus Ungarn, Polen und Russland. Die Brüder waren meistens deutschsprachig, nur etwa ein Viertel von ihnen gehörte der tschechischen Sprachgruppe an. Die tschechischsprachigen Franziskaner bildeten also in Böhmen und im gesamten Vikariat eine klare, aber bedeutende Minderheit. Auf demselben Provinzkapitel in Brünn gab der Generalkommissar Johannes von Sigestro eine Verordnung heraus, die besagte, dass jeder, der über eine Teilung des böhmischen Observantenvikariats spräche, bestraft werden solle.[31]

Seit den neunziger Jahren des 15. Jahrhunderts konsolidierte sich die Vertretung der Tschechen in der Leitung des Vikariats erheblich, obwohl kein Tscheche das Amt des Provinzvikars oder später des Provinzministers erreichte. Im Definitorium wirkten damals der franziskanische Bischof Jan Filipec († 1509), der Jurist Alexander von Chrudim, Georg von Roudnice/Raudnitz († 1504) und Wenzel von Úterý († 1521), der auch *monarcha et corona omnium Bohemorum* genannt wurde. Auf dem Provinzkapitel in Liegnitz im Jahre 1500 wurden in das vierköpfige Definitorium gleich zwei Tschechen gewählt, Alexander von Chrudim und Georg von Raudnitz. Zur Beruhigung der Spannungen zwischen den Tschechen und Deutschen trug neben dem positiven Einfluss des Bischofs Filipec auch die Tatsache bei, dass in der Zeit der Abwesenheit des böhmischen Provinzvikars dieser von einem böhmischen Kommissar vertreten wurde. Seit 1498 hatte dieses Amt der Pilsener Guardian und spätere Prediger in Glatz, der Tscheche Georg

---

29 Chronica Fratrum, S. 169–172. Im Kloster in Brünn ist bereits 1490 Peter von Neuhaus als *predicator Bohemorum* erwähnt: Chronica Fratrum, S. 161.

30 Chronica Fratrum, S. 171–172; GRIEGER, Rudolf: Filipecz. Johann Bischof von Wardein – Diplomat der Könige Matthias und Wladislaw (Studia Hungarica 20), München 1982, S. 47–88, S. 369–409; MACEK, Josef: Víra a zbožnost jagellonského věku [Glaube und Frömmigkeit der Jagiellonenzeit], Prag 2001, S. 163–171; WÖRSTER, Peter: Humanismus in Olmütz, Marburg 1994, S. 28.

31 Chronica Fratrum, S. 172; TEICHMANN: Die franziskanische Observanzbewegung, S. 215f.

von Raudnitz inne.[32] Der Wandel der Atmosphäre war auch durch die notwendige Konzentration auf wesentliche Probleme, die Territorialkonflikte mit den sächsischen Franziskanern und insbesondere auf den kirchenpolitischen Kampf mit der lutherischen Reformation im Herzen der böhmischen franziskanischen Provinz motiviert. Die deutsch-tschechische Rivalität repräsentierte im Wesentlichen den Kampf um Einfluss auf die Amts- und Rangverteilung im Vikariat, und so verstanden es auch die Zeitgenossen. Zu praktischer pastoraler Bedeutung (Visitation, Predigt, Beichte, Beratung) kamen die Volkssprachen darüber hinaus in den einzelnen Klostergemeinschaften, während auf den Provinzkapiteln dagegen Latein als universale Sprache der römischen Kirche vorherrschte. Die Volkssprache war überdies für die Identität der nationalen Minderheiten von großer Bedeutung. Die Deutschen beobachteten die Aspirationen ihrer tschechischen Mitbrüder mit Misstrauen. Ihre eigene Hegemonie in der Leitung des böhmischen Observantenvikariats hielten sie für die nötige Konsequenz der Wahlfreiheit auf den Provinzkapiteln. Die deutschen Franziskaner betrieben jedoch niemals programmatisch die Beschränkung der tschechischen Nationalinteressen. Die Deutschen fühlten sich überdies als keine einheitliche Nationalgruppe, sondern neigten vielmehr zu verschiedenen Formen des Landespatriotismus, wie zum Beispiel die schlesischen Brüder. Unterschiede in der Einstellung gegenüber dem nationalen Problem lassen sich aber auch am Kriterium des Bildungsstandes beobachten. Die gelehrten Franziskaner zogen einen anationalen Universalismus vor, womit sie dem Vermächtnis ihrer italienischen Patres, den Gründern des böhmischen Observantenvikariats, treu blieben. Zur tieferen Konsolidierung der nationalen Verhältnisse kam es jedoch leider nicht, bevor die böhmische Franziskanerprovinz durch die lutherische Reformation zerrüttet wurde. [33]

---

32 Chronica Fratrum, S. 170, 178, 185, 192–193, 200, 256 und 260, passim.

33 Doelle, Ferdinand: Die Observanzbewegung in der sächsischen Franziskanerprovinz bis zum Generalkapitel von Parma 1529, Münster 1918, S. 79–200. Zur Geschichte der böhmischen Franziskaner im Mittelalter vgl. Šmahel, František: Intra et extra muros. Spoleczna rola franciszkanów obserwantów i klarysek na ziemiach czeskich od polowy XIV do końca XV wieku [Intra et extra muros. Die gemeinsame Rolle der Franziskaner-Observanten und Klarissen in den böhmischen Ländern seit der 1. Hälfte des 14. bis Ende des 15. Jahrhunderts], in: Kłoczowski, Jerzy (Hg.): Zakony franciszkańskie w Polsce I., Lublin 1983, S. 275-325; Hlaváček, Petr: Der Bildungsstreit unter den böhmischen Franzikanern-Observanten am Ende des Mittelalters, in: Šmahel, František (Hg.): Geist, Gesellschaft, Kirche im 13.–16. Jahrhundert (Colloquia mediaevalia Pragensia 1), Prag 1999, S. 241–247; Hlaváček, Petr: Errores quorumdam Bernhardinorum: Franciscans and the Bohemian Reformation, in: David, Zdeněk V./Holeton, David R. (Hg.): The Bohemian Reformation and Religious Practice 3 (Papers from the XIXth World Congress of the Czechoslovak Society of Arts and Sciences – Bratislava 1998), Prague 2000, S. 119-126; Hlaváček, Petr: (Anti)intelektuální postoje v české františkánské observanci na sklonku středověku [Die (anti)intellektuelle Position in der böhmischen franziskanischen Observanz im ausgehenden Mittelalter], in: Český časopis historický 100,1 (2002), S. 1–32; Hlaváček, Petr: Der (Anti)intellektualismus der böhmischen franziskanischen Observanz im ausgehenden Mittelalter, in: Wissenschaft und Weisheit. Franziskanische Studien zu Theologie, Philosophie und Geschichte 65,2 (2002), S. 242–266.

István Perczel

Language of religion, language of the people, languages of the documents: the legendary history of the Saint Thomas Christians of Kerala[1]

The present paper is a report on a research project that, although conducted already for six years, has yielded only its preliminary results. Thus it will not describe how things are among the Syrian Christians of Kerala; rather, it will ask some questions that, as far as I know, have not been asked in the standard literature. Why in the 'standard literature'? Indeed, more generally, can one speak at all about any 'standard literature' on this question? In fact, there is no one comprehensive monograph on the Syrian Christians of Kerala, or the Christians of Saint Thomas, as they like to call themselves, or the Nazranies, as they are also called in Kerala. What there is is dispersed in a number of publications belonging to the most disparate academic and non-academic disciplines and published in the most diverse parts of the world. Naturally, a good number of them have been published in India, and, as a matter of fact, many of these studies are rarely – if ever – available in European libraries. To establish a detailed and quasi-exhaustive bibliography just on the publications related to the history and the culture of the St. Thomas Christians would be an important scholarly task in itself.

Thus, this paper proposes to ask some, mainly methodological, questions and indicate some future research directions on the basis of the preliminary results of an international research project, conducted with the participation of a number of

1   The present paper owes much to the contribution of other persons and is far from being any individual achievement. First and foremost, not a single word of it could have been written without the Revd. Prof. Jacob Thekeparampil, who involved me in his long-prepared project of surveying the Syriac manuscripts in India and several times offered the hospitality of the Saint Ephrem Ecumenical Research Institute, nor without Prof. Alain Desreumaux, who helped me to take the first steps in this field. The field-trips to India were mostly financed by Central European University, but also helped by a Dumbarton Oaks (Trustees of Harvard University) Project Grant. At present, the finances come from the *Deutsche Forschungsgemeinschaft* through a grant given to the *Orientalisches Seminar* of Tübingen University. The Mannanam manuscript that I will treat here in greater detail was kindly provided to me by the Revd. Prof. Antony Vallavanthara, CMI, who also permitted its photography. Prof. Hubert Kaufhold was so kind to read the paper and correct some of the mistakes that have found their way into it. Fr. Antony Vallavanthara also read the text and suggested substantial emendations, for which I am extremely grateful. Some of the solutions to philological and historical problems were suggested by Dr. Alexander Toepel, whose contributions are acknowledged in the notes. Fr. Ignatius Payyappilly, Dr. Susan Thomas and Mr. Yesudas Chovokkaran translated Malayalam texts for me. The English text of this paper was thoroughly checked by Matthew Suff. Last but not least, I would not have conceived of the problem treated here without the kind invitation by and discussions with Prof. Michael Richter. I extend my heartfelt gratitude to all these persons and institutions.

institutions and individual scholars and aiming at the survey, the cataloguing and the digitisation of the Syriac manuscript stock, preserved in a number of private and ecclesiastical libraries in Kerala(m), that is, "the Land of the Coconut-Trees," situated on the south-western coast of India. The project extends to as much out of the entire Syriac manuscript collection of India – containing several thousand manuscripts – as can be approached, depending on several human factors. However, the present paper is also my first general and non-specialist report on the results of my own studies within this quite ambitious team-project, results that I believe to have at least some little bearing on our knowledge on the history of local Christianity in India.[2]

1. Some preliminaries on Indian oral history

Who are these St. Thomas Christians? And what can we know in general about their history? It is appropriate to ask these questions at the outset, given that whatever can be known about this people is known in the West only to a narrow stratum of erudite scholars. The widespread ignorance even in otherwise learned circles, even as to the very existence of any indigenous Christians in India, is manifestly undeserved if we consider that this people constitutes up to the present day the easternmost branch of massive Christian populations, converted long before the colonial period. Certainly, properly speaking, the Nestorians of China,[3] whom Matteo Ricci and his Jesuit companions still found there at the beginning of the sixteenth century,[4] constituted the real easternmost branch of autoch-

---

2   On an earlier stage of the project see Françoise BRIQUEL-CHATONNET, Alain DESREUMAUX, István PERCZEL and Jacob THEKEPARAMPIL: The Kerala Manuscripts on CD-ROM: A Joint Indian-French-Hungarian Mission, in: Symposium Syriacum VII, ed. by Rifaat EBIED, Journal of Eastern Christian Studies 56/1–4 (2004), 245–256. See also the following studies: I. PERCZEL: Syriac Manuscripts in India: The Present State of the Cataloguing Process, in: The Harp: A Review of Syriac and Oriental Ecumenical Studies 15 (2002); pp. 289–98; A. PALMER/I. PERCZEL: A New Testimony from India to the Syriac Version of Pseudo-Dionysius (Pampakuda, Konat Collection, MS. 239), in: Iran and the Caucasus 6, 1–2 (2002); pp. 11–26, and the first text edition issuing from the project: The Nomocanon of Metropolitan Abdisho of Nisibis: A Facsimile Edition of MS 64 from the Collection of the Church of the East in Thrissur, ed. by I. PERCZEL, with a new Introduction by Hubert KAUFHOLD, transl. by I. PERCZEL (with a CD of the original digital photos of the MS), Syriac Manuscripts from Malabar 1, Piscataway, NJ 2005. See also the website of the project at www.srite.de.

3   Naming the East Syrian Christians has become a difficult issue. The Chinese East Syrian Christians are traditionally known in the West as 'Nestorians'. On the impraticability of the term 'Nestorians' for whatever belongs to the Church of the East, or the Persian Church, see Sebastian P. BROCK: The Nestorian Church: A Lamentable Misnomer, in: Bulletin of the John Rylands Library 78,3 (1996), pp. 23–35. Still, it is possible to use the term without the implication of any value-judgement, as is the usage of Mar Aprem, Metropolitan of the Church of the East for India, who candidly and unproblematically uses the term "Nestorian" along with other expressions.

4   See the following: Matteo RICCI: Storia dell'Introduzione del Cristianesimo in Cina, ed. by Pasquale M. D'ELIA, S.J., 3 vols., Rome 1942–49, vol. 2, p. 141 and p. 323; id.: Opere storiche, ed. by P. T. VENTURI, S.J., vol. 2: Le lettere dalla Cina (1580–1610), con appendice di documenti inediti,

thonous Christians, but they survived only in traces even in Ricci's time and by now have become totally extinct. But the St. Thomas Christians still constitute a seven million-strong, dynamic minority, doing well socially and economically, in southern India and in their worldwide diaspora. And the ignorance is even more undeserved if one considers this people's intriguingly unique history and social status.

About the early history of the St. Thomas Christians, besides the sparse testimonies of some Late Antique and medieval Western travellers ('Western traveller' here means anybody from the vast territory stretching from the British Isles to Persia), for the time being, we possess only data from the local traditions recorded at different times, first when the Portuguese arrived in southern India and noted them. It can be expected that the international research project that we have been trying to set up for a while will change this situation and will finally provide confirmation or negation of some of these traditional elements. Here I shall only present a couple of documents, preserved in India and Europe, which, in an interesting manner, are likely to illuminate some elements of the local tradition. However, this is just a modest contribution, which, moreover, refers to the much later colonial period. We must still wait for real discoveries shedding light on the Late Antique and medieval history of the Kerala Christians.

1.1. Traditions about Saint Thomas the Apostle

According to tradition, Christianity in Kerala was founded by Saint Thomas the Apostle, who landed on the Malabar Coast, at Maliankara near Cranganore (Kodungallur), in 52 AD. Why precisely in 52 is difficult to say, but this date is firmly held in the present *traditio communis* of the St. Thomas Christians. For how long the date has been established is an interesting question in itself. The modern Malayalam ballad *Thoma Ramban Pattu* ("The Song of Rabban Thomas"),[5] which gives absolutely precise data about the details of the Apostle's activity, dates his arrival to 50 AD, in the month of *Dhanu* (December/January) and his death in Mylapore (Mailapuram) to 72 AD, the 3rd day of the month of *Karkadakam* (July), corresponding to the traditional memorial day of the Apostle in the Church of the East,[6] at 4:50 p.m. The author/redactor of the song says in

Macerata 1913, pp. 289f.; Henri BERNARD, S.J.: La découverte de Nestoriens mongoles aux Ordos et l'histoire ancienne du Christianisme en Extrême-Orient, Tientsin 1935. I did not have the opportunity to consult these sources, and all my information is from Jonathan D. SPENCE: The Memory Palace of Matteo Ricci, New York 1984, pp. 119f.

5   An Italian translation of the song was published by F.X. ROCCA: La leggenda di S. Tomaso Apostolo, in: Orientalia Christiana 32 (1933), pp. 168–79. Rocca says (on p. 169) that he took the song from a further, unspecified, Malayalam book written by Fr. Bernard O.T.C.D., "the most accurate historian of the religion among his folk." This is the two-volume Malayalam book of BERNARD of ST. THOMAS: The Christians of St Thomas 1–2, Pala, 1916 and Mannanam 1921.

6   ROCCA: La leggenda di S. Tomaso Apostolo, p. 177. This day originally commemorates the transfer of the Apostle's relics from India to Edessa.

the last stanza that he is 'the father of the 48th Thomas', that is, a priest in the lineage of Thomas Maliyakal Ramban, a disciple of Saint Thomas, who had written the original. The author/redactor also claims that he only "changed the rhymes", that is, transposed the song from an archaic language to the Malayalam vernacular, in 1601, or, according to some manuscripts, 1101 or even 1061 AD.[7] However, none of these dates can be considered reliable, and I would propose 1653 AD as a *terminus post quem* for the redaction translated by Rocca, because it contains not only obvious elements due to Portuguese influence, but also others which cannot antedate the *Kunan Kurishu Satyam* (Bent Cross Oath) in 1653, an event that I shall treat later. Thus the information in the 'colophon' of the ballad should not be taken at face value. Naturally, this *caveat* concerning the redaction does not preclude the possibility that the kernel of the ballad may be much earlier. Recently I found another tradition in a palm-leaf manuscript in the collection of the Major Archbishop's House of the Syro-Malabar Church in Ernakulam; the manuscript contains eighteen Malayalam apocrypha, among which the Malayalam version of the *Acts of Thomas*. The introduction to this apocryphon, written in the second half of the seventeenth century by a Catholic author(s), dates the death of Saint Thomas to 21 December and says that on that very day the Apostle's memorial day (*Dukhrana*) was celebrated in the Malankara Church.[8] Interestingly, the Indian Jacobite Church still celebrates this on 21 December, while the *Dukhrana* itself is held, by the Jacobites as well, on 3 July.[9]

On his arrival, the Apostle converted several Brahmin families, from whom a good part of the present-day Nazranies descend, and founded seven churches: Maliankara (Kodungallur or Cranganore), Palayur, Kottakavu (North Paravur), Kokamangalam (Pallipuram), Niranam, Chayal and Kollam (Quilon).[10] There is a beautiful story vividly recounted among the local Christians and invoked in many books about the foundation of the Palayur church, not far from Cranganore, where

---

7 ROCCA: La leggenda di S. Tomaso Apostolo, p. 179, quoting the remarks of T. K. JOSEPH: The Saint Thomas Traditions of South India, in: Bulletin du Comité International des Sciences historiques 10 (1938), p. 565.

8 Ernakulam, Major Archbishop's House, MS Palmleaf No. 1, f. 56r: "On Mar Thoma the Apostle. On the 21st of the month of *Dhanu* (December) the commemoration (*Dukhrana*) of Saint (*Qadisha*) Mar Thoma the Apostle is celebrated. In our Malankara Church diocesis the 21st of the month of *Dhanu* is his death date. On 3 *Karkadakam* (July) his disciples took his holy dead body to his country. The people from the city of the Romans (*Rhomaye*) understood that Saint Mar Thoma the Apostle lived before Mar Addai and here is written regarding Mar Thoma the Apostle's acts and miracles." I thank Fr. Ignatius Payyappilly and Mr. Yesudas John Chovokkaran for translating the Malayalam text for me.

9 I will return to this manuscript and the dating of the redaction it contains at the end of the present study.

10 A Syrian Catholic: A Synopsis of the History of the Syrian Church in Malabar, Kottayam 1910, reprinted in G. MENACHERY (ed.): Indian Church History Classics, vol. 1: The Nazranies, Pallinada-Ollur-Thrissur 1998, p. 265. (The volume edited by George Menachery is a goldmine for finding otherwise virtually unfindable publications from India.) See also BERNARD OF ST. THOMAS: A Brief Sketch of the History of the St. Thomas Christians, Trichinopoly 1924 (reprinted in MENACHERY: op. cit.), p. 294.

Saint Thomas is believed to have landed, and close to Guruvayur, the famous center of Krishna worship. According to this tradition, the Apostle arrived there and found several *nambudhiri* (or *namputhiri*) Brahmins (that is, Kerala Brahmins) bathing in a tank and throwing up handfuls of water as an offering to their Sungod. He asked them whether they were able to throw the water up so that it could stay suspended in the air without falling back down. The Brahmins replied this was impossible; the Apostle performed a miracle and the water remained in the air, proving that Christ has accepted the offering. This convinced the Brahmins who accepted baptism from the Apostle in the same tank. Their temple was transformed into a Christian church, while those who stuck to their Hindu faith fled from the place. They cursed the land and called it *Chapakatt* (or Chowghat in the Anglicised version, now Chavakkad), "the Cursed Forest".[11]

Some sixteenth-century Portuguese sources, partly edited but for the most part unedited, studied by the very learned Fr. Mathias Mundadan, speak about converted kings, from whom another name of the community, Tarijanel, derives, which tradition interprets as "sons of kings"[12] Later, the Apostle went to the eastern Coromandel Coast, where he also converted people, and finally died on the Little Mount in Mylapore, nowadays a suburb of Chennai (Madras). There are several versions of the details of the Apostle's death, the most fantastic of which states that one day a hunter out hunting peacocks saw a group of them seated on a flat stone. He shot an arrow at the leader of the group, which was transformed into a man and fell down dead. This was the Apostle.[13] Other accounts, emphasising the point that Saint Thomas died a martyr's death, speak about furious Brahmins who pierced the Apostle with a lance, either when he was praying in rapture in a cave or when he destroyed, by means of his cross, a temple dedicated to the god-

---

11 It is useless to give precise sources for this story. It is known to almost every St Thomas Christian and is also written on a board near the tank, which is still preserved and venerated. Besides the tank there is a well with fresh water, opened miraculously by the Apostle. According to the faith of the St Thomas Christians, drinking this water or washing oneself with the water of the tank has miraculous healing power. I have also read the story in J. C. PANJINIKARAN: The Syrian Church in Malabar (A historical dissertation submitted for the Master of Arts Degree of the University of Madras), Trichinopoly 1914 (reprinted in G. MENACHERY: The Nazranies, on pp. 277–92), p. 290, n. 8.

12 A. Mathias MUNDADAN: History of Christianity in India, vol. 1: From the Beginning up to the Middle of the Sixteenth Century (up to 1542), Bangalore 1984, pp. 43f. and 173f.

13 This version was told to Duarte Barbosa and to Manuel Gomes at the very beginning of the sixteenth century; for Barbosa, see Mansel Longworth DAMES (tr. and ed.): The Book of Duarte Barbosa: An Account of the Countries Bordering on the Indian Ocean and their Inhabitants Written by Duarte Barbosa and Completed Around the Year 1518 A. D., 2 vols., London 1918–21; (repr. Nendeln, Liechtenstein 1967), vol. 2, p. 125; for Gomes, see Antonio DA SILVA REGO (ed.): Documentação para a história das missões do padroado português do Oriente: India, 12 vols., Lisbon 1947–58, vol. 1, p. 298, and MUNDADAN: History of Christianity in India, vol. 1, pp. 44f. A bit different is the version given by Marco Polo, who knows about the hunter and the peacocks, but says that the hunter did not recognise the saint among the peacocks. This seems to be a rationalised version of the original local legend.

dess Kali.[14] His tomb is venerated in Mylapore up to the present day, and pilgrimage to the tomb has always been an important element in the religious life of the St. Thomas Christian community.

The tradition that locates the Apostle's activity in two places, Kerala on the western and Coromandel on the eastern coast of southern India, corresponds to the historical existence of two communities. However, some calamities have destroyed the eastern community, which at some time (differently specified in the different sources) had to migrate westward and to unite with the one in Kerala. A version of the tradition transmitted by Francisco Roz, the first Latin bishop (residing in Angamaly) of the St. Thomas Christians, does not know about the preaching of the Apostle on the Malabar Coast, but holds that all the St. Thomas Christians emigrated there from the east.[15] An interesting element of the local traditions is that – at least in Portuguese times – the same stories were told on the western and on the eastern coast, but connected to different localities.[16] At present there is no autochthonous Christian community on the Coromandel Coast.

As one of my informants – eventually a student of sociology in Delhi – told me, every village has its local Saint Thomas tradition, full of miraculous elements. Just to collect them would be a very important task of anthropological research.

Most of the literature on the question treats the historicity of the Apostle's presence and activities in India, trying to combine the different western and eastern testimonies with elements of local tradition and archaeological findings. The general outcome of these investigations is that the question of the historicity of the tradition is unsolvable for the scholarly methods that we have at our disposal. The strongest argument in favour of the historicity remains nothing else but the tradition itself, an unanimous tradition held not only in India, but also in the whole Christian Orient. Here we also face something quite extraordinary, which deserves a different approach. The very existence of the traditions concerning the Apostle, divergent in their details but unanimous in their core message, and the role of these traditions shaping the self-identity of the community are objective facts. Setting aside the question of how true historically the tradition is, we should

---

14 The former version is contained in several Portuguese documents; the latter is the version of the "Song of Rabban Thomas" (see above, n. 5). See also BERNARD OF ST. THOMAS: A Brief Sketch, cited above in n. 10, p. 312, n. 1, and MUNDADAN: History of Christianity in India, vol. 1, pp. 29–32 and 45. According to T. K. JOSEPH: The Saint Thomas Traditions of South India, p. 562, these versions about the Apostle killed by a Brahmin are all derived from a Latin hagiographic text, the *Passio Thomae*, propagated in Malabar by the Portuguese missionaries, which succeeded in eliminating the earlier local versions.

15 Francisco ROZ, S.J., in his unpublished *Relação da Serra*, British Library, additional MS, 9853, ff. 86–99v. Mundadan studied this manuscript and reports on it and other Portuguese sources, MUNDADAN: History of Christianity in India, vol. 1, pp. 71–75.

16 See MUNDADAN: History of Christianity in India, vol. 1, p. 44: "There is a list of miracles in both traditions which are similar in almost every respect, the main difference being that while the Malabar tradition would maintain that they were performed in Kerala itself, the Mylapore tradition locates them in the Coromandel and links them with the building of the church or house [built by Saint Thomas]."

recognise the Saint Thomas legends as constituting an important, if not the most important, factor in the formation of the Nazranies' communal identity. The tradition of Saint Thomas preaching and converting in India and apparently converting nobody but members of the higher castes, kings and Brahmins,[17] expresses both the Nazranies' embeddedness in the surrounding majority Hindu society and their separation. It explains why they find themselves integrated into the Indian culture, speaking the same language – Malayalam – as their neighbours, at the upper edge of the caste system, being equal to the *Nair* south Indian warrior class and subjected only to the Brahmins. But it also explains why they are separate, professing a different faith, Christianity. It also explains their ambiguous but traditionally well-established position in the society. Being Christians, they believe in the absolute truth and the sole saving power of their religion. At the same time, they live in a society that has been able to accept them as one among its organic strata, while also accepting Christ and the saints as belonging to the community of the many divinities legitimately worshipped by the different segments of the Hindu society. It considered the Christians as one element belonging to the same society, and permitted them to practise their professions (mainly trade and agriculture and, to a lesser extent, military service), which were highly regarded by others. Many Hindus also venerate the Christian holy places, and hold the priests of the St. Thomas Christians in very high esteem, considering them holy men. This might not have always been the case, and the remembrances in the tradition about earlier persecutions may point to less tolerant periods and neighbourhoods. All this and much more is admirably expressed in the founding legends of the community, connected to Saint Thomas.

1.2. Traditions of Thomas of Kana and the earliest Syrian connections

The identity of the St. Thomas Christians is not exhausted by their being Indian and Christian. They are also Syrian. As Placid Podipara says in an emblematic writing of his, "they are Hindu or Indian in culture, Christian in religion and

---

17 From this point of view, the "Song of Rabban Thomas" contains an interesting sentence (ROCCA: La leggenda di S. Tomaso Apostolo, p. 177). It says the following: "Among those whom he [that is, Saint Thomas] converted, altogether 17.550 souls, there were 6.850 Brahmins, 2.500 best Kshatriyas, 3.750 Vaishyas, and 4.250 Shudras. In this manner, he conquered for the right Way the higher castes." The sentence is surprising, given that the four *varnas*, mentioned in this text, in principle comprise the entire caste system, including the higher and the lower castes. However, one should bear it in mind that in south India, where the caste system was implanted much later than in the north, the whole social structure is different. The four *varnas* were not effectively present, but besides the Nambudhiri Brahmins and the Varmas, the royal caste, all those integrated into the caste system were considered as Shudras, among whom there were high castes, such as some of those sub-castes that in the nineteenth century were integrated into the Nair warrior caste, in principle equal to the Nazranies. The greater part of the society remained *avarna*, that is out of the caste system, and had to live in a humiliated position. See Sathya Bai SIVADAS P. Prabhakara Rao: Narayana Guru: The Social Philosopher of Kerala, Mumbai 2002, pp. 11–19 (chapters "The Caste Structure of Kerala" and "The Condition of the Ezhavas").

Syro-Oriental in worship".[18] How they came under Syrian influence is again told by legends preserved by the oral tradition. This speaks about the arrival of another Thomas, Thomas of Kana (*Knayi Thomman* in Malayalam), a rich Syrian merchant from Persia according to one version, but a Christian Jew, originating from Kana in Palestine, a relative of Jesus himself, according to others.[19] The Kerala tradition, which connects its events to absolutely precise dates, knows that this happened in 345 AD. Normally this date is taken for granted both in oral conversation and in writing. However, the early Portuguese witnesses give a wide range of datings. According to some he came earlier, so that he could still meet a servant of Saint Thomas,[20] while others hold that he came later, namely in 752 AD, that is, some 700 years after Saint Thomas.[21] The date 345 seems to come from or at least to be documented by a Syriac text written or copied by a certain Priest Matthew at the beginning of the eighteenth century, in Malabar.[22] With Thomas came seventy or seventy-two families (this number representing the totality of a people, as in the case of the translators of the Septuagint or of the greater circle of the apostles).[23] It is said that he found the St. Thomas Christians in great disarray, and so he reorganised them and put them under the jurisdiction of the Persian Church. In this way the jurisdictional link of the Malabar Coast with the Church of the East in Iraq would originate from this time.

---

18 J. Placid PODIPARA, C.M.I.: Hindu in Culture, Christian in Religion, Oriental in Worship, in: Ostkirchliche Studien 8 (1959), pp. 89–104, reprinted in George MENACHERY (ed.): The St. Thomas Christian Encyclopaedia of India, vol. 2 (Trichur 1973), pp. 107–12. The sentence cited is on p. 89 = 107.

19 For the latter opinion see Jacob VELLIAN: A 'Jewish-Christian' Community, in: The St. Thomas Christian Encyclopaedia of India, p. 73–74.

20 This is the testimony of an East Syrian "Abuna", that is, bishop, interviewed by the Portuguese in 1533. The manuscript about the enquiry is MS Goa 31 in the *Archivum Romanum Societatis Jesu* in the Vatican. The MS was studied by MUNDADAN: History of Christianity in India, vol. 1, p. 91.

21 This is the version recounted by Francisco Dionysio, S.J.: Informação de Christianidade de São Thomé que estam no Malabar, reino da India Oriental, in: Antonio DA SILVA REGO: Documentação, vol. 12, pp. 394–403 (see above, note 9), and Francisco Roz in the documents of a juridical process between the dioceses of Cochin and Angamaly, contained in MS Goa 65, in the archive of the Jesuits mentioned above. All this is the fruit of the archival research of A.M. MUNDADAN, published in his *History of Christianity in India*, vol. 1, pp. 91f.

22 Brevis notitia historica circa Ecclesiae Syro-Chaldaeo-Malabaricae statum, in: Samuel GIAMIL (ed. and tr.): Genuinae relationes inter sedem apostolicam et Assyriorum Orientalium seu Chaldaeorum Ecclesiam: nunc maiori ex parte primum editae, historicisque adnotationibus illustratae, Rome 1902, pp. 552–564, here 554ff.; Giamil took the text over from J.P.N. LAND, Anecdota Syriaca, vol. 1, Leiden 1862, 123f. Giamil thinks its author is "a certain Jacobite Priest, called Matthew" (op. cit. 552, n. 1). However, the only thing we may know from the text is that its author was called Priest Matthew. As to the text itself, it is not of Jacobite but of East Syrian (*vulgo* Nestorian) origin; Giamil, himself a Chaldaean, must have thought that the text was Jacobite, because it is very hostile toward the Franks, that is, the Portuguese and their Latinising tendencies. The text is usually referred to as one written by "Fr. Matthew", see MUNDADAN: History of Christianity in India, vol. 1, pp. 93f.

23 Jacob VELLIAN: A 'Jewish-Christian' Community, in: The St. Thomas Christian Encyclopaedia of India, p. 73.

An important element of the tradition is the famous copper plates that Thomas of Kana is said to have received from the King of Malabar, the Cheruman Perumal. In Kerala in the Middle Ages, up to the end of the eighteenth century royal charters on privileges were written on copper plates in *Vattezhuttu* (literally, "round script") characters, which now very few scholars are able to read either in India or abroad. Communities belonging to different religions possess their own copper plates – so also the Jews, the Christians and the Muslims. At present some of the Christian copper plates are kept at some important ecclesiastical centres, such as the Metropolitanate of the Mar Thoma Church in Thiruvalla and the Indian Syrian Orthodox Seminary in Kottayam. The copper plates are not shown to visitors. Several mutually contradictory decipherings of them have been published. In Portuguese times there seem to have existed the very copper plates that were claimed to contain the privileges that the Cheruman Perumal king gave to Thomas of Kana.[24] In the middle of the sixteenth century the Portuguese acquired them, but by the end of the same century they were lost. According to tradition noted by the Portuguese, these plates briefly related the story of Thomas of Kana arriving in Cranganore and receiving royal privileges from the king. These privileges were the following: he gave his own name, Coquarangon, to Thomas, and he also gave him the "City of the Great Idol", *Magoderpattanam* (or *Mahadevarpatnam*), and a great forest for possession forever, then seven kinds of musical instruments and together with them all honours for the Christians to speak and behave as kings do, so that their brides may whistle during their wedding ceremony, just as the women of the kingly families do, to spread carpets on the grounds, to wear sandals, and to ride elephants. Besides this he gave to Thomas and his people five different taxes that he could collect.[25]

Here is not the place to treat in detail the Thomas of Kana legends. Be that as it may, these traditions are also important formative elements of the Kerala Christians' identity and have an explicative value for their social reality. In fact, it is these legends that explain not only the Syrian affiliation, but also a division between the Nazranies, that is, the division between two endogamous groups, the 'Southists' (*Thekkumbhagar*) and the 'Northists' (*Vadakkumbhagar*). Each group claims legitimate descent from Thomas of Kana and the families that accompanied him, and accuses the other group of being descendants of the noble immigrants' illegitimate children.[26] It is interesting to note that among the Southists there exists the

---

24 For a summary on the copper plates, see MUNDADAN: History of Christianity in India, vol.1, p. 170 ff.

25 Z. M. PARET: The Saint Thomas Christian Copper Plates, in: The St. Thomas Christian Encyclopaedia of India, pp. 134–37. Paret quotes two translations, by A. E. Medlycott and E. R. Hambye, from the manuscript BM Add 9853, which contains the *Relação da Serra* of Francisco Roz. E. M. PHILIP, in: The Indian Church of St Thomas (first published: Kottayam 1908; second edition by Kuriakose Corepiscopa Moolayil, Cheeranchira, Changanessery 2002), p. 58 and p. 70, gives the name *Mahadevarpatnam* and says that this was the name of the Christian quarter in Cranganore.

26 See MUNDADAN: History of Christianity in India, vol. 1, pp. 95 ff.

tradition according to which Thomas' community was Jewish Christian, so that they all have Jewish blood and preserve Jewish Christian traditions.[27]

Thus, it is to the time of Thomas of Kana that the tight jurisdictional and cultural relationship between the Church of Malabar and the Persian Church of the East is traced back. According to the traditional structure, the Indian diocese of the Church of the East was governed by a Metropolitan sent by the Catholicos Patriarch, from Seleucia-Ctesiphon, and later, after the schism of 1552, by the (Uniate) Chaldaean Patriarch. At the same time, at the local level, the church affairs were governed by the Malabar *yogam*, that is 'Assembly'. There was also an indigenous head of the Church of Malabar, called *Jatikkukarthavyan* in Malayalam, which means "the head (or Lord) of the caste", that is, the head of the Saint Thomas Christian community,[28] but also the 'Archdeacon of All India'. Apparently, in his person an indigenous function, characteristic of the St. Thomas Christian community, was combined with an existing function of the Church of the East. According to the canons of the latter Church, the Archdeacon is the highest priestly rank: he is the head of all the clerics belonging to a bishopric; he is responsible for the whole worship of the cathedral church and represents the will of the bishop in his absence.[29] This is an important function indeed. One understands

---

27 See Jacob VELLIAN: A 'Jewish-Christian' Community.
28 The name was found on a palm-leaf document, which, according to J. Kollaparambil, was in the possession of the Pothanikat family in the city of Kothamangalam. See Jacob KOLLAPARAMBIL: The Archdeacon of All India, in: The Syrian Churches Series, vol. 5, Kottayam 1972, pp. 81f. *Jati* means "caste" or "community" and *Kartavian* is "Lord" in Malayalam.
29 See Canon 19 of the synod of Catholicos Ishoyahb I (582–595), held in 585/586, as adopted in Abdisho bar Brikha's *Nomocanon* (written in 1290), Tractate 6, Chapter 8, Canon 1, on pp. 275f. in MS Thrissur 64, corresponding to p. 121 in the Latin translation of L. Assemani in Angelo MAI: Scriptorum Veterum Nova Collectio e Vaticanis codicibus edita, vol. 10, Rome 1838: "The service of the Archdeacon before the bishop is absolutely necessary in the head of the service of the clergymen in all moments of the service and the ecclesiastical gatherings [synods]. And just as it is not befitting that the churches be left without the governance of the bishop, because he is the head of the church, in the same way it is not befitting that the Archdeacon be absent from those moments that are dedicated to the worship or to the ecclesiastical gatherings. So it is good and just that for every bishop in the church of his see necessarily there be an Archdeacon. And the person who is chosen to serve as Archdeacon will be wise and reasonable, watchful and lucid, capable of discernment, self-controlled and good-willed, just and compassionate, expert in the worship and the orders of the church. In all moments he will command according to the will of the bishop over the orders of the worship. And the hidden will of the bishop will become manifest through the tongue and the word of the Archdeacon, so that the priests sit on their seats and that the ranks of the deacons become arranged; he will be the one who reads the Gospel, or it will be upon his command that the one who reads will read; and whoever celebrates will celebrate upon his command, unless the bishop is present. For it is his office to command, if he wants, the one who celebrates, and he designates those who read the readings and those who keep the doors; he will watch over and divide the weeks [that is, the weekly services etc.?] and take care of the businesses of the church; and whatever is not recommended and commanded by the Archdeacon is not in the power of those clerics who receive their supplies from the church [...]." In fact, Abdisho's text combines the canon of Ishoyahb with details taken from the canons of the synod of Mar Isaac, held in 410, but first and foremost with Canon 15 of Mar Isaac (see KOLLAPARAMBIL: The Archdeacon of All India, pp. 69f.). My translation is made on the basis of the Thrissur MS; see its facsimile edition in: The Nomocanon of Metropolitan Abdisho of Nisibis: A Facsimile Edition of MS 64 from the Collection of the Church of

clearly how the appointment of an indigenous Archdeacon of All India served the needs of the ecclesiastical organisation of the Church of the East. While the Catholicos Patriarch of Seleucia-Ctesiphon reserved for himself the right to send his own prelates originating from Iraq to the Indian diocese, the continuous governance of his Indian flock was secured by the indigenous Archdeacon serving as the head of all the priests in Malabar and representing the bishop's will.[30] However, from the local point of view, the rank of the Archdeacon was more important than this; he was not only the most important priest of the community, but fulfilled the role of an Ethnarch. He was "the prince and head of the Christians of St. Thomas"[31] and had such titles as "Archdeacon and Gate of All India, Governor of India".[32] The origin and the meaning of the term 'Gate' is mysterious. According to Kollaparambil, it means the supreme court.[33] I would suppose that it is a Christological title: "I am the Gate of the sheep" [Jn 10:7]. While originally the Archdeacon in the Church of the East was elected by the bishop according to merit,[34] the office of the Archdeacon of India seems to have been hereditary. According to Wilhelm Germann it was the privilege of the Pakalomattam family.[35] Indeed, we know about a number of Pakalomattam Archdeacons, beginning with 1502, when Metropolitan John of India appointed George Pakalomattam. The name of the family varies, and the family is identical with the Parambil family, translated into Portuguese as De Campo.[36] The Archdeacon had all the attributes of a secular leader and was normally escorted by a number, sometimes several thousands, of soldiers.[37] It is important to note that while several bishops could be appointed for the Malabar Coast,[38] there was always only one Archdeacon, a custom contrary

the East in Thrissur, ed. by István PERCZEL, with a new Introduction by Hubert KAUFHOLD (Syriac Manuscripts from Malabar 1) Piscataway, NJ 2005. For other canons concerning the Archdeacon in the *Nomocanon*, see Tractate 6, Chapter 1 (Assemani 107a and b), ibid., Chapter 9 (Assemani 123), Tractate 8, Chapter 19 (Assemani 149), ibid., Chapter 20 (Assemani 151). I owe all these references to Hubert Kaufhold, whom I thank warmly for his help.

30 For the role of the Archdeacon in the Church of the East, see Walter SELB: Orientalisches Kirchenrecht, vol. 1, Vienna 1981, p. 137, but, first and foremost, KOLLAPARAMBIL: The Archdeacon of All India, pp. 38–78.

31 See Andrews THAZHATH: The Juridical Sources of the Syro-Malabar Church, Vadavathoor/Kottayam 1987, p. 38, citing a Portuguese manuscript from the archive of the *Sacra Congregatio de Propaganda Fide* in the Vatican. See also KOLLAPARAMBIL: The Archdeacon of All India, p. 223.

32 KOLLAPARAMBIL: The Archdeacon of All India, pp. 222–26.

33 Ibid., pp. 225f.

34 See the canon of Ishoyahb, cited above in n. 29.

35 See Wilhelm GERMANN: Die Kirche der Thomaschristen: Ein Beitrag zur Geschichte der orientalischen Kirchen, Gütersloh 1877, p. 94, and MUNDADAN: History of Christianity in India, vol. 1, p. 183.

36 KOLLAPARAMBIL: The Archdeacon of All India, p. 162.

37 Ibid., p. 110.

38 Thus, for example, in 1490, Mar Simeon IV (1437–1497) sent two bishops to Malabar, but one of them returned. After that, Mar Eliah V (1502–1503) sent another three bishops in 1503. In India, they found the bishop who had preceded them, Mar John, and in a letter, sent jointly by the three new bishops to the Catholicos, dated 1504, they state that Mar John also sends his greetings. See G. S. ASSEMANI: Bibliotheca Orientalis Clementino-Vaticana, Rome 1719–1728, vol. 3,1, pp. 590–99, and François NAU: Deux notices relatives au Malabar, in: Revue de l'Orient Chrétien

to the canons of the Church of the East. It seems to me that this situation is best explained by the fact that from the point of view of the East Syrian Church structure, the Archdeacon was an ecclesiastical function, but from that of the St. Thomas Christian community it was also a socio-political, princely function, representing the unity of the Christian nation, or caste(s), of Hendo (India).

Belonging to the jurisdiction of the Church of the East, and later to the Chaldaean Patriarchate, meant more to the Kerala Christians than a mere canonical status. It also meant a cultural group identity. As in the Church of the East the language of liturgy, of theology and, in general, of learned discourse was Syriac, this also became the liturgical and religious language of the Malabar Christians. Their services were held in this language, and they stored and deeply appreciated their Syriac manuscripts, partly imported from the Middle East and partly copied in India. However, we have no evidence of books originally written in Syriac in India in this early period. As the language of this people was a dialect of Tamil, which gradually evolved, through the incorporation of Sanskrit, but also Syriac, Arabic, Portuguese and English elements, towards today's Malayalam, evidently Syriac was and has remained up to the present day the language of a learned elite, constituted of the ecclesiastics coming from Iraq and of a stratum of autochthonous Indians. One of the intriguing questions concerning this phenomenon would be to know about the sort of schools where the autochthonous elite learned its Syriac and about their possible localisation. Be that as it may, the vast majority of the St. Thomas Christians in all probability had no knowledge of this language, and one may wonder how many even among their priests knew Syriac beside the basic knowledge of being able to recite the offices. Thus, Syriac was the St. Thomas Christians' 'language of religion', while Tamil and, later, Malayalam must have remained the 'language of the people'. All this said, this is far from being an opposition between the written language of the learned and the spoken language of the people. Tamil and Old Malayalam were written languages with abundant texts engraved either as inscriptions in stone, or as official documents on copper plates, or written on the most widespread carrier of writing – palm-leaf tablets, bound together into codices. Apparently, it was in these written languages and means of writing that the Nazranies communicated with their Hindu, Jewish and Muslim neighbours, while through their language and culture of religion, Syriac, they constituted and still constitute an integral part of the Asia-wide community of the Syrian Christians. Thus, this bilingual situation resulted in a double identity and double embeddedness in two different social, economic and cultural settings. Naturally, to maintain this vernacular culture they also had to have their literate, but this time – in principle – secular, elite, and the two elites must have overlapped to a certain extent. Moreover, my hypothesis, which I shall try to demonstrate on the basis of some documents, is that the identity of this community became in a

---

17 (1912), pp. 82ff. See also J. P. M. VAN DER PLOEG, OP: The Christians of St. Thomas in South India and their Syriac Manuscripts, Rome/Bangalore 1983, pp. 4ff.

way 'Syriacised' during the seventeenth century and that it must have been more Indian before then.

1.3. The Portuguese period

For any element whatsoever, such as the ones mentioned before, of the history of the St. Thomas Christian community before the arrival of the Portuguese colonisers, we have barely any sources other than local traditions and legends. Documented history seems to begin with the arrival of the Portuguese. The European documentation beginning with this period already permits a fairly detailed picture of the social status, life and customs of the Christians whom they found upon their arrival in southern India, and in principle all the following, colonial, history of the community can be traced. However, here as well, although to a lesser extent, history is inextricably interwoven with legend.

At the moment when the Portuguese arrived on the Malabar Coast, the Christian communities that they found there had had longstanding traditional links with the East Syrian Christians in Mesopotamia. During the subsequent period, in 1552, a split occurred within the Church of the East. Part of it joined Rome, so that besides the 'Nestorian' Catholicosate of the East another, 'Chaldaean', Patriarchate was founded, headed by the Patriarch Mar John Sulaqa (1553–1555), claiming to be the rightful heir to the East Syrian tradition. It is very difficult to see the precise influence of this schism on the Church of Malabar. Apparently, both parties sent bishops to India.[39] Over against earlier, somewhat romantic views, which took it for granted that there was a continuous line of Chaldaean bishops, without any Nestorian interference,[40] it is the merit of Joseph Thekkedath to have clarified, on the basis of the Portuguese sources, the real situation, which seems to be the following. The last pre-schism East Syrian Metropolitan, Mar Jacob (1504–1552), died just when the schism occurred. Apparently the first among the two Patriarchs to send a prelate to India was the Nestorian Catholicos, Simeon VII Denkha. The person whom he sent was Mar Abraham, who, in one of fate's ironies, was to be the last Syrian Metropolitan of Malabar, after having gone over to the Chaldaean side. When he arrived in Malabar is not known, but he must have been there already in 1556.[41] Approximately at the same time, the suc-

---

39 See Mar Aprem: The Chaldean Syrian Church in India, Thrissur 1977, p. 24: "Both patriarchs were interested to send bishops to India, the Nestorian line to retain their domination and the new line to establish control over the Indian Church. The Indian Church also was only glad to receive them, perhaps not knowing the split that occurred in the East Syrian Church in 1552 A.D."

40 Such are, among many others, the following: Eugène Tisserant: Eastern Christianity in India: A History of the Syro-Malabar Church from the Earliest Time to the Present Day, Bombay 1957, p. 40; Leslie W. Brown: The Indian Christians of St. Thomas: An Account of the Ancient Syriac Church of Malabar, Cambridge 1956, p. 22; Jonas Thaliath: The Synod of Diamper (Orientalia Christiana Analecta 152) Rome 1958, p. 10 (repr. in Bangalore 1999); J. P. M. van der Ploeg, OP: The Christians of St. Thomas, pp. 8–15.

41 Joseph Thekkedath: History of Christianity in India, vol. 2: From the Middle of the Sixteenth Century to the End of the Seventeenth Century (1542–1700), Bangalore 1988, pp. 37–40. The story

cessor of John Sulaqa, who had been murdered in 1555, Abdisho IV (1555–1567), sent the brother of John, Mar Joseph, to Malabar as Chaldaean bishop; although consecrated in 1555 or 1556, Mar Joseph could not reach India before the end of 1556, nor Malabar before 1558, when the Portuguese were finally alerted by the presence of Mar Abraham and allowed Mar Joseph, accompanied by another Chaldaean bishop, Mar Eliah, to occupy – very briefly – his see, before the Inquisition also sent him to Lisbon in 1562. In this way, nominally there were two rival Syrian Metropolitans in Kerala until 1558, when Mar Abraham was captured, forced to confess the Catholic faith in Cochin and sent back to Mesopotamia, to the Chaldaean Patriarch Abdisho, who (re-)consecrated him Metropolitan and sent him to Rome. There Mar Abraham was ordained Metropolitan a third time in 1565 by Pope Pius IV, who wanted him to reign jointly with Mar Joseph, who in the meantime returned to Malabar in 1564, only to be deported a second time in 1567 and die in Rome in 1569. From Rome, Mar Abraham returned to Mesopotamia and reached the Malabar Coast for the second time in 1568. Although he was once again detained in Goa, in 1570 he managed to escape, and governed the Malabar Christians until his death in 1597.[42] Given the passage of Mar Abraham to the Chaldaeans, the Nestorian Catholicos Patriarch, Mar Eliah VIII (1576–1591), sent another bishop, Mar Simeon, to Kerala. Mar Simeon probably arrived there in 1576.[43] He stayed there until 1584, when he was captured and sent to Rome,

---

is excellently recounted and well argued on the basis of the Portuguese primary sources by Thekkedath, but he is not the first to have discovered the original Nestorian allegiance of Mar Abraham. J. Kollaparambil also mentions this fact in a brief sentence, KOLLAPARAMBIL: The Archdeacon of All India, p. 83. However, the earlier – manifestly mistaken – received wisdom was that Mar Abraham first arrived in Malabar in 1562 as a Chaldaean bishop.

42 The above reconstruction is a synthesis based on two accounts, that of THEKKEDATH (History of Christianity in India, vol. 2, pp. 37–49) and of VAN DER PLOEG (The Christians of St. Thomas, pp. 8–15). These two scholars worked simultaneously on very different primary sources and could not know about each other's work. Here I present the basic line of the events according to the reconstruction of Thekkedath, but correct his dates on the basis of those given by van der Ploeg, who studied the colophons written by Mar Joseph in the books that he copied during his long trip to Malabar, which lasted more than two years. Thekkedath, on the basis of the Portuguese documents that he studied, erroneously thought that Mar Joseph arrived in Goa already in 1555 and was retained there until 1558. However, the colophons in the autographs copied by Mar Joseph clearly indicate the stages of his trip: on July 8, 1556, when he finished copying Vat. Syr. 45, he was in Mozambique, waiting for favourable winds towards India; having reached Goa, he was deported and confined in a Franciscan monastery in Bassein, north of Bombay, where he finished copying Vat. Syr. 128 on December 17, 1556. From there, he was allowed to go to Cochin in 1558, to assist at the 'conversion' of Mar Abraham. Thekkedath also confuses two Nestorian patriarchs, Simeon VI bar Mama and Simeon VII Denkha. On the other hand, van der Ploeg erroneously states that Mar Abraham was first sent to India by Patriarch Mar Abdisho in order to replace the deported Mar Joseph. As he knows about the presence of a Nestorian bishop in Malabar during the first mission of Mar Joseph, he identifies this prelate with Mar Simeon, another Nestorian bishop, sent much later, by Mar Eliah VIII (1576–91).

43 This date is suggested by J. Thekkedath on the basis of a letter written by Francisco Dionysio, the Rector of the Jesuit college in Cochin, dated January 23, 1577, where Dionysio mentions Mar Simon. Cf. THEKKEDATH: History of Christianity in India, vol. 2, p. 50 and n. 88. This is, therefore, a *terminus ante quem*. See also Giuseppe BELTRAMI: La Chiesa caldea nel secolo dell'unione (Orientalia Christiana 29), Rome 1933, p. 103.

where it was discovered that he was a Nestorian and, on account of this fact, his ordination as priest and bishop was declared invalid.[44] He was confined to a Franciscan friary in Lisbon, where he died in 1599.[45]

It is reported that before leaving Malabar, Mar Simeon appointed a priest as his 'vicar general', Jacob by name, who, according to the Portuguese testimonies, resisted all the Latin innovations introduced under Mar Abraham and was finally excommunicated by Archbishop Menezes of Goa before he died in 1596.[46] However, as this priest is also called Archdeacon,[47] I would suggest that his role should be reconsidered. The Archdeacon during the first part of the reign of Mar Abraham was George of Christ, who was on friendly terms with the Latin missionaries and who was to be appointed the successor of Mar Abraham as Metropolitan of India. Thus he should have become, according to the plans of Mar Abraham, supported by the Jesuits, the first indigenous Chaldaean Metropolitan of the St. Thomas Christians. However, the last letter of Mar Abraham where he requests the Pope to confirm George's ordination as Bishop of Palayur and his coadjutor, is dated January 13, 1584, while from another letter of the same Mar Abraham we learn that the consecration of George failed because of the latter's death.[48] After this, we

---

44 This seems to be the correct interpretation of the documents. See Mar APREM: The Chaldean Syrian Church in India, p. 23: "In 1585 A.D. he was declared by the Roman Curia as neither a bishop nor a priest." Unfortunately, many historians still echo the tendentious words of BELTRAMI: La Chiesa caldea nel secolo dell'unione, p. 107, who somewhat overzealously writes as follows: "Dal Raulin apprendiamo che egli [that is, Mar Simeon] fu smascherato dalla sagacia di Sisto V. Alcune lettere che gile vengono perquisite svelano infatti che è nestoriano; che non è vescovo e neppure sacerdote! Certamente Mar Simone meritava pene ben gravi; ma il papa fu benigno e si contentò che venisse relegato in un convento." This summary judgement seems to be misguided. Antonio de Gouvêa, the contemporary historian of the infamous Synod of Diamper and eulogiser of its main author, Alexis de Menezes, although himself a very biased witness, still gives a much more reliable story in his *Iornada do arcebispo de Goa Dom Frey Aleixo de Menezes, primaz da India oriental* (Coimbra 1606), p. 10, where he writes as follows: "[...] et feyto processo, foy sentenceado polo papa que nam era bispo, nem uzasse das officios pontificaes, nem ainda dixesse missa, por nam constar da ordenaçao de sacerdote". These words permit us to reconstruct the situation: as the investigation revealed, on the basis of letters that Mar Simeon obviously had received from Seleucia-Ctesiphon, that he was a Nestorian, Sixtus V declared [foy sentenceado polo papa] that Mar Simon's ordinations as a bishop, and even as a priest, were invalid [por nam constar da ordenaçao da sacerdote], so that he was deprived of the right to say the mass [nem ainda dixesse missa]. Obviously, his ordination was declared invalid, not because it had not occurred, but because it was performed within the Nestorian Church, deemed heretical from the Roman point of view. If we consider that for this sin of his Mar Simeon was condemned to *life detention* in a Franciscan monastery in Lisbon, Beltrami's enthusiasm for the humaneness of the procedure seems to be somewhat exaggerated. See the letter, dated December 15, 1593, of the Jesuit Abramo di Giorgio, cited in BELTRAMI: La Chiesa caldea nel secolo dell'unione, p. 108: "Simone, il quale sta in Lisboa *in carcere perpetua*, in uno monasterio di Santo Francesco, per essere scacciato da questa Serra per falso vescovo."

45 See BELTRAMI: La Chiesa caldea nel secolo dell'unione, p. 107; THEKKEDATH: History of Christianity in India, vol. 2, pp. 50f.; KOLLAPARAMBIL: The Archdeacon of All India, pp. 83 and 105, and Mar APREM: The Chaldean Syrian Church in India, p. 24.

46 KOLLAPARAMBIL: The Archdeacon of All India, pp. 95f., THEKKEDATH: History of Christianity in India, vol. 2, p. 51, and Mar APREM: The Chaldean Syrian Church in India, p. 24.

47 KOLLAPARAMBIL: The Archdeacon of All India, p. 96.

48 Ibid., p. 93.

hear about an Archdeacon with Roman allegiance, perhaps John, the brother of George of Christ, appointed in 1591.[49] As Archdeacon Jacob appears on the scene as a leader of the Church of Malabar in 1584, I would suggest that he was the one who inherited the office of the Archdeacon from George. Rather than being appointed by Mar Simeon, the Nestorian Metropolitan, he inherited the office by family right and sided with Mar Simeon against Mar Abraham, which resulted in a very tense situation. The Roman side seems to have tried to solve this problem by appointing a rival Archdeacon, a first one in 1591, and a second, George of the Cross, in 1593. In this way, although from 1552 rival Metropolitans sent by the two East Syrian Patriarchs contended for the allegiance of the St. Thomas Christians, still, until 1656, the date of the consecration of Kunju Mathai (Matthew) as Archdeacon of the Latin allegiance against the rebellious Mar Thoma, the former Archdeacon, there was only a very brief period (between 1591 and 1596) when two rival Archdeacons contended against each other.

Alexis de Menezes, Archbishop of Goa from 1595 until his death in 1617, together with his Jesuit advisers, decided to bring the Kerala Christians under obedience, an obedience which they conceived as complete conformity to the Roman or 'Latin' customs. This meant separating the Nazranies not only from the Nestorian Catholicosate of Seleucia-Ctesiphon, but also from the Chaldaean Patriarchate of Babylon and subjecting them directly to the Latin Archbishopric of Goa. The most important stage of their activity was the famous Synod of Diamper (Udayamperur) in 1599, when the local Christians' customs were officially anathematised as heretical and their manuscripts were condemned to being either corrected or burnt.[50] The oppressive rule of the Portuguese *padroado* ('patronage') provoked a violent reaction on the part of the indigenous Christian community. This was the *Kunan Kurishu Satyam* (Bent Cross Oath) in Matancherry, Cochin, in 1653, when the rebels, headed by their Archdeacon, made a vow not to accept any allegiance unless to a Syrian Church. In the same year, Archdeacon Thomas was ordained, by the laying on of hands of twelve priests, as the first indigenous Metropolitan of Kerala, under the name Mar Thoma I. This movement later, in 1665, on the arrival of Mor Grigorios Abd'ul-Jalil, a bishop sent by the Syrian

---

49 KOLLAPARAMBIL: The Archdeacon of All India, p. 95.
50 On this synod there is a great number of studies. See, among others, THALIATH: The Synod of Diamper, and Scaria ZACHARIA (ed. and trans.): The Acts and Decrees of the Synod of Diamper, 1599, Edamattam/Kerala 1994, and George NEDUNGATT (ed.): The Synod of Diamper Revisited (Kanonika 9), Rome 2001. For a recent defense of the Diamper Synod, see K. J. JOHN: The Synod of Diamper, in: Journal of South Indian History 2,1 (March 2005), pp. 24–40. The Portuguese text of the Synod of Diamper was published in: Synodo diocesano da Igreja e Bispado de Angamale dos antigos Christaõs de Sam Thome das Serras do Malauar das partes da India Oriental, celebrado pello Reverendissimo Senhor Dom Frey Aleixo de Menezes Arcebispo Metropolitano de Goa, Primaz da India e partes Orientales Sede vagante do dito Bispado..., Coimbra 1606. The text of Session III, Decree XIV containing the list of condemned books is on ff. 12–14. For an English translation of this text, see Scaria ZACHARIA: The Acts and Decrees of the Synod of Diamper 1599, pp. 101f. See also J.-B. CHABOT: L'autodafé des livres syriaques du Malabar, in: Florilegium Melchior de Vogüë, Paris 1909, pp. 613–623.

Orthodox Patriarch of Antioch, resulted in the Mar Thoma party's joining the Antiochian (Syrian Orthodox) Patriarchate and in the gradual introduction of the West Syrian liturgy, customs and script on the Malabar Coast.

As this famous story has been retold so many times, I shall not enter into its details. What interests me here is the role played by the Archdeacons, because this element, seen in the light of some Indian Syriac manuscripts, can give us an insight into the intricate relationship between history and legend. Another aspect that interests me is what I would call a 'Syriacisation' of the Malabar Christian identity during these events. All this gives sufficient material for musing on the role of the different languages of religion and of the people on the Malabar Coast.

During the entire period beginning with the intervention of Archbishop Menezes of Goa in the affairs of the Church of Malabar in 1598, up to the consecration of Archdeacon Thomas as Mar Thoma I in 1653 and his joining the Antiochian Patriarchate in 1665, events were dominated by a constant tension between the Latin Archbishops designated by the Portuguese and the Archdeacons leading the St. Thomas Christian community. In 1597, Mar Abraham, the last Chaldaean Metropolitan of India, died. Mar Abraham, although originally a Nestorian and accused by the Jesuit Francisco Roz of holding 'Nestorian' views, seems to have remained a faithful Chaldaean bishop, that is, in sincere community with Rome, to which his copy of the *Nomocanon* of Abdisho bar Brikha of Nisibis, which he carried to Malabar and which is still preserved in the Library of the Major Catholic Archbishop's House in Ernakulam, testifies. Already the scribe who copied the *Nomocanon* for Mar Abraham included the Nicaeo-Constantinopolitan Creed in its Latin form, with the *Filioque*, and on the first folio of the book one can read a anathema by Mar Abraham on Nestorius.[51]

Thus, if there was strife between the Portuguese missionaries and the indigenous Christians and their Iraqi prelates, it was not of a truly doctrinal, but of an ecclesiological and jurisdictional character. However, something else was also involved: the identity of the St. Thomas Christians. In their striving to preserve their identity, after the death of Mar Abraham in 1597, the most important role was given to Archdeacon George of the Cross, appointed by Mar Abraham in 1593. Archbishop Alexis de Menezes, who was both an ambitious and violent person and a very able Church politician, succeeded in bringing the Archdeacon to obedience and in abolishing the Chaldaean jurisdiction on the Malabar Coast. How perfectly he succeeded is another question, where legends once again begin to play their role. Be that as it may, under his immediate successors this apparent success proved to be more ephemeral and less complete than it appeared after the Synod of Diamper in 1599.

---

51 On this manuscript, now Ernakulam Syr. 10 according to our handlist, see VAN DER PLOEG: The Christians of St. Thomas, pp. 13–14 and pp. 126–28. For a detailed description of the manuscript, see Hubert KAUFHOLD: Syrische Handschriften juristischen Inhalts in südindischen Bibliotheken (Österreichische Akademie der Wissenschaften, Philosophisch-Historische Klasse, Sitzungsberichte, 535. Band), Vienna 1989, pp. 48–51. Kaufhold has published the Syriac text of Mar Abraham's *Anathema on Nestorius* on p. 50 with a German translation and a detailed commentary.

The strife between the Latin Archbishops and the Archdeacons – first George of the Cross and then his nephew, Thomas Parambil (de Campo) – continued and resulted in several revolts of the latter against the former, whenever the Archbishop tried to curtail the traditional rights of the Archdeacon. In this way George of the Cross revolted against Francisco Roz, Archbishop of Angamaly (1601–24), first in 1609, upon which event the latter excommunicated him, and also in 1618. Although George had more friendly relations with Roz's successor, Stephen Britto (1624–1641), he also revolted against the latter in 1632. The rule of the next Archbishop, Francis Garcia (1641–59), again was dominated by constant tension between him and the Archdeacon, Thomas Parambil, until the latter apparently decided definitively to break away from Roman jurisdiction. In 1648–49 he sent a number of letters to several oriental Patriarchs and thus to the Coptic Patriarch of Alexandria, to the Syrian Orthodox Patriarch of Antioch and most probably also to the Chaldaean Patriarch of Babylon, requesting them to send bishops to Malabar.[52]

As an answer to these letters a certain Mar Aꜥtallah, a bishop who termed himself Mor Ignatius, Patriarch of India and China, arrived in India, but the Portuguese detained him in Mylapore and the rumour spread that he was drowned in the sea. His detention so enraged the Archdeacon and his party that they revolted against the Jesuits. On January 3, 1653, the mass of people gathered in Matancherry in Cochin, and swore an oath not to obey the Franks, that is, the Portuguese, but only the Archdeacon, who on May 22 of the same year was ordained bishop, under the name Mar Thoma, twelve priests laying their hands on him. This was the famous Bent Cross Oath, during which almost the entire St. Thomas Christian community seceded from Rome. From the history preceding this event, it is rather clear that this secession cannot be explained by its immediate pretext, that is, the detention of Mar Aꜥtallah, but was the fulfilment of a long-nurtured wish of the Archdeacon, who could not accept his subjugation, and by the local Christians, who wanted to preserve their traditions and autonomy.[53]

This event was followed by a rather troubled period, further complicated by the fact that the Dutch gradually conquered the Malabar Coast. In 1663 they conquered Cochin and expelled all the Portuguese and other European missionaries, with the exception of some Franciscans. At this moment the Apostolic Commissary, Bishop Joseph Sebastiani, had no other choice than to consecrate an indigenous prelate for the remaining party that did not obey Mar Thoma, the former Archdeacon and current bishop. For this purpose he could not but choose another

---

52 On this period see THEKKEDATH: History of Christianity in India, vol. 2, pp. 75–86; THAZHATH: The Juridical Sources of the Syro-Malabar Church, pp. 148–173; Curien Chorepiscopa KANIAMPARAMPIL, The Syrian Orthodox Church in India and Its Apostolic Faith, Detroit, MI 1989, pp. 78ff.

53 See J. KOLLAPARAMBIL: The St Thomas Christians' Revolution in 1653, Kottayam 1981; THEKKEDATH: History of Christianity in India, vol. 2, pp. 91–96; THAZHATH: The Juridical Sources of the Syro-Malabar Church, pp. 171ff.; KANIAMPARAMPIL: The Syrian Orthodox Church in India and Its Apostolic Faith, pp. 80–90; PHILIP: The Indian Church of St Thomas, pp. 133–138.

member of the same Parambil family, considered as being the leader of the community: Alexander de Campo, or Mar Chandy Parambil, who was the cousin of Mar Thoma and originally one of his main four helpers or advisers during the Bent Cross Oath. He made Mar Chandy Parambil a Vicar Apostolic and a titular bishop only, but Mar Chandy Parambil considered himself a Metropolitan and signed his documents as "Metropolitan of All India". Moreover, in 1678, he also appointed an Archdeacon, who happened to be his own nephew, Mathew Parambil (or De Campo). Thus, at this point, due to the binding force of the events and the strategic thought of Bishop Sebastiani, there were to be found two bishops of the St. Thomas Christian community, who were close relatives of each other, both from the traditional leading family of the Nazranies.[54]

2. Tradition as historical source: the testimony of some Syriac manuscripts

The history recounted in the previous section is a – rather deficient and simplifying – summary, with the involvement of a modicum of source criticism, of what is generally known about the early colonial period of the St. Thomas Christians' Church history. I have taken it from the secondary sources available to me, duly cited in the notes above. It is important to bear it in mind that this history was and is written mainly on the basis of a non-systematic selection of contemporary and later Portuguese, Dutch and British documents. At the same time the documents written before, but mainly during, the colonial period by the St. Thomas Christians themselves, in languages other than Portuguese, partly in their own language, Old Malayalam or Malayanma (often in Syriac letters, that is, in Malayalam/nma Garshuni) and partly in Syriac, are hardly if ever exploited for a deeper understanding of this history. Among the aims of the international effort, initiated and instigated by such outstanding Indian scholars as the Revd. Dr. Jacob Thekeparampil and His Grace Dr. Mar Aprem, to survey, explore and treat the rich Syriac manuscript funds of the Malabar Coast, is first to preserve and secondly to open up this repository of potential historical knowledge for two communities: first and foremost for the St. Thomas Christians, who have preserved it and whose cultural heritage it is, but secondly also for the international scholarly community.

As a modest contribution to this task encompassing, in perspective, several thousand Syriac manuscripts, here I shall briefly invoke the testimony of only two Indian Syriac manuscripts that I have had the opportunity to study, one kept in the Bodleian Library (Bodl. Or. 667),[55] already known to the narrower scholar-

---

54 See THEKKEDATH: History of Christianity in India, vol. 2, pp. 96–109; THAZHATH: The Juridical Sources of the Syro-Malabar Church, pp. 173–179; KANIAMPARAMPIL: The Syrian Orthodox Church in India and Its Apostolic Faith, pp. 90–102; PHILIP: The Indian Church of St Thomas, pp.139–150.

55 R. PAYNE-SMITH: Catalogi Codicorum Manuscriptorum Bibliothecae Bodleianae. Pars sexta codices Syriacos, Carshunicos, Mendaeos complectens, Oxford 1864, no. 72.

ly community,[56] and one in Mannanam, Kerala, in the wonderful library of the
monastery of the Carmelites of Mary Immaculate (C.M.I.), hitherto completely
unknown (Mannanam 090-248-4S).[57] The two manuscripts contain brief narratives, one each, on the history of the Church in Malabar, narratives that I consider
to be relevant and illuminating for the study of Indian Church history. However,
although they tell concisely the entire story of the Indian Church until the time
of their writing, they have a positive heuristic value for the colonial period only,
while as far as the pre-colonial period is concerned their relevance is rather negative: they allow us to eliminate some false concepts and give points of departure
for dating certain traditional texts, such as the currently known redaction of the
"Song of Rabban Thomas", invoked at the beginning of this paper. For an understanding of these testimonies, their literary genre should first be clarified.

Both texts are anonymous and without a title. Only William Mill, for whom
the entire manuscript Bodl. Or. 667 was copied in 1821-140, gave the text included in his MS a title: *Historiola Ecclesiae Syro-Malabaricae*.[58] However, a parallel
reading of the two texts, that is, the one preserved in Oxford and the one preserved
in Mannanam, shows that these "histories" are topical writings, linked to specific circumstances: they were composed on the occasion of – or at least relative to
– the ordination of certain Indian bishops. In the previous sections of the present
study we have seen that the ordination of indigenous bishops was an entirely modern phenomenon on the Malabar Coast. When the Portuguese arrived, the age-
old custom was that the Indian Church had Syrian prelates coming from Iraq,
assisted by the actual Ethnarch of the St. Thomas Christians, the Archdeacon,
filling a local hereditary, even dynastic, function, incorporated into the hierar-
chical structure of the Persian Church through the office of the Archdeaconate.
It was Mar Abraham, the last Syrian prelate of Chaldaean allegiance, who made
the first attempt to ordain an indigenous bishop as his successor on the throne of
Angamaly and All India in the 1580s. His attempt was obviously prompted by the
Portuguese pressure aiming at replacing the Syrian hierarchy with a Latin one. In
order to avoid this threat, Mar Abraham tried to have ordained the then Archdeacon, George of Christ, Bishop of Palayur, and to appoint him to be his successor on the Metropolitan see of Angamaly. We have seen that although Rome
agreed to this plan, it nevertheless failed, because of the premature death of Arch-

---

56 Besides Payne-Smith's catalogue, this manuscript is also briefly described in VAN DER PLOEG, The
    Christians of St. Thomas, pp. 228f.
57 The first detailed checklist of the Mannanam holdings, compiled by Fr. Emmanuel Thelly, was
    recently published: Emmanuel THELLY: Syriac Manuscripts in Mannanam Library, in: Symposi-
    um Syriacum VII, Journal of Eastern Christian Studies, 56 (2004), ed. by Rifaat EBIED, pp. 257–
    270. Fr Thelly's checklist does not mention the text discussed here.
58 The text of the *Historiola* was edited with a French translation by François NAU: Deux notices rela-
    tives au Malabar et trois petits calendriers, d'après les manuscrits Bodl. Or. 667, et Paris Syr. 25,195
    et Suppl. Grec. 292, in: Revue de l'Orient Chrétien (Deuxième Série) 7 (1912), pp. 74–99. The
    Syriac text is on pp. 75–79 and its French translation on pp. 79–82. In fact, Nau's edition conflates
    two texts, which are independent of each other. Nau erroneously attributed them to the same per-
    son, who, in reality, was only the copyist of the texts.

deacon George. Thus, it was only later and in a radically different form that Mar Abraham's plan – most probably corresponding to a real and natural desire of the St. Thomas Christians – could come about: this happened with the extraordinary elevation, in 1653, of Archdeacon Thomas to the bishopric by the laying on of hands of twelve priests, invoking a letter of Mar Aʿtallah who, as we will see, was to be considered in later times to be none other than Ignatius, Jacobite Patriarch of Antioch. We have also seen that ten years later, when the Dutch conquered Cochin and expelled the Roman Catholic missionaries, Bishop Joseph Sebastiani found himself in a situation ironically reminiscent of that of Mar Abraham, and was prompted to do the same as what Mar Abraham had wished in vain to do, that is, to ordain a rival indigenous bishop from the same family, in order to counteract the influence of Mar Thoma. After this event there were two rival indigenous hierarchies in Kerala, although not for long: Mar Chandy Parambil's case was not repeated on the Catholic side until the late eighteenth century.

Apparently it was this situation that prompted the composition of our documents. They were meant to legitimise the ordination of certain bishops, retelling the whole history of the Church of Malabar. They did so in an entirely and charmingly legendary manner, proving to be historiographical works whose starting point is not the past but the present. Thus we might call them 'teleological histories'. At this point, of course, one might muse on the question of how many historical works in general would fall outside this category...

2.1. An Apology for Mar Chandy Parambil and the 'Syriacisation' of the St. Thomas Christians

As these texts are either little known or unedited, I shall briefly present them, beginning with the older one, the one in the Mannanam manuscript. It is a small manuscript, measuring 150 x 95 x 15 mm, in blue paper binding. Although at first sight it seems to display several handwritings, closer scrutiny seems to show that the whole manuscript was partly copied, partly written by the same hand, that of Priest Thomas Paltutam, as indicated in the colophon, who used slightly different types of script. The manuscript contains the following items.

1. ff. 1v–74v	A catechesis, manifestly Roman Catholic, in the form of questions and answers, entitled *The True Law that All Christians Should Know*.
2. f. 75 rv	A colophon by the scribe.
3. ff. 77–99v	Diverse homilies on learning
4. ff. 100r–104r.	A brief treatise on Papal primacy, also containing a brief history of the Church of Malabar.
5. ff. 104v–106r.	A metric hymn to Christ, mainly in octosyllabic verse

Unfortunately, the colophon does not give any date, so only the last treatise is datable, precisely because it ends with the date of the ordination of the bishop for whose sake the entire treatise was written: this is Alexander De Campo, that is, Mar Chandy Parambil (1663–1687).

Although one might think that a Syriac translation of a Roman Catholic catechesis, containing the traditional data, is of little historical interest, this is far from being the case. In fact the colophon says the following odd thing:

> [Priest Thomas Paltutam][59] translated this concise little explanation of the law of the living God, which all Christians should know by all means in their intelligence, from the Indian (*Hendwaya*, that is, Malayalam or, rather, Malayanma) to the Syriac language, for the instruction and learning of the simple-minded children, asking from every person of discernment, every trained and learned brother who reads this translation from the Indian [*Hendwayutha*:] language to the Syriac language, [...][60] and simple children, which is necessary for a Christianity that is to attain discernment, that if any mistake or error or something else that is not correct [...] is found in the truth, he [the reader] should not make an outcry against him [the scribe] and should not cover him with mockery, and he should not be grudging and embittered, but will recognise in truth that every creature is deficient and nobody is perfect, but only the living God, in whom only perfection is to be found...

Now what need could there be for – or what would have prompted – Thomas Paltutam, an indigenous Malayali Roman Catholic priest in the seventeenth century, to translate from Malayalam into Syriac a catechesis that either had been originally translated from Latin or Portuguese into Malayalam, or had been composed directly in Malayalam on the basis of European models? It seems to me that an answer to this question can be found on the basis of an analysis of the last but one item in the manuscript, a justification of the Papal claims for primacy (in Kerala as elsewhere) and, attached to this, a brief history of the Church of India, from the time of Saint Thomas the Apostle up to the time when the manuscript was written. Moreover, since we know that Francisco Roz, the first Latin bishop of Angamaly, has written a catechesis in Malayalam, the promulgation and diffusion of which was decided by a decree of the Synod of Diamper,[61] I tend to suppose that

---

59 These data were given by the scribe, most probably Thomas Paltutam himself, encoded in numbers: "[This book was written] by a man whose name is signified in an encoding, in the collection of the number of the signs that are 6 before 41 after 401 [*Thoma*]. And his election [that is, ecclesiastical rank] is signified in the collection of the number 25, which stands before 51 [*kohana*], which was hidden [*g-nida* standing for *g-niza*] from knowledge and whose family is in what the numbers of 30 after 80 and 400 and 6 and 400 and 40 give in pronunciation [*Paltutam*], who translated this concise little explanation of the law of the living God..." Given that the family name is also given in this form, the vocalisation of this Malayalam name remains uncertain.

60 Here part of the manuscript is unfortunately not readable on the scanned copy.

61 See J. Castets, S.J., "Introduction" to the *De erroribus Nestorianorum* of Francisco Roz in: I. Hausherr (ed.): *De erroribus Nestorianorum qui in hac India orientali versantur auctore Francisco Roz S. I.*: Inédit latin-syriaque de la fin de 1586 ou du début de 1587, retrouvé par le P. Castets S.I., missionaire à Trichinopoly, annoté par le P. Irénée Hausherr S.I., in: Orientalia Christiana 11,1 (40) (1928), p. 9: "Le P. Roz n'était pas moins versé dans la langue malayalam ou malabare. Il rédigea les premiers livres religieux en malayalam, une doctrine et un formulaire de prières pour l'instruction des fidèles [...] Le concile de Diamper prescrivit de répandre le texte de cette *Doctrine* et il ordonna à tous les cassenars de l'enseigner et de l'expliquer à leurs ouailles." See

the catechesis found in the Mannanam manuscript might be a Syriac translation of Roz's work.

However, now my main interest is the pamphlet on Papal primacy. This hitherto unpublished pamphlet, whose text in English translation can be found in the *Appendix* of the present study, consists of three parts, all of which are closed by an anathema. The first adduces scriptural proofs for the primacy of Rome; the second begins with an interesting speculation – once again supported by a scriptural illustration from Saint Paul – on the vanity of distinguishing the Christians of Peter from those of James or Thomas: an obvious reference to the 'Jacobitism' of the Antiochian Patriarchate on the one hand and to the common claim on the Malabar Coast, according to which there is a 'Law of Peter' valid in Europe and a 'Law of Thomas' valid in India, so that the two should not be mixed,[62] on the other. Having thus established that there should not be several 'laws' observed in the Church, the author refutes the claim that the unique Head is the Patriarch of Antioch, one of his interesting arguments being that the Patriarch is even not the canonical one – this being the Maronite Patriarch in Lebanon – but a usurper.

Finally the third part, containing a concise history of the Church of Malabar, starts with the Apostolate of Saint Thomas in India and continues with the foundation of the Archdeaconate, by the priest George (Giwargis) from the Pālamaram family. Apparently Pālamaram is an earlier version of Pālamattam, of which Pakalomattam is another variant.[63] If this George is identical with George Pakalomattam, appointed Archdeacon in 1502, and if the story of the foundation of the Archdeaconate by George may be trusted, one may muse on the following question: how old at all is the institution of the Archdeaconate in India? My hypothesis, on the basis of what I have said about the Archdeacon's original princely function, is that earlier there must have existed this princely function of the community, which later, perhaps in the time of George Pakalomattam/Pālamaram, for the sake of the canonical order of the Persian Church, became identified with the ecclesiastic function of the Archdeacon.

---

also the short notice of van der Ploeg: The Christians of St. Thomas, p. 266, entirely based on the Introduction to Roz's writing by P. J. Castets.

62 This was already part of Mar Abraham's argumentation, as reported by Francisco Roz in a letter dated September 30, 1594: "He [Mar Abraham] has the law of St. Thomas and we that of St. Peter and it would be a grave sin and dishonour for these Christians to abandon the law in which they have lived until now, that is, the law of Thomas, and to adopt another in its place.", in: Archivum Romanum Societatis Jesu, Goa-Malabar, vol. 32, f. 531v, as quoted by A. Thazhath: The Juridical Sources, p. 145.

63 I owe this suggestion to Fr. Mathias Mundadan, whom I visited on 5 January 2006. This suggestion is further corroborated by the fact that in Malayalam there occurred a shift from *r* to *t* and *d*. Thus, present-day Kaduthuruthy is mentioned in seventeenth-century Syriac manuscripts as Karuthuruthy, so also present-day Edapally is mentioned in a seventeenth-century Syriac document as Erpelly. The traditional martial art of Kerala is called Kalaripayattu, at least so is it spelled in English transcription, but in fact people pronounce it as Kaledipayett. As a testimony to this – rather recent – phonetic change, even in the modern Malayalam alphabet double *t* is written by two *ra* signs (ᄋᄋ), placed either besides or underneath one another.

Our anonymous document lays great emphasis on the fact that George was from Kuravilangad, the home of the Pakalomattam family, which migrated there from its original home in Kodungallur, the great Christian city. At the same time it knows about no Mesopotamian connection before Mar Abraham, whose original allegiance to the (Nestorian) Church of the East, like his – forced – conversion and his re-ordination in Rome, is well known to the author. The document briefly lists the Latin Archbishops, in order to arrive at Mar Chandy Parambil, whom it calls "Metropolitan and Apostolic Head". We know that Bishop Joseph Sebastiani ordained Mar Chandy Parambil only as Vicar Apostolic, but the latter termed himself "Metropolitan of All India". Apparently, just as the first part of the Mannanam document aimed at proving that only the "Lord Pope" (*Mar Papa*) should be obeyed in the entire Church, and the second aimed at proving that the Jacobite Patriarchate of Antioch had no legitimate claim on the Malabar Coast, so the third part's aim is to prove that Mar Chandy Parambil, coming from the Archdeacons' family and – just like George Pālamaram – originally of Kuravilangad, is the only rightful (Metropolitan) bishop in India, over against the claim of Mar Thoma, the Metropolitan of Antiochian allegiance.

Given that the whole treatise is apparently written for this polemical purpose and that Mar Thoma, although Metropolitan of the dissident party from 1653, joined Antioch only in 1665, when Alexander De Campo had been his rival for two years, so not only this anonymous document, but also the whole Mannanam manuscript should be dated between 1665 and 1687 (the latter date being that of the death of Mar Chandy). The manuscript, consisting of a Syriac translation of a Roman Catholic catechesis – perhaps *the* authoritative Roman catechesis written by Francisco Roz and promulgated by the Synod of Diamper – on the 'True Law of the Christians' from Malayalam, some standard Syriac homilies on learning, the apologetic treatise discussed here and, finally, some octosyllabic devotional verses to Christ, is there to prove, in eloquent seventeenth-century Syriac, that there is only one 'Law' of the Christian Church, the one defined by the Roman Pontiff, and that the only rightful representative of this Law on the Malabar Coast is Mar Chandy Parambil. Thus, this manuscript seems to constitute a most important testimony to the fact that after the revolt of Mar Thoma and his new connections with the Church of Antioch, the Syriac language and an enhanced feeling of Syrian identity gained new importance among the St. Thomas Christians. Apparently, Mar Thoma's party, in order to find legitimation, played, on the one hand, on the conscience of a longstanding Syrian connection of the Church of India, which they were soon to see – as will be shortly shown – as an unquestionable Antiochian allegiance, dating from the times of early Christianity. On the other hand, this party also played on the traditional role of the Archdeacon as Ethnarch, leading to repeated attempts – beginning with the one of Mar Abraham in the 1580s – at ordaining an indigenous bishop from the Archdeacon's family.

The Roman Catholics, who had lost most of their constituency as a result of Mar Thoma's revolt, had to realise, be it for a short period only, the failure of their previous aggressive Latinising policy, which also oppressed, as the documents show, the local Syriacising elite. Now they had to face this challenge, which was also reinforced by the pressure of the Dutch who expelled the Latin missionaries from Malabar. Apparently, their strategic decision was, on the one hand, to ordain Mar Chandy Parambil from Mar Thoma's own family and, on the other, also to enter the ideological battlefield of Syriac learning. According to my hypothesis, this is the explanation for the odd phenomenon, witnessed by the Mannanam manuscript, of translating a Malayalam catechesis into Syriac, and this, as the colophon states, "for the instruction and learning of the simple-minded children". Obviously, the really 'simple-minded' faithful on the Malabar Coast would have known Malayalam rather than Syriac – it is hardly conceivable that translating from Malayalam into Syriac would have answered any popular demand. So I would suggest rather that this expression refers to a very learned indigenous ecclesiastical elite, with good knowledge of Syriac, whom the scribe and the author of the manuscript's colophon, Thomas Paltutam, considers as the simple-minded (and thus easily misleadable, even misled) children of the Roman Catholic church. Most probably it is in the same context that we should understand the appearance of an indigenous Indian hymnographer, Alexander the Indian (Alexandros Hendwaya), praised by none other than Joseph Maria Sebastiani, whose Syriac poetry was also highly appreciated in Rome, and one of whose metric sermons is contained in another manuscript of the Mannanam collection.[64] This Alexander the Indian, or Kadavil Chandy Kattanar from Kaduthuruthy participated in the Bent Cross Oath in 1653 and was elected a member of the four-member council governing the Malabar Church and assisting Metropolitan Mar Thoma I, who separated from Rome and joined the Jacobite Syrian Church of Antioch. Later, Chandy Kattanar returned to the Roman side and was entrusted with the completion of Roz's Syriac translation of the Latin Pontifical, meant to replace the East Syriac ordination book, which had been in use before the Latinisation.[65]

---

64 On the Mannanam manuscript containing the verse treatise of Alexander the Indian, see Emmanuel THELLY: Syriac Manuscripts in Mannanam Library, p. 261.

65 See THEKKEDATH: History of Christianity in India. Vol. 2, p. 92: in February 1653, a month after the *Kunan Kurishu* oath, "during the *munnu noyambu* celebrations at Idappalli, Archdeacon Thomas was once again acclaimed by the assembled crowds as the governor of the archdiocese, and four of the most prominent cattanars [that is, priests] were appointed as his councillors. The four were: Parambil Chandy of Kuravilangad, Bengur George of Agapparambu, Kadavil Chandy of Kaduthuruthy and Anjlimoottil Ittithomen of Kallicherry." On Chandy Kadavil Kattanar, seen from the Roman point of view, see P. J. THOMAS: Malayala Sahityavum Christyanikalum (Malayalam Literature and the Christians), Athirampuzha 1935; second edition with additions by Scaria ZACHARIA: Kottayam 1989, pp. 143–144. I owe this information to Fr. Antony Vallavanthara, who looked for it and kindly translated the relevant passage for me. For an evaluation of his personality and his role on the Jacobite side, see E. M. PHILIP: The Indian Church of St. Thomas, pp. 135ff., and KANIAMPARAMPIL: The Syrian Orthodox Church in India and Its Apostolic Faith, pp. 90ff.

2.2. Malabar Church history as the Orthodox saw it in the intermediate period after the Bent Cross Oath

The Oxford manuscript Bodl. Or. 667 is a small quire, in which William Mill, an English gentleman with good knowledge of Latin, had had copied by several local scribes some texts found in Malabar, in Jacobite possession; apparently Mill was in contact with the Jacobites (the *Yakuba* in Malayalam). Thus, on fol. 21r–23v of the manuscript one finds a small history, similar in genre to the one in the Mannanam manuscript, of the Christian Church in Malabar, a text that Mill entitled *Historiola Ecclesiae Syro-Malabaricae.* On fol. 25r one finds another short note, interesting from our point of view, entitled by Mill *Historiola Romanarum Partium in Malabari.* An English translation of both texts can be read in Appendix 2 below. The two texts are separated by another, written in Malayalam, on fol. 24rv. For both texts, Mill noted in Latin, in a fading, barely legible handwriting, *Descripsit Malpan Abraham [Cotyamensis].*[66] The first title also brings a date, 1821, and so we may conclude that the two texts were copied by Malpan Abraham from Kottayam in 1821, but were not written by him. Rather, they may be much earlier; they are manifestly from two different authors and are independent of each other.[67] Moreover, as we will see, the first text, a short apologetic history, written to justify the consecration of a bishop, belongs as such to the same literary genre as the little Mannanam history written to legitimate Mar Chandy Parambil. Thus, it is well datable to the period between the ordination of the bishop whom it legitimises, that is, Mor Yuhannōn Christophoros of Mosul, ordained in April 1752, and the ordination of Metropolitan Dionysius I in 1770,[68] which put an end to the internal schism within the Jacobite group, an event about which the text does not know yet. More precisely, the text must have been written before the death of one of the bishops whose prayers it invokes as a "bulwark", Mor Basilios Shukr'allah, who died in 1764. Thus, in all probability, the text was written between 1752 and 1764.

2.2.1. First text: *Historiola Ecclesiae Syro-Malabaricae*

The *Historiola* begins, as it should, with the preaching of Saint Thomas in Malabar. It gives the traditional date of his arrival, 52 AD, but instead of the generally accepted seven churches, it knows about only five churches founded by the Apos-

---

66 *Cotyamensis* can be read only in the second title.
67 This clarification was necessary, because François Nau, who published these texts, attributed both of them to "Abraham, prêtre de Travancore", assuming that they were written in 1821. This supposition is in fact due to a misreading of the notice of Payne-Smith in the Catalogue of the Oxford Syriac manuscripts: "Descripsit Guillelmo H. Mill Abraham, presbyter Travancorensis, Dec. 1821". Nau's attribution went unhindered into the standard literature, thus Kollaparambil: The Archdeacon of All India, p. 81: "a letter of a Jacobite priest, Abraham by name, to Mr. William H. Mill in December 1821" (where Kollaparambil means in fact the text copied by Malpan Abraham), and Mundadan: History of Christianity in India, vol. 1, p. 182.
68 Mar Thoma VI (1765–1709), in the line of the Mar Thoma's was ordained Metropolitan under the name Mor Dionysius I in 1770. Even in his lifetime, he was called Mor Dionysius the Great.

tle. It states that there were two privileged families from among which Saint Thomas chose the main priests of the community. It continues with the arrival of Thomas of Kana and the foundation of the Archdeaconate, which, according to our text, was conferred on members of the two leading families – an important correction to what we read elsewhere about the privileged position of only the Pakalomattam family. After a brief mention of another Syrian colonisation in 845, our text states that the Malabar Christians were "Orthodox Jacobite Syrians" from the very time of the first preaching in India of Saint Thomas the Apostle. Odd as this expression may sound, its anachronism is only apparent: in fact it expresses the conviction that the Jacobite Syrian teachings and customs are the legitimate heirs to the pure Apostolic traditions; however, it also expresses the deep attachment of the community to its Syrian identity, apparently very much reinforced by the Antiochian connection in the seventeenth and eighteenth centuries.[69] The text describes in vivid terms the vicissitudes of Mar Abraham, whose original Nestorian allegiance and subsequent forced conversion are apparently well known to the author, although he erroneously supposes that it was the Catholicos Patriarch Mar Elias VIII (1576–91) who originally sent Mar Abraham to Malabar. Then the *Historiola* briefly mentions the Synod of Diamper, which put a – temporary – end to the Syrian customs and introduced the forced celibacy of the clergy. Also, our text indicates in a nicely allusive manner that the newly adopted Latin canons deprived the clergy of legitimate marriage only, simply making illegal the persisting marriages of the priests.[70]

The most emphatic part of the story is dedicated to the antecedents and events of the Bent Cross Oath. According to the text's version, no less a person than Mor Ignatius, the Patriarch of Antioch, came to India in order to venerate the tomb of Saint Thomas, and it was he who, having recognised the difficult situation of the Church, gave an official letter to two deacons, permitting the elevation to the Metropolitanate of Archdeacon Thomas. The drama is enhanced by Mor Ignatius' murder by the Franks, that is, the Portuguese. The whole setting explains why the revolt was necessary, even unavoidable, and why the ordination of the first Mar Thoma was absolutely legitimate. The *Historiola* also presents the ordination, on the Roman Catholic side, of the rival indigenous bishop, Mar Chandy Parambil, laying great emphasis on the fact that he was from the same family as Archdeacon,

---

69 In fact, the claim that the original tradition of the St. Thomas Christians was Antiochian and Jacobite before becoming Nestorian in the fifteenth century remains a well attested opinion within the Jacobite Church in India. See E.M. PHILIP, The Indian Church of St Thomas, Chapter XIII/II "Was the Syrian Church Nestorian?" pp. 111–132. Unfortunately, this thesis is almost never being treated in Western scholarship although at least it should deserve our attention.

70 See also the letter of Mor Grigorios Abd'ul Jalil to the parish priests of Mulanthuruthy, Kandanad and Paravur, dated May 5, 1668: "Till now, priests were allowed to marry according to the canons. The Romanists forbade the marriage of priests and deacons. Many of them fall into the impurity of fornication. ... These unholy people now curse holy matrimony and love adultery. The wrath of God awaits them. Know that marriage is holy and the marriage bed is undefiled and that God judgeth all adulterers and fornicators ..." The quotation is from E.M. PHILIP: The Indian Church of Saint Thomas, p. 146.

later Mar, Thoma. It is also interesting to see that, despite all the activities of the Latin Archbishops, such as Alexis de Menezes, Francisco Roz, Stephen Britto and Joseph Sebastiani, the text makes the permanent schism in the fold of the St. Thomas Christians originate from the moment when two rival indigenous bishops were in function, that is, from 1663. Apparently, at the time of writing of this document the memory that only Mar Chandy Parambil's desertion of Mar Thoma's side was able substantially and permanently to divide the thitherto unified community of the Indian Nazranies was still very much alive.

The text then presents more vicissitudes that the Church of Malabar had to undergo in the period after 1653 and 1663, until it arrives at the ordination of the last bishop in its list, that of Mor Yuhannōn in April 1752, at the hands of Maphrian Basilios Shukr'allah. Here an absolutely precise date and a detailed presentation of the circumstances can also be found, clearly showing that the whole little history was written in order to arrive at this point: apparently at the text's time of writing the ruling bishops of the Jacobite community were Mor Basilios Shukr'allah, Mor Grigorios Hanna Bahudaidi and Mor Yuhannōn Christophoros, whose prayers the author invokes as a protective bulwark for the community. It is conspicuous that after Mar Thoma I none of his followers, that is, the other Mar Thoma's, is mentioned, although the Metropolitanate of the community became a hereditary custom, passing from uncle to nephew, down to 1809, the death of Mar Thoma VII., Mor Basilios Shukr'allah died in 1764. Thus, the writing of our text is safely datable to the period between 1752 and 1764 and can be attributed to a Jacobite milieu, which, during these times, was alienated from the Mar Thoma's of the times (Mar Thoma V and VI) and found legitimation in sticking to the Middle Eastern bishops residing in India, that is, Mor Basilios Shukr'allah, Mor Grigorios Hanna Bahudaidi and Mor Yuhannōn Christophoros of Mosul.[71]

The identification of the milieu where the document was written explains the detailed justification of the events as it stands in the text: the author had to distance his position first from the Catholic one – showing the unquestionable legitimacy of Mar Thoma's revolt and ordination – but secondly from that of the group around the current Mar Thoma's. Thus, although it mentions the Malabar Christians' previous wish to have indigenous bishops, it lays all the emphasis on the 'imported' culture, that is, on the Syriac customs, but also language.

2.2.2. Second text: *Historiola Romanarum Partium in Malabari*

The second text published by Nau and treated here, a short notice on a supposed split between the Jacobites and the Maronites in 1127 and the Synod of Diamper, does not belong to the former one; most probably it was not written by the same

---

71 On Mor Basilios, Mor Grigorios and Mor Yuhannōn, see E.R. HAMBYE: History of Christianity in India, vol. 3: Eighteenth Century, Bangalore 1997, pp. 51ff. For Bahudaidi, Hambye uses the spelling Bakiddide. "'Bahudaidi' is an adjective derived from the placename 'Bahudeida' (= Beth Hudaida = Qaraqosh in Iraq). He was Metropolitan of the Monastery of Mor Behnam in Iraq and, later, of Jerusalem, before he came to India." (from a personal letter of Hubert Kaufhold, dated 9 January, 2005).

author either, because the first text dated Diamper to 1598, while this second one dates it to 1595. In fact, both datings are incorrect, because the Synod of Diamper was held in 1599. The text first condemns in unequivocal terms what it calls Patriarch Maron's secession "from the Petrine See of Antioch", which it connects to the year 1127, and then briefly mentions the leading personalities of the Synod of Diamper. Nau, who first published this fragment, already wondered about the possible meaning of such a vehement inclusion of the Maronites in Indian Church history.[72] In fact, once again, it is the Mannanam history, first published here, that permits us to solve the riddle: the notice about an illegitimate secession of Patriarch Maron from the Patriarchate of Antioch serves to refute the Roman Catholic denial of the Antiochian claims on the Malabar Coast, the argument of which, as we have seen, was based on a denial of the canonicity of the Syrian Orthodox Patriarchate, claiming that the only legitimate Antiochian Patriarch was the Maronite Patriarch on Mount Lebanon. Thus apparently a vilification of the Maronites had become a standard element in the self-legitimising argument of the Jacobites in Kerala.

3. Some conclusions related to the role of languages and to methodology

Having presented first the general setting of the history of the Church of Malabar and second the testimony of two Syriac manuscripts, one preserved in India and one in Europe, one should ask what their bearing is, if any, on our knowledge of the St. Thomas Christians' history in particular and on the complicated interrelations of the languages of the people and the languages of religion in general.

3.1. The early colonial history of the Malabar Christians and some points of repair for dating the undated documents

As far as the St. Thomas Christians' history is concerned, without offering much new information on concrete events, our documents teach us a great deal about the mentality that gave rise to, and the ideological debates that accompanied, the early modern divisions and strife of the Indian Nazrani community, caused by the colonial and missionary interventions in the life of the Christian people of Malabar. Moreover, these documents allow us to recognise a literary genre, that of a brief justificatory Church history, written to legitimise the ordination of a bishop in rivalry with others and competing for the loyalty of the entire community of the St. Thomas Christians.

---

72 See NAU: Deux notices relatives au Malabar, p.74: "La première notice est un résumé jacobite de l'histoire du Malabar dans lequel nous trouvons une phrase assez inattendue consacrée au Maronites", and p. 82, n. 2: "Nous ne pouvons comprendre ce que cette mention vient faire ici, mais nous l'éditons telle quelle."

3.1.1. Dating the *Thomas Ramban Pattu*

Secondly, the recognition of this genre has also given us a methodological tool to date certain documents according to the episcopacy of the person for whose sake the 'teleological history' was written. This allows us to date both the first such document treated here and the Mannanam manuscript in which it is found, to the period between 1665 and 1687, as well as the notice in Mill's Oxford manuscript, to the period between 1752 and 1764. The same methodology may be extended to further documents, an interesting example of which is the *Thomas Ramban Pattu* ("The Song of Rabban Thomas"), the popular Malayalam epic song invoked at the beginning of this study. This ballad does not strictly belong to the genre of the 'teleological Church histories' analysed here, but it is akin to them. Although its 'colophon' dates it to 1061, or 1101, or 1601, none of these datings can be accepted. In fact, not only is the ballad dedicated to "the Mother of all divine virtue, Mary, the Mother of God,"[73] an expression which presupposes at least Portuguese, if not Syrian Orthodox influence, and not only is the story of the death of the Apostle influenced by a Latin *Passio Thomae* propagated by the Portuguese missionaries,[74] but it also contains some apologetic elements, which make it impossible that the song, in the redaction and form in which Rocca published it, could be earlier than the time of the Mar Thoma's and their closer Antiochian allegiance in the period following 1665. In fact, the ballad reports the ordination, by Saint Thomas, of indigenous bishops, one of whom was Paul, "one of the two princes of Chandrapury",[75] ordained for the converts on the eastern Coromandel coast, the other being Thomas in Malabar. Most significantly, the Apostle, just before his departure for and death in Mylapore, regulates the episcopacy and its succession on the Malabar Coast in the following way: "He has commanded that the second heir to the [princely] throne in the paternal line becomes the bishop and that he bears the name Thomas; he has ordered the succession of the priests and, above all, he invoked much grace upon him [that is, upon Bishop Thomas] as a privilege".[76] To me it seems that the inclusion of these verses clearly points to the much later habit of ordaining indigenous bishops from a Malabar princely family, that of the Parambils, and the transmission of this function from uncle to nephew, from one Mar Thoma to another – a custom established in 1653 and followed until the extinction of the direct line of the Mar Thoma's family on 20 June 1809, when Mar Thoma VII died. The erudite Italian translator of the text, F. X. Rocca, also observed this similarity, but, because he firmly believed in the historicity of the account contained in the ballad, thought that the seventeenth-century custom of the succession of the Mar Thoma's was a late survival of the original custom established by the Apostle.[77] However, as we have seen that the ordination of

---

73 Rocca: La leggenda di S. Tomaso Apostolo, p. 170, lines 9–12.

74 Ibid., p. 177, note to line 325.

75 Ibid., p. 175, lines 181–192.

76 Ibid., pp. 175f., lines 243–248.

77 Ibid., p. 175, note to line 243: "Qui abbiamo la regola stabilita dall'Apostolo per la successione episcopale. Il vescovo sara preso della famiglia reale, sarà il secondogenito; e porterà il nome di

indigenous bishops from the Archdeacon's, that is, a princely, family is strictly an early modern phenomenon on the Malabar Coast, practised both as a reaction to colonial pressure and as a means of smartly exerting such pressure, we should consider this element as a projection of a seventeenth-century situation into the first-century story. The recognition of this fact once again permits us to identify the approximate date and the milieu of creation of the ballad or, at least, of the version of it published by Rocca.

On this basis I would suggest that the ballad received its present form between 1665 and 1770, in the hands of a group closely related to the Mar Thoma's and in rivalry both with the Roman Catholics and with the Syrian prelates coming from Antioch. Thus, the ballad's value as a source on early Indian Church history is rather restricted, while, together with the Syriac histories analysed above, it teaches us a great deal about the intellectual situation of the seventeenth and eighteenth centuries in Kerala. With all this, naturally, I do not want to prejudge the value of the traditions constituting the original kernel of the ballad, which are, most probably, much earlier.

3.1.2. Dating the redaction of eighteen newly found Malayalam Apocrypha
During the digitisation of the collection of the Ernakulam Major Archbishop's House in July-August 2005,[78] our team made a quite astonishing discovery. The archives also contain a number of palm-leaf manuscripts of miscellaneous provenience, partly treating Ayurvedic medicine and partly containing official documents of Christian churches, church orders, accounts etc. One among them (now Ernakulam PL 1) is of particular interest: it contains eighteen Christian apocrypha in Malayalam, namely the following:

1. Acts of Peter
2. Acts of Paul
3. Acts of James the Greater
4. Acts of John
5. Acts of Andrew
6. Acts of Thomas
7. Acts of Philip
8. Acts of James the Smaller, the Brother of the Lord
9. Acts of Bartholomew

Tomaso. Una regole questa del nome, che troviamo applicata anche nel secolo XVII, ai principio del movimentto giacobita. Nel poema è detto che trattesi del secondogenito in linea paterna, perchè è ancora costume tra i Bramini e tra le famiglie reali, e anche altre caste, di seguire per l'eredità in legge del *Marumakattayam*, o sistema matriarcale, par cui l'erede è sempre il figlio della sorella del defunto. Invece per successione episcopale dovevano seguire il modo solito di generazione paterna, chiamato nel Malabar: *Makkakattayam*."

78 It is my pleasant duty here to thank the kindness and the helpfulness of all those who permitted this work: His Eminence, Cardinal Varkey Joseph Vittayathil, Major Archbishop of Ernakulam, His Grace, Bishop Thomas Chakiath, Vicar General and Revd. Fr. Ignatius Payyappilly, the Curator of the Archdiocesan Archives.

10. Acts of Matthew
11. Acts of Taddaeus Juda
12. Acts of Matthias
13. Acts of Mark the Evangelist
14. Acts of Luke the Evangelist
15. Life of Mary
16 On the Annunciation
17. On the birth of Mary
18. On the birth of Christ

Thus the manuscript contains a whole cycle of the Acts of the Twelve Apostles, supplemented by the lives of the two other Evangelists – besides Matthew and John – and apocryphal stories and calculations about the lives of Christ and Mary. All these stories are arranged according to the ecclesiastic calendar. Often the texts are introduced or – at the end – commented by somebody who is obviously the redactor of the whole collection. The manuscript was examined by an expert in palm-leaf manucripts, Mr. Dinesan Vadakinniyil,[79] from whom I learned that it was written in the second half of the nineteenth century; both the script used and its linguistic characteristics date it to the same period. However, according to Mr. Dinesan Vadakinniyil, this does not give any information about the date of the texts themselves, because, as these manuscripts are so easily perishable, they were frequently recopied and every such time their text was also adapted to the contemporary language. The same happened to the Ramayana or the Ayurvedic texts as well. Therefore, in order to date the texts themselves and the redaction of the compilation, we need different methods. The first question is to date the redaction contained in the manuscript and so also the notes of the redactor. Such a date will also constitute a *terminus ante quem* for the translation and original redaction of the apocrypha themselves.

I believe that the methods outlined and the basic data gathered in the present study provide a fairly good framework for dating the redaction of the apocryphal collection.

At the beginning of this paper I already mentioned the note on the memorial day of the Apostle Thomas, which the redactor fixes at 21 December, corresponding to the death day of St Thomas still celebrated in the Indian Jacobite and Syrian Orthodox Churches but not in the Indian Catholic Church. The redactor was obviously a Catholic, in fierce polemics with those who had seceded from the Catholic Church and joined the Antiochian Patriarchate – that is, with the Syrian Orthodox. This immediately gives 1665 as *terminus post quem* for the time of the redaction. For a *terminus ante quem* the first point of repair is the fact that the Catholic redactor speaks of a universal custom in the Malankara Church of celebrating the *Dukhrana*, that is, the main memorial day of St Thomas, on 21 Decem-

---

79 Mr Vadakinniyil is presently writing a Ph. D. thesis at the University of Bergen, Department of Social Anthropology.

ber. The origin of this custom is obscure, all the more so, because 21 December coincides with the celebration of the memory of the Martyrdom of St Thomas in the Roman Catholic Church. Thus, rather than an early local custom, the celebration of the *Dukhrana* on 21 December, still alive in the Jacobite Church, seems to be a remnant of a Latinising introduction, probably sometime after Diamper and before the secession of the Jacobites. This custom was subsequently changed in the Catholic Church. As the Synod of Diamper indicated 3 July as the memory day and as this is also the prescription of the Breviary of Francisco Roz,[80] one might suppose that the Western custom of celebrating 21 December was introduced by Bishop Francisco Garcia (1641–1659), famous for his extreme Latinising tendencies.[81] The redactor must have lived in a period when Mar Thoma's party had already joined the Jacobite Church, but when Francisco Garcia's innovations were still alive, not yet reversed, and when Roz's Breviary was not yet universally used in the Malankara Catholic Church or, perhaps, when it was not yet completed. According to Curien Kaniamparambil,[82] the liturgical books, the translation of which was started by Roz, were not completed until the second half of the seventeenth century, when their completion was entrusted to Chandy Kadavil Kattanar (alias Alexandros Hendwaya) who, after the Bent Cross Oath, together with Mar Chandy Parambil deserted the camp of Mar Thoma I and joined the Catholic side. As far as the redaction of the apocrypha is concerned, all this points to a period when the organisation of the Catholic community was not yet entirely tight. Thus, all these factors point toward dating the redaction to the period between 1665 and 1700.

There is one more element corroborating this approximate dating. The *Acts of Peter* finish with the shorter ending of this apocryphon, also found in the Syriac version, one of whose witnesses can be found in a manuscript kept in Thrissur (*MS Thrissur 9*).[83] After the last sentence of the Acts, the redactor added a note of polemical content. This note, alien from the original text of the Acts, corresponds

---

80 See *MS Ernakulam 33* containing this Breviary, f. 311r. Ff. 308r–313v contain the full calendar of the stable feasts according to the months. The manuscript was copied in 1782, in Putthensira, by Deacon Joseph Bar Quriaqos Kannanbully.

81 I owe this suggestion to Dr. Alexander Toepel.

82 KANIAMPARAMPIL: The Syrian Orthodox Church in India and Its Apostolic Faith, p. 91: "Kadavil Kathanar in addition to the dream of a pastoral staff had attractions for certain pecuniar benefits. He was offered the post of translator to complete the translation of the pontifical into Syriac, begun by Fr. Roz, and as a reward he was given 400 puthens." It is true that Fr. Kaniamparambil speaks only about the pontifical. However, I wonder whether this also holds for the Breviary.

83 On the Thrissur MS see Mar APREM I, 221; II, 357; Van der PLOEG, 146; F. BRIQUEL-CHATON-NET, A. DESREUMAUX, and J. THEKEPARAMPIL, "Découverte d'un manuscrit très important contenant des textes apocryphes dans la bibliothèque de la métropolie de l'Église de l'Est à Trichur, Kérala, Inde" in: R. Lavenant (ed.), Symposium Syriacum VII, Uppsala août 1996, Orientalia Christiana Analecta 256, Rome, 1998, pp. 587–597. The authors are inclined to think that the manuscript, which contains an interjected colophon that does not give the place of writing, was written in the Middle East. Their hypothesis has been proven by Hubert Kaufhold, who has found out that the manuscript was brought from the Middle East to India by Mar Timotheos Abimalek, Metropolitan of India residing in Thrissur, in 1908 (from a private letter of Prof. Hubert Kaufhold to the author, dated March 2006).

in almost every point to a section of the treatise on Papal primacy contained in the Mannanam manuscript analysed above. So I give here a parallel translation of three texts. An English translation of this Malayalam note can be read in the left column, while in the right column I give first an English translation of the last sentences of the *Acts of Peter* as found in *MS Thrissur 9* and, second, the parallel text from the Mannanam manuscript.

Note from the end of the Malayalam *Acts of Peter*, f. 12v

After the soul of Shimon left his body and went to the salvation (*moksha*) of God, his students, whose names were Kelmis, Mazlis and others[84] took his holy body from the cross. The many people buried it full of sadness.[85] **Shimon Keppa became the Pope and ruled in the city of Antioch for seven years, and in Rome for twentyfive years.** *And from then on there has been no change in the Roman throne and, as Christ proclaimed, there will be no change in it till the end of the world. And the Satan-worshippers,*[86] *the Jews, the Kappiars*[87] *and the heretics are the doors of Hell. They have been punished and will be punished. Attempts to destroy the Roman Church and to hinder it will be of no use, because it will stand like a rock in the stormy sea. **Those who attack it will be destroyed and it is seen that they are becoming the slaves of the Ruk** [**that is, of the Turks**]. **That is why the Syrian teachers call the Roman Church the Virgin Church. The Roman Church has never changed from this.***[88]

End of the *Acts of Peter* in MS Thrissur 9, f. 163v

And when the soul of the saint ascended, there came Markellos without asking the advise of anybody and took Shimᶜun from the cross and washed him. And he ground spices of myrrh and aloe, embalmed him and put him in a splendid stone coffin, bought for a great price, and put him in his own crypt. Thus was completed the martyrdom (lit. crowning) of the blessed Mar Shimᶜun, the first-born of the Apostles, through the grace of Christ our Lord. To him be glory and to us his love to the ages. Amen.

Treatise on the Papal primacy, MS Mannanam 090-248-4S, ff. 101v–102v

*It is in ignorance that those people from Antioch say – for they are heretics – that the Head of the Church is the patriarch who is in Antioch, for the mere reason that Kephas stayed for a little time in Antioch. But this is a great trap. **The true Antiochian patriarch nowadays stays in the Mountain of Lebanon; he left Antioch because of the occupation of Antioch by the Turks, after the Turks conquered Antioch, so that it is manifest that one** [**of the so-called Antiochian patriarchs**] **rules in treachery, he is only self-ordained, so that he is a patriarch in madness who has troubled all the Christians in the Empire of the Turks** [**lacuna**] **up to the present day.** Peter stayed for seven years in Antioch and, again, he stayed for twenty-five years in Rome and died there, as well as Paul. After the death of Kephas there ruled Linus and he stayed in Rome; and after Linus there ruled Callistus;*

---

84 Kelmis corresponds to Clement (Clemens) and Mazlis to Marcellus.
85 Here end the Acts of Peter and begins the note of the redactor.
86 *Chaytanmar*: the pagans.
87 Kappiar must mean the Muslims, from the Arabic word Kafir, "unbeliever".
88 Translation by Dr. Susan Thomas and by Mr. Yesudas Chovokkaren.

> *after that there ruled Clemens who humbly restrained himself from ruling after Kephas. Therefore it is manifest that in every manner the Head is the Lord Pope who stays in Rome. Let all those who say that he is not* [the Head], *be anathema!*

The above comparison is intended to show that, first, the Malayalam *Acts of Peter* ends where the Thrissur version of the *Acts* ends: Marcellus took the body of Shimᶜon Kepha from the cross and buried it. However, the Malayalam version shortens the story and to the name of Marcellus adds that of Clement, perhaps in order to emphasise the continuity of the Papacy from Peter to Clement and beyond. After that there comes an apologetic note on papal primacy, against some heretics who apparently bring forward the tradition that before going to Rome Peter stayed in Antioch. These are manifestly the Jacobites, against whom the author of the note brings up 1) that Peter stayed in Antioch only for 7 years, while he spent 25 in Rome and 2) that as a divine punishment the Antiochians have become the servants of the Turks. Both arguments can be found with identical content, but with a more detailed explanation, in the treatise on Papal primacy found in the Mannanam manuscript, which we were able to safely date to the time of the episcopacy of Mar Chandy Parambil. Thus it seems to me that the two texts, that of the Mannanam manuscript and that written by the redactor of the Ernakulam Malayalam apocrypha are roughly contemporary and contain the same standard Roman Catholic arguments against Mar Thoma's party and its Antiochian connections. For this reason I would also date the redaction of the Malayalam apocrypha to Mar Chandy Parampil's time, that is, to the period between 1665 and 1687, with a slight possibility of a later, but still seventeenth-century date.

3.2. The languages of religion versus the language of the people

The documents presented and analysed here also contain a lesson for understanding a complicated linguistico-cultural change in seventeenth-century colonial southern India. The intervention of the Portuguese in the life of the local Christian community acted on an intricate system of overlapping cultural influences. As I tried to show in the introductory part of this study, the Indian Nazranies belonged to two worlds: socially, culturally and linguistically they belonged to the neighbouring Hindu society, wholly integrated in its system based on a separation and also protection of the different castes, indeed, of different vocational and cultural sub-entities. At the same time their ecclesiastical and liturgical, but also commercial, bonds integrated them into the Syriac-writing diaspora of the Middle East, more specifically into the East Syrian Church of the East. Through their local leader, the Archdeacon, they integrated into the ecclesiastical structure of the Persian Church, but the Archdeacon also served as the prince of the entire Christian community, dispersed among different Hindu kingdoms. The Portuguese ecclesiastical authorities acted on this sensitive equilibrium without fully recognising it; moreover, they were motivated by their own ideological imperatives, based on the radical ideas of the Counter-Reformation as expressed in the documents of the Council of Trent. So they simultaneously attacked the local social structure of the community, expressed in the function of the Archdeaconate, and the ties linking these Christians to both their Middle Eastern mother Church and their Syrian ecclesiastical customs. This was a blind attack, bringing about disastrous consequences, not only for the St. Thomas Christian community, but also for the Portuguese mission itself. Due to the community's violent Syriacising reaction, led by its princely person, the Archdeacon, whose privileges and prerogatives were contested, the Padroado mission risked losing all its footing; it could stand only through recognising the leading Parambil family's importance (with the consecration of Chandy Parambil) and through entering the Syriacising mood (expressed in such phenomena as the translation of a Malayalam catechesis into Syriac in our Mannanam manuscript). All these changes, also connected to the growing influence of the Antiochian Jacobite Patriarchate, led to a re-Syriacisation of the St. Thomas Christians' culture in the seventeenth and eighteenth centuries.

In fact, there is no evidence that Syriac would have been a literary language used by any more than a very thin elite before the seventeenth century. The virtual non-existence of early Syriac documents, other than liturgical, written on the Malabar Coast is perhaps not only due to the flames of the Synod of Diamper, or the silverfish eating the manuscripts, but also to the fact that the real literary language of the people was Malayalam (or pre-Malayalam, in all its historical versions) and not Syriac. So my working hypothesis, to be verified or falsified by subsequent research, is that Syriac emerged as a real literary language of the community only in the seventeenth century, so much so that the growing Syrian consciousness of the Nazranies gradually resulted in forgetting their own Indian culture and in a disruption in their historical memory. So the Syriac documents, largely unexploited hitherto, will give us many new insights into the early colonial history of the Malabar Coast and, perhaps, also will shed some faint light on earlier times. However, if we want to know more about the pre-colonial period, we will have to turn to the documents written in the local languages and preserved in Vattezhuttu or Kolezhuttu scripts on stone inscriptions, copper plates and palm-leaf manuscripts. If this hypothesis were to prove correct, the palm-leaf manuscript from Ernakulam, containing the eighteen Malayalam apocrypha presented shortly before, may be just a first witness of ancient Malayalam Christian literature, lying buried in these documents. I am convinced that a study of these documents, needing very different skills and the co-operation of a wide scholarly team, will bring about much new information about the past.

Appendix

1. MS Mannanam 090-248-4S, ff. 100r–104r: An untitled Apologetic treatise on Papal Primacy with a brief history of the Malabar Church

[100r] Other

For Simeon Peter is the Head of all the Christians. Let all those who say that he is not, be anathema. To him alone our Lord has said: "You are Peter; I will build up the Church and the gates of Hell will not prevail over it. I give you the key of the Kingdom of heaven and whatever you will bind on earth will be bound in heaven" (Mt 16:18–19). And again, our Lord said to Simeon: "Go to the sea, throw your hook and of the first fish that comes up [100v] open the mouth and you will find a stater; take this and give on behalf of me and of yourself." (Mt 17:27). Our Lord said so: "give it on behalf of me and of yourself" [as he said this {in rasura}] and that they do not give [it] also on behalf of the other apostles, because the others do not need it. Why? Because Simeon is their Head and when their Head gives, it is also sufficient for them. And also after our Lord died and was buried, when Simeon and John went to the tomb, John ran before Simeon and arrived first at the tomb, [but] did not enter within. Simeon Peter came after him and then John entered. Why did John wait outside until Simeon came and why did he not enter? This is because Simeon is the Head of John, the beloved of our Lord and of all the apostles. John is not before Simeon, but waited for his Head. And again, whom among the Apostles did our Lord ask three times: "Do you love me?" and to whom did he say: "tend my sheep" and "tend my flock" and "tend my lambs"? But he told this to Simeon alone. And the explanation [101r] of the fact that our Lord said to Simeon "tend my sheep" is: "tend my apostles" and "tend my flock" means "tend all my disciples" and "tend my lambs" means "tend for me all my Christians". So if our Lord entrusted all the Christians to the hands of Simeon – for it is known that he is Peter, the Head of all the Christians, who is sitting on the See that is in Rome – *then let all those who do not obey the Lord Pope, the heir to Peter, who sits on the See that is in Rome, be anathema!*

But ignorant and foolish people say: "I am a Christian of Peter," "I am one of Jacob", and: "I belong to Thomas." For those who are speaking of such division are lawless and deceitful and envious. This is why the Tongue of the Church said in his First Letter to the Corinthians, in the first chapter: "Thus, there are among you who say, I belong to Paul, and others [101v] who say, I belong to Apollos, and there are who say, I belong to Kephas, and there are who say, I belong to Christ. So has Christ been divided? Or was Paul crucified for you? Or were you baptized in the name of Paul? I give thanks to God that I did not baptize any one of you, except for Crispus and Gaius, so that nobody might say that I baptized in my own name" (1 Cor 1:12–15). So it is clear that there is no division for the Church and that one is the Head of all the Churches, just as Paul said in his Letter to the

Romans: "Thus, we are many, but we are one body in Christ, and each of us is a member of the other" (Rm 12:5). So as we are one body in Christ and as all of us are in the one Church and the Head of the Church is the Lord Pope, the heir to Peter, who sits on the See that is in Rome, whom alone I obey, then it is in ignorance that those people from Antioch say – for they are heretics – [102r] that the Head of the Church is the Patriarch who is in Antioch, for the mere reason that Kephas stayed for a little time in Antioch. But this is a great trap [lit.: captivity]. The true Antiochian patriarch nowadays stays in the Mountain of Lebanon;[1] he left Antioch because of the occupation of Antioch by the Turks, after the Turks conquered Antioch, so that it is manifest that one [of the so-called Antiochian patriarchs] rules in treachery, he is only self-ordained, so that he is a patriarch in madness who has troubled all the Christians in the Empire of the Turks [lacuna] up to the present day. Peter stayed for seven years in Antioch and, again, he stayed for twenty-five years in Rome and died there, as well as Paul. After the death of Kephas there ruled Linus and he stayed in Rome; and after Linus there ruled Callistus; after that there ruled Clement [102v] who humbly restrained himself from ruling after Kephas. Therefore it is manifest that in every manner the Head is the Lord Pope who stays in Rome. *Let all those who say that he is not [the Head], be anathema!*

After our Lord Jesus Christ ascended to heaven and the Apostles received the Holy Spirit, Lord Thomas, the Apostle and beloved of our Lord, also the one who touched the side of the Lord of Life, came to our land of India and went about preaching the holy Gospel; he sowed faith, love and hope, removed the demoniac darkness and lighted the light of the Sun of Righteousness in all India. In fact, to many he taught all that pertains to the true Law and he made them heirs to the Kingdom of Heaven. When the Lord Thomas was taken away from our Indian land and much time had evolved, for a while [India] was darkened from the light of the faith, because there was nobody able to shepherd, and the learning of the Law fainted away. Later, the priest George, also called Pālamaram [103r] from Kuravilangad,[2] was the teacher of the Christians, and taught to everybody the good knowledge, and also built many churches, and shepherded all the Christians. After that, men from his family became the Archdeacons and they also built many churches and taught all the Nazranies and shepherded them. Then, there came Abraham from Babilon, who was driven away from the faith. When he learned the truth, he went to Rome and obeyed the Lord Pope. Then he was ordained a priest, a bishop and a metropolitan a second time. After this, he came here and ruled beautifully. When Metropolitan Mar Abraham died, there came Mar Alesh, Metropolitan of Goa.[3] He opened the door of truth and lighted the light of faith and

---

1 That is, the Maronite Patriarch of Antioch, now residing in Jounieh, north of Beirut, in union with Rome.
2 Is this George identical with George Pakalomattam, appointed Archdeacon in 1502?
3 Alexis de Menezes, S.J., Archbishop of Goa, 1595–1617.

gathered a synod in the holy church of St Gervasius and Protasius, which is in the blessed city of Udayyanpur (Udayamperur: Diamper) and submitted all [103v] Christians to the truth of the faith. And again, [there came] Metropolitan Mar Franciscus, who was also called "of the Rose" and Honorable and Great Teacher,[4] and he also made arise the Sun of righteousness and of the faith, and from him all India was enlightened, just as [from] Saint Thomas, our illustrious father. After this, [came] Metropolitan Mar Stephen;[5] he also ruled beautifully, earnestly and becomingly and without any disorder, when came Metropolitan Mar Franciscus, also called Garcia and Honorable and Righteous Teacher[6] and he ruled righteous-ly, but the Devil raised opposition to him because of his righteousness and justice and sowed tares in his flock and many went astray from the true faith; they aban-doned the obedience to the Head of the Church. When the Lord Pope, the Head of the Church heard about this sedition, he was very much saddened, because his members fell ill. For this reason he sent Bishop Mar Joseph, also called of Saint [104r] Mary, who was from [for?] being a leader of all, who was from the order of the discalced Carmelites.[7] After this bishop came to this region, upon the order of the Lord Pope he gave the episcopacy to the priest Alexander whose name in the Church was Bar Giwargis, from Kuravilangad,[8] on a Thursday, the first of February (Shebat), in the year 1663[9] of our Lord. Therefore, whosoever has ears to hear, should hear that *all those who do not obey and listen to Mar Alexander, Metropolitan and Apostolic Head, will be anathema!*

2a. Bodleian Oriental 667, ff. 21r–25r: A Brief History of the Malabar Church

Historiola Ecclesiae Syro-Malabaricae. Descripsit Malpan Abraham [...] 1821.

In the name of the Father, the Son and the Holy Spirit, one true God. Amen.

[21r] In the year 52 of our Lord, St Thomas the Apostle came to India; he con-verted many people[10] and founded[11] five churches. And he appointed over these churches men from two renowned families.[12] Then he went to Mylapore, he

---

4 Francisco Roz, S. J., Archbishop of Angamaly, 1601–24.

5 Stephen Britto, S. J., Archbishop of Angamaly, 1624–41.

6 Francisco Garcia, S. J., Archbishop of Angamaly, 1641–59.

7 Joseph Maria Sebastiani, O. C. D., Apostolic Comissary, 1655–58, 1661–63.

8 Mar Chandy Parambil (Alexander De Campo), Vicar Apostolic of Malabar, self-styled "Metropoli-tan of All-India", 1663–87.

9 The date is precise: Mar Chandy Parambil was ordained by Bishop Sebastiani on February 1, 1663.

10 I read here ܡܥܡܕ; the reading of Nau is ܐܚܡܥ; he translates accordingly: "il baptisa beaucoup d'hommes."

11 Literally: "made," ܥܒܕ.

12 ܣܥܡ ܚܠܐ ܓܒܪܐ ܠܠ ܚܠܡ ܘܗܕ ܠܠܩܒ ܠܘܘܢܩܬܠ ܠܩܢܝ ܡܢܬܚܗܢܐ. Nau's translation: "il préposa à ces églises deux hommes illustres de sa nation" seems to me incorrect here. The author speaks about the two privileged Nazrani families, which, according to tradition, received a (hereditary!) ordination from St Thomas.

preached, died and was buried there. After this, in the year 345, upon the order of our Father Mor Ignatius, Patriarch of Antioch, a Christian merchant, Thomas by name, came to India and with him also came bishops, priests, deacons and Christians; they settled in this land and preached to us the true ways. And [they selected] from among the men who belonged to the families that had precedence and had received ordination from St Thomas the Apostle and appointed them to be leaders over the flocks in India and he [that is, Thomas the merchant] gave them the Archdeaconate.[13]

In the year 845 of our Lord a merchant, whose name was Job, and with him two bishops came and settled in this land. And according to our customs we were orthodox Jacobite Syrians from the very beginning of the preaching of St Thomas the Apostle, up to the year 1545.

After this, there came a bishop, Mar Abraham by name, appointed by Mar Eliah[14] and he brought with him many books. And from him we took ordination, because we had no bishops. In that time the King of the Portuguese reigned in Fort Cochin,[15] so he caused Mar Abraham to be led by force to Cochin, and after this, he [Mar Abraham] went to Rome and he [the King of Portugal] sent him to the Pope and he [the Pope] appointed him to be over the whole flock of India and again he came here and preached the customs of the Franks to us.

After the death of Mar Abraham, the Portuguese governor of Cochin (?)[16] gave much money to the King of Cochin, and the King caused much distress to the Archdeacon and to the people in the Syrian churches. In the year 1598 of our Lord we abandoned the Syrian customs and adopted the Frankish customs. In this time the priests were hindered from legal marriage.

In the year 1653 of our Lord there came to Mylapore our Father, Mor Ignatius, Patriarch of Antioch, the Father of the Fathers. Two deacons went from Malabar to the Mylapore church to venerate the tomb of Saint Thomas the Apostle. When our Father, Mor Ignatius, saw the deacons and recognised [them], he wept and with him wept the deacons. When the Franks saw this, they set up guards, so that the deacons might not meet and speak with our Father, Mor Ignatius, because there was no bishop from among our nation who would govern the flock of India. Then our Father, Mor Ignatius, with a sign secretly called the deacons and gave them an official letter,[17] in order that they should make Archdeacon Tho-

---

13 Nau translates here: "parmi les hommes des générations précédentes qui avaient reçu l'imposition des mains de l'apôtre Mar Thomas, ils en établirent (certains) pour gouverner les fidèles de l'Inde et ils leurs donnèrent un archidiaconat" – which, again, seems to me imprecise.

14 Mar Eliah VIII, Catholicos Patriarch of the East (1576–91).

15 ܘܩܘܡܝ ܗܘܡܐ seems to be one of the Syriac translations in our document of Fort Cochin. Nau translates: "sur le mur de Cochin."

16 ܩܘܦܘܪ ܣܝܡ ܗܟܠܒܐ. Cf. Nau: "Pourgis, chef de Cochin". I would suggest that this expression means 'the Portuguese governor of Cochin', although some lines above the Syriac word for 'Portuguese' (in plural) was ܦܪܗܬܠܐ܆. In fact, our text is quite inconsistent in the Syriac transcription of foreign words.

17 *Systatikon*, in Syriac, *statikon*, literally "a letter of recommendation". The *systatikon* testifies to the legitimacy of a bishop sent by a patriarch.

mas a bishop and he sent them away. When these deacons came to Malabar, they gave this official letter to Archdeacon Thomas. He sent out letters to the churches. And when all the priests, deacons and Christians who were in Malabar gathered together in front of him and heard that our Father Mor Ignatius came to Fort Cochin,[18] they went there in haste and made it known to the pagan King of Cochin that he should take our Father Mor Ignatius from the violent hands of the Franks and give him to us. And the King told us: "Tomorrow I will send for him to come and go to you".[19] But the Franks knew about this and gave much money to the King of Cochin and he consented to them that they act according to their will. In that very night the Franks bound a big stone to the neck of the blessed man and hurled him into the depth of the sea. And in the same moment when the blessed man died, the pagan King also died.

After these events, [the representatives of] all the families of the Syrians gathered together in the church of Mattancherry and made an oath, one by one, in the name of the Father, the Son and the Holy Spirit, that thenceforward we have no love, agreement, or community with the Franks. After all this, they made Archdeacon Thomas a bishop over all the churches of the Syrians, according to the order of our Father, Patriarch Mor Ignatius.

After this, in the year 1660, Bishop Joseph[20] came to Malabar, but we did not obey him. [So], after a little while this Bishop Mar Joseph called for a certain priest, Alexander, who was from the family of Bishop Mar Thomas. He lured him in through fraud and flattery and gave him the rank of a bishop. After this, the Syrians in Malabar split into two factions.

In the year 1[...][21] came our Father Patriarch Mor Grigorios; and again, in the year 1685 there came to us Maphrian Mor Basilios and Bishop Mor Ivanios,[22] who removed from us the customs of the Franks and took us back to the customs of the first Fathers; and from that time until the present day we have not taken away from those, nor have we added to them.

Again, in the year 1708 of our Lord [there came] Bishop Mar Gabriel[23] upon the command of Catholicos Mar Eliah[24] and preached to us two natures and two

---

18 ܚܣܝܐ ܘܚܦܝܗ.

19 ܡܚܣܪ: ܐܓܒܪ ܐܢܠܐ ܘܐܢܠܐ ܠܚܩܐ; Nau reads the text otherwise: ܡܚܣ. ܐܡܪܙ ܐ ܠܐ ܘ ܐ ܠܐ ܠܚܩ ܠܠܐ ܗ.

20 Joseph Maria Sebastiani, see above, n. 7.

21 The manuscript has a lacuna here; apparently the scribe wanted to fill it after knowing the exact date. Mor Gregorius Abd'ul-Jalil, delegate of Moran Mor Ignatius Abd'ul Masih I, Syrian Orthodox Patriarch of Antioch (1662–1686), arrived in Malabar in 1665. He stayed there until his death in 1671.

22 In 1685 Mor Basilios Yaldo and Mor Ivanios [Yovannis, according to the way he himself spelled his name] Hidaytullah were sent in India by Patriarch Moran Mor Ignatius Abd'ul Masih I. Mor Basilios died soon after arriving in India; Mor Ivanios died in 1693.

23 Mar Gabriel was originally an East Syrian bishop, bearing the rank of the Metropolitan of Mar-Shalita in Azerbaijan. He joined the Chaldaean church under the Chaldaean Patriarch Joseph II. However, without any permission from Rome, he went to Malabar, carrying the *systatikon* of Mar Eliah, Catholicos Patriarch of the Church of the East. He won over almost forty churches to accept his jurisdiction. He died in 1731, in Kottayam.

24 Eliah XI Maroghin (1700–22), Catholicos Patriarch of the Church of the East, residing in Mosul.

hypostases in Christ. Because of this matter there arose great strife between us and a few people from among us and also from among the Franks who followed him. He celebrated the Eucharist with [both] leavened and unleavened bread[25] and established a fast according to the Syrian customs. After the death of this bishop those people who followed him turned back to their earlier customs.

Later, in the year 1751, the 23rd of the month Nissan [April] on a Tuesday, Maphrian Mor Basilios, Metropolitan Mor Grigorios and Chorepiscopa Giwargis [came[26] and made] that Rabban Yuhannōn become a bishop through the hands of Mor Basilios.[27] Let their prayers become a bulwark for us!

2b. A notice on the Maronites and the Synod of Diamper

Historiola Romanarum Partium in Malabari (Descripsit Malpan Abraham Cotyamensis)

In the year 1127, the Syrian Jacobite Metropolitan, Maron,[28] because of the insolence and evil of his heart seceded, together with the members of his flock, the inhabitants of Mount Lebanon, from the Petrine See of Antioch and obeyed the Pope of Rome.[29]

In the year 1595 a council was held in the church of Uttinperur[30] and the heads of the gathering were Bishop Mar Alesos[31] and the Priest Franciscus, also called the Erudite,[32] Priest Andoskon and Priest Jacob from the church of Pallurty in the land of Malabar, and also Archdeacon Giwargis, the leader of the holy churches that are in Malabar.

(Translated by István Perczel)

---

25 ‏ܘܡܢܐ ܟܠܗ ܡܘܢܚܐ ܚܣܡܐ ܘܦܠܝܓܐ‎. A reference to Mar Gabriel's hesitation, known also from other sources, between the Latin and the Syrian customs, the Catholic and the Nestorian allegiance. Nau apparently mistranslates the expression: "avec du pain fermenté et levé".

26 On April 23, 1751, upon the invitation of Mar Thoma V, Maphrian Basilios Shukr'allah Qasabgi, in the company of Chorepiscopa George Nament'allah Tambargi and others, sent by Patriarch Moran Mor Ignatius George III (1745–1768), landed in Cochin. Bishop Grigorios Hanna Bahudaidi arrived alone, eleven months later, and joined them in Kerala. An original of the *systatikon* of these bishops can be found in the Metropolitan's Palace of the Chaldaean Church in Thrissur.

27 Mor Basilios ordained a Syrian monk, Rabban Yuhannōn Christophoros of Mosul, to be a bishop by the name Mor Yuhannōn, in April 1752. From these events a schism within the Orthodox resulted, which definitively concluded only in 1770. Maphrian Mor Basilios died on 9 October 1764, Mor Grigorios died on 27 June 1774.

28 The author most probably means John-Maron II, who in 938 founded his patriarchal see in Akoura, Lebanon.

29 See Nau's note: "Nous ne pouvons comprendre ce que cette mention vient faire ici, mais nous l'éditons telle quelle".

30 A Syriac transcription for Udayamperur or Diamper. In fact, the Synod of Diamper was held in 1599.

31 Alexis de Menezes.

32 Francisco Roz, S.J.

Abbreviations

ACL	Archiv für Celtische Lexikographie
Adj.	Adjektiv/adjective
ae.	altenglisch/Old English
Ags	Altsächsische Genesis
ags.	angelsächsisch/Anglo Saxon
ahd.	althochdeutsch/Old High German
alem.	alemannisch/Alemannic
AL/ALI	Ancient Laws of Ireland
as.	altsächsisch/Old Saxon
B	Benediktinerregel
CCSL	Corpus Christianorum – Series Latina
CDB	Codex diplomaticus Brandenburgensis
Celtica	Celtica, The Dublin Institute for Advanced Studies
CLCLT	Cetedoc Library of Christian Latin Texts
CPL	Clavis Patrum Latinorum
CSEL	Corpus Scriptorum Ecclesiasticorum Latinorum
CV	Communication verticale
DCR	De correctione rusticorum
DEO	De ecclesiasticis officiis
Deut	Deuteronomium/Deuteronomy
DIL	Dictionary of the Irish Language
Ériu	Ériu, Royal Irish Academy
Ex	Exodus/Exodus
F.	Femininum/feminine
FRB	Fontes Rerum Bohemicarum
germ.	germanisch/Germanic
griech.	griechisch/Greek
Hel	Heliand
Hs./Hss.	Handschrift(en)
HUCA	Hebrew Union College Annual
I	Isidor
ie.	indoeuropäisch/Indoeuropean
J	Johannesevangelium/Gospel of John
JAOS	Journal of the American Oriental Society
JRSAI	Journal of the Royal Society of Antiquaries of Ireland
lat.	lateinisch/Latin
LEIA	Lexique Étymologique de l'Irlandais Ancien
LexMA	Lexikon des Mittelalters (Studienausgabe)
Lk	Lukasevangelium/Gospel of Luke
LTI	Lingua tertii imperii
M.	Maskulinum/masculine

MEAH	Miscelánea de Estudios Árabes y Hebraicos
MF	Monseer Fragmente
MGH	Monumenta Germaniae Historica
AA	Scriptores, Auctores antiquissimi
LL	Leges
SS	Scriptores (in folio)
SS rer. Germ.	Scriptores rerum Germanicarum in usum scholarum
MH	Murbacher Hymnen
mhd.	mittelhochdeutsch/Middle High German
MITECS	MIT encyclopedia of the cognitive sciences
MMFH	Magnae Moraviae Fontes historici
Mt	Matthäusevangelium/Gospel of Matthew
N.	Neutrum/neuter
O	Otfrids von Weißenburg liber evangeliorum
OHG	althochdeutsch/Old High German
OI	Old Irish
PAAJR	Proceedings of the American Academy for Jewish Research
Part.	Partizip/participle
Pl.	Plural/plural
PL	Patrologia Latina
RC	Revue Celtique
REMMM	Revue du Monde Musulman et de la Méditerranée
SC	Sources Chrétiennes
st.	stark/strong
sw.	schwach/weak
T	Tatian
Wb	Würzburg
WK	Weißenburger Katechismus
ZCP	Zeitschrift für Celtische Philologie
V.	Verb/verb
*	erschlossene Form/generated form
<	ist entstanden aus/emerged from
>	hat sich entwickelt zu/evolved into

Contributors

Dr. Esperanza Alfonso
Departamento de Estudios Hebreos y Arameos
Facultad de Filología, Edificio A
Universidad Complutense
Ciudad Universitaria
E-28040 Madrid
ealfonso@filol.ucm.es

Prof. Michel Banniard
La Métairie d'en Haut
F-09350-Fornex
michel.banniard@wanadoo.fr

Prof. Ernst Bremer
Fakultät für Kulturwissenschaften
Fach: Germanistik
Universität Paderborn
Warburger Str. 100
D-33098 Paderborn
bremer@zitmail.upb.de

Dr. Charles Burnett
Warburg Institute
Woburn Square
GB-London WC1H 0AB
charles.burnett@sas.ac.uk

Dr. Jonathan P. Decter
Edmond J. Safra Professor of Sephardic Studies
Department of Near Eastern and Judaic Studies
MS 054
Brandeis University
US-Waltham, Ma 02454-9110
decter@brandeis.edu

Dr. Cleophea Ferrari
Georg-Krauss-Str. 40
D-91056 Erlangen
ferrariMCF@aol.com

Prof. Michele C. Ferrari
Friedrich-Alexander-Universität
Mittellatein und Neulatein
Kochstr. 4/3
D-91054 Erlangen
Michele.C.Ferrari@as.phil.uni-erlangen.de

Dr. Martin Fuß
Rotdornweg 1
D-53343 Wachtberg
fuss.m@web.de

Eckhard Hauswald
Cherisy-Str. 20
D-78467 Konstanz
eckhard.hauswald@lycos.de

Dr. Petr Hlaváček
Prodekan Hussitische Theologische Fakultät
Karlsuniversität Prag
Pacovská 350/4, P. O. BOX 56
CZ-14021 PRAHA 4
hlavacek@htf.cuni.cz (hlavacek@rz.uni-leipzig.de)

Prof. Jörg Jarnut
Fakultät für Kulturwissenschaften
Historisches Institut
Universität Paderborn
Warburger Str. 100
D-33098 Paderborn
jjarnut@zitmail.upb.de

Dr. Hanna E. Kassis
Professor *emeritus*
Department of Classical, Near Eastern and Religious Studies
University of British Columbia
CA-Vancouver V6T 1Z1
hek@interchange.ubc.ca

Dr. Martha Keil
Institut für Geschichte der Juden in Österreich
Dr. Karl Renner-Promenade 22
A-3100 St. Pölten
martha.keil@injoest.ac.at

Dr. Anna Kuznetsova
PhD, Senior Researcher
Russian Academy of Sciences
Institute of Slavic Studies
RU-117334, Moscow
Leninskii prospekt, 32A
APHKUA01@alumni.ceu.hu

Dr. Svetlana I. Luchitskaya
Institute of general history
Leninski pr. 89-346
RU-119313 Moscow
svetlana@mega.ru

Prof. Roman Michałowski
ul. Dunikowskiego 1 m. 8
PL-02-784 Warszawa
michalowski.roman@acn.waw.pl

Dr. Hermann Moisl
School of English Literature, Language and Linguistics
Percy Building
University of Newcastle
GB-Newcastle upon Tyne NE1 7RU
http://www.ncl.ac.uk/elll/staff/profile/hermann.moisl
hermann.moisl@newcastle.ac.uk

Prof. Próinséas Ní Chatháin
69, Larchfield Road
Goatstown
IE-Dublin, 14

Dr. Johannes Niehoff-Panagiotidis
Dept. of Medieval Studies
CEU-Budapest
Nádor utca 9
HU-Budapest
niehoffj@ceu.hu

Prof. Morfydd E. Owen
Bryn Eithin
Llanfarian
GB-Aberystwyth
SY23 4BY
owen@arcetsal.fsnet.co.uk

Dr. Johannes Pahlitzsch
Johannes Gutenberg-Universität Mainz
Fachbereich 07: Kultur- und Geschichtswissenschaften
Historisches Seminar
Abteilung V: Byzantinistik
D-55099 Mainz
pahlitz@zedat.fu-berlin.de

Dr. Mayte Penelas
Escuela de Estudios Árabes, CSIC
Cuesta del Chapiz 22
E-18010 Granada
mpenelas@eea.csic.es

Dr. István Perczel
Associate Professor
Philosophy and Byzantine History
Dept. of Medieval Studies
CEU-Budapest
Nádor utca 9
HU-1051 Budapest
perczeli@ceu.hu.

Prof. Jean-Michel Picard
UCD School of Languages, Literatures and Film
Faculties of Arts and Celtic Studies
Room D 306
John Henry Newman Building
University College Dublin
Belfield
IE-Dublin 4
jm.picard@ucd.ie

Prof. Michael Richter
Universität Konstanz
Fachbereich Geschichte und Soziologie
Fach D 13
D-78457 Konstanz
michael.richter@uni-konstanz.de

Prof. Dušan Třeštík
Centrum medievistických studií
Jilská 1
CZ-110 00 Praha 1
trestik@hiu.cas.cz

Prof. David J. Wasserstein
Department of History
Vanderbilt University
VU Station B #351802
2301 Vanderbilt Place
US-Nashville TN 37235-1802
david.wasserstein@vanderbilt.edu

Prof. Roger Wright
Department of Modern Languages
University of Liverpool
GB-Liverpool L69 3BX
roger.wright@liverpool.ac.uk

Volume 9:
Emotion, Gewalt und Widerstand. Spannungsfelder zwischen geistlichem und weltlichem Leben in Mittelalter und Früher Neuzeit, ed. by Ansgar Köb and Peter Riedel, 2007.

Volume 10:
Klosterforschung. Befunde, Projekte, Perspektiven, ed. by Jens Schneider, 2006.

Volume 11:
Language of Religion – Language of the People. Medieval Judaism, Christianity and Islam, ed. by Ernst Bremer, Jörg Jarnut, Michael Richter and David Wasserstein with the assistance of Susanne Röhl, 2006.

Volume 12:
Jean de Mandeville in Europa. Neue Perspektiven in der Reiseliteraturforschung, ed. by Ernst Bremer with the assistance of Susanne Röhl, 2007.

Volume 13:
Vom Umbruch zur Erneuerung? Das 11. und beginnende 12. Jahrhundert – Positionen der Forschung, ed. by Jörg Jarnut and Matthias Wemhoff with the assistance of Nicola Karthaus, 2006.

Volume 14:
Text – Bild – Schrift. Vermittlung von Information im Mittelalter, ed. by Andres Laubinger, Brunhilde Gedderth and Claudia Dobrinski, 2007.

Volume 15:
Kloster und Wirtschaftswelt im Mittelalter, ed. by Claudia Dobrinski, Brunhilde Gedderth and Katrin Wipfler, 2007.

Further volumes in preparation.

www.ieman.de